Lecture Notes in Computer Science   **12195**

More information about this series at http://www.springer.com/series/7409

Gabriele Meiselwitz (Ed.)

Social Computing and Social Media

Participation, User Experience, Consumer Experience,
and Applications of Social Computing

12th International Conference, SCSM 2020
Held as Part of the 22nd HCI International Conference, HCII 2020
Copenhagen, Denmark, July 19–24, 2020
Proceedings, Part II

 Springer

Editor
Gabriele Meiselwitz
Towson University
Towson, MD, USA

ISSN 0302-9743 ISSN 1611-3349 (electronic)
Lecture Notes in Computer Science
ISBN 978-3-030-49575-6 ISBN 978-3-030-49576-3 (eBook)
https://doi.org/10.1007/978-3-030-49576-3

LNCS Sublibrary: SL3 – Information Systems and Applications, incl. Internet/Web, and HCI

This Springer imprint is published by the registered company Springer Nature Switzerland AG
The registered company address is: Gewerbestrasse 11, 6330 Cham, Switzerland

Foreword

The 22nd International Conference on Human-Computer Interaction, HCI International 2020 (HCII 2020), was planned to be held at the AC Bella Sky Hotel and Bella Center, Copenhagen, Denmark, during July 19–24, 2020. Due to the COVID-19 coronavirus pandemic and the resolution of the Danish government not to allow events larger than 500 people to be hosted until September 1, 2020, HCII 2020 had to be held virtually. It incorporated the 21 thematic areas and affiliated conferences listed on the following page.

A total of 6,326 individuals from academia, research institutes, industry, and governmental agencies from 97 countries submitted contributions, and 1,439 papers and 238 posters were included in the conference proceedings. These contributions address the latest research and development efforts and highlight the human aspects of design and use of computing systems. The contributions thoroughly cover the entire field of human-computer interaction, addressing major advances in knowledge and effective use of computers in a variety of application areas. The volumes constituting the full set of the conference proceedings are listed in the following pages.

The HCI International (HCII) conference also offers the option of "late-breaking work" which applies both for papers and posters and the corresponding volume(s) of the proceedings will be published just after the conference. Full papers will be included in the "HCII 2020 - Late Breaking Papers" volume of the proceedings to be published in the Springer LNCS series, while poster extended abstracts will be included as short papers in the "HCII 2020 - Late Breaking Posters" volume to be published in the Springer CCIS series.

I would like to thank the program board chairs and the members of the program boards of all thematic areas and affiliated conferences for their contribution to the highest scientific quality and the overall success of the HCI International 2020 conference.

This conference would not have been possible without the continuous and unwavering support and advice of the founder, Conference General Chair Emeritus and Conference Scientific Advisor Prof. Gavriel Salvendy. For his outstanding efforts, I would like to express my appreciation to the communications chair and editor of HCI International News, Dr. Abbas Moallem.

July 2020   Constantine Stephanidis

HCI International 2020 Thematic Areas and Affiliated Conferences

Thematic areas:

- HCI 2020: Human-Computer Interaction
- HIMI 2020: Human Interface and the Management of Information

Affiliated conferences:

- EPCE: 17th International Conference on Engineering Psychology and Cognitive Ergonomics
- UAHCI: 14th International Conference on Universal Access in Human-Computer Interaction
- VAMR: 12th International Conference on Virtual, Augmented and Mixed Reality
- CCD: 12th International Conference on Cross-Cultural Design
- SCSM: 12th International Conference on Social Computing and Social Media
- AC: 14th International Conference on Augmented Cognition
- DHM: 11th International Conference on Digital Human Modeling and Applications in Health, Safety, Ergonomics and Risk Management
- DUXU: 9th International Conference on Design, User Experience and Usability
- DAPI: 8th International Conference on Distributed, Ambient and Pervasive Interactions
- HCIBGO: 7th International Conference on HCI in Business, Government and Organizations
- LCT: 7th International Conference on Learning and Collaboration Technologies
- ITAP: 6th International Conference on Human Aspects of IT for the Aged Population
- HCI-CPT: Second International Conference on HCI for Cybersecurity, Privacy and Trust
- HCI-Games: Second International Conference on HCI in Games
- MobiTAS: Second International Conference on HCI in Mobility, Transport and Automotive Systems
- AIS: Second International Conference on Adaptive Instructional Systems
- C&C: 8th International Conference on Culture and Computing
- MOBILE: First International Conference on Design, Operation and Evaluation of Mobile Communications
- AI-HCI: First International Conference on Artificial Intelligence in HCI

Conference Proceedings Volumes Full List

1. LNCS 12181, Human-Computer Interaction: Design and User Experience (Part I), edited by Masaaki Kurosu
2. LNCS 12182, Human-Computer Interaction: Multimodal and Natural Interaction (Part II), edited by Masaaki Kurosu
3. LNCS 12183, Human-Computer Interaction: Human Values and Quality of Life (Part III), edited by Masaaki Kurosu
4. LNCS 12184, Human Interface and the Management of Information: Designing Information (Part I), edited by Sakae Yamamoto and Hirohiko Mori
5. LNCS 12185, Human Interface and the Management of Information: Interacting with Information (Part II), edited by Sakae Yamamoto and Hirohiko Mori
6. LNAI 12186, Engineering Psychology and Cognitive Ergonomics: Mental Workload, Human Physiology, and Human Energy (Part I), edited by Don Harris and Wen-Chin Li
7. LNAI 12187, Engineering Psychology and Cognitive Ergonomics: Cognition and Design (Part II), edited by Don Harris and Wen-Chin Li
8. LNCS 12188, Universal Access in Human-Computer Interaction: Design Approaches and Supporting Technologies (Part I), edited by Margherita Antona and Constantine Stephanidis
9. LNCS 12189, Universal Access in Human-Computer Interaction: Applications and Practice (Part II), edited by Margherita Antona and Constantine Stephanidis
10. LNCS 12190, Virtual, Augmented and Mixed Reality: Design and Interaction (Part I), edited by Jessie Y. C. Chen and Gino Fragomeni
11. LNCS 12191, Virtual, Augmented and Mixed Reality: Industrial and Everyday Life Applications (Part II), edited by Jessie Y. C. Chen and Gino Fragomeni
12. LNCS 12192, Cross-Cultural Design: User Experience of Products, Services, and Intelligent Environments (Part I), edited by P. L. Patrick Rau
13. LNCS 12193, Cross-Cultural Design: Applications in Health, Learning, Communication, and Creativity (Part II), edited by P. L. Patrick Rau
14. LNCS 12194, Social Computing and Social Media: Design, Ethics, User Behavior, and Social Network Analysis (Part I), edited by Gabriele Meiselwitz
15. LNCS 12195, Social Computing and Social Media: Participation, User Experience, Consumer Experience, and Applications of Social Computing (Part II), edited by Gabriele Meiselwitz
16. LNAI 12196, Augmented Cognition: Theoretical and Technological Approaches (Part I), edited by Dylan D. Schmorrow and Cali M. Fidopiastis
17. LNAI 12197, Augmented Cognition: Human Cognition and Behaviour (Part II), edited by Dylan D. Schmorrow and Cali M. Fidopiastis

38. CCIS 1224, HCI International 2020 Posters - Part I, edited by Constantine Stephanidis and Margherita Antona
39. CCIS 1225, HCI International 2020 Posters - Part II, edited by Constantine Stephanidis and Margherita Antona
40. CCIS 1226, HCI International 2020 Posters - Part III, edited by Constantine Stephanidis and Margherita Antona

http://2020.hci.international/proceedings

12th International Conference on Social Computing and Social Media (SCSM 2020)

Program Board Chair: **Gabriele Meiselwitz, Towson University, USA**

- Sarah Alhumoud, Saudi Arabia
- Andria Andriuzzi, France
- Francisco Javier Álvarez Rodríguez, Mexico
- Karine Berthelot-Guiet, France
- James Braman, USA
- Adheesh Budree, South Africa
- Adela Coman, Romania
- Isabelle Dorsch, Germany
- Panagiotis Germanakos, Germany
- Tamara Heck, Germany
- Hung-Hsuan Huang, Japan
- Aylin Ilhan, Germany
- Carsten Kleiner, Germany
- Ana I. Molina Díaz, Spain
- Takashi Namatame, Japan
- Hoang D. Nguyen, Singapore
- Kohei Otake, Japan
- Carlos Alberto Peláez, Colombia
- Daniela Quiñones, Chile
- Cristian Rusu, Chile
- Christian W. Scheiner, Germany
- Simona Vasilache, Japan
- Giovanni Vincenti, USA
- Yuanqiong Wang, USA
- Brian Wentz, USA

The full list with the Program Board Chairs and the members of the Program Boards of all thematic areas and affiliated conferences is available online at:

http://www.hci.international/board-members-2020.php

HCI International 2021

The 23rd International Conference on Human-Computer Interaction, HCI International 2021 (HCII 2021), will be held jointly with the affiliated conferences in Washington DC, USA, at the Washington Hilton Hotel, July 24–29, 2021. It will cover a broad spectrum of themes related to Human-Computer Interaction (HCI), including theoretical issues, methods, tools, processes, and case studies in HCI design, as well as novel interaction techniques, interfaces, and applications. The proceedings will be published by Springer. More information will be available on the conference website: http://2021.hci.international/.

General Chair
Prof. Constantine Stephanidis
University of Crete and ICS-FORTH
Heraklion, Crete, Greece
Email: general_chair@hcii2021.org

http://2021.hci.international/

Contents – Part II

Social Computing and User Experience

Social Media Marketing and Consumer Experience

Social Computing for Well-Being, Learning, and Entertainment

Contents – Part I

Ethics and Misinformation in Social Media

User Behavior and Social Network Analysis

Participation and Collaboration in Online Communities

Knowledge Sharing and Community Promotion in Online Health Communities: Examining the Relationship Between Social Support, Community Commitment, and Trust Transfer

Zaenal Abidin[1], Achmad Nizar Hidayanto[2]($\boxtimes$), Dedi I. Inan[3],
Amira Luthfia Fitriani[2], Atikah Zahrah Halim[2], M. Farhan Mardadi[2],
and Rizkah Shalihah[2]

[1] Universitas Negeri Semarang, Gunungpati, Semarang,
Jawa Tengah 50229, Indonesia
z.abidin@mail.unnes.ac.id
[2] Universitas Indonesia, Depok, West Java 16424, Indonesia
nizar@cs.ui.ac.id
[3] The University of Papua, Manokwari, West Papua 98314, Indonesia
d.inan@unipa.ac.id

Abstract. Online health communities (OHCs) have now become a valuable platform for people to seek health-related information. Knowledge sharing and community promotion in the OHCs are critical to sustain their continuous use and improve their engagement. This study aims to investigate factors influencing knowledge sharing and community promotion in the OHC in the perspectives of social support, commitment-trust, and trust transfer theory. A questionnaire survey is employed as a collection data technique. The study results reveal that informational support influences trust transfer, trust towards community and members of the community. In addition, emotional support has a positive impact on community commitment and trust in community members but not in the community itself. Further, community commitment is positively related to both knowledge sharing and community promotion. While trust towards the community is only positively related to community promotion, trust towards members of the community does not have a positive influence on both knowledge sharing and community promotion. This study contributes to the understanding of the relationships among social support, community commitment, and trust transfer towards knowledge sharing and community promotion in the OHC. The findings of the study provide a research model that could be implemented in other contexts that share similar technology landscape.

Keywords: Online health community · Knowledge sharing · Community promotion · Social support · Community commitment · Trust transfer

© Springer Nature Switzerland AG 2020
G. Meiselwitz (Ed.): HCII 2020, LNCS 12195, pp. 3–15, 2020.
https://doi.org/10.1007/978-3-030-49576-3_1

1 Introduction

People increasingly make use of online platforms to look for health-related information. The proliferation of online platforms such as social media has led to an increasing number of OHCs. The OHC is a virtual space for people who search for health information and exchange their experiences regarding medical treatment [1]. The OHC is also called as the online health-related online forum [2] under which people can exchange their knowledge, ask for and provide assistance, discuss and find solutions to health problems, and share stories to others who have similar health issues.

Social support can be considered as an essential factor in the OHC. Social support, in this regard, relates to the members of the OHC that provide information and exchange knowledge on health-related topics to give the community the support and encouragement [1]. However, they do not expect reciprocation, e.g. monetary gifts or enjoyment in sharing information [3, 4]. Their active participation and motivation in giving relevant guidance and facilitating ongoing discussions through knowledge sharing will keep the OHC sustained [5].

Although some previous studies have examined the influence of motivation on individuals in conducting knowledge sharing in the OHCs [6] and in various online communities [7–9], there are still limited numbers of studies that measure the motivation of knowledge sharing and community promotion at the same time. While the relationship between the trust transfer theory [10] and the commitment-trust theory [11] has also not widely explored, trust is believed to be an important factor in the successfulness of the OHC. Therefore, an understanding of these factors: social support, community commitment, and trust transfer need to be extended to examine their relationships.

2 Theoretical Background and Hypotheses Development

The proposed research model shown in Fig. 1. It shows the role of *social support* (i.e., informational support and emotional support), and its impact on the formation of 1) *trust*, both to the members and the community itself, and 2) *community commitment*.

The proposed research model also illustrates the process of trust transfer from the OHC's members and their impact on the formation of community commitments. Furthermore, the proposed research model also outlines hypotheses regarding the role of trust and commitment in the process of sharing knowledge and promoting the OHC.

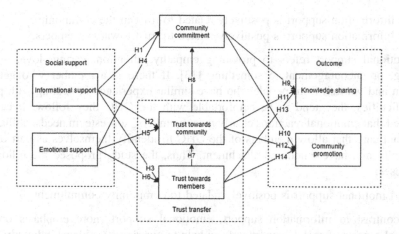

Fig. 1. The proposed research model.

2.1 Social Support

The rapid increase in internet usage over the past decade has changed the way people communicate and interact. They tend to connect with their communities online. Moreover, social networking sites are increasingly popular between them as a means to interact online one and another. In this respect, offline social support gradually changes to the social supportive communication in an online context [12]. Online social support usually refers to information exchange and emotional interaction in virtual space. Therefore, information and emotional support are the two main approaches to providing online support. In this study, information and emotional support are believed to offer relational benefits to the parties involved and help them to facilitate the development and maintenance of relationships in the OHC.

Information support is a type of support that offers individuals with advise, guidance, or information that is useful to help them solving their problems, generating new ideas, or making good decisions [13]. Relational benefits are often seen as the need to build cooperative relationships. In this respect, if there are several members who can benefit from the suggestions and opinions of others in the OHC, they will tend to recognize the value of the community and focus on the desire to maintain a long-term relationship with that community. Thus, the study proposed the following hypothesis:

H1: Information support is positively related to community commitment.

It is easy to understand if someone gets consistently instrumental help, such as valuable advice and direct assistance from members of the OHC. They will be more likely to have trust in those who share the information. Such instrumental assistance will form a sense of trust towards members who contributed to the OHC [13]. In this respect, the members' trust in the OHC will contribute positively to the availability of good information to other community members. Thus, the study proposed the following hypotheses:

H2: Information support is positively related to trust in the community.

H3: Information support is positively related to trust towards members.

Emotional support refers to providing empathy, attention, caring, love, under-standing, or encouragement to something [13]. If there is a member who gets an attention and warmth from people who have similar experience in dealing with pains and difficulties, they tend to be comfortable with the OHC they follow. It can be explained that emotional reactions clearly meet members' self-esteem needs, affiliation, and social care that allow members of the OHC to identify themselves as part of the community and have emotional attachment. Thus, the study proposed the following hypotheses:

H4: Emotional support is positively related to community commitment.

In contrast to information support, emotional support more emphasis on the emotional aspects of social support and can help to overcome problems indirectly [12]. Emotional support helps a member in an OHC to open and seek help from other members in the community. In particular, some members have shown caring attitudes towards other members and consciously know that these attitudes are the basis for developing a sense of trust. Therefore, through emotional exchange and connections with other members in a community, people will develop their trust in other members. Thus, the study proposed the following hypotheses:

H5: Emotional support is positively related to trust in the community.

H6: Emotional support is positively related to trust towards members.

2.2   Trust Transfers

Based on the theory of trust transfer, it is believed that trust in members can be developed through an interpersonal trust for two reasons. First, trust between members will make users believe that the provision and transfer of information in the community tend to be governed by the established principles. This helps members to ensure that the community will continue to improve service quality and offer effective management to build a trusted communication environment [14]. Second, previous research shows that there is a planned level of interpersonal trust for the development of institutional trust [13]. Members of an OHC that builds strong mutual trust will consider the community followed as the right place to communicate. For that, a good communi-cation becomes important in dealing with a community. This gives direction to the following hypothesis:

H7: Trust in members is positively related to trust in the community.

Trust in the community refers to one's perception so that the focus becomes a place that can be relied upon and predicted in social interaction. According to the theory of trust commitment, trust is believed to have a positive impact on a relationship [11]. Recent studies have shown that trust is the main determinant in committing to a virtual community [15]. If members develop trust in the OHC, uncertainty and communicative-related risks will be reduced. Relationships marked by the trust will be highly valued and members will have the desire to continue and strengthen relationships with the community. Thus, the study proposed the following hypotheses:

H8: Trust in society is positively related to community commitment.

2.3 Community Commitments

A committed relationship reflects a desire to maintain a long-term relationship with other individuals [13]. It is believed that the higher the commitment to an OHC, the more individuals will contribute to and participate in that community. Previous research has shown a positive relationship between commitment and user retention. In the context of the OHC, the online platform provides a shared space for users to communicate with each other and users can share their consumption experiences with or receive useful product recommendations from other online users. In this case, if a person is committed to having an ongoing relationship with the OHC, then he/she must make maximum efforts to maintain and participate in discussion activities undertaken to help the community grow and develop. Thus, the study proposed the following hypotheses:

H9: Community commitment is positively related to knowledge sharing intentions.
H10: Community commitment is positively related to community promotion intentions.

2.4 Impact of Trusts and Commitments on Knowledge Sharing and Community Promotion

Trust is often recognized as an important element in building a successful relationship [13]. In particular, the relationship between the trust of the admin responsible for an OHC and the intentions of users as followers or part of that community is intensively examined in recent research. With more and more information on the internet, users will tend to seek advice from the OHC and individuals they can trust. In return, users will be more likely to share their own information with trusted parties because of privacy concerns. Therefore, in this section, we will discuss the effects of one's trust in the context of the OHC, with insights from both trusts in members and trust in the OHC.

Online communities sometimes have a standard for accepting a member, in general, to ensure that it will provide mutual benefits and mutual benefits for its members [13]. As a reciprocal nature of virtual communication, the OHC can apply rules set directly to determine the participatory activities of its members. In addition, the integrity policy of the OHC will reduce concerns for users regarding opportunistic behavior, such as fraudulent advertisements or the use of personal information that is misused. The relationship between community trust and user loyalty is well established in the literature [16]. In this case, if someone has a strong perception of trust in a community, he will be more likely to seek recommendations from the community and share that experience. Thus, the study proposed the following hypotheses:

H11: Trust in society is positively related to knowledge sharing.

H12: Trust in society is positively related to community promotion.

In this study, trust in members is defined as the willingness of individuals to rely on the words, actions, and decisions of other members in the OHC. Previous studies have found that trust in members positively influences online participatory behaviour such as obtaining and providing information in the community [13]. This is because in an trusted environment, a person will tend to help each other and engage further joint discussion activities. In particular, information obtained from credible sources will be considered more useful and used as aids in making decisions [17]. In discussions, someone is more interested in sharing their own experiences when the other party has several related topics. This will make them communicate easily based on general background knowledge and help to reduce the possibility of opportunistic behaviour. Thus, the study proposed the following hypotheses:

H13: Trust in members is positively related to knowledge sharing.

H14: Trust in members is positively related to community promotion.

3 Research Methodology

The questionnaire used in this research consisted of 24 Likert-scale question items. The question items were measured on a five-point Likert scale from strongly disagree to strongly agree (scored from 1 to 5). The question items were adapted from Chen and Shen [13], Yuan, Lin and Zhuo [18], Yan, Wang, Chen and Zhang [19], Casaló, Flavián and Guinalíu [20], and Chen and Hung [21]. Once the design of the research instrument was prepared, we conducted a readability test to prospective research respondents to ensure the questionnaire was feasible to be distributed from various perspectives such as definition, writing conventions, relevance to the study, and the meaning of each question and statement contained in the questionnaire. We conducted a readability test on one expert respondent and five casual respondents. The selected experts already have experience in compiling instruments in a study, while the other respondents are members of the OHC on social media. After obtaining input from the respondents on the readability test, the authors refine the research instrument and distribute the research questionnaire.

The population in this study is the Indonesian who have joined as members of the OHC on social media. The author uses a convenience sampling technique for the sampling method. Data collection is done online via Google Form. The questionnaire was distributed through various social media, namely Twitter, Line Square, Facebook, and online health communities in these social media. These social medias are chosen as they are considered to be able to reach more groups both in terms of age, occupation, and education level.

In this study, the data analysis method used is the PLS-SEM method, by the help of SmartPLS 3.0 software [22]. PLS-SEM is chosen as this method can overcome problems in modelling that often arise, such as data that is not normally distributed and complex research models. PLS-SEM is also chosen because this study only has a few, that is 151 respondents. We follow the SEM procedures suggested by Hair, Sarstedt, Hopkins and Kuppelwieser [23].

4 Results and Discussion

4.1 Demographics of Respondents

The demographics of respondents are summarized in Table 1. Respondents in this study consist of 70.4% women and 29.6% men. Most of them in this study are women because, in fact, more women join the OHC. The majority of respondents in this study are aged 20–30 years (46.1%). This is followed by respondents who are less than 20 years old (35.5%). Most of the respondents have an undergraduate background (53.3%) and followed by those with elementary/junior high school/high school education background or equivalent (29.6%). Most of the respondents are students (67.8%), then followed by private employees (15.1%). Table 1 also informs that most of the respondents have been the members of the OHC for 4–12 months (48%) and less than 4 months (42.1%). Respondents in this study mostly spent time in the OHC for 1–4 h a day (50%), less than 1 h a day (43.4%), and more than 4 h a day (6.6%).

Table 1. The demographic information of the respondents.

	Frequency	Percentage
Gender		
Female	106	70.4
Male	45	29.6
Total	151	100
Age		
Under 20	54	35.5
20–30	69	46.1
31–40	13	8.6
Over 40	15	9.9
Total	151	100
Education		
Secondary school	45	29.8
Undergraduate	94	62.3
Postgraduate	12	7.9
Total	151	100
Social media used for OHC		
Facebook	24	15.8
Instagram	34	22.4
Line square	82	54.6

(continued)

Table 1. (*continued*)

Others	11	7.2
Total	151	100
Employment		
Student	102	67.8
Entrepreneur	9	5.9
Employee	37	24.3
Not working	3	2
Total	151	100
Time spent in OHC per day		
Less than 1 h	66	43.4
1–4 h	75	50
More than 4 h	10	6.6
Total	151	100
Duration of joining OHC		
More than 4 months	64	42.1
4–12 months	72	48
13–24 months	9	5.9
More than 24 months	6	4
Total	151	100

4.2 Measurement Model Testing

In the convergent validity test, the first criterion is to look at the outer loading value of each indicator on each variable. The outer loading value must be above 0.70. The high outer loading value indicates that each related indicator has many similarities and has described the variables [23]. By looking at the loading factor value, there is one indicator that has a value of less than 0.70, namely the KS2 indicator. This indicator was removed to meet the convergent validity test. After the KS2 indicator is deleted, all the outer loading values meet the criteria as can be seen in Table 2.

Besides looking at the outer loading values, the convergent validity test is also evaluated by looking at the Average Variance Extracted (AVE) values. AVE values must be greater than 0.5. As can be seen in Table 2, these results indicate that each variable used in this study has fulfilled the minimum AVE requirement, which is >0.5. Therefore, it can be concluded that convergent validity has been fulfilled.

In the internal consistency reliability test, the Cronbach's Alpha (CA) and Composite Reliability (CR) values must meet the requirements which are greater than 0.7. Table 2 shows that all variables contained in this study meet the criteria of CA and CR values >0.7. Therefore, internal consistency reliability tests are met.

For discriminant validity test, we use two methods for conducting the test, namely the Fornell and Larcker criteria and cross-loading checks. The computation results show that the square root of the AVE values is already higher than the correlations

Table 2. Values of outer loading, CA, CR, and AVE.

Parameter	Outer loading (>0.7)	CA (>0.7)	CR (>0.7)	AVE (>0.5)
CC1	0.798	0.829	0.887	0.663
CC2	0.859			
CC3	0.858			
CC4	0.735			
CP1	0.827	0.884	0.920	0.742
CP2	0.871			
CP3	0.895			
CP4	0.850			
ES1	0.846	0.825	0.896	0.741
ES2	0.885			
ES3	0.852			
IS1	0.768	0.712	0.839	0.635
IS2	0.838			
IS3	0.782			
KS1	0.797	0.785	0.875	0.700
KS3	0.845			
KS4	0.866			
TTC1	0.814	0.795	0.880	0.709
TTC2	0.827			
TTC3	0.883			
TTM1	0.735	0.754	0.860	0.673
TTM2	0.873			
TTM3	0.847			

between each construct, thus they have met Fornell and Larcker criteria [23]. The cross-loadings test also shows that each indicator used in this study has a higher value of the load than the cross load with other variables. Therefore, the discriminant validity test was fulfilled.

4.3 Structural Model Testing

A hypothesis can be accepted when its p-value is smaller or at least equal to 0.05 or equal to 95% significance level and its t-statistics value must be greater than 1.96 [23]. Table 3 shows that out of 15 proposed hypotheses, there are 10 accepted. The other five hypotheses are rejected because they have p-values greater than 0.05 and t-statistics less than 1.96. The original sample row shows the path coefficient value. The value of the path coefficient can describe the degree to which each variable has a significant relationship, either positive or negative, based on the hypothesized relationship.

Table 3. Hypotheses testing results.

Hypothesis		Original sample (O)	T Statistics (|O/STDEV|)	P-Value	Accepted/Rejected
H1	IS → CC	0.009	0.106	0.916	Rejected
H2	IS → TTC	0.361	4.507	0.00001	**Accepted**
H3	IS → TTM	0.369	3.978	0.0001	**Accepted**
H4	ES → CC	0.307	3.132	0.002	**Accepted**
H5	ES → TTC	0.097	1.277	0.202	Rejected
H6	ES → TTM	0.255	3.073	0.002	**Accepted**
H7	TTM → TTC	0.334	4.456	0.00001	**Accepted**
H8	TTC → CC	0.488	6.217	0.000000001	**Accepted**
H9	CC → KS	0.499	5.691	0.00000001	**Accepted**
H10	CC → CP	0.310	3.085	0.02	**Accepted**
H11	TTC → KS	0.090	0.876	0.381	Rejected
H12	TTC → CP	0.329	3.071	0.02	**Accepted**
H13	TTM → KS	0.073	0.703	0.482	Rejected
H14	TTM → CP	0.092	1.223	0.221	Rejected

The R-square value is used to see all the effects of the combined exogenous variables on endogenous variables. The R^2 values used as a standard in this study are 0.75, 0.50, and 0.25 respectively which describe whether the model in this study is classified as strong, moderate, and weak. Q^2 is one of the criteria in testing structural models because the model used in research must be able to adequately predict each indicator of its endogenous latent variables [23]. Q2 values obtained through blind-folding techniques with omission distance or D values between 5 and 10. Q^2 values successively 0.02, 0.15 and 0.35 indicate that exogenous variables have small, medium, and large predictive relevance to an endogenous variable. This study uses a blind-folding technique with an omission distance of 7. Table 4 shows the values of R2 and Q2 on endogenous variables in this study.

Table 4. R-square and Q-square values.

Variable	R-square	Q-square
CC	0.475	0.289
CP	0.408	0.275
KS	0.369	0.226
TTC	0.442	0.288
TTM	0.304	0.188

4.4   Discussion and Implications

This research has identified factors that allow members of OHC to share their health-related knowledge and promote others to join that particular community. In previous studies, examining the motivation that influences individuals in knowledge sharing on various online communities have been carried out [7–9]. But only few of them did investigate the motivation of knowledge sharing and community promotion simultaneously.

The results of this research show that community commitment can directly influence its members to share their knowledge. These results are consistent with the results of previous studies in which committed relationships reflect a desire to maintain a long-term relationship with other individuals [13]. The higher the commitment to an OHC, the more individuals will contribute and participate in the community to share their experiences.

Information support is a type of support that offers individuals with advice, guidance, or information that is useful to help them solve problems, generate new ideas, or make good decisions [13]. The results of this study confirm that information support itself is not enough to build the commitment of community members to the communities they participate in. However, this research can show that information support is positively related to trust towards community and members. This is consistent with previous research that that particular factor is more likely to have confidence in benevolence and integrity, and subsequently form a sense of trust towards information providers [13].

In contrast to the information support, emotional support places more emphasis on the emotional aspects of social support and can help to overcome problems indirectly [12]. The influence of emotional supports the community commitment. If there is a member who gets the attention and warmth of people who experience the same pain and difficulties, they tend to feel comfortable to live in the community they follow, in this case, the OHC. This is caused by emotional reactions such as care and attention given by other members which cause them to be emotionally attached.

Trust in members directly influences trust in the community. This is consistent with the trust transfer theory, it is believed that trust in members can be developed through trust between members will make users believe that the provision and transfer of information in the community tend to be governed by established principles [14]. However, this study does not show that trust in members influences knowledge sharing and community commitment. This is different from the results of previous studies which state that information obtained from credible sources will be considered more useful and used as aids in making decisions [17].

Subsequent results from this study indicate that trust in members can influence trust in the community, and subsequently increase the intention to OHC promotion to others. These results indicate conformity with the results of the study which states that trust is the main determinant in commitment to a virtual community [15].

5 Conclusions

This study aims to look at the impact of information and emotional support on trust towards members and community, as well as community commitment. The conclusions obtained from this study are as follows, first, we showed that the information support provided by members of the OHC affects trust in community members and the community itself. Furthermore, emotional support from community members influences community commitment and trust in community members. Second, the results of this study also indicate the existence of trust transfers in OHC, where trust in members influences trust in the community and subsequently affects community commitment. Third, the results of this study also show the important role of community commitment as the only variable that directly affects knowledge sharing. Morevoer, community promotion is influenced by community commitment and community trust.

Notwithstanding these, in this study the number of collected samples is relatively small, hat is only 151 respondents. This might influence the generality of the findings of this study. Therefore, a larger sample size is sought for a further research to strengthen the findings of this study. In addition, the paper also informs that exploring to what extent the role of the human aspect for example by integrating the health belief model (HBM) or protection motivation theory (PMT) that influence the motivation of the use of technology will be our future research direction.

Acknowledgement. This research has been supported by PDUPT as part of the project entitled "Pengembangan Konsep Tourism Information Service Untuk Smart Experience Pariwisata di Indonesia". It also has been supported by Ministry of Research, Technology and Higher Education of the Republic of Indonesia through a "Penelitian Kompetitif National – Penelitian Pasca Doktor".

References

1. Fan, H., Lederman, R., Smith, S.P., Chang, S.: How trust is formed in online health communities: a process perspective. Commun. Assoc. Inf. Syst. **34**(1), 531–560 (2014)
2. Tanis, M.: Health-related on-line forums: what's the big attraction? J. Health Commun. **13** (7), 698–714 (2008)
3. Papadopoulos, T., Stamati, T., Nopparuch, P.: Exploring the determinants of knowledge sharing via employee weblogs. Int. J. Inf. Manag. **33**(1), 133–146 (2013)
4. Park, J.H., Gu, B., Leung, A.C.M., Konana, P.: An investigation of information sharing and seeking behaviors in online investment communities. Comput. Hum. Behav. **31**, 1–12 (2014)
5. Ardichvili, A., Page, V., Wentling, T.: Motivation and barriers to participation in virtual knowledge-sharing communities of practice. J. Knowl. Manag. **7**(1), 64–77 (2003)
6. Zhang, X., Liu, S., Deng, Z., Chen, X.: Knowledge sharing motivations in online health communities: a comparative study of health professionals and normal users. Comput. Hum. Behav. **75**, 797–810 (2017)
7. Kankanhalli, A., Tan, B.C., Wei, K.-K.: Contributing knowledge to electronic knowledge repositories: an empirical investigation. MIS Q. **29**(1), 113–143 (2005)
8. Lai, H.-M., Chen, T.T.: Knowledge sharing in interest online communities: a comparison of posters and lurkers. Comput. Hum. Behav. **35**, 295–306 (2014)

9. Wasko, M.M., Faraj, S.: Why should I share? Examining social capital and knowledge contribution in electronic networks of practice. MIS Q. **29**(1), 35–57 (2005)
10. Stewart, K.J.: Trust transfer on the world wide web. Organ. Sci. **14**(1), 5–17 (2003)
11. Morgan, R.M., Hunt, S.D.: The commitment-trust theory of relationship marketing. J. Mark. **58**(3), 20–38 (1994)
12. Pfeil, U., Zaphiris, P.: Investigating social network patterns within an empathic online community for older people. Comput. Hum. Behav. **25**(5), 1139–1155 (2009)
13. Chen, J., Shen, X.-L.: Consumers' decisions in social commerce context: an empirical investigation. Decis. Support Syst. **79**, 55–64 (2015)
14. Lu, Y., Zhao, L., Wang, B.: From virtual community members to C2C e-commerce buyers: trust in virtual communities and its effect on consumers' purchase intention. Electron. Commer. Res. Appl. **9**(4), 346–360 (2010)
15. Wu, J.-J., Chen, Y.-H., Chung, Y.-S.: Trust factors influencing virtual community members: a study of transaction communities. J. Bus. Res. **63**(9), 1025–1032 (2010)
16. Shen, J.: Understanding user's acceptance of social shopping websites: effects of social comparison and trust. In: Zhang, R., Zhang, J., Zhang, Z., Filipe, J., Cordeiro, J. (eds.) ICEIS 2011. LNBIP, vol. 102, pp. 365–373. Springer, Heidelberg (2012). https://doi.org/10.1007/978-3-642-29958-2_24
17. Sussman, S.W., Siegal, W.S.: Informational influence in organizations: an integrated approach to knowledge adoption. Inf. Syst. Res. **14**(1), 47–65 (2003)
18. Yuan, D., Lin, Z., Zhuo, R.: What drives consumer knowledge sharing in online travel communities? Personal attributes or e-service factors? Comput. Hum. Behav. **63**, 68–74 (2016)
19. Yan, Z., Wang, T., Chen, Y., Zhang, H.: Knowledge sharing in online health communities: a social exchange theory perspective. Inf. Manag. **53**(5), 643–653 (2016)
20. Casaló, L.V., Flavián, C., Guinalíu, M.: Determinants of the intention to participate in firm-hosted online travel communities and effects on consumer behavioral intentions. Tour. Manag. **31**(6), 898–911 (2010)
21. Chen, C.-J., Hung, S.-W.: To give or to receive? Factors influencing members' knowledge sharing and community promotion in professional virtual communities. Inf. Manag. **47**(4), 226–236 (2010)
22. http://www.smartpls.com. Accessed (2015)
23. Hair, J.F., Sarstedt, M., Hopkins, L., Kuppelwieser, V.G.: Partial least squares structural equation modeling (PLS-SEM): an emerging tool in business research. Eur. Bus. Rev. **26**(2), 106–121 (2014)

Compliment Rules or Compliments Rule? A Population-Level Study of Appearance Commenting Norms on Social Media

Erica Åberg, Aki Koivula[✉], Iida Kukkonen, Outi Sarpila, and Tero Pajunen

Economic Sociology, Faculty of Social Science, University of Turku, Turku, Finland
{ermaab, akjeko, iltkuk, outi.sarpila, teaapa}@utu.fi

Abstract. This study examines norms concerning appearance-related commenting on social media. More specifically, the focus of this study is on the approvability of positively commenting on other people's physical appearance, commenting on other people's dressing style and commenting on the appearance of public figures. We examined how these norms are predicted by gender and social media usage patterns, while considering also a set of control variables, including age. We approach these questions with unique data, which is nationally representative of the Finnish population aged 18–74 (N = 3,724). Our study offers insights into the discussion on the relationship between social media and appearance-related norms. Our findings suggest a generally positive attitude towards commenting on other people's appearance if the comment is positive, with almost half of the respondents approving such commenting. By contrast, commenting on someone's clothing or commenting on the appearance of public figures is considerably less acceptable, with only 20% approving. Our findings reveal that gender, preferred social networking site and age are associated with appearance commenting norms. Women are more likely to approve of positive appearance commentary on social media. However, the propensity to agree on the approvability of appearance commentary is higher for men when it comes to commenting on other people's dressing or public figures' appearances. Overall, the users of Instagram and Facebook seem more liberal towards appearance-related comments as compared to those who do not use social media or use other platforms. Additionally, young people were more positive about appearance commenting in all of these aspects.

Keywords: Appearance-related norms · Online communities · Social media · Instagram · Facebook

1 Introduction

Recent research on body image and social media has emphasized that social networking sites (SNS) offer a central space for engaging in appearance-related social comparisons and appraisals [1, 2]. In the era of so-called selfie culture, internet users are thus considered to face increasing appearance-related pressures and dissatisfaction

G. Meiselwitz (Ed.): HCII 2020, LNCS 12195, pp. 16–28, 2020.
https://doi.org/10.1007/978-3-030-49576-3_2

with their bodies [3]. Just like the consumption of more traditional media such as magazines, exposure to images of idealized bodies online has been associated with the internalization of thin body ideals, appearance comparison and weight dissatisfaction [2, 4].

At the same time, social media has become an important arena for challenging norms regarding physical appearance and binary gender norms. Pertaining to body image, social movements such as fat activism and body positivity are thriving on social media, and are challenging narrow definitions of heteronormative beauty ideals, celebrating bodily diversity, and importantly, advocating for self-acceptance [5, 6]. While social media offers a wide range of different bodily references, it also predisposes individuals to appearance commenting. It may be argued that our extremely visual culture combined with the basic idea of social media - enabling dialogue between people - composes a paradox of people's appearance being evaluated and discussed freely.

Previous research has mainly concentrated on individual responses to appearance commenting. There is a lack of research considering societal-level social rules, i.e. norms, related to appearance-related commenting on social media. More precisely, we do not know to what extent it is normatively allowed to comment on other people's appearance on social media. Previous studies have mostly focused on the effects that exposure to photographs and receiving appearance-related comments have on an individual's body image. These studies have shown that appearance feedback has a crucial impact on appearance satisfaction [1, 7–10]. Thus, it is crucial to examine the acceptability of appearance-related commenting as these attitudes maintain the status quo, where especially women's physical appearance is subject to constant evaluation and comments.

We begin with a brief discussion about the role of physical appearance and gendered norms regarding it in contemporary society. After that, we discuss the impact of social media on individual body image. Then, we move on to describe our data and present the results. We end with a summarising discussion and conclusions.

2 The Norms Concerning Appearance Comments on Social Media

2.1 The Importance of Physical Appearance in Visualised Culture

Appearance is an integral part of everyday interaction. People make inferences and judgements of others based on looks, and utilize their own appearances to communicate belonging to social groups and to make distinctions on the other hand. While this is not new, certain social, economic and political tendencies of contemporary consumer cultures appear to increase the significance of physical appearance [11]. Scholars of consumer culture proclaim that physical appearance has become an essential expression of personal identity in postmodern societies. Individuals are thought to project their inner selves with their looks and construct their very identities through consumption [12, 13]. This logic of consumer culture is considered universal and gendered: everyone is called upon to invest in their appearances in order to comply with the appearance-related norms, i.e. social rules of consumer society, such as having a fit body [14]. Much like any norms, appearance-related norms are upheld through social sanctions. These sanctions range from subtle, non-verbal or verbal hints to more tangible perks and penalties for (non-)adherence to norms, including social and economic ones (for a review, see e.g. [15]). On social media, adherence to appearance-related norms is often verbalized in the forms of comments or likes.

2.2 The Gendered Logic of Appearance Commenting

Despite the ethos of consumer culture, there is a widespread consensus that physical appearance is a more constitutive part of life for women than it is for men. The most often used and generally accepted framework for understanding the centrality of physical appearance for women is the sociocultural theory, which claims that contemporary beauty ideals are reinforced and sustained by sociocultural influences, most notably parents, peers and media [16]. Feminist scholars, in particular, have long proclaimed physical appearance is more salient to identities and self-esteem of women, as women are socialized to be more concerned with their appearances than men and more often judged by their appearance [17]. Women face stricter societal norms when it comes to physical appearance [11], and failing to fulfil the societal ideals of beauty comes with psychological costs [17].

Prior research reveals a tendency for women to receive compliments on their appearance and to compliment on each other's appearance [18], whereas men seem more likely to trade insults [19]. Actually, "competitive verbal abuse" among men and boys may be regarded as signs of male solidarity [20]. A study about appearance commentary in prime-time television [21] found that although male and female characters comment equally on other characters' appearance, female characters are twice as likely to be the recipients of those comments. Male characters more likely insult other males and compliment females, whereas female characters insult and compliment female and male characters with equal frequency (ibid.).

These gendered discourse patterns also carry over to social media use. For example, Hyart, Lesser & Azran (2017) found evidence of men's assertive and dominant discourse style and social role versus on social media, as compared to women's more cooperative and supportive discourse style: men wrote more posts, while women commented on other people's posts. Another study confirmed that females are significantly more likely to 'Like' posts, to post a public reply and express stronger emotional support towards a Facebook status update than males [22] as well as post twice as many comments and updates on Facebook in comparison to men [23].

2.3 Physical Appearance and Social Media

A casual scroll through Instagram will offer a glimpse to the seemingly perfect lives of women with perfect bodies. These photos are usually accompanied by admiring sighs of (usually female) followers; "I wish I had your body", "I love your hair", "You are so #goals". Previous research on physical appearance and social media has mainly relied on objectification theory [24], which claims that women see themselves as objects, i.e. are dependent upon the approving gaze of others. Additionally, women are said to make social comparisons of themselves [25, 26], and consequently, the socially con- structed, normative ideals of beauty are more critical to the self-images of women. Some claim that in a contemporary individualistic culture, selfies' characteristic focus on the body reifies hegemonic beauty norms and invokes the male gaze [27].

Scholars of body image, such as Tiggemann and Barbato [28] claim that objecti- fication theory may be particularly relevant in the context of a photographic social media site like Instagram. According to their study, Instagram is inherently objecti- fying, as its main function is to post photographs of oneself precisely to be looked at and commented on. The photos and the comments received are publicly visible to one's audience, which may increase the experienced dissatisfaction towards one's appear- ance. Instagram is known for its visual features and pervasive commenting norms (ibid.).

However, previous research has mainly concentrated on individual responses on the norms regarding the acceptability of commenting on other people's appearance seem a rather understudied subject in this field. The social acceptability of (mainly positive) commenting on other people's appearance in online forums could also be the driving force on normalizing these conventions on social media, not because people insist other people commenting on them. The comments possibly aim to not make the person feel bad about his/her appearance for the lack of positive comments, but also to obey the platform's commenting norms. These norms appear rather different from offline con- texts, where positive appearance commenting is less frequent and normatively less expected in peer communication.

Despite the prevailing norm of giving positive feedback to friends for their appearance, it is worth noting that positive appearance-related comments can also cause body dissatisfaction. The consequences for negative appearance comments in adoles- cent girls and adult women are well documented: commenting causes, for example, body dissatisfaction, reduced psychological wellbeing and eating disorders [7, 8]. Somewhat counterintuitively, positive appearance-related comments on Instagram photos can also cause body dissatisfaction and have been associated with self- objectification in adolescent and young adult women [1, 10, 28]. Comments lead to increased awareness of appearance and thus encourage girls and women to adopt an objectifying perspective of themselves (on objectification theory, see [24]). Moreover, it appears that just as offline appearance conversations among friends play a pivotal role in the reinforcement of appearance ideals [29], appearance comments on social net- working sites might merely offer a novel medium with negative consequences for women's body dissatisfaction. Studies involving both boys and girls suggest that conversations about appearance-related topics bolster the idea that emulating the ideal appearance of media figures would lead to various positive things, such as popularity and romantic success [30].

It is also apparent that different individuals use social media for different purposes and therefore react to comments and other feedback differently. Fox and Vendemia [31] posited that selective self-presentation on social media enables women with negative body image and low self-esteem to get positive feedback from their peers. Additionally, it has been stated that highly visual social media has the ability to empower users [32], as networked technologies allow for capturing and sharing embodied experience. It has been stated that groups that have previously been objectified and denied agency may take charge of the way they are portrayed [27]. Young women, in particular, may use networked technologies to develop "selfie esteem", building confidence by successful online self-presentation [6].

Despite such enabling and empowering features, there is a reason to be critical. For example, Mills et al. [33] claim that the possibility for selective self-presentation, i.e. retaking and retouching a selfie before posting it on social media for others to see and comment on, actually harmed self-image. Tiggemann and Miller [4] state, that even though photo-editing might increase a sense of control for one's online appearance for a while, it actually made women feel more dissatisfied about the digitally altered aspects of their appearance. Solely browsing through other people's images with positive appearance comments on Instagram photos had negative consequences on women's body image and lead to greater body dissatisfaction [28].

To conclude, a great abundance of the studies on the outcomes of (positive or negative) appearance commenting focus on women, who appear to be more prone to give and receive such comments. Appearance-related comments are usually intended to make a woman feel good or to lift her spirit (for example "You look good", "I would love to have your body", or "That looks good on you"), and usually, the commentators are female peers. The comments are clearly gendered, as directed at a man they might seem a bit peculiar, whereas posed for a woman they appear as normal "girl talk" on social media. Further, selfie-culture and the possibility to encouragingly comment or "like" other people's photos, incorporates a (dis)empowerment paradox, where "personal expressions of beauty may feel empowering at the same moment as those expressions may conform to, and thus reinforce, hegemonic and oppressive cultural norms" [27]. Additionally, compliments, especially ones associated with weight and shape, have negative outcomes also beyond the individuals giving and receiving them. The seemingly innocuous comments also reflect societal norms regarding physical appearance, such as fat prejudice [9, 34].

3   This Study

With this previously introduced literature in mind, we propose the following research questions:

RQ1: Do men and women equally approve of appearance-related commenting on social media?

RQ2: Do social media platforms differ in the extent to which their users approve of appearance-related commenting on social media?

RQ3: Is the approval of appearance-related commenting on social media equally gendered among users of different social media platforms?

4 Data and Methods

4.1 Participants

Our data are derived from the survey "Finland in the digital age". A total of 2,470 participants aged 18–74 were from the initial sample of 8,000 Finnish-speakers collected randomly from the Finnish census. Additionally, the data were improved with 1,254 participants (also aged 18–74) from a nationally representative online panel of volunteer respondents administrated by a market research company. The final data included a total of 3,724 respondents of which 66% comes from the probability sample and 34% from the nonprobability sample.

4.2 Measures

We provide information on the measurements and descriptive statistics for all the variables used in the further analyses in Table 1. As for the dependent variable, we used three variables formed on the basis of the following statements:

- It's alright to comment on another person's appearance on social media if the comment is positive
- It's alright to comment on another person's appearance on social media if the comment concerns dressing rather than physical traits
- It's alright to comment on another person's appearance on social media if that person a public figure

In the formation of statements, we consider the potential social desirability bias by inquiring into general commentary instead of the respondent's own commentary. The first statement takes into account that also positive commentary can be problematic for social media users and make them feel dissatisfied and insecure [28]. The second statement assumes that it may be more acceptable to comment on dressing, which is more related to people's own choices, whereas physical attributes may have elements that people cannot choose. The final statement consists of the idea that people can, in a certain way, view public figures free of general norms and rules, which may make commenting on their appearance more acceptable than usual [35].

The responses were asked via 5-point Likert scales in which "1 = Completely disagree", "2", "3 = Do not disagree", "4", and "5 = Completely agree". In the analysis, we recoded the variable by combining values 1–2 into the category "Disagree", 3 into the category "Neutral", and 4–5 into the category "Agree".

As for independent variables, we used gender and the preferred social network site. Gender was asked via three categories, but due to lack of observations from others than men or women we focused only binary level differences and deleted the "other" category from the analyses. We were especially interested in differences between the users of Facebook and Instagram platforms. Accordingly, we separated the respondents who only use Facebook from those who use both Facebook and Instagram or solely Instagram. Moreover, those respondents who did not use Facebook or Instagram, but used some other SNS, we classified into the category "Other".

Table 1. Descriptive statistics for the applied variables

Variable	Obs.	Prop./Mean	Min	Max
Variable 1	3,634		1	3
It's alright to comment on another person's appearance on social media if the comment is positive				
Disagree		.25		
Neutral		.38		
Agree		.37		
Variable 2	3,647		1	3
It's alright to comment on another person's appearance on social media if the comment concerns dressing rather than physical traits				
Disagree		.44		
Neutral		.39		
Agree		.18		
Variable 3	3,642		1	3
It's alright to comment on another person's appearance on social media if that person a public figure				
Disagree		.45		
Neutral		.39		
Agree		.16		
Gender	3,706		0	1
Male		.50		
Female		.50		
The preferred SNS	3,724		1	3
Else/None		.38		
Facebook		.31		
Instagram		.31		
Age	3,711	51.5	18	74

We controlled for the age of participants throughout the analyses. We determined respondents' age via an open-ended question in which the respondents reported their year of birth.

4.3 Analysis Strategy

In the first phase of the empirical study, we analyzed the gender and platform differences in experiencing appearance-related pressures on social media. Secondly, we analyzed the modifying effects of the preferred SNS on the gender differences by comparing whether the association of SNS is similar among men and women. Finally, in the statistical model, we tested the associations by employing multinomial logistic regression and held the control variable (age) as constant. Accordingly, the models were equated with respect to each hypothesis:

$$H1:\ P(Y) = X1 + C1$$
$$H2:\ P(Y) = X2 + C1$$
$$H3:\ P(Y) = X1 + X2 + X1 * X2 + C1$$

Here the Y refers to the probability of agreeing with appearance-related commenting on social media. X1 stands for gender. C1 means age, and it is handled as a covariate in each model. Finally, X2 means the preferred social network site.

The analyses were performed with the Stata 15.1 program. We presented the main results of hypotheses as relative risk ratios (rrr) with statistical significances. In order to illustrate the effects in more interpretable and descriptive manner, we post-estimated the estimations as predicted probabilities and showed them in figures by utilizing the coefplot package [36].

5 Results

5.1 Descriptive Analysis

We begin our analysis by descriptively examining the distribution of variables. The results are presented in Fig. 1. As shown in the figure, there is a generally positive attitude towards commenting on appearance, with over 40% agreeing with a claim if

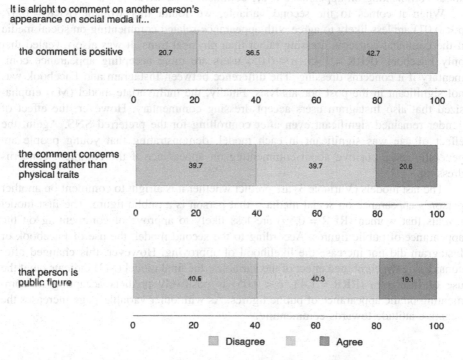

Fig. 1. Appearance-related commenting on social media: descriptive distribution of responses for three categories, %

the comment is positive. By contrast, commenting on dressing is generally not considered very acceptable, with only 21% agreeing to the claim. Similarly, only 19% approved commenting on the appearance of public figures.

5.2 Explorative Analysis

Table 2 reveals the results of multinomial logit models alternately for each dependent variable from 1–3. We begin with variable 1. According to model 1, women (RRR = 1.42; p < 0.01) are more likely to agree with appearance-related commenting on social media if the comment is positive. The model 2 indicates that both Facebook (RRR = 1.90; p < 0.01) and Instagram (RRR = 2.27; p < 0.01) users are more accepting appearance commentary. Post hoc analysis revealed that the difference between Instagram and Facebook users was not statistically significant. The model 3 is made up to indicate the multivariate effects of gender, the preferred SNS and their interaction. The model reveals that the effect of gender was indirect through the social media platform as women (RRR = 1.09; p > 0.05) were less likely to approve of positive commentary. However, we could not find a significant interaction effect between gender and social media platform. In this sense, we can argue that women are more active in using SNS, which partially explains their attitude towards positive commentary when compared to men. As the table shows, the effect of age was significant in each model, demonstrating that young people are generally more positive about commenting on appearance if the comment is positive.

When it comes to the second variable, we found that women (RRR = 0.57; p < 0.01) are less likely to agree with appearance-related commenting on social media if the comment concerns dressing rather than physical traits. It was also revealed that only Facebook (RRR = 1.45; p < 0.05) users are more accepting appearance commentary if it concerns dressing. The difference between Instagram and Facebook was not significant in the post hoc analysis. Finally, the multivariate model (M3) emphasized that also Instagram users accept dressing commentary. However, the effect of gender remained significant even after controlling for the preferred SNS. Again, the effect of age was significant in each model, demonstrating that young people are generally more positive about commenting on appearance if the comment concerns dressing.

The last models (Variable 3) are predict whether it is alright to comment on another person's appearance on social media if that person is a public figure. The first model reveals that women (RRR = 0.39) are less likely to approve of commenting on the appearance of public figures. According to the second model, the use of Facebook or Instagram did not increase the likelihood of approving. However, this changed after considering the combined effect of the variables: the final model (M3) indicates that the use of Instagram (RRR = 1.43, p < 0.05) is positively predicts accepting of commenting on the appearance of public figures. As with other variables, age increases the negative attitude towards commenting.

Table 2. Predicting agreeing with an appearance-related commenting on social media. Relative risk ratios with standard errors derived from multinomial logit models.

	Variable 1			Variable 2			Variable 3		
	M1	M2	M3	M1	M2	M3	M1	M2	M3
Female	1.42**		1.09	0.57**		0.55**	0.40**		0.39**
	(0.14)		(0.18)	(0.05)		(0.11)	(0.04)		(0.09)
Facebook		1.90**	1.58**		1.45**	1.47*		1.12	1.20
		(0.23)	(0.26)		(0.19)	(0.24)		(0.15)	(0.20)
Instagram		2.27**	2.05**		1.26	1.45*		1.13	1.43*
		(0.29)	(0.37)		(0.17)	(0.25)		(0.15)	(0.24)
Female #Facebook			1.43			1.05			1.04
			(0.34)			(0.28)			(0.30)
Female #Instagram			1.13			0.95			0.94
			(0.28)			(0.24)			(0.26)
Age	0.94**	0.94**	0.94**	0.95**	0.95**	0.95**	0.94**	0.94**	0.94**
	(0.00)	(0.00)	(0.00)	(0.00)	(0.00)	(0.00)	(0.00)	(0.00)	(0.00)
Observations	3,616	3,624	3,616	3,629	3,637	3,629	3,624	3,632	3,624

Variable 1: "It's alright to comment on another person's appearance on social media if the comment is positive"
Variable 2: "It's alright to comment on another person's appearance on social media if the comment concerns dressing rather than physical traits"
Variable 3: "It's alright to comment on another person's appearance on social media if that person a public figure"
Relative risk ratios for response "Agree" when "Disagree" is held as a base category
Standard errors in parentheses **$p < 0.01$, *$p < 0.05$

6   Discussion

In this study, we examined the approvability of commenting on other people's physical appearance in a variety of situations on social media. We examined how these norms are predicted by gender and social media usage patterns, while also considering a set of control variables.

We found that men are more likely to approve appearance-related commenting on social media when it comes to comments that concern style or a public figure. This might reflect a "male gaze" on the online content. Men may perceive appearance-related commenting differently from women, as they are not exposed to appearance commenting to the same extent that women are. They might consider these comments as something that has relevance for women, as women place more importance on how they look. Women, on the other hand, are more likely to make social comparisons and objectify themselves, which results in feelings of appearance dissatisfaction. As such feelings are more familiar to women, who are socialized to place more importance on their appearance, they even might feel morally obligated to give appearance-related compliments. Indeed we found that women are more approving of appearance-related compliments on social media.

It is well known that women face stricter appearance-related norms than men, and that women are more likely than men to form their self-esteem on social comparisons [28, 33]. Normative ideals of beauty reinforce a very narrow definition of beauty which is almost impossible to achieve and as such, creates bodily dissatisfaction. Appearance-related comments are partly responsible for bolstering these norms on social media, as they verbally define the socially approved content by complimenting on certain appearances and thus causing appearance pressures for those who are unable to meet these requirements [28].

We found users of Instagram and Facebook are more liberal when it comes to appearance-related comments, as compared to those who use other platforms or are not active social media users. Users of Instagram were the most approving towards appearance-related commenting, however, the differences between Instagram and Facebook users were not statistically significant. This is somewhat surprising, seeing that Instagram is considered *the* platform for appearance-related social comparisons. Instagram also allows for larger imagined audiences and is more "selfie-centred" than Facebook. According to previous research, it also generates more appearance-related pressures than Facebook [37].

Overall, we found the norms regarding appearance commenting seem rather unambiguous: appearance commenting on social media is considered acceptable by the relative majority of our respondents if the comment is positive. Yet according to previous studies, this norm too endangers the wellbeing of many people, who are at the risk of experiencing appearance-related disturbances, such as body dissatisfactions, eating disorders or lowered mood [7, 8]. Therefore, our findings merit consideration and need to be addressed in more detail.

It is worth noting that our results do not reveal whether our respondents themselves comment on other people's appearances online, or had just paid attention to other people's behaviour. Thus, the responses reveal the normative status quo on social networking sites, not personal behaviour or preferences. Platforms like Instagram have their own established practices that encourage appearance commenting, which may reinforce the acceptability of such commenting, as comments can become customary and even a necessary part of communication. In a social environment where appearance-related commenting is customary, not receiving compliments may also be a source of appearance dissatisfaction. Thus, users may comment on their peers' appearances to make peers feel good about themselves and also to obey the platform's commenting norms. These norms appear rather different from offline contexts, where positive appearance commenting is less frequent and normatively less expected in peer-to-peer communication. Instagram has rather frequently discussed possibilities of hiding the number of "likes" and blocking unwanted commentary in order to keep Instagram "a positive space for self-presentation". Considering the results of this study, as well as previous studies concerning the harms of appearance-related commenting, the development of policies to limit likes and commenting or to make it private appear worth considering for platforms such as Facebook as well.

The novelty value of our research lies in applying nationally representative data to study the unexplored topic of appearance commenting norms on social media. Future research could delve deeper into these gendered social media norms, and for example, use split-ballot designs to consider whether norms are different depending on the gender of the commentator and the gender of the person receiving the comment.

References

1. Slater, A., Tiggemann, M.: Media exposure, extracurricular activities, and appearance-related comments as predictors of female adolescents' self-objectification. Psychol. Women Q. **39**(3), 375–389 (2015)
2. Holland, G., Tiggemann, M.: A systematic review of the impact of the use of social networking sites on body image and disordered eating outcomes. Body Image **17**, 100–110 (2016)
3. Tiggemann, M., Slater, A.: NetGirls: the internet, facebook, and body image concern in adolescent girls. Int. J. Eat. Disord. **46**(6), 630–633 (2013)
4. Tiggemann, M., Miller, J.: The Internet and adolescent girls' weight satisfaction and drive for thinness. Sex Roles **63**(1–2), 79–90 (2010)
5. Sastre, A.: Towards a radical body positive: reading the online "body positive movement". Fem. Media Stud. **14**(6), 929–943 (2014)
6. Gill, R., Elias, A.S.: 'Awaken your incredible': love your body discourses and postfeminist contradictions. Int. J. Media Cult. Polit. **10**(2), 179–188 (2014)
7. Melioli, T., Rodgers, R.F., Rodrigues, M., Chabrol, H.: The role of body image in the relationship between Internet use and bulimic symptoms: three theoretical frameworks. Cyberpsychol. Behav. Soc. Netw. **18**(11), 682–686 (2015)
8. Webb, H.J., Zimmer-Gembeck, M.J.: The role of friends and peers in adolescent body dissatisfaction: a review and critique of 15 years of research. J. Res. Adolesc. **24**(4), 564–590 (2014)
9. Calogero, R.M., Herbozo, S., Thompson, J.K.: Complimentary weightism: the potential costs of appearance-related commentary for women's self-objectification. Psychol. Women Q. **33**(1), 120–132 (2009)
10. Tiggemann, M., Boundy, M.: Effect of environment and appearance compliment on college women's self-objectification, mood, body shame, and cognitive performance. Psychol. Women Q. **32**(4), 399–405 (2008)
11. Sarpila, O., Koivula, A., Kukkonen, I., Åberg, E., Pajunen, T.: Double standards in the accumulation and utilisation of 'aesthetic capital'. Poetics (2020, accepted for publication)
12. Bauman, Z.: Consuming Life. Polity Press, Cambridge (2007)
13. Featherstone, M.: Consumer Culture and Postmodernism. Sage, Thousand Oaks (2007)
14. Sassatelli, R.: Fitness Culture: Gyms and the Commercialisation of Discipline and Fun. Palgrave Macmillan, Hampshire (2010)
15. Anderson, T.L., Grunert, C., Katz, A., Lovascio, S.: Aesthetic capital: a research review on beauty perks and penalties. Sociol. Compass **4**(8), 564–575 (2010)
16. Thompson, J.K., Heinberg, L.J., Altabe, M., Tantleff-Dunn, S.: Sociocultural theory: the media and society. In: Exacting Beauty: Theory, Assessment, and Treatment of Body Image Disturbance, pp. 85–124 (1999)
17. Wolf, N.: The Beauty Myth: How Images of Beauty Are Used Against Women. Random House, New York (1991)
18. Janet, H.: Complimenting: a positive politeness strategy. In: Language and Gender: A Reader (1998)

19. Holmes, J.: Compliments and compliment responses in New Zealand English. Anthropol. Linguist. **28**, 485–508 (1986)
20. Talbot, M.M.: Language and Gender. An Introduction. Polity Press, Cambridge (1998)
21. Lauzen, M.M., Dozier, D.M.: You look mahvelous: an examination of gender and appearance comments in the 1999–2000 prime-time season. Sex Roles **46**(11–12), 429–437 (2002)
22. Joiner, R., et al.: Publically different, privately the same: gender differences and similarities in response to Facebook status updates. Comput. Hum. Behav. **39**, 165–169 (2014)
23. Wang, Y.C., Burke, M., Kraut, R.E.: Gender, topic, and audience response: an analysis of user-generated content on Facebook. In: Human Factors in Computing Systems (2013)
24. Fredrickson, B.L., Roberts, T.: Objectification theory: toward understanding women's lived experiences and mental health risks. Psychol. Women Q. **21**(2), 173–206 (1997)
25. Leahey, T.M., Crowther, J.H., Mickelson, K.D.: The frequency, nature, and effects of naturally occurring appearance-focused social comparisons. Behav. Ther. **38**(2), 132–143 (2007)
26. McMullin, J.A., Cairney, J.: Self-esteem and the intersection of age, class, and gender. J. Aging Stud. **18**(1), 75–90 (2004)
27. Barnard, S.R.: Spectacles of self(ie) empowerment? Networked individualism and the logic of the (post)feminist selfie. In: Communication and Information Technologies Annual: [New] Media Cultures, pp. 63–88. Emerald Group Publishing Limited (2016)
28. Tiggemann, M., Barbato, I.: "You look great!": the effect of viewing appearance-related Instagram comments on women's body image. Body Image **27**, 61–66 (2018)
29. Clark, L., Tiggemann, M.: Appearance culture in nine- to 12-year-old girls: media and peer influences on body dissatisfaction. Soc. Dev. **15**(4), 628–643 (2006)
30. Trekels, J., Ward, L.M., Eggermont, S.: I "like" the way you look: how appearance-focused and overall Facebook use contribute to adolescents' self-sexualization. Comput. Hum. Behav. **81**, 198–208 (2018)
31. Fox, J., Vendemia, M.A.: Selective self-presentation and social comparison through photographs on social networking sites. Cyberpsychol. Behav. Soc. Netw. **19**(10), 593–600 (2016)
32. Tiidenberg, K., Cruz, E.G.: Selfies, image and the re-making of the body. Body Soc. **21**(4), 77–102 (2015)
33. Mills, J.S., Musto, S., Williams, L., Tiggemann, M.: "Selfie" harm: effects on mood and body image in young women. Body Image **27**, 86–92 (2018)
34. Vartanian, L.R., Peter, H.C., Janet, P.: Implicit and explicit attitudes toward fatness and thinness: the role of the internalization of societal standards. Body Image **2**(4), 373–381 (2005)
35. Marwick, A.E.: Scandal or sex crime? Gendered privacy and the celebrity nude photo leaks. Ethics Inf. Technol. **19**(3), 177–191 (2017)
36. Jann, B.: Plotting regression coefficients and other estimates. Stata J. **14**(4), 708–737 (2014)
37. Åberg, E., Koivula, A., Kukkonen, I.: A feminine burden of perfection? Appearance-related pressures on social networking sites. Telemat. Inf. **46**, 101–319 (2020)

Understanding Open Collaboration
of Wikipedia Good Articles

Huichen Chou[1]([⊠]) [iD], Donghui Lin[1] [iD], Toru Ishida[2] [iD],
and Naomi Yamashita[3]

[1] Department of Social Informatics, Kyoto University, Kyoto 606-8501, Japan
chou.huichen.33e@st.kyoto-u.ac.jp
[2] School of Creative Science and Engineering, Waseda University,
Tokyo 169-8555, Japan
[3] NTT Communication Science Labs, Kyoto 619-0237, Japan

Abstract. Contents created by open collaboration online is an important knowledge source to the modern society nowadays. Wikipedia is a prime example which can match the quality of professional encyclopedias. Yet the percentage good quality articles are low. So how different sized teams yield similar quality work is unclear such as articles of the same Wikipedia category. By identifying different editors and studying the collaboration with the work process of Wikipedia Good Articles (GAs), one can understand how different teams create quality work in open collaboration online. To distinguish editors, this research denotes their editing activity categories and subject the editing activities to factor analysis to obtain editor characteristics in the form of quantitative scores. Then we study the collaboration by investigating editors' engagement in the work creation process along with the article size changes. The result shows the GAs creation are largely done by editors of high scored in content-shaping characteristic. In a short period prior to GA nomination, these editors suddenly appear to work and increases the article's size to the completed GA level. Editors without dominate editor characteristics are causing the differences in team size. This research contributes to propose a new method to understand how open collaboration creates quality work and the method can easily extend to study more Wikipedia article categories. Last, the research result implies quality work can be assured by expert to work at the end of the creation process in the open collaboration.

Keywords: Crowd intelligence · Collaborative content creation · Wikipedia

1 Introduction

People working collaboratively on online platforms are an important resource for creating social assets [1]. People of different ability and knowledge work together without physical constraints. The "wisdom of crowds" and can tackle highly complex tasks such as creating knowledge and Wikipedia is a prime example [2]. Wikipedia has huge participation numbers and creates hundreds of thousands of articles every year [3]. Wikipedia's content can match the quality of professional encyclopedias [4] but the overall quality issue is a concern [6]. According to a Wiki quality project [5],

G. Meiselwitz (Ed.): HCII 2020, LNCS 12195, pp. 29–43, 2020.
https://doi.org/10.1007/978-3-030-49576-3_3

Wikipedia articles can be graded into different quality levels and only around 0.6% of the articles are recognized as Good Articles (GA) level or above. GA requirement includes: well written with no obvious mistakes and approaching the quality of a professional encyclopedia. Wikipedia articles quality has attracted much research interests. Previous researches have focused on the composition of editing activities and type of editors in yielding better quality [2, 7–9] and some have examined the impact of additional editors and editor diversity on article quality [8, 13]. Yet it is not known how different sized teams yield similar quality work – the GAs of the same Wikipedia categories which can provides us a better understanding of how open collaboration works.

To find the answer, we propose, in addition to identify different editors, we also study the collaboration with work process. This is because work process has impact on performance [14]. For Wikipedia, however, the work process and how it can yield good quality content remains unidentified. In order to gain more understanding on how open collaboration can achieve Wikipedia GA, and to provide references for open collaboration system design, we propose to fill the previous research gap by focusing on single Wikipedia category to represent similar quality works and we choose a general topic - the "US state parks" which do not require specific knowledge to demonstrate our approach. Our research approach can be easily extended to study other categories and different quality levels of Wikipedia articles.

To distinguish editors, we denote their editing activities categories based on Pfeil's method which has semantic considerations [10]. In addition, we are inspired by the psychology research of Cattell-Horn-Carroll with their theory of human cognitive ability [11], we subject the editing activities to factor analysis to obtain editor characteristics in the form of quantitative scores. We have identified the following editor characteristics: content-shaping for creating article content; copy-editing that improves the writing; indexing that links articles to the Wikipedia category; reversion, which fights vandalism; vandalism, which damages articles; and link fixing which is the activity of fix link. Each editor receives scores in each editor characteristics.

Our result shows the GAs creation work are largely done by editors of high scored in content-shaping characteristic. In addition, editors without dominate editor characteristics are causing the differences in team size. We found that it can be years, these editors perform scant editing activities each on the article and the article size generally remains low. Then in few months prior to GA nomination, the strong content-shaping characteristic editor suddenly appears to work and increases the article's size to the completed GA level. In some cases, this editor might also have strong copy-editing ability that allows her/him to finish the GA singlehandedly. In some cases, another editor with high copy-editing ability appears to improve the writing during this pre-nomination period. This finding is in line with previous research by Zhang et al. who found there is sudden increasing and centralized in editing activities before GA nomination passed. Their research also confirms this phenomenon only exist in GA creation and does not exist in the Wikipedia articles of lower quality levels [12].

This main contributes to of this paper are as follows:

- We contribute a new method to understand how open collaboration creates quality by identifying editor's characteristics and exploring editor appearance sequence in the working process along article size changes.
- The research finds quality work can be assured by expert-the high scored content-shaping characteristic editor who mainly work at the end of the GA can finish of GA creation in Wikipedia "US state park" GA case. A large number of different participants might not be needed for creating quality work.
- The strong content-shaping characteristic editors can be recruited to create more GAs of the same Wikipedia category so to increase the overall quality of Wikipedia articles in the Wikipedia US state park case.

2 Related Work

2.1 Wikipedia Quality Measurement

This study exploits the advantages of the Wikipedia:WikiProject Wikipedia/Assessment as many related work of Wikipedia quality. Wikipedia/Assessment is a WikiProject that focuses on assessing the quality of Wikipedia-related articles [5]. The project department evaluates the quality of articles with a rating system and gives them banners on their talk page to reflect assessment results. This system helps users recognize an article's quality and the excellent contributions of editors as well as identifying articles that need further work.

The rating system consists of the following seven levels written in ascending order of quality: Stub, Start, C-class, B-class, Good Articles (GA), A-class, and Featured Articles (FA). Wikipedia gives a detailed list of the criteria for these levels. A Featured Article is defined as follows: "A featured article exemplifies the very best work and is distinguished by professional standards of writing, presentation, and sourcing." GAs are "Useful to nearly all readers, with no obvious problems; approaching (but not equaling) the quality of a professional encyclopedia." B-class: "Readers are not left wanting, although the content may not be complete enough to satisfy a serious student or researcher." The assessment is done by impartial reviewers.

In our paper, we also use the quality assessment categories defined by Wikipedia: WikiProject Wikipedia/Assessment. Previous Wikipedia quality studies [2, 7] using this quality assessment rating system have been performed. Especially we focused on GA as being indicative of quality work present in online open collaboration output. The GA assessment is "well-written, comprehensive in coverage, well-researched with proper verifiable references, neutral in viewpoint, stable without any need to be updated often, compliance with Wikipedia style guidelines, and appropriate images and length. We consider FA level is too demanding to meet our research purposes and take GA to indicate practical content of sufficient quality.

2.2   Collaboration Studies for Achieving Higher Quality Wikipedia Articles

Collaboration on Wikipedia and quality relationships have been studied for decades. Wikipedia's success depends on volunteer editors, each of whom does a little bit of work that contribute to slow growth in coverage and article size [15]. Some early study on Wikipedia found that the editors and collaboration are the primary factors determining work quality [7, 16]. Early studies on collaboration tried to find metrics that could quantify article quality such as the number of editors and edits, and types of editing activities etc. These studies did find that quality generally improved with more words, more edits [17], and more surface edits [18]. Subsequent studies started to argue that good editors were needed to produce quality work and focused on understanding them by extracting editors by clustering or identifying their expertise or reputation [9]. Several studies addressed editor diversity and introduced various diversity measurements for achieving better quality [7, 8]. They found that large teams might not produce better work, and were unable to explain how various-sized teams could create similar quality work.

However, no previous work considered how different sized teams could produce content of the same quality – the GAs of the same Wikipedia category. Some works studied Wikipedia quality with focus on editors and sought collaboration patterns of different quality levels. Liu and Ram [7] first classified editors based on their editing activities and identified various collaboration patterns that yielded different levels of article quality. They defined and annotated editing activities into the following four categories: reversion and the insertion, modification, and deletion of sentences, links, and references. They used K-means clustering to identify different types of editors and as well as to identify collaboration patterns based on what types of editing activities were performed by whom. Last, they reported on five types of collaboration patterns and the percentage of different levels of Wikipedia articles that exhibited them. Unfortunately, the research failed to identify a clear collaboration pattern that yielded better quality regardless of editor type; it also provided no clear recommendations for Wikipedia or other open collaboration systems.

The attribute of time is another important element in the creation of quality group works. Only Zhang et al.'s [12] research on Wikipedia editor group behavior considered time; it suggested a common collaboration pattern for GA creation. That is the team increases its activities and focuses on the content a few months before GA nomination expires. Their study, however, did not study how different editors collaborate across the GA creation process timeline. Our approach to understanding the collaboration that yields quality Wikipedia articles is an extension of previous works in several aspects. First, we focus on the GA quality level to investigate the collaboration patterns of different editors. Second, we use factor analysis to extract editor abilities based on their editing activities, and thus find the editor contributions that can clearly identify the differences among editors. Last, we incorporate the sequential activities of editors in the article creation process to represent the collaboration among editors.

3 Method

We propose a two-phase method to study collaboration within teams of editors: phase one: "Distinguish editors" and phase two: "Analyze the collaboration". In phase one, we find out the difference in editors with the factor scores of factor analysis based on their involvement in the creation of GAs in the same Wikipedia category. Then we plot the sequence of their appearance together with article size changes in phase two. We show the overview of our method in Fig. 1. In the following, we detail our approach in Sects. 3.1 and 3.2.

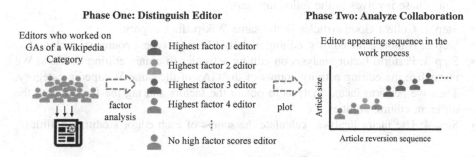

Fig. 1. Two phase method for understanding GAs creation

3.1 Phase One: Distinguish Editor

Editors bring different skills and knowledge to their projects and using such aspects to differentiate the editors helps us understand the source of quality discrepancies [7]. This, however, is difficult to achieve by just observing editing activity type. Since each editor is involved in different activities, it is difficult to explain the differences among them from just the counts of their different editing activities.

We borrow an approach from the psychology field - the "Cattell-Horn-Carroll model" of human cognitive abilities [11]. The model is used to measure human cognitive abilities by performing factor analysis on the correlation of different data sets such as psychological tests, school marks and competence ratings to produce factors - a taxonomy of cognitive abilities. Factor analysis is a multivariable statistical approach for grouping large numbers of primary features and finding their linear combination that yields a global factor. Factor analysis can explore the possible underlying factor structure. Factors are latent variables that observed variables have similar patterns of responses to. Factor loading, the relationship of each variable to the underlying factor, is represented by each variable's contribution to the factor score; it shows on how strongly that variable relates to the factor. By embedding taxonomy as one factor, the factor scores can represent the differences in individual ability for each cognitive ability [19].

Similarly, we use factor analysis techniques to obtain editing abilities from the editing activities of each editor of the same Wikipedia categories. Based on the factor scores of the editing ability of each editor, we can identify editor differences. The factor analysis technique is more suitable for our research than the clustering method. Factor analysis is a multivariable statistical technique that uses the correlation among variables to potentially reduce the number of unobserved variables called factors that can subsequently explain the data. With exploratory factor analysis we can find the editing abilities as the data merge onto factors and score each editor's editing abilities. The k-means technique clusters groups of editors into different types and so limits how well we can understand each editor. In addition, ambiguity exists when choosing the number of clusters. Therefore, we choose a more robust approach that uses factor analysis to obtain editor abilities and thereby gain a better understanding of each editor based on their factor scores.

This phase involves in the following step:

- Step 1: Collect Good Articles in the same Wikipedia category.
- Step 2: Annotate the editors' editing activity (different types) counts of each editor.
- Step 3: Perform factor analysis on editing activities to obtain editing abilities. We normalize the editing activity counts of the GAs of the same Wikipedia category. Then we perform factor analysis to obtain the factors and tag the factors with the different editing abilities.
- Step 4: Use factor analysis, calculate the scores of each editor's editing abilities.

3.2   Phase Two: Analyze Collaboration

Previous studies on the collaboration yielding Wikipedia contents proposed many different metrics [7, 20]. Our approach to collaboration analysis uses the reversion sequences of editors as they appear in the GA creation process. This research investigated team collaboration with the sequence of editors' appearances in the work process from an article's start until it is accepted as a GA candidate. We rank the editors according to their editing ability scores. We highlight the editors of highest scores of each editing ability in the team and present the rest of the editors as one type of editor – low score editor. We also plot the article size over time to give more information for understanding how GAs are created. Last, we compare the collaboration of editors for different Wikipedia articles in the same Wikipedia categories, and perform analyses to conclude how different-sized teams yield work of similar quality yielding a better understanding of how GAs are created.

In phase two, our collaboration analysis method proceeds in the following step:

- Step 1: Plot the sequences of editors as they appear in the GA reversion process. Based on the editing ability scores, we identify the highest score editors of each editing ability and plot the reversion sequence of their appearance in the GA creation process.
- Step 2: Plot the editor sequence together with article size changes.
- Step 3: Find the relationship of major editor (highest content-shaping characteristic editor) appearance in the work sequence and article size changes.
- Step 4: Compare collaboration patterns (Step 3) of different teams.

Our method introduces a novel approach to investigate open collaboration that involves in distinguishing the differences among editors and studying their appearance sequence in the quality work creation. In addition, to the best of our knowledge, we are the first research aim to obtain editing ability of editors of Wikipedia and give each editor factor scores based on factor analysis. This method can also be used as an editor reputation system for other future Wikipedia research as well as other open collaboration research in understanding the worker.

4 Data Setting and Annotation

4.1 Data Selection

To focus on how open collaboration creates quality content, this research exploits the Wikipedia:WikiProject Wikipedia/Assessment; we select Good Articles as quality content. We investigate GAs of the same article category together to eliminate topic related differences. We chose GAs from a general topic, the subcategory of "US state park" from the "Geography and places" category. As it is an example of a topic that does not need editors with deep knowledge and to which anyone can contribute.

We used the 20 GAs of the US state parks of Wikipedia from the Wikipedia Good Articles list as of April 1, 2018 from the Wikipedia GA category list of "national and state parks, nature reserves, conservation areas, and countryside routes" under "Geography and places." We omitted national parks because those articles are much longer than those of state parks.

We also provide the statistical details of the GAs of the research in the Sect. 5 result; they include article names, the number of reversions in the history page, and GA size in bytes.

4.2 Edit Category Construction

Wikipedia editing is regarded as the process of "applying expertise" and the value of performing research based on editing activities is recognized. In addition, we consider semantic labels for editing activity categories since previous research finds that semantic differences can impact article quality [18]. The annotation of articles to analyze editors and collaboration activities started with article creation and continued to their acceptance as a GA nominee.

To determine appropriate categories, we examined the history entries of the view and talk pages of several GAs and observed the changes in the articles between revisions. Based on Pfeil et al.'s [10] defined activity categories, we also followed Pfeil's approach and used the grounded theory approach and extracted the possible categories of editing activities semantically. Since we also performed the category extraction process several times until saturation was reached, our category construction is a variant of Pfeil et al.'s research. We discarded the annotations of style/typography and mark-up language since neither impacts the GA standard, and the US state park GAs do not have these activities. This paper adds a semantic of link activity with finer granularity of add links in the content, add links in the reference, and add links in the category of the article. We also added a talk page, which is a critical editing activity that represents collaboration cost. This yielded the following 14 activity categories:

- Format: contribution that alters the appearance or structure of the whole page.
- Add information: additions to topic-related information.
- Delete information: removal of topic-related information.
- Clarify Information: rewording of existing information.
- Correct spelling: correction of spelling.
- Correct grammar: correction of grammar.
- Reversion: reuse of earlier version, which is normally triggered by the undo button on the editing history page.
- Fix link: modification of existing links and changing dead links to correct web address links, including changing the text of link addresses.
- Delete link: removal of existing links.
- Vandalism: entries/actions that damage the page.
- Use of talk page: messages left by editors on it.
- Add links to the category: addition of links in the article's category section.
- Add links in content: addition of them in article's main content.
- Add links in reference: addition of them to the article's reference section.

We manually annotated these activities from the differences among revision pages in this research. This is because the current automated categorization system offers accuracy of 0.643 in terms of the semantic annotation on Wikipedia articles [21]. We expect with the continuous advancement of automation on sematic annotation, the extension of this research can cover much larger numbers of Wikipedia categories in the future.

In addition, our annotation is based on the revision history pages and the record of different activities on each page. If there were two "add information" activities in different parts of the content of one revision history page, we counted them as one activity to reduce the counting ambiguity created by extracting multiple bits of information to describe one single issue.

4.3   Using Factor Analysis to Obtain Editing Characteristics

In order to perform factor analysis on the data, we normalized the editing activity counts based on the article and activity categories. Since the numbers of editors and editing activities exhibit a large variance among articles, we normalized the original data of the edit activity counts by dividing them by the total number of such editing activity of each article. This is the same method used in a previous study [7]. Accordingly, the variance of factor scores is 1 and the mean of factor scores of each factor is 0. We used IBM SPSS premium software for factor extraction.

We firstly confirm our data is suitable for factor analysis with Kaiser-Meyer-Olkin (KMO) and Bartlett's test two parameters [19]; all three categories yielded a KMO Measure of Sampling Adequacy near 1 and a Bartlett's Test of Sphericity of significance close to zero. We used Principal Component Analysis (PCA) for the latent factor extraction and eigenvalues equal or greater than 1 to determine the number of factors. We also performed Varimax rotation to minimize the number of variables that have high loadings on each factor, which helps to simplify the interpretation of the factors [19].

5   Result

This section details our experiment and describes the results gained. This section is organized to cover the three Wikipedia categories. For each Wikipedia category, we first statistically overview the data we annotated from the GAs of the Wikipedia category which includes the titles, numbers of editing activities manually annotated per article, numbers of editors per article, and article sizes. The information offers a surface observation of the differences among editor teams and article size for the same GA category. Then we present our factor analysis results and factor extraction, and report the editing ability categories. After that, we present three typical GA creation processes for each Wikipedia category. Finally, we conclude with the collaboration pattern of GA creation.

5.1   Statistics Overview of GAs of the US State Parks

There are a total of 20 GAs covering US state parks. Table 1 shows the large variance in the GAs of this category. The smallest team consisted of 4 editors while the largest team had 108 editors. The editing activity counts are proportional to team size. While article size also varies, the variance is much less than that for team size.

Table 1. Statistics of US state parks GAs.

Good Articles title	Number of activities	Number of editors	Article size (bytes)
Above All State Park	73	6	8,166
Albany Pine Bush	347	62	37,899
Beaver Brook State Park	56	4	8,811
Becket Hill State Park Reserve	69	7	6,458
Brown County State Park	299	56	38,444
Clark State Forest	150	22	7,589
Cloudland Canyon State Park	257	35	12,265
Farm River State Park	77	7	8,757
Haddam Island State Park	82	4	9,334
Haley Farm State Park	62	5	9,687
Hopeville Pond State Park	55	3	9,893
Kayak Point County Park	77	6	17,942
Minneopa State Park	156	40	28,623
Pettigrew State Park	200	24	19,425
Piedmont Park	462	108	31,647
Pomeroy State Park	45	4	4,985
Silver Springs State Fish and Wildlife Area	137	6	12,935
Tualatin River National Wildlife Refuge	145	12	21,721

5.2   Factor Analysis of Editor's Characteristics

Table 2 shows the factor analysis result for the US state park GAs. F1 to F6 are the six factors extracted as the basic dimensions of editing abilities. The numbers in the matrix represents the loading of the editing activities to the factor. Numbers closer to 1 indicate a higher loading of the activity in the factor. We use bold format to highlight the editing activity with the highest loadings. We also explain the details of each factor below.

- F1 is content-shaping ability with five activities focusing on content information coverage: format, add information, delete information, add link in content, and add link for reference. Since these activities mainly target content-information enrichment, they are called content shaping.
- F2 is the copy-editing ability that emphasizes clarifying information, spelling, grammar, and use talk page. All target writing improvement.
- F3 is indexing ability and links articles to the Wikipedia category index page as add link in the category.
- F4 is reversion activity.
- F5 is vandalism, which is the activities of vandalism to damage articles.
- F6 is link fixing ability, which is the activity of fix link.

Table 2. Rotated factor matrix of the US state parks category: 14 editing activities

Editing activities categories	F 1	F 2	F 3	F 4	F 5	F 6
Format	**0.85**	0.40	0.06	−0.01	−0.02	0.14
Add information	**0.90**	0.36	0.10	0.04	−0.01	0.17
Delete information	**0.90**	0.30	0.14	0.08	−0.01	0.16
Clarify information	0.55	**0.71**	−0.08	0.01	−0.02	0.17
Spelling	0.54	**0.69**	0.09	0.09	−0.02	0.09
Grammar	0.38	**0.80**	0.10	0.01	−0.01	0.25
Reversion	0.07	0.04	0.03	**1.00**	−0.01	−0.01
Fix link	0.41	0.32	0.19	−0.02	−0.02	**0.83**
Delate link	0.66	0.60	0.09	0.01	−0.01	0.21
Vandalism	−0.02	−0.02	−0.03	−0.01	**1.00**	−0.01
Use of talk page	0.63	0.62	0.00	0.05	−0.02	0.04
Add links to the category	0.17	0.04	**0.97**	0.03	−0.03	0.12
Add links in content	**0.78**	0.28	0.23	0.04	−0.02	0.25
Add links in reference	**0.86**	0.41	0.09	0.06	−0.01	0.16

5.3   Collaboration in GA Creation Process

In this section, we present the result of plotting the editor's sequence of appearance in the reversion history when creating a GA. In Fig. 2, we give three examples of GAs of different sizes to show the collaboration that occurred when creating the US state park GAs. It gives the creation period and reversion counts in GA creation.

We mark the editors according to their highest score work of the six editing abilities of the team. For editors with editing ability scores all below 0, we indicate them as low score editor using a grey circle dot since their score is below average. Here we only indicate the editor with the highest content-shaping score. We also give information of number reversion and the dates of such GA creation and the reversion sequences of editors as they appear in the GA creation process.

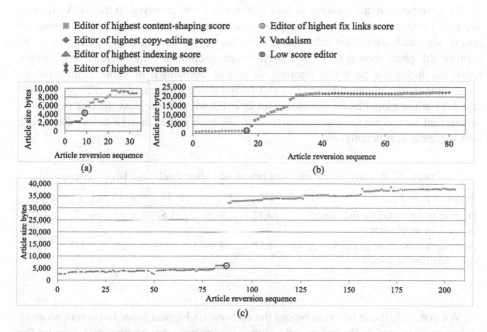

Fig. 2. Three examples of GA collaboration creation process for US state park subcategory. (a) Small GA: Farm River State Park created from 2013-01-22 to 2014-11-20 with 33 reversions, the 9th reversion on 2014-05-23 is circled. (b) Median sized GA: Tualatin River Nation Wildlife Refuge created from 2006-07-28 to 2009-03-27 with 80 reversions, the 14th reversion on 2009-02-21 is circled. (c) Large GA: Albany Pine Bush created from 2005-06-12 to 2010-09-23 with 203 reversions, the 81th reversion on 2010-07-19 is circled.

For *Farm River State Park* GA in Fig. 2(a), the whole GA creation process took almost two years. The highest content-shaping ability editor only started to work six months before successful GA nomination. He/she pretty much finished the work without much help from others. For the *Tualatin River Nation Wildlife Refuge* in Fig. 2 (b) the highest content-shaping ability editor only worked for one month and ten days before successful GA nomination. For *Albany Pine Bush* GA in Fig. 2(c) the highest content-shaping ability editor only started to work two months, continuously, prior to GA completion. This editor also has the highest copy-editing ability score of the team. In the same period, there was an editor with the second highest copy-editing score who helped in GA completion. This editor also had the highest score in link fixing ability, but due to the significance of the copy-editing ability, we mark this editor as having the highest copy-editing score. We indicate when this editor started to work with a red circle in the figure and report details of the number of reversions and the date of the reversion. The result indicates editors with the highest score in content-shaping (represented by the orange square) mainly appeared just prior to GA completion. They increases the article size suddenly and work continuously towards GA nomination passed. We also observe their activities were performed only for a few months regardless of GA size.

To give better representation of how different editors involved in the work process. We also present the six factors' average scores of editors before the sudden increases in article size and after. The calculation uses the revision frequency of editors so to capture the phenomenon of high content-shaping characteristics editors work many revisions during the prior GA nomination period. As shown in Table 3, the average factor scores of content-shaping (F1) and copy-editing characteristics (F2) are at 1.88 and 1.91 while global factor scores are set at 1. F3 which represents the link the article to external source are the main activity as it has high scores at 1.57 before the article size increase significantly.

Table 3. Average factor scores of before and after article size large increase

Revision period	F 1	F 2	F 3	F 4	F 5	F 6
From creation to before the largest increase in article size	0.42	−0.39	**1.57**	0.07	0.12	−0.05
From largest increase in article size to GAs nomination passed	**1.88**	**1.91**	−0.09	0.28	0.11	0.40

We conclude it can be years before the editor with highest score in content-shaping ability appears, and in the meantime various editors perform minimal revisions on the articles and the article size remains low. The low score editors have no dominant editing abilities other than link GAs to external source. There can be many such kind of editors and they are the cause of large difference in team size and activity count.

5.4   Implication and Discussion

This research chose Wikipedia GAs of a general topic to demonstrate an approach to investigate collaboration in creating GAs. We found there is common collaboration exists in most of the GA examples analyzed in this research. Prior to achieving GA nomination, an editor with strong content-shaping ability expands the article and continuously works on it. They mainly work on the GA for few months and during this period, there is little involvement of the other editors. In just a few cases, a strong copy-editing ability editor was present there and could help out. In addition, before they started to work, the revision history mainly involved editors who perform scant activities. The presence of quiescent low editing activity editors explains why team attributes appear different in creating GAs in the same Wikipedia category.

We argue that our findings imply that Wikipedia GA creation relies less on the sheer number of editors, most whom will only nominally engage in collaboration, and more on strong content-shaping editors who can enhance articles at the final stage of the GA creation process. Similar open collaboration systems should pay attention to the different workers and the work creation process in yielding quality output.

We acknowledge we demonstrate our research method with three Wikipedia categories are limited to represent the other categories of Wikipedia in quality work creation. Yet our research achieves to demonstrate that the editing abilities and collaboration patterns are different among different categories. Our method can be extended with automized annotation and study large amount of Wikipedia articles of different categories as well different quality levels. The method can obtain more understanding of the open collaboration of Wikipedia articles and provide recommendations to the future open collaboration system design.

6 Conclusion

Although open collaboration provides unlimited opportunity to society, it also faces some challenges. A good example is Wikipedia. While its importance to modern society is beyond question, the quality issue has long been studied but how quality articles are created remains unclear. This paper proposed a novel method that eliminates the Wikipedia quality research gap. We first considered how different size teams yielded similar quality GAs in the same Wikipedia categories. Then we used factor analysis to differentiate the editors through their editing abilities. Last, we studied the roles and collaboration of editors' throughput of the GA creation process.

While we analyzed GAs in the US state parks to demonstrate our method, the method can be easily extended to study other Wikipedia categories. Our second contribution is that we found collaboration patterns for creating GAs from we can make recommendations to Wikipedia and other open collaboration systems. The key one being to secure a strong content-shaping ability editor who will continuously for a few months to secure GA acceptance. Sometimes another editor with strong copy-editing skills would be recommended to support the writing quality. At other times, if the strong content-shaping editor is also top-notch in copy editing, he or she might single-handedly improve the writing. Years might pass before this editor starts to work, and low editing activity editors (those might with little editing abilities) contributes to the article. Such editors are the reason for differences in team-size and team diversity.

Last, as for the aspects of open collaboration and system design, this research also contributed a method that allows consideration of workers and work processes and provided design considerations for Wikipedia and other open collaboration systems in facilitating quality work creation.

Acknowledgement. This research was partially supported by a Grant-in-Aid for Scientific Research (A) (17H00759, 2017-2020) and a Grant-in-Aid for Scientific Research (B) (18H03341, 2018-2020) from the Japan Society for the Promotion of Science (JSPS).

References

1. Viégas, F.B., Wattenberg, M., McKeon, M.M.: The hidden order of Wikipedia. In: Schuler, D. (ed.) OCSC 2007. LNCS, vol. 4564, pp. 445–454. Springer, Heidelberg (2007). https://doi.org/10.1007/978-3-540-73257-0_49
2. Stvili, B., Twidale, M.B., Smith, L.C., Gasser, L.: Information quality work organization in Wikipedia. J. Am. Soc. Inf. Sci. Technol. **59**(6), 983–1001 (2008)
3. https://en.wikipedia.org/wiki/Wikipedia:Statistics. Accessed 19 Jan 2020
4. Giles, J.: Internet encyclopedias go head to head. Nature **438**(15), 900–901 (2005)
5. https://en.wikipedia.org/wiki/Wikipedia:WikiProject_Wikipedia/Assessment. Accessed 19 Jan 2020
6. Deng, H., Tarigan, B., Grigore, M., Sutanto, J.: Understanding the 'quality motion' of Wikipedia articles through semantic convergence analysis. In: Nah, F.F.-H., Tan, C.-H. (eds.) HCIB 2015. LNCS, vol. 9191, pp. 64–75. Springer, Cham (2015). https://doi.org/10.1007/978-3-319-20895-4_7
7. Liu, J., Ram, S.: Who does what: collaboration patterns in the Wikipedia and their impact on article quality. ACM Trans. Manag. Inf. Syst. (TMIS) **2**(2), 11 (2011)
8. Robert, L., Romero, D.M.: Crowd size, diversity and performance. In: Proceedings of the 33rd ACM Conference on Human Factors in Computing Systems, pp. 1379–1382. ACM (2015)
9. Kane, G.C.: A multi-method study of information quality in wiki collaboration. ACM Trans. Manag. Inf. Syst. (TMIS) **2**(1), 4 (2011)
10. Pfeil, U., Zaphiris, P., Ang, C.S.: Cultural differences in collaborative authoring of Wikipedia. J. Comput. Mediat. Commun. **12**(1), 88–113 (2006)
11. Carroll, J.B.: Human Cognitive Abilities: A Survey of Factor-Analytic Studies. Cambridge University Press, Cambridge (1993)
12. Zhang, A.F., Livneh, D., Budak, C., Robert Jr., L.P., Romero, D.M.: Crowd development: the interplay between crowd evaluation and collaborative dynamics in Wikipedia. In: Proceedings of the ACM on Human-Computer Interaction, CSCW, p. 119 (2017)
13. Arazy, O., Nov, O., Patterson, R., Yeo, L.: Information quality in Wikipedia: the effects of group composition and task conflict. J. Manag. Inf. Syst. **27**(4), 71–98 (2011)
14. McGrath, J.E.: Time matters in groups. In: Intellectual Teamwork, pp. 37–76. Psychology Press (2014)
15. Kittur, A., Kraut, R.E.: Harnessing the wisdom of crowds in Wikipedia: quality through coordination. In: Proceedings of the ACM Conference on Computer Supported Cooperative Work, San Diego, USA, pp. 37–46 (2008)
16. Bryant, S.L., Forte, A., Bruckman, A.: Becoming Wikipedian: transformation of participation in a collaborative online encyclopedia. In: Proceedings of the International ACM SIGGROUP Conference on Supporting Group Work, Sanibel Island, Florida, USA, pp. 1–10 (2005)
17. Wilkinson, D.M., Huberman, B.A.: Assessing the value of cooperation in Wikipedia. First Monday **12**(4), (2007)
18. Jones, J.: Patterns of revision in online writing: a study of Wikipedia's featured articles. Written Commun. **25**(2), 262–289 (2008)
19. Child, D.: The Essentials of Factor Analysis. Cassell Educational, London (1990)

20. Klein, M., Maillart, T., Chuang, J.: The virtuous circle of Wikipedia: recursive measures of collaboration structures. In: Proceedings of the 18th ACM Conference on Computer Supported Cooperative Work & Social Computing, Vancouver, Canada, pp. 1106–1115 (2015)
21. Daxenberger, J., Gurevych, I.: A corpus-based study of edit categories in featured and non-featured Wikipedia articles. In: Proceedings of COLING, pp. 711–726. ACL, Mumbai (2012)

Federated Artificial Intelligence for Unified Credit Assessment

Minh-Duc Hoang[1], Linh Le[2], Anh-Tuan Nguyen[2], Trang Le[2],
and Hoang D. Nguyen[3(✉)]

[1] University of New South Wales Sydney, Sydney, Australia
MinhDuc.Hoang@student.unsw.edu.au
[2] BeU Research Group, Hanoi, Vietnam
{Linh.Le,Tuan.Nguyen,Trang.Le}@beu.ai
[3] University of Glasgow, Singapore, Singapore
HarryNguyen@glasgow.ac.uk

Abstract. With the rapid adoption of Internet technologies, digital footprints have become ubiquitous and versatile to revolutionise the financial industry in digital transformation. This paper takes initiatives to investigate a new paradigm of the unified credit assessment with the use of federated artificial intelligence. We conceptualised digital human representation which consists of social, contextual, financial and technological dimensions to assess the commercial creditworthiness and social reputation of both banked and unbanked individuals. A federated artificial intelligence platform is proposed with a comprehensive set of system design for efficient and effective credit scoring. The study considerably contributes to the cumulative development of financial intelligence and social computing. It also provides a number of implications for academic bodies, practitioners, and developers of financial technologies.

Keywords: Credit scoring · Artificial intelligence · Federated learning · Financial risk · Social reputation

1 Introduction

The recent decades have witnessed a rapid pace of change with the advance of the Internet and new technologies. Having all these digital technologies available at their fingertips, people are using them in everyday life, making them ubiquitous [23]. The financial industry, therefore, has been undergoing digital transformation; in which new types of data, products and services have been continuously developed [16].

To date, there are approximately 1.7 billion adults that are unbanked according to The Global Findex database [4], especially those who are living in developing countries where transactions are predominantly facilitated in cash. It is significantly challenging for financial institutions to evaluate credit inquiries or loan applications; nevertheless, digital footprints such as social network or mobile

© Springer Nature Switzerland AG 2020
G. Meiselwitz (Ed.): HCII 2020, LNCS 12195, pp. 44–56, 2020.
https://doi.org/10.1007/978-3-030-49576-3_4

data have become increasingly promising to address this challenge in digital transformation. These new types of data can be used to cover this deficiency of available data in financial risks assessment with broader coverage of information [12]. The past studies have shown that behavioural insights on digital data are a good supplement to the traditional credit scoring approach as it can help banks to predict fraud, reduce defaults and avoid leaving out potential credit inquiry [2,7,19].

Digital footprints involve dealing and collecting enormous amounts of data from a great variety of sources in different types and semantics, creating a significant challenge to unify, aggregate, classify and fulfil all data fields in one system. Moreover, they are often associated with issues of data reliability, especially in the measure of soft factors and risks of complex fraudulent data. The use of artificial intelligence (AI), hence, plays a vital role to harness big data for better financial products and services. This paper aims to address major boundaries of credit scoring on fiscal and social footprints by introducing a federated credit assessment framework with a comprehensive set of system concepts and design guidelines.

Based on theoretical foundations, the research contributes to the cumulative development of financial artificial intelligence and risk scoring systems. It draws out many implications for academic bodies, industrial practitioners, and developers.

The structure of the paper is as follows. Firstly, we review the literature background of our paper in Sect. 2. Secondly, we discuss the existing challenges of the credit assessment in Sect. 3. Next, we present our federated credit assessment framework with system design and concepts. Lastly, Sect. 5 concludes our paper with findings and contributions.

2 Literature Background

2.1 Financial Creditworthiness Scoring

Credit scoring has been defined as a set of models that supports the process of financial decision making in regard to the granting of credit for individuals by lenders [20]. Since the 1950s, the concept and techniques of credit assessment have evolved swiftly, supported by the development of expertise and technology to match the increase in customer demand after the advent of credit card [13]. Advanced technologies such as data mining, machine learning and AI have been providing tremendous support to the creation of new models that ensure better accuracy to predict individual's risk performance. Furthermore, the application of credit scoring has also transformed beyond its initial use in the lending industry to predictive analytics on how likely a customer will churn, which patients might be posing a higher risk of a specific kind of disease or whose tax submission should be investigated further [20].

Empirical studies have shown a great variety of models being applied to generate credit scores for bank users throughout the last several decades [3,9,13].

Table 1. Common financial predictors

Category	Description	Example indicators	Ref
Demographic	Personal details that matter to the assessment of an individual's creditworthiness	**Numerical:** age, number of children, number of dependent, monthly income; **Categorical:** gender, marital Status, residential status, postcode, home/mobile phone, education, profession	[6, 26]
Tenure	Variables that are related to time	Time at current address, time at present job, time in employment, time with the bank, account longevity, duration of loan in months	[5, 10, 17]
Trade	Variables related to an individual's trading activities	**Numerical:** number of active accounts, number of open accounts, percent trades that delinquent/never delinquent, ratio of payment/total income, ratio of debt/total income; **Categorical:** type of bank accounts, loan from other banks	[5, 17]
Balance	Variables that help access the financial situation of an individual	Past and current amount of loans received, saving account status, current account status	[6, 17]
Inquiry	These variables illustrate the underlying factors related to every credit application	**Numerical:** number of inquiries in the past months, credit limit; **Categorical:** inquiry purpose, loan guarantors, collateral type, credit rating	[5, 9, 17]

In general, there is a certain level of similarity between these models in terms of the predictors being used to produce the response. However, different models will have their own selection for the number of predictors used, and there are also some distinct predictors that are considered to add novel values to the existing models. Table 1 lists out some of the most commonly used predictors in popular financial credit scoring models.

Nevertheless, with the increasing ubiquity of digital technologies, the finance industry has been facing unprecedented challenges in assessing credit risk. Hence, there is an emerging trend for application of social data into many aspects of credit scoring.

2.2   Social Reputation Scoring

With the average worldwide Internet penetration of 59% today [18], digital footprints are being created by billions of monthly active users, which contribute to the pool of an enormous amount of social data. Hence, combining social and financial data into the assessment of credit risks has become a new trend with great potentials of social data in the lending industry. Social data serve as a valuable and supplementary data source to enhance predictive models in credits.

A large number of studies have extensively investigated the use of digital footprints for credit scoring [7,8,12,19]. Social footprints include user demographics (e.g., age, gender, relationship status), user-generated contents (e.g., Twitter tweets or Facebook posts), and social relationships (e.g., friends or followers) on social networking sites. Guo et al. (2016) demonstrated significant improvement by 17% with the use of social features in their personal credit scoring model [8]. In addition, mobile data (e.g., call and messaging events) and browsing behaviours (e.g., websites and browsing duration) have also been explored to improve credit models [14]. San et al. (2015) employed Gradient Boosting Tree in their real-time approach using mobile behaviours, which outperformed credit bureaus, such as Experian or Equifax, by a large margin [15]. With a huge amount of unstructured data, these social data sources provide capabilities to track and evaluate individuals and businesses for trustworthiness, not only in a financial credit sense but also in a behavioural sense, i.e. sincerity, honesty, and integrity.

As human interactions are now taking place more and more often on the Internet, social data have not only been utilised by private sectors in sharing economy and collaborative economy, but also by public sectors in social credit scoring. Social credit has become increasingly beneficial in the identification and dissemination of reputational information, which has become a crucial element of the 21st-century digital transformation. With the recent advancement of big data and artificial intelligence technologies, social-based credit systems have evolved beyond traditional credit scoring approaches into massive and complex modelling systems with the utilisation of technological data (e.g., facial recognition or movement trackings).

3   Emerging Challenges in Credit Assessment

With the advents of new technologies and the development of expertise across the industry, the traditional credit scoring methods have now transformed to become automated as banks started looking for a way to utilise their limited resources to no longer have to "treat each small exposure individually" [21]. However, along this much-needed digital transformation are concerns about different obstacles that can challenge the implication of these new approaches. Hereby, this paper will look into several challenges that current credit assessment systems are facing as the following.

Big and heterogeneous data. It is without a doubt that big data is playing an imperative role in improving the accuracy of credit scoring given the values it can create by providing accesses to a larger pool of information over a broader target audience. However, big data is also a double-edged sword that poses a variety of challenges due to its complex and dynamic characteristics. Collecting this enormous amount of data requires the contribution from a great variety of sources/websites/applications in different languages and formats, targeting various segmentation of users. Thus, it creates a significant challenge to unify, aggregate, classify and fulfil all data fields in a scoring system [24]. Even though this can be partially overcome by certain methods, it is laborious to choose proper objective functions for a specific data heterogeneity problem [11]. Moreover, existing approaches might overlook the actual context and interpretation of the data, thereby compromising the performance of the system with a significant impact on the targeted users.

- **Reliability.** The social-financial credit scoring has commonly been criticised for issues of data reliability, particularly in the measurement of soft factors and risks of a monopolistic system lacking cross-referencing. It is possible for individuals or platform providers might deliberately manipulate data resulting in inaccurate social-based credit ratings. Or simply, another issue regarding data reliability lies on human errors of the input data. Working with a model that heavily relies on the quality of the input, especially historical data in this case, requires proper data validation techniques. Moreover, getting up-to-date data plays a crucial role to improve system performance [20].

- **Security and Privacy.** Credit scoring also raises controversy for its potential infringement on privacy. Currently, data protection law through Council of Europe convention and EU Directive, and most recently General Data Protection Regulation in EU (GDPR), which introduce a framework for the regulation of rating and reputation data, has been growing in significance. Data protection laws also elaborate further on the conditions of legal processing of personal data. Nevertheless, from a policy perspective, it is suggested that a review of security and privacy should be in place as a means of safeguarding individual rights as well as exercising checks and balances of the design and operation of the credit assessment systems. It is important to highlight any problems of information security, data privacy and flaws, particularly with respect to ratings by financial institutions.

- **Explainability.** A credit assessment system will not be trusted without transparent. Interpretability was the key selling point in traditional credit models; nevertheless, AI-based models with new types of data have been tagged with a lower degree of explainability. This has become a technological challenge of explaining AI decisions. Credit ratings of individuals based on social and financial data are prone to errors due to data, algorithms, or manipulation issues. Therefore, explainable and accountable credit assessment is necessary to build and engage sincerity and honesty in consumer networks.

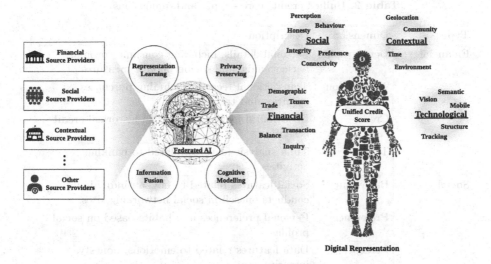

Fig. 1. Federated artificial intelligence for credit assessment

4 Federated Artificial Intelligence for Unified Credit Assessment

In this paper, we propose a federated credit assessment framework with the use of artificial intelligence to address the existing challenges in credit scoring. It utilises a state-of-the-art machine learning engine to integrate heterogeneous data sources and to produce high-dimensional digital representations of consumers. The dimensionality of these digital representations may range from 20,000 to 30,000 data features; which encompass social, financial, contextual, and technological characteristics optimised under millions of artificial neurons according to the criterion based on credit decisions. Figure 1 provides an overview of the federated artificial intelligence for unified credit assessment.

The framework consists of FIVE (5) key components: (1) Unified credit score, (2) Information fusion, (3) Privacy-preserving, (4) Cognitive Modelling, and (5) Representation learning. The following sub-sections discuss these components in great details.

4.1 Unified Credit Score

Credit score is traditionally assessed based on hard data denoting to contextual and financial information of borrowers such as age, name, address, credit history, and transactions. Nevertheless, due to the advent of social media and technology advancement, personal credit score has been evaluated using multiple categories of data, including hard and soft information [8,15]. This research paper proposes a unified credit score which is assessed based on wider sets of

Table 2. Unified credit score - types and dimensions

Type	Dimension	Description
Financial	Demographic	Personal details, including consumer profile, backgrounds, and socioeconomic measures
	Transaction	Transactional records, including purchases, inquiries and transfers
	Credit	Behavioural features related to historical credit activities
	Tenure	Time analysis features related to banking activities
Social	Behaviour	Social features related to how an individual conducts oneself in social networking sites
	Preference	Personal preferences and habits based on social profile
	Perception	Data features related to emotions, honesty, integrity, etc
	Connectivity	Social relationships including social networks associated with credit ratings and communications
	Content	Unstructured data features generated by consumers in social networking sites
Contextual	Geolocation	Geographical features, including location-based conditions and networks
	Time	Temporal and seasonal features
	Environment	Environmental features, including epidemiological and pollution conditions
	Community	Physical context features, including neighbourhood, groups and businesses
Technological	Semantic	Linguistic and philosophical features based on natural language modelling
	Vision	Visual features, including facial features and user-generated images/videos
	Mobile	Activity data features based on mobile usage and browsing behaviours
	Tracking	Movement-based features including sensor-based movements and positioning measures

data. We suggest the construction of a credit score based on four types with multiple dimensions: financial, social, contextual and technological characteristics, as shown in Table 2.

It aims to provide integrated and comprehensive aspects of the digital representation for each individual. Both hard data (financial and contextual data) and soft data (social and technological information) are included in the computation of the unified credit score. For instance, the financial data include but not limited to credit records (e.g., credit score, debt to income ratio and annual income) and transactions (e.g., number of successful sale, days from last purchase, and transaction ratio). In the social category, a useful credit model needs to investigate behaviours such as trends in commercial transactions or social network characteristics in online platforms. Moreover, content-related features, including numbers of friends, posts, messages, or interactions, are good supplement to enhance credit scoring. Also, contextual dimensions such as geolocation, time, environment, and community play a crucial role in predicting the likelihood of default behaviours. Semantic, visual, mobile and tracking features are promising predictors of the technological dimensions, which enrich other types of data sources for better interpretability and performance.

4.2   Information Fusion

Unified credit assessment entails individual-level data analysis from multiple, heterogeneous data sources. An enormous amount of financial, social, contextual and technological data are collected from a vast variety of sources/websites/applications. They are diverse in languages, types, formats, and even unit levels; thus, it is essential to employ information fusion strategies to eliminate uncertainty and reliability issues in the big data. The process of information fusion integrates multiple data sources into a robust, accurate and consistent body to be used in the federated AI. This component involves many data processing techniques such as aggregation, selection, cleaning, construction, and formatting. For instance, a hierarchical decomposing method can be adopted to handle the data at multiple levels, such as individual and contextual categories. Moreover, we introduce the use of multilayer network (MLN) analysis to model social data from multiple perspectives for higher efficiency [22].

Furthermore, digital footprints of consumers are typically widespread on multiple financial information systems and social networking sites. These data traces are found and collected in a disconnected and fragmented manner. User entity resolution, therefore, plays a crucial role to interconnect the data traces into single digital identities. Transfer models for cross-domain user matching are proposed to incorporate consumer activity data into user entity resolution with deep neural networks [1]. This technique outperforms similarity-based matching models to provide a mechanism for recognising and merging consumer profiles. We propose the use of deep user activity transfer to prevent duplicated profiles and synthetic data, thereby increasing the reliability of the data.

4.3   Federated Representation Learning

This paper introduces federated representation learning that builds deep neural network models across decentralised data providers. This approach enables multiple organisations to optimise the learning pathways with a unified objective without sharing data. The heterogeneity and security issues of data sources,

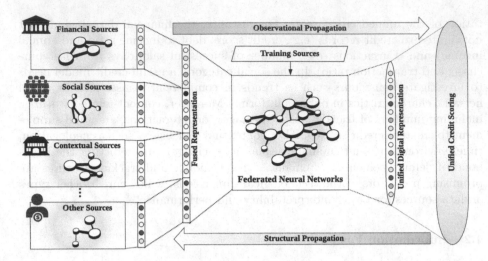

Fig. 2. Federated representation learning

therefore, are taken care of in the federated AI. Figure 2 illustrates how federated representation learning works across multiple data source providers.

The federated learning aims to orchestrate data representations from various sources into a unified digital body for credit scoring in an iterative manner. Each organisational unit has dynamic and local neural networks with a standardised objective function to observe incoming data samples for producing high-dimensional representations, which typically range between 2,048 and 4,096 data features. This approach harnesses parallelised computing powers to learn distributed and heterogenous data effectively. Moreover, the use of artificial neural networks allows federated AI to handle complex and non-linear data structures.

The main principle of federated representation learning consists in the dynamic nature of neural networks with constant observational and structural propagation. On the one hand, observational propagation is a forward process that represents and computes data observations through a system of millions of neurons in order to elicit the loss in credit assessment. On the other hand, structural propagation happens with the training of labelled data sources to provide the exchange of neural network weights and reconfigurations between a central node and local nodes. As a result, multiple data sources from various organisations can be efficiently integrated in harmony to score personal credits.

4.4   Privacy-Preserving

The key advantage of federated AI is to ensure data secrecy, in which it is by design that no local data is transmitted externally for machine learning. Nevertheless, there is a possibility for individual re-identification based on high-

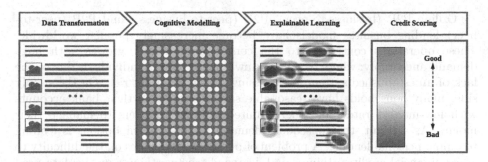

Fig. 3. Cognitive modelling for credit assessment

dimensional feature matching. With the use of publicly available information, a reverse-engineering process can be done to discover consumer profiles.

We propose the use of user-level differentially private representations to balance the trade-off between privacy and data utility [27]. Our federated AI employs state-of-the-art neural network architecture to capture the sensitivities of consumer data and to decide the degree of representation learning while achieves good performance for credit scoring.

4.5 Cognitive Modelling

In recent years, cognitive intelligence has been widely explored as an advancement of brain-inspired systems in artificial intelligence [25]. Although the mechanism of human brains remains largely unknown, simulating cerebral activities creates new ways of understanding data and making decisions, especially for credit scoring. In this study, the ultimate objective is to develop a brain-inspired artificial intelligence to assess personal credits similar to human-based decisions. Figure 3 provides the general concept of cognitive modelling for credit assessment.

We propose several steps to develop our explainable, federated AI. First, transforming different types and formats of data into relevant data embeddings. Second, projecting data embeddings into user-level cognitive maps with multiple distributed data features. Cognitive modelling happens at a deeper level of computational consciousness in alignment with human judgements in investigating personal credits. Furthermore, explainable learning is introduced to provide stakeholders of the cognitive intelligence system an interpretation of the predictions made by the deep learning model using the state-of-the-art approaches.

4.6 Discussion

Unified credit assessment is promising to provide integrated and comprehensive representation for each individual. With the support of federated AI, the proposed approach can be applied in determining individual creditworthiness for many applications, including property loan or personal lending.

Online B2P (business-to-peer), P2B (peer-to-business), and P2P (peer-to-peer) lending business models have become increasingly popular worldwide. These operations contribute to the considerable market growth with huge demand and supply; where banks are unwilling to lend to individuals due to the lack of an established system for assessing consumer credit risk. On the supply side, many households have reasonable savings sitting in their bank accounts with low-interest rates, and there limited options for avers to manage their money. As a result, the consequent demand for investment options is leading to online personal lending. A problem of personal lending lies on the difficulty to assess financial creditworthiness and degree of trustworthiness on the data used in the analysis. The problem persists more burdensome in developing countries; in which the majority of people do not use bank accounts, leaving social traces even more critical in assessing individual creditworthiness.

The proposed framework will help B2P, P2B, P2P lending providers easier in making credit decisions. It is essential for lenders to identify creditworthiness by investigating the digital representations of their potential customers with the use of financial and social data. Unified credit scoring, therefore, will be a useful tool to improve both customer ratings and transaction monitoring. Moreover, it has the potential to improve the effectiveness of anti-money laundering programs; which meaningfully contributes to the economic and social stability.

5   Conclusion

Our study has several implications for theoretical literature and development of financial technologies. First, we propose a new paradigm of unified credit assessment supported by federated artificial intelligence. Second, we elaborate this paradigm to recommend a novel distributed system to produce digital representations for individual credit scoring with the privacy-preserving mechanism. Last but not least, we designed the federated AI platform, which is capable of reshaping current credit assessment approaches towards data and decision orchestration. It unveils the capability of building a unified credit score based on financial, social, contextual, and technological data for effective credit evaluation.

This paper is not an end, but rather a beginning of future research. We are looking into ways of further refining machine learning through the process of state-of-the-art brain-inspired technologies.

Acknowledgment. This study is a part of the BeU AI research initiative.

References

1. Ahangama, S., Poo, D.C.C.: Application of deep user activity transfer models for cross domain user matching. In: ICIS 2019 on Analytics and Data Science (2019)
2. Björkegren, D., Grissen, D.: The potential of digital credit to bank the poor. In: AEA Papers and Proceedings, vol. 108, pp. 68–71 (2018)

3. Chen, C., Lin, K., Rudin, C., Shaposhnik, Y., Wang, S., Wang, T.: An interpretable model with globally consistent explanations for credit risk. arXiv preprint arXiv:1811.12615 (2018)
4. Demirguc-Kunt, A., Klapper, L., Singer, D., Ansar, S., Hess, J.: The Global Findex Database 2017: Measuring Financial Inclusion and the Fintech Revolution. The World Bank, Washington (2018)
5. Desai, V.S., Crook, J.N., Overstreet Jr., G.A.: A comparison of neural networks and linear scoring models in the credit union environment. Eur. J. Oper. Res. 95(1), 24–37 (1996)
6. Dinh, T.H.T., Kleimeier, S.: A credit scoring model for Vietnam's retail banking market. Int. Rev. Financ. Anal 16(5), 471–495 (2007)
7. Ge, R., Feng, J., Gu, B., Zhang, P.: Predicting and deterring default with social media information in peer-to-peer lending. J. Manag. Inf. Syst. 34(2), 401–424 (2017)
8. Guo, G., Zhu, F., Chen, E., Liu, Q., Wu, L., Guan, C.: From footprint to evidence: an exploratory study of mining social data for credit scoring. ACM Trans. Web (TWEB) 10(4), 1–38 (2016)
9. Lee, T.S., Chen, I.F.: A two-stage hybrid credit scoring model using artificial neural networks and multivariate adaptive regression splines. Expert Syst. Appl. 28(4), 743–752 (2005)
10. Malhotra, R., Malhotra, D.K.: Evaluating consumer loans using neural networks. Omega 31(2), 83–96 (2003)
11. Mandreoli, F., Montangero, M.: Dealing with data heterogeneity in a data fusion perspective: models, methodologies, and algorithms. In: Data Handling in Science and Technology, vol. 31, pp. 235–270. Elsevier (2019)
12. Masyutin, A.A.: Credit scoring based on social network data. Bus. Inform. 3(33), 15–23 (2015)
13. Mays, E.: Handbook of Credit Scoring. Global Professional Publishing, London (2001)
14. Óskarsdóttir, M., Bravo, C., Sarraute, C., Vanthienen, J., Baesens, B.: The value of big data for credit scoring: enhancing financial inclusion using mobile phone data and social network analytics. Appl. Soft Comput. 74, 26–39 (2019)
15. Pedro, J.S., Proserpio, D., Oliver, N.: MobiScore: towards universal credit scoring from mobile phone data. In: Ricci, F., Bontcheva, K., Conlan, O., Lawless, S. (eds.) UMAP 2015. LNCS, vol. 9146, pp. 195–207. Springer, Cham (2015). https://doi.org/10.1007/978-3-319-20267-9_16
16. Scardovi, C.: Digital Transformation in Financial Services. Springer, Cham (2017). https://doi.org/10.1007/978-3-319-66945-8
17. Sinha, A.P., May, J.H.: Evaluating and tuning predictive data mining models using receiver operating characteristic curves. J. Manag. Inf. Syst. 21(3), 249–280 (2004)
18. Statista: global digital population 2020 (2020). https://www.statista.com/statistics/617136/digital-population-worldwide/
19. Tan, T., Phan, T.Q.: Social media-driven credit scoring: the predictive value of social structures (2018). Available at SSRN 3217885
20. Thomas, L.C., Crook, J.N., Edelman, D.B.: Credit Scoring and Its Applications. SIAM Society for Industrial and Applied Mathematics, Philadelphia (2017)
21. Vojtek, M., Koèenda, E., et al.: Credit-scoring methods. Czech J. Econ. Finan. (Financ. Uver) 56(3–4), 152–167 (2006)

22. Vu, X.S., Santra, A., Chakravarthy, S., Jiang, L.: Generic multilayer network data analysis with the fusion of content and structure. In: 20th International Conference on Computational Linguistics and Intelligent Text Processing, 7–13 April 2019, La Rochelle, France (2019)
23. Wang, F.Y., Carley, K.M., Zeng, D., Mao, W.: Social computing: from social informatics to social intelligence. IEEE Intell. Syst. **22**(2), 79–83 (2007)
24. Wang, L.: Heterogeneous data and big data analytics. Autom. Control Inf. Sci. **3**(1), 8–15 (2017)
25. Wang, Y., et al.: Cognitive intelligence: deep learning, thinking, and reasoning by brain-inspired systems. Int. J. Cogn. Inform. Nat. Intell. (IJCINI) **10**(4), 1–20 (2016)
26. West, D.: Neural network credit scoring models. Comput. Oper. Res. **27**(11–12), 1131–1152 (2000)
27. Vu, X.S., Tran, S.N., Jiang, L.: dpUGC: learn differentially private representation for user generated contents. In: Proceedings of the 20th International Conference on Computational Linguistics and Intelligent Text Processing, 7–13 April 2019, La Rochelle, France (2019)

Exploring TikTok Use and Non-use Practices and Experiences in China

Xing Lu[1], Zhicong Lu[2(✉)], and Changqing Liu[3]

[1] Ningxia University, Yinchuan, China
lxncs@nxu.edu.cn
[2] University of Toronto, Toronto, Canada
luzhc@dgp.toronto.edu
[3] Guangdong University of Foreign Studies, Guangzhou, China
liucq@gdufs.edu.cn

Abstract. Short-form video sharing mobile applications like TikTok (Douyin) have been gaining traction globally in recent years. These video sharing platforms have transformed how users consume online content in a drastic way. The recommendation algorithms of these applications form a "ludic loop" for users – the more users watch videos, the better the algorithms work, and the more users are exposed to content of their interest. Although prior research has explored how and why users watch short-form videos, relatively little research has studied those who choose not to use Douyin. To address this, we conducted a survey study with Internet users in China (N = 192), focusing specifically on Douyin and those who have abandoned or never adopted Douyin. Our results show that various perceptions of these users shape diverse practices of engagement with and disengagement from Douyin. Those who choose not to use Douyin are mostly motivated by the fear of addiction, or the stigmatized perceptions of videos on Douyin that deemed low-quality. Those who are using Douyin and those who choose to quit Douyin have different perceptions of the efficacy of Douyin's recommendation algorithms. We situate our findings with prior research on technology non-use, and provide design implications for future video-based social media.

Keywords: Short video sharing · Uses and gratifications · User engagement · Social computing · Non-use · TikTok

1 Introduction

TikTok (or Douyin, 抖音, for its Chinese version) is a short-form video sharing mobile application launched in autumn 2016. As of January 2020, Douyin boasts 400 million daily active users in China [24], and TikTok is still gaining great traction around the globe, among the most downloaded non-game apps of iOS App Store and Google Play App Store globally [14]. It allows users to produce and browse quick-fire short-form videos lasting from 15 s to a few minutes, to share funny and even nonsense videos widely online. Douyin's influence has also

G. Meiselwitz (Ed.): HCII 2020, LNCS 12195, pp. 57–70, 2020.
https://doi.org/10.1007/978-3-030-49576-3_5

extended to people's offline life: many commodities, places of interest, cultural practices, fancy food, and songs become widely spread on the platform, and users eagerly pursue such things in their real life as a fashionable life style [8]. Because of its worldwide popularity, some early research has explored the use of TikTok or Douyin, examining the roles such platforms play in their users' social lives. However, most of the existing literature are qualitative in its nature, and mainly focuses on specific use scenarios, such as sharing content of intangible cultural heritage on Douyin [9] or outdoor experiences on Douyin [10].

In this paper, we are interested in both the use and non-use of Douyin. It is worth exploring why some Internet users in China choose not to use Douyin or to quit using Douyin given that more than half of the Internet users in China (400 million) are using Douyin daily [24]. As shown in prior research that using Douyin is seen as 'a fashionable lifestyle' in China [8], refusing Douyin could exclude a user from information access and social interactions in a way that refusing few other technologies would in China, thus making Douyin non-use an important area of study. To our knowledge, no extant research has examined the prevalence of leaving or not using TikTok, the commonality of the desire to leave TikTok, types of opinions about leaving TikTok, or other practices of limiting TikTok use without leaving entirely. Furthermore, little is known about what the leaving process of TikTok entails or its personal and social ramifications. Specifically, we are interested in the following questions:

RQ1: What motivates users to use Douyin and to not use Douyin?
RQ2: How do users use Douyin and how do users abandon using Douyin?
RQ3: How do users perceive the efficacy of Douyin's recommendation algorithms, and how does the perception influence their use and non-use?

More specifically, we are interested in the following four types of users:

– *current user*, who currently has Douyin app on their device and uses Douyin;
– *deleted with no intention to come back*, who has deleted Douyin and is very unlikely to come back;
– *temporarily deleted*, who has temporarily deleted Douyin but could technically reinstall at any time; and
– *never used*, who has never had used Douyin.

This paper aims to address this gap by a survey study of 192 participants in China about their use and/or non-use of Douyin. Our results shed light on the prevalence of non-using or leaving Douyin, in what contexts users are using Douyin, what features of Douyin users make use of, what content and genres of videos users watch on Douyin, and how users perceive the user experience of the recommendation algorithms. We relate our results to prior research in video interaction and video sharing platforms, live streaming, and social computing theories. We also discuss design and social implications from our investigation in the situated cultural context of China.

2   Background and Related Work

Sharing videos online have been adopted by Internet users and communities since the birth of online video or image sharing platforms such as YouTube and Instagram. Compared with these popular online video sharing platforms, Douyin has some unique features, such as emphasizing short-form videos, background music, and special visual effects and filters. Given the traction it has been gaining in the past few years, we chose to focus on Douyin to understand the specific practices of using short video sharing platforms, and to investigate the affordances of such platforms in the unique social media landscapes and social contexts of China.

Motivations for use of online video sharing platforms such as YouTube, Instagram and Snapchat are well studied. For example, a survey of online videos found that adult content producers mostly post videos of family and friends doing everyday things, themselves or other people behaving in funny ways, and events they attend [6]. Research has also found that video sharing platform users often want to present themselves differently from their social life [13], and youth content providers want to perform, tell stories, and express their opinions and identities in a performative way [25]. Several research has also explored motivations, e.g., aspirational, educational, inspirational, entertainment, community, and ambience [20], and use practices of live streaming, e.g., video gaming [4], information behavior on social live streaming services [18,26], mobile live streaming [19], live streaming in China [7,11,12], gamification in live streaming [17], and live streaming shopping. Several research also focuses on different stakeholders of live streaming, e.g., how viewers support streamers [22] and how moderators get involved in helping streamers [21].

However, non-use of video sharing platforms have been less explored, mostly because there are many different video-sharing platforms available in the world, and not using one specific platform may result from arbitrary reasons. However, as Douyin has its unique features and has become almost a dominating video sharing platform in China, refusing Douyin could exclude a user from information and social interactions in a way that refusing few other technologies would in China, thus making Douyin non-use an important and interesting area of study. Researchers have studied non-use of technology more generally [1,3], and have provided typologies of non-users. For example, Wyatt's proposed four dimensions of non-users (i.e., resisters, rejectors, the excluded, and the expelled) [23], and Satchell and Dourish proposed a more nuanced six varieties of non-use particular to HCI (i.e., lagging adoption, active resistance, disenchantment, disenfranchisement, displacement, and disinterest) [16].

To the best of our knowledge, this paper is one of the first to examine the use and non-use of short video sharing practices on Douyin using a quantitative method. We also provide a nuanced understanding of how perceptions of recommendation algorithms influence use and non-use of Douyin.

3   Methods

3.1   Data Collection: Survey

We adapted the methods of Rader et al. [15] and Baumer et al. [1], who used an online survey-based methodology to collect stories about issues related to computer security and Facebook non-use, respectively. We developed an online questionnaire in a similar manner, using two types of questions. The questionnaire was first developed in English with the research team, then translated into Chinese by one of the native Chinese authors and validated by another.

The first line of questioning probed the use or non-use of Douyin. These questions included mostly yes/no, multiple choice, or 5 point Likert-style questions and focused on understanding whether the respondent is currently actively using Douyin, when s/he first started using Douyin, which features s/he uses most often, whether s/he had ever deactivated or deleted her or his account, or deleted the mobile app, whether s/he had ever considered deleting or deactivated her or his own account, how they perceived the usefulness of Douyin's recommendation algorithms, and how they perceived their privacy using Douyin, and other similar questions. The items were adapted from the framework of evaluating user experience of recommender system from Knijnenburg et al. [5], which includes questions probing users' perceptions of recommendation quality and variety.

The second set of questions were open-ended and probed the experience and practices of deactivating or deleting Douyin. Similar to Baumer et al. [1], all respondents were asked to tell a story about a time when they or someone they knew either left/delete Douyin or systematically limited their use in some way.

Additionally, certain parts of the questionnaire were either shown or hidden depending on responses to certain questions. For example, respondents who had deleted their Douyin app were asked to describe how they made the decision and what happened afterward. Those who had not deactivated their account or deleted their app but had considered doing so were asked to describe a time that made them consider leaving. Respondents who had never used Douyin were asked why they did not. The factual questions about use and non-use similarly adapted to respondents' answers. For example, respondents who did not currently use Douyin were not shown questions about their most used features. Those who had deactivated their account or deleted Douyin app were asked how satisfied they were with that decision. Respondents who had not deleted Douyin app were asked if they had ever considered deleting it. The survey concluded with demographic information, including age, gender, occupation, and city.

The questionnaire was distributed mainly through WeChat, where the authors posted the link to online survey in many chat groups on WeChat, followed by a brief description of the study goals. In addition, respondents were asked to forward the questionnaire to anyone they thought might be interested.

3.2   Analysis of Open-Ended Data

Responses to the open-ended questions were analyzed using an open coding method [3]. The authors coded the first 20% of responses and met to gain consensus on the codes. One author coded the remaining responses and met with the other coder to reach agreement. All the codes were then discussed by all the authors using affinity diagramming to group and find emerging themes.

4   Results

The survey was completed by 192 respondents. In what follows, we first provide the demographic data of the respondents, then we report on their motivations and practices of use/non-use of Douyin. After that, we detailed their perceptions of the recommendation algorithms of Douyin.

Most respondents in our study (81.2%) were between 15–25 years old, and 78.7% were college or university students, with 56.3% being male, 39.1% being female, and 4.7% not disclosed. Although our sample skewed a little young, it aligns with Douyin's target – young users. In terms of education, over half of the respondents (69.3%) either were studying for a bachelor's degree or already got one, while 17.7% either were studying for a master's degree or already got one, which aligns with previous market report of Douyin users in China. Our respondents also spanned 15 different provinces in China, although they were mostly located in Guangdong (18.8%) and Ningxia (57.3%) due to the limitation of our sampling method.

Of all the respondents, 34.9% (N = 67) were current users of Douyin, 44.3% (N = 85) never used Douyin, 13.5% (N = 26) had temporarily deleted Douyin, and 7.3% (N = 14) had used Douyin but quitted Douyin without an intention to come back. So in total, 55.7% (N = 107) respondents were using or had used Douyin.

4.1   Usage of Douyin

When asked about how often the current users use Douyin, about two thirds of the respondents (65.7%) use Douyin at least once a day. Only 7.5% respondents use Douyin less than once per week (Fig. 1). The results demonstrated that many respondents arc dedicated Douyin users.

In terms of different Douyin features the respondents use, we found that over 90% of respondents focus on watching Douyin videos and liking videos posted by others (Fig. 2). About 65.7% respondents also often search for Douyin videos or specific music. Surprisingly, over half of respondents (62.7%) also often download Douyin videos to keep the record or share the videos to other social media, however, less than 30% of respondents share videos to other users regularly. This could partly be due to the fact that sharing Douyin video links directly is banned on WeChat, and the workaround for users to share Douyin videos with friends is to download the video on the device and send it as a video message. It also indicates that Douyin users are highly motivated to keep a record

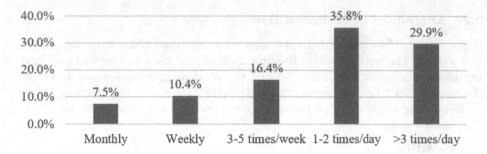

Fig. 1. Frequency of using Douyin (N = 67).

of the videos they watched on their devices, especially those videos that catch their attention. Our respondents also regularly look for local videos (44.8%), comment on Douyin videos by other users (44.8%), and watch livestreams on Douyin (43.3%). However, only about one third of our respondents (34.3%) regularly make videos and upload to Douyin. Further, less than 30% respondents send messages to other Douyin users and comment on livestreams on Douyin, even lesser purchase commodities on Douyin (14.9%) or send virtual gifts for livestreamers (7.4%).

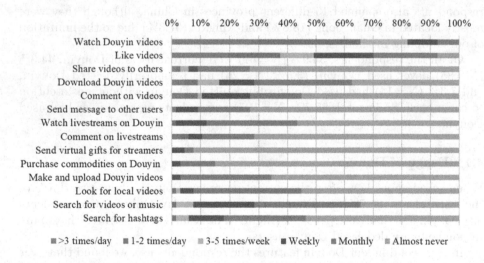

Fig. 2. Frequency of using Douyin features (N = 67).

We adapted items from the study of Bentley and Lottridge [2] on situations where people watch mobile TV to ask about different situations where respondents used Douyin. Over half of the respondents watch Douyin before going to bed (Fig. 3). Other commonly reported situations include when using the restroom, when waiting shortly, when traveling, when eating, and when nothing to do. It seems that the short-form nature of Douyin videos fits the spontaneous

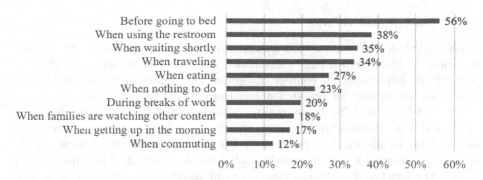

Fig. 3. The situations where people watched Douyin videos (N = 67).

nature of these situations. It also implicates that dedicated users use Douyin in various situations throughout the day, mostly in a short period of time.

4.2 Motivations and Gratifications of Using Douyin

We asked the respondents to describe what they think is the most valuable in using Douyin in their own words. We analyzed their free-text responses and aggregated similar responses into themes. The most prevalent themes include entertainment (e.g., for fun and killing time), knowledge (e.g., information), positive energy, intelligent recommendation, music, social, and commercial, see Fig. 4. It is surprising that about 28% of respondents reported knowledge or educational value as the most valuable gratification of using Douyin, even approaching those who reported entertainment or fun. There were also 11.2% respondents reported positive energy Douyin provided as the most valuable. This implicates that besides fun and happiness, a lot of dedicated Douyin users are motivated by Douyin's educational value or the positivity it brings to users, which seems to be an unique phenomenon considering the actual affordances of short-form video (producing eye-catching, joking, or even nonsense videos).

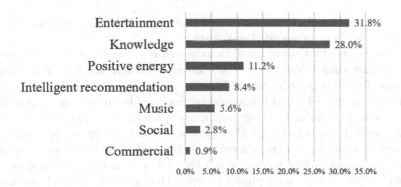

Fig. 4. The most important and valued motivation of using Douyin (N = 107).

4.3 Content and Genres

With regards to the content that was most favored by respondents, there were a variety of video genres that users had a high interest in watching (Fig. 5). The survey items used for content categories and genres of videos on Douyin were adapted from prior research about Douyin and live streaming by Lu et al. [8] and Lu et al. [12]. Again, many respondents (68.2%) reported that they enjoy watching videos about *positive energy*, i.e., where the content providers share videos to advocate for pro-social behaviors or charity engagement. Music and songs, knowledge sharing, movie-related, food-related, and life tips are also among the top favorite content genres by our respondents. Funny videos were only reported by 11.2% respondents as one of their favorite genres of videos.

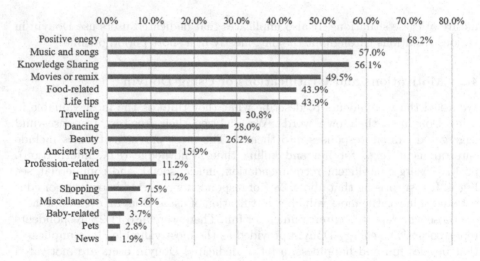

Fig. 5. Genres of videos respondents liked to watch on Douyin (N = 107).

4.4 Motivations and Practices of Douyin Non-use

We now reported on the motivations and practices of Douyin non-users through the analysis of their open-ended responses.

For those who had never used Douyin before (N = 85), the most reported reasons for not using Douyin include the anticipation that using Douyin costs too much time, fear of being addicted to Douyin, an impression that Douyin is full of 'vulgar' videos, fear of being influenced by low-quality content or inappropriate values, fear of toxicity of the community, and preferring text or image to video. Several respondents noted that they saw a lot of news on social media that some content providers on Douyin create vulgar or low-quality content, or share videos with inappropriate values, which they thought deemed to have negative influence on users, especially young people. They got stigmatized impressions from other channels and eventually choose to stay away from using Douyin, and even ask people around not to use Douyin. As noted in the following quote,

"From my impression on Douyin videos shared from my friends who are using Douyin, I think many Douyin videos are boring and low-quality videos uploaded by people who have too much free time, or are just for commercial purposes and they produce videos to catch your attention. I think using Douyin to watch such videos is like reducing IQ for me."

For those who had used Douyin but deleted it (N = 40), the most reported reasons for deleting Douyin mobile app include feeling that Douyin 'wastes' too much time, having to focus on work or study, continuously seeing homogeneous videos, fear of being addicted, taking up too much memory of the mobile device, using up too much mobile data, distrusting videos that use filters, fear of health getting affected by overusing Douyin, and dissatisfaction with the recommended videos. For example, one respondent noted,

"When using Douyin, I often stayed up late at night watching those videos, which caused me not having enough energy to study the next day. Later I felt that some videos on Douyin are vulgar and homogeneous. Douyin's filters are so powerful that those good-looking girls may not really be beautiful in real life. After deleting Douyin, I have enough mobile data, go to bed earlier, and I no longer have unrealistic fantasy about beautiful girls."

When asked whether they had adopted any practices to limit their use of Douyin, 69.2% of respondents (N = 74) who had used Douyin reported they had deleted Douyin app, and 37% reported that they had used other approaches to reduce Douyin use. Among the 74 respondents who had deleted Douyin, 41.9% were neutral (neither satisfied nor unsatisfied) with the decision, 18.9% satisfied, and 31.1% very satisfied. This indicates that for some users, simply deleting Douyin did not make them happier – although they could save time, they might still miss the joy or value provided by Douyin after deleting it. Several respondents who were students reported that during the end of semesters they usually delete Douyin to focus on study. Some also reported that they used some time management tools to limit the time they spend using Douyin every day, or set up alarm to stop using Douyin before going to bed. Basically, most strategies they adopted were to combat their addictions with Douyin.

Several responses also revealed several unique cases where they persuade or even force their friends or families to limit the use of Douyin or quit using Douyin. For example, some people think watching Douyin videos too much could influence adolescents' values, so they would persuade young people limit their use of Douyin, as noted by the following quote, *"Many videos on Douyin could twisted young people's perceptions of life and values. I think they should focus more on learning than watchign Douyin"*. In another case, a respondent reported that one of his female friends urged her boyfriend to stop using Douyin, because she did not want him to be involved with too many beautiful female content providers on Douyin, which could bring risks to their relationship, "*A girl noticed that her boy friend followed many female content providers on Douyin. She felt a little offensive, so she forced her boyfriend to delete Douyin*". This indicates that Douyin has become so influential in China that many people begin to control the use of Douyin in their close-tie relationships to avoid being negatively influenced by Douyin in real life.

4.5   Experience with Recommendation Algorithms of Douyin and Its Relationship to Non-use

We also asked all the respondents who had used Douyin (current users or quitted users; N = 107) to rate their user experience of the recommendation algorithms of Douyin. We now report on the differences on their user experience between those who are currently still using Douyin (N = 67; Group A) and those who quit Douyin (N = 40; Group B, see Table 1).

We found that between the two groups, they had no significant difference in their perceptions of relevance of the recommended videos on Douyin, perceptions of the variety of content recommended by Douyin, perceptions of the relevance of content providers of the recommended videos, and confidence in Douyin's respect for their privacy. On the other hand, current users agreed more on the statements that the recommended videos on Douyin fit their preference, are fun and of good quality, and they like the recommended videos. Current users also agreed that the recommended videos on Douyin are less similar, have various genres, and they would like to recommend Douyin to their friends. Those who had used Douyin but deleted it also agreed more than current Douyin users that Douyin discloses their private information and invades their privacy.

Our results show that the perceived quality of user experience of Douyin's recommendation algorithms influence Douyin users' use or non-use. Those who abandon Douyin in general perceived that Douyin's recommendation algorithms work worse than current Douyin users perceived, and they were more concerned about their privacy using Douyin's recommendation algorithms. This implicates that the perceived efficacy of recommendation algorithms of Douyin play an important role for its users to decide whether to keep using Douyin.

5   Discussion

Our results describe the varying degrees and types of dis/engagement with/from Douyin, and the motivations and justifications respondents gave for their choices. We reflect on our findings and relate to prior work on the negation of technology.

5.1   Use and Non-use of Social Media

Our findings echoed several findings of prior work on non-use. Respondents who did not use Douyin could be described as actively resisting Douyin [16]. Such users include not only those who had never installed Douyin on their mobile

Table 1. Descriptive statistics for scales and variables used in survey instrument

	A Current users N = 67 Mean(SD)	B Deleted N = 40 Mean(SD)	Difference between A & B
Recommended videos are relevant	3.25 (0.68)	3.05 (0.78)	n.s.
Recommended videos fit my preference	3.48 (0.73)	3.20 (0.72)	$p < 0.1$
Recommended videos are fun	3.49 (0.66)	3.08 (0.69)	$p < 0.01$
Recommended videos are of good quality	3.27 (0.62)	2.98 (0.62)	$p < 0.05$
I like recommended videos	3.30 (0.60)	2.90 (0.59)	$p < 0.01$
Recommended videos are not from favorite content providers	3.00 (0.67)	3.00 (0.72)	n.s.
Recommended videos have various content	3.40 (0.55)	3.23 (0.73)	n.s.
Recommended videos are similar	3.04 (0.64)	3.45 (0.75)	$p < 0.01$
Recommended videos have various genres	3.25 (0.59)	2.90 (0.78)	$p < 0.01$
I would recommend Douyin to others	3.21 (0.79)	2.65 (0.89)	$p < 0.001$
Douyin discloses private information about me	3.00 (0.83)	3.35 (0.70)	$p < 0.05$
Douyin invades my privacy	2.67 (0.75)	3.17 (0.64)	$p < 0.001$
I feel confident that Douyin respects my privacy	3.09 (0.60)	2.85 (0.74)	n.s.

device, but also those who had used Douyin but decided to delete the app, i.e., resistors and rejectors [23]. Disenchantment [16] aligns with several respondents who reported that they thought the content on Douyin is banal, and prevalence of videos with filters on Douyin makes them distrust content on Douyin. We also found that many users have a strong opinion that they wanted to influence people in their close-tie relationships (children, parents, or intimate relationship), which are seldom reported in prior research. This might be partly due to the nature of collective culture, which worth further exploration.

We also saw something we term *conditional* or *contextual resistance*, that several respondents only quit temporally but return to using Douyin after certain conditions are cleared, e.g., those who wanted to focus on studying during the exams deleted Douyin temporally but installed Douyin after finishing the exams. This could partly be explained by that people easily get addicted to Douyin and it is hard to quit, and that they may find value in the content on Douyin that totally leaving Douyin will make them feel lost. However, future research should further explore this group of users and their motivations and practices.

We also found a interesting conflicting perceptions from those who keep using Douyin and those who do not use or quit Douyin in that the former reported that they found that many videos on Douyin which has **positive energy** were valuable to them, while the latter reported that they thought a lot of videos are low-quality and have twisted values. Although it might be true that they had different channels which took them to different types of content, there is also a chance that they actually had different standards for 'positive energy', especially considering that many videos with 'positive energy' may not be that visually pleasant to watch (e.g., some organizations helping homeless people or those in poverty in rural areas). Future research should better probe how different people perceive positive energy, and how their perceptions on positive energy influence their social media use.

5.2   User Perceptions on Recommendation Algorithms

Our results empirically show that users who perceived better user experience with recommendation algorithms of Douyin tend to keep using Douyin, which highlights the important role recommendation algorithms of Douyin plays in engaging users. We also show that those who quitted using Douyin had more concerns with privacy issues regarding the recommendation algorithms of Douyin. However, due to the limitation of our method, we could not conclude the low perceptions of recommendation algorithms and Douyin non-use have causality, nor that privacy concerns and Douyin non-use have causality.

Our result also raises an interesting question regarding user perceptions on recommendation algorithms: how Douyin use influence users perceptions and concerns on privacy? From the open-ended data, it seems that those dedicated Douyin users seemed to be more tolerant to privacy issues. They experienced the benefits of Douyin's recommendation algorithms which could accurately provide interesting content for them to watch whenever they want. They might gradually perceive privacy intrusion as "normal" and even grant more access of their personal data to Douyin if they want more 'convenience' from Douyin. Future work should explore the long-term influence of recommendation algorithms – would such ludic recommendation algorithms of Douyin make users more tolerant to privacy issues? How should we design better privacy mechanisms for platforms like Douyin to make people more aware of privacy risks?

5.3   Limitations and Outlook

Our study has several limitations. The survey data is based on self-reported use, and is subject to the usual biases that can appear when people are asked to remember their behaviors. Since this exploratory study include many open-ended questions, where we simply collected stories rather than ask about specific motivations or experiences. Thus, the proportions for each theme may not be representative; a respondent not mentioning does not mean s/he has not experienced it. Our sampling is also not ideal, since it is a combination of snowball sampling and convenient sampling. Our sample skewed a little young in Chinese population, and did not proportionally cover people in different areas of China.

In addition to aforementioned research opportunities, the medium of prepared questions yielded responses that were often ambiguous and hinted at more insights "under the surface". Future work should use techniques such as in-depth interviews, focus groups, diaries, and other methods to explore deeper. Larger-scale quantitative data could also be leveraged to investigate Douyin non-use at scale.

References

1. Baumer, E.P., et al.: Limiting, leaving, and (re)lapsing: an exploration of facebook non-use practices and experiences. In: Proceedings of the SIGCHI Conference on Human Factors in Computing Systems, CHI 2013, pp. 3257–3266. ACM, New York (2013). https://doi.org/10.1145/2470654.2466446
2. Bentley, F., Lottridge, D.: Understanding mass-market mobile TV behaviors in the streaming era. In: Proceedings of the 2019 CHI Conference on Human Factors in Computing Systems, CHI 2019. ACM, New York (2019). https://doi.org/10.1145/3290605.3300491
3. Birnholtz, J.: Adopt, adapt, abandon: understanding why some young adults start, and then stop, using instant messaging. Comput. Hum. Behav. **26**(6), 1427–1433 (2010)
4. Hamilton, W.A., Garretson, O., Kerne, A.: Streaming on twitch: fostering participatory communities of play within live mixed media. In: Proceedings of the SIGCHI Conference on Human Factors in Computing Systems, CHI 2014, pp. 1315–1324. ACM, New York (2014). https://doi.org/10.1145/2556288.2557048
5. Knijnenburg, B.P., Willemsen, M.C., Gantner, Z., Soncu, H., Newell, C.: Explaining the user experience of recommender systems. User Model. User-Adap. Inter. **22**(4–5), 441–504 (2012). https://doi.org/10.1007/s11257-011-9118-4
6. Purcell, K.: Online video 2013. Pew Research Center, Washington (2013). http://www.pewinternet.org/2013/10/10/online-video-2013/
7. Lin, J., Lu, Z.: The rise and proliferation of live-streaming in China: insights and lessons. In: Stephanidis, C. (ed.) HCI 2017. CCIS, vol. 714, pp. 632–637. Springer, Cham (2017). https://doi.org/10.1007/978-3-319-58753-0_89
8. Lu, X., Lu, Z.: Fifteen seconds of fame: a qualitative study of Douyin, a short video sharing mobile application in China. In: Meiselwitz, G. (ed.) HCII 2019. LNCS, vol. 11578, pp. 233–244. Springer, Cham (2019). https://doi.org/10.1007/978-3-030-21902-4_17
9. Lu, Z., Annett, M., Fan, M., Wigdor, D.: "I feel it is my responsibility to stream": streaming and engaging with intangible cultural heritage through livestreaming. In: Proceedings of the 2019 CHI Conference on Human Factors in Computing Systems, CHI 2019. ACM, New York (2019). https://doi.org/10.1145/3290605.3300459
10. Lu, Z., Annett, M., Wigdor, D.: Vicariously experiencing it all without going outside: a study of outdoor livestreaming in China. Proc. ACM Hum. Comput. Interact. **3**(CSCW), 1–28 (2019). https://doi.org/10.1145/3359127
11. Lu, Z., Heo, S., Wigdor, D.J.: Streamwiki: enabling viewers of knowledge sharing live streams to collaboratively generate archival documentation for effective in-stream and post hoc learning. Proc. ACM Hum. Comput. Interact. **2**(CSCW), 1–26 (2018). https://doi.org/10.1145/3274381
12. Lu, Z., Xia, H., Heo, S., Wigdor, D.: You watch, you give, and you engage: a study of live streaming practices in China. In: Proceedings of the 2018 CHI Conference on Human Factors in Computing Systems, CHI 2018. ACM, New York (2018). https://doi.org/10.1145/3173574.3174040

13. McRoberts, S., Ma, H., Hall, A., Yarosh, S.: Share first, save later: performance of self through snapchat stories. In: Proceedings of the 2017 CHI Conference on Human Factors in Computing Systems, CHI 2017, pp. 6902–6911. ACM, New York (2017). https://doi.org/10.1145/3025453.3025771

14. Nelson, R.: The top mobile apps for November 2018 TikTok reached a new high (2018). https://sensortower.com/blog/top-apps-november-2018

15. Rader, E., Wash, R., Brooks, B.: Stories as informal lessons about security. In: Proceedings of the Eighth Symposium on Usable Privacy and Security, SOUPS 2012. ACM, New York (2012). https://doi.org/10.1145/2335356.2335364

16. Satchell, C., Dourish, P.: Beyond the user: use and non-use in HCI. In: Proceedings of the 21st Annual Conference of the Australian Computer-Human Interaction Special Interest Group: Design: Open 24/7, OZCHI 2009, pp. 9–16. ACM, New York (2009). https://doi.org/10.1145/1738826.1738829

17. Scheibe, K.: The impact of gamification in social live streaming services. In: Meisel-witz, G. (ed.) SCSM 2018. LNCS, vol. 10914, pp. 99–113. Springer, Cham (2018). https://doi.org/10.1007/978-3-319-91485-5_7

18. Scheibe, K., Fietkiewicz, K.J., Stock, W.G.: Information behavior on social live streaming services. J. Inf. Sci. Theory Pract. 4(2), 6–20 (2016)

19. Tang, J.C., Venolia, G., Inkpen, K.M.: Meerkat and periscope: I stream, you stream, apps stream for live streams. In: Proceedings of the 2016 CHI Conference on Human Factors in Computing Systems, CHI 2016, pp. 4770–4780. ACM, New York (2016). https://doi.org/10.1145/2858036.2858374

20. Taylor, T.: Watch Me Play: Twitch and the Rise of Game Live Streaming, vol. 24. Princeton University Press, Princeton (2018)

21. Wohn, D.Y.: Volunteer moderators in twitch micro communities: how they get involved, the roles they play, and the emotional labor they experience. In: Proceedings of the 2019 CHI Conference on Human Factors in Computing Systems, CHI 2019. ACM, New York (2019). https://doi.org/10.1145/3290605.3300390

22. Wohn, D.Y., Freeman, G., McLaughlin, C.: Explaining viewers' emotional, instrumental, and financial support provision for live streamers. In: Proceedings of the 2018 CHI Conference on Human Factors in Computing Systems, CHI 2018. ACM, New York (2018). https://doi.org/10.1145/3173574.3174048

23. Wyatt, S.M., Oudshoorn, N., Pinch, T.: Non-users also matter: the construction of users and non-users of the internet. In: Now Users Matter: The Co-construction of Users and Technology, pp. 67–79 (2003)

24. Xu, T.: Bytedance's Douyin reaches 400 million users (2020). https://technode.com/2020/01/06/bytedances-douyin-reaches-400-million-users/

25. Yarosh, S., Bonsignore, E., McRoberts, S., Peyton, T.: YouthTube: youth video authorship on youtube and vine. In: Proceedings of the 19th ACM Conference on Computer-Supported Cooperative Work & Social Computing, CSCW 2016, pp. 1423–1437. ACM, New York (2016). https://doi.org/10.1145/2818048.2819961

26. Zimmer, F., Scheibe, K.: What drives streamers? Users' characteristics and motivations on social live streaming services. In: Proceedings of the 52nd Hawaii International Conference on System Sciences (2019)

Building an Integrated Comment Moderation System – Towards a Semi-automatic Moderation Tool

Dennis M. Riehle$^{(\boxtimes)}$, Marco Niemann , Jens Brunk ,
Dennis Assenmacher , Heike Trautmann , and Jörg Becker

ERCIS, University of Münster, 48149 Münster, Germany
dennis.riehle@ercis.uni-muenster.de

Abstract. The past decade has been characterized by a strong increase in the use of social media and a continuous growth of public online discussion. With the failure of purely manual moderation, platform operators started searching for semi-automated solutions, where the application of Natural Language Processing (NLP) and Machine Learning (ML) techniques is promising. However, this requires huge financial investments for algorithmic implementations, data collection, and model training, which only big players can afford. To support smaller or medium-sized media enterprises (SME), we developed an integrated comment moderation system as an IT platform. This platform acts as a service provider and offers Analytics as a Service (AaaS) to SMEs. Operating such a platform, however, requires a robust technology stack, integrated workflows and well-defined interfaces between all parties. In this paper, we develop and discuss a suitable IT architecture and present a prototypical implementation.

Keywords: Comment moderation · Machine learning · Business model · IT platform · Analytics as a service

1 Introduction

The internet and especially the web 2.0 disrupted the way how people communicate and exchange information. Where sporadic letters to the editor have been the most prominent form of reader feedback for decades, newspapers nowadays offer discussion fora and comment sections, allowing their audience to directly interact and engage with each other and the journalists [23,32,34]. In times of decreasing sales of physical newspaper copies, reader engagement in the digital realm (and hence dwelling time) is perceived as central for economic sustainability [34]. However, the promising concept turned out to be less shiny in reality: instead of being spaces for lively exchange that create value for the reader, many comment sections turned out to be collections of appalling and vile content [23]. With estimates ranging from 2% to 80% of abusive user-generated comment

© Springer Nature Switzerland AG 2020
G. Meiselwitz (Ed.): HCII 2020, LNCS 12195, pp. 71–86, 2020.
https://doi.org/10.1007/978-3-030-49576-3_6

content [4,11,23,28,36,44], many journalists and newspapers turn their back on comment sections and even urge their readers to refrain from reading comments at all [3,23]. Despite being an unpleasant experience that might scare off people (and hence subscription and advertisement money), especially hateful or insulting comments can even cause substantial legal issues [48]. Considering the massive amounts of incoming comments that newspapers face (e.g., The New York Times reports 9,000 comments per day [17]), manual filtering and moderation turn out to be a *"great deal of extra work"* [48]. The necessary workforce to handle these comments is a substantial investment without any direct returns (as comments are typically a free feature). Consequently, many newspapers either decided to lock the comment sections for the most debated topics or even closed them completely [4,31,48,57]. While economically reasonable, many journalists prefer to refrain from these radical approaches because of ethical considerations [4,14,23,47]. However, if newspapers decide to keep the functionalities for direct user feedback, enforcing the typically more rigid guidelines often worsens the already problematic expenses. For example, moving from post-moderation (*checking when reported*) to strict pre-moderation (*checking before publishing*) can be a prohibitive investment for many newspapers, especially if comments should be released timely. While some – especially large – newspapers might be able to afford this type of debate, many other opportunities for exchange with readers will disappear eventually. To keep these virtual spaces of discourse available, both practitioners and academics began to investigate, whether comment moderation could be (semi-)automated [3,41]. Recent advances in the areas of machine learning (ML) and natural language processing (NLP) show promising results and provide reason to believe that such a solution is indeed feasible. However, there are still several substantial challenges left that range from a precise definition of the problem at hand to the actual training of the ML models and ensuring their acceptance. Furthermore, competent analysts and developers that could create and maintain such a tool are sparse and expensive. This situation makes it hard for small- and medium-sized enterprise (SME) media companies to benefit from these developments that could make comment sections more economically promising again. To address the mentioned challenges, we propose the creation of a novel Analytics as a Service (AaaS) platform, which would help to bundle extant resources to both speed up the problem-solving process as well as to reduce the cost and competencies required from SME newspapers. After introducing the business model in [6], we shed some light on the proposed technical architecture and its implementation.

2   Current Challenges

Despite the fact that abusive language received increasing interest from academia over the last decade, there are still some open research challenges left.

One of the open challenges is the fundamental question of *what constitutes abusive language*. While being widely discussed, no consistent and commonly used definition emerged [41,60] so far, which is partly due to the complexity of clearly delineating those concepts [22,25,40,52]. As a consequence, there is neither uniformity regarding the terms used to name the concepts nor regarding the use of the terms themselves. To ensure a common terminological ground we propose to increasingly work towards a standard definition or at least to agree on a common process to create definitions as, e.g., proposed by [40]. Since abusive language detection tools will be applied by a diverse set of platforms, this process should be able to integrate platform-specific restrictions [46] as well as the (inter-)national legal perspective(s) under which they are operating [20,40].

A second, closely related, challenge is the *accurate labeling* of large data sets. The underlying issue is the abundance of user comments generated each day that are not only natural language and hence unstructured data, but also lack any form of natural labeling. As abusive comments are usually filtered by algorithms that require those labels to train a suitable model (supervised learning algorithms), this implies a lack of necessary data for algorithms to separate clean from problematic comments. To overcome this issue, data is currently often manually annotated record by record which is time-consuming, expensive, and prone to biases [31,41]. Even though options such as crowd-sourcing exist and have been shown to be effective for the problem at hand [13,29,60], only financially powerful actors will be able to afford a substantial amount of labeling—plus the diversity of the annotating people is often detrimental to the annotation quality and consistency. As the quality of any detection tool substantially depends on the quality of its training material, we propose to use "custom crowds" [35] with carefully selected and curated annotators—which, however, increases the already substantial financial cost. Furthermore, pre-labelled data only reflects the status quo at a specific point in time.

Even with a suitable data set at hand further pitfalls and challenges await. Similar to many other machine learning problems, a plethora of different algorithms and algorithm classes are used to obtain promising results. These range from classical algorithms, such as logistic regression [1,7,13], tree-based approaches [8,10,13,15,37,49], Naïve Bayes [10,13,15,33], and SVMs [7,10,13,15,33,37,49,55,61] to neural networks, e.g. Recurrent Neural Networks [39,46,53], Convolutional Neural Networks [37,45,46,56] or Long Short-Term Memory Networks [1,32,37,56]. Currently, many publications do not report all major metrics (precision [1,7,37,41], recall [1,7,9,37,41], F-score [1,7,37,41], accuracy [16,46,60]), nor does the domain have an agreed-upon representation for the comments [41,50]. Furthermore, questions such as classifier configuration, parameter tuning or even interpretability [59] are still largely unanswered. Our proposal is to ensure greater clarity in result communication by incentivizing the reporting of all relevant parameters and metrics while assessing the potential of AutoML as an option to reduce the human bias [18,19,30].

The concluding challenge will revolve around achieving acceptance of all stakeholders which are primarily the community managers and the community members. In countries with codified freedom of speech many people—so far—perceive (semi-)automatic moderation as censorship and opinion dictatorship. Extant research tells us that people are more likely to trust and accept systems they can understand [12,24,38,54,59]—especially in cases where they behave in an unexpected manner (e.g., by blocking a comment) [27]. The EU regulation on algorithmic transparency, which grants every user of an "intelligent system" the right to receive an explanation for each automated decision, will further increase the need for interpretable results [5,21,26,43]. However, the associated domain of explainable artificial intelligence [51] is still in its early stages, respectively in its infancy considering abusive language detection.

3   A Business Model Canvas for an Integrated Platform

The aforementioned challenges require the adoption of (semi-) automated comment moderation tools. Especially for smaller and medium sized organizations, which do not have the human resources to perform a post-moderation of all user comments, (semi-) automated comment moderation is essential. First successful attempts to deploy such a tool have been reported in the literature (e.g., [56]). However, most of the published solutions only address some of the four challenges outlined above. While some seminal papers like [41] handle up to three of the challenges, many others at best deal with two [2], leaving large parts of the overall issue unaddressed. Additionally, especially for SMEs, further issues arise. Not every website operator or newspaper organization is capable of developing a system of their own. Therefore, the question arises, how a viable service-oriented business model could look like that provides this analytic functionality also to SME customers.

In previous work [6], we have adopted the Business Model Canvas (BMC) by Osterwalder [42] to develop a business model for operating a central comment moderation platform. The BMC is a strategic management tool, which uses a visual chart of nine building blocks to describe a business' value propositions, infrastructure, customer and finances. The resulting canvas is depicted in Fig. 1, where the nine building blocks identify as follows (cf. [6]):

"The **Customer Segments** building block defines the different groups of people or organizations an enterprise aims to reach and serve" [42, p. 20]. In this case, the AaaS platform serves a segmented market, because it distinguishes between different types of customers with different needs and problems. There will be small, medium and large enterprise customers. These customer types differ in the amount of comments that need to be processed as well in the frequency of performing additional ad-hoc analyses.

The **Value Proposition** building block describes which value the platform offers the customers through products or services. The AaaS platform creates value for its differently sized customers in three ways: First, since manual moderation reflects a major cost factor, automatic comment processing reduces costs for the customers. Second, the platform supports its customers in processing comments in a structured and documented manner to ultimately improve the quality of comment moderation. Third, the platform allows its customers to re-open comment sections on topics which had to be closed before and, as such, resurrects and increases their interaction within the community.

Key Partners	Key Activities	Value Propositions	Customer Relationships	Customer Segments
Provider for IT infrastructure, i.e., server hardware including CPU and CPU	Research & development Model building and training	Process of comment moderation follows a clear structure and is well documented Manual effort reduces, as comments are pre-scored and optionally filtered by the	Platform is used as a self-service by moderators Models are trained and adapted based on invividual customer needs	Customers can be split in three different segments: Small customers, only individual requests on demand, pay-by-use
Hosting provider, i.e., supply with bandwidth and network	Provision of API Scoring of new data			Medium-sized customers, integrated comment moderation workflow via API, purchasing packages with a given amount of requests
Cooperating partners from media industry, who provide comment data	**Key Resources** Open-source machine learning frameworks, e.g., Keras & Tensorflow Scored data sets	analysis system Increased engagement with visitors, as comment sections do not need to be closed further Clean comment sections more attractive for advertisers	**Channels** Digital communication and data exchange via the API Data can be exchanged by push or pull principle	Large customers, unlimited requests, fixed price

Cost Structure	Revenue Streams
Rental of hardware and hosting	Income through subscription-based plans
Research & development costs	Income through consultation and model adaption
Effort for consultation and model adaption for customers	

Fig. 1. Business Model Canvas for an integrated platform [6]

The **Channels** building block explains how a firm delivers its value proposition to their customers but also how it reaches new customers and communicates with existing ones. In this work we abstract from communication and marketing channels, as this is an issue of the exact instantiation of this conceptual business model. The delivery of the value proposition, which is the comment evaluation and the ability to moderate comments in an appropriate dashboard, is provided digitally. The data of the customers' own content management system and the AaaS platform is exchanged live through pre-defined application programming interfaces (API), which use push, pull and receive protocols.

The building block of **Customer Relationships** describes which kind of relationships the business maintains with its respective customer segments. In general, all customer segments (small to large customers) are provided with a self-service interface. They can submit the comments that need to be evaluated, receive and display the results and possibly manage them in the provided interface. On top of that, however, specific customers may want the trained evaluation models to be adapted to particular needs. This represents a second type of customer relationship that goes beyond the previously mentioned self-service infrastructure.

The **Revenue Streams** represent all incoming turnover that the business generates from its customers. Similar to the previous building block, the revenue stream is twofold. The first includes consulting, adapting and also implementing on a customer basis; e.g., the previously mentioned customization of the evaluation models or an API-provision for individual content management systems. The second and major revenue stream represents the subscription model that the different customer segments utilize to receive evaluations for their comments.

The essential resources needed to implement the business model are reflected in the building block of the **Key Resources**. The AaaS platform makes use of a variety of machine learning methods, tools, frameworks and libraries to calculate the evaluation models. Many of the applied assets are open source or available under different accessible licenses. Besides, training data sets are needed. These data sets include real world comments annotated with labels and additional information that the machine learning algorithms leverage to extract their decision making patterns. These data sets can stem from partners, customers or might be even self-developed.

Key Activities. The key activities building block describes the most important tasks that the business needs to perform in order to deliver its business value to the customers. For our platform, the most important activity is the evaluation of comments submitted by the customers. To be able to do this, two secondary activities need to be performed. On the one hand, the APIs need to be implemented and provided beforehand. And on the other hand, the evaluation model needs to be trained, which is a continuous challenge, as language is not a static but evolving construct.

Key Partnerships include all the relations and strategic partnerships that enable the business model to function. Considering the previous two building blocks, a strategic partnership with the developers of the machine learning tools and frameworks is of importance. Through this, the platform can ensure a timely and continuous delivery of necessary updates. Similarly, data set providers can be important partners. For example, some customers might also be data deliverers at the same time and therefore the relationship should receive special attention. Another more basic, but as important, partnership is the IT infrastructure and hosting of the platform. The calculation and provision of the machine learning evaluation models requires great amounts of calculation power and the availability of the service must always be guaranteed.

Last but not least, the **Cost Structure** includes all the cost that accumulate by executing the business model. Of course, the previously mentioned infrastructure, hosting, and computing power incurs major costs on the business. Furthermore, research and continuous development on how to improve, adapt, and optimize the evaluation models are very important. And ultimately, the staff that executes the consulting and adaption actions with (future) customers must be noted here as well.

4   Building an IT Architecture

To address the previously outlined challenges and to implement the presented AaaS business model a suitable IT artifact is needed. Given the aaS approach the platform needs to be web-based and multi-tenant-ready (#tenants=n) (each tenant being a media operator). As most media companies cater their content (and hence comments) to multiple systems (#systems=m) (ranging from proprietary CMS to social media platforms such as Facebook) the AaaS platform will have to support up to $n \times m$ interfaces. The concept of the platform is depicted in Fig. 2.

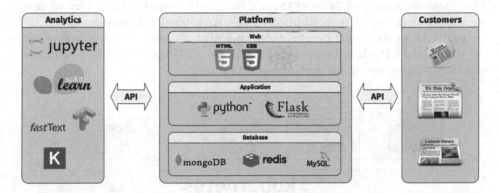

Fig. 2. Conceptualization of an integrated platform

Between these systems and the IT platform, data needs to be exchanged via Application Programming Interfaces (API). Here, two different data exchange patterns need to be distinguished: Following the *push principle*, the data sources actively push new user comments to the platform. This likely requires customization and/or programming on the side of the data source, as the software there needs to implement the API of the platform. An advantage of the push principle is the immediate availability of user comments on the platform, as the push activity can be triggered right after the comment was posted by the user. In contrast, the *pull principle* does not require programming on the data source's side but on the side of the platform. While this may be beneficial in case of closed-source software, where the website/weblog of the tenant cannot be adapted to implement the platform's API, the downside is that new comments are only periodically imported by the platform (e.g., every couple of minutes) and, hence, are not immediately available for processing.

The platform itself requires a database system for storing and processing user comments, where both `mongoDB` and `MySQL` are used. An additional Redis server is used for internal event processing. The web application's front-end uses modern technologies, namely HTML5 and CSS3 and is built using the web framework React. For the middleware (or application layer) we selected the Python-based framework `flask`[1]. The decision to go for a Python-based backend originates in the primarily Python-based analytics component. Hence, going for

---

[1] https://www.palletsprojects.com/p/flask/.

a full Python stack is supposed to reduce integration issues while simultaneously increasing the maintainability.

For the implementation of different classification algorithms and machine learning models, plenty of open-source tools and libraries are available. For development purposes, `jupyter notebook` is available. We use `fastText` to convert our textual input data into machine-processable word embeddings, which can be further utilized in machine learning models, e.g., by using `scikit-learn`. The libraries `Keras` and `TensorFlow` are included to add the capability to create deep-learning models in addition to the traditional ML models offered by `sklearn`. As an additional benefit, these specialist libraries do not only support the traditional CPU-based execution but the use of GPUs and TPUs which have been found more potent for such classification tasks.

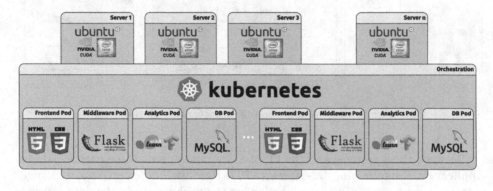

Fig. 3. IT architecture of an integrated platform

Based on the conceptualization of an integrated platform providing AaaS (cf. Fig. 2), we derive a suitable IT architecture. Since the platform supports different tenants, new data sources may be added or deleted at any time. Similarly, the amount of users as well as the amount of comments these users are posting may change over time. Consequently, the platform needs to be scalable to accomodate the changing computational load. To account for this, we have to implement our AaaS platform as virtualizable microservices. Nowadays, containerization is the most common virtualization, since it is light-weight and easy to deploy. Here, every microservice runs isolated in a separate container using a containerization engine like `Docker` or `containerd`. For orchestration of containers, i.e., the management of containers running and scaling the amount of running containers to the actual computation demand, usually a separate tool is used. We have chosen `Kubernetes`[2] for this purpose, since it is both open-source and industry-stable. While we exclusively discussed the software-stack so far, some of the included tools set limitations regarding the usable hardware, as, e.g., `tensorflow` can only compute on GPUs with `CUDA`, restricting our servers

---

[2] https://kubernetes.io/.

to use nvidia chips[3]. As the base operating system we chose Ubuntu, which is currently the most common Linux distribution for web services [58]. **Kubernetes** integrates all physical servers into a single cluster, where services can be executed as "pods" (technically containers). Figure 3 visualizes all involved components. The frontend pod serves the website's front-end, i.e., the HTML, CSS files etc. to the client's browser. The middleware pod does the processing of web requests in the back-end and maps all HTTP requests to an actual service. The analytics pod performs background tasks related to data processing like, for instance, the training of machine learning models with new data. Lastly, the DB pod serves and manages the database instance for data storing. All pods can be replicated, i.e, they can be executed multiple times, which allows the platform to scale to the actual computation demand.

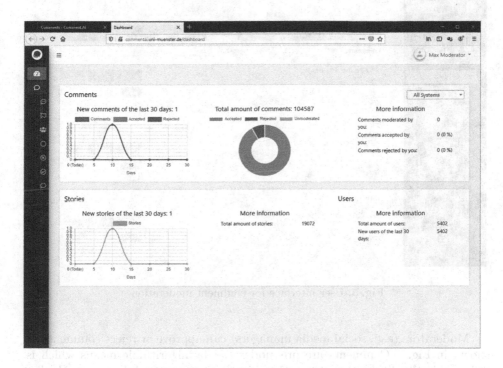

Fig. 4. Dashboard of the moderation platform

Currently, we have developed a prototypical implementation of the designed integrated platform according to the principles mentioned above. Figure 4 shows a screenshot of that implementation. In this example, we have imported user comments from two different sources: A Wordpress blog and the proprietary

---

[3] The decision for Intel CPUs is acknowledging Intel's leading market position for server processors.

CMS of a large German newspaper. The dashboard shows the amount of comments that were composed recently and visualizes the share of rejected comments among the amount of total comments. Furthermore, it provides an overview of newly created stories/articles as well as the development of users participating in the discussions. Combining this diverse information, the dashboard should cater to the needs of community managers as well as their superior (social media) managers.

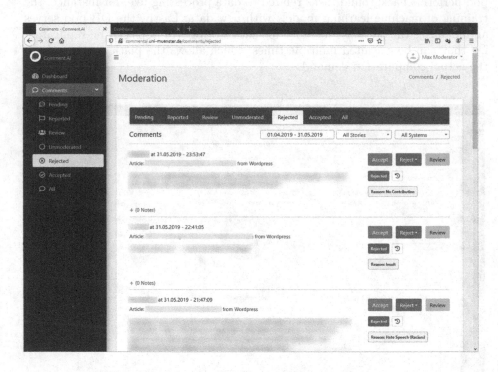

Fig. 5. User interface for comment moderation

Moderators (e.g., social media managers) can approve or reject comments as shown in Fig. 5. Comments are pre-moderated by algorithmic means which is reflected in the different queues depicted in the horizontal tab bar above the list of comments. Here, moderators can quickly jump into different queues to focus on comments which need attention. When comments are rejected, one rejection reason can be selected out of a list of pre-defined reasons. These pre-defined reasons are subject to specification by the site administrator. Besides approving or rejecting comments, moderators can also forward comments to other moderators by requesting a review. This supports discussing comments with colleagues in cases where decisions are hard to take. An exemplary, simplified moderation process with the AaaS platform is depicted in Fig. 6.

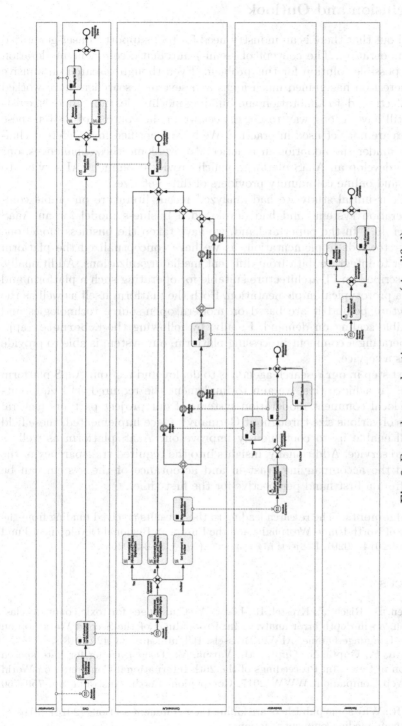

Fig. 6. Exemplary moderation process (simplified)

5   Conclusion and Outlook

We pointed out that there is an industry need for tool support in user-generated comment moderation. The concept of (semi-) automatic comment moderation provides a possible solution for this problem. Even though research on abusive language detection has gained much focus and several researchers have worked on data collection, data annotation and building machine learning models, existing tools still have a long way to go. Especially in the context of SMEs, these technologies are not yet used in practice. We have identified four different challenges that hinder the adoption in practice. To overcome these challenges, our goal was to develop an AaaS platform, which provides comment AI services to newspaper and online community providers of different sizes.

Within our initial study we had analyzed recent literature on online comment moderation systems and had developed a business model for an AaaS platform (cf. [6]). In the paper at hand, we have taken the business model one step further towards implementation, as we have conceptualized the platform in a manner to integrate data from different media organizations. Additionally, we have described an IT architecture suitable for operating such a platform and developed a prototypical implementation. Both the platform itself as well as the IT architecture behind it are based on modern open-source technologies and enable flexible scaling on demand. Finally, by following the Kubernetes approach of operating a comment processing platform, our system is able to provide analytics as a service.

The next step in our research agenda is to deploy and test our AaaS platform in practice. To achieve this, we aim to implement the required API endpoints within the local comment moderation systems of our project partners (several newspapers of various size throughout Germany). Once implemented, these field studies will enable us to continuously improve our AaaS platform as well as the provided service. Additionally, insights into the required transparency of the system and the accompanying trust in and acceptance of the system can be evaluated from a first hand perspective for the first time.

Acknowledgements. The research leading to these results received funding from the federal state of North Rhine-Westphalia and the European Regional Development Fund (EFRE.NRW 2014–2020), Project: M●DERAT! (No. CM-2-2-036a).

References

1. van Aken, B., Risch, J., Krestel, R., Löser, A.: Challenges for toxic comment classification: an in-depth error analysis. In: Proceedings of the Second Workshop on Abusive Language Online, ALW2, Brussels, Belgium, pp. 33–42 (2018)
2. Badjatiya, P., Gupta, S., Gupta, M., Varma, V.: Deep learning for hate speech detection in tweet. In: Proceedings of the 26th International Conference on World Wide Web Companion, WWW 2017, Companion, Perth, Australia, pp. 759–760 (2017)
3. Bilton, R.: Why some publishers are killing their comment sections (2014). https://digiday.com/media/comments-sections/

4. Boberg, S., Schatto-Eckrodt, T., Frischlich, L., Quandt, T.: The moral gatekeeper? Moderation and deletion of user-generated content in a leading news forum. Media Commun. **6**(4), 58–69 (2018)
5. Brunk, J., Mattern, J., Riehle, D.M.: Effect of transparency and trust on acceptance of automatic online comment moderation systems. In: Proceedings of the 21st IEEE Conference on Business, Informatics, Moscow, Russia, pp. 429–435 (2019)
6. Brunk, J., Niemann, M., Riehle, D.M.: Can analytics as a service save the online discussion culture? - the case of comment moderation in the media industry. In: Proceedings of the 21st IEEE Conference on Business Informatics, CBI 2019, Moscow, Russia, pp. 472–481 (2019)
7. Burnap, P., Williams, M.L.: Cyber hate speech on Twitter: an application of machine classification and statistical modeling for policy and decision making. Policy Internet **7**(2), 223–242 (2015)
8. Chatzakou, D., Kourtellis, N., Blackburn, J., De Cristofaro, E., Stringhini, G., Vakali, A.: Mean birds: detecting aggression and bullying on Twitter. In: Proceedings of the 2017 ACM Web Science Conference, WebSci 2017, Troy, New York, USA, pp. 13–22 (2017)
9. Chen, H., Mckeever, S., Delany, S.J.: Harnessing the power of text mining for the detection of abusive content in social media. In: Angelov, P., Gegov, A., Jayne, C., Shen, Q. (eds.) Advances in Computational Intelligence Systems. AISC, vol. 513, pp. 187–205. Springer, Cham (2017). https://doi.org/10.1007/978-3-319-46562-3_12
10. Chen, Y., Zhou, Y., Zhu, S., Xu, H.: Detecting offensive language in social media to protect adolescent online safety. In: Proceedings of the 2012 ASE/IEEE International Conference on Social Computing, 2012 ASE/IEEE International Conference on Privacy, Security, Risk Trust, SOCIALCOM-PASSAT 2012, Amsterdam, Netherlands, pp. 71–80 (2012)
11. Cheng, J.: Report: 80 percent of blogs contain "offensive" content (2007). https://arstechnica.com/information-technology/2007/04/report-80-percent-of-blogs-contain-offensive-content/
12. Cramer, H., Wielinga, B., Ramlal, S., Evers, V., Rutledge, L., Stash, N.: The effects of transparency on perceived and actual competence of a content-based recommender. In: Proceedings of the Semantic Web User Interaction: Workshop CHI 2008 Exploring HCI Challenges, SWUI 2008, Florence, Italy, pp. 1–10 (2008)
13. Davidson, T., Warmsley, D., Macy, M., Weber, I.: Automated hate speech detection and the problem of offensive language. In: Proceedings of the Eleventh International Conference on Web Social Media, ICWSM 2017, Montreal, Canada, pp. 512–515 (2017)
14. Diakopoulos, N.: Picking the NYT picks: editorial criteria and automation in the curation of online news comments. #ISOJ, Off. Res. ISOJ J. **5**(1), 147–166 (2015)
15. Dinakar, K., Reichart, R., Lieberman, H.: Modeling the detection of textual cyberbullying. In: Social Mobile Web, Paper from 2011 ICWSM Workshop, ICWSM 2011, Barcelona, Spain, pp. 11–17 (2011)
16. Djuric, N., Zhou, J., Morris, R., Grbovic, M., Radosavljevic, V., Bhamidipati, N.: Hate speech detection with comment embeddings. In: Proceedings of the 24th International Conference on World Wide Web, WWW 2015 Companion, Florence, Italy, pp. 29–30 (2015)
17. Etim, B.: The Most Popular Reader Comments on the Times (2015). https://www.nytimes.com/2015/11/23/insider/the-most-popular-reader-comments-on-the-times.html

18. Feurer, M., Klein, A., Eggensperger, K., Springenberg, J.T., Blum, M., Hutter, F.: Efficient and robust automated machine learning. In: Proceedings of the 28th International Conference on Neural Information Processing Systems, NIPS 2015, Montreal, Canada, pp. 2755–2763 (2015)

19. Feurer, M., Klein, A., Eggensperger, K., Springenberg, J.T., Blum, M., Hutter, F.: Auto-sklearn: efficient and robust automated machine learning. In: Hutter, F., Kotthoff, L., Vanschoren, J. (eds.) Automated Machine Learning. TSSCML, pp. 113–134. Springer, Cham (2019). https://doi.org/10.1007/978-3-030-05318-5_6

20. Fišer, D., Erjavec, T., Ljubešić, N.: Legal framework, dataset and annotation schema for socially unacceptable online discourse practices in Slovene. In: Waseem, Z., Chung, W.H.K., Hovy, D., Tetreault, J. (eds.) Proceedings of the First Workshop on Abusive Language Online, ALW1, Vancouver, Canada, pp. 46–51 (2017)

21. Fleischmann, K.R., Wallace, W.A.: A covenant with transparency. Commun. ACM **48**(5), 93–97 (2005)

22. Fortuna, P., Nunes, S.: A survey on automatic detection of hate speech in text. ACM Comput. Surv. **51**(4), 1–30 (2018). https://doi.org/10.1145/3232676

23. Gardiner, B., Mansfield, M., Anderson, I., Holder, J., Louter, D., Ulmanu, M.: The dark side of Guardian comments (2016). https://www.theguardian.com/technology/2016/apr/12/the-dark-side-of-guardian-comments

24. Gefen, D., Karahanna, E., Straub, D.W.: Trust and TAM in online shopping: an integrated model. MIS Q. **27**(1), 51–90 (2003)

25. Gelber, K.: Differentiating hate speech: a systemic discrimination approach. Crit. Rev. Int. Soc. Polit. Philos. 1–22 (2019)

26. Goodman, B., Flaxman, S.: European union regulations on algorithmic decision-making and a "Right to Explanation". AI Mag. **38**(3), 50 (2017)

27. Gregor, S., Benbasat, I.: Explanations from intelligent systems: theoretical foundations and implications for practice. MIS Q. **23**(4), 497–530 (1999)

28. Hine, G.E., et al.: Kek, cucks, and god emperor trump: a measurement study of 4chan's politically incorrect forum and its effects on the web. In: Proceedings of the 11th International Conference Web Social Media, ICWSM 2017, Montral, Canada, pp. 92–101 (2017)

29. Howe, J.: The rise of crowdsourcing. Wired Mag. (2006)

30. Hutter, F., Kotthoff, L., Vanschoren, J. (eds.): Automated Machine Learning: Methods, Systems, Challenges. Springer, Heidelberg (2018, in press). http://automl.org/book

31. Köffer, S., Riehle, D.M., Höhenberger, S., Becker, J.: Discussing the value of automatic hate speech detection in online debates. In: Tagungsband Multikonferenz Wirtschaftsinformatik 2018. MKWI 2018, Lüneburg, Germany (2018)

32. Kolhatkar, V., Taboada, M.: Constructive language in news comments. In: Proceedings of the First Workshop on Abusive Language Online, ALW1, Vancouver, Canada, pp. 11–17 (2017)

33. Lee, Y., Yoon, S., Jung, K.: Comparative studies of detecting abusive language on Twitter. In: Proceedings of the Second Workshop on Abusive Language Online, ALW2, Brussels, Belgium, pp. 101–106 (2018)

34. Lewis, S.C., Holton, A.E., Coddington, M.: Reciprocal journalism: a concept of mutual exchange between journalists and audiences. J. Pract. **8**(2), 229–241 (2014)

35. Lukyanenko, R., Parsons, J., Wiersma, Y., Wachinger, G., Huber, B., Meldt, R.: Representing crowd knowledge: guidelines for conceptual modeling of user-generated content. J. Assoc. Inf. Syst. **18**(4), 297–339 (2017)

36. Mansfield, M.: How we analysed 70m comments on the Guardian website (2016). https://www.theguardian.com/technology/2016/apr/12/how-we-analysed-70m-comments-guardian-website
37. Mathur, P., Sawhney, R., Ayyar, M., Shah, R.R.: Did you offend me? Classification of offensive Tweets in Hinglish language. In: Proceedings of the Second Workshop on Abusive Language Online, ALW2, Brussels, Belgium, pp. 138–148 (2018)
38. McKnight, D.H., Choudhury, V., Kacmar, C.: The impact of initial consumer trust on intentions to transact with a web site: a trust building model. J. Strateg. Inf. Syst. 11(3–4), 297–323 (2002)
39. Mehdad, Y., Tetreault, J.: Do characters abuse more than words? In: Proceedings of the 17th Annual Meeting of the Special Interest Group on Discourse and Dialogue, SIGDIAL 2016, Los Angeles, CA, USA, pp. 299–303 (2016)
40. Niemann, M., Riehle, D.M., Brunk, J., Becker, J.: What is abusive language? Integrating different views on abusive language for machine learning. In: Grimme, C., Preuss, M., Takes, F.W., Waldherr, A. (eds.) MISDOOM 2019. LNCS, vol. 12021, pp. 59–73. Springer, Cham (2020). https://doi.org/10.1007/978-3-030-39627-5_6
41. Nobata, C., Tetreault, J., Thomas, A., Mehdad, Y., Chang, Y.: Abusive language detection in online user content. In: Proceedings of the 25th International Conference on World Wide Web, WWW 2016, Montreal, Canada, pp. 145–153 (2016)
42. Osterwalder, A., Pigneur, Y.: Business Model Generation: A Handbook for Visionaries, Game Changers, and Challengers. Wiley, Hoboken (2010)
43. Owotoki, P., Mayer-Lindenberg, F.: Transparency of computational intelligence models. In: Bramer, M., Coenen, F., Tuson, A. (eds.) SGAI 2006, pp. 387–392. Springer, London (2007). https://doi.org/10.1007/978-1-84628-663-6_29
44. Papacharissi, Z.: Democracy online: civility, politeness, and the democratic potential of online political discussion groups. New Media Soc. 6(2), 259–283 (2004)
45. Park, J.H., Fung, P.: One-step and two-step classification for abusive language detection on Twitter. In: Proceedings of the First Workshop on Abusive Language Online, ALW1, Vancouver, Canada, pp. 41–45 (2017)
46. Pavlopoulos, J., Malakasiotis, P., Androutsopoulos, I.: Deep learning for user comment moderation. In: Proceedings of the First Workshop on Abusive Language Online, ALW1, Vancouver, Canada, pp. 25–35 (2017)
47. Plöchinger, S.: Über den Hass (2016). http://ploechinger.tumblr.com/post/140370770262/%C3%BCber-den-hass
48. Pöyhtäri, R.: Limits of hate speech and freedom of speech on moderated news websites in Finland, Sweden, the Netherlands and the UK. Annales–Series historia et sociologia izhaja štirikrat letno 24(3), 513–524 (2014)
49. Reynolds, K., Kontostathis, A., Edwards, L.: Using machine learning to detect cyberbullying. In: Proceedings of the 10th International Conference on Machine Learning and Applications and Workshops, ICMLA 2011, Honolulu, Hawaii, USA, pp. 241–244 (2011)
50. Sahlgren, M., Isbister, T., Olsson, F.: Learning representations for detecting abusive language. In: Proceedings of the Second Workshop on Abusive Language Online, ALW2, Brussels, Belgium, pp. 115–123 (2018)
51. Samek, W., Wiegand, T., Müller, K.R.: Explainable artificial intelligence: understanding, visualizing and interpreting deep learning models. ITU J. ICT Discov. 1(1), 39–48 (2017)
52. Schmidt, A., Wiegand, M.: A survey on hate speech detection using natural language processing. In: Ku, L.W., Li, C.T. (eds.) Proceedings of the Fifth International Workshop on Natural Language Processing for Social Media, SocialNLP 2017, Valencia, Spain, pp. 1–10 (2017)

53. Serrà, J., Leontiadis, I., Spathis, D., Stringhini, G., Blackburn, J.: Class-based prediction errors to categorize text with out-of-vocabulary words. In: Proceedings of the First Workshop on Abusive Language Online, ALW1, Vancouver, Canada, pp. 36–40 (2017)
54. Sinha, R., Swearingen, K.: The role of transparency in recommender systems. In: Extended Abstracts on Human Factors in Computing Systems, CHI 2002, Minneapolis, MN, USA, pp. 830–831 (2002)
55. Sood, S.O., Antin, J., Churchill, E.F.: Using crowdsourcing to improve profanity detection. In: AAAI Spring Symposium Series, Palo Alto, CA, USA, pp. 69–74 (2012)
56. Švec, A., Pikuliak, M., Šimko, M., Bieliková, M.: Improving moderation of online discussions via interpretable neural models. In: Proceedings of the Second Workshop on Abusive Language Online, ALW2, Brussels, Belgium, pp. 60–65 (2018)
57. The Coral Project Community (2016). https://community.coralproject.net/t/shut ting-down-onsite-comments-a-comprehensive-list-of-all-news-organisations/347
58. W3Techs: Usage Statistics and Market Share of Linux for Websites (2020). https:// w3techs.com/technologies/details/os-linux
59. Wang, C.: Interpreting neural network hate speech classifiers. In: Proceedings of the Second Workshop on Abusive Language Online, ALW2, Brussels, Belgium, pp. 86–92 (2018)
60. Wulczyn, E., Thain, N., Dixon, L.: Ex Machina. In: Proceedings of the 26th International Conference on World Wide Web, WWW 2017, Perth, Australia, pp. 1391–1399 (2017)
61. Yin, D., Xue, Z., Hong, L., Davison, B.D., Kontostathis, A., Edwards, L.: Detection of harassment on web 2.0. In: Proceedings of the Content Analysis in the WEB, CAW 2.0, Madrid, Spain, pp. 1–7 (2009)

Understanding Moderation in Online Mental Health Communities

Koustuv Saha[✉], Sindhu Kiranmai Ernala, Sarmistha Dutta, Eva Sharma, and Munmun De Choudhury

Georgia Institute of Technology, Atlanta, USA
{koustuv.saha,sernala3,sdutta65,evasharma,munmund}@gatech.edu

Abstract. Online Mental Health Communities (OMHCs) enable individuals to seek and provide support, and serve as a safe haven to disclose and share stigmatizing and sensitive experiences. Like other online communities, OMHCs are not immune to bad behavior and antisocial activities such as trolling, spamming, and harassment. Therefore, these communities are oftentimes guided by strict norms against such behavior, and moderated to ensure the quality and credibility of the content being shared. However, moderation within these communities is not only limited to ensuring content quality. It is far more complex—providing supportive spaces for disclosure, ensuring individuals' privacy, etc.—because of the sensitive population that they cater to. By interviewing 19 moderators across 12 such OMHCs on Reddit, this paper studies the practices and structure of moderation in these communities to better understand their functioning and effectiveness. Our research questions primarily revolve around three major themes—moderation, support, and self-disclosure. We find practices of moderation hierarchy, and several distinctions in motivations and responsibilities of the moderators individually and as a group. We also notice that these communities predominantly encourage emotional support, and provide supportive spaces that encourage self-disclosure on stigmatized concerns. Our findings highlight the necessity of awareness corresponding to (currently lacking) privacy concerns, and raises the importance of the presence of mental health experts (counselors and psychiatrists) in these communities. On the basis of the insights drawn from this work, we discuss the implications and considerations for designing OMHCs.

Keywords: Online mental health communities · Subreddit · Reddit · Moderation · Support · Self-disclosure

1 Introduction

Online mental health communities (OMHCs) provide dedicated online spaces for individuals to discuss, seek, and share information, advice, and support related to mental health challenges faced by themselves or their near and dear ones

© Springer Nature Switzerland AG 2020
G. Meiselwitz (Ed.): HCII 2020, LNCS 12195, pp. 87–107, 2020.
https://doi.org/10.1007/978-3-030-49576-3_7

[21,22,61]. The enduring success of these communities has essentially established the potential of computer-mediated communication to enable sensitive and personal discussions. Given the socio-economic dimensions and prevailing social stigma associated with mental health, OMHCs are particularly benefiting because of a variety of affordances, such as facilitating anonymity, peer connections, candid self-disclosures, and asynchronous participation [1,2,7,18,54].

However, like other online communities, OMHCs are not immune to internet-related bad and antisocial behaviors, such as trolling, harassment, and spamming [13,16,17,39]. By lifting the moral constraints and social etiquette that regulate our behavior in physical world situations, online communities may espouse abrasive reactions. Such antisocial behaviors can not only spark arguments in online communities but can also damage members' self-esteem, confidence, and mental health, such as exacerbate their psychological stress [17,67]. In fact, these consequences are compounded because OMHCs cater to sensitive population of individuals (ones possibly struggling with mental health challenges). For instance, diagnosing, suggesting, and adopting drugs and alternative treatments without clinical corroboration can adversely affect individuals [14,45,67]. Further, since OMHCs are largely peer-driven platforms, it is essential to ensure the quality, credibility, and supportiveness of content being shared, so that these communities facilitate positive health and behavior change [12].

Reddit, one of the most popular social media sites [60], consists of several online communities (called as subreddits) where people share and discuss on specific topics of interests, and among these, there are subreddits dedicated to mental health (such as depression, anxiety, stress, suicidal ideation, schizophrenia, etc.). Typically, these subreddits serve as supportive space for mental health, and the discussions in these subreddits are around thoughts, intents, and apprehensions of individuals struggling with mental health concerns [2,21,22,70,72].

Amidst the heavily polarized, hate speech landscape on the internet, these Reddit OMHCs have thus been acknowledged to serve as a "safe haven" for people who are struggling with mental health conditions [21,23]. In particular, to maintain the civility, and to ensure that their sensitive and plausibly vulnerable populations are not adversely served, these OMHCs set norms and guidelines of member behaviors, and regulate the same through moderation [12,44]. However, there is no clear knowledge on what works and what does not work with respect to moderation practices in these OMHCs. Such an understanding would not only benefit both existing and new OMHCs, but would also potentially help to recommend guidelines and to design interventions and customized changes for online mental health communities. In order to contribute towards the broad research interest of what makes an OMHC effective in terms of transparency in moderation practices [38,44], this article presents the first study of moderation and functioning of these communities, via the following research questions:

RQ1. How are the moderators enrolled, and what factors motivate a moderator? How do individual moderators function together as a group?

RQ2. What kind of support is sought and received in OMHCs? How do the moderators deem themselves fit to provide support in sensitive discussions?

RQ3. How do OMHCs facilitate the members to open up about their self-experiences? What aspects contribute towards sensitive disclosures? At the same time are there any privacy concerns, and how are they addressed?

We interview 19 OMHC moderators spanning across 11 subreddits, and examine the data using a qualitative inductive coding approach. Our findings reveal three major themes cutting across the research questions: moderation, support, and self-disclosure. Along these three themes, we discuss the factors that help these communities thrive and the challenges faced by both these communities and their moderators. Finally, we conclude with design implications and recommendations to help improve the functioning and efficacy of OMHCs.

2   Background and Related Work

2.1   Online Mental Health Communities

Online support groups have been around since 1982, they offer social contact and information to people coping with stress, diseases, and disabilities [48,54]. Several studies have found that participating in online support groups fosters personal empowerment due to the psychological impact of writing, expressing emotions, sharing information, interpersonal relationships, and being helped in decision-making and taking action [7,11,47,59,81]. Besides, a considerable fraction of online users seek mental health-related information on the Internet [62].

In recent years, there has been a growing focus on understanding the characteristics and dynamics of OMHCs. Online communities enable self-disclosure around mental health challenges, which are otherwise socially stigmatizing [4,21,57,82]. Several platform affordances such as anonymity and asynchronous participation, have been found to support candid and disinhibiting discourse [2,30,48,54,73]. By participating in these communities, individuals with difficult and sensitive experiences can build rapport, trust, and intimacy, fulfilling those needs that may be unmet otherwise in offline settings [6,33,55,63].

2.2   Social Support in Online Communities

Kaplan defines social support as *"degree to which an individual's needs for affection, approval, belonging, and security are met by significant others"* [46]. Erving Goffman notes that individuals in distress particularly benefit from interactions with and support from "sympathetic others" who share the same social stigma and have had similar experiences [32]. Essentially, social support provides a range of benefits, such as developing coping strategies from distressful events, psychological adjustment, illness recovery, and reduced mortality [19,53].

OMHCs facilitate individuals to seek and gather peer-to-peer psychosocial support [72]. OMHC members receive emotional support either directly via messages of caring and concern, or indirectly via comparisons with others who have had similar experiences [2,5,26]. For instance, Andalibi et al. [2] studied how survivors of sexual abuse seek support in Reddit online communities. Community members also seek informational support by exchanging information and advice around their experiences, identifying possible explanations, and building social capital [10,36]. Other research has studied the efficacy of these two forms of support in concert: Wang and colleagues explored how emotional and informational support received in an online breast cancer community impacted group members' participation and satisfaction [78,79]. De Choudhury et al. quantified the effectiveness of various support seeking behaviors in decreasing depression and increasing self-efficacy and quality of life [22].

2.3 Self-disclosure in Online Communities

Self-disclosure as an act of revealing personal information to others, is an integral part of social interaction. It provides an opportunity to express one's thoughts and feelings, develop trust, and build intimacy in personal relationships [43]. However, self-disclosure is a much more complex and critical process for those with a concealable, stigmatized identity such as mental illness [64]. The stigma around these conditions may risk unfavorable outcomes such as social rejection and discrimination, and might be detrimental to wellbeing. Experimental manipulation studies found that participants do not experience the benefits of disclosure when confidant reactions are neutral or negative [65]. However, positive outcomes of disclosure due to opening up, include a wide range of therapeutic benefits leading to both physical and mental wellbeing, such as lowered psychological distress [28,58]. For instance, studying post-traumatic stress experiences of rape and sexual assault victims, Ullman and Filipas found that disclosures lead to more positive social reactions [75]. This complex nature of both possibilities are nested within an ongoing process of *"stigma management"*—coping with the psychological and social consequences of their identity [32].

A rich body of work in the Computer Mediated Communication (CMC) literature has studied self-disclosures and the socio-cognitive processes centered around them. Through several experimental and anecdotal evidence, internet-based behaviors have been characterized to exhibit high levels of self-disclosure [41]. Self-disclosure in CMC contexts is also argued to be beneficial, having been linked to trust and group identity [40,42], as well as playing an important role in social interactions by reducing uncertainty [20,27].

An emergent line of research has investigated the nature of self-disclosures on social media and online communities. Several quantitative studies have focused on modeling and characterizing differences in multimodal (textual, visual) forms of self disclosure on social media [21,24,27,28,51,69,78]. Similarly, from a qualitative perspective, prior work has studied how individuals undergoing gender transition use Facebook to engage in sensitive disclosures of their experiences [35]. In another study, Andalibi et al. found that individuals struggling with negative emotions, such as that related to depression or self-harm, use Instagram to self-disclose and engage in social exchange and storytelling about their stigmatized experiences [4]. Existing literature has also investigated unique design affordances of social media like anonymity, "throwaway" accounts, and selective audiences enhance self-disclosure [2,3,77].

2.4   Reddit as a Platform for Online Mental Health Communities

Reddit is a widely used online forum where registered users share content in the form of text, links and images. Users can create a new post or comment on existing posts. These posts are organized by topic of discussion into many sub-communities called "subreddits", such as politics, programming, science etc.

Reddit is also known to support and facilitate mental health discourse [21] through a variety of subreddits (or communities) related to specific challenges, such as depression ($r/depression$), anxiety ($r/anxiety$), psychosis ($r/psychosis$), stress ($r/stress$) and suicidal ideation ($r/SuicideWatch$) [70,72]. These and other similar communities have also been observed to provide support, such as emotional and informational [4] to individuals coping with mental illnesses (e.g., $r/helpmecope$, $r/rapecounseling$, $r/MMFB$ (Make Me Feel better)).

Generally, OMHCs on Reddit range from small subreddits with as low as 100 users to large ones with more than 1000 users. These subreddits function as any other subreddits, facilitating individuals to post and comment, upvote or downvote content, share links, pictures and videos, etc. However, the dynamics between the members are seemingly different from other subreddits. Posts in these communities can be seen as a *means to ask for help, share problems, and struggles* by individuals approaching these subreddits. On the other hand, comments provide a means to other members to respond, advice, show kindness and love, share their experiences, and emphatize with the author of the post.

As noted earlier, support and self-disclosure are the two integral elements of making support communities work better [25]. Reddit is no exception: as a platform it provides both of these dimensions through its design and features, such as the community-based structure it holds, and the pseudonymity it offers to its members. The semi-anonymous nature of Reddit is known to enable candid self-disclosure around stigmatized topics like mental health [21]. Moreover, Reddit communities are moderated, and follow certain norms, which help in keeping the discussions in relevance, and minimizes spamming and offensive content [16,34].

However, prior work has also demonstrated that anonymity is often associated with the prevalence of a multitude of antisocial behaviors, including trolling, offensive and hateful speech, and online harrassment to name a few [39,41], which is also observed on Reddit [8,15,76]. Such activities can have severe consequences to the psychological wellbeing of the community members [9,67]. Saha et al. found that the exposure to such hateful content can lead to an increase in stress of the community members [67]. Moreover, in the case of mental health communities, which serve vulnerable populations, the risks can be far more devastating [31]. Furthermore, privacy challenges in the space of online social media is well-known [49]. Fabian et al. noted that users are not often aware of the possibilities to indirectly gather a lot of information about them by analyzing their contributions and behavior online [29].

Together, we envision the need to better understand the dynamics of OMHCs in general, and on Reddit as a case example. We present a multi-community case study of OMHCs, and with our research questions centered around moderation, support, disclosure, and privacy, we examine what makes these communities thrive, and what are the challenges that remain to be addressed.

3   Overview of Reddit OMHCs

Fig. 1. An example OMHC page.

This study considers a variety of online mental health communities (OMHCs) on Reddit with varied sizes of both number of members and number of moderators (see Fig. 1). To identify a set of subreddits, we adopted a snowball sampling approach starting with a few known subreddits already studied in prior work [2,21,70,72], and then using Reddit's subreddit search feature looking for keywords such as "mental health", "support", "counseling", "depression", "anxiety", etc. We iterated on these mental health related keywords, and subsequently augmented them based on frequently occurring keywords that co-appeared in subreddit descriptions, including keywords such as "trauma", "abuse", "suicide", "therapy", "coping", etc. We identified 26 such subreddits that are related to mental health. These include r/depression, r/anxiety, r/mentalhealth, r/depressed, r/Bipolar2, r/KindVoice, r/dysthymia, r/schizophrenia, etc. These subreddits widely vary in the number of members and the number of moderators, and some of them also have "auto-moderators" [37]. Auto-moderators are bots that are programmed to automatically filter and remove unwanted activities, such as spam, troll posts, and posts that do not adhere to community norms.

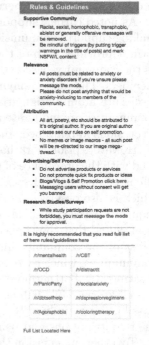

Fig. 2. An example norms page.

Fig. 3. An example page defining the FAQs of a community.

Norms and Guidelines. Norms and guidelines of these communities are listed on the landing pages of these communities (see Fig. 2 for example). These guidelines describe the kind of posts that are welcomed in the community and that posts should not harm other members in any way.

For example *r/anxiety* norms say, *"All posts must be related to anxiety or anxiety disorders [..] Please do not post anything that would be anxiety-inducing to members of the community.".* For supportive responses, the community members are generally reminded to write meaningful and helpful comments. For example community guidelines in r/depression say, "Encouragement is not helpful unless it integrates real, personal understanding of the OP's feelings and situation". Communities also discourage hurtful and racist comments, and may also discourage research survey, advertisements, and other propaganda on the community without approval of the moderators (Fig. 3).

Wikis and FAQs. Many OMHCs contain Wikis and FAQs (Frequently Asked Questions) sections where moderators share useful resources for the mental health issues relevant for their community. They also share information about other related communities that could be useful for individuals looking for help.

Sister Communities. Many OMHCs identify sister communities. These are Internet Relay Chats, discord chatrooms, or private related communities. We observed that these communities serve specific purposes such as synchronous support, or detailed and privacy-preserving social exchanges.

4   Methods

4.1   Choosing Interviewees

We note that over the years, social computing researchers have studied data unobtrusively gathered from Reddit communities for various problems [23,52, 68,69,74]. Regarding their perspective towards research, we observed that while some communities explicitly encourage researchers about studying their community, others warn researchers about not doing so. However most of these communities generally prefer approval from moderation teams [71]. For instance, the

Table 1. Summary statistics of the Reddit OMHCs studied in this paper.

Community	# Members	# Moderators	Community age	# Interviews
r/Depression	177,682	11	7 years	2
r/Anxiety	112,415	11	5 years	3
r/adhd	71,890	16	5 years	1
r/BipolarReddit	16,376	7	7 years	1
r/KindVoice	8,939	7	3 years	1
r/schizophrenia	6,959	5	4 years	1
r/MaladaptiveDreaming	4,229	8	3 years	5
r/depressionRegimen	4,161	7	2 years	1
r/AvPD	2,758	2	4 years	1
r/DID	1,830	8	6 years	1
r/dysthymia	643	1	5 years	1
r/mentalhealth	27,996	2	5 years	1

r/anxiety community says, *"While study participation requests are not forbidden, you must message the mods for approval."* Therefore, we were cautious in not posting about our research publicly in the community, and we contacted the moderators in getting approval for conducting research on their community.

4.2 Recruitment Process

Following approval from our institution's Institutional Review Board (IRB), we used interviewing as our qualitative research method to study moderation in OMHCs. All the interviewers are familiar with research in social media and mental health. Three coauthors already owned a Reddit handle and one of them created a new handle for this study. The interviewers began by actively observing the chosen 26 Reddit communities (ref: previous section) for two weeks before embarking on recruiting interviewees. We did not actively participate in these communities because of their sensitive nature and posting norms. As posting just for participation would seem disingenuous, we refrained from commenting or posting, and only made field observations.

For contacting the moderators of the chosen communities, we drafted a single message introducing ourselves, the purpose of our research study, our reddit user handles and urls to our personal/academic webpages. This was to establish trust with the moderators and enhance our credibility. Relatedly, one of the moderators later informed during the interview – *"We get spam mails asking for interviewing members. However, yours had college name and website and you did not ask to interview the members, so we were okay with it."*.

We faced obstacles while contacting the moderators. Initially, our recruitment strategy consisted of contacting each moderator separately using the direct message feature on Reddit. However, some of the moderators responded back with the feedback that the best way to contact moderators is by using the "modmail" feature. Modmail is essentially a common mail feature which when used, forwards messages to all the moderators in the subreddit. We used this modmail feature to contact the moderators thereafter. Out of a total of 106 moderators (across 26 OMHCs) who were contacted, 34 moderators responded, 10 of whom rejected participating in our study outright. To the remaining 24 moderators who expressed interest, we sent a consent form to participate. Based on the 21 signed consent forms that we received, we conducted three skype interviews, two email interviews, two phone interviews, 13 Reddit chat interviews, and one face-to-face interview conducted on the authors' college campus, with a participant who happened to live in the same city. Two participants abruptly dropped out in the middle of their interviews (one each on chat and email), and our rest of the study concerns the remaining 19 completed interviews. All the interviews lasted between 30 to 90 min. These interviews were conducted in Spring 2017, and Table 1 gives an overview of the OMHCs (as of Spring 2017) whose moderators were interviewed for the purposes of the study.

5   Findings

5.1   RQ1: What It Takes to Be a Moderator

We describe the basic moderation methodology followed in our chosen OMHCs. For this, we centered our interviews around enrollment policy, motivation, roles, and responsibilities of moderators. This section presents our observations on these high level constructs.

Moderator Enrollment Policy. OMHCs administer community-specific policies to enroll moderators. While some communities have subjective and selective appointment of moderators, other communities follow a more formal application process that includes documentation and background verification. The themes of enrollment can be broadly grouped under – 1) Members approached existing moderation team; 2) Moderators approached members; and 3) Founded the community.

Members Approached Moderators. Out of the 16 moderators interviewed, 7 participants responded that they volunteered in becoming a moderator. The participants' interest in applying for the role of a moderator had varied purposes, such as improving the community in terms of activity, engagement, and new features. This category involves active members who were self-motivated for moderating in the community.

Moderators Approached Members. For 7 out of the 16 participants, they were approached by the existing subreddit moderation team to moderate in the community. Like in the above case, the members were active members of the communities, which drew the attention of the moderators.

Founded the Community. The remaining three participants created their respective communities. These moderators felt the need of having a designated community for their corresponding purpose. One of the moderators said, *"I created this subreddit. There was a subreddit in depression, but I didn't find any subreddit on specific condition*[1]*, so I created this for focused discussions.*

Motivation of the Moderators. Next, we discuss the motivation of the members in becoming a moderator of the mental health community. The responses were mostly grouped under the following categories:

Altruism. Altruism is one of the most dominating factors of collaboration in online communities [80]. Our findings suggest similar observation as most of our participants agreed to moderate solely on altruistic reasons. They answered that it does feel good in helping fellow members undergoing mental health challenges. One participant attributed moderation as a form of "community service", and an excerpt of interview response demonstrating altruistic reasons, goes like, *"I have gone through depression myself. Knowing what depression can do to someone, I aspire to offer support where I can because nobody deserves to feel so low. Being able to support others also greatly improves my self-confidence and overall makes me feel better about myself. This motivates me to support more people.".*

Leadership Opportunity. Moderating a subreddit provides an opportunity to showcase one's leadership and management skills. This is what motivated two participants in accepting the role of a moderator. He participants felt they feel a sense of ownership in moderating a community as one's own, similar to what has been observed in prior work [50].

Improving the Community. Another notable pattern in motivation we observed among our participants, was their desire to improve the community in some regard. This included the cases when, they felt that the community lacked an active moderator, or they felt they could contribute new ideas, thoughts or design changes. One of the moderators, who was enthusiastic about bringing in design and customization changes in the subreddit, commented, *"The subreddit is important to me, and I wanted to improve it. I emailed the mods. I wanted to include a list of symptoms on the sidebar and also have an announcement that talked about a 'treatment' of specific condition. The moderators invited me to be a mod so I could make the changes I talked about."*

Awareness About Treatment. While the community norms of many OMHCs discourage alternative medicine, treatment, and diagnosis related discussion in their forum, many moderators were motivated to spread a awareness, for example, *"I felt I could help some people being a moderator by spreading information about available therapy or training such as mindfulness or the use of supplements like omega-3, for example, that could be beneficial for people dealing with some mental health issues.".*

---

[1] The mental health condition/community name has been obfuscated to safeguard the identity of the community.

Roles, Responsibilities of Moderators. Moderators of OMHCs take up several roles and responsibilities. One of the most prevalent roles (among our participants) included cleaning up spam and troll posts. In particular, we asked the moderators how they defined spam, for which they responded – 1) posts which are offensive and derogatory to community members; 2) posts which violate community norms by any means (e.g., diagnosis-related posts in some communities); and 3) posts relating to commercials and irrelevant content. Besides removing such content, moderators also ban or warn members posting such content. Other roles included implementing Reddit features such as triggers and design changes for their community.

One theme we found was the way moderators deal with posts on self-harm and suicidal thoughts. Interestingly, such posts are a "strict no" for most communities because of the consequences they may have on fellow members. However, certain OMHCs employ strategies to specially handle such cases. For example, one common tactic was that although such posts are removed, the moderators personally follow up with the member over private chat to help counsel. At times, it may be difficult for the moderators to find resolution, such as one moderator expressed, *"I do remove them, and I try to message them but I haven't found a way to PM them in a tactful and sensitive way."*.

Notably, a particular OMHC has a methodological follow-up questionnaire, for every suicide-related posts, with questions centered around *"Plan", "Means", "Time set", and "Intention"*. This OMHC further provides and recommends suicide hotline number. Some OMHCs employ certain design mechanisms, such as *suicide chatlines*, where any suicide related posts are diverted, such as a moderator mentioned, *"about suicide chat - suicide textline, we were wondering if we can put it on the side bar or like as a permanent thing"*, and triggers, which label any self-harm related posts with relevant markers about the content, like one of the participants commented, *"We have a trigger system - You put trigger in the title - suicide warning"*. Finally, moderators also cater to redirecting posts to more specific suicide related support communities like, *r/SuicideWatch*.

Moderation Group Structure. OMHCs have varying hierarchical structure among moderators. By hierarchy, we do not mean explicitly assigned moderator designations but rather the implicit power balance amongst them. We observe four kinds of hierarchical equations—1) distinct head moderator, 2) flat hierarchy, 3) single moderator, and 4) demarcated roles.

Distinct Head Moderator. Some communities have a distinct head moderator who functions as the final decision-maker. This person is typically the most active moderator or the creator the community. As one moderator says, *"I feel like there is a hierarchy but it is never really discussed. For example one moderator is the founding member and he has an upper say"*. As is evident from the interview excerpt, we found that although head moderators existed in some cases, it was very implicit and oftentimes not apparent at all.

Flat Hierarchy. Most OMHCs in our study maintain a flat hierarchy, like one moderator narrated *"if I and other person are disagreeing then other opinions are sought and decisions are taken on majority vote"*.

Single Moderator. Small communities may prevail with a single moderator. These are typically communities in their early stage and are relatively simplistic models of moderating.

Demarcated Roles. One OMHC assigned every moderator with different duties and demarcated roles: *"Every one of the moderators have full permissions so there isn't any difference. However, I recruited mod1 because she is the most active user on the sub. She makes sure content is on topic and is flaired properly. I recruited mod2 for doing research and building a Wiki page."*

5.2   RQ2: Social Support

Our next research question is centered around support sought and received in OMHCs, need of medical experts.

Regulating Support Sought and Received. Our interviews suggest that OMHCs play an integral role in helping individuals who often lack social contact in their physical world lives. We find that individuals who approach OMHCs usually look for others who are experiencing or have experienced similar problems. People not only seek emotional support, but also seek advice on alternative ways to handle pain, stress, side effects of their treatment, etc. Some of the communities explained that comments giving drug suggestions are taken down, but they encourage people to share information about what worked for them.

One moderator who started the community said, *"I created it is as I wanted people to analyze and contribute to solutions to their everyday situations [..] it turned on its own into a support group. People started posting about their issues and received warm responses from others who offered empathy more than anything else."*. This shows the ways in which a support community caters to the varying needs of its members.

Need of Medical Experts. Since these communities relate to extending support on mental health conditions, we also asked the moderators if they feel the need of having medical experts. One OMHC had an expert who was pursuing her doctorate in psychotherapy. As described by a moderator of this community, this expert was active only once in four months and thus was not actively involved in moderation. Nevertheless, her presence was important as she helped individuals to understand specifics of their conditions and treatment.

Another community frequently hosts AMAs (which stands for "Ask Me Anything"), where medical experts are invited to answer community members' questions regarding their diagnosis, treatment, medication etc. One of the moderators of this community explained the helpfulness of these open sessions, *"Before I became a mod, there was an AMA where a psychologist fielded questions by members. I believe it was a success. Something like that could be very useful again in the future."*

Except these two instances, no other community has any moderators who were medical experts. Moreover, some of these communities did not feel the need of having medical experts. They argued that their communities only provide a supportive space whose purpose was not to provide any medical advice. For example, one moderator commented, *"It is a support community because it consists of people who have experiences with the same problem (mental health disorder) in this case [...] The community is there to offer advice and share experiences, and not to diagnose."*, and another noted, *"We don't allow actual medical advice as deciding what kind of treatment needs can't be done through an internet forum [..] treatment cannot and should not be decided through internet forums, that's not the most major concern we have."*

However, some interviews showed inclination towards having experts, especially when more authority is required to help an individual, and one of the moderators expressed the need of experts when their community grows bigger, *"Maybe, I want in the future, when there are more members"* This moderator described that trained professional is necessary to identify individuals needing immediate attention or to provide tailored help.

5.3   RQ3: Disclosure and Privacy

For our final research question, we describe moderators' perspective on self-disclosure and privacy in OMHCs.

Moderator Perspectives on Mental Health Disclosures. We begin by investigating what features of the community enable and encourage self-disclosures regarding mental health concerns. First, aligning with prior research [4], we find that the pseudonymous nature on Reddit appears to be helping people candidly disclose their experiences around mental health challenges. The second design feature that enables candid disclosures is "throwaway accounts". Throwaways are temporary accounts that users create to dissociate from their primary identity. Most throwaway accounts are used exactly once; thus their use disallows user behavior to be tracked historically, or through postings made from primary Reddit accounts [57].

Alongside the aforementioned design features, responses from moderators revealed motivations for community members' disclosures. One motivation is that disclosing or opening up leads to a "sense of belonging". The social isolation that one encounters in the offline world is reduced by participating in such online communities where there is a notion of group membership. Next, according to the moderators, other motivations involved gaining a notion of personal empowerment. One interviewee mentioned that opening up about their mental health concerns provides them the strength to fight the challenge in the offline world. Being able to articulate their experiences also allows them to gain clarity which further enables in dealing with the challenges. This relates to how self-disclosure is allowing individuals to gain perspective and enabling them to fight the mental health challenges they face [58].

Finally, we found moderators to be optimistic regarding more people freely opening up on their communities. One moderator attributed this optimism to the progress made by the community over the years. Specifically, with an increasing number of members, the community was becoming more active. By seeing others opening up and finding positive outcomes, more members are inclined to open up. The same moderator also observed a decrease in the usage of throwaway accounts over time, *"I don't have any statistics off the top of my head, but just from my observations, it seems like more people are posting with their original accounts instead of making one-time-only accounts."*

Privacy Concerns. Interestingly, a striking majority of moderators whom we interviewed did not note any privacy concerns within their respective communities. Some attributed the lack of privacy concerns to the pseudonymous nature of Reddit, and others appeared to be incognizant of privacy violations within their community. Moderators, in general, seemed very respectful of the privacy concerns of community members. We also obtained responses that related this to a change in the mindset of people in general about mental health challenges. One moderator commented on the growing awareness around mental health issues and how it enables individuals to easily open up on online communities, and another expressed that the privacy provided by anonymous online communities empowers people to conduct sensitive discussions, *"I think more people in general are being open about their struggles, whether it is online or in person. I'm seeing more things like celebrities all over the world opening up about having mental illness(es) and/or being diagnosed."*

However, moderators noted isolated incidents of privacy violations. For instance, a thread asked members to share their location, so they could find and connect with each other in the physical world. Another incident involved a member being stalked on Reddit by another user, who upon investigation was also a moderator of the mental health community. The interviewed moderator faced difficulty in resolving the issue between a member and another moderator. Such contrasting experiences, despite a lack of privacy concerns reveals limited perceptions of risk that one encounters when privacy is compromised.

6   Discussion and Conclusion

6.1   Overview of Findings

By interviewing moderators of online mental health communities (OMHCs), we examined the moderation practices and perspectives on the functioning of Reddit OMHCs. Our findings primarily revolve around three major themes—moderation, support, and self-disclosure in Reddit OMHCs. First, we presented insights on the various motivations, roles, and responsibilities of OMHC moderators. We note several distinctions—these include altruistic motivations of moderators and unique responsibilities such as moderating sensitive posts on self-harm and suicidal ideation. Next, we draw insights on how support is sought and provided. We observe that alongside emotional support, these communities provide a space for individuals undergoing mental health challenges to seek and provide advice on experiences and coping mechanisms. Finally, we note how these communities provide online spaces for self-disclosure on stigmatized concerns.

6.2   Challenges of Moderation

Based on our interviews with moderators of OMHCs, we identify three major challenges faced by these communities that seek to provide a safe haven of information seeking and support to individuals in need.

Privacy. With sensitive and stigmatized mental health concerns being shared in these communities, it is important to balance that against privacy-related concerns. We note a striking discord in the notion of privacy as revealed by the moderators. While a majority of them did not acknowledge any serious privacy concerns present in the communities they moderate, some moderators expressed the importance of privacy concerns and expected the community members to be cautious about what they reveal. While certain design features may enhance the sense of belonging and can lead to positive outcomes, it is important to weigh the benefits against concerns regarding an individual's privacy and potential negative consequences. Intentional or inadvertant release of personally identifiable information may be exploited by bad actors or targeted advertisers. Because there is a perceived safety on the grounds of pseudonymity on Reddit, rather than a cautionary approach, most responses elicited an incognizant view towards privacy. This calls into questioning the efficacy of the various community affordances in supporting moderation and intervention.

Along similar lines, there is a constant negotiation between the goals of self-disclosure and privacy. Our work suggests the necessity to educate and raise awareness about privacy-related concerns and subsequent consequences to community members in a better fashion—this could be driven both at social computing platform level (Reddit), and at community-specific level by the moderators. While it is important that individuals feel comfortable to open up about their experiences on these communities, it is also crucial that they do so in an informed manner with regards to potential consequences associated with the reveal of sensitive and personally identifiable information.

Moderating Content. Our work contributes to understanding transparency of moderation practices broadly in online communities [38,44], and particularly in OMHCs. OMHCs have unique moderation goals. In terms of mitigating trolling behavior, spam, harassment, or even unhelpful content, these communities need to be extra cautious given the sensitive nature of discussions. These bad behaviors may become additional triggers to such a sensitive vulnerable population [67]. These communities also see a range on posts on self-harm and suicidal ideation which could negatively affect other members. Therefore, in contrast to regular online communities, moderation in OMHCs comes with an increased sense of liability, responsibility, and opportunity to have significant impact.

Wellbeing of Moderators and Volunteers. The wellbeing of OMHC moderators is an important aspect that is often ignored. They read through several posts daily, many of which are psychologically triggering. These moderators have struggled with some form of mental illness at some point of time, or in the present. In fact, our participant pool included moderators who acknowledged that they felt suicidal in the past. One moderator claimed that they were aware of their own mental health condition, and reckoned that they intentionally should not go through too much of negative content at a single go, and they limited the duration of moderation activities per day. To curb negative outcomes such as moderators being distressed by reading enormous volumes of negative content, our work implies the need of appropriate measures within OMHC moderation paradigm to ensure their wellbeing.

6.3   Design Implications

Building on our findings and insights into the challenges faced by OMHCs on Reddit, we propose the following two design directions.

Improved Triaging of Posts. As discussed before, triaging posts is an extremely important task on these communities. Beyond tackling trolling, harassment, and spam, members who post about sensitive expect back a response from the community. Especially, in cases when one posts a critically urgent concern, they need to be responded back as immediately as possible with peer-support and coping strategies. Further, it is crucial that the response is positively affirming and helpful [56]. However, it is a difficult task for a limited number of moderators to address the concerns in every post throughout the day. The ever-growing nature of these communities corresponds to further aggravation of the problem. Some communities have existing features like an auto-mod to ensure that posts with urgency are flagged and that every post gets an automated response. To extend these efforts, automated mechanisms could be recommended to provide scalability and personalized support through efficient triaging of posts. These communities can additionally collaborate with crisis helpline organizations to implement strategies of triaging and effective interventions.

Early Detection of Mental Health Concerns. In addition to the above, automated approaches can facilitate early detections of the adversity of mental health using longitudinal data of the individuals [28,66]. While automated approaches may lack clinical accuracy and relevance, they can assist in instrumenting tailored and timely support efforts by recommending consultation with clinicians and counselors. Similarly, some of the seasoned peer-supporters can be made aware in advance regarding the concerns of those members struggling with severity in their mental health conditions.

AMAs with Experts. Ask me anything (AMAs) are popular interaction medium on Reddit where experts answer questions raised by community members. For OHMCs, our findings from RQ2 suggest that AMAs with clinical experts might help members of these communities to get access to informational resources and raise awareness. However, this recommendation does not apply for specific medical questions related to diagnosis or prescriptions.

Designing for Support Provisioning. Presently, OMHCs rely on the structure and design of post-comment discussion threads for provisioning and reaching out for support. The same discussion thread structure is used for asking questions, raising awareness, sharing experiences and discussing community-related topics. By designing different interaction mechanisms for reaching out and provisioning social support, we believe the community can better manage support matching. For instance, someone who is seeking emotional support can request a listener who is comfortable with the others' disclosure. Similarly, someone with a comorbid condition might be looking for similar others to understand their experiences. Such a design can help in delegating responsibilities that are currently taken up by moderators to other members.

Acknowledgements. This project was approved by the Institutional Review Board (IRB) at Georgia Tech. We thank Eric Gilbert and Michaelanne Dye for their valuable feedback.

References

1. Andalibi, N.: Social media for sensitive disclosures and social support: the case of miscarriage. In: Proceedings of the GROUP. ACM (2016)
2. Andalibi, N., Haimson, O.L., De Choudhury, M., Forte, A.: Understanding social media disclosures of sexual abuse through the lenses of support seeking and anonymity. In: Proceedings of the CHI (2016)
3. Andalibi, N., Morris, M.E., Forte, A.: Testing waters, sending clues: indirect disclosures of socially stigmatized experiences on social media. PACM HCI, 2(CSCW), 1–23 (2018)
4. Andalibi, N., Ozturk, P., Forte, A.: Sensitive self-disclosures, responses, and social support on Instagram: the case of# depression. In: CSCW (2017)
5. Bambina, A.: Online Social Support: The Interplay of Social Networks and Computer-Mediated Communication. Cambria Press, Amherst (2007)
6. Barak, A., Boniel-Nissim, M., Suler, J.: Fostering empowerment in online support groups. Comput. Hum. Behav. 24(5), 1867–1883 (2008)
7. Beaudoin, C.E., Tao, C.-C.: Benefiting from social capital in online support groups: an empirical study of cancer patients. CyberPsychol. Behav. 10(4), 587–590 (2007)
8. Bergstrom, K.: "Don't feed the troll": shutting down debate about community expectations on Reddit.com. First Monday 16(8) (2011)
9. Bishop, J.: Examining the Concepts, Issues, and Implications of Internet Trolling. IGI Global, Hershey (2013)
10. Burleson, B.R., MacGeorge, E.L., Knapp, M.L., Daly, J.A.: Supportive communication. Handb. Interpers. Commun. 3, 374–424 (2002)

11. Caplan, S.E., Turner, J.S.: Bringing theory to research on computer-mediated comforting communication. Comput. Hum. Behav. **23**, 985–998 (2007)
12. Chancellor, S., Andrea, H., De Choudhury, M.: Norms matter: contrasting social support around behavior change in online weight loss communities. In: Proceedings of the CHI (2018)
13. Chancellor, S., Lin, Z.J., De Choudhury, M.: This post will just get taken down: characterizing removed pro-eating disorder social media content. In: Proceedings of the CHI (2016)
14. Chancellor, S., Nitzburg, G., Andrea, H., Zampieri, F., De Choudhury, M.: Discovering alternative treatments for opioid use recovery using social media. In: Proceedings of the CHI (2019)
15. Chandrasekharan, E., Pavalanathan, U., Srinivasan, A., Glynn, A., Eisenstein, J., Gilbert, E.: You can't stay here: the efficacy of Reddit's 2015 ban examined through hate speech. PACM HCI **1**(CSCW), 1–22 (2017)
16. Chandrasekharan, E., et al.: The internet's hidden rules: an empirical study of reddit norm violations at micro, meso, and macro scales. PACM HCI **2**(CSCW), 1–25 (2018)
17. Cheng, J., Bernstein, M., Danescu-Niculescu-Mizil, C., Leskovec, J.: Anyone can become a troll: Causes of trolling behavior in online discussions. In: Proceedings of the CSCW (2017)
18. Chung, J.E.: Social interaction in online support groups: preference for online social interaction over offline social interaction. Comput. Hum. Behav. **29**, 1408–1414 (2013)
19. Cohen, S., Wills, T.A.: Stress, social support, and the buffering hypothesis. Psychol. Bull. **98**(2), 310 (1985)
20. Cozby, P.C.: Self-disclosure: a literature review. Psychol. Bull. **79**(2), 73 (1973)
21. De Choudhury, M., De, S.: Mental health discourse on reddit: self-disclosure, social support, and anonymity. In: ICWSM (2014)
22. De Choudhury, M., Kıcıman, E.: The language of social support in social media and its effect on suicidal ideation risk. In: ICWSM (2017)
23. De Choudhury, M., Kiciman, E., Dredze, M., Coppersmith, G., Kumar, M.: Discovering shifts to suicidal ideation from mental health content in social media. In: Proceedings of the CHI (2016)
24. De Choudhury, M., Sharma, S., Logar, T., Eekhout, W., Nielsen, R.: Quantifying and understanding gender and cross-cultural differences in mental health expression via social media. In: CSCW (2017)
25. Donath, J.S.: We need online alter egos now more than ever. Wired Mag. (2014)
26. Dunkel-Schetter, C.: Social support and cancer: findings based on patient interviews and their implications. J. Soc. Issues **40**(4), 77–98 (1984)
27. Ernala, S.K., et al.: Characterizing audience engagement and assessing its impact on social media disclosures of mental illnesses. In: Twelfth International AAAI Conference on Web and Social Media (2018)
28. Ernala, S.K., Rizvi, A.F., Birnbaum, M.L., Kane, J.M., De Choudhury, M.: Linguistic markers indicating therapeutic outcomes of social media disclosures of schizophrenia. Proc. ACM Hum.-Comput. Interact. **1**(CSCW), 43:1–43:27 (2017)
29. Fabian, B., Baumann, A., Keil, M.: Privacy on reddit? Towards large-scale user classification. In: ECIS (2015)
30. Forte, A., Andalibi, N., Greenstadt, R.: Privacy, anonymity, and perceived risk in open collaboration: a study of tor users and wikipedians. In: Proceedings of the 2017 ACM Conference on Computer Supported Cooperative Work and Social Computing, pp. 1800–1811 (2017)

31. Goebert, D., Else, I., Matsu, C., Chung-Do, J., Chang, J.Y.: The impact of cyber-bullying on substance use and mental health in a multiethnic sample. Matern. Child Health J. **15**(8), 1282–1286 (2011)
32. Goffman, E.: Stigma: Notes on the Management of Spoiled Identity. Simon and Schuster (2009)
33. Greene, J.A., Choudhry, N.K., Kilabuk, E., Shrank, W.H.: Online social networking by patients with diabetes: a qualitative evaluation of communication with Facebook. J. Gener. Internal Med. **26**, 287–292 (2011)
34. Grimmelmann, J.: The virtues of moderation. Yale JL & Tech. **17**, 42 (2015)
35. Haimson, O.L., Brubaker, J.R., Dombrowski, L., Hayes, G.R.: Disclosure, stress, and support during gender transition on Facebook. In: CSCW, pp. 1176–1190. ACM (2015)
36. Helgeson, V.S., Cohen, S., Schulz, R., Yasko, J.: Long-term effects of educational and peer discussion group interventions on adjustment to breast cancer. Health Psychol. **20**(5), 387 (2001)
37. Jhaver, S., Birman, I., Gilbert, E., Bruckman, A.: Human-machine collaboration for content regulation: the case of Reddit automoderator. ACM TOCHI **26**, 1–35 (2019)
38. Jhaver, S., Bruckman, A., Gilbert, E.: Does transparency in moderation really matter? User behavior after content removal explanations on Reddit. Proc. ACM Hum.-Comput. Interact. **3**(CSCW), 1–27 (2019)
39. Jhaver, S., Chan, L., Bruckman, A.: The view from the other side: the border between controversial speech and harassment on Kotaku in action. First Monday **23**(2) (2018)
40. Joinson, A.: Causes and implications of disinhibited behavior on the internet (1998)
41. Joinson, A.N.: Self-disclosure in computer-mediated communication: the role of self-awareness and visual anonymity. Eur. J. Soc. Psychol. **31**, 177–192 (2001)
42. Joinson, A.N., Paine, C.B.: Self-disclosure, privacy and the internet. The Oxford Handbook of Internet Psychology, p. 2374252 (2007)
43. Jourard, S.M.: Self-disclosure: an experimental analysis of the transparent self (1971)
44. Juneja, P., Subramanian, D.R., Mitra, T.: Through the looking glass: study of transparency in Reddit's moderation practices. Proc. ACM Hum.-Comput. Interact. **4**(GROUP), 1–35 (2020)
45. Kang, R., Dabbish, L., Sutton, K.: Strangers on your phone: why people use anonymous communication applications. In: Proceedings of the CSCW (2016)
46. Kaplan, B.H., Cassel, J.C., Gore, S.: Social support and health. Med. Care **15**(5), 47–58 (1977)
47. Klein, K., Boals, A.: Expressive writing can increase working memory capacity. J. Exp. Psychol. Gener. **130**(3), 520 (2001)
48. Lawlor, A., Kirakowski, J.: Online support groups for mental health: a space for challenging self-stigma or a means of social avoidance? Comput. Hum. Behav. **32**, 152–161 (2014)
49. Liu, Y., Ferreira, D., Goncalves, J., Hosio, S., Pandab, P., Kostakos, V.: Donating context data to science: the effects of social signals and perceptions on action-taking. Interact. Comput. **29**, 132–146 (2016)
50. Luther, K., Bruckman, A.: Leadership in online creative collaboration. In: Proceedings of the CSCW (2008)
51. Manikonda, L., De Choudhury, M.: Modeling and understanding visual attributes of mental health disclosures in social media (2017)

52. Nathan Matias, J.: Going dark: social factors in collective action against platform operators in the reddit blackout. In: Proceedings of the 2016 CHI Conference on Human Factors in Computing Systems, pp. 1138–1151. ACM (2016)

53. Mattson, M., Hall, J.G.: Health as communication nexus: a service-learning approach (2011)

54. Naslund, J.A., Aschbrenner, K.A., Marsch, L.A., Bartels, S.J.: The future of mental health care: peer-to-peer support and social media. Epidemiol. Psychiatr. Sci. **25**(02), 113–122 (2016)

55. Newman, M.W., Lauterbach, D., Munson, S.A., Resnick, P., Morris, M.E.: It's not that i don't have problems, i'm just not putting them on Facebook: challenges and opportunities in using online social networks for health. In: Proceedings of the ACM 2011 Conference on Computer Supported Cooperative Work, pp. 341–350. ACM (2011)

56. Norcross, J.C., Lambert, M.J.: Psychotherapy relationships that work III. Psychotherapy **55**(4), 303 (2018)

57. Pavalanathan, U., De Choudhury, M.: Identity management and mental health discourse in social media. In: Proceedings of the WWW Companion (2015)

58. Pennebaker, J.W.: Writing about emotional experiences as a therapeutic process. Psychol. Sci. **8**(3), 162–166 (1997)

59. Pennebaker, J.W., Chung, C.K.: Expressive writing, emotional upheavals, and health. Foundations of health psychology, pp. 263–284 (2007)

60. Pew (2018). pewinternet.org/fact-sheet/social-media. Accessed 18 Apr 2018

61. Potts, H.W.W.: Online support groups: an overlooked resource for patients. He@ lth Inf. Internet **44**(1), 6–8 (2005)

62. Powell, J., Clarke, A.: Internet information-seeking in mental health. Br. J. Psychiatry **189**(3), 273–277 (2006)

63. Pruksachatkun, Y., Pendse, S.R., Sharma, A.: Moments of change: analyzing peer-based cognitive support in online mental health forums. In: Proceedings of the CHI (2019)

64. Quinn, D.M., Chaudoir, S.R.: Living with a concealable stigmatized identity: the impact of anticipated stigma, centrality, salience, and cultural stigma on psychological distress and health. J. Pers. Soc. Psychol. **97**, 634 (2009)

65. Rodriguez, R.R., Kelly, A.E.: Health effects of disclosing secrets to imagined accepting versus nonaccepting confidants. J. Soc. Clin. Psychol. **25**, 1023–1047 (2006)

66. Saha, K., Chan, L., De Barbaro, K., Abowd, G.D., De Choudhury, M.: Inferring mood instability on social media by leveraging ecological momentary assessments. In: Proceedings of the ACM IMWUT (2017)

67. Saha, K., Chandrasekharan, E., De Choudhury, M.: Prevalence and psychological effects of hateful speech in online college communities. In: WebSci (2019)

68. Saha, K., De Choudhury, M.: Modeling stress with social media around incidents of gun violence on college campuses. Proc. HCI **1**(CSCW), 1–27 (2017)

69. Saha, K., et al.: The language of LGBTQ+ minority stress experiences on social media. PACM HCI **3**(CSCW), 1–22 (2019)

70. Saha, K., Sugar, B., Torous, J., Abrahao, B., Kiciman, E., De Choudhury, M.: A social media study on the effects of psychiatric medication use. In: ICWSM (2019)

71. Seidman, I.: Interviewing as Qualitative Research: A Guide for Researchers in Education and the Social Sciences. Teachers College Press, New York (2013)

72. Sharma, E., De Choudhury, M.: Mental health support and its relationship to linguistic accommodation in online communities. In: Proceedings of the CHI (2018)

73. Sharma, E., Saha, K., Ernala, S.K., Ghoshal, S., De Choudhury, M.: Analyzing ideological discourse on social media: a case study of the abortion debate. In: Proceedings of the CSS. ACM (2017)

74. Shelton, M., Lo, K., Nardi, B.: Online media forums as separate social lives: a qualitative study of disclosure within and beyond Reddit. In: iConference 2015 Proceedings (2015)

75. Ullman, S.E., Filipas, H.H.: Predictors of PTSD symptom severity and social reactions in sexual assault victims. J. Trauma. Stress **14**, 369–389 (2001)

76. van der Nagel, E., Frith, J.: Anonymity, pseudonymity, and the agency of online identity: examining the social practices of r/Gonewild. First Monday **20**(3) (2015). https://doi.org/10.5210/fm.v20i3.5615

77. Vitak, J.: The impact of context collapse and privacy on social network site disclosures. J. Broadcast. Electron. Media **56**, 451–470 (2012)

78. Wang, Y.-C., Burke, M., Kraut, R.: Modeling self-disclosure in social networking sites. In: CSCW, pp. 74–85. ACM (2016)

79. Wang, Y.-C., Kraut, R., Levine, J.M.: To stay or leave?: the relationship of emotional and informational support to commitment in online health support groups. In: CSCW, pap, 833–842. ACM (2012)

80. McLure Wasko, M., Faraj, S.: "It is what one does": why people participate and help others in electronic communities of practice. J. Strateg. Inf. Syst. **9**(2), 155–173 (2000)

81. Yang, D., Kraut, R., Levine, J.M.: Commitment of newcomers and old-timers to online health support communities. In: Proceedings of the CHI (2017)

82. Yang, D., Yao, Z., Kraut, R.: Self-disclosure and channel difference in online health support groups. In: ICWSM (2017)

User-Generated Short Video Content in Social Media. A Case Study of TikTok

Aliaksandra Shutsko[✉]

Heinrich Heine University Düsseldorf, Düsseldorf, Germany
aliaksandra.shutsko@uni-duesseldorf.de

Abstract. According to Alexa's ranking of the top 500 sites on the web, YouTube takes the second place, demonstrating the importance of online services focused on sharing of short self-shot videos. With growing popularity of mobile phones, mobile only short video sharing social media applications appeared on the market. One of such applications is TikTok, probably the most talked-of video sharing platform of 2019, similar to its twin service for the Chinese market, called Douyin. The content on YouTube varies greatly in topic: from music and toys to science and technologies, from computer games and cooking to education and politics. But does the content on mobile short video platforms differ that much too? The content of 1,000 videos on TikTok as a prominent representative of mobile short video sharing social media services was analyzed to find out which content is common and popular on TikTok. Content analysis was applied as the main research technique. Comedy videos and musical performances turned out to be the most popular and the most frequent categories among both male and female performers. Comedy videos are, however, especially frequent among male creators. At that, videos related to beauty and DIY are common for females, but not for males. Additional attention in this study was paid to the potential law infringements on the platform. The cases of potential violations of copyright and personal rights were observed. Videos containing inappropriate contents such as violence, sexual activity, or consumption of drugs and alcohol were, by contrast, not revealed.

Keywords: TikTok · Video sharing · Content analysis · Gender differences · Law infringements

1 Introduction

Video as a type of user-generated content online becomes more and more popular, which can be confirmed by the second place of YouTube among top websites worldwide, leaving behind among others the social networking site Facebook (#6), the knowledge base Wikipedia (#13), and the microblogging service Weibo (#16)[1]. Furthermore, on example of YouTube high rank the preference of short videos on a wider variety of topics created by ordinary (non-professional) users can be observed as the service also outperforms the traditional Video-on-Demand systems such as Netflix (#21 in Alexa's ranking as of February 2020). With that, YouTube is not the only one

---

[1] The top 500 sites on the web, www.alexa.com/topsites.

© Springer Nature Switzerland AG 2020
G. Meiselwitz (Ed.): HCII 2020, LNCS 12195, pp. 108–125, 2020.
https://doi.org/10.1007/978-3-030-49576-3_8

representative of video sharing industry concentrated on user-generated contents, as the variety of such services is dramatically extending. Some platforms such as Vimeo concentrate on professionally generated contents. On social live streaming services (SLSSs), such as YouNow, Twitch, Periscope, people can broadcast their programs in real time and chat with each other during the stream [1]. With the growing importance of smart phones, video sharing applications available for mobile users only, i.e. Snapchat or Vine, appeared. The last ones are additionally characterized by ultra-short video length, varying from six seconds limit on the former Vine to 60 s limits on Snapchat. Attractiveness of videos of short content for users could be additionally evidenced in the subsequent extension of Instagram's functionality with "stories." Similar to the aforementioned services in the video length, but different in the functionality is the mobile video sharing social media application TikTok, probably the most talked-of video sharing platform of 2019.

"Make Your Day" states on the homepage of TikTok over funny creative user-created videos (see Fig. 1). Launched in August, 2017 by the Chinese technology company ByteDance [2], TikTok (#501 in Alexa's ranking) became especially popular after merging with another short video sharing platform musical.ly [2, 3]. Both applications concentrate on production of short videos by their users. musical.ly, which emerged four years before TikTok, was famous with lip-synch effect, when users created videos with the help of the in-app synchronization functionality singing their favorite songs. However, as our study will further demonstrate, the content on TikTok is no more limited to lip-synch performances. Another particularity of TikTok is that it has a twin application in China which was launched by ByteDance even earlier than TikTok itself, namely in September, 2016, and is called Douyin (#12,930 in Alexa's ranking) [2].

Make Your Day
Real People. Real Videos.

Fig. 1. Screenshot of some videos appearing on TikTok Homepage (TikTok Homepage, www.tiktok.com)

Recent rankings demonstrate that the application continues to win the popularity worldwide, being the most downloadable social media app in September, 2019 in both App and Play Stores [4]. Though the application is especially popular in Asian region, i.e., India, Indonesia, Malaysia [5] and a lot of people in China even "identify themselves as Douyiner" [6], recent statistics from Digiday indicate the user growth also in Europe with the largest market in Germany, where the number of monthly active users increased from 4.1 Million in January, 2019 to 5.5 Million in November, 2019 followed by the United Kingdom with the 5.4 Million in November, 2019 [7].

The main feature of TikTok is shooting and sharing short videos of 15 up to 60 s of any content except for "harassment or cyberbullying, harmful or dangerous content, nudity or sexual activity" [8], outlined as "don'ts" in the TikTok community guidelines. The application offers its users the functionality to apply numerous video and music filters and effects (e.g., photo templates, slow motion, bit rate sound, lip-sync, etc.) as well as to create special kinds of cooperative videos, i.e. duets and reactions [9]. A lot of videos appear as a reaction to the challenges launched by other users, TikTok itself or well-known brands and celebrities, who also start using TikTok for social media marketing campaigns. Along with functionality dedicated to the video production, the service provides functionality for networking, i.e. messaging, following other users, evaluation of videos with likes, shares and comments, which makes the application not only a video sharing platform, but additionally a social networking service. The use of application is also simple for users who use it for watching rather than for content creation and sharing. Similarly to Vine, which was characterized by users' batch and passive view [10], users on TikTok are also exposed to a large amount of short videos that change each other with a simple screen scroll.

Generally, it can be concluded that TikTok is a comfortable place for its users where creativity and self-expression take leading positions. However, although being popular and frequently downloadable, on one hand, and promoting creativeness among its users, on the other hand, TikTok gained a very controversial fame in mass media, wherein the main critiques lay on problems around the young people, who are believed to be the majority of active users on TikTok. Inability to control the age of young to very young users by registration [11], child data use [12], copyright issues [13], cyberbulling and cyber-grooming [14]. Unfortunately, all of those notions appear in the mass media in connection with the use of TikTok. Additionally, one special issue in Germany became videos of young sometimes lightly dressed girls, who are at the most risk of misuse by strangers because of such contents, even though those young girls do not tend to attract the opposite sex attention [15]. But is TikTok really that dangerous for its audience? Are the contents on TikTok inappropriate for younger users? With these questions in mind we undertook a case study applying content analysis to reveal what do the users of TikTok in Germany as the largest market in Europe create and like.

2   Background and Related Work

Social media applications such as Instagram and Vine "encourage the generation and consumption of user generated content (UGC) on a large scale" [16]. Studies confirm that younger users are more active in using Internet for social connections and entertainment and younger age has "the predominant sociodemographic effect on content creation" [17]. The use of some video sharing platforms with limited built-in editing functionality, i.e. YouTube, is associated with some limitations, when it comes to the younger group of content creators. Although youth actively engage in video creation on YouTube, they mostly neither edit nor minimally cut their videos, as that requires familiarity with video editing and sometimes financial investments [18]. Thus, TikTok with its numerous free editing options allowing to perfect created content and all that with a few clicks on smart phone, which is practically always at hand, is potentially attractive for younger persons.

In spite of its popularity with impressive numbers of downloads and active users and also in spite of its constant appearance in the mass media even though in gloomy tones, a small number of research articles with the focus on TikTok is currently available, and those available are dedicated to Douyin or its predecessor musical.ly. With this study we contribute to research on mobile short video sharing social media applications taking TikTok as a prominent representative.

Searching for "TikTok", "Douyin" and "musical.ly" in articles' titles, abstracts, key words and topics, we found a total of twelve articles in Scopus and Web of Science. Three of those articles concentrated on modeling of micro-video recommendation services and mentioned TikTok as they took datasets from the platform for analysis. Two more articles were considered as irrelevant as they investigated a video-AI based visual destination image extraction method and reforms in online brand building in Chinese state-owned enterprises.

Another two articles concentrated on children's safety, which is somewhat closer to our research as we investigate whether contents on TikTok are inappropriate for younger generation. Milkaite and Lievens [19] underlined that social media apps such as Instagram, Snapchat and TikTok, which are popular among children, have still not enough transparent and clear privacy policies and should enhance them applying "legal visualization, co-design, co-creation techniques and participatory design methods." Badillo-Urquiola et al. [20] investigated children's view on social media apps design taking TikTok as an example and found that children are interested in learning potential online dangers as well as in being able to mitigate online risks.

Furthermore, Rettberg [21] investigated video-based communication and suggested that hand signs largely used in lip-syncing videos on musical.ly "constitute a codified, non-verbal language of pictograms that is equivalent to emoji in text-based communication," thus indirectly emphasizing the importance of lip-syncing videos for the application. Literat and Kligler-Vilenchik [22], however, added that the content on musical.ly diversified with times and the application had been even used for "youth collective political expression" during the 2016 US presidential elections.

Two more articles focused directly on Douyin and its characteristics. Chen et al. [23] investigated the "fundamental characteristics" (video length, video bitrate, and video size) of the application and the distribution of video's popularity metrics (views, likes, shares, and comments) with the application for the cashing mechanisms. They confirmed that most of the videos (95%) do not exceed 15 s and that 65% of videos have the length of 14–16 s. In terms of popularity it was discovered that similarly to videos on other platforms Zipf's law can be applied to the most popular videos in terms of views and likes on Douyin.

Lu and Lu [6] conducted a qualitative study of Douyin concentrating on user's motivations to use the application and challenges and concerns its users face. They found that people relax and have fun while they watch videos. Another important factor was socialization. Similar to the usage of SLSSs [1], people on Douyin like to communicate with others, find friends from strangers or appropriate communities and even engage into virtual intimate relationship with the creators, i.e. become involved in "parasocial interactions" [24]. However, some people watch videos in order not to be left out of conversations (i.e., not to be "discriminated") in offline everyday life. As to the challenges in application, users were not satisfied with the search functionality as well as with the recommendation system. Privacy issues, addiction and extreme use of the service for both sharing and watching videos were among main users' concerns.

Beyond the Douyiner's motivations, Lu and Lu's study [6] revealed the content categories the users engage in. In popular videos, performers often show fashionable items or cosmetics, demonstrate romantic behavior "narrating lover's prattle," or give practical recommendations to their fans in matters of "good-looking profile images" or "fancy nicknames." Although not being representative, the category "prosocial behaviour" of humans was named by the Douyiners as important due to its association with "positive energy." Additionally, the category of knowledge sharing was mentioned as category with videos of high production value. Among other "engaging" contents were categories dedicated to popular nature and social sciences, education (e.g., "learning notes about Maths"), arts and skills (calligraphy, dancing, painting, etc.), professional life, life hacks, tourism, as well as videos related to babies (e.g., "baby raising," "early education" or showing babies' "talents").

To sum up the existing literature on TikTok, the application was involved into the studies that concentrated on technical parameters of videos on sharing platforms, children's online safety, motives to use the service and content generated by users on Douyin and to some extent on the former musical.ly. With that, indication of such topics as knowledge sharing raises special interest to Douyin and TikTok, as in English and German mass media the use of short videos platforms like Vine, musical.ly, or TikTok itself is almost exclusively associated with funny, music, and dancing videos. Yarosh et al. [25] in their research on youth-authorship on Vine and YouTube also mention the categories related to fun and self-presentation as more typical for youth. Although a lot of short video content categories were named above, some of the categories common for video sharing services were not yet mentioned. Among them are pets and animals, news and politics, autos and vehicles, computer games [26–28], and toys [27]. Also sexy self-presentation of adolescents is no exception on social networking sites [29] and young people often have access to and can even appear in videos of inappropriate content, i.e. related to bullying, sexual behavior, drugs, etc. [30].

Another important point of social media services usage, yet not touched in research on short video applications, is gender differences. Despite that, some studies on SLSSs as well as on YouTube provide hints, that gender differences take place on short video sharing platforms. Thus, differences were indicated gender differences in practically all aspects of SLSSs usage, i.e. in content preferences, motivations to stream and to watch, tendencies in law infringements, and perception of gamification elements [31]. A study on YouTube found that males differ from females in their participatory behavior. More precisely, males tend to dislike and comment more than females, whereas females are more exposed to sharing [32]. As to the sexy contents on SNSs in general, young girls tend to post themselves with a sexy appearance more often than males [29].

One more important aspect of studies on video sharing services, namely potential law infringements, also remained uncovered in the literature on TikTok, although previous research demonstrated that the use of video sharing platforms is often connected with violations related to copyright, personal rights, as well as inappropriate contents [33–35]. As TikTok is largely based on videos supported with music and Germany has one of the strictest copyright legislation, we checked whether potential copyright issues arise on TikTok in the light of German *Urheberrecht*. Another frequently observed law infringement is violation of personal rights [35]. In this study we analyzed whether TikTok creators film third parties without their evident permission. Taking into account that most of the TikTok users are believed to be underage persons, we additionally checked whether sexual or violent contents as well as videos showing drug or alcohol consumption (all of which cause harm to younger audience) are found on TikTok as it is the case on other video sharing services [35, 36].

In line with above literature review, the following research questions were formulated:

(RQ1) Which content post users on TikTok?
(RQ2) Are there gender differences among creators in the content preferences?
(RQ3) Videos of which content are the most popular on TikTok?
(RQ4) Do potential law infringements occur on TikTok?

At this point, it should be mentioned that this study refers to the videos originated from Germany. That is caused by the fact that one of the technical requirements of TikTok is setting up the country, when creating an account. We therefore had to limit our research to one country. However, since video sharing platforms are popular for a long time in Germany [37] and the chosen country has the highest number of TikTok users among other European countries, the study is viewed as representative.

3   Methods

Content analysis was used as the main research technique allowing researchers to achieve reliable and valid results by coding and, therefore, quantifying qualitative contents (i.e., texts, images, sounds, signs, etc.) [38, pp. 18–19]. The content analysis was conducted in five most common steps identified in literature by McMillan [39]. First, the research questions were formulated. After that as the second step of the content analysis, the sample was selected. Sampling frame consisted of 1,000 videos appearing on TikTok's main feed ("for you page"), which randomly proposes videos to its users. As videos appearing on the main feed become customized depending on what content had been already watched and liked, we additionally searched for videos using hashtags #foryou, #foryourpage, and #fürdich. Those hashtags are described as the most neutral ones and unlike many other hashtags are not restricted to any specific content, thus covering a wide range of video themes.

At the third step, the content categories were defined, which resulted in appearance of the codebook. In line with the RQ1 to identify the content categories on TikTok in general, the categories in this study were collected inductively. For that, a preliminary study of videos on TikTok was conducted. Each of the eight coders had to watch the videos on TikTok during two weeks and mark possible content categories. After that, the categories proposals from all coders were aggregated, sorted and extended with the descriptions, videos of which content should be assigned to a specific category. This resulted firstly in 26 content categories. The 27th category "Sexy/Flirting" was added to the codebook in view of the critique of the mass media around TikTok. Videos should be assigned to that category, when performers show off their bodies (i.e., scantily or skin-tight dressed or wear very short cloths) and/or perform or pose provocatively, which is in line with previous studies [29]. The content by itself does not show sexual scenes and cannot be viewed as inappropriate for underage users, but can draw attention of opposite sex, which in its turn can potentially lead to cyber-grooming. Finally, the 28th category "Not assignable" was added covering the contents that could not be assigned to any of the 27 categories. Beyond that, ten formal categories were defined to enable researchers to answer RQ2 to RQ4. They included a category of gender, five categories related to potential law infringements (copyright and personal right violations, demonstration of inappropriate contents such as violence, sexual activity, drugs or alcohol consumption). Four more formal categories covered statistics data, i.e. number of likes, shares, and comments to a video, and number of user's followers, all of which served for evaluation of video popularity. Regarding the category of gender, it should be clarified that it referred to the gender of the performer depicted in the video, not to the user who shared the video, as no demographic data, including gender, is available in the user's profile and relaying on the profile's photo did not always provide evidence about user's gender.

At this step, it was also important "to define the time period of the study" [39]. The research team decided to analyze the content on TikTok during two months from May 1, 2019 to June 30, 2019, thus ensuring wider range of video contents and increasing the representativeness of the study as new videos appear every day. The time period was divided into four parts, so that each group of two coders collected and coded the videos during two weeks.

The fourth step involved training coders and checking the reliability of their coding skills. The research team consisted of eight coders (master students at a German university) from which four groups of two coders each were created. To save the coding results, a Google spreadsheet with all content and formal categories included was created. Each coder had access to the document and had to put the results of his or her coding into the document. Each coder within the group had to code independently. For that, two TikTok accounts were created using which the coders could watch and code videos. Each coder had to choose and analyze 125 videos and send them to the partner for parallel coding. That was ensured by sending the videos via direct messages. That way was additionally guaranteed that the coders worked with identical data. Totally, each group coded 250 videos and each video was coded twice. The binary coding was used, where "1" meant that a video belongs to a category and "0" – does not. The coders were allowed to assign a video to several categories. The observation that one video can combine different types of content was mentioned also in the previous research [25]. The formal categories were coded only by one of the coders, e.g. the coder who sent the video. To check the reliability of the cross-coding results, Krippendorf's alpha was applied [38, p. 226]. As the values calculated for each group and for each category exceeded the reliability minimum of 0.8, the coding data were accepted as reliable [38, p. 241]. If disagreements occurred, the coding values were reviewed in groups to jointly meet the final decision on the coding value. In the final fifth step of the content analysis, the research team analyzed and interpreted the collected coding data.

4 Results

4.1 User-Generated Content on TikTok

In the frame of this content analysis, 1,000 videos on the mobile video sharing application TikTok were analyzed allowing to determine which contents appear on TikTok (RQ1). As it can be seen on Fig. 2, the highest number of videos (32.4%) belongs to the category "Comedy & Joke." The second most frequently observed category with 137 videos is "Musical performance." Further on, the categories "DIY & Tutorials" (89 videos) and "Dance" (88 videos) stand very close to each other taking the third and the fourth places, accordingly. With that, those two categories as well as all other categories individually amounted to less than 10%. Although in very small amount (0.02%), the videos showing no content in fact ("Nothing") were also observed. The categories "Games" and "Travel" also appeared to be among the less frequent content categories. The much-talked-of category "Sexy/Flirting" occurred 19 times. In most of the videos of this category, the performers were skin-tight dressed and posed with a sexy gaze. In two videos, girls wore a swim suit only. At that, the contents were combined with musical performances or doing everyday things.

To reveal the differences in content preferences among male and female content creators (RQ2), the data about gender of video performers was collected. Generally, in a total of 405 videos female performers were observed; male persons performed in only 201 videos. Relatively frequently, i.e. in 240 videos, groups of two or more people were shot. In 154 videos no persons, but animals, nature, food, or other objects were presented.

The results on the frequency of content occurrence depending on the gender of the performer are present in the Table 1. It is remarkable that "Comedy/Joke" is the most frequent category among both female and male creators. However, the named category is especially frequent among males, as more than 40% of videos with male performers were assigned to that category as opposed to 29.63% by females. In addition to that,

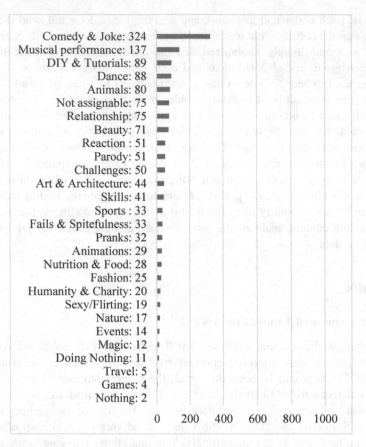

Fig. 2. Distribution of content categories on TikTok by occurrence frequency (N = 1,000)

both genders seem to like to create the content referring to the categories "Musical performance" and "Dance." Also relatively frequently among both genders are the videos where performers parody other people (mostly their relatives, i.e. parents or older/younger sisters/brothers, or teachers). Though rather rarely observed, the videos of the category "Pranks," where the scenes of rather inappropriate behavior are shot, have remarkably comparable relative frequency among both genders. Not surprisingly, the categories "Beauty" and "DIY & Tutorials" are among the most frequent by females, but are rather rare by males. Next to comedies and musical performances, males in their turn prefer to generate the content showing their reaction to something, including other videos ("Reaction"), or taking up the challenges ("Challenges"). With that, the category "Relationship," often showing persons from their romantic side, occurs more frequently among males than females. Remarkable is the distribution of videos in the category "Sexy/Flirting," as girls appeared in 18 out of 19 videos. The prevalence of sexy self-presentation by female persons is, however, in line with previous studies [29].

To identify the categories which are the most popular among TikTok users (*RQ3*) we analyzed 100 videos with the highest numbers of likes, shares, and comments, respectively. Chen et al. [23] concluded that popularity metrics on Douyin are distributed by Zipf's law, which means that very view videos get the most of the likes and, vice versa, most of the videos get very few likes. Our analysis also confirmed such inhomogeneous distribution of popularity metrics. Thus, 100 out of 1,000 videos got 63.25% of all likes, 81.37% of all comments, and 76.73% of all shares. It was, therefore, sufficient to analyze only 100 most popular videos to reveal the most popular categories.

Table 1. Distribution of content categories on TikTok depending on the performer's gender

Category	Female performers			Male performers		
	Rank	Number of videos (N = 405)	Relative frequency	Rank	Number of videos (N = 201)	Relative frequency
Comedy/Joke	1	120	29.63%	1	88	43.78%
Musical Performance	2	69	17.04%	2	30	14.93%
Beauty	3	53	13.09%	11	6	2.99%
DIY & Tutorials	4	47	11.60%	11	6	2.99%
Dance	5	42	10.37%	4	15	7.46%
Not assignable	6	35	8.64%	6	11	5.47%
Parody	7	26	6.42%	5	13	6.47%
Sexy/Flirting	8	18	4.44%	14	1	0.50%
Challenges	8	17	4.20%	4	15	7.46%
Skills	9	17	4.20%	5	13	6.47%
Animals	10	16	3.95%	7	10	4.98%
Animations	11	15	3.70%	13	2	1.00%
Fashion	12	14	3.46%	11	6	2.99%
Relationship	12	13	3.21%	8	9	4.48%
Sports	12	13	3.21%	9	8	3.98%
Fails & Spitefulness	13	13	3.21%	10	7	3.48%
Pranks	13	9	2.22%	11	6	2.99%
Doing Nothing	14	9	2.22%	14	1	0.50%
Reaction	14	8	1.98%	3	18	8.96%
Art & Architecture	15	8	1.98%	11	6	2.99%
Nature	16	7	1.73%	12	3	1.49%
Events	17	6	1.48%	14	1	0.50%
Nutrition/Food	18	5	1.23%	6	11	5.47%
Magic	19	4	0.99%	12	3	1.49%
Humanity/Charity	19	3 ·	0.74%	8	9	4.48%
Games	20	2	0.49%	14	1	0.50%
Travel	20	2	0.49%	14	1	0.50%
Nothing	–	0	–	14	1	0.50%

Generally, it can be observed that videos on TikTok main feed appear not only in case of their high popularity. On the contrary, the number of likes, shares, and comments to clips recommended for viewing by the system varied greatly from 0 to several billions (see Table 2). The results of correlation analysis are basically congruent with Chen et al.'s study [23], as correlations tend to be predominantly positive moderate. At that, the correlation between the number of likes and shares is positively high, signalizing that the more likes collected a video, the more shares it gets. Thus, people tend to share videos that they liked. Further on, recipients of those videos will also most probably like the shared video. Close to that, is the highly moderate correlation between likes and comments: Users rather relatively leave their comments to videos they liked. Additionally, we analyzed whether the number of user's followers positively effects video popularity, as one can suggest, that the more followers a user has, the more likes, shares and comments collect his or her videos. That being said, the resulted low correlation with all metrics rather indicates the absence of such effect, meaning that the high number of followers contributes to the popularity of a video only to a low degree.

Table 2. Distribution of popularity metrics to the analyzed videos (N = 1,000) on TikTok and correlation between parameters

Popularity metrics	Likes	Comments	Shares	Followers
Maximum value	9,700,000	1,200,000	1,100,000	18,000,000
Minimum value	0	0	0	0
Median	109,450	942	2,000	78,200
Correlations				
Likes	1	.463**	.746**	.244**
Comments	.463**	1	.341**	.100**
Shares	.746**	.341**	1	.114**
Followers	.244**	.100**	.114**	1

**: correlation is significant at the level of 0.01.

The top seven highly ranked, i.e. most popular, content categories can be found in the Tables 3a, 3b, and 3c. The ranks were assigned to categories depending on how many times a video of a specific category occurred in the top 100 videos.

The absolute winner by the number of likes, comments, and shares is the category "Comedy/Joke" followed by the categories "Musical performance" and "Art & Architecture." With that, remarkable is the high popularity of the category "Art & Architecture," as videos of this category unlike the above mentioned categories were not among the most frequently observed. Similar to that are the categories "Animals" and "Humanity/Charity." Opposite to that are the frequent categories "Beauty" and

"Parody," which do not occur among most liked, commented, and shared videos with relative frequency of not less than 5%. All other popular categories were also among the frequently observed. With that, the categories which are typical for mostly liked videos, also appear in the ranking of mostly commented and mostly shared videos, being in line with the results of correlation analysis. Special attention was paid to the category "Sexy/Flirting," which actually appeared among 100 most liked, commented, and shared videos, but only twice, triply, and twice, accordingly. Similar to that is the problematic category "Pranks," which was three times highly liked and once highly shared, although it did not occur among the highly commented videos.

The further look into the distribution of popularity metrics, however, indicated that, although some categories were among most frequently observed, they did not obligatory get the highest number of likes, comments, or shares. In terms of likes, videos of the categories "Humanity/Charity," "Fails & Spitefulness," and "Challenges" got even more likes than "Comedy/Joke" and "Musical performance". Similarly, videos of the categories "Relationship," "Art & Architecture," "Humanity/Charity," and "Dance" appear to be more actively commented than the category "Comedy/Joke," although being less frequent in the top 100 videos. As to the shares, the category "Comedy/Joke" keeps its leading positions in terms of both frequency and popularity. Outstanding are the categories "Relationship" and "Skills" with the lowest ranks, but practically highest numbers of shares.

Table 3a. Most popular content categories on TikTok depending on the number of likes

Rank	Category	Number of videos (n = 100)	Median: Number of likes
1	Comedy/Joke	33	2,300,000
2	Musical performance	14	2,200,000
	Art & Architecture	14	1,850,000
3	Dance	9	2,300,000
	Relationship	9	1,800,000
4	Animals	8	1,700,000
	Challenges	8	2,400,000
	Humanity/Charity	8	2,850,000
5	DIY & Tutorials	7	1,900,000
	Skills	7	2,000,000
6	Not assignable	6	2,300,000
7	Fails & Spitefulness	5	2,600,000

Table 3b. Most popular content categories on TikTok depending on the number of comments

Rank	Category	Number of videos (n = 100)	Median: Number of comments
1	Comedy/Joke	30	27,000
2	Art & Architecture	16	31,300
3	Musical performance	14	18,700
4	DIY & Tutorials	10	20,000
	Dance	10	29,150
5	Humanity/Charity	9	30,800
	Not assignable	9	15,200
6	Animals	7	25,400
	Challenges	7	16,500
	Animations	7	17,100
7	Relationship	6	42,400

Table 3c. Most popular content categories on TikTok depending on the number of shares

Rank	Category	Number of videos (n = 100)	Median: Number of shares
1	Comedy/Joke	32	2,200,000
2	Musical performance	17	54,350
3	Art & Architecture	14	46,650
4	Animals	11	48,700
	DIY & Tutorials	11	48,700
5	Dance	9	54,500
	Challenges	9	60,000
6	Relationship	8	101,750
7	Skills	6	83,200

4.2 Potential Law Infringements on TikTok

The analysis of collected data additionally confirmed that some potential law violations can be observed on TikTok (*RQ4*). The results are present in the Table 4. To find out whether the copyright violations take place on TikTok we first analyzed if music was playing in videos, which resulted in that 262 out of 1,000 videos, which were not supported with any music. In 304 out of the remaining 738 videos with music (i.e., in 30.4% of all videos), there were observed cases of copyright violations. The main reasons were the absence of a proper title to a played song or playback of songs from private collections in the background. However, it should be noted that such kinds of copyright violations are seen as potential law infringements in terms of very strict German legislation. At the same time, those cases could be treated as "fair use" in the USA. The personal rights violations were observed in 19 videos, most of them filming people in background. In one case, a teacher was the object of the video shot with a hidden mobile phone. As to inappropriate content, the analyzed videos do not show either violence or drug and alcohol consumption. The sexual content was also not found.

Table 4. Potential law infringements in videos on TikTok (N = 1,000)

Potential law infringement	Copyright	Personal rights	Inappropriate contents		
			Violence	Sexual	Drug or alcohol consumption
Number of videos	304	19	0	0	0

5 Discussion

In this study, 1,000 videos were analyzed to reveal which contents are common and popular on TikTok. The content analysis demonstrated that a few categories, i.e. "Comedy & Joke," "Musical performance," "DIY & Tutorials," and "Dance," stand out in terms of relative frequency, while numerous other categories take only small percentage of shares in the videos distribution. Especially prominent turned out to be videos where creators show comedic content. The category left behind musical videos, where people sing or dance, in terms of both frequency and popularity, although musical videos are also highly ranked.

With the category "Comedy" being on the top, TikTok is very similar to other video sharing platforms, including YouTube, YouNow, and Vine, each being representative of different types of video sharing applications. This result is also in line with the study on Douyin [6], stating that having fun is one of the most common user motives. Musical clips and creative dances along with beauty, fashion, relationships, prosocial behavior, life hacks, animals, food: All those categories have TikTok and Douyin in common. At the same time, videos oriented at political issues as well as travelling are rather exceptional on TikTok. Unlike Douyin, videos addressing educational needs as well as content related to the professional life did not occur on TikTok. Thus, categories related to knowledge sharing are not the specific for TikTok and are only partially present in the categories "DIY & Tutorials" and "Beauty," which in turn can be characterized as entertaining. Also baby related videos on TikTok could be assigned to funny videos and not to educational content as it is the case on Douyin [6]. Beyond that, not typical for TikTok are videos focused on computer games as distinct from SLSSs [28] and YouTube [27]. In contrast with YouTube, videos dedicated to vehicles [26] or aimed at children [27] are also not found on TikTok. We suggest that the absence of the named categories is connected with the age of TikTok users, who are believed to be predominantly adolescents. This especially refers to the categories related to politics, professional life, vehicles, or parenting, which are more relevant for adults. In addition to that, a limit in length can influence the absence of videos, where users share their knowledge on topics such as education or technologies. To present such content in a short, interesting and understandable form requires additional mental preparation and, moreover, can remind on school classes, whereas youth may rather want to relax and have fun.

Comparing TikTok with Vine [25], further confirms that people tend to use short videos platforms for entertainment, posting videos with jokes, funny moments, singing, and dances. Selfie-like videos also tend to be peculiar on short video sharing services.

At the same time, unlike Vine [25], inappropriate harmful contents were not observed on TikTok. As to other law infringements, the cases of potential copyright violations, which are typical for all social networking services [17], were observed relatively frequently. However, the cases were treated as potential infringements in terms of very strict German legislation. In the USA, it would be rather viewed as "fair use." Similarly to SLSSs [35], issues related to personal rights were observed in a small amount.

The content analysis additionally revealed that the much-talked-of content where young people appear in a sexy manner is not that frequent on the platform. However, harms, which can be potentially inflicted to younger users by strangers, are enormous, and even if they happen to one person only, they can be crashing and intolerable for that person. Therefore, more work should be undertaken with the performers as those could not be aware of the consequences to which can lead sexy posing on platforms where content is publicly available.

6 Limitations

As it was already mentioned, the videos in this study originate from Germany due to TikTok technical requirements, which pose some limitations on the implications of the results, as cultural aspects can influence users' preferences in contents. Also due to the absence of demographic information in users' profiles, the age of the users was not analyzed. Although, overall observations of the coders allow to conclude that TikTok is especially popular among adolescents, but not children. Moreover, the representatives of the "Generation X" [40] also find place on TikTok, often appearing together with their younger relatives.

7 Conclusion and Future Work

With this study we started to investigate TikTok as a prominent representative of mobile video sharing social media applications. The content analysis demonstrated that videos on TikTok are aimed at entertainment combined with self-expression and self-presentation. Appearance of mostly non-serious topics as opposed to politics and education (i.e., knowledge sharing) further confirm the tendency that TikTok is rather used to relax and have fun same as Douyin [6] and former Vine [25]. Furthermore, the study supports previous findings on the use of short video sharing services by younger individuals, stating that they view such platforms "as a stage to perform, tell stories, and express their opinions and identities in a performative way" [25].

Though, the service stipulates a lot of directions for future research. To improve users experience in the application, more work should be done to evaluate TikTok as an information service. The focus could be laid on the perceived and objective quality of TikTok as an information system measured by its perceived ease of use and perceived usefulness, on one hand, and by its functionality, usability, degree of gamification and efficiency, on the other hand, with all of the elements being important for evaluation of information services [41]. Not less important is to understand what motivates users to use the service. Do people use it exclusively to create and watch videos on the platform and why they spend their time on those activities? Does the factor of socialization or the fear to be an outlier in offline life drive TikTok users as it is the case on YouNow [1] and Douyin [6], accordingly? In the light of strong criticism on TikTok because of the high possibility of cyber-grooming cases, a study aimed at the named problem should be additionally undertaken contributing to the safety of younger persons in online space. For that, videos of sexual contents could be intentionally searched for with the goal to further analyze the comments to them and, if possible and ethical, its effect on users.

Acknowledgements. The data in this project were collected and coded by Aliaksandra Shutsko, Alon Borenshtein, Elisabeth Levin, Fabian Birghan, Jennifer Storms, Neil Suárez Rodríguez, Robert Hettenhausen, Sebastian Blaszczok. The supervisors of the project were Kaja J. Fietkiewicz and Wolfgang G. Stock. The author would like to thank all the participants of the project.

References

1. Scheibe, K., Fietkiewicz, K.J., Stock, W.G.: Information behavior on social live streaming services. J. Inf. Sci. Theory Pract. **4**(2), 6–20 (2016)
2. ByteDance. https://www.bytedance.com/en/about. Accessed 20 Dec 2019
3. TikTok Newsroom: musical.ly and TikTok unite to debut new worldwide short-form video platform upgraded app, titled TikTok, now available globally. https://newsroom.tiktok.com/en-us/musical-ly-and. Accessed 20 Dec 2019
4. TikTok continues to lead social app download rankings in September. https://www.socialmediatoday.com/news/tiktok-continues-to-lead-social-app-download-rankings-in-septemb er/565692/. Accessed 20 Dec 2019
5. TikTok Statistics That You Need to Know in 2020. https://www.oberlo.com/blog/tiktok-statistics. Accessed 20 Dec 2019
6. Lu, X., Lu, Z.: Fifteen seconds of fame: a qualitative study of Douyin, a short video sharing mobile application in China. In: Meiselwitz, G. (ed.) HCII 2019. LNCS, vol. 11578, pp. 233–244. Springer, Cham (2019). https://doi.org/10.1007/978-3-030-21902-4_17
7. TikTok mit 5,5 Mio. aktiven Nutzern in Deutschland. https://www.futurebiz.de/artikel/tiktok-nutzerzahlen-deutschland/. Accessed 20 Dec 2019
8. Making Smart Content Choices on TikTok. https://newsroom.tiktok.com/de-de/newsroom/making-smart-content-choices-on-tiktok. Accessed 20 Dec 2019
9. TikTok Newsroom: DIY: Duets & Reactions on TikTok. https://newsroom.tiktok.com/en-gb/diy-duets-reactions-on-tiktok. Accessed 20 Dec 2019
10. Zhang, L., Wang, F., Liu, J.: Understand instant video clip sharing on mobile platforms: Twitter's vine as a case study. In: Proceedings of Network and Operating System Support on Digital Audio and Video Workshop, pp. 85–90. ACM, New York (2014)
11. TikTok: Record fine for video sharing app over children's data. https://www.bbc.com/news/technology-47396767. Accessed 20 Dec 2019
12. TikTok under investigation over child data use. https://www.theguardian.com/technology/2019/jul/02/tiktok-under-investigation-over-child-data-use. Accessed 20 Dec 2019
13. TikTok Transparency Report. https://www.tiktok.com/safety/resources/transparency-report. Accessed 20 Dec 2019

14. TikTok Has a Predator Problem. A Network of Young Women is Fighting Back. https://ww w.buzzfeednews.com/article/ryanhatesthis/tiktok-has-a-predator-problem-young-women-are -fighting-back. Accessed 20 Dec 2019

15. Warum Tik Tok für Kinder gefährlich werden kann. https://www.focus.de/digital/handy/cyb ergrooming-warum-tik-tok-fuer-kinder-gefaehrlich-werden-kann_id_10407806.html. Accessed 20 Dec 2019

16. Gurbani, V.K., Migliosi, A., State, R., Payette, C., Cilli, B., Engel, T.: A characterization of short-video and distributed hot-spot activity in Instagram. In: Proceedings of the Principles, Systems and Applications on IP Telecommunications, pp. 28–34. ACM, New York (2015)

17. Hoffmann, C.P., Lutz, C., Meckel, M.: Content creation on the Internet: a social cognitive perspective on the participation divide. Inf. Commun. Soc. **18**(6), 696–716 (2015)

18. McRoberts, S., Bonsignore, E., Peyton, T., Yarosh, S.: Do it for the viewers!: audience engagement behaviors of young YouTubers. In: Proceedings of the 15th International Conference on Interaction Design and Children, pp. 334–343. ACM, New York (2016)

19. Milkaite, I., Lievens, E.: Child-friendly transparency of data processing in the EU: from legal requirements to platform policies. J. Child. Media **14**(1), 5–21 (2019)

20. Badillo-Urquiola, K., Smriti, D., McNally, B., Golub, E., Bonsignore, E., Wisniewski, P.J.: Stranger danger!: social media app features co-designed with children to keep them safe online. In: Proceedings of the 18th ACM International Conference on Interaction Design and Children, pp. 394–406. ACM, New York (2019)

21. Rettberg, J.W.: Hand signs for lip-syncing: the emergence of a gestural language on musical. ly as a video-based equivalent to emoji. Soc. Media+ Soc. **3**(4) (2017)

22. Literat, I., Kligler-Vilenchik, N.: Youth collective political expression on social media: the role of affordances and memetic dimensions for voicing political views. New Media Soc. **21** (9), 1988–2009 (2019)

23. Chen, Z., He, Q., Mao, Z., Chung, H., Maharjan, S.: A study on the characteristics of Douyin short videos and implications for edge caching. In: Proceedings of the ACM Turing Celebration Conference – China, pp. 1–6. ACM, New York (2019)

24. Zimmer, F., Scheibe, K., Stock, W.G.: A model for information behavior research on social live streaming services (SLSSs). In: Meiselwitz, G. (ed.) SCSM 2018. LNCS, vol. 10914, pp. 429–448. Springer, Cham (2018). https://doi.org/10.1007/978-3-319-91485-5_33

25. Yarosh, S., Bonsignore, E., McRoberts, S., Peyton, T.: YouthTube: youth video authorship on YouTube and vine. In: Proceedings of the 19th ACM Conference on Computer-Supported Cooperative Work & Social Computing, pp. 1423–1437. ACM, New York (2016)

26. Che, X., Ip, B., Lin, L.: A survey of current YouTube video characteristics. IEEE Multimed. **22**(2), 56–63 (2015)

27. A Week in the Life of Popular YouTube Channels. https://www.pewresearch.org/internet/ 2019/07/25/a-week-in-the-life-of-popular-youtube-channels/. Accessed 14 Oct 2019

28. Friedländer, M.B.: Streamer motives and user-generated content on social live-streaming services. J. Inf. Sci. Theory Pract. **5**(1), 65–84 (2017)

29. van Oosten, J.M., Vandenbosch, L., Peter, J.: Gender roles on social networking sites: investigating reciprocal relationships between Dutch adolescents' hypermasculinity and hyperfemininity and sexy online self-presentations. J. Child. Media **11**(2), 147–166 (2017)

30. García Jiménez, A., Montes Vozmediano, M.: Subject matter of videos for teens on YouTube. Int. J. Adolesc. Youth **24**(1), 63–78 (2020)

31. Scheibe, K., Zimmer, F.: Gender differences in perception of gamification elements on social live streaming services. Int. J. Interact. Commun. Syst. Technol. **9**(2), 1–15 (2019)

32. Khan, M.L.: Social media engagement: what motivates user participation and consumption on YouTube? Comput. Hum. Behav. **66**, 236–247 (2017)

33. Agrawal, S., Sureka, A.: Copyright infringement detection of music videos on YouTube by mining video and uploader meta-data. In: Bhatnagar, V., Srinivasa, S. (eds.) BDA 2013. LNCS, vol. 8302, pp. 48–67. Springer, Cham (2013). https://doi.org/10.1007/978-3-319-03689-2_4

34. Zimmer, F., Fietkiewicz, K.J., Stock, W.G.: Law infringements in social live streaming services. In: Tryfonas, T. (ed.) HAS 2017. LNCS, vol. 10292, pp. 567–585. Springer, Cham (2017). https://doi.org/10.1007/978-3-319-58460-7_40

35. Honka, A., Frommelius, N., Mehlem, A., Tolles, J.N., Fietkiewicz, K.J.: How safe is YouNow? An empirical study on possible law infringements in Germany and the United States. J. MacroTrends Soc. Sci. 1(1), 1–17 (2015)

36. Livingstone, S., Kirwil, L., Ponte, C., Staksrud, E.: In their own words: What bothers children online? Eur. J. Commun. 29(3), 271–288 (2014)

37. Huguenin, K., Kermarrec, A.M., Kloudas, K., Taïani, F.: Content and geographical locality in user-generated content sharing systems. In: Proceedings of the 22nd International Workshop on Network and Operating System Support for Digital Audio and Video, pp. 77–82. ACM, New York (2012)

38. Krippendorff, K.: Content Analysis: An Introduction to its Methodology, 2nd edn. Sage, Thousand Oaks (2004)

39. McMillan, S.J.: The challenge of applying content analysis for the World Wide Web. In: Krippendorff, K., Bock, M.A. (eds.) The Content Analysis Reader, pp. 60–67. Sage, Los Angeles (2009)

40. Fietkiewicz, K.J., Lins, E., Baran, K.S., Stock, W.S.: Inter-generational comparison of social media use: investigating the online behavior of different generational cohorts. In: Proceedings of the 49th Hawaii International Conference on System Sciences, pp. 3829–3838. IEEE Computer Society, Washington, DC (2016)

41. Schumann, L., Stock, W.G.: The information service evaluation (ISE) model. Webology 11(1), 1–20 (2014)

Review of Electronic Word-of-Mouth Based on Bibliometrics

Peihan Wen and Ruiquan Wang[✉]

Chongqing University, Chongqing, China
wenph@cqu.edu.cn, 376876185@qq.com

Abstract. The Electronic word-of-mouth (eWOM) is recognized as one of the most influential resources of information transmission, especially in consumer purchase decisions. There exists an increasing trend in the number of publications related to the eWOM these years. In order to explore the specific developments in this field, a detailed overview of eWOM is presented. Different from other reviews focusing on qualitative analysis, we quantitatively analyze the relevant articles of eWOM with the bibliometric method, using 1000 eWOM-related publications retrieved from Web of Knowledge during 1998 and 2019, to ensure the objectivity and effectiveness of the results. To reveal the contributions of journals, authors, institutions and regions, leading individuals and collaboration patterns were identified. Furthermore, the topic-method mapping network (TMMN), a relationship network with two types of nodes for topic keywords and method keywords, was presented to demonstrate the hot research topics and corresponding methods as well as the relationships between them. Finally, some suggestions were provided for review websites. This study offers a valuable orientation for scholars focusing on eWOM processes.

Keywords: eWOM · Bibliometric method · TMMN · Collaboration network

1 Introduction

The word-of-mouth (WOM) is the process which allows consumers to share information and opinions that direct buyers towards and away from specific products, brands and services [1]. This process has been demonstrated that personal conversations and informal communications among acquaintances not only influence consumers' choices and purchase decisions, but also shape consumer expectations [2], pre-usage attitudes [3], and even post-usage perceptions of a production or services [4]. A unique aspect of the WOM effect that distinguishes it from more traditional marketing effects is the positive feedback mechanism between WOM and product sales. That is, WOM leads to more product sales, which in turn generate more WOM and then more product sales [5].

With the advent of the Internet era, it is possible for consumers to share the opinions and experience towards a product through the internet, and this kind of process is described as electronic word-of-mouth (eWOM) [1].

Due to the fact that eWOM is recognized as one of the most influential resources of information transmission [6], this field attracts a large number of researchers.

© Springer Nature Switzerland AG 2020
G. Meiselwitz (Ed.): HCII 2020, LNCS 12195, pp. 126–144, 2020.
https://doi.org/10.1007/978-3-030-49576-3_9

A research has shown that word of mouth is goal driven and serves five key functions: impression management, mood regulation, information acquisition, social connections, and persuasion [7]. This five motivations drive the contents of the personal conversations without their awareness. In term of sentiment of online review, some researches have clarified the impact of sentiment on the validity and perceived helpfulness of consumer reviews. The findings demonstrate that although reviews with higher levels of positive sentiment in the title receive more readerships [8], negative sentiment, such as anxiety and anger, will enhance readers' perception of the content of the review [9]. Furthermore, some scholars have focused on the factors that affect the perceived usefulness of online consumer reviews [10], revealing that the extent of subjectivity, informativeness, readability, and linguistic correctness in reviews matters in influencing sales and perceived usefulness [11]. In terms of trust, some findings indicate that moderating variables such as consumer involvement and experience as well as the type of website affects the way consumers assess trustworthiness [12], and information quality, website quality and consumer satisfaction influence consumer trust towards consumer-generated media (CGM) [13].

As consumers' online reviews play an important role in generating electronic word of mouth, some online platforms have begun to consciously regulate consumer reviews. To explain what the online platforms should do, effect of organizational response to negative consumer reviews is explored [14] and the results show that the provision of an online response (versus no response) link enhanced inferences that potential consumers draw regarding the business's trustworthiness and the extent to which it cares about its customers. To collect more reviews, many websites encourage user interaction, such as allowing one user to subscribe to another and the benefits are significant: as users become more popular, they will generate more reviews and more objective reviews [15], which in turn attract more potential consumers. Besides, a number of online platforms, such as Airbnb, tend to contain very limited linguistic resources of reviews, thereby establishing a norm for highly positive reviews on the site [16]. The research on eWOM applications is mainly concentrated in the fields of hotels [17–22], tourism [23–25], accommodation [26], and restaurant [27].

Currently, there are a number of reviews in the eWOM field, and some of them are overviewed by collecting and analyzing published articles. For example, Cantallops identified the factors of comments and the impact of eWOM in the hotel industry [28], King and Racherla conducted a multi-dimensional analysis of eWOM communications [29], and Alalwan outlined the main topics and trends in social media and marketing related areas [30]. In addition, some scholars have conducted a meta-analysis of the existing research results [31–33].

These reviews, however, focus on qualitative analysis. In contrast, this paper quantitatively analyzes the relevant articles of eWOM by bibliometric method Bibliometrics was defined as "the application of mathematics and statistical methods to books and other media of communication" by Pritchard [34], and described as a knowledge-generating system that helps to explore, organize and analyze large amounts of historical data helping researchers to identify "hidden patterns" that may help researchers in the decision-making process [35]. Compared with Meta-analyses, bibliometrics evaluate papers by analyzing data provided from the database more quantitatively and qualitatively [36]. Some common tools such as authors keyword analysis, affiliations, conceptual maps, cluster and factor analysis, citation and co-citation analysis was applied to reflect research trends [37]. The use of bibliometrics is gradually extending to all disciplines [38], such as medical insurance [39, 40], latent semantic analysis (LSA) [41], virtual and remote labs [42], fuzzy decision making [43], operational research & management science (OR&MS) [44] and circular economy [45].

The paper is organized as follows. In the Sect. 2, the data source, search strategy and analysis methods are described. In the Sect. 3, leading journals, leading authors, leading institutions, leading regions as well as collaboration network among them are provided. The topic-method mapping network (TMMN) is presented in the Sect. 4. Section 5 draws the conclusions and implications.

2   Data Source and Analysis Methods

2.1   Data Source

To quantitively overview the development of the eWOM, we considered 1,000 articles focusing on eWOM. These papers were published in the period from 1998 to 2019 in the Web of Science database. Web of Science (previously known as Web of Knowledge) is an online subscription-based scientific citation indexing service that provides a comprehensive citation search. It gives access to multiple databases that reference cross-disciplinary research, which allows for in-depth exploration of specialized subfields within an academic or scientific discipline [46]. The retrieval was determined by the expressions of the topic. Several possible expressions of eWOM, such as "electronic word-of-mouth", "eWOM" and "e-word-of-mouth" were used as topic keywords. Therefore, the retrieval expression was: TS = ("e* word-of-mouth" OR "eWOM"). A total of 1,279 documents were retrieved, and 1,000 documents were selected according to the cited frequency from high to low.

Although most of the documents retrieved in this way had a high correlation with eWOM, there were still some documents that are totally unrelated with eWOM. Through simply browsing the information of these documents (including title, abstract and keywords), 4 irrelevant documents were eliminated, and another 4 papers (ranked 1001–1004) were selected to supplement documents to 1,000.

2.2   Analysis Methods

With the help of data analysis software, the characteristics and trends of eWOM related research were quantitatively analyzed by bibliometric method. Full record and cited references of all selected documents were exported from Web of Science to InCites and CiteSpace.

InCites is a comprehensive scientific assessment and analysis tool based on Web of Science. Some indicators of documents and journals, such as times cited and journal impact factor, were analyzed by InCites.

CiteSpace, a Java based application that help to recognition and visualization of developments in the scientific literature, has become an influential information visualization software in the field of information analysis [47]. In this paper, due to its powerful functions to facilitate the understanding and interpretation of network patterns, CiteSpace was used to build collaboration networks for authors, institutions and regions and visualize collaboration patterns.

In addition to cooperation networks, bar charts were used to compare the number of documents for leading authors, leading institutions and leading areas, and tables were used to demonstrate the specific indicators from these three aspects, such as times cited, percentage of cited documents and citation impact.

In the part of TMMN, the LDA (Latent Dirichlet Allocation) was applied to label the documents, especially for those without keywords or with totally unrelated keywords with topic and method, according to the title, abstract and introduction; keywords co-occurrence networks were adopted to figure out high frequency keywords as well as the relationship between them; and mapping network was presented to reveal the degree of relevance between the major topic keywords and method keywords.

3   Index Information Analysis and Results

From the Web of Science, totally 1,000 documents were retrieved and the annual releases of these documents in the period of 1998 to 2019 are shown in Fig. 1.

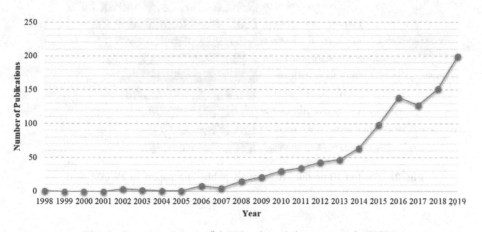

Fig. 1. Annual releases of 1,000 selected documents of eWOM

Stood at approximately 0 at 1998, the number of annual publications remained stable until 2007. After that, the figure for annual releases experienced an increase, from 5 documents at 2007 to just under 50 documents at 2013. Although the number of documents declined by 10 documents from 2016 to 2017, that figure rose sharply, peaking at 200 documents at 2019. It was noticeable that number of documents published in 2019 constituted nearly 20% of the total value, indicating that an increasing number of researchers were attracted by eWOM related research recently years.

In this section, collaboration networks of authors, institutions and regions were built to reveal collaborations in the field of eWOM among them, and leading journals, leading authors, leading institutions and leading regions were also been displayed.

3.1   Leading Journals

The traditional academic communication has a long history, and journals, as a formal means of academic communication, play an important role in disseminating scientific research results, leading the development of disciplines and consolidating scholars. The identification and analysis of leading journals can help researchers in a specific academic field to find the best source of papers quickly and accurately, and guide their submissions, contributing to the academic communication. The top 10 productive journals publishing papers in eWOM are shown in Fig. 2 and detailed indicators of these 10 journals are list in Table 1.

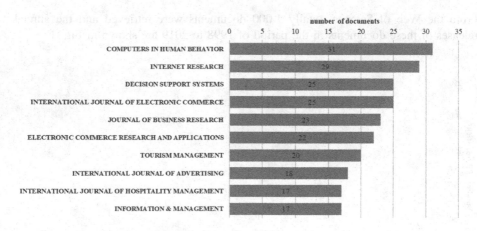

Fig. 2. The top 10 productive journals publishing papers in eWOM field

Table 1. Detailed indicators of top 10 productive journals publishing papers in eWOM field

Rank	Journal	ND	TC	% DC	IF
1	COMPUTERS IN HUMAN BEHAVIOR	31	710	90.23%	4.31
2	INTERNET RESEARCH	29	972	93.10%	4.11
3	DECISION SUPPORT SYSTEMS	25	1113	88.00%	3.85
4	INTERNATIONAL JOURNAL OF ELECTRONIC COMMERCE	25	1770	84.00%	3.44
5	JOURNAL OF BUSINESS RESEARCH	23	1331	86.96%	4.03
6	ELECTRONIC COMMERCE RESEARCH AND APPLICATIONS	22	911	86.36%	2.91
7	TOURISM MANAGEMENT	20	2403	90.00%	6.01
8	INTERNATIONAL JOURNAL OF ADVERTISING	18	745	88.89%	2.23
9	INTERNATIONAL JOURNAL OF HOSPITALITY MANAGEMENT	17	1018	94.12%	4.47
10	INFORMATION & MANAGEMENT	17	360	94.12%	4.12

Abbreviations: ND = number of documents; TC = times cited; % DC = percentage of documents cited; IF = impact factor.

It is clear that these 10 journals all have high impact factors and could be regarded as the leading journals in field of eWOM during 1989 to 2019. Ranked the first, COMPUTERS IN HUMAN BEHAVIOR has the most published documents among these 10 journals, with 4.31 as impact factor. It is followed by INTERNET RESEARCH, with 4.11 as impact factor. DECISION SUPPORT SYSTEMS, INTERNATIONAL JOURNAL OF ELECTRONIC COMMERCE, JOURNAL OF BUSINESS RESEARCH and ELECTRONIC COMMERCE RESEARCH AND APPLICATIONS have similar number of published documents (about 25), with 3.85, 3.44, 4.03, 2.91 as impact factors, respectively. Among these 4 journals, INTERNATIONAL JOURNAL OF ELECTRONIC COMMERCE has the highest times of citation (1,770 times), but has the lowest percentage of cited document. Although only has 20 documents, TOURISM MANAGEMENT has the highest impact factor (6.01) and citation times (2,403 times). Ranked ninth and tenth, the impact factors of INTERNATIONAL JOURNAL OF HOSPITALITY MANAGEMENT and INFORMATION & MANAGEMENT have relatively high impact factors (4.47 and 4.12, respectively), and both have the highest percentage of cited documents (94.12%).

3.2 Author Collaborations and Leading Authors

In most subject areas, the role of cooperation in research is showing increasing significance. Stefan Wuchty et al. used 19.9 million papers over 5 decades and 2.1 million patents to demonstrate that teams increasingly dominate solo authors in the production of knowledge [48]. Teams typically produce more frequently cited research than individuals do, and this advantage has been increasing over time.

Generated by CiteSpace, the collaboration network of authors, shown in Fig. 3, totally has 75 authors and 51 connections by selecting top 30 levels of most cited authors of each year from 1989 to 2019. Each author is represented by one point and the size of the points shows the counted times in this network. The links in the figure demonstrate the cooperation between authors and the thickness of the line represents the frequency of cooperation.

As can be seen from Fig. 3, although cooperation is not very popular in eWOM, there is still some cooperation patterns. Small group is the main model of cooperation, and one possible explanation is that eWOM is a field with massive scale and various research directions. The authors linked by the lines are defined as collaborative authors. The most collaborative authors in this network are Cheung, C. M. K. and Martinez-Torres, M. R.

Fig. 3. Author collaboration network of annual top 30 cited authors from 1989 to 2019

Figure 4 and Table 2 show top 10 most productive authors and top 10 authors with the highest impact factors in eWOM research, respectively. Cheung, C. M. K. is the most productive authors and have 10 documents, followed by Law, R., Martinez-Torres, M. R., and Lee, M. K. O. with 8 documents. By contrast, Lee, J. and Ahn, J. own least papers among these authors, with only 5 documents.

It is clear from the Table 2 that the top 10 highest impact factors are all exceed 500, of which Dellarocas, C. had the highest impact factors of 986. These 10 authors share the same pattern—each person has published only one paper, but has an extremely high number of citations. Except for Dellarocas, C., other 9 authors have similar impact factors, ranging from 669 of Pan, B. to 514 of Forman, C.

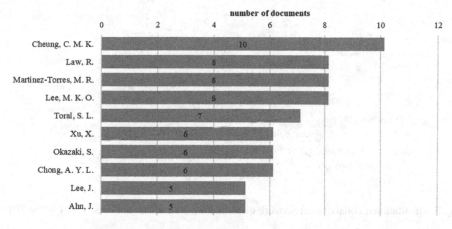

Fig. 4. Top 10 most productive authors in eWOM field

Table 2. The top 10 authors with the highest impact factors in eWOM field

Rank	Author	ND	TC	CI	Affiliation
1	Dellarocas, C.	1	986	986	Massachusetts Institute of Technology (MIT)
2	Pan, B.	1	669	669	College of Charleston
3	Pauwels, K.	1	663	663	Dartmouth College
4	Bucklin, R. E.	1	663	663	University of California Los Angeles
5	Chowdury, A.	1	662	662	n/a
6	Sobel, K.	1	662	662	Penn State University
7	Schuff, D.	1	647	647	Temple University
8	Mudambi, S. M.	1	647	647	Temple University
9	Wiesenfeld, B.	1	514	514	New York University
10	Forman, C.	1	514	514	Georgia Institute of Technology

Abbreviations: ND = number of documents; TC = times cited; CI = citation impact.

3.3   Institution Collaborations and Leading Institutions

The collaboration network of institutions, shown in Fig. 5, totally has 123 institutions and 72 connections by selecting top 30 levels of most cited institutions of each year from 1989 to 2019. Each institution is represented by one point and the size of the points shows the counted times in the network. The links demonstrate the cooperation between institutions and the thickness of the line represents the frequency of cooperation.

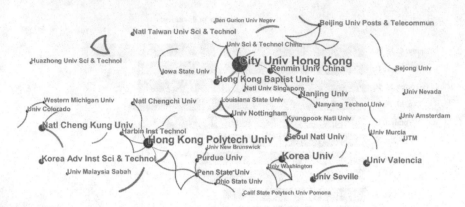

Fig. 5. Institutional collaboration network of annual top 30 cited documents from 1989 to 2019

There exists a great number of institutions involved in eWOM related research. The most striking points on the map are City University of Hong Kong, Hong Kong Polytechnic University and Korea University, showing the great contributions of these three institutions to this research field. Besides, the patterns on the graph show that there are pretty obvious clusters centered on the core institutions, which illustrates the dominant position of these research institutions in eWOM.

Table 3 lists top 10 most productive institutions in eWOM field. It is noticeable that three of top 10 most productive institutions, City University of Hong Kong, Hong Kong Polytechnic University and Hong Kong Baptist University, are located in Hong Kong, which respectively ranked the first (30 documents), the fourth (18 documents) and the sixth (14 documents). Although ranked the third, California State University System has the lowest citation impact (11.85) among these 10 institutions. Ranked the fifth, PCSHE has the highest citation times (2295 times), while National Cheng Kung University has the lowest citation times (144 times).

Table 3. The top 10 most productive institutions in eWOM field

Rank	Institution	ND	TC	%DC	CI
1	City University of Hong Kong	30	1628	83.33%	54.27
2	State University System of Florida	21	1079	95.24%	51.38
3	California State University System	20	237	80.00%	11.85
4	Hong Kong Polytechnic University	18	492	88.89%	27.33
5	Pennsylvania Commonwealth System of Higher Education (PCSHE)	18	2295	100.00%	127.5
6	Hong Kong Baptist University	14	1079	100.00%	77.07
7	University System of Georgia	14	869	92.86%	62.07
8	University of Texas System	13	792	92.31%	60.9
9	Korea University	12	456	83.33%	38
10	National Cheng Kung University	12	144	100.00%	12

Abbreviations: ND = number of documents; TC = times cited; % DC = percentage of documents cited; CI = citation impact.

3.4   Region Collaborations and Leading Regions

The collaboration network of regions, shown in Fig. 6, totally has 43 regions and 76 connections by selecting top 30 levels of most cited regions of each year from 1989 to 2019. Each region is represented by one point and the size of the points shows the counted times in the network. The links demonstrate the cooperation between regions and the thickness of the line represents the frequency of cooperation.

Figure 6 shows that several dominant countries, such as China and the USA, play a leading role in regional cooperation. Different from the "small group" cooperation model between authors, there is a close connection between regions. Most of the regions in the map have cooperation with other regions, indicating the diversity of inter-regional cooperation in the eWOM field.

Figure 7 compares the number of documents of the top 10 most productive regions in field of eWOM during 1989 to 2019. The percentage of the documents of the USA represents the most part (33%) of the total value, followed by that figure for China (32%). The percentage of South Korea, the United Kingdom and Spain constitute 9%, 8%, 7%, respectively, ranked third to fifth. By contrast, Germany, Canada and Australia only account for 4%, 4% and 3%. More specifically, in the part of China, the proportion of China mainland accounts for a half of total value of Chinese documents, while that figure for Taiwan and Hong Kong represent for one-third and one-sixth, respectively.

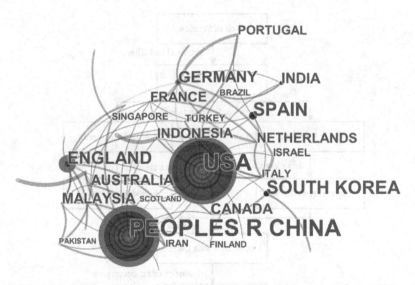

Fig. 6. Regional collaboration network of annual top 30 cited documents from 1989 to 2019

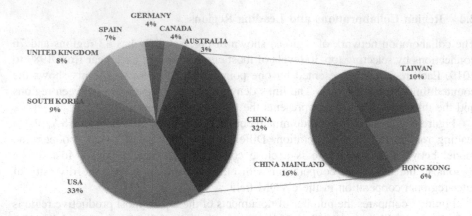

Fig. 7. The top 10 most productive regions in eWOM field

4   Content Information Analysis and Results

To reveal the connections between research topics and research methods in the field of eWOM, a topic-method mapping network (TMMN) was constructed with the biblio-metric method. TMMN is a relationship network with two types of nodes for topic keywords and method keywords, respectively. These two kinds of keywords were both

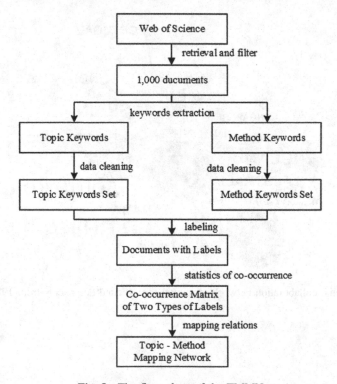

Fig. 8. The flow chart of the TMMN

mined from 1,000 related papers, and the mappings between each two keywords reveal the degree of connection of them. The process of TMMN could be divided into five specific steps: retrieval, keywords extraction, data cleaning, labeling, building a mapping network. The flow chart of TMMN is presented in Fig. 8.

Retrieval. The data source and retrieval criteria are given in Sect. 2.

Keywords Extraction. For most scientific papers, the keywords given by the author can summarize the research topic of the article. Some author keywords, however, fail to reasonably summarize the content of the paper. Therefore, in order to obtain accurate topic words and method words, the LDA (Latent Dirichlet Allocation) and regular expression were both applied to extract the feature words related to the topics and methods according to the title, abstract and introduction of the papers.

Data Cleaning. Keywords were cleaned by according to the following guidelines:

- Delete meaningless words and words with duplicate meanings, such as "internet" and "online".
- Delete words that are too broad, such as "electronic word-of-mouth", "eWOM" and "influence".
- Don't care about regions, data sources (website), and the differences between positive and negative. The words such as "America" and "Facebook" were deleted and the words such as "untrustworthy" and "incredible" were replaced by "trust".
- Replace synonyms to form a unified standard expression. For example, "gender differences" would be replaced by "gender gap", "online complaints" would be replaced by "negative comments" and "online healthcare" would be replaced by "medical service".

Fig. 9. Topic keyword network of annual top 30 cited documents from 1989 to 2019

The next step was to build word sets with a limited number of keywords. Figure 9 and Fig. 10 show the topic keyword network and method keyword network, respectively, of annual top 30 cited documents from 1989 to 2019, from which the representative keywords can be clearly identified. Each node represents a keyword, and the higher the frequency of words, the larger the label of the nodes. According to the topic keyword network and method keyword network, top 12 topic words and method words were listed in the Table 4. These two types of keywords formed topic word set and method word set, respectively.

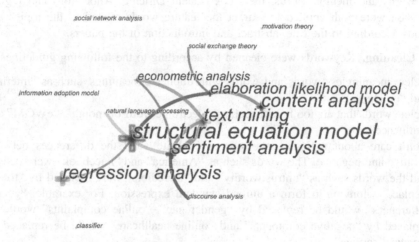

Fig. 10. Method keyword network of annual top 30 cited documents from 1989 to 2019

Table 4. The top 12 topic words and method words in keyword networks

Rank	Topic keyword	Frequency	Rank	Method keyword	Frequency
1	Trust/credibility	126	1	Structural equation model	39
2	Social media	118	2	Regression analysis	22
3	Purchase intention	65	3	Sentiment analysis	22
4	Marketing	63	4	Content analysis	21
5	Hospitality industry	61	5	Text mining	18
6	Tourism industry	50	6	Elaboration likelihood model	11
7	Consumer behavior	45	7	Econometric analysis	6
8	brand building	40	8	Dual-process theory	4
9	Customer satisfaction	32	9	Information adoption model	2
10	Sentiment	23	10	Natural language processing	2
11	User engagement	21	11	Classifier	2
12	E-commerce	17	12	Social exchange theory	2

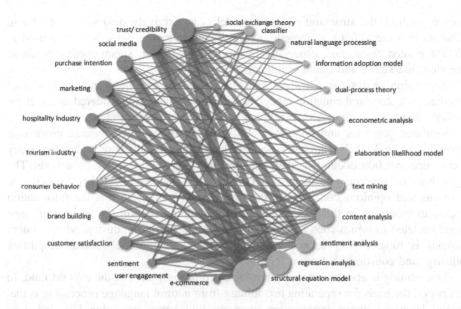

Fig. 11. Topic-method mapping network in field of eWOM

Labeling. This step was in preparation for building a mapping network. If the keywords of a paper contain keywords that exist in the topic word set or method word set, the paper would be marked corresponding to this keyword. For example, if a paper has keywords "trust", "fraud reviews" and "regression analysis", then it would be marked with labels "trust" and "regression analysis".

Building a Mapping Network. First, a keyword co-occurrence matrix was constructed based on the labels of the papers. The keyword co-occurrence matrix is a two-dimensional matrix with 12 topic words and 12 method words as its two dimensions, respectively. The number of times these keywords appear in pairs is the co- occurrence value. Then, according to the keyword co-occurrence matrix, the topic-method mapping network was built, shown in Fig. 11. In the figure, each dot represents a keyword. The dots on the left half are topic words, and the dots on the right half are method words. The higher the number of times this word appears in papers, the larger the dots are. The relationships between the topic words and method words are represented by lines with different thicknesses. The thick lines indicate that the two keywords appear frequently together, that is, they are closely related. In turn, thin lines indicate that their relationship is not so close.

TMMN reveals the mappings between research topics and research methods in the field of eWOM, providing scholars hot topics of eWOM and corresponding available methods.

The most commonly used method in the eWOM field is the structural equation model, which is related to 12 popular research directions to varying extents. As a social science method, the structural equation model can effectively deal with some latent variables that are difficult to directly and accurately measure, so it is widely used in eWOM related researches, especially in the topics of trust, social media, purchase intention, marketing and brand building.

Regression analysis is a widely used data processing method and is often used together with structural equation model. Regression analysis is considered an excellent analysis method, which can analyze the relationship between different variables.

Sentiment analysis and content analysis belong to natural language processing methods, but in TMMN, they are separated due to their much more higher frequency occurrence in 1,000 documents than other natural language processing methods. The algorithms of sentiment analysis and content analysis can effectively identify the emotions and opinions contained in the review information, so that the information related to emotions in the text could be fully obtained. Sentiment analysis is most closely related to topics such as sentiment, trust, and tourism industry, while content analysis is most closely related to topics such as trust, social media, hospitality industry, and consumer behavior.

Text mining is also one of the technologies commonly used in the eWOM field. In this paper, the basis for separating text mining from natural language processing is that natural language processing focuses more on linguistics, involving knowledge of vocabulary, semantics, grammar, etc., while text mining focuses more on technical means, including algorithms time complexity, algorithm space complexity, data storage, etc.

Other methods and technologies, such as elaboration likelihood model, econometric analysis, dual-process theory and information adoption model are also widely used in eWOM related research fields.

5   Conclusions and Implications

This paper quantitatively clarified the research development of the eWOM field from 1998 to 2019 based on the 1,000 documents retrieved from Web of Science. To reveal the contributions of journals, authors, institutions and regions, leading individuals and collaboration patterns were identified. Furthermore, the TMMN, which determines the relationships of between different research topics and research methods, were built to providing the guidelines of hot topics and corresponding methods, contributing to offer a valuable orientation for scholars focusing on eWOM processes.

5.1   Promotion of Subject Development

The collaboration between authors and institutions needs to be further strengthened. Although eWOM is a wide-ranging research area, there are certain similarities and portability in the processes and methods in this area. Small groups are currently the main form of collaboration, and there is little communication between different research groups. The author cooperation map shows that although there are productive and high-cooperative authors, these authors are limited to small-scale collaborations, failing to contribute globally. Similarly, although there are three highly cooperative leading institutions in Hong Kong, their cooperation with each other is not close, which limits their influences on this field.

Scholars from different countries or institutions should work together to break the barriers of various disciplines, which is considered the most effective way to promote research progress in the eWOM research field.

5.2 Guidance to Review Websites

According to the TMMN, popular research contents and applied methods in this field were demonstrated. The 12 listed research topics and methods show that the focus of research in the eWOM field is the relationship between customers and service providers by analysis of the data collected from surveys, websites and databases. For example, the most popular research topic is trust, including customers' trust in service providers, customers' trust in evaluation sites, and, in turn, service providers' trust in customers. Besides, the most applied methods are structural equation model and regression analysis, which are used to explore the relationship between factors based on statistics. Therefore, for the majority of researches in this field, the review websites are considered the most important part.

Undoubtedly, these websites, including online stores and social network sites, should lay great significance to the credibility of online reviews as well as the way to avoid fake comments. Objective and credible evaluation is the foundation of a review website, because they can enhance mutual trust and customer involvement. As a result, higher customer engagement will generate more interaction and feedback, which will contribute positively to the relationships between customer and review site.

Another key point in enhancing customer-site relationships is the management of negative reviews. Appropriate online complaint management is necessary for successful electronic customer relationship management [49], which relate great significance to complaint resolving. Providing excellent online customer services and responding to complaints quickly are considered two helpful approaches.

Besides, according to the mapping network, detailed analysis of customer-generated reviews, including sentiment analysis and content analysis, is a challenging task of these websites for the purpose of taking advantage of the potential value of electronic word of mouth. For some service providers, the online review are regarded as the best way to help them find out the drawbacks in their products or services. Therefore, it cannot be overemphasized to fully analyze the content of customer reviews and discover potential information.

References

1. Jalilvand, M.R., Esfahani, S.S., Samiei, N.: Electronic word-of-mouth: challenges and opportunities. Procedia Comput. Sci. **3**(8), 42–46 (2011)
2. Anderson, E., Salisbury, L.: The formation of market-level expectations and its covariates. J. Consum. Res. **30**(1), 115–124 (2003)

3. Herr, P.M., Kardes, F.R., Kim, J.: Effects of word-of-mouth and product-attribute information on persuasion: an accessibility-diagnosticity perspective. J. Consum. Res. **17**(4), 454–462 (1991)
4. Bone, P.F.: Word-of-mouth effects on short-term and long-term product judgments. J. Bus. Res. **32**(3), 213–223 (1995)
5. Godes, D., Mayzlin, D.: Using online conversations to study word-of-mouth communication. Mark. Sci. **23**(4), 545–560 (2004)
6. Chen, Y.F., Law, R.: A review of research on electronic word-of-mouth in hospitality and tourism management. Int. J. Hosp. Tour. Adm. **17**(4), 347–372 (2016)
7. Berger, J.: Word of mouth and interpersonal communication: a review and directions for future research. J. Consum. Psychol. **24**(4), 586–607 (2014)
8. Salehan, M., Kim, D.J.: Predicting the performance of online consumer reviews: a sentiment mining approach to big data analytics. Decis. Support Syst. **81**(C), 30–40 (2016)
9. Yin, D., Bond, S.D., Zhang, H.: Anxious or angry? Effects of discrete emotions on the perceived helpfulness of online reviews. MIS Q. **38**(2), 539–560 (2014)
10. Liu, Z., Park, S.: What makes a useful online review? Implication for travel product websites. Tour. Manag. **47**, 140–151 (2015)
11. Ghose, A., Ipeirotis, P.: Estimating the helpfulness and economic impact of product reviews: mining text and reviewer characteristics. IEEE Trans. Knowl. Data Eng. **23**(10), 1498–1512 (2011)
12. Filieri, R.: What makes an online consumer review trustworthy? Ann. Tour. Res. **58**, 46–64 (2016)
13. Filieri, R.: Why do travelers trust tripadvisor? Antecedents of trust towards consumer-generated media and its influence on recommendation adoption and word of mouth. Tour. Manag. **51**, 174–185 (2015)
14. Sparks, B.A., So, K.K.F., Bradley, G.L.: Responding to negative online reviews: the effects of hotel responses on customer inferences of trust and concern. Tour. Manag. **53**, 74–85 (2016)
15. Janze, C., Siering, M.: 'Status effect' in user-generated content: evidence from online service reviews. Soc. Sci. Electron. Publ. **25**(2), 222–238 (2015)
16. Bridges, J., Vásquez, C.: If nearly all Airbnb reviews are positive, does that make them meaningless? Curr. Issues Tour. **21**(18), 2057–2075 (2018)
17. Mauri, A.G., Minazzi, R.: Web reviews influence on expectations and purchasing intentions of hotel potential customers. Int. J. Hosp. Manag. **34**, 99–107 (2013)
18. Xu, X., Li, Y.: The antecedents of customer satisfaction and dissatisfaction toward various types of hotels: a text mining approach. Int. J. Hosp. Manag. **55**, 57–69 (2016)
19. Berezina, K., Bilgihan, A., Cobanoglu, C., Okumus, F.: Understanding satisfied and dissatisfied hotel customers: text mining of online hotel reviews. J. Hosp. Mark. Manag. **25**(1), 1–24 (2016)
20. Ladhari, R., Michaud, M.: Ewom effects on hotel booking intentions, attitudes, trust, and website perceptions. Int. J. Hosp. Manag. **46**, 36–45 (2015)
21. Zhao, Y., Xu, X., Wang, M.: Predicting overall customer satisfaction: big data evidence from hotel online textual reviews. Int. J. Hosp. Manag. **76**, 111–121 (2019)
22. Hu, Y.H., Chen, Y.L., Chou, H.L.: Opinion mining from online hotel reviews – a text summarization approach. Inf. Process. Manage. **53**(2), 436–449 (2017)
23. Sparks, B.A., Perkins, H.E., Buckley, R.: Online travel reviews as persuasive communication: the effects of content type, source, and certification logos on consumer behavior. Tour. Manag. **39**(Complete), 1–9 (2013)
24. Sotiriadis, M.: Sharing tourism experiences in social media: a literature review and a set of suggested business strategies. Int. J. Contemp. Hosp. Manag. **29**(1), 179–225 (2016)

25. Luo, Q., Zhong, D.: Using social network analysis to explain communication characteristics of travel-related electronic word-of-mouth on social networking sites. Tour. Manag. **46**, 274–282 (2015)
26. Gossling, S., Zeiss, H., Hall, C.M., Martin-Rios, C., Ram, Y., Grotte, I.P.: A cross-country comparison of accommodation manager perspectives on online review manipulation. Curr. Issues Tour. **22**(14), 1744–1763 (2019)
27. Zhang, Z., Ye, Q., Law, R., Li, Y.: The impact of e-word-of-mouth on the online popularity of restaurants: a comparison of consumer reviews and editor reviews. Int. J. Hosp. Manag. **29**(4), 694–700 (2010)
28. Cantallops, A.S., Salvi, F.: New consumer behavior: a review of research on ewom and hotels. Int. J. Hosp. Manag. **36**, 41–51 (2014)
29. King, R.A., Racherla, P., Bush, V.D.: What we know and don't know about online word-of-mouth: a review and synthesis of the literature. J. Interact. Mark. **28**(3), 167–183 (2014)
30. Alalwan, A.A., Rana, N.P., Dwivedi, Y.K., Algharabat, R.: Social media in marketing: a review and analysis of the existing literature. Telematics Inform. **34**(7), 1177–1190 (2017)
31. Floyd, K., Freling, R., Alhoqail, S., Cho, H.Y., Freling, T.: How online product reviews affect retail sales: a meta-analysis. J. Retail. **90**(2), 217–232 (2014)
32. You, Y., Vadakkepatt, G.G., Joshi, A.M.: A meta-analysis of electronic word-of-mouth elasticity. J. Mark. **79**(2), 19–39 (2015)
33. Babić Rosario, A., Sotgiu, F., De Valck, K., Bijmolt, T.H.A.: The effect of electronic word of mouth on sales: a meta-analytic review of platform, product, and metric factors. J. Mark. Res. **53**(3), 297–318 (2016)
34. Pritchard, A.: Statistical bibliography or bibliometrics? J. Doc. **25**(4), 348–349 (1969)
35. Morris, S., Deyong, C., Wu, Z., Salman, S., Yemenu, D.: Diva: a visualization system for exploring document databases for technology forecasting. Comput. Ind. Eng. **43**(4), 841–862 (2002)
36. Moher, D., Liberati, A., Tetzlaff, J., Altman, D.G.: Preferred reporting items for systematic reviews and meta-analyses: the PRISMA statement. Ann. Int. Med. **151**(4), 264–269 (2009)
37. Chen, C., et al.: The structure and dynamics of co-citation clusters: a multiple-perspective co-citation analysis. JASIST **61**(7), 1386–1409 (2010)
38. Aria, M., Cuccurullo, C.: Bibliometrix: an r-tool for comprehensive science mapping analysis. J. Inform. **11**(4), 959–975 (2017)
39. Faust, O., Hagiwara, Y., Hong, T.J., Lih, O.S., Acharya, U.R.: Deep learning for healthcare applications based on physiological signals: a review. Comput. Methods Programs Biomed. **161**, 1–13 (2018)
40. Gu, D., Li, J., Li, X., Liang, C.: Visualizing the knowledge structure and evolution of big data research in healthcare informatics. Int. J. Med. Inform. **98**, 22–32 (2017)
41. Tonta, Y., Darvish, H.R.: Diffusion of latent semantic analysis as a research tool: a social network analysis approach. J. Inform. **4**(2), 166–174 (2010)
42. Heradio, R., Luis, D.L.T., Galan, D., Cabrerizo, F.J., Herrera-Viedma, E., Dormido, S.: Virtual and remote labs in education: a bibliometric analysis. Comput. Educ. **98**, 14–38 (2016)
43. Blanco-Mesa, F., Lindahl, J.M.M., Gil-Lafuente, A.M.: A bibliometric analysis of fuzzy decision making research. In: 2016 Annual Conference of the North American Fuzzy Information Processing Society (NAFIPS). IEEE (2017)
44. Laengle, S., et al.: Forty years of the European journal of operational research: a bibliometric overview. Eur. J. Oper. Res. **262**(3), 803–816 (2017)
45. Homrich, A.S., Galvao, G., Abadia, L.G., Carvalho, M.M.: The circular economy umbrella: trends and gaps on integrating pathways. J. Clean. Prod. **175**, 525–543 (2018)

46. Drake, M.: Encyclopedia of Library and Information Science, First Update Supplement. CRC Press, Boca Raton (2005)
47. Chen, C.: CiteSpace II: detecting and visualizing emerging trends and transient patterns in scientific literature. J. Am. Soc. Inform. Sci. Technol. **57**(3), 359–377 (2006)
48. Wuchty, S., Jones, B.F., Uzzi, B.: The increasing dominance of teams in production of knowledge. Science **316**(5827), 1036–1039 (2007)
49. Cho, Y., Im, I., Hiltz, R., Fjermestad, J.: An analysis of online customer complaints: implications for web complaint management. In: HICSS. IEEE Computer Society (2002)

Social Computing and User Experience

Identifying User Experiences
for Decision-Making in Service Science

Silvana Aciar[1,2(✉)], Mayela Coto[3], and Gabriela Aciar[2]

[1] CONICET, Buenos Aires, Argentina
saciar@unsj-cuim.edu.ar
[2] Universidad Nacional de San Juan, San Juan, Argentina
gaby_aciar@yahoo.com.ar
[3] Universidad Nacional Costa Rica, Heredia, Costa Rica
mcoto@una.ac.cr

Abstract. The purpose of this paper is to propose a method based on text mining techniques that employs user comments on the Web to clarify users' experiences of a service. The method classifies user experiences into the categories of instrumental qualities, non-instrumental qualities, and emotional reactions. The Text-Miner Software Kit (TMSK) and Text Rule Induction Kit (RIKTEXT) were used to obtain the classification rule sets. A case study on the tourist domain was conducted to assess the rules' precision in classifying sentences into the three user experience categories. One thousand hotel reviews from the website www.tripadvisor.com were used in the evaluation process. Two datasets were built: one for training and one for testing. For validation, 100 new opinions were used to assess the rules' precision. The results are considered good because there was only a 10% error in automatic classification versus manual classification. Based on this result, we argue that the automatic identification of information about user experience of a service can be done accurately using text mining techniques, such as those presented in this work.

Keywords: User experience · Opinion mining · Ontology

1 Introduction

Service providers must have the capacity to adapt to the dynamic, globalized market with greater access to technology [1, 2], and services should be oriented to customers and their expectations. Tools that help convert data into useful information for decision-making play an important role in knowing the value of use that customers give to services [2, 3]. Analyzing this value provides important indicators for evaluating and improving the services. In this sense, it is relevant to identify the sources containing user information that can be used to obtain useful indicators for decision-making.

Currently, one of the main sources of information is the Web, where most information is in the form of unstructured text, emails, personal or institutional webpages, comments on social networks, digital books, newspapers, and databases. The process for extracting this information was developed approximately 80 years ago [4–6]. Given the amount of information that exists, it is almost impossible to retrieve it, index it, and

© Springer Nature Switzerland AG 2020
G. Meiselwitz (Ed.): HCII 2020, LNCS 12195, pp. 147–157, 2020.
https://doi.org/10.1007/978-3-030-49576-3_10

interpret it manually. Therefore, text mining techniques are used to identify patterns, predict usage trends, identify semantic structures, and classify instances and entities automatically [5, 7]. Text mining allows service providers to obtain relevant information for decision-making, for example, by analyzing customers' comments and opinions, which are available on the Web, and adapting their services according to the customers' needs and preferences [8–10].

The purpose of this paper is to propose a method based on text mining techniques that will allow for understanding users' experiences of a service on the basis of their written comments on the Web. For this, user experiences were conceptualized, recovered, and quantified. The user's experience of a service was classified into the categories of instrumental qualities, non-instrumental qualities, and emotional reactions [11]. A case study on the tourist domain was conducted to assess the accuracy of the rules in the classification of sentences in the three categories.

This study contributes to the growing literature on service science, and especially to the field of user experience, by introducing an automatic method for obtaining and presenting the key factors that influence the success of a service focused on the experiences of its users. The remainder of this paper will proceed as follows. Sections 2 and 3 present the main theoretical concepts related to the study, while Sect. 4 provides an overview of the methods for establishing the sets of rules. Section 5 presents the controlled experiment that was conducted to assess the validity of the rules. The paper ends with concluding remarks and future work in Sect. 6.

2   Science of Services and User Experience

In general terms, a service has an economic value but lacks material consistency [2, 3]. The science of services is the application of scientific disciplines to add value to services while satisfying the needs of their users [11]. Through the application of models and theories, the science of services fosters innovation, competition, and quality through the joint creation of value by providers and users [12].

One of the most important challenges in the science of services is to obtain information to feed the analysis process, which allows the decision-making associated with continuous improvement of the service design [2, 3, 11]. The more user information that can be obtained or more variables that can be measured, the greater the opportunity to improve the service. For example, a variable such as the user's previous behavior can contribute to improving new versions of a service. Continually innovating services benefits both providers and users, who will continue to use a service if they are satisfied with it.

The design of services has migrated from a design specified by specialists to one that is focused on the user. Previously, most companies and entities providing services focused on analyzing the economic benefits or quality of products and overlooked the internal processes that produced those results [13]. A user-centered design refers to the use of methods that ensure that services have high levels of usability [13, 14]. A service's degree of usability is influenced, to a large extent, by the user's experience of interacting with the service or previous interactions with similar services.

The user experience is defined as an integrating concept of the interaction between the end-user and the company, its services, and products [15, 16]. User satisfaction is the result of the actual user experience and user expectations of the service. As mentioned earlier, one of the most important challenges in designing services is how to obtain information about users' expectations and experiences of a service to optimize its design.

3   Evaluation of User Experience and Opinion Mining

Numerous methods have been developed to obtain information on user experience, including laboratory studies with users, surveys, and evaluation by experts [17–19]. Laboratory methods involve inviting participants to use prototype versions of products or services. Psychophysical variables are measured, and experts observe all user actions to detect usability problems as well as the emotions associated with the product or service in a possible context of use. Surveys are generally used to obtain information from users after they have interacted with a product or service. Online surveys facilitate obtaining comments from a large number of users in a short time. Another method of evaluation is using expert knowledge. Usability experts are recruited to inspect a product or service design according to usability heuristics. This method is typically used in the early design stages, before the product or service is evaluated by users, and can be more expensive in both time and money.

Of the aforementioned methods, the most popular are surveys [17, 18], which consist of a group of questions specially designed to a certain how users use a product or service. The main advantage of surveys is that they elicit concrete answers, allowing for a statistical treatment to analyze the results. However, there are some drawbacks. For example, (1) there are few opportunities for the user to express themselves about other aspects not considered in the survey and (2) people are generally reluctant to answer surveys, resulting in few or incomplete answers. Given these problems, alternative means of obtaining information about user experience are social networks, forums, and opinion blogs [20, 21].

Extracting user experience from these sources allows the providers to make good decisions, improve versions of the product/service, or correct any problems detected from customer experiences. The essential difference in the information obtained from networks compared to that obtained by surveys is the immediacy. This information is spontaneous and unstructured and has great value for companies and their business strategies, customer service, and trend detection [5–7].

However, manually analyzing all these opinions would take a long time given their volume and variety. Therefore, opinion mining arises with the purpose of automating the analysis of user opinion information. Opinion mining is an extension of text mining. While text mining entails automatically analyzing any text, opinion mining automatically analyzes user opinions about a product, person, entity, or service [6]. There are numerous applications of opinion mining [5], such as the analysis of opinions on a product or service in marketing, analysis of opinions on a political candidate, or the compilation of opinions considered as "potential threats" to society, as in the case of the fight against terrorism or in the defense industry.

The objective of opinion mining is to classify positive, negative, and neutral opinions on the basis of certain criteria indicating to which of these three categories a given expression belongs. For this, it is necessary to identify what is most likely to indicate that an opinion is considered positive or negative. The methods used for opinion processing can be divided into two categories—lexical-based and learning-based [3, 4]—although both are currently used together to improve the performance of opinion mining algorithms.

Some of the techniques used in these methods are machine learning (ML), natural language processing (NLP), and information retrieval (IR). These three techniques are not mutually exclusive. The most common strategy is applying several of them to obtain stronger results than those obtained by applying only one technique [3, 5, 6]. My Opinion Tools is a tool that can process large volumes of data in a short time, with high accuracy, at a low cost.

4 Text Mining to Extract User Experience Information

The objective of this study was to identify user experience automatically based on the opinions written by users. To achieve this goal, it was necessary to obtain association rules that would allow for discovering the words in a text associated with user experience.

4.1 User Experience Categories

To classify text relating to user experience, categories or classes of user experience had to be identified. In this paper, the dimensions defined in [22] are taken as categories of user experience: instrumental qualities, non-instrumental qualities, and emotional reactions.

The instrumental qualities are related to the technical characteristics and effectiveness of the function provided by the product, system, or service; self-description; and the ability to control its operation. Non-instrumental qualities refer to design features, such as materials, shapes, colors, and location. Emotional reactions include emotions, which consist of motor expressions and subjective feelings, which can be positive or negative. Figure 1 shows the text mining process for obtaining rules enabling the classification of user opinions into categories of user experience.

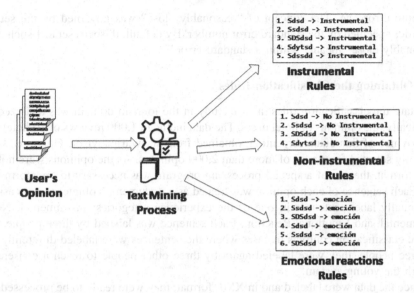

1. Sdsd -> Instrumental
2. Ssdsd -> Instrumental
3. SDSdsd -> Instrumental
4. Sdytsd -> Instrumental
5. Sdssdd -> Instrumental

Instrumental Rules

1. Sdsd -> No Instrumental
2. Ssdsd -> No Instrumental
3. SDSdsd -> No Instrumental
4. Sdytsd -> No Instrumental

Non-instrumental Rules

User's Opinion

Text Mining Process

1. Sdsd -> emoción
2. Ssdsd -> emoción
3. SDSdsd -> emoción
4. Sdsd -> emoción
5. Ssdsd -> emoción
6. SDSdsd -> emoción

Emotional reactions Rules

Fig. 1. Text mining to obtain information about user experience from opinions written on the Web.

4.2 Text Mining Process

Once the user experience categories were defined, the next step was the classification process, which followed the text extraction process described in [23]. Each sentence of the user's opinion was classified by means of rules-based classification techniques into either the "Instrumental", "Non-instrumental", or "Emotional Reaction" category. The Instrumental category included all sentences containing information on objective aspects of the service, such as if it fulfilled the objectives for which it was created. The Non-instrumental category grouped together all sentences containing information about the physical characteristics of the service, such as location, access to it, and payment method. Finally, the Emotional Reaction category contained all sentences describing the feelings caused by the user's interaction with the service.

The Text-Miner Software Kit (TMSK) and Text Rule Induction Kit (RIKTEXT) were used to obtain the classification rule sets [24]. TMSK generates a dictionary from a set of documents (opinions in our case) and converts a set of sentences into vectors, which creates a dictionary of relevant words. Preprocessing must be done to place user opinions in an XML file. This format is required by TMSK. The "Vectorize" function of TMSK creates the vectors from the XML documents. Documents are converted into an array format where each row corresponds to a document and each column corresponds to a word in the dictionary. RIKTEXT uses the dictionary and vectors representing each category to train a classifier, consequently returning the set of rules for each category.

The best set of rules was selected on the basis of the complexity and error rate of each rule. RIKTEXT found the set of rules with the minimum error rate and then identified a less complex set of rules whose error rate was reasonably close to the minimum error rate. The concept of "reasonably close" was governed by the set of properties specified by the standard error number. By default, this was set to 1 such that "reasonably close" meant "within a standard error."

4.3   Obtaining the Classification Rules

To obtain the classification rules, a case study in the tourism domain was analyzed— specifically, the opinions of hotel users. The data included 1,000 reviews of 10 hotels in the province of San Juan, Argentina, obtained from www.tripadvisor. Opinions were randomly selected from a set of more than 2,000 opinions. As the opinions were not in XML format, the use of a special processing program was necessary to transform the data. Each sentence of each opinion was treated as a document. Volunteers were asked to manually label sentences in one of the experience categories: Instrumental, Non-instrumental, and Emotional Reaction. Each sentence was labeled by three people. To resolve classification conflicts in cases where the sentences were labeled differently by the three people, they were labeled again by three other people to reach a consensus through the voting system.

Once the data were labeled and in XML format, they were ready to be processed by TMSK to generate the dictionary and a set of tagged vectors. A 950-word dictionary was generated, which was used to generate the vectors. The vectors were divided into portions of training and tests. Test cases were randomly selected in RIKTEXT to determine how many cases should be used for testing. Two thirds of the cases were defined for training and the rest for validation tests. Figures 2, 3, and 4 present the sets of rules obtained to classify sentences within the categories of Instrumental, Non-instrumental, and Emotional Reaction, respectively.

Rule Set	Number of Rules	Variables	Training error	Test error	Test standard deviation	Error/ variable
1	23	26	0,1696	0,3650	0,0449	0,00
2	23	25	0,1736	0,3650	0,0449	1,01
3	22	23	0,1795	0,3450	0,0435	2,34
4	18	18	0,2091	0,3250	0,0421	3,34
5	12	12	0,2249	0,3050	0,0397	4,34
6	10	10	0,2308	0,2850	0,0393	5,04
7	8	8	0,2409	0,2700	0,0321	5,74
8*	6	6	0,3222	0,2567	0,0265	6,44
9	5	5	0,3201	0,2799	0,0378	7,14
10	1	1	0,3470	0,6319	0,0423	1,33

*best rule set according to error rate and simplicity

```
Selected Rule Set
1. fácil & comunicarse -> Instrumental
2. eficientes -> Instrumental
3. novedoso -> Instrumental
4. seguro & no -> Instrumental
5. tradicional -> Instrumental
6. amistoso -> Instrumental
```

Fig. 2. Set of rules for classifying sentences in the Instrumental category of user experience

Rule Set	Number of Rules	Variables	Training error	Test error	Test standard deviation	Error/ variable
1	23	24	0,1096	0,2571	0,0360	0,00
2*	13	13	0,1136	0,2571	0,0360	0,61
3	11	11	0,1195	0,2733	0,0365	1,94
4	10	10	0,1491	0,3059	0,0374	2,94
5	9	9	0,1649	0,2896	0,0370	3,94
6	8	8	0,1708	0,4115	0,0390	0,18
7	1	1	0,1809	0,4059	0,0404	0,12

*best rule set according to error rate and simplicity

Selected Rule Set
1. limpieza -> No instrumental
2. ubicación -> No instrumental
3. restaurant -> No instrumental
4. habitaciones -> No instrumental
5. servicios -> No instrumental
6. propietarios -> No instrumental
7. ruido -> No instrumental
8. baños -> No instrumental
9. desayuno -> No instrumental
10.transporte & aeropuerto -> No instrumental
11.atracciones -> No instrumental
12.desayuno -> No instrumental
13. recepción -> No instrumental

Fig. 3. Set of rules for classifying sentences in the Non-instrumental category of user experience

Rule Set	Number of Rules	Variables	Training error	Test error	Test standard deviation	Error/ variable
1	19	33	0,4696	0,3050	0,0549	0,00
2	16	27	0,4736	0,3050	0,0549	1,41
3	12	17	0,4795	0,2850	0,0349	2,74
4*	8	8	0,5091	0,2650	0,0149	3,74
5	6	6	0,5249	0,2950	0,0449	4,74
6	5	5	0,5308	0,3250	0,0749	5,44
7	4	4	0,5409	0,3550	0,1049	6,14
8	3	3	0,6222	0,3850	0,1349	6,84
9	2	2	0,6201	0,4150	0,1649	7,54
10	1	1	0,6470	0,4450	0,1949	8,45

*best rule set according to error rate and simplicity

Selected Rule Set
1. feliz -> Instrumental
2. furioso -> Instrumental
3. sorpresa -> Instrumental
4. contento -> Instrumental
5. asco -> Instrumental
6. fantástico -> Instrumental
7. horrible -> Instrumental
8. muy & bueno -> Instrumental

Fig. 4. Set of rules for classifying sentences in the Emotional Reaction category of user experience

The chosen rules were those that had a minimum error rate or were very close to the minimum, but perhaps simpler than the minimum (*). The result of the rules validation is shown in Table 1, which depicts the measurements of precision, recall, and F-measure for the training data and test data.

Table 1. Classification process evaluation

Measures	Categories					
	Instrumental		Non-instrumental		Emotional reaction	
	Training data	Test data	Training data	Test data	Training data	Test data
Precision	71.6189	67.5816	73.0299	70.3844	74.0881	60.0140
Recall	89.2448	76.9371	54.1316	44.2000	64.5301	37.5140
F-Measure	79.4661	71.9564	62.1762	54.2997	68.9795	46.1678

5 Validation

Once the set of rules for classifying sentences in the different user experience categories was obtained, a controlled experiment was conducted to assess the validity of the rules. For this, 100 new opinions about San Juan hotels from www.tripadvisor.com were used. A computer algorithm was created to automatically apply the classification rules. The rules were applied to each hotel opinion, and sentences were obtained for each of the user experience categories. An example is shown in Table 2.

Table 2. Sample sentences containing information about the user's experience of the hotel

Category	Hotel reviews sentences
Instrumental	I was satisfied by the presence of a guard, very attentive. Highly recommended
Non-instrumental	The beds made noise. It is very close to the city center
Emotional reaction	Very dirty, disgusting, and depressing

Additionally, the same group of three volunteers made a manual classification of the 100 new opinions to identify whether they contained instrumental, non-instrumental, emotional reaction, or irrelevant information. Table 3 shows a comparison of the results obtained with the automatic classification and the manual classification, measured by the mean absolute error in each category. There was an average automatic classification error of 0.10.

Table 3. Automatic classification Vs manual classification results

Sentences	Automatic classification	Manual classification	Absolute average error
Non-instrumental	355	367	0.12
Instrumental	98	106	0.08
Emotional reaction	124	115	0.09
Irrelevant	123	112	0.11
Total sentences	**700**	**700**	**0.10**

Of the success cases, more than 96.7% of the sentences that were manually classified in the non-instrumental category were also classified in this category by the automatic method using the defined rules. Likewise, 92.4% of the sentences in the instrumental category were classified well by the automatic method, and 100% of the sentences classified manually in the Emotional Reaction category were also classified in this category by the automatic method. As these data demonstrate, in general terms, the defined rules had a high degree of effectiveness in the three categories of user experience.

An analysis of the error cases revealed that they were generated mainly for two reasons. First, there were words in the sentences that were not considered in the rules or in the synonyms dictionary. For example, a sentence classified by the automatic method as irrelevant contained the word "windows," which was not synonymous with the word "room" in the rules of the Non-instrumental category. Second, some sentences that were automatically classified into a single category were classified into two categories in the manual classification because they were too long and contained information from more than two categories of user experience.

6 Conclusion

This paper presents an automatic classification process of user experience based on text mining techniques. Information about user experience of a service can be obtained using this process, but identifying such information is not an easy task.

A case study on the tourist domain was analyzed to assess the rules' precision for the process of classifying sentences in three categories of user experience defined in the literature: Instrumental, Non-instrumental, and Emotional Reaction. One thousand reviews of hotels in the province of San Juan, Argentina were obtained from the website www.tripadvisor.com. Two data sets were built: one for training and one for testing. To evaluate the rules' precision, 100 new opinions were used. The results obtained are considered good because there was only a 10% error against a classification made manually. On the basis of this result, we can conclude that the automatic identification of information about users' experience of a service can be done accurately using text mining techniques, such as those presented in this work.

That is, the proposed method allows for automatically filtering relevant information regarding user experience of services/products from thousands of opinions written in comments on the Web. As mentioned in this paper, such techniques are less intrusive and less expensive than conducting surveys of end users. Filtering user experience information using text mining techniques goes beyond just knowing if the opinion is positive or negative; relevant comments should be filtered from user experience information that involve physical, objective, and emotional qualities. The rules obtained through the text mining techniques in this study are a first step toward obtaining that kind of information about user experience.

In future work, the rules will be refined by updating the synonyms dictionary to improve the classification process. A way to deal with sentences that may belong to more than one category will also be analyzed. In addition, an interface will be created to summarize and provide this information in an understandable way for decision-makers of the entities that provide services. This interface must provide relevant information, for decision-making, about the experiences of users who have used a product or service. Once the interface is created, it must be validated with future users (service providers).

References

1. Maglio, P.P., Kieliszewski, C.A., Spohrer, J.C., Lyons, K., Patrício, L., Sawatani, Y. (eds.): Handbook of Service Science, Volume II. SSRISE. Springer, Cham (2019). https://doi.org/10.1007/978-3-319-98512-1
2. Peters, C., et al.: Emerging digital frontiers for service innovation. CAIS 1(39) (2016). https://doi.org/10.17705/1cais.03908
3. Netzer, O., Feldman, R., Goldenberg, J., Fresko, M.: Mine your own business: market-structure surveillance through text mining. Mark. Sci. 31(3), 521–543 (2012)
4. Hsiao, Y.H., Chen, M.C., Liao, W.C.: Logistics service design for cross-border E-commerce using Kansei engineering with text-mining-based online content analysis. Telematics Inform. 34(4), 284–302 (2017)
5. Aggarwal, C.C., Zhai, C. (eds.): Mining Text Data. Springer, Boston (2012). https://doi.org/10.1007/978-1-4614-3223-4
6. Mostafa, M.M.: More than words: social networks' text mining for consumer brand sentiments. Expert Syst. Appl. 40(10), 4241–4251 (2013)
7. Amado, A., Cortez, P., Rita, P., Moro, S.: Research trends on big data in marketing: a text mining and topic modeling based literature analysis. Eur. Res. Manag. Bus. Econ. 24(1), 1–7 (2018)
8. Gan, Q., Ferns, B.H., Yu, Y., Jin, L.: A text mining and multidimensional sentiment analysis of online restaurant reviews. J. Qual. Assur. Hosp. Tour. 18(4), 465–492 (2017)
9. Ravi, K., Ravi, V.: A survey on opinion mining and sentiment analysis: tasks, approaches and applications. Knowl.-Based Syst. 89, 14–46 (2015)
10. Sun, S., Luo, C., Chen, J.: A review of natural language processing techniques for opinion mining systems. Inf. Fusion 36, 10–25 (2017)
11. Vargo, S.L., Wieland, H., Akaka, M.A.: Innovation in service ecosystems. J. Serviceol. 1(1), 1–5 (2016)
12. Ostrom, A.L., et al.: Moving forward and making a difference: research priorities for the science of service. J. Serv. Res. 13(1), 4–36 (2010)
13. Lin, C.J., Cheng, L.Y.: Product attributes and user experience design: how to convey product information through user-centered service. J. Intell. Manuf. 28(7), 1743–1754 (2017)

14. Chilana, P.K., Ko, A.J., Wobbrock, J.: From user-centered to adoption-centered design: a case study of an HCI research innovation becoming a product. In: Proceedings of the 33rd Annual ACM Conference on Human Factors in Computing Systems, pp. 1749–1758. ACM, New York, April 2015

15. Bilgihan, A.: Gen Y customer loyalty in online shopping: an integrated model of trust, user experience and branding. Comput. Hum. Behav. **61**, 103–113 (2016)

16. Lallemand, C., Gronier, G., Koenig, V.: User experience: a concept without consensus? Exploring practitioners' perspectives through an international survey. Comput. Hum. Behav. **43**, 35–48 (2015)

17. Trischler, J., Scott, D.R.: Designing public services: the usefulness of three service design methods for identifying user experiences. Public Manag. Rev. **18**(5), 718–739 (2016)

18. Weast, J.C., et al.: US Patent Application No. 15/168,084 (2016)

19. Helms, K., Brown, B., Sahlgren, M., Lampinen, A.: Design methods to investigate user experiences of artificial intelligence. In: 2018 AAAI Spring Symposium Series. Stanford University, Palo Alto, California USA, March 2018

20. Milovanovic, S., Bogdanovic, Z., Labus, A., Barac, D., Despotovic-Zrakic, M.: An approach to identify user preferences based on social network analysis. Future Gener. Comput. Syst. **93**, 121–129 (2019)

21. Khalaj, J., Pedgley, O.: A semantic discontinuity detection (SDD) method for comparing designers' product expressions with users' product impressions. Des. Stud. **62**, 36–67 (2019)

22. Van Der Linden, J., Amadieu, F., Vayre, E., Van De Leemput, C.: User experience and social influence: a new perspective for UX theory. In: Marcus, A., Wang, W. (eds.) HCII 2019. LNCS, vol. 11583, pp. 98–112. Springer, Cham (2019). https://doi.org/10.1007/978-3-030-23570-3_9

23. Aciar, S., Zhang, D., Simoff, S., Debenham, J.: Informed recommender: basing recommendations on consumer product reviews. IEEE Intell. Syst. **22**(3) (2007)

24. Weiss, S.M., Indurkhya, N., Zhang, T., Damerau, F.: Text Mining: Predictive Methods for Analyzing Unstructured Information. Springer, New York (2004). https://doi.org/10.1007/978-0-387-34555-0

Customer eXperience in e-Learning:
A Systematic Mapping Study

Iván Balmaceda Castro[1]([⊠]) [iD], Cristian Rusu[2] [iD],
and Silvana Aciar[1] [iD]

[1] Consejo Nacional de Investigaciones Científicas y Técnicas (CONICET),
San Juan, Argentina
ibalmaceda89@gmail.com, saciar@unsj-cuim.edu.ar
[2] Pontificia Universidad Católica de Valparaíso,
Av. Brasil 2241, 2340000 Valparaíso, Chile
cristian.rusu@pucv.cl

Abstract. This article investigates the application of the concept of Customer eXperience (CX) in the education and presents the results of Systematic Mapping Study (SMS) of the literature on CX specifically in e-Learning, also User Experience (UX) and Usability. Studies show that usability and UX in such platforms may influence in this process. The aim of this work aims to analyze scientific publications to characterize this context of CX. Existing studies on the subject were identified, specifying the type of research, its purpose, the use of techniques and method. The literature shows that the concept of CX has different definitions. The purpose of CX is identified as to deliver satisfaction throughout the customer experience that, in turn, leads to brand loyalty and advocacy, but results show there are few publications concerning the subject, especially in the domain of e-learning, and therefore is clear the need to encourage research and academic production.

Keywords: Customer eXperience · User eXperience · Education · E-learning · Systematic Mapping Study

1 Introduction

In recent years, e-learning has evolved by giant steps in terms of educational content, technological resources and possibilities of interaction. Today, many institutions add this form of learning as a complement to traditional teaching. Also, provides new possibilities for professors, students, and university staff through new forms of training and learning innovations [1]. Among them are educational content management, activities, assessment and communication between students and teachers [2].

When evaluating the quality of the teaching-learning process, usability and User eXperience (UX) is of great importance. But institutions, today, seek not only to evaluate the teaching-learning process, but also the institution as a whole, and that is where we focus on Customer Experience (CX).

ISO 9126-1 defines "Usability refers to the ability of software to be understood, learned, used and attractive to the user, under specific conditions of use" [3].

© Springer Nature Switzerland AG 2020
G. Meiselwitz (Ed.): HCII 2020, LNCS 12195, pp. 158–170, 2020.
https://doi.org/10.1007/978-3-030-49576-3_11

Meanwhile, Dilon A. defines the User Experience as "the sum of three levels: action, what the user does; result, what the user gets; and emotion, what the user feels" [4].

Evaluation methods should be able to identify the emotional, functional and rational factors that come into play in each interaction, in a specific cultural context of the service. The aim of CX is to enhance relationships with customers and build customer loyalty [5].

The objective of this document is to describe a systematic mapping study related to CX in e-Learning, in its form of interaction, and to identify the evaluation techniques of usability, UX, CX in this context. In this paper we present some conclusions about the state of art in this field and we hope to contribute to further research.

This document is organized by: Sect. 2 presents background. Section 3 describes the method applied to carry out this investigation. Section 4 presents the results. Section 5 presents the discussion of our results. Finally, Sect. 6 concludes the document.

2 Backgrounds

2.1 User eXperience and Usability: Their Relationship with e-Learning

User experience (UX) plays the role to identify the users feeling which can result in either positive or negative results. [6, 7] ISO 9241 standard defines how "user's perceptions and responses that result from the use and/or anticipated use of a system, product or service". [8], taking an entire view of a person's emotions, attitudes, and expectations. Whereas, Usability is the facility, satisfaction with which they can use a product; [8] defined as "The extent to which a product can be used by specified users to achieve specified goals with effectiveness, efficiency and satisfaction in a specified context of use".

E-Learning is "A teaching and learning modality, which may represent all or part of the educational model in which it is applied, which exploits electronic means and devices to facilitate access, evolution and improvement of the quality of education and training" [9]. These concepts, Usability and UX, in e-Learning are very important, because if the system is not usable, it obstructs learning.

2.2 Customer eXperience

CX is increasingly discussed but not yet clearly defined. The Customer eXperience (CX) expresses the feelings customers have about the extent to which their experiences with a company have met their needs [10]. CX is considered as "the set of physical and emotional experiences that occur in the interactions with products and/or services offered by a certain brand and/or company from the first contact with the consumer, including the entire "journey" of the consumer, up to the final post-consumer stage" [11].

CX influences customers' perceptions and opinions of value and service quality and therefore affects customer loyalty [12]. CX focusses on new dimensions of products and services, besides the traditional marketing.

Human Computer Interaction (HCI) and particularly User eXperience (UX) design and research focuses on the interactions that take place during the customer lifecycle. UX analyzes customer's sensations resulting from any interaction with an interactive software system.

CX has a holistic approach, focusing on any interaction between the costumer and the company, in so-called "touchpoints" [13]. In each touchpoint CX should be assessed using both quantitative and qualitative methods; this is the only way to understand the "journey" of the costumer.

3   Research: Applied Method

A systematic mapping study is a defined method to build classifications in order to perform thematic analysis to obtain a visual map of the existing knowledge on a particular topic [14]. With the information obtained, it allows us to answer more specific research questions, following a strategy or protocol based on a systematic review process of scientific production. With the use of this tool, it also allows us to identify topics where there are sufficient primary studies to conduct systematic reviews and topics where more primary studies need to be generated. [15].

We have done a systematic mapping on CX in e-Learning, based on the method proposed by Petersen [16], following a procedure that includes 5 stages, A) Define research questions, B) Perform literature search, C) Select studies, D) Classify articles and E) Extract and aggregate data.

3.1   Researh Questions

We oriented the systematic mapping to understand that motivates the Customer eXperience in the e-learning domain, for that we defined three concrete research questions (see Table 1) to set the scope of the research, more detailed knowledge and a comprehensive view of the subject.

Table 1. Research questions defined in this work

ID	Research question
RQ1	What is the CX in e-learning?
RQ2	What kinds of studies were published about the CX, UX and Usability in E-learning?
RQ3	What evaluation methods are used in these studies?

3.2   Data Source and Search Strategy

For the searches, we selected five different academic repositories: ACM Digital Library, Springer Link, ScienceDirect, IEEE Xplore Digital Library and Google Scholar to determine the main results of the application of this procedure, indicating the main findings obtained from this analysis. They are specialized in the field of Software Engineering and Human-Computer Interaction and in them we will find hundreds of scientific articles.

The search strings (see Table 2) were defined attending to the research questions proposed aiming to identify studies related to CX, UX, Usability and educational computing or approaches in general concerning Virtual Learning environment or e-learning.

Table 2. Search string

ID	Search string
ST1	"Customer experience" and "educational computing"
ST2	(("customer experience" AND ("e-learning" OR "virtual learning environment" OR "learning") AND usability) OR ("user experience" AND "e-learning) and "education")

These strings were applied to the specified search sources and the number of articles that were found was too high to be analyzed.

3.3 Select Studies

The search for articles for study selection we used the inclusion criteria stated in Table 3. And we also considered the exclusion criteria described in Table 4, for refining the list of primary studies with high contribution.

Table 3. Inclusion criteria for the Systematic Mapping Study

ID	Inclusion criteria
I1	Scientific articles, Reports and Conference Proceedings
I2	Studies published in the last 5 years. Between January 2015 and December 2019
I3	Papers written in English

Table 4. Exclusion criteria for the Systematic Mapping Study

ID	Exclusion criteria
E1	Articles that do not address Customer eXperience, User eXperience and Usability specifically in education
E2	Articles available only as abstract or PowerPoint presentations
E3	Duplicate studies, whose main contribution is not related to research focus.
E4	Articles written in a language other to English

3.4 Classify Articles

The selection of the primary studies was done in two stages: First, applying the inclusion and exclusion criteria, reading the title, abstracts and keywords of the studies found in the search.

Then, a validation process was carried out by reading the full text of each of the studies selected in the first stage, among which there were studies included as well as those discarded from this mapping.

3.5   Extract and Aggregate Data

We developed data extraction sheets for each of the search strings considered in the study where the findings are recorded along with all the corresponding bibliographic information. Then, all the forms are joined in a single form by removing the duplicated articles.

For the analysis, tables and graphs with the collected data have been used as a basis for answering each research question. In the case of the graphs, the numbers presented are equivalent to the Quantity/Percentage of the selected studies.

4   Results

4.1   Study Selection

The search strings applied in all the specified sources gave a total of 1264 articles between the years 2015 and 2019.

The Table 5 presents the summary of the number of studies obtained as a result of applying the search chain in each library.

Table 5. Summary of primary studies obtained

Digital library	Results obtained
ACM Digital Library	53
Springer Link	383
ScienceDirect	45
IEEE Xplore Digital Library	21
Google Scholar	762
TOTAL	1264

From the total of results in the searches of digital libraries, we found that 324 articles were duplicated, leaving 873 for analysis.

After applying the inclusion and exclusion criteria and when the results of the different search chains are combined, a total of 43 works are obtained that apply to the research topic (see Table 6). The results of the systematic mapping of the literature are presented as answers to each of the questions posed in the planning.

Table 6. Selected studies

Id	Title	Author	Year
[A1]	Digital game elements, user experience and learning: A conceptual framework	Alexiou, A. - Schippers, M.	2018
[A2]	Factors of E-Learning System Affecting Students' Satisfaction: Empirical Evidence from Virtual Campuses of Southern Punjab	Amir Rizwan, M. - Ali, N - Asad, A. Hasnain, A. - Punjab, M.	2018
[A3]	In the journey of user center design for the virtual environment	Antumano N.	2019
[A4]	Evaluating user experience in joint activities between schools and museums in virtual worlds	Barneche Naya, V. - Hernández Ibáñez, L.	2015
[A5]	Quality Management of Learning Management Systems: A User Experience Perspective	Zaharias, P. - Pappas, C.	2016
[A6]	FI-AR learning: a web-based platform for augmented reality educational content	Coma-Tatay, I. - Casas-Yrurzum, S. - Casanova-Salas, P.- Fernández-Marín, M.	2019
[A7]	Multisensory games-based learning - lessons learnt from olfactory enhancement of a digital board game	Covaci, A. - Ghinea, G. - Lin, C. - Huang, S. - Shih, J.	2018
[A8]	User experience of academic staff in the use of a learning management system tool	De Kock, E. - Van Biljon, J - Botha, A.	2016
[A9]	Gamifying education: what is known, what is believed and what remains uncertain: a critical review	Dichev, C. - Dicheva, D.	2017
[A10]	From massive access to cooperation: lessons learned and proven results of a hybrid xMOOC/cMOOC pedagogical approach to MOOCs	Fidalgo-Blanco, Á. - Sein-Echaluce, M. - García-Peñalvo, F.	2016
[A11]	Mixed-methods research: a new approach to evaluating the motivation and satisfaction of university students using advanced visual technologies	Fonseca, David Redondo, Ernest Villagrasa, Sergi	2015
[A12]	High school learners' continuance intention to use electronic textbooks: A usability study	Gelderblom, H. - Matthee, M. - Hattingh, M. - Weilbach, L.	2019
[A13]	Tertiary student attitudes to invigilated, online summative examinations	James, R.	2016
[A14]	UX based adaptive e-learning hypermedia system (U-AEHS): an integrative user model approach	Jeong, H.	2016
[A15]	A framework for customer relationship management strategy orientation support in higher education institutions	Khashab, B. - Gulliver, S. - Ayoubi, R.	2018
[A16]	Proposing a new pedagogy-based website design: A usability test with lifelong learners	Khlaisang, J.	2017
[A17]	The roles of academic engagement and digital readiness in students' achievements in university e-learning environments	Kim, H. - Hong, A. - Song, H.	2019

(continued)

Table 6. (*continued*)

Id	Title	Author	Year
[A18]	Enhancing e-learning systems with personalized recommendation based on collaborative tagging techniques	Klašnja-Milićević, A. - Ivanović, M. - Vesin, B. - Budimac, Z.	2018
[A19]	A checklist for assessing blind users' usability of educational smartphone applications	Lee, Y. Lee, J.	2019
[A20]	CBET: design and evaluation of a domain-specific chatbot for mobile learning	Liu, Q. - Huang, J. - Wu, L. - Zhu, K. - Ba, S.	2019
[A21]	Finding the right elements user experience elements for educational games	Nagalingam, V. - Ibrahim, R.	2017
[A22]	MB-PBA: Aprovechando Merkle Tree y Blockchain para mejorar la autenticación basada en el perfil del usuario en los sistemas de E-Learning	Pham, H. - Nguyen, D. - Luu, H. - Huynh-Tuong, N.	2019
[A23]	The megaclass as a service production system and the challenge of facilitating its continuous quality improvement: Towards a research agenda in a complex domain	Ograjenšek, I, - Gal, I.	2018
[A24]	Student information system satisfaction in higher education: the role of visual aesthetics	Ramírez-Correa, P. - Rondán-Cataluña, F. - Arenas-Gaitán, J.	2018
[A25]	Adopting an Omnichannel Approach to Improve User Experience in Online Enrolment at an E-learning University	Rebaque-Rivas, P. - Gil-Rodríguez, E.	2019
[A26]	Measuring User Experience of the Student-Centered e-Learning Environment	Santoso, H. - Schrepp, M. - Isal, Y. - Utomo, A. - Priyogi, B.	2016
[A27]	What leads people to keep on e-learning? An empirical analysis of users' experiences and their effects on continuance intention	Rodríguez-Ardura, I. - Meseguer-Artola, A.	2016
[A28]	Geo-located teaching using handheld augmented reality: good practices to improve the motivation and qualifications of architecture students	Sánchez Riera, A. - Redondo, E. - Fonseca, D.	2015
[A29]	Users' domain knowledge prediction in e-learning with speech-interfaced augmented and virtual reality contents	Sathia Bhama, P. - Hariharasubramanian, V. - Mythili, O. - Ramachandran, M.	2017
[A30]	Cultural influences moderating learners' adoption of serious 3D games for managerial learning	Siala, H. - Kutsch, E. - Jagger, S.	2019
[A31]	Enhancing human-computer interaction and user experience education through a hybrid approach to experiential learning	Talone, A. - Basavaraj, P. - Wisniewski, P.	2017
[A32]	E-LEARNING Ergonomic criteria for evaluating the quality of e-learning	Todorova, M. - Karamanska, D. - Koleva, E. - Koleva, L.	2017
[A33]	Demographic variables and Online Customer Experience of Educational Websites users	Trivedi, A. - Deshwal, P. - Soni, U. - Mani, N.	2018
[A34]	Exploring user satisfaction for e-learning systems via usage-based metrics and system usability scale analysis.	Harrati, N. - Bouchrika, I. - Tari A. - Ladjailia, A.	2016

(*continued*)

Table 6. (*continued*)

Id	Title	Author	Year
[A35]	Assessing The Influence of Big Five Personalities at The Level of Student Engagement and Lostness on The Faculty Website	Wardhana, A.- Sandiwarno, S.	2019
[A36]	Online Learning Experience Scale Validation and Its Impact on Learner's Satisfaction.	Deshwal, P. – Trivedi, A. – Himansgi H.	2017
[A37]	Online Learning Self-Efficacy in Students With and Without Online Learning Experience	Whitney Alicia Zimmerman & Jonna M. Kulikowich	2016
[A38]	Engineering education for sustainable development: using online learning to support the new paradigms	Sivapalan, S. - Clifford, M.J. – Speight, S.	2016
[A39]	Practical guidelines for designing and evaluating educationally oriented recommendations	Santos, O.C. - Boticario, J. G.	2015
[A40]	Exploring Online Learners' Interactive Dynamics by Visually Analyzing Their Time-anchored Comments	Sung, C.-Y. - Huang, X.-Y. - Shen, Y. - Cherng, F.-Y. - Lin, W.-C. - Wang, H.-C.	2017
[A41]	Setting accessibility preferences about learning objects within adaptive elearning systems: User experience and organizational aspects	Rodriguez - Ascaso, A. -, Boticario, J. G. – Finat C. -Petrie, H.	2017
[A42]	Emotions ontology for collaborative modeling and learning of emotional responses,	Gil, R. –Virgili-Goma, J. - García, R. – Mason, C.	2015
[A43]	Automatically learning topics and difficulty levels of problems in online judge systems	Zhao, W.X.- Zhang, W. – He, Y.- Xie, X - Wen, J.R.	2018

Figure 1 shows the distribution of the studies according to the year of publication. The number of studies published in 2016 doubled that of 2015, while in 2017, 2018 there were fewer than the year before. In 2019 they are higher than 2017 and 2018 but the same as in 2016.

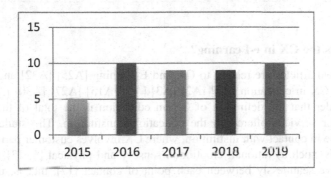

Fig. 1. Distribution of primary studies by year.

The Fig. 2 shows the distribution of primary studies by the type of forum in which they have been published. Table 7 shows the primary studies for each type of forum. The classification shows that 18% of them were published as conference or workshop papers; the 77% of them were more complete papers published in journals and 5% in Others.

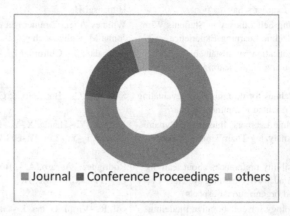

Fig. 2. Distribution of primary studies by type of forum.

Table 7. Distribution of primary studies by type of forum.

AREA	Studies
Journal	[A1] [A2] [A4] [A5] [A6] [A7] [A10] [A11] [A12] [A13] [A14] [A15] [A16] [A17] [A18] [A19] [A20] [A23] [A24] [A26] [A27] [A28] [A29] [A30] [A34] [A35] [A37] [A38] [A39] [A40] [A41] [A42] [A43]
Conference Proceedings	[A3] [A8] [A21] [A22] [A25] [A31] [A33] [36]
Others	[A9] [A32]

4.2   What Is the CX in e-Learning?

Specifically two articles are related to CX and E-learning [A25] [A32] and another 8 are related to CX in education [A1] [A2] [A3] [A5] [A15] [A27] [A30] [A33].

We consider that the definition of CX in education is the total of the products, systems and/or services offered in the educational institution. The students pass a prolonged time in contact with institution, where CX involves customer participation at different levels, such as rational, emotional, sensory and physical [5, 13]. Customers expect to move seamlessly between each point of contact [17], that is, through the channels according to their preferences, needs and behavior. To do this, it is necessary to trace the customer's journey through the different processes to determine which channels are involved and how they are involved [18].

The literature suggests that whatever the service, system or indeed product, a customer is buying or receiving, that customer will have an experience; good, bad or indifferent.

E-learning is the way to carry out distance education, distributing learning material and processes over the Internet [19]. Also, making data and tools available to users requires considering their different characteristics cultural background, technical experience, technological equipment, and physical/cognitive abilities, that will allow creating a more pleasurable experience in the user [20].

Actually, e-Learning, indicates online experience is affected by perceptual fluency [21]. Earlier barriers to education were limited access to study material and course content. High reliability of connectivity solves this problem as digital modes of education provide all the necessary information, where learning is accelerated. Becoming in one of the optimistic as well as a fulfilling experience of an individual's life [17, 22, 23].

4.3 What Kinds of Studies Were Published About the CX, UX and Usability in e-Learning?

In terms of this research question, our aim was to investigate what types of studies were made (see Table 8) we analyze what kind of contexts.

Table 8. Type of research and methodology used

Methods		Total	Type methods	Studies
Type of research (n = 43)	Quantitative methods	10		
			Experiment	[A4] [A7] [A20] [A31]
			Quasi experiment	[A22]
			Survey	[A5] [A27] [A32] [A33] [A37]
	Qualitative methods	25	Case study	[A3] [A24] [A26] [A29] [A40] [A41]
			Observation	[A1] [A13] [A17] [A35] [A39] [A43]
			Document analysis	[A6] [A9] [A10] [A12] [A14] [A16] [A18] [A19] [A21] [A23] [A28] [A38] [A42]
	Mixed methods	8		[A2] [A8] [A11] [A15] [A25] [A30] [A34] [A36]

4.4 What Evaluation Methods Are Used in These Studies?

Concerning this research question, we analyzed the included studies in terms of methods that are used to evaluated. (see Table 9). We found 39 studies that provide some method of evaluation.

Table 9. Evaluation methods

METHOD	Studies	f
User profile	[A4] [A22] [A37]	3
Technical models for the assessment of emotions	[A1] [A2] [A4]	2
Surveys	[A27] [A32] [A35] [A36] [A37] [A38]	6
Demographic questionnaires	[A17] [A30] [A33] [A38]	4
Interviews	[A25] [A38] [A39] [A40] [A42]	5
Comparative methods for analyzing the collected data	[A2] [A10] [A21] [A36]	4
Inspection	[A8] [A11] [A17] [A24] [A26] [A31] [A34] [A37] [A40]	9
Test	[A6] [A7] [A11] [A20] [A27]	5
Checklist	[A19]	1

5 Discussion

This systematic mapping aimed to identify the Customer eXperience in e-Learning. Also evaluation techniques of CX, UX and Usability in the context of education, specifically in e-learning.

The results showed that there are several studies regarding the techniques used to evaluate the usability and UX. However, there are still some gaps that can be explored in Customer eXperience, by further studies:

- Few studies were conducted in the context customer experience. Among the studies that were found, none presented a new technique. Altogether, 7 contained evaluation.
- Few techniques performs the usability/UX evaluation process in an automated way;
- There were no studies relating the influence of the usability/UX improvement in the learning process.

These identified gaps may contribute to give an insight to further research in order to improve the quality of the evaluation techniques of Customer eXperience in e-Learning.

6 Conclusions

In this Systematic Mapping Study (SMS), we analyzed the publications regarding the CX in e-Learning, as well as evaluation techniques of CX, UX and Usability based on research published during the last 5 years and available on the relevant scientific databases. From a starting set of 1264 publications, a total of 43 publications were selected.

These researches were published mainly in journals, achieving 77% of the total.

Through the research questions it was possible to specify the relationship between the CX concept and e-Learning. Also what kind of studies were published, in which 58% use qualitative methods, 23% quantitative methods and 19% mixed methods. And what methods are being used to evaluate Usability, UX and CX, where we found 39 studies that provide some method.

This SMS revealed that there is still a need for more research in this area.

The literature indicates that there are several techniques to evaluate UX and Usability in e-learning, but there is no one technique that is more adequate in CX. This identified gap in SMS may be the starting point for further research.

Acknowledgment. Authors from Pontificia Universidad Católica de Valparaíso (Chile) and Universidad Nacional de San Juan (Argentina) are participating in the HCI-Collab Project – The Collaborative Network to Support HCI Teaching and Learning Processes in IberoAmerica (http://hci-collab.com/). And Iván Balmaceda Castro is a beneficiary of one CONICET (Argentina) doctoral scholarship since 2019 at 2023.

References

1. Rodrigues, H., Almeida, F., Figueiredo, V., Lopes, S.L.: Monitoring e-learning through published articles: a systematic review. Comput. Educ. **136**, 87–98 (2019)
2. Freire, L.L., Arezes, P.M., Campos, J.C.: A literature review about usability evaluation methods for e-learning platforms. In: 18th World congress on Ergonomics - Designing a sustainable future (IEA 2012), pp. 1038–1044. IOS Press, Recife (2012)
3. ISO/IEC 9126-1. Software Product Evaluation – Quality characteristics and guidelines for their use. International Organization for Standardization (1991)
4. Dillon, A.: Beyond Usability. Process, Outcome and Affect in human computer interactions. Faculty of Information Studies, University of Toronto (2001)
5. Frow, P., Payne, A.: Towards the "perfect" customer experience. J. Brand Manag. **15**(2), 89–101 (2007). https://doi.org/10.1057/palgrave.bm.2550120
6. Montuwy, A., Cahour, B., Dommes, A.: Using sensory wearable devices to navigate the city: effectiveness and user experience in older pedestrians. Multimodal Technol. Interact. **3**, 17. https://doi.org/10.3390/mti3010017
7. Hu, K., Gui, Z., Cheng, X., Wu, H., McClure, S.: The concept and technologies of quality of geographic information service: improving user experience of GIServices in a distributed computing environment. ISPRS Int. J. Geo-Inf. **8**, 118 (2019)
8. ISO 9241-210: Ergonomics of human-system interaction—Part 11: Usability: Definitions and concepts. International Organization for Standardization, Geneva, Switzerland (2018)
9. Adam, M.R., Vallés, R.S., Rodríguez, G.I.M.: E-learning: características y evaluación. Ensayos de economía **23**(43), 143–159 (2013)
10. Hill, N., Roche, G., Allen, L.: Customer Satisfaction. The Customer Experience Through the Customer's Eye. Congent Publishing, London (2007)
11. Laming, C., Mason, K.: Customer experience—an analysis of the concept and its performance in airline brands. Res. Transp. Bus. Manag. **10**, 15–25 (2014)
12. Petre, M., Minocha, S., Roberts, D.: Usability beyond the website: an empirically-grounded e-commerce evaluation instrument for the total customer experience. Behav. Inf. Technol. **25**(2), 189–203 (2006)

13. Stein, A., Ramaseshan, B.: Towards the identification of customer experience touch point elements. J. Retail. Consum. Serv. **30**, 8–19 (2016)
14. Petersen, K., Feldt, R., Mujtaba, S.: Systematic mapping studies in software engineering. In: Proceedings of the 12th International Conference on Evaluation and Assessment in Software Engineering (2017)
15. Kitchenham, B., Budgen, D., Pearl Brereton, O.: Using mapping studies as the basis for further research – a participant-observer case study. Inf. Softw. Technol. **53**(6), 638–651 (2011)
16. Petersen, K., Feldt, R., Mujtaba, S., Mattsson, M.: Systematic mapping studies in software engineering. In: Visaggio, G., Baldassarre, M.T., Linkman, S., Turner, M. (eds.) Proceedings of the 12th International Conference on Evaluation and Assessment in Software Engineering (EASE 2008), pp. 68–77. British Computer Society, Swinton (2008)
17. Rebaque-Rivas, P., Gil-Rodríguez, E.: Adopting an omnichannel approach to improve user experience in online enrolment at an e-learning university. In: Stephanidis, C. (ed.) HCII 2019. CCIS, vol. 1034, pp. 115–122. Springer, Cham (2019). https://doi.org/10.1007/978-3-030-23525-3_15
18. Antunano, N.: In the journey of user center design for the virtual environment. In: Ahram, T. Z., Falcão, C. (eds.) AHFE 2018. AISC, vol. 794, pp. 583–592. Springer, Cham (2019). https://doi.org/10.1007/978-3-319-94947-5_59
19. Zimmerman, W.A., Kulikowich, J.M.: Online learning self-efficacy in students with and without online learning experience. Am. J. Distance Educ. **30**(3), 180–191 (2016)
20. Todorova, M., Karamanska, D., Koleva, E., Koleva, L.: Criterios ergonómicos para evaluar la calidad del e-learning. Revista - Electrotechnica Electronica (E + E) **52**(5–6), 24–29 (2017)
21. Sivapalan, S., Clifford, M., Speight, S.: Engineering education for sustainable development: using online learning to support the new paradigms. Australas. J. Eng. Educ. **21**(2), 61–73 (2017). https://doi.org/10.1080/22054952.2017.1307592
22. Todorova, M., Karamanska, D., Koleva, E., Koleva, L.: E-LEARNING Ergonomic criteria for evaluating the quality of e-learning (2017)
23. Trivedi, A., Deshwal, P., Soni, U., Mani, N.: Demographic variables and online customer experience of educational websites users. Procedia Comput. Sci. **132**, 965–970 (2018)

Customer eXperiences in Retail: Case Studies in Physical and Virtual Channels

Camila Bascur$^{(\boxtimes)}$, Cristian Rusu$^{(\boxtimes)}$, and Daniela Quiñones$^{(\boxtimes)}$

Pontificia Universidad Católica de Valparaíso, Av. Brasil 2241,
2340000 Valparaíso, Chile
cbascurbarrera@gmail.com,
{cristian.rusu,daniela.quinones}@pucv.cl

Abstract. Customer eXperience (CX) is a relatively new concept in the industry and generally related to marketing. It is focused examining the entire client's journey and experiences with various systems, products or services offered by a company. Lately, there is a growing interest in CX by organizations, since it is one of the most important factors when it comes to maintaining a competitive advantage with their peers. Adding to this, that customers nowadays seek to create an experience beyond the acquisition of a product.

The article examines a specific case study of a Chilean retail store through two Customer Journey Map (CJM) of the main sales channels (physical and virtual). In which the stages of the purchasing process are identified, considering the activities within these stages, the touchpoints and the elements present in the touchpoints, in order to make a comparison of the trips of the clients in their different channels of sale.

Keywords: Customer eXperience · Customer Journey Map · Touchpoint

1 Introduction

Nowadays, the use of the Customer eXperience (CX) concept has been increasing. This is because many companies are concerned with delivering value to their customers through their products/systems/services in order to generate a competitive advantage that allows them to differentiate themselves from their peers.

The client has become an important part of the company, due to the greater power and influence they exert. Customers have more knowledge about the products and prices offered by companies, so they not only look for a product, but they also look for unique and memorable experiences that accompany the delivery of products, systems and/or services [1]. The relationship between customers and companies is covered by several stages, ranging from the initial knowledge of a potential customer, the shopping experience, to the subsequent use of the product [2]. This relationship is marked by different touchpoint, which are generated through different interactions between clients-company, whose main objective is to change the perception of the client with respect to the brand or organization that offers them [3].

The article shows the results obtained after examining the case of a Chilean retail store (with presence in Peru). This store is of the departmental type, since it is large and

© Springer Nature Switzerland AG 2020
G. Meiselwitz (Ed.): HCII 2020, LNCS 12195, pp. 171–180, 2020.
https://doi.org/10.1007/978-3-030-49576-3_12

offers a large number of products, which seek to cover a wide range of needs: clothing, footwear, furniture, decoration, among others [4]. This article seeks to demonstrate how the customer interacts with the aforementioned store through two Customer Journey Map (Map), which represent its two main sales channels (physical and virtual), identifying the purchase stages, and its main activities, including touchpoint present at each stage of purchase and its elements.

The document is organized as follows: Sect. 2 briefly discusses relevant concepts: CX, touchpoint, nature of touchpoints, among others. Section 3 describes the case study, highlighting the purchase stages, activities within the stages, touchpoint and touchpoint elements. Finally, Sect. 4 presents conclusions and future work.

2   Theoretical Background

Customer eXperience (CX) is a broad concept that covers both clients and companies and studies the physical and emotional experiences that occur through interactions with the products and/or service of a brand present in an organization. These experiences occur from the first direct and conscious contact to the post-consumer phase [5], therefore it is understood that the client's experience is strictly personal and involves the client's participation at different levels [6–8], and it transcends the moment of purchase as the only interaction with an organization.

To better understand what CX means, we must consider the stages that the client goes through when purchasing a product. In general, these stages are [9, 10]:

- Pre-purchase: It is the first stage in the purchase process, where customers identify the alternatives, evaluate the benefits and risks and finally make a purchase decision. Then, they identify the potential suppliers, evaluating in the same way benefits and risks of each option before making a final decision.
- Purchase: During this stage, the client has already defined the product and company in which it will acquire it, this after having evaluated all the options and having identified which is the one that will provide the most value.
- Post-purchase: In this stage the clients evaluate the quality of service and their satisfaction/dissatisfaction with the experience of the service granted. The result of this process will affect your future intentions, such as whether or not to remain loyal to the company (provider), or transmit recommendations (positive or negative) to your environment or others.

If during these stages, everything goes as expected, that is, that the product and service provided by the company has met its expectations, that the price/quality ratio is acceptable, and other influential factors in the purchase process, it is likely that customers are satisfied and become loyal customers.

It should be noted that during all the stages mentioned above, touchpoint between customer and the company are present. These touchpoints occur through the products/systems or services, and correspond to any interaction (including encounters where there is no physical interaction) that could alter the way the client feels about the product, brand, business or service [11]. The touchpoints are extremely important for companies, since they are the means by which organizations disclose information to their clients, both previous and future, helping to cultivate trust and the relationship between the client and the company. The interaction can be active, passive, direct or indirect, and perceived by any of the senses that the human being possesses.

The authors Stein and Ramaseshan identified seven types of elements present in the touchpoints [12]:

- Atmospheric: These are the physical characteristics that customers observe when they interact with any part of the company. For example, amenities, environment, attractiveness, layout, store design.
- Technological: They are the direct interactions that a client has with any form of technology during a meeting with the company. For example, technology, ease of use, convenient technology and self-service technology.
- Communicative: Corresponds to any unidirectional communication from the company to the client, including promotional and informative messages. For example, advertising.
- Process: These are all the actions or steps that clients must take to achieve a particular result. For example, waiting time, navigation and service process.
- Employee-client interaction: Corresponds to the direct and indirect interactions that customers have with employees when they interact with any part of the company: For example: useful and argumentative employee, personalized service, friendly greeting.
- Client-client interaction: These are the direct and indirect interactions that customers have with other clients when they interact with any part of the company. For example, customer comments, direct and indirect interactions with customers.
- Interaction with the product: Corresponds to the direct or indirect interactions that customers have with the tangible intangible product offered by the company: For example, quality, variety, direct and indirect interactions with the product.

Touchpoints can interact through the different channels a company has. Most companies have two main channels, the physical and the virtual, the first corresponds to the physical place where the purchase process is generated, on the contrary, in the virtual channel where the entire purchase process of online way. In ancient times they used to be completely different channels that did not talk to each other, but as companies strive to improve customer experience, these channels have achieved the unification of the experience delivered, what is known today as omnichannel.

3   Customer Journey Map: Physical and Virtual Channels in Retail

Usually, companies carry out a CJM, which is a tool that helps to better understand the concept of CX in an organization [13]. Its objective is to make a diagram of the steps from beginning to end that the client follows when interacting with a certain organization.

Figures 1 and 2 present the main channels, both physical and virtual, present in the retail store, which are used to market their products. In these images you can see the stages, both main and secondary, the main contact points and the elements present in them.

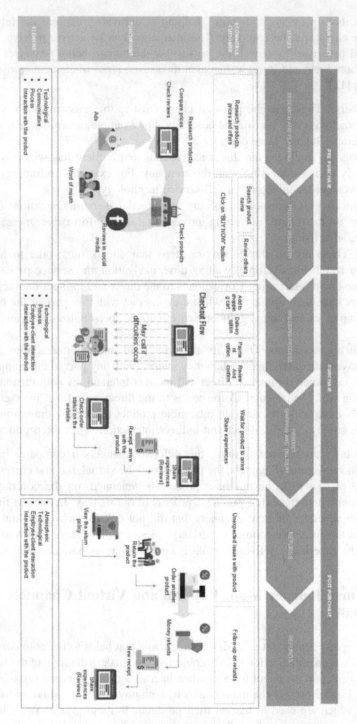

Fig. 1. Customer Journey Map of virtual channel

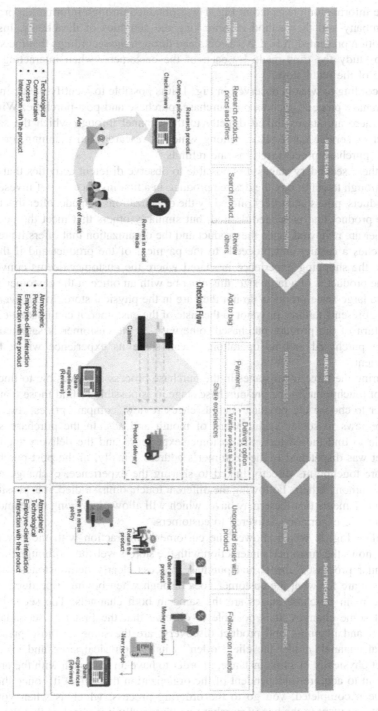

Fig. 2. Customer Journey Map of physical channel

The information presented in Fig. 1 was obtained through information provided by the company and the method of observing the activities of the clients. Instead, the information presented in Fig. 2 was obtained through the recordings that the store itself uses to study the trips made by each of the customers, when interacting with the website of the retail store.

According to what is observed in Fig. 1, it is possible to identify the main stages in the purchase process, such as pre-purchase, purchase and post-purchase. Within these stages there are stages linked directly to the channel through which the sale of the product or service takes place, among which is research and planning, product discovery, purchase process, returns and refunds.

In these secondary stages it is possible to observe different activities that the client goes through to get to buy the desired product, in a first instance a brief investigation of the products, prices and offers offered by the organizations is made, after this the search for the product that is needed/desired, but similarly others that meet the needs of the customer are reviewed, once the product and the organization that offers it are found, it approaches a cashier and proceeds to the payment of the product and if the user so wishes, the shopping experience is shared where the customer deems convenient, in case the product is of a large size, this must be with an office at the customer's address, because large-scale products do not they are in the physical store. In the event that the product presents failures or is not to the taste of the customer, it can make the exchange and return of the product purchased, otherwise, if the customer is satisfied with the product purchased and its operation, it can share its experience where he deems convenient.

During the three main stages in the purchase process it is possible to find different types of touchpoint. In the pre-purchase stage, it is possible to find those that will help the user to choose the product, such as check review, compare prices, research products, reviews in social media, word of mouth and ads. In the purchase stage it is possible to find the cashier, the customer experience and the delivery method if the product was dispatched to the customer's address. Finally, in the post-purchase stage there are touchpoints directly linked to sharing the experience, exchange and return policies, among others. Following the different touchpoints studied, it is possible to find different elements that these may have, which will allow classifying them and focusing better on the experience delivered to customers.

Unlike Fig. 1, which showed the customer's interaction with the physical store, Fig. 2 shows the customer's interaction with the store's website. Although they seem to be similar processes, the virtual purchase process clearly demonstrates what all the processes are for what the customer goes through when buying a product.

The main purchase stages are the same in both channels. The secondary stages present some changes. It is possible to observe that the first two secondary stages, research and planning and product discovery, are the same as those present in the physical channel, unlike the client often visits the physical store and visualizes the product physically in a first instance, in order to have an approach with the product that you want to acquire (independent of the organization that offers it), once these stages have been completed, you go to the ordering process, which is when you add the product you want to the bag of purchase and internally it is checked that the product is available, if so, the purchase order is issued, otherwise, the customer is notified of the steps for the return or exchange of the product, after this it is passed to the next stage, product shipping and delivery, where the client, in certain opportunities, can choose the type of delivery that suits him, this can be, withdrawal in store (without cost to the client) or dispatch to address (with cost associated with the customer), as in the previous channel, if the product is large, the customer has no choice and must choose home delivery. In the event that the product presents failures or is not to the taste of the customer, it can make the exchange and return of the product purchased, otherwise, if the customer is satisfied with the product purchased and its operation, it can share its experience where he deems convenient.

Each of these stages is marked by the activities that are present in this purchase channel, which is generally marked by the actions that the client follows, the main difference between the physical and virtual channel, is when it is desired to carry out the purchase, this because in the physical channel is close to a box, payment is made and the product is already from the customer, instead in the virtual channel, this process is somewhat different, and it occurs since the customer presses the buy button and There are a series of verifications that the customer must go through in order to have the purchase confirmation, once this is completed, it is passed to the delivery of the product, which can be withdrawn by the customer personally or dispatched to the address of East.

During the three main stages in the purchase process it is possible to find different types of touchpoints, which do not present much difference compared to the physical channel in the pre-purchase stage, only that they can be presented in the various channels that the company has. On the other hand, in the purchase stage in case of any inconvenience with the purchase it is possible to have virtual assistance (only), and all confirmations and validations are made internally with subsequent notification to the customer's mail. Finally, in the post-purchase stage there are touchpoints directly linked to sharing the experience, exchange and return policies, among others.

In the same way that in the physical channel it is possible to find the different elements that touchpoints can have, which will allow them to be classified and focus better on the experience delivered to customers.

According to the CJM presented in Fig. 1 and 2, the secondary stages of the purchase process is detailed in Table 1.

As it was observed in the CJM of the main sales channels offered by the store studied, it is not possible to find great differences just by looking at the figures. As a result of this, it is that in Table 1, the secondary stages of the purchase process can be observed, where the research and planning present similarities, independent of the channel that the client chooses in the beginning, this can perform its investigation in the multiple channels offered by the different stores that offer the desired product, in the next stage product discovery, is somewhat similar to the previous one, and it is where the customer decides the store where they want to buy their product, being the one that delivers the best conditions, the That will be chosen. Next, the secondary stages are presented where the differences in the purchase process are more evident, which is directly related to the channel that the customer chooses to make the purchase, that is, in the physical channel, just look for the product and proceed to the payment, however in the virtual channel they go through different verifications and confirmations before finally receiving the final confirmation of the purchase.

Table 1. Comparison between the purchasing stages of the virtual and physical channel.

Physical	Virtual
Research and planning	**Research and planning**
• You have a need that you want to be covered, either by a product, system or service that is capable of satisfying it. It mostly occurs through the different websites that companies offer and physical stores.	
Product discovery	**Product discovery**
• According to the whole range of products/systems/services able to satisfy the need, the client chooses the most suitable one for him.	
	Ordering process
	• Once the product/system/service has been chosen, the purchasing process begins, which ends with the payment of the product.
Purchase process	
• Once the product/system/service has been chosen, the customer approaches a box to make the purchase. It ends when the customer makes the payment of the product. If the product is of a larger size, we proceed to deliver the product at the customer's address	**Product shipping and delivery**
	• Once the payment process is finished, the company begins to process the purchase and manage the delivery of the product, either at the customer's home or in the company's premises.
Returns	**Returns**
• In case the product is defective, that is not the requested product or that does not satisfy the client completely; This, you can start the process of returning the purchase. It is mostly necessary to approach the physical store (of the company that offers its online services) to make the return.	
Refunds	**Refunds**
• If the return of the product corresponds, a refund is made, either by changing the product for the same or another, or simply delivering the total amount of the product.	

Finally, in case of acquiring a product in a physical way, the most common way to make a change or return of a small product is to approach the store, in case of a large product the supplier must approach to find the product at the customer's address; in case of acquiring a product in a virtual way and this is of small size, the customer must approach the store, in case the product is large, the supplier is the one who must take care of removing the product at home the client's.

Generally, and according to customer comments, it is possible to generate greater contact in the physical store, since it is attended by the workers themselves, feeling a certain degree of empathy with the work done by them, trying to avoid unnecessary conflicts; The relationship with online shopping is not the same, this is because people who do not have a person in a physical way to consult or claim, feel they have the right to request things in an unfriendly way.

4 Conclusion

Currently, there are multiple companies that offer their products through multiple channels. The case studied does not escape this, so it is interesting to fully study the entire purchase process, to understand where the customer has its main satisfactions and frustrations.

It is evident that although the channels seem to be similar, there are still differences that are proper to the channel through which the products are marketed, that is, that in the physical channel there may be greater inconveniences in customer service or in not finding the product desired (by the dimensions of this), however in the virtual channel, the main frustration of the client is to have no one to respond immediately to the questions that he has regarding the product or simply have the need to observe physically what you will buy virtually.

According to a study by the Chilean Chamber of Commerce in 2018, online sales have increased by 39.4% [14], which shows an upward trend in electronic sales. This explains why in the near future there should not be large differences in the process of buying customers, and must unify it, in such a way, that regardless of the channel chosen by the customer, the experience should be the same in both channels.

As a result, it is necessary to understand all the stages of the purchase process and where it is necessary to intervene to deliver a good customer experience, and thus achieve customer loyalty.

As future work, it is expected to perform an analysis of the store studied using the SERVQUAL scale as a method to study the quality of service delivered by the Chilean retail store.

References

1. Maital, S.: The experience economy: work is theatre & every business a stage. MIT Sloan Manag. Rev. **40**, 93 (1999)
2. Jantsch, J.: Duct Tape Marketing: The World's Most Practical Small Business Marketing Guide. Thomas Nelson Inc., Nashville (2011)
3. WOW Customer Experience. https://www.wowcx.com/que-es-un-touchpoint-o-punto-de-contacto/. Accessed 15 Jan 2020
4. Wikipedia. https://es.wikipedia.org/wiki/Grandes_almacenes. Accessed 15 Jan 2020
5. Laming, C., Mason, K.: Customer experience—an analysis of the concept and its performance in airline brands. Res. Transp. Bus. Manag. **10**, 5–25 (2014)
6. Vanharanta, H., Kantola, J., Seikola, S.: Customers' conscious experience in a coffee shop. Procedia Manuf. **3**, 618–625 (2015)
7. LaSalle, D., Britton, T.A.: Priceless: Turning ordinary products into extraordinary experiences. Harvard Business School Press, Brighton (2003)
8. Schmitt, B.: Experiential marketing. J. MARK. manag. **15**(1–3), 53–67 (1999)

9. Frambach, R., Roest, H., Krishnan, T.: The impact of consumer Internet experience on channel preference and usage intentions across the different stages of the buying process. J. Interact. Mark. **21**, 26–41 (2007)
10. Wisdom Jobs. https://www.wisdomjobs.com/
11. The CEO Refresher. http://www.refresher.com/alrpmtouchpoint.html. Accessed 15 Oct 2019
12. Stein, A., Ramaseshan, B.: Towards the identification of customer experience touchpoint elements. J. Retail. Consum. Serv. **30**, 8–19 (2015)
13. Rosenbaum, M.S., Otalora, M.L., Ramírez, G.C.: How to create a realistic customer journey map. Bus. Horiz. **60**(1), 143–150 (2017)
14. Cámara Nacional de Comercio. https://www.cnc.cl/ventas-online-crecen-un-394-durante-2018-mostrando-una-tendencia-al-alza/. Accessed 15 Jan 2020

Evaluation of Customer eXperience and Behaviour: A Literature Review

Sandra Cano[✉] ⓘ, Cristian Rusu ⓘ, and Daniela Quiñones ⓘ

Pontificia Universidad Católica de Valparaíso,
Av. Brasil 2241, 2340000 Valparaíso, Chile
{sandra.cano, cristian.rusu, daniela.quinones}@pucv.cl

Abstract. This article presents a review of the literature from the last 5 years in research related to methods they have used to evaluate the Customer eXperience. Following the area of computer science, we observe how different works have integrated artificial intelligence or physiological signals to evaluate the emotional state or perceptions of a customer. However, most of these works are very oriented towards a single channel of communication. Models and evaluation methods have also been implemented, where the interest of researchers in deepening the customer experience from different disciplines can be observed.

Keywords: Customer eXperience · User eXperience · Consumer behaviour

1 Introduction

Customer eXperience (CX) is related to the different interactions that a user can have with a system, products or services. CX is derived from user experience, which is defined by ISO 9241-11 *as a user's perceptions and responses that result from the use and/or anticipated use of system, product or service* [1]. In 2003 LaSalle and Britton [2] defined CX, as a *set of interactions between a customer and a product, a company, or part of its organization, which provoke a reaction*. Klaus and Maklan [3] defined CX as *the customer's cognitive and affective assessment of all direct and indirect encounters with the firm relating to their purchasing behaviour*.

The growth of technologies, new markets, services and channels have been created for a customer, with the purpose of offering an experience. De La-Hoz in his book "Customer Experience" [4], states that customers live experiences whenever they interact with the company, using a product or service and that these interactions can become stimuli and are related to the brand. However, it is important to ask: *What relationship do emotions have with the product/service, and why are they important?*. According to the **"Somatic Marker"** hypothesis, emotions can influence decision making [5].

However, identifying the emotional states of a client involves monitoring the different interactions he makes with a particular brand through personnel, system, product or service. One of the problems in CX is measurement. For a customer who has not had incidents in the process of purchasing a product, his satisfaction is positive. Therefore,

G. Meiselwitz (Ed.): HCII 2020, LNCS 12195, pp. 181–192, 2020.
https://doi.org/10.1007/978-3-030-49576-3_13

it searches to generate a memory in the experience of the purchase, in such a way that it can influence his behaviour to future, to return to buy with the same company.

In 2007, a group of researchers [6] proposed a CX framework composed of six components: sensory, emotional, cognitive, pragmatic, lifestyle and relational. They also mention that there are two types of values when the client interacts with the company - perception and expectation. The appearance of CX is nothing new, since with Schmitt (1999) [7] the term **experiential marketing** appears, defining it as *"products, communications and marketing campaigns that awaken senses and reach the heart of the consumer, that they manage to generate a type of stimulation in people"*. Schmitt identifies a set of factors that should be taken into account such as Strategic Experiential Modules: sense (sensory experiences), feel (affective experiences), think (cognitive experiences), act (physical experiences behaviours and lifestyle) and relate (social-identify experiences).

Evaluating CX is a challenge, according to Rusu et al. [8], indicating that CX is built through a touch-point sequence; and the nature of each touch-point is different: the experience of one touch-point could be highly influenced by the experiences of the other touch-point. Therefore, to evaluate CX is to consider different types of customer interaction with the product/service, so it can be evaluated on different qualitative and quantitative techniques. In 1985, Parasuraman et al. [9] proposed a model called SERVQUAL to measure service quality, which it is composed of ten dimensions of service quality: tangibles, reliability, responsiveness, communication, credibility, security, competence, courtesy, understanding the customer, and access. In 2011, Maklan and Klaus [10] proposed a customer experience quality scale called EXQ (EXperience Quality measurement). EXQ is grouped by 4 dimensions: product experience, outcome focus, moments-of-truth, and peace-of-mind.

In 2012 Klaus and Maklan [11] introduced the term *Customer Service Experience* where involve customer emotion and perception. This term is related with experience quality, where Chang and Horng [12] proposed an experience quality model composed by five dimensions: physical surrounding, customers themselves, services provider, other customers, and customer companions. Therefore, customer experience quality should be evaluated at the affective level because emotion is strongly related to feelings. However, in 2013 Klaus et al. [13] customer experience quality was redefined as *customer cognitive and affective assessment of all direct and indirect encounters with the firm relating to their purchasing behaviour.*

Neurophysiology studies have related the experience with sensory, cognitive and emotional components [14, 15], showing that some regions of the brain are activated during the presentation of stimuli [16]. A study made by Lu et al. [17] to measure CX has used psychophysiological responses to measure the quality of a service in real time. It has also been supported by the Think-Aloud technique to obtain the subjective experience of customers. They have captured psychophysiological responses as EDA and neurophysiological responses as EEG with the aim of measuring emotional experience and mental workload. Both instruments of evaluation used - qualitative and quantitative - showed a high consistence with the data. They have thus shown that the psychophysiological response can be used to measure the user experience in using the service. to reflect service quality. Other studies have meanwhile integrated theory of mind and empathy in consumer behaviour [18], beginning with the actions made by consumers involve a number of mental processes organized in complex ways.

Therefore, a literature review was conducted to identify how authors have implemented techniques or methods (qualitative and quantitative) for measuring CX, and the behaviour when a customer interacts with a product or service. The literature review identifies a set of publications relevant to the research questions. This study was carried out by following the guidelines and framework proposed by [19, 20] for performing a literature review in software engineering.

2 Background

2.1 Customer eXperience (CX)

CX is related to both the company and the customer. Therefore, a set of interactions exists between both. The type of interaction can be through physical or digital channels and the relationship can be offering, customer service, brand, or ad campaigns, among others. Today customers are accustomed to the use of technology during everyday activities such as e-commerce, where they prefer to buy using the online-service. However, the customer has several ways to interact and certain touch-points with a device and a brand.

Therefore, when a customer interacts with a product/service their emotions can have an influence on the decision to buy. Based on the Somatic Maker Theory [5] the decision-making process is related with emotions and feelings. Moreover, Klaus and Maklan [3] have defined CX, as: *"The customer's cognitive and affective assessment of all direct and indirect encounters with the firm relating to their purchasing behaviour"*. Another definition is defined by [21] as: *"emotional/affective, cognitive, sensorial, relational/social and physical/behavioural responses to stimuli during the consumer journey"*. Therefore, some authors [17, 18] have been interested in studying the use of psychophysiological measures. Meanwhile, other authors [10, 21] have studied techniques related with formative and summative measures by means of satisfaction questionnaires, direct observation, and focus groups, among others.

A study was carried out by Veiga et al. [22] about a systematic review, in which measuring customer experience in service, called *"service experience"*, is a consequence of delivery, where it can include different areas such as: psychology, sociology, marketing and consumer behaviour. However, this service can be measured with cognitive, emotional and behavioural responses. LaSalle and Briton [2] indicate that the experience is strictly personal and implies such aspects as: rational, emotional, sensorial, physical, and spiritual. Its evaluation depends on the comparison between customer and stimuli coming from the interaction with the company and different **moments of contact** or **touch-points.**

2.2 Consumer Behaviour

Consumer behaviour is a new scientific discipline under study in the context of marketing theory. Consumer behaviour can be defined as *a marketing discipline that studies the behaviour of individuals, groups or organisations and the processes they use to select, secure, use and dispose of products and services, experiences or ideas to satisfy needs and the impacts that these processes have on the consumers and society* [23]. Consumer behaviour includes several disciplines from psychology, sociology, social, ethnography, marketing and behavioural economics. Consumer behaviour thus implies the use of concepts and tools from other disciplines to understand consumers better.

A model proposed by Schiffman and Kanuk [24] presents a set of stages of the consumer process, such as: external influence (input), decision-making (process) and post-decision behaviour (output). In the decision-making process, there are psychological inputs such as: emotions, learning, personality, perception and attitudes. However, the articles most found in engineering areas evaluate consumer physiological responses using sensors and devices to capture responses.

The analysis of consumer behaviour is key to knowing which aspects influence in the selection of product/service, shopping for a product, among others. Advances made in technology have allowed researchers to research how to study of human behaviour in real and daily life. There are a set of aspects that influence the consumer to purchase, such as: emotions, perceptions, needs, etc. Hernández et al. [25] analysed consumer perceptions that lead to purchase over the internet. Bandura (1986) [26] mentions that it is related with the skills obtained through internet use. Therefore, users with more experience in use of the technology prefer online shopping.

The use of physiological techniques has generated interest in some researchers to study the consumer's emotions and cognitive responses. Shaw and Bagozzi [18] analysed from the neuroscience field how these may contribute to understanding consumer psychology in such aspects as: attention, memory, emotional processing, and reward processing. Caruelle et al. [27] conducted a literature review of electrodermal activity as one option for understanding consumer emotions. Another technique used is eye-tracking, Webel et al. [28], based on the theory of visual attention and eye-movements to evaluate consumer behaviour. Mazaherri et al. [29], proposed a model of online consumer behaviour in services marking where they carried out a study for comparing the Canadian and Chinese cultures, in which the authors found stronger attitudes for the Chinese compared to Canadians, while Canadians make decisions based on self-interest.

However, the studies presented do not measure all aspects related to consumer behaviour. The study of consumer behaviour includes social, personal and psychological factors. In the consumer they studied aspects such as: (1) How consumers think and feel about a product, brands, services or retailers; (2) How consumers reason and select between different options; (3) the behaviour of consumers while they search and shop; (4) How consumer behaviour is influenced by the environment; (5) How marketing can be adapted and improved to influence the consumer more strongly.

Therefore, neuro-marketing appears to be dedicated to the study of consumer behaviour in order to understand purchase decisions, preferences and behaviour.

3 Research Method

To guide this research, a literature review method was applied based on a framework and literature review in software engineering proposed by [19, 20], which sets out the stages to be followed:

Stage 1:   Identify the research question
Stage 2:   Identify relevant studies
Stage 3:   Study selection
Stage 4:   Charting the data

3.1 Identify the Research Questions

RQ1:   What techniques are used to evaluate CX?
RQ2:   What techniques are used to evaluate consumer behaviour?
RQ3:   What are the limitations of current research?
RQ4:   What research topics are being addressed?

3.2 Identify Relevant Studies

Using the keywords "customer experience", "measurement" and "evaluation", in the last 5 years (2016–2020), 14 documents were found in SCOPUS by subject area, including Engineering (16%) and Computer Sciences (32%).

Scopus was limited to the keywords "customer satisfaction", "quality of service", "quality of experience" (QoE), "quality of service", "customer experience" and 9 documents were found. These were used to evaluate customer experience in such online services as: cloud providers, mobile devices, and the healthcare industry.

Science Direct database produced 10 documents, wherein one document was found for evaluating user preferences through brain responses [30] using the ERP method applied to the development of user experience measurement and product evaluation to understand the decision-making mechanism.

ACM gave up 260 documents, using only the keywords "customer experience" and "evaluation". One article found presented customer experience from a holistic perspective. The authors thus defined user experience related to customer experience and brand experience [31]. Another study found is an emotion recognition system on online shopping capturing biometric data and facial expressions [32].

Sage Database resulted in 361 documents, wherein only 3 documents are related (subject) with engineering & computing. One document used machine learning techniques for quality control in a manufacturing environment [33].

On changing the keywords for "customer experience" and "physiological" in the last 5 years, 5 articles were found. A study made by Caruelle et al. [27] used electrodermal activity to measure and understand consumer emotions. Lara et al. (2019) [34] proposed a methodology that integrates physiological data by facial expression to identify emotions in patients, taking into account the specific client of health services, i.e. the patient. In 2016, a study was proposed to evaluate the customer experience during online shopping [35], wherein the authors used physiological data to measure emotional arousal and an eye tracker.

A search was carried out for papers written in English during the last five years (2016–2020). The search was made in electronic databases with very specific keywords and filtering criteria. Table 1 below shows the databases used and the number of articles found. The literature review shows that the terms used related to customer experience are: service experience, customer satisfaction, quality of service, customer service, and consumer behaviour [3, 18, 36].

Table 1. Journals (publications) using keywords: *Customer experience, Evaluation* and *Measurement*

Journal	Number of articles	% articles
IEEE Xplore	19	4.7
Science Direct	10	2.4
Sage Journals	361	89
ACM Digital Library (http://dl.acm.org)	0	0
Scopus	14	3.5

3.3   Study Selection

Evaluating customer experience can include a number of approaches, such as: customer satisfaction scores, product/service quality metrics, and physiological responses.

The most commonly found methods to evaluate customer experience are shown in Table 2, where a search was made in the *Scopus* database.

Table 2.   Methods to evaluate the Customer eXperience

Data collection	Questionnaire	No. of documents	Area	Method
Survey	SERVQUAL	687	Logistics, Transportation online, Health, Online shopping, Tourism	Subjective
Survey	SITEQUAL	255	Online shopping and websites	Subjective
Survey	EXQ	119	Hotels, retail Banks	Subjective
Interviews	Thinking - Aloud			Subjective
Pyschophysiological	EEG-EDA, Eye Tracking		Online shopping and websites	Objective

SERVQUAL is a questionnaire most often used to evaluate CX in different areas. SERVQUAL was created in 1985 by a team of academic researchers. It is designed to capture aspects such as: reliability, assurance, tangibles, empathy, and responsiveness. Some researchers created other questionnaires based on SERVQUAL focused on special services, such as HEALTHQUAL in the health context and EDUQUAL in the educational context. SITEQUAL was created to evaluate ecommerce websites. This instrument includes four aspects: aesthetic design, ease of use, processing speed and security.

EXQ is a measuring scale of the customer, which incorporates key attributes of CX such as: product experience, outcome focus, moments-of-truth and peace-of-mind.

Answering the research questions:

RQ1: What techniques are used to evaluate CX?

Evaluating customer experience can use two approaches: objective and subjective. Objective measurement is based on how well someone can perform a set number of tasks in a controlled environment, while subjective measurement is how experts measure what people say.

Subjective assessment methods can be qualitative and quantitative. Articles found in different journal databases have used techniques such as: survey [2, 37]; SERVQUAL, a questionnaire to measure service quality [38], which contains 22 items in Likert Scale; WebQual [39] is an extension of SERVQUAL, which is composed of 24 measurements items, including service quality aspects such as: reliability, competence, responsiveness, access, credibility, communication, and understanding the individual. Yoo and Donthu [40] proposed an instrument for e-commerce sites called SITEQUAL, which includes four dimensions (ease of use, aesthetic design, processing speed and security). Another instrument used is to measure customer experience quality is EXQ scale [3] with four dimensions (product experience, focus, moment-of-truth and peace-of mind).

Objective assessment methods have been applied, using Artificial Intelligence algorithms to detect emotions using pattern recognition techniques or capturing physiological responses through sensors. AQuA is used as an automatic quality analysis of conversation scripts in real-time, applying deep learning [41]. Others studies put more emphasis on measuring emotions in the customer experience, where Seng and Ang (2018) [42] proposed an audio-visual emotion recognition system to detect six emotions (happy, angry, sad, disgust, surprise and fear). In 2019, Lu et al. [17] conducted a study to measure the online service quality in real-time utilizing psychophysiological responses. In the experiment, participants were reminded to use the think-aloud method to express their operation, emotion and feelings, while psychophysiological responses were measured using EEG (Electroencephalography) and EDA (Electrodermal activity) signals. The aim of the experiment was to find the "customer service interface" webpage in five minutes. In 2018, Ceccacci et al. [32] proposed a tool to analyse customer emotions along the customer journey in a nonintrusive way. The authors therefore used three methods: facial recognition, speech recognition, and biofeedback analysis, employed in a retail context. Other studies, such as McColl-Kennedy et al. in 2017 [43], focused on health and measured emotions of the patient during health care experiences.

RQ2: What techniques are used to evaluate consumer behaviour?

Emotions in the consumer have been of interest in studies because factors such as emotional states or perceptions can determine decisions while shopping.

The relationship with other sciences such as psychology, economy, engineering and neurosciences have shown that it can be a support in discovering ways to evaluate consumer behaviour, where instruments have been created to understand consumers better. However, many existing techniques are very subjective and new ways are being sought to obtain more reliable results.

Objective techniques meanwhile are beginning to be of greater interest to researchers from the computer sciences, but any research found has applied to online services.

It is important to mention that in experiments, between the observations in a natural and an artificial one, results may change, which cannot be monitored in a natural situation. Therefore, the need arises to use technical apparatus such as: psychgalvanometer, which measures resistance in the skin: pupil-metre which follows pupil dilation; eye-tracking camera, which monitors horizontal and vertical eye movements; voice, which shows the emotional reaction, and EEG, based on monitoring brain activity. The use of technology has resulted in researchers using a number of different approaches to obtain more data on consumers.

RQ3: What are the limitations of research?

Most research to evaluate customer experience comprise the use of models and methodologies, whose theories are transferred to different questionnaires. Most articles published are not published in computer & engineering journals. The few works found in computer journals are applied more to online services. Therefore, customer experience involves more than one channel.

Moreover, the proposed questionnaires have too many categories to be evaluated and are too long, which may cause the client to be unavailable to answer the questions.

RQ4: What research topics are being addressed?

The growth of technology has led to the creation of new communication channels for customers. Companies are therefore trying to improve the processes of interaction with the customer, with the aim of achieving greater customer loyalty, bearing in mind that customers can be diverse, from those who prefer to use technology, to older people suspicious of technology and who prefer traditional processes. As technology and marketing strategies are incorporated, the channels grow more and evaluating that experience can often become a challenge.

The website may include online stores or care services using chatbots. Therefore, the interaction being totally digital allows in an easier way to capture some answers in the customer, like knowing what he does before, during and after the purchase in online shopping services. Until now, the researches that have been found have been oriented to understand the consumer more on the web and have created more web oriented technologies. However, there are still customers who prefer traditional shopping methods without the use of the internet. Therefore, tools in this type of environment that include technology are not very common to find. Therefore, the following question appears: How do digital and physical elements interact to form the customer experience?

3.4 Charting Data

It is cause for some concern that almost none of the research is from Latin America. Figure 1, shows the number of publications by country. Of most interest is that almost 50% of the articles come from engineering journals. This is because it is a topic that no longer involves only one science, but several (See Fig. 2).

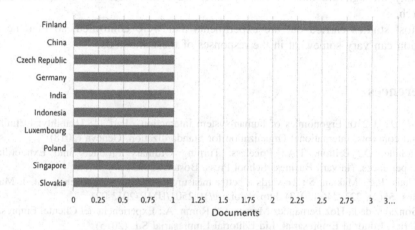

Fig. 1. Research found by country in Customer eXperience.

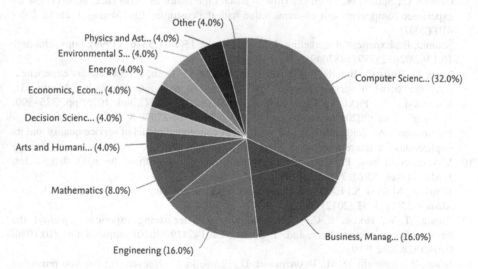

Fig. 2. Publications by subject in Customer eXperience.

4 Conclusions

The concept of customer experience appeared in the mid-1980s and today is gaining interest from researchers in a number of different areas. From the computer sciences, several studies have been conducted in which techniques for evaluating customer experience were implemented. From techniques in which questionnaires were created, to techniques where artificial intelligence concepts were used in order to recognize the customer's emotions or sensors used in order to obtain physiological responses.

However, most of these research works are associated more with customer experience through the Internet. Customers however not only interact with the product or company through the Internet but by other ways that were not considered in the research.

Most studies carried out are experiments that were controlled, so that the real situation can vary somewhat in the responses of these methods.

References

1. ISO 9241-210: Ergonomics of human-system interaction—Part 11: Usability: Definitions and concepts, International Organization for Standardization, Geneva (2018)
2. LaSalle, D., Britton, T.A.: Priceless: Turning Ordinary Products into Extraordinary Experiences. Harvard Business School Press, Boston (2003)
3. Klaus, P.P., Maklan, S.: Towards a better measure of customer experience. Int. J. Market Res. **55**(2), 227–246 (2013). https://doi.org/10.2501/IJMR-2013-021
4. Gonzalez de la-Hoz Fernandez Marcos, G., Romn, A.: Experiencia del Cliente. Empresarial Series. Editorial Empresarial. Lid Editorial Empresarial S.L (2015)
5. Damasio, A.R.: El error de Descartes. Crítica, Barcelona (2004)
6. Gentile, C., Spiller, N., Noci, G.: How to sustain the customer experience: an overview of experience components that co-create value with the customer. Eur. Manag. J. **25**(5), 395–410 (2007)
7. Schmitt, B.: Experiential marketing. J. Mark. Manag. **15**(1-3), 53–67 (1999). https://doi.org/10.1362/026725799784870496
8. Rusu, V., Rusu, C., Botella, F., Quiñones, D., Bascur, C., Rusu, V.Z.: Customer experience: a bridge between service science and human-computer interaction. In: Ahram, T., Karwowski, W., Pickl, S., Taiar, R. (eds.) IHSED 2019. AISC, vol. 1026, pp. 385–390. Springer, Cham (2020). https://doi.org/10.1007/978-3-030-27928-8_59
9. Parasuraman, A., Zeithaml, V.A., Berry, L.L.: A conceptual model of service quality and its implications for future research. J. Mark. **49**(4), 41–50 (1985)
10. Maklan, S., Klaus, P.: Customer experience: are we measuring the right things? Int. J. Market Res. **53**(6), 771–792 (2011)
11. Klaus, P., Maklan, S.: EXQ: a multiple-item scale for assessing service experience. J. Serv. Manag. **23**(1), 5–33 (2012)
12. Chang, T.-Y., Horng, S.-C.: Conceptualizing and measuring experience quality: the customer's perspective. Serv. Ind. J. **30**(14), 2401–2419 (2010). https://doi.org/10.1080/02642060802629919
13. Klaus, P., Gorgoglione, M., Buonamassa, D., Panniello, U., Nguyen, B.: Are you providing the "right" customer experience? The case of Banca Popolare di Bari. Int. J. Bank Mark. **31**(7), 506–528 (2013)

14. Pace-Schott, E.F., et al.: Physiological feelings. Neurosci. Biobehav. Rev. **103**, 267–304 (2019)
15. Kastner, S., Ungerleider, L.G.: The neural basis of biased competition in human visual cortex. Neuropsychologia **39**(12), 1263–1276 (2001)
16. Ohme, R., Reykowska, D., Wiener, D., Choromanska, A.: Analysis of neurophysiological reactions to advertising stimuli by means of EEG and galvanic skin response measures. J. Neurosci. Psychol. Econ. **2**(1), 21–31 (2009)
17. Lu, P., Li, L., Ma, L.: Online service quality measurement utilizing psychophysiological responses. In: Ahram, T. (ed.) AHFE 2019. AISC, vol. 965, pp. 347–352. Springer, Cham (2020). https://doi.org/10.1007/978-3-030-20454-9_36
18. Shaw, S.D., Bagozzi, R.P.: The neuropsychology of consumer behavior and marketing. Consum. Psychol. Rev. **1**, 22–40 (2018). https://doi.org/10.1002/arcp.1006
19. Arksey, H., O'Malley, L.: Scoping studies: towards a methodological framework. Int. J. Soc. Res. Methodol. **8**(1), 19–32 (2005). https://doi.org/10.1080/1364557032000119616
20. Kitchenham, B.A.: Procedures for undertaking systematic reviews. Joint Technical report, Computer Science Department, Keele University (TR/SE- 0401) and National ICT Australia Ltd. (0400011T.1) (2004)
21. Lemon, K.N., Verhoef, P.C.: Understanding customer experience throughout the customer journey. J. Mark. **80**(6), 69–96 (2016)
22. Bueno, E.V., Weber, T.B.B., Bomfim, E.L., Kato, H.T.: Measuring customer experience in service: a systematic review. Serv. Ind. J. **39**(11-12), 779–798 (2019). https://doi.org/10.1080/02642069.2018.1561873
23. Husić-Mehmedović, M., Kukić, S., Čičić, M.: Consumer behavior. School of Economics and Business in Sarajevo (2012)
24. Schiffman, L.G., Kanuk, L.L.: Consumer Behavior, 8th edn. Pearson/Prentice Hall, Upper Saddle River (2004)
25. Hernández, B., Jiménez, J., José Martín, M.: Customer behavior in electronic commerce: the moderating effect of e-purchasing experience. J. Bus. Res. **63**(9–10), 964–971 (2010). ISSN 0148-2963
26. Bandura, A.: Social Foundations of Thought and Action: A Social Cognitive Theory. Prentice-Hall, Englewood Cliffs (1986)
27. Caruelle, D., Gustafsson, A., Shams, P., Lervik-Olsen, L.: The use of electrodermal activity (EDA) measurement to understand consumer emotions – a literature review and a call for action. J. Bus. Res. **104**(2019), 146–160 (2019)
28. Wedel, M., Pieters, R.: Eye Tracking for Visual Marketing. Found. Trends® Mark. **1**(4), 231–320 (2008). https://doi.org/10.1561/1700000011
29. Mazaheri, E., Richard, M.-O., Laroche, M.: Online consumer behavior: comparing Canadian and Chinese website visitors. J. Bus. Res. **64**(9), 958–965 (2011)
30. Guo, F., Ding, Y., Wang, T., Liu, W., Jin, H.: Applying event related potentials to evaluate user preferences toward smartphone form design. Int. J. Ind. Ergon. **54**, 57–64 (2016)
31. Lee, H.-J., Lee, K.K., Choi, J.: A structural model for unity of experience: connecting user experience, customer experience, and brand experience. J. Usability Stud. **14**(1), 8–34 (2018)
32. Ceccacci, S., Generosi, A., Giraldi, L., Mengoni, M.: An emotion recognition system for monitoring shopping experience. In: Proceedings of the 11th PErvasive Technologies Related to Assistive Environments Conference (PETRA 2018), pp. 102–103. Association for Computing Machinery, New York (2018). https://doi.org/10.1145/3197768.3201518
33. Escobar, C.A., Morales-Menendez, R.: Machine learning techniques for quality control in high conformance manufacturing environment. Adv. Mech. Eng. (2018). https://doi.org/10.1177/1687814018755519

34. Reinares-Lara, P., Rodríguez-Fuertes, A., Garcia-Henche, B.: The cognitive dimension and the affective dimension in the patient's experience. Front. Psychol. **10**, 2177 (2019)

35. Kvasnicova, T., Kremenova, I., Fabus, J., Babusiak, B.: E-commerce user experience: do we feel under pressure during online shopping? In: Proceedings of the 20th World Multi-Conference on Systemics, Cybernetics and Informatics. WMSCI 2016, vol, 2, pp. 41–44 (2016)

36. Yang, Z., Jun, M., Peterson, R.T.: Measuring customer perceived online service quality: scale development and managerial implications. Int. J. Oper. Prod. Manag. **24**(11), 1149–1174 (2004). https://doi.org/10.1108/01443570410563278

37. Torres, E.N., Zhang, T., Ronzoni, G.: Measuring delightful customer experiences: the validation and testing of a customer delight scale along with its antecedents and effects. Int. J. Hosp. Manag. (2019)

38. Kettinger, W.K., Lee, C.C.: Pragmatic perspectives on the measurement of information systems service quality. MIS Q **21**(2), 223–240 (1997)

39. Barnes, S.J., Vidgen, R.: An evaluation of cyber-bookshops: the WebQual method. Int. J. Electron. Commer. **6**(1), 11–30 (2001)

40. Yoo, B., Donthu, N.: Developing a scale to measure the perceived quality of Internet shopping sites (SITEQUAL). Q. J. Electron. Commer. **2**(1), 31–47 (2001)

41. Abhinav, K., Dubey, A., Jain, S., Arora, V., Puttaveerana, A., Miller, S.: AQuA: automatic quality analysis of conversational scripts in real-time. In: Rutkowski, L., Scherer, R., Korytkowski, M., Pedrycz, W., Tadeusiewicz, R., Zurada, Jacek M. (eds.) ICAISC 2019. LNCS (LNAI), vol. 11509, pp. 489–500. Springer, Cham (2019). https://doi.org/10.1007/978-3-030-20915-5_44

42. Seng, K.P., Ang, L.: Video analytics for customer emotion and satisfaction at contact centers. IEEE Trans. Hum.-Mach. Syst. **48**(3), 266–278 (2018). https://doi.org/10.1109/thms.2017.2695613

43. McColl-Kennedy, J.R., Danaher, T.S., Gallan, A.S., Orsingher, C., Lervik-Olsen, L., Verma, R.: How do you feel today? Managing patient emotions during health care experiences to enhance well-being. J. Bus. Res. **79**, 247–259 (2017). ISSN 0148-2963

User eXperience Heuristics for National Park Websites

Dania Delgado[1], Daniela Zamora[1], Daniela Quiñones[1],
Cristian Rusu[1], Silvana Roncagliolo[1(✉)], and Virginica Rusu[2]

[1] Pontificia Universidad Católica de Valparaíso, Valparaíso, Chile
dania.carolina.dm@gmail.com,
danielaa.zamora4@gmail.com, {daniela.quinones,
cristian.rusu,silvana.roncagliolo}@pucv.cl
[2] Universidad de Playa Ancha, Valparaíso, Chile
virginica.rusu@upla.cl

Abstract. A national park website extends (in certain way) a physical national park. It does not have a physical location so its elements and information can be appreciated from anywhere in the world. Usability is a well-known concept, for decades. User eXperience (UX) is a broader concept that encompasses usability. The usability and UX evaluation are important tasks to perform when developing any kind of websites. In this regard it is important to evaluate whether a national park website is intuitive, easy to use, and allows users to complete their objectives. National park websites have their own features that differentiate them from other systems, so it is necessary to use a set of appropriate heuristics for these types of websites. The article presents a set of 14 heuristics to evaluate the UX of national park websites. The heuristics were developed using the methodology proposed by Quiñones et al. [2]. To validate and refine the UX heuristics for national park websites, we performed two iterations. In the first iteration the heuristics were validated through heuristic evaluation and expert judgment (survey), while in the second iteration the heuristics were validated through user tests (co-discovery and focus group). Based on validation results, we concluded that the proposed set of heuristics are effective.

Keywords: National park websites · User eXperience · Usability · Heuristics

1 Introduction

A national park website extends, in certain way, a physical national park. It does not have a physical location so its elements and information can be appreciated from anywhere in the world. After reviewing the literature, we identified that there is no formal definition for national park websites. Based on the review that we performed, we can define a national park website as a collection of web pages that deliver information of a physical national park through multimedia resources. Depending on the type of national parks, their websites offer users information on flora and fauna, images, common activities in the area, recommendations, maps, among others.

© Springer Nature Switzerland AG 2020
G. Meiselwitz (Ed.): HCII 2020, LNCS 12195, pp. 193–204, 2020.
https://doi.org/10.1007/978-3-030-49576-3_14

Usability is a well-known concept, for decades. User eXperience (UX) is a broader concept that encompasses usability. The usability and UX evaluation are important tasks to perform when developing any kind of websites. It is necessary to assess whether the websites meet the needs of the users and whether it fits properly in the physical, social and organizational context in which it will be used. In this regard it is important to evaluate whether a national park website is intuitive, easy to use, and allows users to complete their objectives. UX should be explicitly considered, since the information, the content, the, presentation and the structure of the website should generate a user-friendly experience, motivating people to learn about the characteristics of the physical national park.

In general terms, usability/UX evaluations methods can be classified into: (1) inspections, where expert evaluators inspect a product to detect potential usability/UX problems; and (2) tests, where real or representative users interact and complete tasks using a product, system, or service. Heuristic evaluation is probably the most common usability inspection method. Expert evaluators detect potential usability problems, based on heuristics [1]. Nielsen's heuristics allow evaluators to inspect a website in a general way, without focusing on specific domain features. However, the above makes it difficult to detect usability domain-specific problems.

National park websites have their own features that differentiate them from other products, so it is necessary to use a set of appropriate heuristics for these types of websites. Moreover, we think that heuristics can help detecting problems related to UX, and not limited to usability aspects [2, 3].

This article presents a set of 14 heuristics to evaluate the UX of national park websites. The heuristics were developed using the methodology proposed by Quiñones et al. [2]. The methodology proposes 8 stages to develop and validate a new set of heuristics. To validate and refine the UX heuristics for national park websites, we performed two iterations. In the first iteration the heuristics were validated through heuristic evaluation and expert judgment (survey), while in the second iteration the heuristics were validated through user tests (co-discovery and focus group). Based on validation results, we concluded that the proposed set of heuristics are effective.

The article is organized as follows: Sect. 2 presents the theoretical background; Sect. 3 shows the methodology used to develop the set of heuristics for national park websites; Sect. 4 presents the final set of User eXperience heuristics for National Park Websites; Sect. 5 details the heuristics' validation; and finally Sect. 6 presents the conclusions and future works.

2   Theoretical Background

2.1   Usability

According to ISO 9241-210 [4], usability is defined as "the extent to which a product, system, or service can be used by specific users to achieve specific goals with effectiveness, efficiency and satisfaction in a specific context of use". This definition focuses on the concept of quality and the use of a certain product, system or service. Usability focuses on how the user achieves their specified goals, the resources used to achieve the goals and the degree to which the user needs are met. Jakob Nielsen indicates that the nature of usability is multidimensional [5]. Nielsen states that usability has the following 5 attributes [5]:

1. Learnability: The ease of learning the operation and behavior of the system for inexperienced users.
2. Efficiency: The level of productivity attainable once the expert user has already learned the system. The greater the usability of a system, the faster the user is using it, and the work is done faster.
3. Memorability: The ease of remembering the functionality of the system, so that the occasional user when returning to the system after an inactive period, does not have the need to learn how to use it again.
4. Errors: The system must have a low error rate, that is, users make few mistakes while using the system, and in case they make them help them recover easily.
5. Satisfaction: This is the most subjective attribute. It is the extent to which the user finds the system pleasant to use.

For the development of heuristics for national park websites, all the Nielsen's usability attributes were considered.

2.2 User eXperience

Different authors have defined the User eXperience (UX) from different perspectives, so there is no single term that defines it. A user-centered approach would involve not only analyzing the factors that influence the purchase or choice of a product, but also analyzing how customers use the product and the experience resulting from its use [6].

The ISO 9241-210 standard [4] defines the UX as "the perceptions and responses of the person resulting from the use and/or anticipated use of a product, system or service". On the other hand, Nielsen and Norman consider the UX as "an integrating concept of all aspects of the interaction between the end user, the company, its services and products" [6].

Today the UX is being studied, mainly with a multidisciplinary approach. The UX is composed of different aspects or factors. Peter Morville proposes a model with 7 factors that explains the UX [7]:

1. Useful: the content must be original and satisfy a need.
2. Usable: The product or system must be easy to use.
3. Desirable: Image, identity, brand and other design elements are used to evoke emotion and gratitude.
4. Valuable: The product or system must add value to the interested user.
5. Findable: The product or system must have a good navigation and its content must be easily found, so that the user always finds what he/she needs.
6. Accessible: The content must be accessible to various types of people, including those with disabilities.
7. Credible: Users must trust and believe what is presented to them.

For the development of heuristics for national park websites, 6 of the 7 factors mentioned above were considered: useful, valuable, credible, usable, desirable, and findable. The accessible factor was not considered since there are already clear rules and automatic tools that allow to assess it (such as the rules proposed by the World Wide Web Consortium community) [8].

2.3 Heuristic Evaluation

The heuristic evaluation is an expert inspection method that identifies the usability/UX problems that users may encounter when using a product or an interface [9]. The heuristic evaluation is one of the most used methods; it is low cost and allows finding fast usability errors on a website, application or any system that interacts with the user. The expert evaluators (between 3 and 5) evaluate the interface by detecting usability/UX using heuristics.

The product or system is evaluated based on usability heuristics, which can be generic (as Nielsen's Heuristics [10]) or specific (to evaluate usability, UX and specific application domains). According to the set of heuristics chosen, the evaluators are responsible for detecting potential usability/UX problems that a user might encounter when interacting with the system interface being evaluated.

Initially, evaluators work independently to find and document the problems detected. The previous experience that each evaluator has with the system can influence the number of problems encountered. Subsequently a work in group is carried out where the evaluators gather in a single list the problems identified. Then, an individual work continues in which each evaluator independently qualifies the severity, frequency and criticality of each of the problems in the common list. Finally, they return to work in group to consolidate and interpret the results. A ranking of usability/UX problems is established that allows determining which problems are more serious, and therefore more urgent in being corrected.

2.4 National Park Websites

The National Forestry Corporation (CONAF, as abbreviated in Spanish) in charge of national parks in Chile defines a physical national park as a generally large area, where there are several unique or representative environments of the country's natural biological diversity, not significantly altered by human action, capable of self-perpetuation and in which species of flora and fauna or geological formations are of special educational, scientific or recreational interest [11].

Other authors define a national park as terrestrial, marine areas, or a combination of both, in a natural or semi-natural state, with slight or no human population, designated to protect the ecological integrity of one or more ecosystems of international, regional or national importance and managed primarily for ecosystem conservation purposes [12].

In the United States, the concept of a national park is understood as a protected area through a law of the United States Congress, managed by the National Park Service. This concept includes all areas designated national parks and most national monuments, as well as other types of protected areas in the country. Only 58 elements of the 395 units of the US National Park System (March 2009) are properly national parks [13].

Although a formal definition of a national park website has not been found, from the literature review we infer that it is a concept that complements the physical national park; therefore, it does not have a location and its elements and information can be appreciated anywhere in the world. In this sense, for this research a national park website has been defined as a collection of web pages that provide information on the physical national park through multimedia resources. In these websites it is possible to find information about flora and fauna, images, common activities of the area, recommendations, maps, among others.

The area protected by a national park usually has a scientific interest for: (1) the presence of native and landscape species; and (2) the beauty of its landscapes. In addition to their importance for the protection of ecosystems, they become important tourist destinations [14]. Through websites, each park seeks to provide information on its main attractions, as well as characteristics of its climate, rates, services offered and activities to be carried out. The images play a critical role in this because they reflect the beauty of the place and encourage visitors to know them.

According to the purpose of the site we have classified a national park website as informative, educational, nature preservation and/or commercial:

- Informative: It allows the user to obtain information about the characteristics and relevant data about a national park.
- Educational: Teach users about characteristics, dangers, historical places, etc. from the physical national park.
- Preservation and conservation of nature: Proposes strategies to protect the physical park from hazards such as destruction, degradation, theft and pollution of the environment.
- Commercial: They seek to recommend and promote some lodgings and places to eat that are associated with the park.

Based on the literature review, we proposed the following features that define a national park website:

1. Updated information: Information about the latest news in the physical park is published in order to keep users updated.
2. Virtual experience: Allows to visit a place without the user moving, offering the user a virtual experience through different resources.
3. Multimedia resources: The way of presenting information is varied, usually through text, images, audios and videos.
4. Permissions, restrictions and recommendations: The website should present clearly the activities allowed within the physical park, recommendations and restrictions before and during a visit; either about the state of the road, the dangers or the accessibility of the park.
5. Information credibility: The information present in the various sections of the national park website should be reliable and credible for the user.
6. Asynchronous interaction: It should allow users to communicate over the Internet asynchronously, that is, temporarily independently, such as forums and blogs.
7. Useful and interesting content: The information and content presented by the website must be useful and fulfill purposes that arouse interest in users.

8. Multi-language content: The website must offer several language options in all its sections.

For the development of heuristics for national park websites, all the previous features were considered.

3 Methodology

To develop the set of UX heuristics for national park websites we applied the methodology proposed by Quiñones et al. [2, 3]. The methodology has 8 stages that can be applied iteratively to develop and validate a new set of heuristics. Table 1 shows the 8 methodology stages.

Table 1. Stages of the methodology to develop usability/UX heuristics proposed by Quiñones et al. [2, 3].

Stage	Definition
Step 1: Exploratory stage	Perform a literature review
Step 2: Experimental stage	Analyze data that are obtained in different experiments to collect additional information that has not been identified in the previous stage
Step 3: Descriptive stage	Select and prioritize the most important topics of all information that was collected in the previous stages
Step 4: Correlational stage	Match the features of the specific application domain with the usability/UX attributes and existing heuristics (and/or other relevant elements)
Step 5: Selection stage	Keep, adapt and/or discard the existing sets of usability/UX heuristics that were selected in Step 3 (and/or other relevant elements)
Step 6: Specification stage	Formally specify the new set of usability/UX heuristics
Step 7: Validation stage	Validate the set of heuristics through several experiments in terms of their effectiveness and efficiency in evaluating the specific application
Step 8: Refinement stage	Refine and improve the new set of heuristics based on the feedback that was obtained in Step 7

3.1   The National Park Websites Heuristics Development Process

Generic Nielsen's heuristics [10] are useful for evaluating systems, products or services, but they do not cover all the specific features of a national park website. Given the above, we developed a new set of heuristics using the methodology proposed by Quiñones et al. [2]. To develop the heuristics, we perform two iterations (see Fig. 1). Table 2 summarizes the stages and activities performed in the first and second iteration.

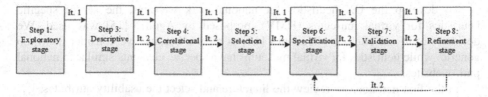

Fig. 1. Iterations performed to develop the set of UX heuristics for national park websites.

Table 2. Stages and activities performed in the two iterations to develop UX heuristics for national park websites.

Stage	Activities performed in Iteration 1	Activities performed in Iteration 2
Step 1: Exploratory stage	− Problem statement − Literature review of key concepts, such as: usability, user experience, national park websites, features	Not performed
Step 2: Experimental stage	− Not performed due to available time	Not performed
Step 3: Descriptive stage	− Selection of set of heuristics to use (Nielsen's heuristics and virtual museums heuristics) − Selection of usability and UX attributes to use (5 and 6 attributes respectively) − Selection of specific features of national park websites to use	− Identification of missing specific feature of national park websites − Selection of specific features of national park websites to use (8 features)
Step 4: Correlational stage	− Association of usability attributes and UX factors to the specific features of national park websites identified	− Association of usability attributes and UX factors to the new specific feature
Step 5: Selection stage	− Selection of the heuristics to maintain, adapt, eliminate and create using the set of heuristics for virtual museums [15] − Maintain and/or adapt: 12 heuristics − Eliminate: 3 heuristics − Create: 6 new heuristics	− Modification of 13 heuristics selected from the first proposal − Elimination of 5 heuristics of the first proposal − Creation of 1 new heuristic
Step 6: Specification stage	− Specification of 18 UX heuristics for national park websites (first proposal)	− Specification of 14 UX heuristics for national park websites (second and final proposal)
Step 7: Validation stage	− Validation of heuristics through heuristic evaluation and expert judgment (survey)	− Validation of heuristics through user tests (co-discovery and focus group)
Step 8: Refinement stage	− Detection and documentation of improvements to be made (refine 7 heuristics) − Planning of the second iteration (we decided to iterate from stage 3)	− Detection and documentation of improvements to be made (refine 4 heuristics) − Improvement of the writing of the heuristics based on the results obtained in the validation stage

To develop the UX heuristics for national park websites, the set of specific heuristics for virtual museums (HMV), proposed by Aguirre [15] was used. We decided not to use Nielsen's heuristics [10] as a basis because we consider them too generic; while heuristics for virtual museums have specific elements similar to national park websites.

In the first iteration, we review the literature and select the usability attributes, UX factors and specific application features (see Table 2). To specify the heuristics, we used the template proposed by the methodology of Quiñones et al. [2] including 13 elements: ID, priority, name, definition, explanation, application feature (national park websites), examples, benefits, problems, checklist, usability attributes, UX factors, and related heuristics. In this iteration we proposed a set of 18 heuristics. As a result of the validations performed in the first iteration, we detected redundant elements in the definition, description and elements of the checklist.

We decided to iterate to refine the proposed set. In the second iteration we detected that several heuristics shared elements in common, so we decided to review the specification of the heuristics and join those that were similar. The second and final version of the proposal ended with 14 heuristics to evaluate national park websites.

More details about the stages and activities performed to develop, validate and refine the heuristics can be find in [2] and [3].

4   User eXperience Heuristics for National Park Websites

As mentioned above, we proposed a set of 14 heuristics to evaluate the UX on national park websites. Table 3 shows the final set of heuristics including their ID, name and definition. More details about the set proposed can be find in [2] and [3].

Table 3. Set of UX heuristics for national park websites.

ID	Name	Definition
NPH1	Visibility of system	The national park website should keep the user informed about any process and change of status, within a reasonable time
NPH2	Multimedia resources	The national park website should be attractive to the user by providing a virtual experience when browsing through different multimedia resources, such as images, videos or audios
NPH3	Information of interest	The national park website should provide visible and useful information for the user, such as allowed activities, recommendations, and restrictions
NPH4	Match between system and the real world	The national park website should offer several language options and be familiar to the user, using words, phrases and concepts that are known to him/her
NPH5	User control and freedom	The national park website should allow the user to navigate freely and should provide options to do and undo some action

(*continued*)

Table 3. (*continued*)

ID	Name	Definition
NPH6	Consistency and standards	The national park website should be consistent in all its pages, following a coherent structure
NPH7	Information credibility	The information presented in the sections of the national park website should generate user confidence
NPH8	Error prevention	The national park website should be able to prevent or warn the occurrence of problems that may cause errors
NPH9	Minimize the user's memory load	The user should always have all the information available and not be forced to use his/her memory to follow the thread of the interaction
NPH10	Flexibility and efficiency of use	The national park website should be designed so that novice and expert users are able to achieve their objectives when browsing the website
NPH11	Aesthetic and minimalist design	The national park website should show relevant elements, with a design that is pleasing to the eye and that has a logical structure without redundant elements
NPH12	Help the user recover from errors	Whenever an error occurs, clear and simple messages should be shown to the user with the origin of the problem and suggestions to solve it
NPH13	Help and documentation	The national park website should offer help and documentation that is geared towards the specific tasks that the user performs
NPH14	Asynchronous interaction	Users should be allowed to communicate over the Internet asynchronously, that is, temporarily independently, such as forums and blogs

5 Heuristics Validation

The methodology proposed several methods to validate a new set of heuristics [2]. The experiments performed make it possible to check the effectiveness and efficiency of the new set of heuristics when evaluating the UX of national park websites.

To validate the set of heuristics proposed, we performed two iterations. In the first iteration we validated the heuristics through heuristic evaluation and expert judgment. In the second iteration we validated the heuristics through user test, specifically, co-discovery and focus group.

In the heuristic evaluation, we checked the new set of UX heuristics for national park websites (NPH) against heuristics for virtual museums [15] (VMH). The Yellowstone National Park Website (https://www.nps.gov/yell/index.htm) was evaluated by evaluators with similar experience performing heuristic evaluations. The "control group" (3 evaluators) used the VMH to identify usability/UX problems, and the "experimental group" (3 evaluators) used the new set of heuristics proposed, NPH. With the results, we evaluated the effectiveness of the heuristics in terms of the 5 criteria [2,

3]: (1) number of correct and incorrect associations of problems to heuristics; (2) number of usability/UX problems that were identified; (3) number of specific usability/UX problems that were identified; (4) number of identified usability/UX problems that qualify as more severe; and (5) number of identified usability/UX problems that qualify as more critical. The new set of heuristics performs well, and it is an effective instrument when better results than the control heuristics (VMH) are obtained in terms of the 5 criteria.

NPH obtained better results than VMH in the criteria (1) (NPH has a higher percentage of correct associations and a lower percentage of incorrect associations); (3) (NPH finds more specific usability/UX problems than VMH); (4) (NPH finds more usability/UX problems qualify as more severe than VMH); and (5) (NPH finds more usability/UX problems qualify as more critical than VMH). For criterion (2), NPH did not identify the highest amount of problems, so it was necessary to perform additional experiments to review and improve NPH (we performed a second iteration). The detailed results obtained in the heuristic evaluation can be reviewed in [3].

In addition, in the first iteration we applied a survey to 3 experts performing heuristic evaluations. We applied a questionnaire that assesses evaluators' perceptions of PNH, concerning 4 dimensions (D1 – Utility, D2 – Clarity, D3 – Ease of use, D4 – Necessity of an additional checklist) and 3 questions (Q1 – Easiness, Q2 – Intention of use, Q3 – Completeness) [3].

Based on the results, we refined several heuristics. We eliminated 4 heuristics as there were similarities to others. In addition, the experts gave some comments regarding heuristics. In general, experts commented that heuristics covered the specific features of national park websites. One of the evaluators stated that there were similarities between the heuristics "Content visualization" and "Aesthetic and minimalist design"; and between the heuristics "Virtual Experience" and "Multimedia Resources", so we joined some heuristics into one and we refined their specifications.

In the second iteration, we validated the heuristics through Co-discovery and Focus group. Co-discovery (also named "constructive interaction") is a user test method where users work collaboratively to complete tasks when interacting with a system. Users can help each other through difficulties, learn from each other and solve problems together to complete different tasks [16]. Focus group is a technique where a group of users participate in a discussion, in this case, to discuss about their perception using a system in order to identify usability/UX problems.

The Co-discovery test was designed based on the usability/UX problems identified by the control group that were not detected by the experimental group in the heuristic evaluation performed in the first iteration (Yellowstone National Park Website). To design the tasks, those usability/UX problems with a severity greater than 2 and/or a criticality greater than 4 were selected (these problems were: "difficulty finding information due to the English language", "high content of static and theoretical information", "difficulty to use the search engine due to confusing options", "little representation of the calendar icon", and "small size of the images").

In the experiment participated 16 students (8 couples) between 20 and 26 years old of the Multilingual Tourism Administration program, from the University of Playa Ancha, Chile. As a result, most users were satisfied with the information found on the website and would visit it again at another time. In addition, in general the participants maintained a neutral stance in view of the difficulty of the work done, but the results obtained were mostly effective.

The same users who participated in the Co-discovery test participated in the Focus group. The participants were divided into two groups (one group of 8 people and another group of 6 people, since 2 people could not participate). The objective of the focus group was to collect qualitative information about the perception of users regarding the use of the Yellowstone National Park Website, and then verify if the problems mentioned were possible to evaluate and identify with the set of UX heuristics proposed for evaluating national park websites.

Both groups commented that it would be essential for a national park website to have audios, videos, images, maps and recommendations that complement each other to improve the virtual user experience. The perceptions mentioned indicate that users consider the presence of multimedia resources important, feature covered by the heuristic "Multimedia Resources" (NPH2). Both groups had a negative perception about the amount of information the national park website presented on a single page, which caused them disgust. This problem is covered by the heuristic "Aesthetic and minimalist design" (NPH11).

In addition, the users highlighted positively the presence of content of interest, such as the main information of the park, the map of its extension, recommendations, places to visit and rates. Although, they pointed out that there should be a section that notifies or shows the closest events to make them easier to find. The above is covered by the heuristic "Information of interest" (NPH3). On the other hand, users highlighted that the contents were updated and came from a reliable source, which is related to the heuristic "Information credibility" (NPH7).

Both groups stated that one aspect that the national park website does not consider and that they find highly relevant to deal with is the variety of languages, which is directly related to the heuristic "Match between system and the real world" (HPN4).

Finally, one group positively highlighted the search engine that owns the website, which they considered easy to use and helpful to find what they need, an aspect that is covered by the heuristic "Flexibility and efficiency of use" (NPH10). In addition, they stated that it would be very useful to have a section with the comments and opinions of other users who have visited the park, both virtual and physical, as it gives them greater information security. The above is covered by the heuristic "Asynchronous Interaction" (NPH14). We concluded that all perceptions, opinions and problems discussed by the two groups were evaluated by the set of heuristics proposed.

6 Conclusions

The User eXperience (UX) is an important element to consider when designing products, systems and services. In this sense, the UX evaluation is critical to detect those problems that generate frustration, to improve the interaction and the overall user experience.

National park websites are a type of website aimed at delivering information about the physical national park. After reviewing the literature, we did not find a definition about these types of websites, so we proposed a definition based on the description of a physical national park, adding relevant elements related to websites.

The website of a national park does not attempt to replace physical visits, but is aimed at those users who cannot access in person. The website allows them to interact and learn about national parks.

We proposed a set of 14 heuristics to evaluate the user experience on national park websites. We performed two iterations to validate and refine the proposed set. The results obtained allow us to verify that the heuristics are effective, since they allow to detect specific usability/UX problems related to national park websites.

As future work we intent to further validate the heuristics through heuristic evaluations in other case studies, and user tests considering other user profiles.

References

1. Nielsen, J., Molich, R.: Heuristic evaluation of user interfaces. In: Proceeding of Conference on Human factors in Computing Systems. SIGCHI 1990, pp. 249–256 (1990)
2. Quiñones, D., Rusu, C., Rusu, V.: A methodology to develop usability/user experience heuristics. Comput. Stand. Interfaces **59**, 109–129 (2018)
3. Quiñones, D., Rusu, C.: Applying a methodology to develop user experience heuristics. Comput. Stand. Interfaces **66**, 103345 (2019)
4. ISO 9241-210. Ergonomics of Human-system Interaction—Part 210: Human-centred Design for Interactive Systems. International Organization for Standardization (2010)
5. Nielsen, J.: Usability 101: Introduction to Usability (2012). https://www.nngroup.com/articles/usability-101-introduction-to-usability/. Accessed 29 Jan 2020
6. Montero, H., Fernández, M., Francisco, J.: La Experiencia del Usuario. http://www.nosolousabilidad.com/articulos/experiencia_del_usuario.htm. Accessed 29 Jan 2020
7. Morville, P.: User Experience Design (2004). http://semanticstudios.com/user_experience_design/. Accessed 29 Jan 2020
8. World Wide Web Consortium (W3C): Making the Web Accessible (2020). https://www.w3.org/WAI/. Accessed 29 Jan 2020
9. Usability Partners: Methods. http://www.usabilitypartners.se/about-usability/methods#heuristic-evaluation. Accessed 29 Jan 2020
10. Nielsen, J.: Ten Usability Heuristics. https://www.nngroup.com/articles/tenusability-heuristics/. Accessed 29 Jan 2020
11. Conaf: Parques de Chile. http://www.conaf.cl/parques-nacionales/parques-de-chile. Accessed 29 Jan 2020
12. EcuRed: Parque Nacional. https://www.ecured.cu/Parque_Nacional. Accessed 29 Jan 2020
13. Parque nacional (Estados Unidos). https://es.wikipedia.org/wiki/Parque_nacional_(Estados_Unidos). Accessed 29 Jan 2020
14. Definición de parque nacional. http://definicion.de/parque-nacional/. Accessed 29 Jan 2020
15. Aguirre, N.: Experiencia de Usuario en Museos Virtuales, Undergraduate Thesis Pontificia Universidad Católica de Valparaíso, Chile (2015)
16. Jordan, P.W.: Designing Pleasurable Products: An Introduction to the New Human Factors. CRC Press, Boca Raton (2002)

Programmer eXperience: A Set of Heuristics for Programming Environments

Jenny Morales[1]([✉]) [ID], Cristian Rusu[2] [ID], Federico Botella[3] [ID], and Daniela Quiñones[2] [ID]

[1] Facultad de Ingeniería, Universidad Autónoma de Chile, Av. 5 Poniente 1670,
3460000 Talca, Chile
jmoralesb@uautonoma.cl
[2] Pontificia Universidad Católica de Valparaíso, Av. Brasil 2241,
2340000 Valparaíso, Chile
{cristian.rusu,daniela.quinones}@pucv.cl
[3] Universidad Miguel Hernández de Elche, Avinguda de la Universitat d'Elx s/n,
03202 Elche, Spain
federico@umh.es

Abstract. The definition of user experience (UX) is broad and covers several aspects. The job of any programmer is very specific and demanding. He/she uses different systems or tools to carry out their programming tasks. We consider a programmer as a specific case of user, who employs programming environments and other software development artifacts. We therefore consider this particular kind of UX as Programmer eXperience (PX). Several authors have defined different aspects of PX, including, among others, language features, programming learning factors or programmer performance. Usability is a relevant aspect of UX, as well as an important aspect of programming environments. Heuristic evaluation is an inspection method that allows evaluating the usability of interactive software systems. We developed a set of heuristics following the methodology proposed by Quiñones et al. We defined a new set of 12 specific heuristics that incorporate concepts of UX and usability of programming environments. These heuristics have been validated following also that methodology. The results obtained in different effectiveness criteria were satisfactory. However, the set of heuristics could be further refined and validate in new scenarios or case studies.

Keywords: Programmer eXperience · User eXperience · Usability · Heuristic evaluation · Programming environments

1 Introduction

Programming environments are systems that provide different tools that facilitate the work of a programmer. The definition of UX is quite broad and refers to the perceptions of a user in relation to different products, systems and/or services [1]. In this work, we consider the programmer as a user and Programmer eXperience (PX) a specific kind of UX.

G. Meiselwitz (Ed.): HCII 2020, LNCS 12195, pp. 205–216, 2020.
https://doi.org/10.1007/978-3-030-49576-3_15

In previous works, we found that the PX is related to the motivation and perception of the programmer. PX is also related to the choice of development tools as the programming environments. We also found that most studies focus on the usability of programming environments. One way to evaluate usability is through heuristic evaluation. To perform a heuristic evaluation, a specific set of heuristics is needed to find usability problems in a specific domain.

In this paper, we present a set of heuristics that incorporates aspects of UX and usability to evaluate programming environments. We followed the methodology proposed by Quiñones et al. in 2018 [2] to develop the set of heuristics. This methodology contains 8 stages, which allow the development of heuristics and their validation. We developed a new set of 12 specific heuristics that incorporates concepts of UX and usability of programming environments. The set of heuristics was validated through two experiments established in the methodology used: expert judgment and heuristic evaluation. The results obtained allowed us to establish the effectiveness of the proposed set. In both experiments we evaluated several criteria and dimensions.

The paper is organized as follows. Section 2 introduces the theoretical background. Section 3 describes the methodology followed to develop the set of heuristics and the results obtained. Finally, in Sect. 4 we present conclusions and future work.

2   Theoretical Background

2.1   User eXperience

User eXperience (UX) is defined by the International Organization for Standardization (ISO) 9241-210 as follows: "user's perceptions and responses that result from the use and/or anticipated use of a system, product, or service" [1]. To explain the UX several authors have proposed models, one of them is Morville's "Honeycomb" [3]. This model is composed of seven aspects which are briefly identified below:

- Useful: the system or product must be useful and meet a need, otherwise there is no justification for the product.
- Usable: ease of use is vital. The system must be simple and easy to use. Usability is necessary but is not sufficient.
- Desirable: the visual aesthetics of the product or system should be balanced and in relation to the elements of emotional design.
- Findable: the system must be easy to navigate and incorporate objects easy to find. Users can find what they need.
- Accessible: the system must be accessible for all users, including those with disabilities.
- Credible: companies, products or services must be reliable for users.
- Valuable: the system must deliver value to our sponsors. The user experience must contribute to customer satisfaction and/or advance in the mission depending on the organization.

2.2   Usability

Usability is an important element within the user experience. ISO 9241-11 of 2018 [4] defines usability as follows: "extent to which a system, product or service can be used by specified users to achieve specified goals with effectiveness, efficiency and satisfaction in a specified context of use". Also, this standard defines effectiveness, efficiency and satisfaction as follow:

- Effectiveness: accuracy and completeness with which users achieve specified goals.
- Efficiency: resources used in relation to the results achieved.
- Satisfaction: extent to which the user's physical, cognitive and emotional responses that result from the use of a system, product or service meet the user's needs and expectations.

Nielsen in 1993 [5] explained that the usability has five attributes that allow to evaluate it and possibly measure it:

- Learning: the system can be learned and used quickly by the user.
- Efficiency: related to the level of productivity that the user can achieve when using the system.
- Memorability: related to the ease of being remembered by non-frequent users.
- Errors: related to the number of mistakes a user makes when performing a task. The system must have low rates of errors.
- Subjective Satisfaction: the users must be satisfied when using the system.

2.3   Programmer eXperience

We consider the programmer as a user of different systems and artifacts in their work. One kind of system is the programming environment. In a systematic literature review [6] we found several articles that address usability in programming environments for different users (end users and professional users) [7–10]. Also, we carried out experiments in previous works in order to evaluate the perception of the usability in programming environments used by students and professional programmers. The results obtained showed that two of three Integrated Development Environments (IDE) obtained low usability scores [11]. This indicates that usability is an important aspect that must be developed and improved in programming environments. In addition, we found articles that propose sets of heuristics to evaluate programming environments [12], programming languages and programmer environments [13].

As mentioned earlier, usability is an important element in the programmer experience, when the programmer uses a programming environment. However, it is not the only factor that affects PX, because of we have to consider other elements as the aspects indicated in the "honeycomb" model of user experience.

The programmer experience has a close relationship with the user experience because PX considers the perception of programmers about systems, products and services (in this work the systems are programming environments). In addition, PX has a personal component related to the intrinsic and extrinsic motivations that the programmer has. Other skills like technical and social skills can facilitate their performance in a development group [6].

2.4   Heuristic Evaluation

Heuristic evaluation (HE) is an inspection method that allows us to evaluate the usability of interfaces [14]. HE is carried out by a group of evaluators, who may or may not be experts. The evaluators examine the interface and judge the compliance of the usability principles in the interfaces.

The usability principles are heuristics grouped in sets. A set of heuristics can be general like in Nielsen's heuristics, or specific to the product to evaluate, such as social networks, languages or programming environments.

One HE is less expensive than a test with users and can be performed in a short period of time [14].

3   Methodology

The development of the heuristics to evaluate the programming environments was performed based on the methodology proposed by Quiñones et al. [2]. This methodology contains 8 stages, which can be carried out iteratively, optionally, or overlapped depending on the specific case. Next, we explain briefly each stage:

1. Exploratory stage: perform a literature review.
2. Experimental stage: analyze data that are obtained in different experiments to collect additional information that has not been identified in the previous stage.
3. Descriptive stage: select and prioritize the most important topics of all information that was collected in the previous stages.
4. Correlational stage: match the features of the specific application domain with the usability/UX attributes and existing heuristics (and/or other relevant elements).
5. Selection stage: keep, adapt and/or discard the existing sets of usability/UX heuristics that were selected in Step 3 (and/or other relevant elements).
6. Specification stage: formally specify the new set of usability/UX heuristics.
7. Validation stage: validate the set of heuristics through several experiments in terms of their effectiveness and efficiency in evaluating the specific application.
8. Refinement stage: refine and improve the new set of heuristics based on the feedback that was obtained in previous stage.

This methodology allows obtaining a set of heuristics in a specific domain incorporating aspects of usability and user experience. In this work, the programming environments are the specific domain used by programmers.

3.1   Heuristics Development

We followed the methodology carefully. We collect relevant information from different scientific databases in relation to the specific domain and found several features, usability/UX attributes, and sets of heuristics. Regarding the sets of heuristics found, two sets of heuristics about programming environments were used in the development of our new set and we refer to them as base sets.

The first set evaluates programming environments [12] and has 9 heuristics. This set is an adaptation of the set proposed by Nielsen, to evaluate programming environments. In this work we identified this set with the abbreviation NA (Nielsen Adapted) followed by the corresponding number. In Table 1 we can see the set of heuristics adapted from Nielsen.

Table 1. Set adapted from Nielsen [12].

Id	Heuristic	Definition
NA-1	Visibility	Informs user about program status
NA-2	Real-word match	Speaks developer's language (e.g., dialogs are understandable)
NA-3	Control	Users feels in control of what they are developing (the application), and not just controlling the IDE
NA-4	Consistency	Coherent, predictable system behavior and appearance
NA-5	Error handling	Clear error messages and recovery
NA-6	Recognition, not recall	Minimizes memory load
NA-7	Flexibility	Suits users of varying experience
NA-8	Minimalist design	Shows only relevant information
NA-9	Relevant help	Easy to search and find information

The second set evaluates programming languages and programming environments [13]. This set is more extensive than the previous one and includes aspects of learning, languages and programming environments. We identified this set with the abbreviation EL (Environments and Languages) followed by corresponding number. Table 2 shows EL set with their 13 heuristics.

Table 2. Set of heuristics proposed [13].

Id	Heuristic	Definition
EL-1	Engagement	The system should engage and motivate the intended audience of learners. It should stimulate learners' interest or sense of fun
EL-2	Non-threatening	The system should not appear threatening in its appearance or behavior. Users should feel safe in the knowledge that they can experiment without breaking the system or losing data
EL-3	Minimal language redundancy	The programming language should minimize redundancy in language constructs and libraries
EL-4	Learner-appropriate abstractions	The system should use abstractions that are at the appropriate level for the learner and task. Abstractions

(continued)

Table 2. (*continued*)

Id	Heuristic	Definition
		should be driven by pedagogy, not by the underlying machine
EL-5	Consistency	The model, language and interface presentation should be consistent, internally, and with each other. Concepts used in the programming model should be represented in the system interface consistently
EL-6	Visibility	The user should always be aware of system status and progress. It should be simple to navigate to parts of the system displaying other relevant data, such as other parts of a program under development
EL-7	Secondary notations	The system should automatically provide secondary notations where this is helpful and users should be allowed to add their own secondary notations where practical
EL-8	Clarity	The presentation should maintain simplicity and clarity, avoiding visual distractions. This applies to the programming language and to other interface elements of the environment
EL-9	Human-centric syntax	The program notation should use human-centric syntax. Syntactic elements should be easily readable, avoiding terminology obscure to the target audience
EL-10	Edit-order freedom	The interface should allow the user freedom in the order they choose to work. Users should be able to leave tasks partially finished and come back to them later
EL-11	Minimal viscosity	The system should minimize viscosity in program entry and manipulation. Making common changes to program text should be as easy as possible
EL-12	Error-avoidance	Preference should be given to preventing errors over reporting them. The system should prevent or work around an error
EL-13	Feedback	The system should provide timely and constructive feedback. The feedback should indicate the source of a problem and offer solutions

We considered experiments carried out by other authors to complement the information collected previously. We performed our own experiments in order to incorporate features or usability problems that were not found in the reviewed articles.

We then prioritized the information collected and decided what aspects, attributes and set of heuristics are considered important in the development of our new set. Also, we decided what actions to take over the existing set of heuristics: creating, adapting, maintaining or eliminating. The actions made over these sets of heuristics are shown in Fig. 1.

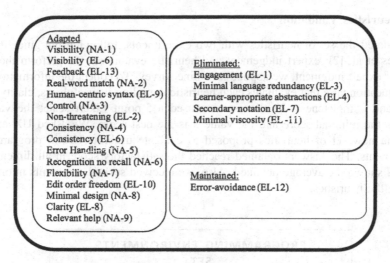

Fig. 1. Actions made with heuristics found.

The first version of the proposed heuristics set is shown in Table 3. The obtained set is composed of 12 heuristics, created by considering the heuristic sets found (base sets), and performing the actions mentioned and explained previously.

The proposed set contains 9 adapted heuristics, one maintained heuristic and two new heuristics. We identify with the abbreviation PE (Programming Environment) and its corresponding number.

Table 3. Set of heuristics for programming environments (1st iteration).

ID	Heuristics	Description
PE-1	Visibility	Inspired by the basic heuristics. Adapted heuristics
PE-2	Programmer Words	Inspired by the basic heuristics. Adapted heuristics
PE-3	Control	Inspired by the basic heuristics. Adapted heuristics
PE-4	Consistency	Inspired by the basic heuristics. Adapted heuristics
PE-5	Error-Avoidance	Maintained heuristic
PE-6	Recognition	Inspired by the basic heuristics. Adapted heuristics
PE-7	Flexibility of Use	Inspired by the basic heuristics. Adapted heuristics
PE-8	Minimalist Design	Inspired by the basic heuristics. Adapted heuristics
PE-9	Error Handling	Inspired by the basic heuristics. Adapted heuristics
PE-10	Help	Inspired by the basic heuristics. Adapted heuristics
PE-11	Configurable Screen	New heuristic created
PE-12	Automatic feedback	New heuristic created

3.2   Heuristics Validation

We validated the set of heuristics with two experiments, following the guidelines of Quiñones et al. [2]: expert judgement and heuristic evaluation. To perform the validation of expert judgment, we applied an online survey. To collect the information, we used a questionnaire that evaluates each heuristic regarding its usefulness, clarity, ease of use and completeness. In all cases we used a 5-point Likert scale; the value 1 indicates the minimal score and the value 5 is the best score. We asked UX experts about the new set of heuristics proposed to evaluate usability/UX in programming environments. The answers obtained reached the satisfactory score in all dimensions. Figure 2 shown the average obtained. Also, we received several comments in order to improve the heuristics.

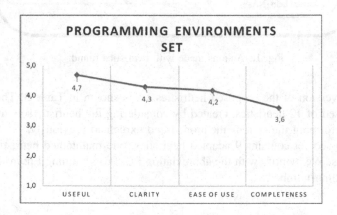

Fig. 2. Results survey experts.

To perform the heuristic evaluation, we consider an IDE as a case study and develop a heuristic evaluation with two groups: the experimental group that worked with the heuristics proposed by us and the control group that worked with a summary version of the heuristics of Kölling and McKay [13]. The results obtained were favorable for our proposed heuristics in various effectiveness criteria, such as Number of correct associations of the problem with the heuristics, Number of specific usability/UX problems identified and Number of usability/UX problems identified qualifies as more severe. For example, Number of correct associations of the problem with the heuristics are shown in Eq. (1) for experimental group and in Eq. (2) for the control group. The experimental group obtained the better results than experimental group in relation to correct association.

$$Correct\,Associations\,(CA1) = (26/30) * 100 = 86.67\%. \tag{1}$$

$$Correct\,Associations(CA2) = (15\,/\,25) * 100 = 60.00\% \tag{2}$$

The comments obtained from the experts in both experiments (expert judgment and heuristic evaluation) were considered. Modifications were made in the set of heuristics. In general, a description of the example image of heuristic compliance was added in each heuristic. In addition, we improve consistency in heuristics in some cases the names, definitions and explanations. These changes in all cases were minor but improved the accuracy of heuristics.

3.3   The Set of Usability/UX Heuristics for Programming Environments

The set of heuristics that we proposed and validated for programming environments is shown in Table 4. In this table we identified each heuristic by means of id, name and definition. The first ten heuristics are adaptations of the heuristics base and the last two correspond to new heuristics created.

The definition of each heuristic must be done in detail, so we used a template with several elements following the methodology used.

An example of a template used to define the heuristics is shown in Table 5. In this table we can see the Automatic Feedback heuristic (PE-12). The elements contained in the template are the indicated by the Quiñones et al. methodology [2]:

- Id: contains the heuristic identifier.
- Name: indicates the name of the heuristic.
- Definition: a brief definition of heuristics.
- Explanation: a more detailed explanation of the heuristic.
- Explanation of the figure: a detailed explanation of the example figure, which represents the accomplishment of the heuristic, incorporating used environment, operating system in addition to the context of the figure.
- Example figure: an image that represents the fulfillment of the heuristic.
- Benefits: identification of the expected benefits associated with the fulfillment of the heuristic.
- Usability attributes and/or UX aspects: aspects associated with the heuristic.

Table 4. A Set of heuristics for programming environments.

ID	Heuristics	Definition
PE-1	Visibility	The programming environment must keep the user informed about its status. In addition, it must deliver timely information
PE-2	Programmer Language	The programming environment must speak the programmer language without ambiguous terminology
PE-3	Control	The programming environments must give control to the programmer on his/her project, in a safe way
PE-4	Consistency	The programming environments must be consistent in appearance and behavior

(continued)

Table 4. (*continued*)

ID	Heuristics	Definition
PE-5	Error-Prevention	The programming environments should favor the prevention of errors over their reporting. If the system can prevent or workaround an error, then it should do it
PE-6	Recognition	Programming environments should minimize the memory load of the programmer, favoring recognition
PE-7	Flexibility of Use	The programming environments must allow different ways of use
PE-8	Minimalist Design	The programming environments must show only important information orderly and clear
PE-9	Error Handling and Recovery	The programming environments should offer clear error messages and facilities to recovery
PE-10	Help	The programming environments must provide aid for programmers in relation to the way they should be used
PE-11	Configurable Interface	The programming environments must allow the programmer to customize its interface
PE-12	Automatic feedback	The programming environment should offer the programmer automatic feedback that facilitates his/her work

Table 5. Example of heuristic specification: Automatic Feedback PE-12.

Id	PE-12
Priority	3
Name	Automatic feedback
Definition	The programming environment should offer the programmer automatic feedback that facilitates his/her work
Explanation	The environment should offer immediate feedback and provide suggestions to complete a sentence, self-documentation, auto code detection, and the use of color-coding
Examples	The picture shows heuristic compliance The programming environment provides different automatic feedback such as recognition of reserved words in specific colors, suggests methods and/or functions of objects or data types This automatic feedback is delivered when the programmer writes or moves the mouse over the object The programming environment used in the image was Visual Studio Code version 1.36 on macOS and the IDE used in this image was Dev-C++ version 5.11 on Windows operating system

(*continued*)

Table 5. (*continued*)

Id	PE-12
Picture	
Benefits	It facilitates the work of the programmer, improving efficiency
Usability/UX attribute	Usable and useful (UX) Memorability, learnability, error and efficiency (Usability)

4 Conclusions and Future Work

A programmer is a specific user of systems, products and services. We focus this work on programmer experience (PX), which we identify as a specific case of the user experience (UX). The PX is affected by the tools that programmers use. One of these commonly used tools are programming environments.

In this work, we present the development of a set of heuristics to evaluate programming environments, which includes aspects of usability/UX. The development of the set of heuristics has been carried out under a rigorous methodology that allowed us to obtain a specific set which is made up of 12 specific heuristics. This set was subjected to validation through two experiments: expert judgment and heuristic evaluation. In both cases, the results obtained allowed us to validate the heuristics and were also refined to obtain a final set presented in this work.

This work focuses on one of the most important artifacts that a programmer uses, the programming environments. As future work we intend to further validate the set of heuristics in new contexts and case studies. We also intend to develop sets of heuristics for other software development artifacts evaluation, such as programming codes, design documents or programming languages.

Acknowledgment. We are grateful to all experts that participated in the survey. We also thank to all participants in the heuristic evaluation. Jenny Morales is a beneficiary of one INF-PUCV doctoral scholarship.

References

1. ISO 9241-210: Ergonomics of human-system interaction - Part 11: Usability: Definitions and concepts. International Organization for Standardization, Geneva (2018)
2. Quiñones, D., Rusu, C., Rusu, V.: A methodology to develop usability/user experience heuristics. Comput. Stand. Interfaces **59**, 109–129 (2018)
3. Morville, P.: User experience honeycomb. http://semanticstudios.com/user_experience_design/. Accessed 14 Dec 2019
4. ISO 9241-11: Ergonomics of human-system interaction - Part 11: Usability: Definitions and concepts. International Organization for Standardization, Geneva (2018)
5. Nielsen, J.: Usability Engineering. AP Professional, Boston (1993)
6. Morales, J., Rusu, C., Botella, F., Quiñones, D.: Programmer eXperience: a systematic literature review. IEEE Access **7**, 71079–71094 (2019)
7. Cao, J., Fleming, S.D., Burnett, M.: An exploration of design opportunities for 'gardening' end-user programmers' ideas. In: Proceedings of the IEEE Symposium Visual Languages and Human-Centric Computing (VL/HCC), Pittsburgh, USA, pp. 35–42 (2011)
8. Kuttal, S.K., Sarma, A., Rothermel, G., Wang, Z.: What happened to my application? Helping end users comprehend evolution through variation management. Inf. Softw. Technol. **103**, 55–74 (2018)
9. Smith, J., Brown, C., Murphy-Hill, E.: Flower: navigating program flow in the IDE. In: Proceedings IEEE Symposium Visual Languages Human-Centric Computing (VL/HCC), Raleigh, USA, pp. 19–23 (2017)
10. Traver, V.J.: On compiler error messages: What they say and what they mean. Adv. Hum.-Comput. Interact. **2010**, 1–26 (2010)
11. Morales, J., Botella, F., Rusu, C., Quiñones, D.: How "friendly" integrated development environments are? In: Meiselwitz, G. (ed.) HCII 2019. LNCS, vol. 11578, pp. 80–91. Springer, Cham (2019). https://doi.org/10.1007/978-3-030-21902-4_7
12. Kline, R.B., Seffah, A.: Evaluation of integrated software development environments: challenges and results from three empirical studies. Int. J. Hum.-Comput. Stud. **63**(6), 607–627 (2005)
13. Kölling, M., McKay, F.: Heuristic evaluation for novice programming systems. ACM Trans. Comput. Educ. (TOCE) **16**(3), 12 (2016)
14. Nielsen, J., Molich, R.: Heuristic evaluation of user interfaces. In: Proceedings of the SIGCHI Conference on Human Factors in Computing Systems, pp. 249–256. ACM (1990)

Understanding User Needs and Customer eXperience in Tourism Area

Luis Rojas, Daniela Quiñones[✉], and Cristian Rusu

Pontificia Universidad Católica de Valparaíso, Valparaíso, Chile
luis.rojas.o01@mail.pucv.cl,
{daniela.quinones, cristian.rusu}@pucv.cl

Abstract. Customer eXperience (CX) is one of the most important factors among companies and organizations to gain a competitive advantage in the area of tourism. To achieve this leadership in this area, it is important that industries focus on understanding the needs of their different customers, because the needs that a customer has and expects to satisfy when using products, systems or services, are not the same than those of another customer. This research presents a review and analysis of several articles related to the customer experience regarding hotels, restaurants and airlines in the tourism area. We classified the needs into these three industries or sectors and for each of them, we present the customer's needs in a general way and then highlight some of these needs for the different classifications as purpose of travel (business or leisure), type of traveler (solo, couple, family, or friends) and cultural differences.

Keywords: Customer eXperience · Customer needs · Tourism · Touchpoints

1 Introduction

Nowadays it is very common to find similar products or services coming from different companies. This generates a lot of competition in the industry and the need to differentiate from the rest in order to be able to attract a greater number of customers. Because of this, companies no longer think only about the price and quality of their various offers, but now focus on a new factor that a few decades ago was not as important as today, the experience, specifically what their customers experience through the different moments and channels of interaction with the company. This experience is called Customer eXperience (CX), but as it is a relatively new concept, there is still confusion about giving it a general definition.

Customers always interact with companies in different ways generating a set of experiences. These different instances/points of contact between customers and companies -through products, systems or services- are called touchpoints. Touchpoints are really important as they are where customers create an image of the company. If customers have a terrible experience/interaction in any touchpoint, it can cause a bad impression of the entire company. For this reason, touchpoints have great value for organizations, because they provide information that allows them to know in which interactions with their customers stand out or need to improve.

© Springer Nature Switzerland AG 2020
G. Meiselwitz (Ed.): HCII 2020, LNCS 12195, pp. 217–225, 2020.
https://doi.org/10.1007/978-3-030-49576-3_16

Tourism industry is a growing economic area which is composed of various types of businesses, such as hotels, museums, restaurants, among others. In this area companies seek to deliver the best kind of experience to their customers to stand out from the competition. However, companies need to realize that there are different types of customers with different needs. There are customers who come from different countries, continents or regions of the world, who have different cultures. As well there are those who travel alone, with friends, family, couple, etc. Each of them traveling for specific purposes such as leisure or business. Therefore, companies must adapt their products, systems or services according to the needs of different customers.

It is important to know how companies and organizations identify customers and their needs, specifically in the tourism area, what are the most used products, systems and/or services and how is the interaction. Thus, it is possible to detect those touchpoints at which customers have a bad experience and seek for ways to improve the interaction and the complete customer experience. This article presents an analysis of different articles related to the CX in the tourism area. We discussed and analyzed the relationship between the different sectors/industries related to the tourism area (hotels, restaurants, and airlines) and the different customer needs according to their type of traveler (solo, couple, family, or friends), purpose of travel (leisure or business), and cultural differences. The document is organized as follows: Sect. 2 presents the concept of customer experience, tourism and its evaluation methods; Sect. 3 presents the customer needs in the tourism area; and Sect. 4 presents the conclusion and future work.

2   Theoretical Background

2.1   Customer eXperience

Customer eXperience (CX) is a concept that currently has aroused the interest of companies from different sectors. However, there is still no generally accepted CX definition. According to Meyer & Schwager [1], CX is "the internal and subjective response customers have to any direct or indirect contact with a company". Klaus & Maklan [2] define CX as "the customer's cognitive and affective assessment of all direct and indirect encounters with the firm relating to their purchasing behavior". Laming & Mason [3] describe CX as "the physical and emotional experiences occurring through the interactions with the product and/or service offering of a brand from point of first direct, conscious contact, through the total journey to the post-consumption stage". It can be observed how different definitions of CX have been proposed over the years. Nevertheless, they share some statements with which certain approximations can be obtained, such as: (1) result of customer-organization interaction through products, services or systems; (2) the interaction can be direct or indirect, positive or negative; and (3) it is totally subjective, as they are the customer's perceptions.

Furthermore, several authors propose different dimensions, attributes and/or aspects that define the CX. Gentile, Spiller and Noci [4] focused their research under a widely-known brands perspective. Authors propose six dimensions of CX: (1) sensorial: aim to provide good sensorial experience through any of the five senses to arise, e.g., aesthetical pleasure, excitement, satisfaction, or sense of beauty; (2) emotional: generation of moods, feelings, emotions to create an affective relation with the company, its brand or products; (3) cognitive: related to customer's thinking and conscious mental processes, engage customers by using their creativity or problem solving abilities; (4) pragmatic: associated to practical act of doing something and the concept of usability through all the product life-cycle stages; (5) lifestyle: refers to values and beliefs shared by the company and the customer through the product, its consumption and/or use; and (6) relational: involves customer's social context, relationship with other people and their own ideals.

For another perspective focused on sport tourism, Klaus and Maklan [5] identify five dimensions of CX: (1) hedonic enjoyment: related to hedonism and excitement which is felt, perceived and experienced by participants at any time; (2) personal progression: refers to making 'progress', improving their skills and technique, giving great value to the participants; (3) surreal feeling: associated to recollections of a dream-like state, an almost altered stage of reality based on a certain activity or encounter; (4) social interaction: sense of belonging to a community where members share common ground; and (5) efficiency: associated with physical attributes and the organizational flow.

Related to the tourism area, Gopalan and Narayan [6] states that "The customer experience in tourism consists of an assorted bundle of experiences, starting with the immigration desk and customs clearance at the airport". While Tung and Ritchie [7] define tourism experience as "An individual's subjective evaluation and undergoing (i.e., affective, cognitive, and behavioural) of events related to his/her tourist activities which begins before (i.e., planning and preparation), during (i.e., at the destination), and after the trip (i.e., recollection)".

2.2 Tourism

Tourism is one of the economic sectors with the greatest impact worldwide, as it creates jobs, drives exports and generates prosperity across the world [8]. The World Tourism Organization (UNWTO) [9] defines tourism as a social, cultural and economic phenomenon involving the movement of persons within or outside their country for different purposes, such as leisure or business.

Within tourism there are multiple classifications, such as (1) by type of traveler: solo, couple, family, or friends; (2) by purpose of travel: leisure or business mainly, although some authors include conferences, education, among others; or (3) by type of travel: domestic or international (inbound – outbound).

Tourism is composed of different sectors/industries such as hotels (e.g. upscale hotels, bed and breakfast, green hotels), restaurants (e.g. local, fine, ethnic), airlines, museums, amusement parks, among others.

Interaction between customers and the tourism industry occurs at multiple touchpoints of the customer's journey. On this journey, customers can relate to different industries through several products, systems or services. This interaction can be direct, indirect, passive or active, and be perceived by any of the human basic senses (sight, hearing, smell, taste or touch) [38].

For example, if a couple wants to do international tourism for leisure purposes, they could interact with any of the following sectors: (1) to travel to their destination, with airlines, trains, or a cruise ship; (2) to stay at their destination, with some type of hotel; (3) to feed, with some type of restaurant; and (4) to have fun, they can interact with shopping centers, museums, city tours, among others. Thus, in each of these encounters, the customer interacts with different companies/sectors -through products, systems or services-.

2.3   Customer Experience Evaluation

Customer experience evaluations are mainly focused into find how customers feel when they interact with some organization/enterprise through their products, services or systems. As with the CX concept, there is no general acceptance by the various authors of the best technique or method for evaluating/measuring CX. However, there are some that are frequently used for their ease of application and good results obtained. These methods for evaluating CX are: Interviews [10], Questionnaires [10], Surveys [10], Focus Group [10], among others. Moreover, different scales are usually applied, such as: Importance Performance Analysis (IPA) [39], SERVQUAL [40], SERVPERF [41], or Customer Experience Quality (EXQ) [42].

In addition to these traditional methods, User eXperience (UX) and usability methods could be used to evaluate some aspects of CX. This is because CX can be considered as an extension of UX and this as an extension of usability [11]. Usability is defined by the ISO-9241-11 [12] as "the extent to which a product can be used by specified users to achieve specified goals with effectiveness, efficiency and satisfaction in a specified context of use". The ISO 9241-210 [13] standard defines the UX as "person's perceptions and responses resulting from the use and/or anticipated use of a product, system or service".

Thus, heuristic evaluation proposed by Nielsen and Molich [14] could be another method to evaluate different aspects of CX and to be able to detect different potential CX problems. However, it may not cover all aspects of CX and should therefore be complemented by alternative evaluation methods [11]. In addition, existing methodologies focused on develop usability/user experience heuristics could be extended, such as the one proposed by Quiñones et al. [15] to create CX heuristics. However, when applying any of the above methods, it should always be considered that the CX evaluation methods should be applied to each of the touchpoints, because in each of these interactions, customers generate their own experiences, opinions and assessments of the company.

3   Customer's Needs in Tourism Area

Customers have different perceptions and needs, not all are equal. Some customers may perceive one service as unnecessary, but for another it may be a fundamental need [21]. That is why the different companies in this industry must focus on delivering the best possible experience to each type of customer that interacts with them. Because the way in which customers experience a service impacts how they will feel about the company that provides the service and how it will behave in the future [3].

Customers' needs depend on several different factors, could be for the type of traveler, where a tourist traveling with family will have different needs than one traveling alone, or even with friends. This can be seen more clearly in the purposes of travel, where there are evident differences whether traveling for leisure or work. However, these are not the only factors affecting customer needs. Another important factor is the culture of customers, because they may be from different countries, continents or regions of the world. Finally, the last factor to mention, which may be obvious, is the industry/area with which customers interacts. Where customers will not have the same needs if they go, for example, to a hotel or restaurant, being able to have completely different needs.

We reviewed and analyzed different studies focused on the evaluation of CX regarding on several attributes/factors. The studies raise different needs that customers seek to meet when using a certain product, system or services offered in the tourism area. Then, authors evaluated these needs with various instruments mainly using surveys, interviews, or questionnaires. However, they also conducted focus groups, used multidimensional scales and reviewed customer opinions on different websites.

Table 1 shows a compilation of the different needs that a customer has and expects to satisfy when using products, systems or services in the tourism area. Based on the articles reviewed, we observed that the most common industries analyzed are: hotels, restaurants, and airlines. We classified the needs into these three industries or sectors and for each of them, we present the customer's needs in a general way and then highlight some of these needs for the different classifications.

Table 1. Customer needs according to the tourism industry or sector

Industry/sector	Customer's needs
Hotels [17–30]	(1) **Room/Bathroom Aspects** (comfortable, spacious, sufficient sunlight, clean, temperature control) (2) **Location** (close to city center, close to local attractions, close to airport/railway station, accessibility, convenient transportation, quiet area, free parking) (3) **Food Aspects** (free breakfast, variety of food, food quality, vegetarian and gluten free options) (4) **Environment** (restaurant, swimming pools, non-smoking policy, conference and meeting room, hotel bar, fitness center, spa, business center) (5) **Staff Aspects** (friendliness, multi-language skills, helpful, efficient check-in/out, reliable reservation, polite) (6) **Security Facilities** (electronic key cards, safe deposits, fire alarms) (7) **Others** (free Wi-Fi, value for money, babysitting, travel advices, self-service laundry, pet friendly)

(continued)

Table 1. (*continued*)

Industry/sector	Customer's needs
Restaurants [22, 30–35]	**(1) Food Quality** (taste, nutrition, freshness, smell) **(2) Food Variety** (variety of drinks, taste preferences, variety of menu, vegan option) **(3) Environment** (interior design, background music, lighting, aroma, cleanliness, calmness) **(4) Location** (close to city centre, parking, outdoor seating, accessibility) **(5) Staff Aspects** (appearance, hygiene, friendliness, linguistic skills, cordiality) **(6) Service Aspects** (attentiveness, menu knowledge, accuracy, speed, attention to customers, complaints handling, sanitation, privacy respect) **(7) Others** (free Wi-Fi, multi-language menu, entertainment, value for money, accept international credit cards, promotional incentives)
Airlines [3, 36, 37]	**(1) Staff Aspects** (attractiveness, performance, courtesy, helpfulness, friendliness, professional, multi-lingual skills) **(2) Cabin/Aircraft** (seat comfort, leg room, baggage space, temperature, air quality, noise) **(3) Ground** (punctuality, baggage handling, efficient check-in, lounge) **(4) Others** (safety/reliability, value of money, reservation, Wi-Fi & connectivity, food & beverages, entertainment)

Reviewing and analyzing several articles, we identify that in general, customers have the same needs when they interact with restaurants and airlines. In the case of restaurants, this is because food is a basic need, independent of the purpose of travel, that is why there are not many studies focused on differentiating their needs. In the case of airlines, although there is a category called "Business", it is not intended for tourist traveling only for business reasons, but for customers who prefer certain facilities. For that reason, no research was found to make a clear differentiation in these industries.

However, regarding hotels although customers can share needs, there are some that are mostly valued according to the purpose of travel. When traveling for leisure they value: travel advices, hotel bar/lounge, multilingual staff, bicycles for free or for rent, security facilities (electronic key cards, safe deposits and fire alarms), free breakfast, location close to attractions, and location close to city center. While traveling for business, they give more importance to: business center, location close to airport/railway station, free parking, spacious suites, efficient reservation, nonsmoking policy, fitness center with gym, spa, babysitting, efficient check-in and check-out, meeting/banqueting facilities, and international calls. The other needs mentioned in Table 1 are important for both such as those related to the rooms/bathrooms, food, environment, among others.

Regarding the different needs according to the type of traveler, a differentiation of customer needs could not be found respect to restaurant and airline industries, as happened in the previous classification. Related to hotel industry Radojevic et al. [25] performed a research focused on the different demographic groups. They indicated that the levels of satisfaction in hotels vary considerably according to the type of traveler, thus: (1) solo travelers appreciate the hotel's location and the presence of free internet;

(2) groups of friends, give importance to the location and the presence of lobby bar; (3) couples prefer free internet; and (4) families appreciate the presence of air conditioning and a lobby bar.

Related to customer's needs according to their culture, Teng [22] focused on restaurants and tourist accommodation, he states that customers with different cultural contexts give importance to various aspects such as: staff (smiling, eye contact, pleasant tone, and personal attention), environment (interior design, artefacts, layout, music, lighting, and aroma), food (taste preferences, and variety of menu), among others. Moreover, Torres, Fu and Lehto [16] performed a research focused on hotel experience and they indicated that American tourists could have different needs, preferences and expectation than Canadian tourist, Northern European tourists or Latin American tourists, where for example: American tourists prefer flexible service along with professionalism; Canadian tourists seek cleanliness; Northern European tourists give greater importance to problem resolution; and Latin American tourists highlighted efficiency and food.

4 Conclusions and Future Work

Within this study, we investigate the customer's needs in relation to the different industries/sectors with which they interact (hotels, restaurants or airlines) through a general classification of needs (Table 1) and then highlighting certain specific needs according to the purpose of travel (business or leisure), type of traveler (solo, couple, family, or friends) and cultural differences. Customer needs were obtained reviewing and analyzing several articles focused on the evaluation of CX regarding on several attributes/factors most valued by customers. Concerning hotels, customer needs were classified into seven categories: (1) room/bathroom aspects, (2) location, (3) food aspects, (4) environment, (5) staff aspects, (6) security facilities, and (7) others. Related to restaurants, customer needs were classified also into seven categories: (1) food quality, (2) food variety, (3) environment, (4) location, (5) staff aspects, (6) service aspects, and (7) others. Regarding airlines, customer needs were classified also into four categories: (1) staff aspects, (2) cabin, (3) service aspects, (4) ground, and (5) others. This general classification can be helpful to industries/sectors to know which customer needs to focus on to generate a positive customer experience regardless of the purpose of travel, type of traveler or cultural differences.

However, this study shows limitations in the area of study, because there is not yet a clear and precise differentiation on the different customer needs according to the purpose of travel, type of traveler, or cultural differences in the industries of the area. In addition, the identification of touchpoints in the area are not indicated, because the articles analyzed did not cover the topic. Therefore, we just explained them and talked about their importance for companies and customer experience evaluation.

As future work, we intent to fill the gaps found in the limitations. First, conduct several studies to identify and classify customer's needs according to the purpose of travel, type of traveler, and cultural differences. Second, differentiate these needs from specific types of business for example, budget hotels, midscale hotels or upscale hotels. Finally, carry the research further than just hotels, airports and airlines, including other sectors that interact with the tourism industry such as museums, theme parks, city breaks, among others, and specify the different touchpoints with which the customer interacts for each of those industries.

References

1. Meyer, C., Schwager, A.: Customer experience. Harv. Bus. Rev. **85**(2), 116–126 (2007)
2. Klaus, P., Maklan, S.: Towards a better measure of customer experience. Int. J. Mark. Res. **55**(2), 227–246 (2013)
3. Laming, C., Mason, K.: Customer experience - an analysis of the concept and its performance in airline brands. Res. Transp. Bus. Manag. **10**, 15–25 (2014)
4. Gentile, C., Spiller, N., Noci, G.: How to sustain the customer experience: an overview of experience components that co-create value with the customer. Eur. Manag. J. **25**(5), 395–410 (2007)
5. Klaus, P., Maklan, S.: Bridging the gap for destination extreme sports – a model of sports tourism customer experience. J. Mark. Manag. **27**(13–14), 1341–1365 (2011)
6. Gopalan, R., Narayan, B.: Improving customer experiences in tourism: a framework for stakeholder collaboration. Socio-Econ. Plan. Sci. **44**(2), 100–112 (2010)
7. Tung, V.W.S., Ritchie, J.R.B.: Exploring the essence of memorable tourism experiences. Ann. Tour. Res. **38**(4), 1367–1386 (2011)
8. World Travel and Tourism Council: Travel & Tourism Economic Impact 2019 (2019)
9. UNWTO: Glossary of Tourism Terms (2014). https://www.unwto.org/glossary-tourism-terms
10. Jordan, P.: Designing Pleasurable Products. An Introduction to the New Human Factors. Taylor & Francis, London (2000)
11. Rusu, V., Rusu, C., Botella, F., Quiñones, D., Bascur, C., Rusu, V.Z.: Customer eXperience: a bridge between service science and human-computer interaction. In: Ahram, T., Karwowski, W., Pickl, S., Taiar, R. (eds.) IHSED 2019. AISC, vol. 1026, pp. 385–390. Springer, Cham (2020). https://doi.org/10.1007/978-3-030-27928-8_59
12. ISO 9241-11: Ergonomic requirements for office work with visual display terminals (VDT's) – Part 11: Guidance on Usability. International Organization for Standardization, Geneva (1998)
13. ISO 9241-210: Ergonomics of human-system interaction—Part 210: Human-centred design for interactive systems. International Organization for Standardization (2010)
14. Nielsen, J., Molich, R.: Heuristic evaluation of user interfaces. In: Proceeding SIGCHI 1990 Conference on Human factors in Computing Systems, pp. 249–256 (1990)
15. Quiñones, D., Rusu, C., Rusu, V.: A methodology to develop usability/user experience heuristics. Comput. Stand. Interf. **59**, 109–129 (2018)
16. Torres, E., Fu, X., Lehto, X.: Examining key drivers of customer delight in a hotel experience: a cross-cultural perspective. Int. J. Hosp. Manag. **36**, 255–262 (2014)
17. Wang, S., Hung, K.: Customer perceptions of critical success factors for guest houses. Int. J. Hosp. Manag. **48**, 92–101 (2015)
18. Lyu, J., Li, M., Law, R.: Experiencing P2P accommodations: Anecdotes from Chinese customers. Int. J. Hosp. Manag. **77**, 323–332 (2019)
19. Ren, L., Qiu, H., Wang, P., Lin, P.M.C.: Exploring customer experience with budget hotels: dimensionality and satisfaction. Int. J. Hosp. Manag. **52**, 13–23 (2016)
20. Peng, J., Zhao, X., Mattila, A.S.: Improving service management in budget hotels. Int. J. Hosp. Manag. **49**, 139–148 (2015)

21. Nasution, H.N., Mayondo, F.T.: Customer value in the hotel industry: what managers believe they deliver and what customer experience. Int. J. Hosp. Manag. **27**, 204–213 (2008)
22. Zhang, Y., Cole, S.T.: Dimensions of lodging guest satisfaction among guests with mobility challenges: a mixed-method analysis of web-based texts. Tour. Manag. **53**, 13–27 (2016)
23. Radojevic, T., Stanisic, N., Stanic, N.: Ensuring positive feedback: factors that influence customer satisfaction in the contemporary hospitality industry. Tour. Manag. **51**, 13–21 (2015)
24. Zhou, L., Ye, S., Pearce, P.L., Wu, M.Y.: Refreshing hotel satisfaction studies by reconfiguring customer review data. Int. J. Hosp. Manag. **38**, 1–10 (2014)
25. Radojevic, T., Stanisic, N., Stanic, N.: Solo travellers assign higher ratings than families: examining customer satisfaction by demographic group. Tour. Manag. Perspect. **16**, 247–258 (2015)
26. Radojevic, T., Stanisic, N., Stanic, N., Davidson, R.: The effects of traveling for business on customer satisfaction with hotel services. Tour. Manag. **67**, 326–341 (2018)
27. Merli, R., Preziosi, M., Acampora, A., Ali, F.: Why should hotels go green? Insights from guests experience in green hotels. Int. J. Hosp. Manag. **81**, 169–179 (2019)
28. Chu, R.K., Choi, T.: An importance-performance analysis of hotel selection factors in the Hong Kong hotel industry: a comparison of business and leisure travellers. Tour. Manag. **21** (4), 363–377 (2000)
29. Liu, S., Law, R., Rong, J., Li, G., Hall, J.: Analyzing changes in hotel customers' expectations by trip mode. Int. J. Hosp. Manag. **34**, 359–371 (2013)
30. Teng, C.C.: Commercial hospitality in restaurants and tourist accommodation: perspectives from international consumer experience in Scotland. Int. J. Hosp. Manag. **30**(4), 866–874 (2011)
31. Nam, J.H., Lee, T.J.: Foreign travelers' satisfaction with traditional Korean restaurants. Int. J. Hosp. Manag. **30**(4), 982–989 (2011)
32. Alhelalat, J.A., Habiballah, M.A., Twaissi, N.M.: The impact of personal and functional aspects of restaurant employee service behaviour on customer satisfaction. Int. J. Hosp. Manag. **66**, 46–53 (2017)
33. Yrjölä, M., Rintamäki, T., Saarijärvia, H., Joensuu, J., Kulkarni, G.: A customer value perspective to service experiences in restaurants. J. Retail. Consum. Serv. **51**, 91–101 (2019)
34. Otengei, S.O., Bakunda, G., Ngoma, M., Ntayi, J.M., Munene, J.C.: Internationalization of African-ethnic restaurants: a qualitative enquiry using the dynamic capabilities perspective. Tour. Manag. Perspect. **21**, 85–99 (2017)
35. Park, C.: Efficient or enjoyable? Consumer values of eating-out and fast food restaurant consumption in Korea. Int. J. Hosp. Manag. **31**(1), 87–94 (2004)
36. Siering, M., Deokar, A.V., Janze, C.: Disentangling consumer recommendations: explaining and predicting airline recommendations based on online reviews. Decis. Support Syst. **107**, 52–63 (2018)
37. Sezgen, E., Mason, K.J., Mayer, R.: Voice of airline passenger: a text mining approach to understand customer satisfaction. J. Air Transp. Manag. **77**, 65–74 (2019)
38. Bascur, C., Rusu, C., Quiñones, D.: User as customer: touchpoints and journey map. In: Ahram, T., Karwowski, W., Taiar, R. (eds.) IHSED 2018. AISC, vol. 876, pp. 117–122. Springer, Cham (2019). https://doi.org/10.1007/978-3-030-02053-8_19
39. Martilla, J.A., James, J.C.: Importance-performance analysis. J. Mark. **41**(1), 77–79 (1977)
40. Parasuraman, A., Zeithaml, V.A., Berry, L.L.: SERVQUAL: a multiple-item scale for measuring consumers' perceptions of service quality. J. Retail. **64**(1), 12–40 (1988)
41. Cronin, J., Taylor, S.: Measuring service quality: a reexamination and extension. J. Mark. **56** (3), 55–68 (1992)
42. Klaus, P., Maklan, S.: EXQ: a multiple-scale for assessing service experience. J. Serv. Manag. **23**(1), 5–33 (2012)

Customer eXperience in Valparaíso Hostels: Analyzing Tourists' Opinions

Virginica Rusu[1]([⊠]) [iD], Cristian Rusu[2] [iD], Daniela Quiñones[2] [iD],
Silvana Roncagliolo[2] [iD], Victoria Carvajal[2], and Martin Muñoz[2]

[1] Universidad de Playa Ancha, Av. Playa Ancha 850, 2340000 Valparaíso, Chile
virginica.rusu@upla.cl
[2] Pontificia Universidad Católica de Valparaíso,
Av. Brasil 2241, 2340000 Valparaíso, Chile
{cristian.rusu,daniela.quinones,
silvana.roncagliolo}@pucv.cl,
victoria.carvajal.videla@gmail.com,
m.a.feldstedt@gmail.com

Abstract. Customer eXperience is one of the key concepts in Service Science, an interdisciplinary research field oriented to the systematic innovation of services. The Tourist eXperience, as customer of specific services, is strongly related to the quality of the services that are offered. Online travel agencies generate online communities, where tourists can quantitatively (scores) and qualitatively (reviews) evaluate the services they received. Their opinions offer information for other fellow travelers when they are choosing tourism-related services. They also offer valuable information for decision makers in tourism entities. Tourist opinions express in fact their experiences as customers. Many researches focus on qualitative tourists' comments, evaluating their reviews with big data and natural language processing techniques. However, we focused our work on quantitative data. The paper presents a quantitative study on the opinions of the tourists that used accommodation services offered through the online travel agency HostelWorld, in hostels from Valparaíso, Chile. We used descriptive statistics to analyze tourists' profile, and inferential statistics to analyze tourists' opinions.

Keywords: Tourist eXperience · Customer eXperience · Service Science · Online travel agency

1 Introduction

Service Science is an interdisciplinary research field oriented to the systematic innovation of services. One of the key concepts in Service Science is Customer eXperience (CX). There is no consensus over the CX definition. A broad definition was proposed by Laming and Mason, which consider that CX includes "the physical and emotional experiences occurring through the interactions with the product and/or service offering of a brand from point of first direct, conscious contact, through the total journey to the post-consumption stage" [1].

© Springer Nature Switzerland AG 2020
G. Meiselwitz (Ed.): HCII 2020, LNCS 12195, pp. 226–235, 2020.
https://doi.org/10.1007/978-3-030-49576-3_17

CX is achieved through a sequence of interactions between the customer and the company (or companies), in all "touch-points" [2, 3]. CX evaluation is challenging [4, 5]. It should be done in each touch-point, it should attend all products/systems/services that the customer interacts with, and it should capture the touch-point specific nature.

CX and Service Science are particularly relevant in tourism. The tourism (and associated) services offer is rapidly growing. Traditional channels for promotion/sales/feedback are replaced by virtual channels: online travel agencies, virtual museums, touristic attractions websites etc. CX includes interactions with software systems (websites), customer service (face-to-face, by phone, by email), as well as other tourists' opinion (shared in specialized websites, social networks, personalized surveys etc.). The Tourist eXperience, as customer of specific services, is strongly related to the quality of the services that are offered [6, 7].

Over the years our work focused on evaluating the User eXperience (UX) of tourism – related websites: online travel agencies, virtual museum, national parks. We used an interdisciplinary approach, focusing on application area (tourism), but also on the specificity of the products involved (software systems).

Online travel agencies generate online communities, where tourists can quantitatively (scores) and qualitatively (reviews) evaluate the services they received. Their opinions (1) offer information for other fellow travelers when they are choosing tourism-related services, and (2) offer valuable information for decision makers in tourism entities. Tourist opinions express in fact their experiences as customers.

Many researches focus on qualitative tourists' comments, evaluating their reviews with big data and natural language processing techniques. However, we focused our work on quantitative data. In previous studies we analyzed quantitative data on travelers' opinion, available at two online travel agencies' websites: www.tripadvisor.cl and www.hotelclub.com [8, 9]. Data relationships and trends were identified.

The paper presents a quantitative study on the opinions of the tourists that used accommodation services offered through the online travel agency *HostelWorld* [10], in hostels from Valparaíso, Chile. Section 2 presents the case study. Section 3 discusses the results of our study. Section 4 highlights conclusions and future work.

2 Case Study: HostelWorld

HostelWorld is an online travel agency that offers accommodation in hostels worldwide. As stated at www.hostelworld.com, it works with around 36,000 properties in 178 countries (see Fig. 1). As declares, the website also offers over 12 million verified guest reviews. Reviews are both qualitative (guests' opinion on the hostel) and quantitative. The quantitative evaluation includes guests' perception on 7 dimensions, which represents variables of service quality:

- *Value for money,*
- *Location,*
- *Atmosphere,*
- *Facilities,*
- *Security,*
- *Staff,*
- *Cleanliness.*

Fig. 1. HostelWorld homepage, indicating their presence and number of reviews worldwide.

Each dimension is qualified in a scale from 1 (worst) to 10 (best). An overall evaluation is also available, as the average scores of the 7 dimensions. The overall score is also associated to a conceptual evaluation, being "Superb" the best one, associated to overall scores from 9.0 to 10.

The website offers an overview of the quests reviews that includes (see Fig. 2):

- The overall score and the associated conceptual evaluation,
- The conceptual evaluation on 3 dimensions: Location, Staff, and Cleanliness,
- The total number of guests' reviews available for the hostel.

As the 3 above mentioned dimensions scores are indicated at first hand, it seems that they have a special meaning for travelers, in HostelWorld's view.

Fig. 2. Guests reviews overview, located in the main presentation of a hostel.

When accessing property's details, one can get access to:

- Scores on all 7 dimensions, as well as overall score and the associated conceptual evaluation (see Fig. 3),

- Overall score and the associated conceptual evaluation of each reviewer (see Fig. 4).

 Moreover, each review is also providing:

- Guest "name" (or "Anonymous" instead),
- Guest(s)' country of residence,
- Type of guest(s),
- Age group,
- Number of reviews that the guest(s) has/have made, and the associated level of "expertise", being "Globetrotter" the highest one,
- Review date.

 Reviews can be sorted by several criteria: "Top Rated", "Lowest Rated", "Newest", "Oldest", and "Age Group". User may choose to display all available reviews, or only English reviews. The level of detail, especially the guest's "expertise", as well as the flexibility in filtering and sorting reviews show the relevance that guests' opinion have.

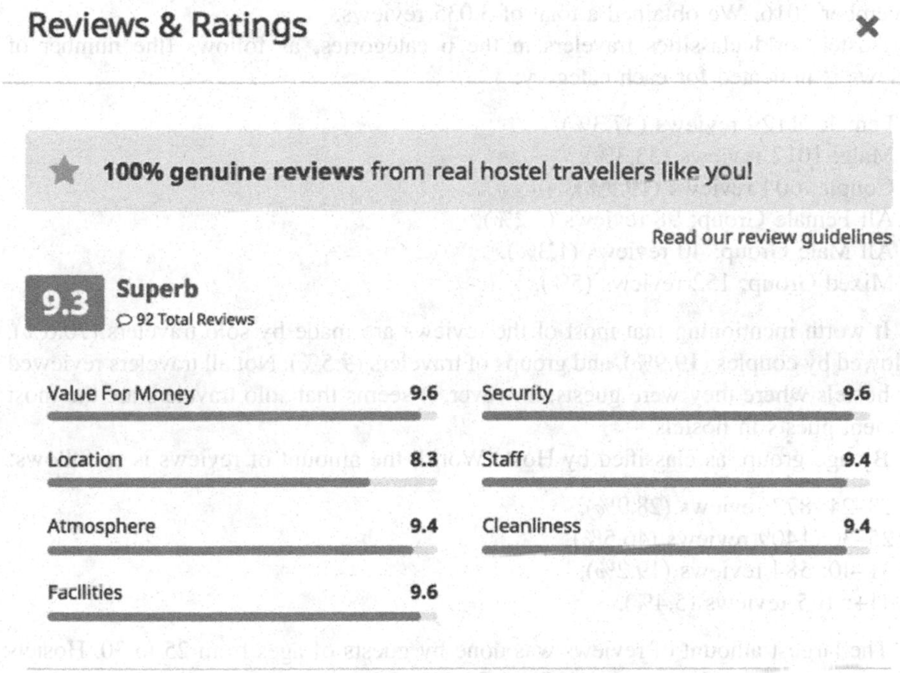

Reviews & Ratings ✕

⭐ **100% genuine reviews** from real hostel travellers like you!

Read our review guidelines

9.3	**Superb**
	💬 92 Total Reviews

Value For Money	**9.6**	Security	**9.6**
Location	**8.3**	Staff	**9.4**
Atmosphere	**9.4**	Cleanliness	**9.4**
Facilities	**9.6**		

Fig. 3. Detailed scores on 7 dimensions, overall score and conceptual evaluation.

Anonymous
USA, Male, 25-30
Globetrotter
32 reviews

8.6 Fabulous   📅 23 Jul 2019

Nice stay! It's kind of a compromise between a hostel and a hotel. There isn't much of a social scene, but you get a more comfortable and private bed than you would in most hostels. The free breakfast (w/coffee) is great. You're a bit far out of town, but it's really easy to catch the bus or order an Uber. The WiFi doesn't work in all areas of the house. The owner was very helpful.

Fig. 4. A guest review frame.

3 Results and Discussion

We extracted all reviews associated to hostels in Valparaíso, Chile, available in late December 2016. We obtained a total of 3,035 reviews.

HostelWorld classifies travelers in the 6 categories, as follows (the number of reviews is indicated for each category:

- Female: 1129 reviews (37.3%),
- Male: 1012 reviews (33.3%),
- Couple: 604 reviews (19.9%),
- All Female Group: 98 reviews (3.2%),
- All Male Group: 40 reviews (1.3%),
- Mixed Group: 152 reviews (5%).

It worth mentioning that most of the reviews are made by solo travelers (70.6%), followed by couples (19.9%), and groups of travelers (9.5%). Not all travelers reviewed the hostels where they were guests; however, it seems that solo travelers are the most frequent guests in hostels.

By age group, as classified by HostelWorld, the amount of reviews is as follows:

- 18–24: 877 reviews (28.9%),
- 25–30: 1409 reviews (46.5%),
- 31–40: 584 reviews (19.2%),
- 41+: 165 reviews (5.4%).

The largest amount of reviews was done by guests of ages from 25 to 30. Hostels seem to be preferred by young people, as 75.4% of the reviews were done by people up to 30 y/o.

By country of origin, most of the reviews were done by foreign travelers:

- 2,924 reviews were done by foreign travelers (96.3%),
- 111 reviews were done by Chilean travelers (3.7%).

Analyzing the country of origin of travelers, most of them come from USA (489 reviews, 16.1%), followed by England (380 reviews, 12.5%), Germany (308 reviews, 10.1%), Australia (284 reviews, 9.4%), France (199 reviews, 6,6%), and Brazil (155 reviews, 5,1%). All other countries represent less than 5% of the travelers.

We also grouped travelers by geographic region, as defined by the World Tourism Organization (UNWTO). By region, the number of reviews is as follows (1 review does not fit into any geographic region):

- Europe: 1491 reviews (49.1%),
- Americas: 1112 reviews (36.6%),
- Asia and Pacific: 401 reviews (13.2%),
- Middle East: 16 reviews (0.5%),
- Africa: 14 reviews, (0.5%).

We check the normality of all 7 dimensions, using the Kolmogorow-Smirnow K-S test (with p-value ≤ 0.05 as decision rule). We checked the hypothesis:

- H_0: the variable has a normal distribution,
- H_1: the variable does not have a normal distribution.

As Table 1 shows, none of the variables have a normal distribution. Therefore we used nonparametric statistic tests to analyze data. In all tests p-value ≤ 0.05 was used as decision rule.

Table 1. Kolmogorow-Smirnow K-S test for checking a normal distribution.

	Value for money	Location	Atmosphere	Facilities	Security	Staff	Cleanliness
p-value	0.000	0.000	0.000	0.000	0.000	0.000	0.000

We used Kruskal–Wallis H tests to check the hypothesis:

- H_0: there are no significant differences between the opinions of different type of travelers,
- H_1: there are significant differences between the opinions of different type of travelers.

As Table 2 shows, there are no significant differences between the opinions of different type of travelers, regarding 3 dimensions: Location, Atmosphere, and Facilities. Significant differences occur in 4 dimensions: Value for money, Security, Staff, and Cleanliness.

Table 2. Kruskal–Wallis H tests by type of travelers.

	Value for money	Location	Atmosphere	Facilities	Security	Staff	Cleanliness
p-value	**0.013**	0.531	0.091	0.245	**0.005**	**0.002**	**0.004**

We also used Kruskal–Wallis H tests to check the hypothesis:

- H_0: there are no significant differences between the opinions of travelers belonging to different age groups,
- H_1: there are significant differences between the opinions of travelers belonging to different age groups.

As Table 3 shows, there are no significant differences between the opinions of travelers belonging to different age groups, in none of the 7 dimensions.

Table 3. Kruskal–Wallis H tests by age group.

	Value for money	Location	Atmosphere	Facilities	Security	Staff	Cleanliness
p-value	0.729	0.460	0.723	0.664	0.370	0.170	0.455

We used Mann–Whitney U tests to check the hypothesis:

- H_0: there are no significant differences between the opinions of Chilean and foreign travelers,
- H_1: there are significant differences between the opinions of Chilean and foreign travelers.

As Table 4 indicates, there are significant differences between the opinions of Chilean and foreign travelers in all 7 dimensions.

Table 4. Mann–Whitney U tests by travelers' origin (domestic vs. international travelers).

	Value for money	Location	Atmosphere	Facilities	Security	Staff	Cleanliness
p-value	0.003	0.000	0.000	0.000	0.001	0.000	0.000

We used Kruskal–Wallis H tests to check the hypothesis:

- H_0: there are no significant differences between the opinions of travelers belonging to different geographic region,
- H_1: there are significant differences between the opinions of travelers belonging to different geographic region.

As Table 5 shows, there are significant differences between the opinions of travelers belonging to different geographical regions in all 7 dimensions.

Table 5. Kruskal–Wallis H tests by geographic region.

	Value for money	Location	Atmosphere	Facilities	Security	Staff	Cleanliness
p-value	0.015	0.002	0.004	0.004	0.006	0.004	0.000

Table 6 presents the average scores by dimensions, as well as the general overall score.

Table 6. Average scores by dimensions.

Categories	Value for money	Location	Atmosphere	Facilities	Security	Staff	Cleanliness	Overall score
By type of travelers:								
Female	8.45	9.03	8.37	7.96	8.62	8.65	8.01	8.44
Male	8.71	9.11	8.52	8.14	8.83	8.96	8.38	8.67
Couple	8.52	9.03	8.32	8.07	8.88	8.72	8.31	8.55
All female group	8.57	9.06	8.41	7.98	8.55	8.65	8.18	8.49
All male group	8.60	8.75	8.70	8.00	8.70	8.95	8.05	8.53
Mixed group	8.61	9.09	8.41	7.92	8.83	8.91	8.17	8.56
By age group:								
18–24	8.52	9.06	8.35	8.01	8.67	8.66	8.16	8.49
25–30	8.57	9.05	8.41	8.05	8.80	8.80	8.19	8.55
31–40	8.61	9.11	8.49	8.09	8.75	8.87	8.33	8.60
41+	8.59	8.97	8.55	8.00	8.80	9.04	8.17	8.59
By origin:								
Domestic (Chilean)	8.95	9.50	9.03	8.85	9.15	9.28	8.77	9.08
International (foreigners)	8.55	9.04	8.39	8.01	8.74	8.77	8.19	8.53
By geographic region:								
Europe	8.51	9.00	8.37	7.96	8.69	8.71	8.06	8.47
Americas	8.67	9.17	8.54	8.19	8.86	8.92	8.39	8.68
Asia and Pacific	8.51	8.95	8.25	7.97	8.74	8.70	8.27	8.49
Middle East	8.00	8.88	7.75	7.88	8.25	8.50	8.50	8.25
Africa	8.29	9.14	8.14	7.86	8.43	8.71	7.86	8.35
All guests	*8.56*	*9.06*	*8.42*	*8.04*	*8.75*	*8.79*	*8.21*	*8.55*

Averages scores by groups are quite homogeneous. In all 7 dimensions, differences are less than 1 point, in a 10 points scale, in almost all cases. Facilities scores the lowest score in all cases, excepting Middle East travelers; in their opinion Atmosphere got the lowest score.

We performed Spearman ρ tests to check the hypothesis:

- H_0: $\rho = 0$, two dimensions are independent,
- H_1: $\rho \neq 0$, two dimensions are dependent.

Table 7. Spearman ρ test for the 7 dimensions.

	Value for money	Location	Atmosphere	Facilities	Security	Staff	Cleanliness
Value for money	1	0.393	0.613	0.641	0.483	0.570	0.606
Location		1	0.358	0.355	0.418	0.368	0.374
Atmosphere			1	0.570	0.401	0.623	0.519
Facilities				1	0.492	0.514	0.643
Security					1	0.438	0.506
Staff						1	0.485
Cleanliness							1

As Table 7 shows, all dimensions are correlated (weakly, moderately or strongly). There are 4 strong correlations:

- "Value for money" is strongly correlated with "Atmosphere", "Facilities" and "Cleanliness"; when travelers think they got a good value for what they paid, they also positively evaluate hostel's atmosphere, facilities that it offers, and its cleanliness,
- "Facilities" is strongly correlated with "Cleanliness"; a positive evaluation of hostel's facilities is accompanied by a positive evaluation of its cleanliness.

4 Conclusions

CX is a key concept in Service Science, but lately the HCI community shows a growing interest in the field. Tourist eXperience focuses on tourist of specific services. Evaluating Tourist eXperience is as challenging as evaluating CX in general.

Online travel agencies generate online communities, where tourists quantitatively (through scores) and qualitatively (trough reviews) evaluate the services they received. Many researches focus on qualitative tourists' comments, but we focused our work on quantitative data. We evaluated over 3,000 reviews of hostels located in Valparaíso, Chile, available at HostelWorld online travel agency.

Guests' reviews seem to be particular important for HostelWorld. The agency offers reviews' overview at first sight, but also detailed information on all available reviews, as well as on the level of expertise of the guests that made that reviews. It also offers options to sort and filter the reviews. 3 of the 7 dimensions assessed by guests seems to be particularly relevant in HostelWorld' view: Location, Staff, and Cleanliness.

Not all travelers make reviews after there are staying in a hostel. However, the available reviews show that Valparaiso's hostels are preferred by solo travelers (70.6% of the reviews), and by young travelers (75.4%). The gender balance is slightly in favor of female travelers. The majority of travelers are foreigners, only 3.7% travelers being Chileans. By geographic region, most of the travelers come from Europe (49.1%); by country of origin most of them come from USA (16.1%).

There are no significant differences between the opinions of travelers by age group, in none of the 7 dimensions. On the contrary, there are significant differences between the opinions of domestic and foreign travelers in all 7 dimensions. There are also significant differences in all 7 dimensions when analyzing travelers' opinion by geographic region. There are significant differences by type of traveler regarding 4 of the 7 dimensions: Value for money, Security, Staff, and Cleanliness.

Guests' opinions are rather homogeneous; in all 7 dimensions, differences are less than 1 point, in a 10 points scale, in almost all cases. Facilities score lowest in almost all cases. All dimensions are weakly, moderately, or strongly correlated.

As future work, we will extend our study to hostels from other cities. It would be particularly interesting to compare travelers' perception on hostels from Valparaíso and Viña del Mar, which are geographically located together, but are quite different in terms of what they offer as tourism attractions.

References

1. Laming, C., Mason, K.: Customer experience – an analysis of the concept and its performance in airline brands. Res. Transp. Bus. Manag. **10**, 15–25 (2014)
2. Interaction Design Foundation: Customer Touchpoints - The Point of Interaction Between Brands, Businesses, Products and Customers. http://www.interaction-design.org/literature/article/customer-touchpoints-the-point-of-interaction-between-brands-businesses-products-and-customers. Accessed 20 Jan 2020
3. Stein, A., Ramaseshan, B.: Towards the identification of customer experience touch point elements. J. Retail. Consum. Serv. **30**, 8–19 (2016)
4. Grigoroudis, E., Siskos, Y.: Customer Satisfaction Evaluation: Methods for Measuring and Implementing Service Quality. Springer, Heidelberg (2010). https://doi.org/10.1007/978-1-4419-1640-2
5. Rusu, V., Rusu, C., Botella, F., Quiñones, D., Bascur, C., Rusu, V.Z.: Customer eXperience: a bridge between service science and human-computer interaction. In: Ahram, T., Karwowski, W., Pickl, S., Taiar, R. (eds.) IHSED 2019. AISC, vol. 1026, pp. 385–390. Springer, Cham (2020). https://doi.org/10.1007/978-3-030-27928-8_59
6. Tussyadiah, I.: Toward a theoretical foundation for experience design in tourism. J. Travel Res. **53**(5), 543–564 (2014)
7. Bosangit, C., Hibbert, S., McCabe, S.: If I was going to die I should at least be havingfun: travelblogs, meaning and tourist experience. Ann. Tour. Res. **55**, 1–14 (2015)
8. Rusu, V., et al.: Assessing the customer eXperience based on quantitative data: virtual travel agencies. In: Marcus, A. (ed.) DUXU 2016. LNCS, vol. 9746, pp. 499–508. Springer, Heidelberg (2016). https://doi.org/10.1007/978-3-319-40409-7_47
9. Rusu, V., Rusu, C., Guzmán, D., Roncagliolo, S., Quiñones, D.: Online travel agencies as social media: analyzing customers' opinions. In: Meiselwitz, G. (ed.) SCSM 2017. LNCS, vol. 10282, pp. 200–209. Springer, Cham (2017). https://doi.org/10.1007/978-3-319-58559-8_17
10. HostelWorld Homepage. http://www.hostelworld.com/. Accessed 20 Jan 2020

Students' Perception on Customer eXperience: A Comparative Study

Cristian Rusu[1]([⊠]) [iD], Virginia Rusu[2] [iD], Federico Botella[3] [iD],
Daniela Quiñones[1] [iD], Bogdan Alexandru Urs[4], Ilie Urs[5],
Jenny Morales[6] [iD], Sandra Cano[1] [iD], Silvana Aciar[7] [iD],
and Iván Balmaceda Castro[8]

[1] Pontificia Universidad Católica de Valparaíso, Av. Brasil 2241,
2340000 Valparaíso, Chile
{cristian.rusu,daniela.quinones,sandra.cano}@pucv.cl
[2] Universidad de Playa Ancha, Av. Playa Ancha 850, 2340000 Valparaíso, Chile
virginica.rusu@upla.cl
[3] Universidad Miguel Hernández de Elche, Avinguda de la Universitat d'Elx s/n,
03202 Elche, Spain
federico@umh.es
[4] Babeş-Bolyai University, Universităţii 7-9, 400084 Cluj-Napoca, Romania
ursbogdan@yahoo.com
[5] Dimitrie Cantemir Christian University, Burebista 2,
400276 Cluj-Napoca, Romania
dr_ursilie@yahoo.com
[6] Facultad de Ingeniería, Universidad Autónoma de Chile, 5 Poniente 1670,
3460000 Talca, Chile
jmoralesb@uautonoma.cl
[7] Silvana Aciar, CONICET, San Juan, Argentina
saciar@unsj-cuim.edu.ar
[8] Iván Balmaceda Castro, CONICET, San Juan, Argentina
ibalmaceda89@gmail.com

Abstract. Traditionally related to Service Science, Customer eXperience (CX) is also becoming a relevant Human-Computer Interaction (HCI) topic. The well-known concepts of usability and User eXperience refer to a single system, product or service. CX extends the UX concepts in a holistic approach, focusing on customer's interactions (touchpoints) with all systems, products and services that a company offers. CX has a highly interdisciplinary nature; our approach on CX comes from HCI, as many of the customer – company interactions are based on interactives software systems and digital products. Forming CX professionals is challenging. We think that including CX as topic in HCI courses is becoming a necessity. The paper presents a 2019 comparative study on students' perception on CX, which follows-up a similar study that we have done in 2018. The survey includes students from Chile, Spain, Romania, Colombia and Argentina, enrolled in CS and Law programs. The results help prioritizing the CX topics and designing a CX course.

Keywords: Customer eXperience · User eXperience · Service Science · Curricula

© Springer Nature Switzerland AG 2020
G. Meiselwitz (Ed.): HCII 2020, LNCS 12195, pp. 236–246, 2020.
https://doi.org/10.1007/978-3-030-49576-3_18

1   Introduction

Traditionally, the Customer eXperience (CX) concept was related to marketing and Service Sciences. However, the Human-Computer Interaction (HCI) community is showing a growing interest on CX. Following this trend, we are working for almost two decades on Usability and User eXperience (UX), but lately we are also focusing on CX.

Most of our work is based on the ISO 9241 standard definitions on usability and UX [1]:

- Usability: "extent to which a system, product or service can be used by specified users to achieve specified goals with effectiveness, efficiency and satisfaction in a specified context of use",
- UX: "user's perceptions and responses that result from the use and/or anticipated use of a system, product or service".

It worth highlighting that both definitions refer not only to (interactive) software systems, but also to products and services. Usability focuses on effectiveness, efficiency and satisfaction when achieving specific goals. It is generally agreed that UX extends the usability concept, referring to all user's perceptions and responses when using (or even intend to use) a system, product or service. We think that CX extends the UX concept (and consequently the usability concept), as it examines the whole customer journey and experiences with several systems, products or services that a company offers, instead of focusing on a single one.

There is still no agreement on a unique UX definition; agreeing on a unique CX definition is even harder, as the CX concept is much more complex than the UX one. Laming and Mason think that CX includes "the physical and emotional experiences occurring through the interactions with the product and/or service offering of a brand from point of first direct, conscious contact, through the total journey to the post-consumption stage" [2].

CX has a highly interdisciplinary nature. Our approach on CX comes from HCI; we think that CX may be the bridge between HCI and Service Science [3–5]. CX is developed through a sequence of "touchpoints" (interactions) between the customer and the company (or companies) that offer the product/system/service [6, 7]. Many of these are based on interactives software systems and digital products. Moreover, CX in one touchpoint usually influence customers' perception in other touchpoints. That is why we think CS students need at least some CX knowledge.

We are teaching HCI for almost two decades, at undergraduate and graduate level, mainly for Computer Science (CS) students. UX is a main topic in all our courses and we are very well aware that including CX as topic in HCI courses is a necessity. We started teaching CX as optional course at graduate and undergraduate level in Chile, in 2018. We designed the course based on our research and teaching experience, feedback from industry, and from our alumni. The holistic CX approach proved to be a necessity especially in a diploma program that we are teaching since 2015, a program that brings together professional of very different background: CS, Design, Psychology, Architecture, Engineering etc.

The paper presents a comparative study on students' perception on CX; it is a follow-up study that continues our previous work [8]. Our 2019 survey included students from Chile, Spain, Romania, Colombia and Argentina, enrolled in CS and Law programs. Section 2 describes the survey that we made. Section 3 discusses the results and compares them with our previous findings. Section 4 highlights conclusions and future work.

2   The Survey

We made an exploratory study regarding students' perception on CX in 2018 [8]. Our goal was to assess Computer Science students' perception on CX. We also tried to compare their opinion with the opinion of students from other fields of study: Tourism, Medical Technology, Law, and Civil Engineering.

We applied a specific questionnaire that we developed iteratively. The questionnaire was first validated through a pilot study, with approximately 20 respondents. It was then applied to 202 students, from Chile, Romania and Spain in 2018 [8]. We applied the same questionnaire in 2019, to 199 students from Chile, Romania, Colombia, Argentina and Spain. The questionnaire is presented in Table 1.

Table 1. The questionnaire.

Section	Question	Type
Demographic	What is your field of study?	Selection
	Do you already get a university degree?	Yes/No
	If so, indicate it.	Open question
	Are you currently working?	Yes/No
	If so, indicate the field you are working in.	Open question
	Gender	Female/Male/Not revealed/identified
	What is your age?	20 y/o or less/21–25/26–30/over 30 y/o
	Country of residence	Chile, Romania, Colombia, Argentina, Spain
The perception of the CX concept and its relevance	Indicate the products/systems/services that you think you'll develop/offer as professional	Open question
	How difficult it is to identify your customers? (P1)	Likert scale with 5 levels (1 - Very difficult, 5 – Very easy)
	How important do you think your customers' experience is? (P2)	Likert scale with 5 levels (1 - Very little important, 5 – Very important)
	How important it is an explicit approach to CX in the curricula? (P3)	Likert scale with 5 levels (1 - Very little important, 5 – Very important)
	Does the current curricula include CX related topics?	Yes/No/I don't know
	If so, indicate them.	Open question

(continued)

Table 1. (*continued*)

Section	Question	Type
Topics that a CX course should include	Products/systems/services that I'll develop/offer as professional (T1)	Likert scale with 5 levels (1 - Very little important, 5 – Very important)
	Costumers of products/systems/services (T2)	Likert scale with 5 levels (1 - Very little important, 5 – Very important)
	Customers' needs (T3)	Likert scale with 5 levels (1 - Very little important, 5 – Very important)
	CX design (T4)	Likert scale with 5 levels (1 - Very little important, 5 – Very important)
	CX evaluation (T5)	Likert scale with 5 levels (1 - Very little important, 5 – Very important)
	The company – customers relationship (T6)	Likert scale with 5 levels (1 - Very little important, 5 – Very important)
	CX importance for the company's success (T7)	Likert scale with 5 levels (1 - Very little important, 5 – Very important)
Comments	Indicate any CX related aspect that you would like to highlight.	Open question

We focused the questionnaire on two main areas: (1) the perception of the CX concept and its relevance, and (2) topics that a CX course should include. Students' perception on CX relevance was assessed through three questions:

- How difficult it is to identify their customers (P1),
- How important their customers' experience is (P2),
- How important it is an explicit approach to CX in the curricula (P3).

The proposed topics for a CX course were:

- Products/systems/services that students will develop/offer as professionals (T1),
- Costumers of the products/systems/services they will develop/offer (T2),
- Customers' needs (T3),
- CX design (T4),
- CX evaluation (T5),
- Company – customers relationship (T6),
- CX importance for the company's success (T7).

All the above mentioned items were evaluated on a Likert scale with 5 levels (1 - Very little important, 5 – Very important). Two open questions included in the questionnaire were particularly important as qualitative assessment instruments: (1) what CX related topics include the current curricula (if includes any), and (2) CX related aspects that students would like to highlight.

3   Results and Discussion

3.1   Students' Background

We collected valid data from 199 students, from:

- Chile: 99 students, 49.7%,
- Romania: 53 students, 26.6%,
- Colombia: 21 students, 10.6%,
- Argentina: 17 students, 8.5%,
- Spain: 9 students, 4.5%.

Students voluntarily participated in the experiment; we did not follow a sampling procedure. Moreover, Chilean students' participation was lower than expected, due to the social crisis that occurred in October 2019. There is why we couldn't collect data from Tourism and Medical Technology students, as we did in 2018. The field study covered in all countries excepting Romania was CS. We managed to also cover Law with a significant number of students, in Chile (78 students) and Romania (53 students).

As students were in the final part of their studies, 72 out of 199 students (36.2%) are working and studying in the same time. Students' distribution by field of study was as follows:

- Law: 131 students, 65.8%,
- CS: 68 students, 34.2%.

As in 2018, gender distribution was relatively balanced, however males were predominant in CS programs:

- Males: 101 students, 50.8%,
- Females: 94 students, 47.2%,
- 4 students did not revealed/identified their gender (2.0%).

Similarly to the 2018 survey, the predominant age group was 21 to 25. In 2019 the age distribution was as follows:

- 20 y/o or less: 17 students (8.5%),
- 21 to 25 y/o: 142 students (71.4%),
- 26 to 30 y/o: 20 students (10.1%),
- Over 30 y/o: 20 students (10.1%).

No CX induction was made prior to the survey, and no CX definition was given to respondents. Students answered the survey based only on their specific (field related) and general knowledge. None of the students was previously enrolled in a CX course. That is why we think the survey results' express students' unbiased perception. The number of participants was unbalanced, and the results cannot be generalized.

3.2   Quantitative Results

Table 2 synthetizes the main quantitative results of the survey, the average scores of students' perceptions on CX relevance (P1, P2, P3), and on CX topics in a CX course (T1, T2, T3, T4, T5, T6, T7).

Table 2. Survey's quantitative results. Averages perceptions on CX, and on topics' relevance in a CX course.

Country (No. of students)	Field of study (No. of students)	Averages scores									
		P1	P2	P3	T1	T2	T3	T4	T5	T6	T7
Chile (99)	CS (21)	3.62	4.43	4.38	4.62	4.57	4.76	4.29	4.29	4.67	4.29
	Law (78)	3.59	4.06	4.42	4.28	4.35	4.50	4.13	4.24	4.38	4.35
Romania (53)	Law (53)	3.04	4.08	4.25	4.15	4.17	4.42	4.28	4.15	4.47	4.55
Colombia (21)	CS (21)	3.62	4.29	4.57	4.71	4.67	4.62	4.87	4.81	4.62	4.71
Argentina (17)	CS (17)	3.23	4.12	4.42	4.59	4.47	4.53	4.71	4.71	3.88	4.76
Spain (9)	CS (9)	3.11	3.89	4.12	3.56	3.67	4.23	4.11	3.78	4.11	4.56
All (199)	All (199)	3.40	4.13	4.37	4.32	4.34	4.51	4.31	4.30	4.41	4.53

Item P1 (how difficult it is to identify their customers) got the lowest averages in all cases. P1 got the lowest score in the case of Romanian law students, but got one of the highest scores in the case of the Chilean Law students; 8 of the 10 items got lower score from Romanian Law students than from their Chilean fellows. Almost all items scored better for Chilean and Colombian CS students.

Table 3 synthetizes the results of the surveys done in 2018 and 2019. Results are very similar. In both cases the major difficulty seems to be identifying customers. All other items got remarkably good scores, over 4.0 (out of 5.0).

Table 3. Averages perceptions on CX, and on topics' relevance in a CX course. A comparison between the 2018 and 2019 surveys.

Year (No. of students)	Field of study	Averages scores									
		P1	P2	P3	T1	T2	T3	T4	T5	T6	T7
2018 (202)	All	3.56	4.36	4.39	4.38	4.29	4.59	4.32	4.36	4.35	4.47
2019 (199)	All	3.40	4.13	4.37	4.32	4.34	4.51	4.31	4.30	4.41	4.53

We used the Kolmogorow-Smirnow K-S test (using p-value $\leq$ 0.05 as decision rule), to check the hypothesis:

- H_0: the variable has a normal distribution,
- H_1: the variable does not have a normal distribution.

Table 4 shows that none of the variables have a normal distribution. That is why we used nonparametric statistic tests to analyze data. In all tests p-value $\leq$ 0.05 was used as decision rule.

Table 4. Kolmogorow-Smirnow K-S test for checking a normal distribution.

	P1	P2	P3	T1	T2	T3	T4	T5	T6	T7
p-value	0.000	0.000	0.000	0.000	0.000	0.000	0.000	0.000	0.000	0.000

We performed Spearman ρ tests to check the hypothesis:

- H_0: $\rho = 0$, the items P(T)m and P(Tn) are independent,
- H_1: $\rho \neq 0$, the items P(T)m and P(Tn) are dependent.

Table 5. Spearman ρ test for P and T items.

	P1	P2	P3	T1	T2	T3	T4	T5	T6	T7
P1	1	I	I	I	I	I	I	I	I	I
P2		1	0.423	0.286	0.293	0.370	0.167	0.329	0.375	0.260
P3			1	0.304	0.427	0.374	0.289	0.227	0.323	0.315
T1				1	**0.749**	0.498	0.466	0.471	0.422	0.415
T2					1	**0.647**	0.552	0.544	0.501	0.504
T3						1	0.475	0.482	0.531	0.430
T4							1	0.546	0.427	0.456
T5								1	0.522	0.492
T6									1	0.535
T7										1

As Table 5 shows, item P1 (how difficult it is to identify your customers) is independent of all other items. It looks like a certain disconnection between how students identify their customers and students' perception on all other assessed CX aspects. All other items are (very) weakly to strongly dependent. The strongest correlations occur between:

- T1 and T2: when students find easy to identify the products/systems/services they will develop/offer as professionals, they also find easy to identify the customers of those products/systems/services,

- T2 and T3: when students find easy to identify the customers of the products/systems/services they will develop/offer, they also find easy their customers' needs.

We used the Mann-Whitney U test to check the hypothesis:

- H_0: there are no significant differences between the perception of students by field of study,
- H_1: there are significant differences between the perception of students by field of study.

As Table 6 indicates, there are significant differences related to the field of study only regarding T4, the perceived relevance of CX design.

Table 6. Mann–Whitney U tests by students' field of study.

	P1	P2	P3	T1	T2	T3	T4	T5	T6	T7
p-value	.291	.336	.633	.115	.229	.560	**.007**	.062	.874	.495

We used the Kruskal–Wallis H tests to check the hypothesis:

- H_0: there are no significant differences between the perception of students from different countries,
- H_1: there are significant differences between the perception of students from different countries.

As Table 7 indicates, there are significant differences by countries the field of study regarding several items: P1 (the perceived difficulty in identifying their customers), T1 (the perceived relevance of the products/systems/services they will develop/offer as professionals), T2 (the perceived relevance of the customer of their products/systems/services), T4 (the perceived relevance of CX design), and T5 (the perceived relevance of CX evaluation).

Table 7. Kruskal–Wallis H tests by countries.

	P1	P2	P3	T1	T2	T3	T4	T5	T6	T7
p-value	**.001**	.966	.199	**.003**	**.010**	.313	**.000**	**.002**	.191	.477

We used the Kruskal–Wallis H tests to check the hypothesis:

- H_0: there are no significant differences between the perception of students belonging to different age groups,
- H_1: there are significant differences between the perception of students belonging to different age groups.

As Table 8 indicates, there are no significant differences by age group in none of the 10 items.

Table 8. Kruskal–Wallis H tests by age group.

	P1	P2	P3	T1	T2	T3	T4	T5	T6	T7
p-value	.282	.506	.217	.972	.720	.741	.245	.084	.565	.819

We used the Kruskal–Wallis H tests to check the hypothesis:

- H_0: there are no significant differences between the perception of students by gender,
- H_1: there are significant differences between the perception of students by gender.

As Table 9 indicates, there are significant differences by gender regarding only P2 (the perceived importance of customers' experience).

Table 9. Kruskal–Wallis H tests by gender.

	P1	P2	P3	T1	T2	T3	T4	T5	T6	T7
p-value	.575	**.024**	.097	.124	.092	.375	.206	.388	.394	.417

We used the Mann-Whitney U test to check the hypothesis:

- H_0: there are no significant differences between the perception of students that are working and studying, and the ones that are only studying,
- H_1: there are significant differences between the perception of students that are working and studying, and the ones that are only studying.

As Table 10 indicates, there are no significant differences related to the employment status regarding none of the 10 items.

Table 10. Mann–Whitney U tests if students are working or not.

	P1	P2	P3	T1	T2	T3	T4	T5	T6	T7
p-value	.531	.156	.880	.997	.597	.871	.654	.113	.874	.674

Students' opinions are rather similar. Significant differences occur in few cases. Most of the differences are related to the country of residence of the students. However, we do not have enough evidence to suspect cultural-related differences.

3.3 Qualitative Results

All students were able to identify the products/systems/services they think they will develop/offer as professionals. However, they are not really sure if their curricula include CX related topics. Even when they are enrolled in the same program, and therefore they have similar background, their perception on the topics that CX includes is variable. This is consistent with the results of our 2018 study [8].

CS students indicated a broad range of CX related topics: HCI, Usability (Engineering), User Interfaces, Requirements Engineering, Software Engineering, Software Quality, Software Design, and Accessibility. It seems that they relating CX with HCI, UX and usability. They are aware of the impact that software quality attributes (and in particular usability) have on CX. They are also aware that the whole process of developing interactive software systems has an impact on users as customers. Topics that CS students indicate in 2019 are more diverse that in our 2018 study. That is probably because the 2018 involved only students from Chile, Spain and Romania. Additionally, in 2019 the survey involved students from Colombia and Argentina.

Law students are also indicating a broader range of topics than in 2018. As in 2018, Civil Law is mentioned, but many other topics are highlighted: Commercial Law, Financial Law, Economic Law, Management, Economy, Customers Rights, Law Education, Taxes Regulations, Professional Ethics, and Litigation. That is probably because the 2018 survey included only 26 Law Romanian students; the 2019 survey included 131 Law students, from Romania and Chile.

As in 2018, very few students answered the open question regarding CX related aspects that they would like to highlight:

- Some CS students referred to customers' opinion, digital marketing, the software developer relationship with the customer, and the creation of postgraduate programs in CX; topics are quite different of those indicated in the 2018 survey, probably because the 2019 survey included CS students from Colombia and Argentina, beside Chile and Spain.
- Some Law students referred to customers' rights, the importance of being correctly informed as customer; topics are recurrent in both Chile and Romania, and were also indicated in the 2018 survey.

As in the previous survey, students highlighted CX related issues based on their background/field of study. All suggested topics worth to be attended in a CX course.

4 Conclusions and Future Work

We consider CX a holistic, interdisciplinary concept, that extends UX, focusing on customer's (cumulative) experience when interacting with all systems, products and services that a company offers. As many of these interactions involve interactive software systems and digital products, the increasing interest on CX from the HCI community make a lot of sense. Actually, CX may build a bridge between HCI and Service Science.

Teaching HCI and UX for years, we noticed an increasing demand on forming CX professionals. That is why we are teaching a CX optional course for CS graduate and undergraduate students since 2018. An exploratory study that we have done in 2018 showed that students of several programs (CS, Law, Tourism, Medical Technology, and Civil Engineering) and countries (Chile, Spain and Romania) are aware of the CX (and related topics) importance.

We conducted a similar survey in 2019. This time it involves fewer fields of study (CS and Law), but more countries (Chile, Spain, Romania, Colombia and Argentina). The 2019 survey led to similar results as the one that we have done in 2018. They both confirmed the students' awareness of the importance of CX, and the importance of a CX course. Studies' quantitative and qualitative findings help us validating the CX course structure and content.

Applying the survey in Chile in 2019 was particularly difficult. As future work, we would like to see if the survey lead to similar results for students from other fields, universities, and countries.

Acknowledgments. We would like to thank to all students involved in the study. Authors from Pontificia Universidad Católica de Valparaíso (Chile), Universidad de Playa Ancha (Chile), and Universidad Nacional de San Juan (Argentina) are participating in the HCI-Collab Project – The Collaborative Network to Support HCI Teaching and Learning Processes in IberoAmerica (http://hci-collab.com/).

References

1. ISO 9241-210: Ergonomics of human-system interaction—Part 11: Usability: Definitions and concepts, International Organization for Standardization, Geneva (2018)
2. Laming, C., Mason, K.: Customer experience – an analysis of the concept and its performance in airline brands. Res. Transp. Bus. Manag. **10**, 15–25 (2014)
3. Lewis, J.R.: Usability: lessons learned… and yet to be learned. Int. J. Hum.-Comput. Interact. **30**(9), 663–684 (2014)
4. Rusu, V., Rusu, C., Botella, F., Quiñones, D.: Customer eXperience: is this the ultimate eXperience? In: Proceedings Interacción 2018. ACM (2018)
5. Rusu, V., Rusu, C., Botella, F., Quiñones, D., Bascur, C., Rusu, V.Z.: Customer eXperience: a bridge between service science and human-computer interaction. In: Ahram, T., Karwowski, W., Pickl, S., Taiar, R. (eds.) IHSED 2019. AISC, vol. 1026, pp. 385–390. Springer, Cham (2020). https://doi.org/10.1007/978-3-030-27928-8_59
6. Interaction Design Foundation: Customer Touchpoints - The Point of Interaction Between Brands, Businesses, Products and Customers. http://www.interaction-design.org/literature/article/customer-touchpoints-the-point-of-interaction-between-brands-businesses-products-and-customers. Accessed 20 Jan 2020
7. Stein, A., Ramaseshan, B.: Towards the identification of customer experience touch point elements. J. Retail. Consum. Serv. **30**, 8–19 (2016)
8. Rusu, C., et al.: Forming customer eXperience professionals: a comparative study on students' perception. In: Ahram, T., Karwowski, W., Pickl, S., Taiar, R. (eds.) IHSED 2019. AISC, vol. 1026, pp. 391–396. Springer, Cham (2020). https://doi.org/10.1007/978-3-030-27928-8_60

An Experimental Study on Promotion of Pro-Environmental Behavior Focusing on "Vanity" for Interactive Agent

Mizuki Yamawaki[1](✉), Kimi Ueda[2] , Yoshiki Sakamoto[2], Hirotake Ishii[2] ,
Hiroshi Shimoda[2] , Kyoko Ito[3,4] , Takuya Fujioka[5], Qinghua Sun[5],
Yasuhiro Asa[5], and Takashi Numata[5]

[1] Faculty of Engineering, Kyoto University, Kyoto, Japan
yamawaki@ei.energy.kyoto-u.ac.jp
[2] Graduate School of Energy Science, Kyoto University, Kyoto, Japan
[3] Graduate School of Human Health Sciences, Tokyo Metropolitan University,
Tokyo, Japan
[4] Office of Management and Planning, Osaka University, Suita, Japan
[5] Research & Development Group, Hitachi, Ltd., Tokyo, Japan

Abstract. Although one of the solutions for environmental issues is to promote our pro-environmental behaviors (PEB) which is one of prosocial behaviors, it has not been done enough. This study focuses on "Vanity" for interactive agents as motivation for PEB. The purpose of this study is to confirm three hypotheses as follows; (1) One have "Vanity" for an interactive agent who is an observer. (2) Pro-social behavior is promoted by "Vanity" for interactive agents. (3) (1) can be also realized even when the prosocial behavior is PEB that are not supposed to be shared as one of our norms. In order to confirm these hypotheses, a comparison experiment employing an interactive agent and non-interactive agent was conducted. In the experiment, participants were asked to communicate with one agent for five minutes. After the communication, they were asked to wash dishes and to donate some money by the agent. Then, they were also asked to communicate with another agent, and they were asked to wash dishes and to donate by the agent as well. The amount of water use and the amount of donation were evaluated as indicators of PEB and prosocial behavior, respectively. Furthermore, the "Vanity" for the agent was measured by a questionnaire. As the result, there was a significant difference in the degree of "Vanity" (p < .001), however there was no significant difference in the amount of water use and donation amount. The interactivity of the agent affected participants' subjective feelings.

Keywords: Interactive agent · Vanity · Pro-environmental behavior · Subject experiment

G. Meiselwitz (Ed.): HCII 2020, LNCS 12195, pp. 247–258, 2020.
https://doi.org/10.1007/978-3-030-49576-3_19

1   Introduction

Energy consumption has been increasing since the Industrial Revolution [1], and it has caused serious global warming issue. Since carbon dioxide, a greenhouse gas, is generated with the consumption of energy, energy saving is necessary to solve the global warming issue. It is therefore necessary for individuals to perform pro-environmental behavior (PEB). Since PEB has a social dilemma structure, strong motivation is necessary to take action. In this study, the authors focused on "Vanity" as a motivation for PEB. "Vanity" is defined as "the desire to show oneself better to the other" in this study. This means that the presence of observer motivates them to behave prosocial activity to improve their reputation. Izuma et al. studied on their prosocial behaviors dealing with donation [2]. They compared donation rate in two cases with and without an observer, and revealed that the donation rate got higher in the case with observer. This can be interpreted that they change their behavior worrying about their reputation. In other words, they have vanity and tend to show themselves better when being observed. It has been known that the target of the vanity should not always human being according to conventional studies. Powell et al. conducted an experiment where they found that the amount of donations with eye figure on a donation box in supermarket increased 48% comparing with that without eye figure [3]. The dictator's game conducted by Haley and Fessler indicated that they provided more dividend under the condition where eye figure was displayed on the screen than that without eye figure [4]. Although above studies suggest that vanity has a possibility to motivate them to do prosocial behaviors which may make them lose over, there have been few study to deal with PEB as one of the prosocial behaviors. In this study therefore the authors have focused on an interactive agent as an observer to tickle their vanity and promote their PEBs. The interactive agent is expected to have strong influence for making them to have vanity and to improve prosocial behaviors comparing with non-interactive agent because they have higher personification. The purpose of this study is therefore to confirm the following hypotheses related to the relationship between an interactive agent as an observer and prosocial behaviors such as PEB.

- Hypothesis 1. They tend to have more vanity for an interactive agent than that for non-interactive agent.
- Hypothesis 2. The vanity for an interactive agent promotes prosocial behaviors which value is shared as norms.
- Hypothesis 3. Hypothesis 2 can be held even when the prosocial behavior is PEB which is not known to be shared as norms.

2   Design Guidelines of Interactive Agents to Promote PEB

Based on the conventional studies mentioned above, the following three factors are supposed to be essential to stir vanity and defined as the design guideline for the interactive agent.

1. The user feels that the agent does evaluate his/her behavior.
2. The user feels that the agent has sense of value for certain activities (PEB/protective activity in this study).
3. The user feels the agent favorable.

3 Experimental Method

3.1 Outline of Experiment

In this study, a comparison experiment was conducted with two experimental conditions of an interactive agent and non-interactive agent, and their vanity for the agents and prosocial behaviors were measured to find whether three hypotheses mentioned in Sect. 1 were held or not. Concretely, in order to verify the hypothesis 1, questionnaires were given after contacting with both agents to investigate how much vanity they had. In order to verify the hypothesis 2, how much amount of donation they made, which was an index of prosocial behavior, was investigated when communicating with both agents and compared the results. And in order to verify hypothesis 3, how much amount of water they saved to do a task, which was an index of PEB, was measured when communicating with both agents and compared the results as well.

3.2 Interactive and Non-interactive Agents

In this study, a chick type CG character "Piyota" was employed as the agent. Piyota has been developed as a non-human-type interactive agent, and it can dynamically form emotional expressions [5,6]. Figure 1 shows the appearance of two types of agents employed in this experiment. In the experiment, one was assigned as an interactive agent while another was as non-interactive agent. And two kinds of agent's speech voice with higher pitch and lower pitch were generated using a prototype of deep neural network-based parametric text-to-speech developed by R&D group of Hitachi, Ltd. Their colors and voices were set to be different for the interactive agent and non-interactive agent in order for the participants to distinguish them. The assignment of their colors and voices were randomly set to each participant in order to counterbalance their influence. The fundamental design of the both agents were the same. Both of the agents talked to the participants that they thought PEB was important in order to realize the design guideline 2. And they talked about their private information to disclose themselves for the participants to feel them favorable in order to realize the design guideline 3. They also talked a short story which showed they sometimes observed and evaluated others' behaviors in order to realize the design guideline 1. The difference of the agents was interactiveness, for example, the non-interactive agent didn't ask questions or do interactive behaviors such as they showed pleasure when they were stroked while the interactive agent did them. Table 1 shows the contents of their dialogues.

Table 1. Dialogue with interactive and non-interactive agents

Element of remark	Interactive agent	Non-interactive agent
Self disclosure	· Tell that the agent's birthday gifts were always hand-me-down	· Tell that the agent's birthday and Christmas were simultaneous cerebrated (the agent wanted to celebrate them separately)
	· Tell that the agent's birthday present hat is still a favorite	· Tell that the agent has big socks, and there is a big present in the socks when the agent gets up in the Christmas's morning
	· Tell that many brothers gathered together on a cold day	
Find values in PEB	· Explain that saving water can save power	· Explain that saving water can save power
	· Explain that detergent use leads to river pollution	· Explain that detergent use leads to river pollution
Evaluate others	· Tell that the agent did not want to see the water meter want up with the agent's friend leaving the shower running	· Tell that the agent's friend was brushing her teeth with water flowing and did not want to see water wasted
	· Tell that friends do not sort garbage	· Tell that the agent's friends set air conditioning to 18°
	· Tell that the agent broke off a relationship with the agent's friend because they acted badly for the environment	· Tell that the agent broke off a relationship with the agent's friends because they acted badly for the environment
Interaction	· Ask for his/her name and call his/her by name	
	· Ask and remember participant's birthday	
	· Ask about transportation and respond according to the answer	
	· Ask whether he/she does PEB and respond according to the answer	
	· Express pleasure when being stroked	
	· Ask whether he/she usually does housework and praise how to wash	

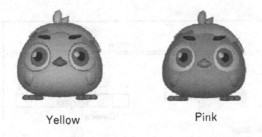

Yellow · Pink

Fig. 1. Appearances of agent. (Color figure online)

3.3 Experimental Period and Participants

The experiment was conducted from December 9th to 20th, 2019. The participants were 33 university undergraduate students or graduate school students who had no communication anomaly.

3.4 Experimental Environment

The experiment was conducted in an experimental room which top view is shown in Fig. 2. One of the agents was displayed on the monitor which was placed in front of the participants and the monitor size was 1.37 m width and 0.87 m height.

3.5 Procedure

Figure 3 shows the experimental procedure. The interaction of the interactive agent was realized in Wizard of Oz method. One of experimenters was hidden behind the partition, monitored their utterances and behaviors by a camera installed at the top of the monitor, and operated the agent speech and behaviors as reactions to them. In order to measure the degree of PEB activity, the participants were asked to wash dishes as an experimental task and amount of water use when washing was measured as an index of PEB. Since it is supposed that the amount of used water got decreased because of learning effect, a practice task for washing was done before the experiment. In the practice task, they were asked to decorate a cake and then wash the used chopping board, a cup, a spoon and a knife using a sponge, dishwashing detergent and water. After the practice task, they took a five-minute break and then conducted experimental condition 1, which was one of the interactive agent condition or the non-interactive condition. When starting the condition 1, they were given one 500 JPY coin, four 100 JPY coins and ten 10 JPY coins as their reward. And they were instructed to use the money when they donated in the later experiment. After that, the agent appeared and talked for five minutes as shown in Fig. 4. They were asked to wash the dishes as well as the practice task and then they were to donate

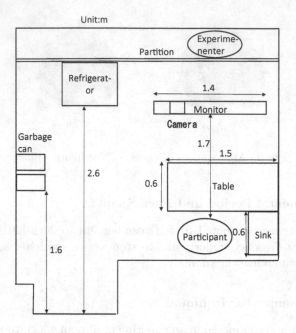

Fig. 2. A layout of an experiment room.

some money. The amount of donated money was measured as an index of their prosocial behaviors. They moved to the waiting room after the donation and answered the questionnaire. Then the condition 2 started where another agent appeared as well as the condition 1. When starting the condition 2, the same amount of coins was given as well as the condition 1. The agent of condition 1 and 2 was one of the interactive agent or the non-interactive agent and they were randomly assigned to each participant in order to counterbalance the order to eliminate the ordering effect.

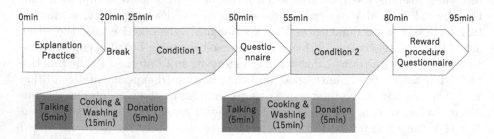

Fig. 3. Experimental procedure.

Fig. 4. A scene of experiment.

3.6   Measurement Items

– Questionnaire
  The following subjective feelings were asked in seven grade Likert scale from 0 to 6.
  1. How they felt they had interacted with the agent (interaction).
  2. How they thought the agent regarded ecological activity valuable (understanding of sense of value for ecological activity).
  3. How they thought the agent regarded protection of endangered species valuable (understanding of sense of value for species protection).
  4. How they felt the agent had evaluated your behavior (evaluated feeling).
  5. How they like the agent (favor).
  6. How they wanted to show themselves better than usual (vanity).
  7. How they felt the agent had its own will (will).
– Amount of donation
  Each agent asked donation for spices protection to the participant. The amount of the donation was measured under each condition as an index of prosocial behavior because its value has been widely shared among people.
– Amount of water use
  The agent talked to them that saving water was important for the environment and then they were asked to wash dishes and the amount of the water use when washing was measured as an index of PEB.
– Feeling to be observed by experimenter
  Because it may be possible that their behaviors based on the vanity was not for the agent but for the experimenter, the feeling how they had been observed by the experimenter was asked by seven grade Likert scale from 0 to 6 as well.

4   Experimental Results and Discussion

4.1   Subjective Feelings for Agents

The results were analyzed by two-tailed paired t-test between the interactive agent condition and non-interactive agent condition, and then the interaction of order and appearance of agents were confirmed by two-way ANOVA. The analysis results are shown below;

– Feeling of interaction
  The average score under the interactive agent condition was 4.24 (S.D. = 1.35) while that under non-interactive agent condition was 2.54 (S.D. = 1.77), and there was a significant difference (p < .001). No interaction of orders and appearances of the agents were found by the result of ANOVA.
– Feeling of having will
  The average in the interactive agent condition was 4.00 (S.D. = 1.64), and the average in the non-interactive agent condition was 3.12 (S.D. = 1.75). A significant difference appeared (p < .001). An interaction in regard to the order was observed(p < .05). Specifically, when the agent in the Condition 2 was the non-interactive agent, the average value in regard to the non-interactive agent was significantly lower than that when the agent in the Condition 1 was the non-interactive agent. When contacting the non-interactive agent after contacting the interactive agent, a feeling that communication was one-sided could be emphasized, and they felt that the non-interactive agent have less will.
– Feeling to be evaluated
  The average score under the interactive agent condition was 4.18 (S.D. = 1.33) while that under non-interactive agent was 2.67 (S.D. = 1.67), and there was a significant difference (p < .001). No interaction of orders and appearances of the agents were found by the result of ANOVA.
– Favor
  The average score under the interactive condition was 4.45 (S.D. = 1.44) while that under non-interactive agent condition was 3.52 (S.D. = 1.48), and there was a significant difference (p < .001). No interaction of orders and appearances of the agents were found by the result of ANOVA.
– Understanding of sense of value for ecological activity
  The average score under the interactive agent condition was 4.94 (S.D. = 1.09) while that under non-interactive agent was 4.76 (S.D. = 1.09), and there was no significant difference. It was supposed that ceiling effect appeared because the scores under both conditions were high. An interaction of orders of the agent was found by the result of ANOVA. In case that they contacted with the interactive agent first, the average score under the non-interactive agent was lower. It was supposed when they listened to the non-interactive agent they only felt weak enthusiasm comparing with the interactive agent.
– Understanding of sense of value for species protection
  The average score under the interactive agent condition was 4.42 (S.D. = 1.12) while that under non-interactive agent was 4.06 (S.D. = 1.41), and there was no significant difference. From the results of understanding of sense of values, their understandings were not depending on the interactiveness of the agents but the contents which they talked. Interaction of appearance of agents was found, where the score of non-interactive agent was lower when its color was pink. It was supposed that the voice pitch of another agent, yellow, was lower

so that they felt its persuasion stronger. Because the average scores of both understandings were more than 4, it was supposed that they understood what they should do to show themselves better.

– Vanity

The result of vanity is shown in Fig. 5. The average score under the interactive agent condition was 3.42 (S.D. $= 1.60$) while that under non-interactive agent was 2.67 (S.D. $= 1.63$), and there was a significant difference ($p < .001$). No interaction of orders and appearances of the agents were found by the result of ANOVA. It was found that the hypothesis 1 was held from these results.

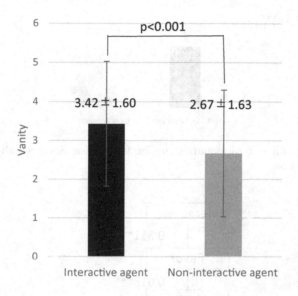

Fig. 5. Average scores of vanity under interactive agent condition and non-interactive agent condition.

– Feeling to be observed by experimenter

The average score was 3.94 (S.D. $= 1.74$) and there was no significant correlation between these scores and vanity, amount of donation or amount of water use. It was supposed that the feeling to be observed by experimenter didn't affect the experimental results.

4.2   Amount of Donation

The average amount of donation is shown in Fig. 6. There was no significant difference between the interactive agent condition and the non-interactive agent condition. No interaction of order and appearance was found by the results of ANOVA. Figure 7 shows the result of Structural Equation Modeling (SEM) from interactiveness to amount of donation. It was found that interactiveness affected favor, favor affected vanity and vanity affected amount of donation. The model however included 500JPY donations which were outliers. When they were excluded, the path coefficient between vanity and donation would be lower.

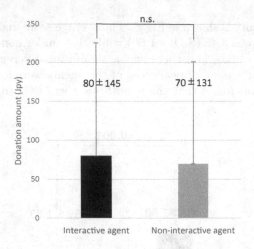

Fig. 6. Average amount of donation under interactive agent condition and non-interactive condition.

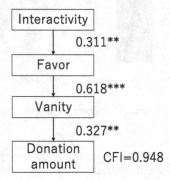

Fig. 7. Result of Structural Equation Modeling for donation.

4.3   Discussion About Donation Amount

There was no significant difference of donation between the conditions even though vanity improved prosocial behavior as the result of SEM. It was because 23 participants out of 33 made the same amount of donations under both the conditions. In the experiment, they made donations twice. It was supposed that they remembered amount of their first donation and tended to give the same amount for their second donation. It was suggested that the experimental design where the degree of prosocial behavior was measured by the amount of donation should be redesigned.

4.4   Amount of Water Use

The average amount of water use is shown in Fig. 8. There was no significant difference between the interactive agent condition and the non-interactive agent condition. No interaction of order and appearance was found by the results of ANOVA. Figure 9 shows the result of SEM from interactiveness to amount of water use. There was no significant path from vanity and amount of water use.

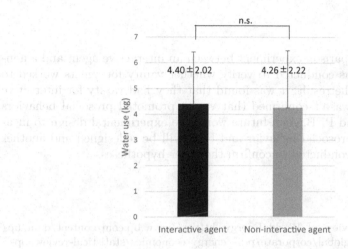

Fig. 8. Average amount of water use.

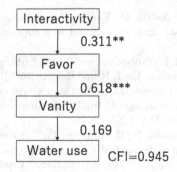

Fig. 9. Result of Structural Equation Modeling for water use.

4.5   Discussion of Water Use

There was weak but significant correlation found between amount of water use and feeling of interaction (Correlation Coefficient $(C.C) = 0.36$, $p < .01$), and weak but significant correlations were also found between amount of water use and favor $(C.C. = 0.31, p < .01)$ and feeling of having will $(C.C. = 0.29, p < 0.01)$.

As the feature of the dish washing task, it was supposed that the more they behaved politely the more they consumed water when they washed dishes. Because the feeling of interaction, favor and feeling of having will might make the behaviors of some participants polite, the amount of water use increased under the interactive agent condition. It was also suggested that the experimental design where the degree of PEB was measured by the amount of water use should be redesigned as well as donation.

5 Conclusion

In this study, a comparison experiment between an interactive agent and a non-interactive agent was conducted to verify whether vanity for agents worked to promote PEB. As the result, it was found that they had vanity for interactive agents, however it wasn't confirmed that vanity promoted prosocial behaviors such as donation and PEB. As a future work, the experimental design to measure the degree of prosocial behavior and PEB will be redesigned and another experiment will be conducted to confirm the other hypotheses.

References

1. BP Statistical Review of World Energy. https://www.bp.com/content/dam/bp/business-sites/en/global/corporate/pdfs/energy-economics/statistical-review/bp-stats-review-2019-full-report.pdf. Accessed 29 Jan 2019
2. Izuma, K., Saito, D.N., Sadato, N.: Processing of the incentive for social approval in the ventral striatum during charitable donation. J. Cogn. Neurosci. **22**(4), 621–631 (2010)
3. Powell, K.L., Roberts, G., Nettle, D.: Eye images increase charitable donations: evidence from an opportunistic field experiment in a supermarket. Ethology **118**(11), 1096–1101 (2012)
4. Haley, K.J., Fessler, D.M.T.: Nobody's watching? Subtle cues affect generosity in an anonymous economic game. Evol. Hum. Behav. **26**(3), 245–256 (2005)
5. Hiroki, S., et al.: An fMRI investigation on the positive consequences of being imitated by a virtual non-human agent. In: Proceedings of Neuroscience 2018, 110, November 2018, San Diego, CA, USA (2018)
6. Numata, T., Asa, Y., Kitagaki, T., Hashimoto, T., Karasawa, K.: Young and elderly users' emotion recognition of dynamically formed expressions made by a non-human virtual agent. In: Proceedings of 7th International Conference on Human-Agent Interaction, T10, pp. 253–255, October 2019, Kyoto, Japan (2019)

Social Media Marketing and Consumer Experience

The Key Role of Social Media in Identifying Consumer Opinions for Building Sustainable Competitive Advantages

Armenia Androniceanu[1], Irina Georgescu[1(✉)], and Jani Kinnunen[2]

[1] Bucharest University of Economic Studies, 010374 Bucharest, Romania
armenia.androniceanu@man.ase.ro,
irina.georgescu@csie.ase.ro
[2] Åbo Akademi University, 20500 Turku, Finland
jani.kinnunen@abo.fi

Abstract. The continuous increase of competition in international markets and the diversification of consumers' interests and expectations of products and services expressed on the social media networks have led us to investigate how the opinions of consumers can significantly influence the changes in the strategy of the organizations. In order to find out the role of social media networks for developing a successful business based on consistent competitive advantages, we chose sentiment analysis and lexicon-based approach. In this paper we used a public dataset Women's Clothing E-Commerce Review, consisting of real commercial data collected by Nick Brooks, but being anonymized, to analyze the customers' reviews on fashion. The original dataset consists of 23486 customer reviews and 10 variables. The data are text and numerical types. First, we will analyze the numerical types to find out existing connections between data. We apply the supervised techniques, known as the corpus-based approach, such as neural networks and logistic regression by means of IBM SPSS Statistics v20 software. Thus, the manufacturing companies can discover in the opinions of the consumers the good parts of their products and services, which should be maintained and developed, but also not as good and totally inadequate characteristics of their products and services, which should be replaced. The results of our research help companies discover the key success factors for a business that can contribute significantly to their competitive advantages and also where they can intervene to change certain characteristics of the products and services offered on the market.

Keywords: Social media · Consumer · Sentiment analysis

1 Introduction

We all know that Amazon is a giant in the area of online commerce. In fact, in the US, Amazon is responsible for 49.1% of online retail sales starting in 2018. Statistics show that 49% of Amazon's consumers come to Amazon first when they buy products online, because Amazon is an excellent portal for generic purchases - it has great variants for each type of product sought.

© Springer Nature Switzerland AG 2020
G. Meiselwitz (Ed.): HCII 2020, LNCS 12195, pp. 261–277, 2020.
https://doi.org/10.1007/978-3-030-49576-3_20

Social media networks can influence consumer attitude and behaviour of the products sold online. In general, social networks are seen mainly as a way of socializing, informing on certain issues of interest. In the last decade, social networks have become a way of promoting products and services in a business community or in a group of people who share the same concerns or hobbies [1–5].

The most popular social media networks on the Internet are the following:

- Facebook is still the largest social network in the world. It is said to have about 2 billion monthly users as of December 2017;
- WhatsApp is a social networking platform for instant messaging mainly used on smartphones. It was recently purchased by Facebook and is estimated to have about 1 billion users as of January 2018;
- LinkedIn is a social network platform used mainly by business professionals. As a registered trademark of Microsoft, LinkedIn has approximately 500 million users in January 2018.
- Google+ is a social network developed by Google and has about 150 million users as of January 2018.
- Twitter has about 320 million users, who can post tweets limited to 280 characters.
- Instagram is a social network for accessing photos and videos. It's part of Facebook and has about 800 million users in January 2018.
- Pinterest is a social network where content is added in the form of pins and has about 200 million users in January 2018.
- Befilo (New) is a new social network where everyone is automatically friends with everyone. Everything that needs friendship requests is now a story. You just have to join the network and automatically connect with all the members.
- Zoimas (New) is a - social network of ads that keeps you online as little as possible. You can only log in once in 12 h, you can log in only 15 min each time you log in, you can only post once every login and you have up to 150 friends.
- Messenger (New) is another social networking platform for instant messaging that works inside Facebook. Its users are estimated to be around $ 1.2 billion in January 2018.

Nowadays, most of the marketing specialists are considering social networks as a suitable medium for promotion, advertising and online sales [6–13].

Social media are no longer simply social networks, they are real sources of information and opinion formation. The role of social media is significantly influenced by large platforms. If in the past the number of consumer interactions with the brand was followed in the social media, at present, the most important role of these platforms is to increase brand awareness. Product reviews from social media are important, because recommendations are among the first three most important sources of consumer information in absolutely all areas in which companies operate.

Social media has become a research medium. This is an important place where companies "listen" to their consumers. Therefore, they must have the appropriate tools for "social listening". Otherwise they lose most of the information about the product or service offered. Overall, the importance of social media for brands increases as consumers' habits change. From this perspective we conducted this research. We chose the fashion field and analysed the behaviour and feelings of the online consumer of these products. Thus, we managed to outline an online consumer profile for clothing products sold in the online environment.

One should emphasize that the data-mining techniques applied on any social media data can lead to conclusions about which products are seen positively or negatively or if the products are seen good enough to be recommended.

In the next section, earlier research literature is reviewed; then, the applied methodology is presented followed by the analysis and discussion of the results. Finally, the paper is concluded with the limitations of the study.

2 Literature Review

A social media network is an informational network of internet users, based on certain websites where users can register and interact with other users, already registered. These social media networks are part of the relatively new, global phenomenon, called Web 2.0. Thus, the members of a social media network are connected informally and contribute actively to the collection and dissemination of information through the web.

A social media network is a web service designed to create virtual links between users, with social, commercial, political and educational applications. So we can say, that a social network is an information network of internet users who subscribe to the social network and interact with other users, already registered.

Social networks are developing user communities with common interests for a variety of specialized web services in certain fields. Sometimes the informational content, which is provided on the social network, is generated by the users themselves. In this case we talk about social media.

The most important members of a social media network include: the moderator; the silent, the enthusiastic, the agitator; the curious, and the influential.

1. The moderator is the one who takes care that the activity of the community is carried out under optimal conditions, its role being particularly important, it is responsible for the content posted, the one approving any comment.
2. The silent person is the one who visits the site to observe, read the comments, very rarely to express his opinion on a particular subject.
3. The enthusiast is the one who posts the most content, frequently expresses his opinion, being the most active of the members.
4. The agitator is indispensable for an online community, it is the one that contradicts everyone, provokes them and initiates numerous contradictory discussions.
5. The curious is the one who generates the content through the frequently asked questions, he is extremely valuable for the dynamics of the discussion group.
6. The influencer is the most connected to the networks, having a large number of online contacts and therefore he will spread any information to a large number of people connected to the Internet as quickly as possible.

One of the main advantages of social media networks is the interaction of brands with consumers. Other important advantages are: cheap transmission environment, high accessibility, the possibility to listen continuously to consumer opinions, attracting fans, market research. Social networks can bring consistent financial benefits and sustainable competitive advantages.

A segmentation of the consumers of social networks helps the brands choose their future consumers in the social media according to their marketing needs. The specialists identified different types of users [14–17]. There are the following four major types of consumers in social networks: Quiet users, Story consumers, Chameleons and Experts.

Quiet users are the least active category. In their circle of virtual friends there are only people well known to them with whom they have close relationships in real life [18]. Their role in a network is that of "gate keepers", who see information, receive it and rarely distribute it to other people.

The story consumers are users more active than the quiet ones. They are very close to those in their contact list and then to people they have met in wider contexts, forming a social circle of 50–100 friends. They read with interest the information posted by other users, express their opinions, but they also express their own opinions and post pictures and information on their profile page. The story consumer is an active information seeker. It does not create its own content but will publish content created by the brand.

Chameleons are active, quite numerous and usually use several social networks, having between 100 and 300 virtual friends. In addition to the profile updates, add comments to different topics, share links or create their own content, occasionally access applications and promote themselves. Chameleons are not reluctant to add people they don't know to their contact list.

Experts are the most active category of users of social networks. In their list we will find more than 300 friends on social media. They spend a lot of time on the network: log in several times a day or leave the site open, often use applications, experiment and communicate a lot. Experts create their own content and filter the content that others distribute. From the perspective of brands, they have the potential to become "trend-setters".

The researches of the specialists show that in social media consumers appreciate the brands already known but who are responsive to their needs and constantly communicate with them. From this perspective we approached the social media networks in our work. For this purpose, we have used a database in which the online consumers of fashion clothing are registered with their opinions and sentiments regarding the products purchased online. The companies will find out how customers perceive their products and services and how they can improve their offers.

3 Methodology

Due to the large volume of information on the internet, it is difficult to find opinion sources and summarize opinions manually. Therefore, machine learning automated this process. On social media, sentiment analysis offers a public opinion about a brand. For companies with e-commerce platforms, extracting important information from customers reviews may have a crucial impact on their success of marketing program. In order to analyze the data, we apply the supervised techniques, known as the corpus-based approach, such as neural networks and logistic regression by means of SPSS. Based on the results, we made a series of correlations and created a consumer profile of online products that may be of real interest to the entire business community in the virtual environment. Sentiment analysis or opinion mining is an automated process by which subjective information is extracted from text by means of machine learning techniques. In business, sentiment analysis is used to exploit unstructured data in order to extract the social sentiment of a brand, product or service.

In this case, the target variable is Recommended taking two values, Yes and No, depending if the product has been recommended or not by the client. The sentiment analysis is viewed as a classification problem. The data is divided into the training set and the test set. By means of confusion matrix and ROC curve we will compute the accuracy of each classifier and we will graphically represent it.

We also apply unsupervised techniques known as the lexicon-based approach. An important aspect in sentiment analysis is the semantic orientation or the polarity of a word or a sentence. First, we build a dictionary or a lexicon. Generally, each word is associated with a polarity value (+1, if the polarity is positive, i.e. word as nice, elegant, −1 if the polarity is negative, i.e. unattractive, bad and 0 if the polarity is neutral, i.e. dress, trousers). We compute the total polarity of the text by adding the polarity of each word from the lexicon. To carry out this experiment we use R environment.

4   Research Results and Analysis

The dataset is called Women's Clothing E-commerce Review and it belongs to Nick Brooks [19, 20]. The dataset contains customers' reviews on clothing and the references on the company have been anonymized. The names of the customers were not disclosed. The company name has been replaced by retailer.

We reduced the number of observations to half: 11031. The attributes of the dataset are: Customer Id, Clothing Id, Age of the reviewer, Title of the review, Review text, Product rating by reviewer, Positive feedback count, Recommendation by reviewer, Name of the division of the product, Name of the department of the product and Type of product. After cleaning the data, we obtained 9092 review cases without any missing data. Of these reviews 82% give a recommendation (*Recommended* = 1) and 18% of the reviews do not give a recommendation (*Recommended* = 0).

4.1   Sentiment Analysis

On this dataset several researches have been made [19–21]. Paper [21] analyzes the attributes of the dataset by descriptive statistics and sentiment analysis. The supervised learning method is a bidirectional recurrent neural network implemented in Python, used to classify the reviewed products. The results of the experiments showed that a recommendation indicates a positive sentiment score.

We start from the previous research [19, 20], where a corpus and a document term matrix have been built. A document term matrix is a matrix which allows the comparison of words and terms. The line represents the document and the column

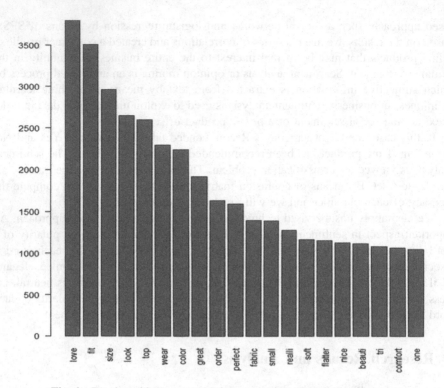

Fig. 1. Barplot with the most 20 frequent words (Our determination)

represents a word. The barplot from Fig. 1 shows the frequency of the first 20 frequent words.

Next, we create a word cloud with the most frequent terms, picking out the top 200 most frequent (Fig. 2) ones. A wordcloud is a collection of words that show the most frequent words of different sizes, according to how often they are used in the text. Wordclouds are powerful data visualization tools, revealing key patterns in the data. As seen in Fig. 2, love, great, perfect, comfortable and wear stand out as positive words, while looked, wanted back, disappointed, returned, and cheap stand out as negative ones.

The next step is the Sentiment Analysis, meaning we have to compute the polarity of the positive and negative words. We will use the Harvard-IV Dictionary, which is a dictionary of positive and negative words. We will select the results of the Harvard-IV Dictionary, according to which each review has a word count, a positivity score (PosGI), a negativity score (NegGI) and an overall score (PosGI – NegGI = SentGI).

Table 1 shows the descriptive statistics of the final used data in our analysis for the 9092 reviews (N). In addition to the three sensitivity variables, we have computed their normalized counterparts: NegGI100, PosGI100, and SentGI100, which are obtained by dividing NegGI, PosGI, and SentGI by the word counts and multiplied by 100. The normalized sensitivity figures, thus, are not dependent on the length of reviews, but give a comparable measure of sensitivity of reviews (per 100 words). This is done due

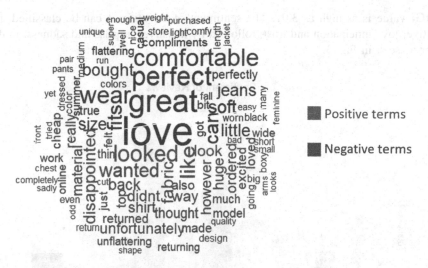

Fig. 2. WordCloud with the most frequent positive and negative terms (Our determination)

to clear dominance of the positive reviews with recommendation (82%) over the negative reviews with no recommendation (18%), which also means that the length of positive reviews are longer, while it is not a-priori know, whether the length of the reviews actually add important positive (or negative) content, while the content is seen in PosGI, NegGI and SentGI; the wordcount-normalized NegGI100, PosGI100, and SentGI100, are computed and later tested to handle such potential bias towards positive review outcomes.

Table 1. Variables and descriptive statistics.

	N	Minimum	Maximum	Mean	Std. dev.
NegGI	9092	0,00	2,17	0,12	0,15
PosGI	9092	0,00	3,04	0,23	0,26
SentGI	9092	−0,67	3,91	0,11	0,22
NegGI100	9092	0,00	22,22	0,55	0,92
PosGI100	9092	0,00	50,00	1,23	2,15
SentGI100	9092	−22,22	50,00	0,70	1,97
Rating	9092	1,00	5,00	4,20	1,11
Age	9092	18,00	93,00	43,14	12,04
Recommended	9092	0,00	1,00	0,82	0,38

(Our determination)

Overall, the reviews are positive, but the minimum score (SentGI) is negative −0.67, the 1st quartile (25th percentile) SentGI = 001, median (50th percentile) SentGI = 008, and 3rd quartile (75th percentile) SentGI = 0.17, while the maximum

SentGI value is as high as 3.91. The sentiment of the reviews can be classified into positive, joy, anticipation and trust, followed by negative, surprise and sadness, in this order as seen in Fig. 3.

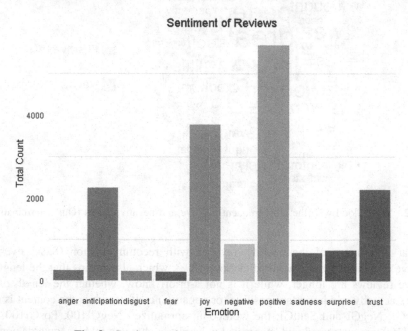

Fig. 3. Sentiment of the reviews (Our determination)

The second part of the text analysis consists of the logistic regression model and neural network classifiers applied to this dataset.

4.2 Logistic Regression

The purpose of the applied logistic regression is to measure the extent to which a class variable depends on explanatory variables. In our case, we have two dependent classes, *recommendation of a product* or *not recommending* the product, for which we will obtain a measure of *probability of success*; model fitting will be reported; measures of pseudo-R-squares will be discussed to find out how well the explanatory variables explain the variation in the dependent variable; further, the statistical significance of each explanatory factor will be obtained. Before these results insignificant variables are removed to obtain the final model, and then, the final model's parameter estimates and the comparable importance of the retained explanatory variables will be analysed.

Logistic regression is applied to the dependent *Recommended* variable, which is a binary class variable, which takes the two possible values: *1* when the reviewer recommends the reviewed product or *0*, when no recommendation is given. We start by testing which potential explanatory variables seen earlier in Table 1 are significant in predicting the recommended class. Firstly, by using IBM SPSS Statistics v20 software, we test a binomial logistic regression model including as explanatory variables only the sensitivity measures, *GI*s and their normalized (divided by word counts of each review) forms *GI*100s, i.e. *NegGI and NegGI100* (measuring negativity), *PosGI* and *PosGI100* (measuring positivity), and their differences *SentGI* and *SentGI100* (sensitivity). We tested several stepwise variable elimination methods resulting in consistent outcome. Using the forward stepwise method based on likelihood ratios, we obtain, after three iteration rounds, the variables left in the equation and the eliminated variables. These are shown in Table 2.

Table 2. The retained and eliminated variables.

Variables in the equation		B	S.E.	Wald	df	Sig.
Step 3	SentGI	3,438	0,262	171,529	1	0,000
	NegGI	−0,916	0,198	21,342	1	0,000
	PosGI	0,308	0,153	4,077	1	0,043
	Constant	1,283	0,041	963,287	1	0,000
Variables not in the equation		Score			df	Sig.
	SentGI100	1,761			1	0,185
	NegGI100	0,879			1	0,349
	PosGI100	0,592			1	0,442
Overall stats		2,937			3	0,401

(Our determination)

It is noticed on the top of Table 2 that the significances (Sig.) of *NegGI, PosGI* and *SentGI* are all under 5%; thus, the variables are significant at 5% level. Similarly, on the bottom of Table 2 it is seen that the corresponding normalized measures per 100 words,

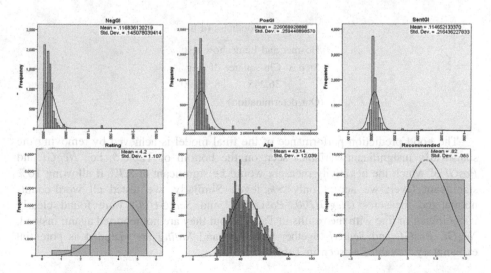

Fig. 4. The distributions of the retained model variables (Our determination)

NegGI100, PosGI100 and *SentGI100,* are all clearly insignificant as the most significant variable, *SentGI100,* is significant at 18.5% level, while larger than 10% (or even
5%) levels are unacceptable. Figure 4 shows the distributions of the retained variables
and the difference from a normal distribution.

In the next step, we proceed to the actual model, where the explanatory variables of
Rating (1–5), the reviewer's *Age* together with the above retained measures of
NegativityGI, PositivityGI and *SensitivityGI* are again tested by the binomial logistic
regression model. After three steps (the last step with eight rounds of iterations), we
achieve 93,8% total accuracy (93,5% for non-recommendation class *0* and 93,9% for
the recommended class *1*) as shown in Table 3.

Table 3. Prediction accuracy of the binomial logistic regression model.

Classification				
Observed		Predicted		
		Recommended		Percentage correct
		0	1	
Recommended	0	1535	106	93,5%
	1	458	6993	93,6%
Overall percentage				93,8%

(Our determination)

One can see from Table 4 that the p-value is less than 0.5, which suggests that the
model would benefit if allowing interactions or non-linearity. We will not introduce
such in the logistic regression model; instead, we let the neural network model of the
next section be trained to find out the more complex relationships.

Table 4. Goodness of fit.

Hosmer and Lemeshow test			
Step 3	Chi-square	df	Sig.
	36,245	8	0,00

(Our determination)

The good prediction performance of the final model is achieved by removing the
statistically insignificant variables seen on the bottom of Table 5, i.e., *NegGI* and
PosGI of which the negativity measure would be significant at 8.7% if allowing 10%
significant level; we accept only 5% level. Similarly, we tested all word-count-
normalized measures (*NegGI100, PosGI100,* and *SentGI100*) were found clearly
insignificant in line with the results in Table 2, but they are not reported again; instead,
NegGI, PosGI, and *SentGI* together with *Age* and *Rating* are included as potential
explanatory variables as seen in Table 5.

Table 5. The retained and eliminated variables.

Variables in the equation		B	S.E.	Wald	df	Sig.
Step 3	SentGI	0,826	0,359	5,286	1	0,021
	Rating	3,317	0,094	1252,899	1	0,000
	Age	0,009	0,004	4,662	1	0,031
	Constant	−10,638	0,36	873,685	1	0,000
Variables not in the equation		Score			df	Sig.
	NegGI	2,935			1	0,087
	PosGI	0,094			1	0,760
Overall stats		3,390			5	0,564

(Our determination)

The final logistic regression model is:

$$Z = ln\left(\frac{p}{1-p}\right) = Constant + \alpha^* Rating + \beta^* SentGI + \gamma^* Age.$$

p is the probability that the review is favourable, and $1 - p$ the probability that the review is unfavourable. The *Recommendation* (0/1) is the dependent variable and *Rating, SentGI and Age* of a reviewer are the retained explanatory variables (as shown on the top of Table 5), which is computed using the logistic regression model:

$$Recommendation = \begin{cases} 1 & if \quad 1/(1+e^{-Z}) \geq 0.5 \\ 0 & if \quad 1/(1+e^{-Z}) < 0.5, \end{cases}$$

where $Z = -10.638 + 3.317 * Rating + 0.826 * SentGI + 0.009 * Age$ is the logistic regression equation, which shows that one unit increase in the rating will increase the odds of having a recommendation by exp(3.317) = 27.57 times; one unit increase in the sensitivity indicator will increase the odds of having a recommendation by exp (0.826) = 2.284 times; and one year increase in a reviewer's age will increase the odds of having a recommendation by exp(0.009) = 1.009 times.

The model is summarized in Table 6. In general, R^2 is not clearly defined in order to measure the variance in the response variable for the logistic regression. The most common pseudo R^2 s have been proposed by Cox and Snell [22] and Nagelkerke [23], respectively. They have values between 0 and 1. For this model, the largest pseudo R^2 is Nagelkerke R Square, meaning that 79.7% is the proportion of variance in the review recommendation associated with the predictors.

Table 6. Goodness-of-fit.

Model summary		
−2 Log likelihood	Cox & Snell R Square	Nagelkerke R Square
2517,434	0,487	0,797

(Our determination)

Next, we study the importance of the considered variables using an artificial neural network.

4.3   Multilayer Perceptron Neural Network

IBM SPSS v20 statistical software is used also to construct the multilayer perceptron, MLP, neural network. We include the same variables as in the previous section with the logistic regression model: *NegGI, PosGI, SentGI, Age* and *Rating* and the same data set is divided into the training set consisting of 70% of the 9092 cases and the 30% test set.

The back-propagation algorithm is used with scaled conjugated gradient optimization over the two hidden layers. The hyperbolic tangent, $f : R \rightarrow (-1, 1)$, $f(c) = \frac{e^c - e^{-c}}{e^c + e^{-c}}$, is selected as the activation function for hidden layers and the activation function in the output layer is softmax, $\sigma : R^K \rightarrow (0, 1)$, $P_j = \sigma(z)_j = \frac{e^{z_j}}{\sum_{k=1}^{K} e^{z_k}}$, *for*

$j = 1, \ldots, K$ *and* $z = (z_1, \ldots, z_K) \in R^K$, where K = 2 as the number of output classes (1 for recommendation and 0 for no recommendation). The output of the softmax function consists of the two probabilities, one for each dependent variable class, and the two probabilities sum up to 1.

Figure 5 shows the constructed model architecture. The explanatory variables are seen on the left. The rating variable is set categorical and, thus, 5 input neurons are devoted to the 5 rating classes. The first hidden layer has 7 neurons (plus a bias) and the second hidden layer has 5 neurons (plus a bias).

The blue and gray lines in Fig. 5 denote weights: the darker (blue) and thicker the lines, the greater the weights, after the input layer, of the explanatory variable inputs and, after then, the weights of the activations from the first hidden layer to the second hidden layer and, finally, the weights of the activations from the second hidden layer to the output layer.

Table 7 summarizes the model performance. The final model has 94.5% (the overall percent for the test set) prediction accuracy, which is slightly higher than the accuracy of the logistic regression model (93.8%). Both classes of the *Recommendation* (0/1) are predicted as well (94.4% accuracy for no recommendation and 94.5% for recommendation).

In machine learning, ROC curve is one of the most important evaluation metrics to measure the classifier's performance. The performance of the model is depicted by the ROC curve in Fig. 6. AUC = 0.976, which tells that there are 97.6% chances that the model will be able to distinguish between the positive class (1) and the negative class (0).

Finally, the importance of the explanatory (independent) variables in predicting the dependent *Recommendation* are depicted in Fig. 7. When importance is normalized so that the most important factor, *Rating*, obtains 100% importance, the next important variables, in decreasing order, are *SentGI* (26.0%), *PosGI* (19.3%), *NegGI* (13.8%), and the least important variable, *Age* (10.0%).

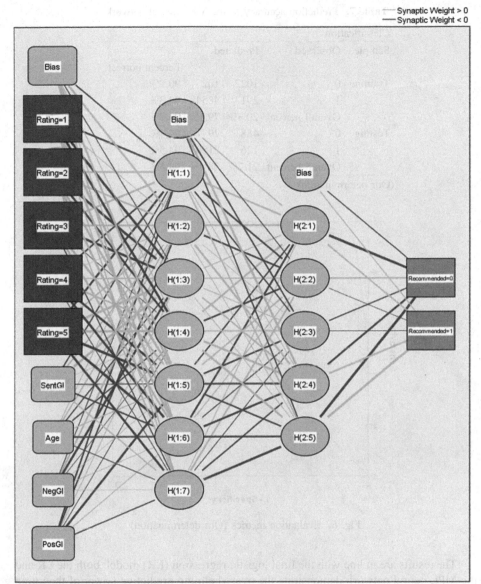

Hidden layer activation function: Hyperbolic tangent

Output layer activation function: Softmax

Fig. 5. The architecture of the applied MLP neural network (Our determination) (Color figure online)

Table 7. Prediction accuracy of the MPL neural network.

Classification				
Sample	Observed	Predicted		
		0	1	Percent correct
Training	0	1022	102	90.9%
	1	291	4854	94.3%
	Overall percent	20.9%	79.1%	93.7%
Testing	0	488	29	94.4%
	1	126	2180	94.5%
	Overall percent	21.7%	78.3%	94.5%

(Our determination)

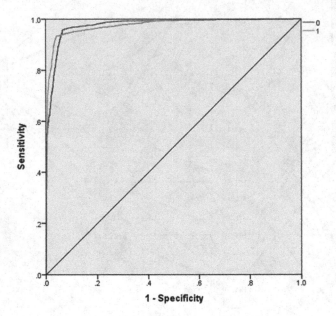

Fig. 6. Evaluation metrics (Our determination)

The results are in line with the final logistic regression (LR) model: both the LR and the MPL neural network demonstrate the overwhelming predictive power of the rating variable over the other variables; both models found the sensitivity measure (*SentGI*) the second powerful explanatory variable and the Age as having only small predictive power; however, the LR model eliminated both *PosGI* and *NegGI* as statistically insignificant, while the neural network is capable to use them in prediction by allowing complex interactions and non-linearities. As seen by very high prediction accuracies of the two applied models, the sensitivity measure of *PosGI* and *NegGI* (and thus also *Age*) were not critical for predicting the reviewers' given recommendation - no-recommendation with high accuracy. *SensitivityGI*, as the difference of *PosGI* and *NegGI*, has predictive power although it is limited compared to *Ratings*.

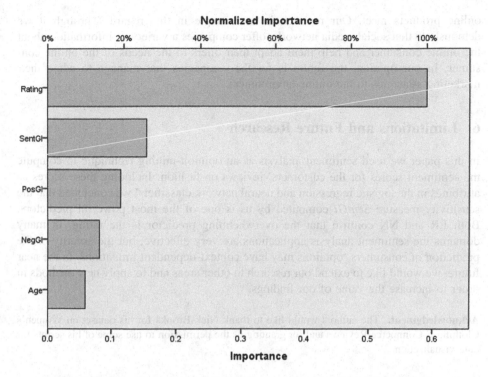

Fig. 7. Relative importance of the explanatory variables (Our determination)

5 Conclusions

Social networks can greatly help both business development in the virtual environment and the improvement of social life, but there must always be a balance between online and real interaction. At the same time, we can point out that the online social networks will change the way of approaching social, economic, political, educational life. That's why companies need to create special marketing strategies to use the benefits that social media offers for their business.

Social media networks contribute to the development of a new type of competitive market in a virtual environment, which will significantly mark the business in all areas. Social networks will reduce communication costs and strengthen active communities in the virtual environment. The advantages of online commerce will increasingly attract more companies but also consumers and a new form of competition between companies in the virtual environment will develop. The virtual market will be dominated by companies that manage to use social networks effectively to promote their products and to attract an increasing number of consumers of products and services in the online environment.

Our research shows that social media networks deliver essential information to companies. These can become the basic source for creating and developing their competitive advantages in the virtual market where the producers and consumers of online products meet. Our research is an example in this regard. Through it we demonstrate that social media networks offer companies a variety of information about the online consumer and help them adapt their offers to the needs of the online consumer. In our opinion, the future is for the companies that manage to adapt their marketing strategies to the online environment.

6   Limitations and Future Research

In this paper we used sentiment analysis as an opinion-mining technique to compute the sentiment scores for the customers' reviews on fashion. Including these scores as attributes in the logistic regression and neural network classifiers, we concluded that the sensitivity measure *SentGI* computed by us is one of the most powerful predictors. Both LR and NN confirm that the overwhelming predictor is the rating. In many domains the sentiment analysis applications are very effective, but the polarity or the prediction of consumers 'opinions may have context-dependent limitations. In the near future, we would like to extend our research to other areas and to apply new methods in order to increase the value of our findings.

Acknowledgment. The authors would like to thank Nick Brooks for his dataset on Women's Clothing E-Commerce Reviews and for granting us the permission to use some of his scripts for data visualization.

References

1. Tvaronavičienė, M.: Insights into global trends of capital flows' peculiarities: emerging leadership of China. Adm. Manag. Public **32**, 6–17 (2019). https://doi.org/10.24818/amp/2019.32-01
2. Vaitkevicius, S., Mazeikiene, E., Bilan, S., Navickas, V., Savaneviciene, A.: Economic demand formation motives in online-shopping. Eng. Econ. **30**(5), 631–640 (2019). https://doi.org/10.5755/j01.ee.30.5.23755
3. Victor, V., Thoppan, J.J., Fekete-Farkas, M., Grabara, J.: Pricing strategies in the era of digitalisation and the perceived shift in consumer behaviour of youth in Poland. J. Int. Stud. **12**(3), 74–91 (2019). https://doi.org/10.14254/2071-8330.2019/12-3/7
4. Yunus, E., Susilo, D., Riyadi, S., Indrasari, M., Putranto, T.D.: The effectiveness marketing strategy for ride-sharing transportation: intersecting social media, technology, and innovation. Entrep. Sustain. Issues **7**(2), 1424–1434 (2019). https://doi.org/10.9770/jesi.2019.7.2(44)
5. Ulewicz, R., Blaskova, M.: Sustainable development and knowledge management from the stakeholders' point of view. Pol. J. Manag. Stud. **18**(2), 363–374 (2018)
6. Kot, S., Brzezinski, S.: Market orientation factors in sustainable development and corporate social responsibility. Asian J. Appl. Sci. **8**(2), 101–112 (2015)
7. Borocki, J., Radisic, M., Sroka, W., Greblikaite, J., Androniceanu, A.: Methodology for strategic posture determination of SMEs - the case from a developing country. Inžinerinė Ekonomika-Eng. Econ. **30**(3), 265–277 (2019)

8. Belas, J., Belas, L., Cepel, M., Rozsa, Z.: The impact of the public sector on the quality of the business environment in the SME segment. Adm. Manag. Public **32**, 18–31 (2019). https://doi.org/10.24818/amp/2019.32-02
9. Gavurova, B., Tucek, D., Kovac, V.: Economic aspects of public procurement parameters in tertiary education sector. Adm. Manag. Public **32**, 42–62 (2019). https://doi.org/10.24818/amp/2019.32-04
10. Kot, S., Tan, M., Dragolea, L.: The use of social media supporting studying. Econ. Sociol. **10**(1), 169–180 (2017). https://doi.org/10.14254/2071-789x.2017/10-1/12
11. Smolag, K., Slusarczyk, B., Kot, S.: The role of social media in management of relational capital in universities. Prabandhan: Ind. J. Manag. **9**(10), 34–41 (2016)
12. Sokół, S., Słupińska, S.: Creative management of the advertising form and content. Entrep. Sustain. Issues **7**(2), 842–861 (2019). http://doi.org/10.9770/jesi.2019.7.2(4)
13. Štefko, R., Bačík, R., Fedorko, R., Oleárová, M., Rigelský, M.: Analysis of consumer preferences related to the use of digital devices in the e-commerce dimension. Entrep. Sustain. Issues **7**(1), 25–33 (2019). https://doi.org/10.9770/jesi.2019.7.1(2)
14. Al-Tkhayneh, K., Kot, S., Shestak, V.: Motivation and demotivation factors affecting productivity in public sector. Adm. Manag. Public **33**, 77–102 (2019). https://doi.org/10.24818/amp/2019.33-05
15. Gavurova, B., Bacik, R., Fedorko, R., Nastisin, L.: The customer's brand experience in the light of selected performance indicators in the social media environment. J. Compet. **10**(2), 72–84 (2018). https://doi.org/10.7441/joc.2018.02.05
16. Raišienė, A.G., Bilan, S., Smalskys, V., Gečienė, J.: Emerging changes in attitudes to interinstitutional collaboration: the case of organizations providing social services in communities. Adm. Manag. Public **33**, 34–56 (2019). https://doi.org/10.24818/amp/2019.33-03
17. De la Hoz-Rosales, B., Camacho, J., Tamayo, I.: Effects of innovative entrepreneurship and the information society on social progress: an international analysis. Entrep. Sustain. Issues **7**(2), 782–813 (2019). http://doi.org/10.9770/jesi.2019.7.2(1)
18. Mura, L., Vlacseková, D: Motivation of public employees: case study of Slovak teaching and professional staff. Adm. Manag. Public **31**, 67–80 (2018). https://doi.org/10.24818/amp/2018.31-05
19. Brooks, N.: Guided numeric and text exploration E-commerce (2018a). https://www.kaggle.com/nicapotato/guided-numeric-and-text-exploration-e-commerce
20. Brooks, N.: Women's e-commerce clothing review (2018b). https://www.kaggle.com/nicapotato/womens-ecommerce-clothing-reviews
21. Agarap, A.F., Grafilon, P.M.: Statistical analysis of e-commerce reviews with sentiment classification using bidirectional recurrent neural network. (2018). https://arxiv.org/abs/1805.03687
22. Cox, D.R., Snell, E.J.: Analysis of Binary Data, 2nd edn. Chapman and Hall/CRC, London (1989)
23. Nagelkerke, N.J.D.: A note on a general definition of the coefficient of determination. Biometrika **78**, 691–692 (1991)

The Digital "Advertising Call": An Archeology of Advertising Literacy

Karine Berthelot-Guiet[✉]

CELSA Sorbonne Université-GRIPIC, Paris, France
karine.berthelot-guiet@sorbonne-universite.fr

Abstract. This paper questions the notion of digital advertising literacy. We first propose a theoretical positioning that tries to think of self-taught literacy, not necessarily linked to education and state intervention, by a daily company with advertising. We will explore the French case, since the nineteenth century, to understand how people developed advertising literacy through different means. In this respect, how can we think of an active receiver, controlling codes instead of manipulated crowds? We will then explore contemporary forms of advertising digital literacy such as online conversation on social networks, algorithmic advertising, and advertising culture

Keywords: Digital discourses · Advertising literacy · Social media · Consumption · Culture

1 Introduction

Today's main overarching view of literacy, including advertising, is a media education issue. This point of view is nourished by the vision of institutions such as UNESCO or French state organization called CLEMI (Centre for Media and Information Education). Thus, the UNESCO website states that media literacy "plus Information Literacy equals Media and Information Literacy," including related literacies amongst which advertising literacy is listed. Media literacy is a growing and expanding system since it is linked to all the new technologies, and it now includes "social networking literacy." The whole set is deeply linked to "social literacies" - scientific, political, family, and cultural literacies [1, 2].

Advertising literacy is also linked to "Combatting Disinformation and Misinformation" and based on the principle that children should be protected from advertising manipulation. This definition must be explored since we are going to propose another way of looking at it; that is to say, we are going to explore how people have developed a kind of advertising literacy by themselves over time, and continue to do so.

2 About Literacy and Advertising: Definitions

2.1 Advertising: Manipulated Crowds

The notion of advertising literacy, in academic researches, has been mostly developed, although poorly, around the idea of a needed education necessary to protect children:

© Springer Nature Switzerland AG 2020
G. Meiselwitz (Ed.): HCII 2020, LNCS 12195, pp. 278–294, 2020.
https://doi.org/10.1007/978-3-030-49576-3_21

advertising literacy has been seen as one of the relatively neglected areas. In his article, Baudrillard moves the question not to evacuate the manipulation but to show that it is far from being crude. In 2010, Malmelin [3] had also pointed out to bewildering paucity of the studies about this subject while he was defining advertising literacy and drawing its frame [4]. "Erdem explains that these few researches were, at first in the 1990s, focused on children and considered advertising literacy as an "integrative part of media literacy." Then, at the turn of the century, the rise of computing, smartphones, and tablets changed the theoretical landscape. It gave less importance to children while maintaining the idea of a necessary education since "the self-propagation of the message also enables the consumer/potential consumer to be persuaded to buy and to be used as an advertising tool for advertising producers." Now, especially with digital devices, everybody is seen as vulnerable to advertising.

The notion of advertising manipulation is not specific to the field of media literacy researches and has to be linked to a long tradition of critical analysis of advertising. Different theoretical paradigms have proposed a reflection on advertising and the relationships it is likely to have with society. These approaches come together in the most negative role they attribute to advertising in its effects [5]. Regardless of the methods, modes of action and final goals, advertising is presented as a powerful means of acting on the crowds. These analyses have as another common point to be based on a particular conception of the modes of reception and receivers of advertising: they are passive, inactive, receiving the messages and reacting mechanically to them, as under hypnosis. The posture denies any individual or collective intelligence in front of the advertising. All is seen from the angle of manipulation and false needs.

This approach has a first theoretical affiliation in works on the effects of mass communications on the public, such as Tchakhotine [6], who demonstrates how the use of advertising techniques has enabled the effectiveness of Hitler's propaganda. The mechanism of persuasion is based on psychological conditioning under the effect of repetition and scanning of slogans.

A second approach is just as mechanistic since it postulates systematic persuasion of the advertising message on the least educated strata of the populations. It has been developed by Frankfurt School researchers who dealt with advertising while working on the cultural industries. This analysis follows the Marxist criticism of advertising. Advertising is supposed to change consumer behavior by dictating preferences [7].

Advertising campaigns help to build a kind of "barrier to entry" for newcomers in business since, in order to change consumers' tastes and lead them to buy their products, new producers must advertise, which is very expansive. Thus, advertising participates in a system of closing the market and would oppose competition by protecting undertakings by monopolistic situations. For Adorno and Horkheimer [7], advertising is entirely part of mass culture, that is to say, a culture stemming from the cultural industries. It participates in the process whereby the introduction of new products into the daily life of the proletariat leads the members of this social class to hope for an improvement in their lot through consumption, and this diverts the members of this social class from the trade union and political struggle. Consumption and advertising act in the manner of anesthetics and derivatives and prevent them from devoting themselves to the essential.

Habermas [8] addresses advertising in his analysis of the public sphere since it is invaded by advertising, which leads private persons to exercise "directly their influence, as owners, on all private persons forming the public." Big companies have adopted their technical infrastructures to mass production, in order to ensure their monopoly, which then prohibits modifying production volumes. Long-term sales strategies are then necessary to ensure the flow of productions; and advertising, using psychological techniques, replaces competition between prices and prevents people from rational comparison on economic criteria and determines the exchange value.

Marcuse [9], in 1968, states that the development of mass culture is accompanied by the development of mass consumption and advertising, which, in synergy with the media in general, exercises power and manipulates the unconscious of consumers to adapt them to the standards of mass culture.

The idea of advertising manipulation and its affinities with the propagandist systems developed by Marcuse echoes the currents of economic analysis devoted to advertising that tend to construct advertising as a means of manipulating the population. In this respect, Galbraith [10] reduces advertising to the manipulative dimension when he develops the idea that the power of advertising conviction allows companies to absorb production surpluses by creating artificial or false needs, if necessary.

Some books, more journalistic, such as The Hidden Persuaders [11], give fuel to the ideas of manipulation and false needs. Furthermore, the research explorations go on with Ewen [12], who focuses on the psychological manipulation aspects of advertising crafted to act on instincts through the creation of desires, habits, and culture.

In response to these analyses of advertising based on the theory of manipulation, but in continuity on the principle of seeing advertising as an effective instrument of social control, Baudrillard [13] moves the question not to evacuate the manipulation but to show that it is far from being rough. The psychological conditioning exists, but it is complex and partly consented. The advertising receiver is no longer conceived as a recipient in the first sense, a simple chamber of recording elements intended to modify and/or create its behaviors. Baudrillard tries to overcome the notion of needs to introduce the idea that advertising produces "distinctive" signs. While consuming, consumers do not exchange objects, but signs and the sign-value of an object are more important than its practical value. Advertising offers people a system of hierarchy of objects that meets their need for social differentiation. Advertising builds a system of industrial production of differences, which, while refuting the thesis of conformity production, confirms that of manipulation. For Baudrillard, advertising is the crowning of the system of objects because it is both discourse on objects and discourse-object: it deals with consumption while being consumed.

Baudrillard is close to post-Marxist approaches, but he qualifies the notion of manipulation; and analyses the system of consumers' conditioning through advertising, as a logic of fable and adhesion. Although one does not believe in advertising discourse, one sticks to it, just as the child can decide to stick "no matter what" to the idea that Santa exists even if he knows that adults make gifts. This "Logic of Father Christmas" must demonstrate the power of conditioning triggered by the recognition of the consumer for the concern and the regression logic in which he enters. Baudrillard goes to a higher degree of generality and emphasizes the autonomous aspect of advertising, stated as "autonomous medium" which transforms consumption as a whole into signs taken in a system of exchange that refers "from one object to another, from one sign to another, from one consumer to another." Advertising produces industrialization of speech and functions, beyond the true and the false, as a self-fulfilling prophecy, which effectively eliminates the question of needs, true or false, and that of manipulation.

At the same time, Morin [14] writes a short text where he keeps the idea of manipulation while affirming the complexity of advertising, which on its part, constitutes, in a way, the nobility as an object of research. We leave a macro approach, overlooking, for one that articulates microanalysis to the overall view. Morin stresses the global penetration of contemporary society by advertising and defines it as a "universal mediator of consumption" in the global system of "production-delivery-consumption." He notes, however, that to truly understand advertising, it must also be seen as a stand-alone system, at the same time a specific action system and a crossroads phenomenon".

First, he writes about the incentive systems of advertising discourse, using the aesthetic, playful, and erotic aspects; then, he goes towards the reception phenomena and gives the receiver credit not to consider as true everything presented to him by advertising. Therefore, Morin states that people can escape the indoctrination while recognizing the power of persuasion to the advertising discourse due to the gratitude people develop for the pleasure it gives them.

2.2 Advertising: Rise of an Active Receiver

From a sociological perspective, other elements challenge approaches that somehow demonize advertising. Thus, the principle of leveling competition is not obvious. If we take the example of advertising for retailers' brands, we can say that conventional brands compete with mass retail, and then "advertising is not consensual." [15] Furthermore, the hypotheses on the modification of public beliefs due to mass cultural productions and advertising are called challenged by research carried out on reception. Researches on "uses and gratification" (the 1980s') postulate an activity of the receiver of media and advertising. They seek to understand how decoding works on the receiver side of mass communication. In this respect, Katz and Liebes' study of Dallas'viewers, decoding, is useful to think about advertising [16]. In their paper, they underline a kind of ignorance, in the late 1980s, about the process of decoding and the lack of "an adequate theory of the nature of viewer involvement." They state how audiences can differ in their decoding of a mass media program, and that reception is not "an individual experience, but something is done -before, during, or after- together with others."

Katz and Liebes then develop the notion of critical reception when people discuss the program as a program and not as a story. They make a distinction between syntactic critical statements that "refer to "themes" and "messages" which figure in the story," pragmatic critical statements expressing "the viewer's awareness of his experience or his "position" about the program, and/or an awareness of the functions and effects of the program on others." In this respect, the decoding of a manipulative message is analyzed as "highly involving," and people are good at it. It led the authors to the idea that "viewers' abilities are seriously underestimated by producers, critics, and academics."

Although these studies do not focus on the advertising discourse but mostly on TV programs and mass media productions in general, we can easily see how they enable us to rethink the approach to advertising. The meaning of programs and advertising messages is not fixed; it varies from one cultural sphere to another. The meaning is no longer conceived as predetermined and fixed. These researches are close to the very principles of the semiotic approaches which establish the polysemia of the message in general and that of the media message and, therefore, of advertising in particular. The meaning is not predetermined, and it results from an interpretation of those who receive the message. The contexts in which messages are sent and received, thus build a probability of meaning. The advertising message is no longer "injected" into the receiver and, at the same time, it is not wholly subject to individual interpretations, and its meaning results from a permanent negotiation of signs. In this regard, the analyses initiated by Eco [17] particularly highlight the process of co-production of the meaning that arises from the encounter between the message and the cultural, social, and personal background of each receiver. The reception of the advertising message, like that of any message, is, therefore, the product of a semiosis, some of which may be anticipated, in particular by the use of widely shared forms, such as stereotypes.

Some thinkers, such as the French essay writer, Lipovetsky [18] are more virulent against critical approaches to consumption and advertising. His work denies advertising the power to dominate consumers and manipulate them and sweeps away the issue of false needs. His formulations, in the manner of advertising claims, stress his point of view: "advertising offers, the consumer does whatever he likes; adverting has powers, but not all powers."

2.3   Advertising Literacy: Knowledge and Control of the Codes

We have seen that the analysis of advertising manipulation is part of researches that probably fed a suspicious point of view applied to mass media productions, such as the educational vision of literacy. With Katz and Liebes, we first encounter analyses take into consideration a common critical activity of the receptors, especially when mass media production tends to be manipulative. Therefore, we can consider, thanks to the reception analysis works that advertising can be treated by receivers in the same way since it is mass-produced and supposedly manipulative. Richard Hoggart, working on reception too, but from a different point of view, commonly called cultural studies, will enable us to pose the hypothesis of another definition for advertising literacy.

The cultural studies researches [19] consider that mass communications, through media and audiences, are linked to broader social and cultural practices. They focus on a global perspective of social life, combining individual intervention and the role played by the production of meaning in the orientation of social action. Culture can be defined as a process of production of meaning instead of a set of reference works. Then popular culture gains a significant place. The question to determine whether some of the audiences who use patterns of interpretation different from those of the dominant social order, can also use them on the mass media. In this research, current and prominent in its constitution is Hoggart and his book "The Uses of Literacy. Aspects of Working-Class Life" [20].

Hoggart explores the notion of literacy and its links with popular culture in ways that can help, once applied to advertising, to consider its literacy both online and outline. Literacy is defined as the use of the mastery of codes, some skills sometimes acquired through education but mostly by experience and socially valued skills. As Jeanneret states it [21], we can say that Hoggart defines literacy as the ability of a person sufficiently educated to recognize and identify documents and their statuses even with oblique attention. Literacy is the double implementation of practical and critical adjustment and works as the ability to have an evaluative view. This is different from the idea of literacy, linked to literature, or "lettrure," as developed by Goody [22], that is to say, linked to letters and lecture and writing.

We share Jeanneret's [21, 23] analysis of Hoggart's literacy. Hoggart's starts with cultural matters that are specific to the working class and shifts the analysis of the cultural powers from the primacy of contents or beliefs towards the postures of adhesion. The actors of the cultural industries base their production on the latter and divert this form of experience to objects and logics that are foreign to it. Nevertheless, this does not lead to the disappearance of popular culture. Jeanneret [23] explains that this point of view makes of Hoggart much more than the supporter of the freedom of the receivers. Hoggart expresses concern about the rise of a "faceless culture," emerging through the combination of systematic instrumentalization and general defiance. Hoggart formulates what Jeanneret calls semiotics of defiance, rooted in oblique attention, a distance in which resides the quality of popular know-how. The distanciation does not end adherence.

Then Jeanneret [21] draws the link with advertising when he explains that one of the sources of renewing advertising semiotics came, in France, in the 80', from the development of a reading of the communicational context based on an active audience of advertising. The public of advertising public is presented as bearing expectations, therefore accessible to a solicitation, provocation, and collective complicity. Advertising messages can be staggered or aberrant, staging adhesions and rejections by the public within messages. The reaction and interpretative activity of audiences are looked for. Practical and critical adjustment regarding advertising is exploited and traps media culture in return. Reception is thought of as an evaluative look at the quality of media production.

Therefore, this paper seeks to explore this alternative approach to advertising literacy: how receivers build, about advertising, knowledge, reading, interpretative, critical, and commenting skills. Overall, this means exploring how advertising audiences build and implement a culture of the domain, and this for several centuries for some European countries and the USA.

3 Forms of Advertising Literacy

In order to address contemporary forms of advertising literacy, it is necessary to trace its implementation through the historical transformations of advertising forms. They will enable us to understand contemporary advertising, how audiences gained and forged the ability to analyze and distanciate. Thus, we will be able to address digital literacy. At the same time, a review of the implementation of forms of reactions and criticism of advertising discourse is also essential for a good understanding of contemporary advertising literacy, its oblique, and defiant receptions. We shall concentrate on the example of France.

3.1 Traditional Forms of Advertising: Posters and Press

The advertising poster is one of the oldest advertising media. It is still an advertising medium of importance today, especially since there seems to be a kind of "French exception." Advertising by display is strongly present, for various historical reasons such as the presence of advertising in the Parisian metro since its creation or that of large billboards in the vicinity of little grocery stores.

In France, it is common to bring back the beginnings of advertising posters (in the sense of making a piece of news public) to 1539, the date on which it was decided that the royal ordinances should "have been published to the sound of the trumpet and public call and be hung to a notice board." The poster had a limited role; it was under the responsibility of the king, practiced by "royal displayers," and the content was very controlled. Advertising was, however, possible in an indoor display to make public a sale. The display is restricted except for the entertainment area; each theatre has its color since white paper was reserved for royal edicts. The first half of the nineteenth century is the reign of the bookseller's poster highlighting novels likely to appeal to a broad audience. New sectors are beginning to use the poster for advertising their products, as evidenced by the poster for perfumery products in César Birotteau de Balzac. The poster is mostly if not only, composed of text, with some typographical variants.

Display companies appear around 1840, while posters start a significant development thanks to the technique of reproduction by lithography that enables the use of images first in black and white, then in color from the 1850s. Jules Chéret will be an essential protagonist since he is also a lithographer and printer and is at the origin of the technology enabling very brilliant colors. The illustrated advertising poster begins its golden age and attracts artists such as Lautrec, Mucha, Bonnard. It is very present in the urban landscape, and Paris is a land of choice for posters since Haussman's urban transformation works to transform the city into a giant wooden palisade very suitable for advertising display. Besides, urban furniture is created for the display of shows, and the start-up of the metro opens a new horizon since it is designed with spaces dedicated to advertising. After a period of decline, the revival of the poster in France takes place after the First World War, illustrators like Loupot, Cassandre, Carlu, Colin are very familiar with artistic currents, and they create recognizable personal styles. After the Second World War, the advertising display needs to adapt to the advent of suburbs and private cars. Locations are put along the main roads, and the posters become giant to ensure that they can be seen from a car. At the same time and for the same reason, drawings become more straightforward, and photography starts its rise with an intense search for sophistication, especially in the 1980s, as in the advertising productions of French artist Jean-Paul Goude.

Beyond the stabilization of different forms of advertising posters, in sizes, formats, and organizations, another literacy emerges, that of connoisseurs who develop an aesthetic appreciation—the posters created by recognized artists and the movement of collectors known as "affichomania" witness it. The recognition of the artistic value of posters is a great reward for advertising. In 1884, a first poster exhibition was organized at the Vivienne passage, specialized galleries opened, and a journal named "La Plume" is entirely dedicated to advertising posters. The "affichomania" collecting movement lasts between 1886 and 1896 and shows an artistic recognition of the advertising poster; it introduces the poster into French heritage. At the same time, Affichomania is part of the bourgeois consumer practices of the late 19th century, since they are kin of novelty and industrial items [24]. Advertising posters appear as one of the places of the avant-garde.

The traditional media of advertising create formats that constrain it and, at the same time, make it recognizable. Some elements are expected, and others are almost mandatory. It transforms the advertising messages into stereotypes, that is to say, a fixed form, which programs their reading and shapes the messages "according to the imperatives of a prefabricated model" [25]. This phenomenon is particularly noticeable in advertising in the press.

Beyond the mandatory formats, advertising is also mostly regulated and constrained by the elements that the advertising message must or may contain. It is, in fact, a discourse that has essential or sometimes necessary constituents, strongly weighing on the elaboration of the message. Press advertisements contain several constituent elements, which can be considered as strong internal constraints, whether they are canonical formatting or the systematic presence of the brand name and/or product, the logo. We will focus here mainly on canonical formats. Since press ads are, with posters, the oldest forms of advertising in France and this long period has allowed a stabilization of its forms and contents.

The first forms of advertising in French newspapers started in the first quarter of the nineteenth century, and, shortly after that, three primary forms of advertising were stabilized: the "English ad," the "Poster ad" and "réclame." The "English ad" was a written advertisement, without pictures, playing with typographies and their size. The "Poster ad" was a kind of small display poster, with black and white image, reproduced identically for sometimes several decades. These two kinds of press advertisements were very small and crowded in the dedicated section of the newspaper, which was the last page or back cover. One can say they are so small that they are genuinely unreadable, let say almost invisible. This is counterbalanced by the sanctuarization of the location that ensures recognition and enables the emergence of literacy. We will come back later on the réclame.

Press advertisements changes at the time of the magazine, when advertisements get closer to posters. There is a gradual set up towards canonical forms of a magazine advertisement, one or two pages, with specific reading circuits. This happens internationally, and today, one can spot an ad in a magazine even when they cannot read the language. The most stable elements of press advertisements are the brand, product or company name, and logotype. They act as an anchor, first-rate, always present; it represents the brand that is the main generator of advertising discourse.

The advertisement usually consists of one or more photographs. It may contain non-mandatory informative linguistic elements, such as editorial content, or by obligation, legal notices in advertisements concerning alcoholic beverages, processed foods, or translations of language elements into foreign languages (French laws). The various elements are predictable, and they can easily be identified in the space of the single or double-page. Moreover, the image most often cohabits with the slogan and the brand signature.

In traditional forms, the press advertisement presents what is called a Z-reading circuit, starting at the top of the image on the left, passing right to descend diagonally to the left, and finish at the bottom right. Usually, points of interest like the slogan, the brand name, the photograph of the packaging are "posed" at the most-watched reading points, namely the beginning and the end of the Z-circuit.

In other advertising media such as cinema, radio, and television, classical advertising is regulated by strong forms of delimitation that can be a short intermission in movie theatres, a change in tone and frequency of voice on the radio, and a dedicated opening and ending with a jingle of the advertising period on French television.

3.2   Anti-advertising Movement and Advertising Literacy

Consumer associations with their implementation of consumer education on the decoding of advertising have been significant in France regarding advertising literacy. Globally, advertising is a very regulated activity, both legislatively and self-regulated; it is also subject to a constant and unfavorable social judgment. French public seems to have made a specialty of it since the beginnings of insertions in the press. As early as 1920, the professionals stressed the discredit that the population throws on their profession and its main productions. They speak of "resistance" of the population as a whole, which they link to a supposed "French spirit" made "of independence of character and refusal to allow themselves to be imposed ready-made judgments." [26]

Where did this come from? French entrepreneurs and manufacturers, in the first part of the twentieth century, are dubious or even hostile to advertising because "a good product is sufficient to itself," they see it as an expense whose usefulness is not certain [27]. The political class and the journalists are also in the mistrust, and the press confines advertising at the end of the issues or in separate notebooks until the 1930s. The remarks of French intellectuals against advertising over the decades are often violent, and they embrace the idea of manipulation too.

However, the preceding elements do not allow us to explain how this negative opinion spread outside Parisian and intellectual circles. On this point, Martin points out that three professional groups were particularly hostile to advertising and participated in the diffusion among the whole population "an anti-advertising" ideology: small merchants, traveling salesmen, family doctors, and pharmacists. Small merchants saw advertising as the armed arm of manufacturers who wanted to turn them into mere depositories, reducing their profits and social role; traveling salespeople did not wish to become mere relays of advertising discourse, while family doctors and pharmacists, prescribers and manufacturers of pharmaceutical specialties, felt endangered by the laboratories and their numerous advertisements. Beyond the financial loss, these three professions, very close to the populations, fought against the social devaluation of their professions: the grocer is part of the trading bourgeoisie, the doctors and pharmacists are notables, and the salesmen enter houses to make the sale.

The beginnings of consumer society in the 1950s in France seem to have erased these problems. However, at the same time, France experiences a specific period called "May 68," which is a month of civil revolution uniting students, workers, and politics in a giant strike that changed deeply French society. At that time, the theoretical works of post-Marxists researchers (see above) were mainly published in France, and they immediately came out of the narrow circle of intellectuals and researchers. Their main arguments, namely manipulation, creation of false needs, and psychological work, have been implanted sustainably in the militant and collective discourses.

At the same time, consumer associations concentrate their activities around two poles: lifting all that can hinder free competition and guaranteeing consumer information. They most often attack advertising as a single information medium issued by producers and intended to serve their sole interest [28]. The goal is to be able to attack advertising in court, which leads them to want to "develop a judgment system that allows activists to sort between advertising messages for consumer interest" [28]. Between 1973 and 1983, the magazine *50 Millions of Consumers* published each month, on its back cover, the decoding of an advertisement. The column was titled "Did you see him like that?" and "invariably began with the same warning: To consumers, advertising shows a particularly attractive face. Maybe it is its business. Ours is to look closer; that is what we try to do here every month." In order of importance; the criticisms concerned the representation of the objective qualities of the product (37%), the respect of the law (14%), the representation of the commercial qualities of the product, the identification of the advertiser or his legal, scientific or medical guarantees (9%) and the accusation of incitement to dangerous or illegal behavior (9.5%) [28].

At the beginning of the 1980s, the associations start to drop the criticism of advertising. It seems mostly because the legal points - the need to give optimal information, the respect by the advertising of standards "intended to make the message a conventional representation of the qualities of the good or service" - on which these positions were based are weakened, and the court judgments less easily agree with associations. For example, in 1982, a television spot for the brand Samsonite is attacked for false advertising; it stages two bulldozers that play football with a suitcase of the brand coming out unscathed from the operation. In May 1984, the court of cassation closes the case by affirming that the film is not lying and produces a discourse about advertising reception, which affirms that "attractive advertising frequently results in a certain use of fantasy." It also pushes back "the limits of the offense of false advertising." It states that courts must "take into account the degree of discernment and critical sense of the average consumer since the law is not intended to protect the weak-minded. The public cannot be spared the slightest effort of attention or reflection" [28].

Moreover, this judgment highlights the fact that the advertising message can be disconnected by audiences from its commercial perspective and considered as a cultural practice. A 1983 judgment by the Paris Correctional Court held that the slogan "The Wonder Battery only wears out if used" cannot be considered a lie and that it has become part of popular culture. During the same period, consumerism started to pause. From the beginning of the 1980s, lawsuits made by associations against advertising decreased. These associations started to focus more on "the quality of the products and the conditions of the market," and their magazines less and less talked about advertising.

In fact, at that time, advertising, in France, became a cultural element, and improving the quality of advertising productions made it a popular show in the 1980s. Advertising was a real mass phenomenon. People praise the creativity of Jean-Paul Goude, and advertisers are invited on television sets. Advertising is considered as a mode of expression reflecting contemporary society, and it is possible to watch commercials or posters for themselves, without an immediate commercial perspective. Newspapers such as "Libération" contribute significantly to this trend since they regularly open their columns to the news of advertising and the life of the media. This logic of spectacle came to fruition in 1981 with the creation of "La Nuit des publivores," a "montage of international commercials and trailers dating from 1935 to 1981", shown at the Kinorama cinema in Paris.

At the end of the 1990s, France resumes its old anti-advertising tradition when joining the international movement criticizing both advertising and brands. Naomi Klein's [29] book "No logo: the tyranny of brands" is a hit in France and benefits from a strong media cover. Since the 2000s, anti-advertising position has been fed either by advertisers, journalists, or members of associations like RAP (Resistance to Advertising Aggression) and "Pub Breakers." Finally, some people involved in the anti-globalization movement take part in criticism, such as Ignacio Ramonet, editor of the Monde Diplomatique, Paul Ariès, and essayist François Brune. They accuse advertising of invading public and private space, extending itself to areas that should be far from it (political, humanitarian), manipulating minds, creating false needs, and limit free will. From then on, advertising is, in France, commonly compared to a drug, a source of pollution, a waste. These ideas are also often taken up by the media system, which sees it as a means of informing, including on comments sometimes hostile to the brands on which their economic model is based.

Associations against advertising and consumption constitute, on an international scale, the French originality. The actions can be individual (stickers "Stop advertising" or "No advertising" on the mailboxes of individuals) or collective (such as degradation of advertising posters and organization of days without brands, without advertising). The advertising industry does not stand idly by, and some advertising people even see it as an opportunity to take over consumer demands. However, as we are going to see, the most common and important mode of reaction has instead led to a redefinition, sometimes hasty, of the contours of advertising under the pretext that advertising had become a problematic mode of communication.

4   Advertising Literacy and Digital

Traditional forms of advertising and anti-advertising allow us, in France, to see the contours of advertising literacy. The discourses against advertising and consumerism have enabled the emergence and the affirmation of an advertising literacy that allows the public to be enlightened. The beginning of online advertising, at the end of the 1990s, starts a new period for advertising literacy since. In addition to the classic forms of advertising, which are taken up globally with online banners and pop-ups, new forms, new discourses, new online advertising formats emerge, researching and producing a displacement of borders, a blurring. These phenomena make it possible to question advertising literacy in the digital age and to understand the difficulties and facilitations.

4.1 Advertising Literacy Blur

The start of online advertising was about basic, recognizable, avoidable forms, thus an advertising literacy transposable from the traditional media to the digital forms. Web 2.0 has generated new opportunities for advertising professionals, and search for a blurring of the classic markers of identification. Thus, they made what was already done in the conventional media visible. These forms of masked digital advertising provoked the re-appearance of old and recent advertising forms of "deception," such as the ancient "réclame" problem.

Historically, in France, advertising forms have not always given themselves as such, due to a lack of regulation. The advertisement, very commonly used by producers from 1850, known as "réclame," is at the origin of the bad opinion. It was presented in the form of a relatively short article, and it was an "ad disguised as an article, an editorial advertisement that is intended to mislead the reader." [30] It was twice as expensive to buy space as other forms of advertising because it was thought that the trust subscribers had in their newspaper made it very effective. Through self-regulation of advertisers, the moralization of newspaper owners, and the law, this form of advertising is now prohibited and must be marked as such by a mention such as advertising, infomercial, or advertorial. However, the notion of deception is difficult to change. In France, at least, the "réclame" is at the origin of perceptions in terms of manipulation and lies due to big financial and pharmaceutical scandals and bankruptcies due to fraudulent réclames.

Nowadays, this kind of blurring is possible with digital communication. Advertising people have, since the beginning of the 2000s, developed a kind of shared belief in the growing inadequacy of classic advertising, based on the escalation of anti-advertising discourses, on the saturation of existing media spaces, on the promotion of the brand. The media appearances of brands were multiplied but also transformed according to two major strategies that can only appear *a posteriori* and with theoretical distance. Overall, these forms are tactics of existence, working on the modalities of the existence of the discourse of the brand according to its degree of distance or rework of advertising statutory professional definition. These are strategies of existence for brands to reduce the advertising content of discourses by an unadvertising work, or increase it and working it qualitatively or attempting to invent media, in a hyperpadvertising movement.

The *unadvertization* [31, 32] brings together a set of productions that have the common characteristic of presenting themselves as non-advertising or outside the field of advertising. The idea is to allow the existence of the message, which is thus supposed to escape the current reproaches and reticence of the audiences against advertising. Professionals in the field base their choices on a supposed "resistance" to advertising that goes with an excellent knowledge, acquired from the earliest age, of the "manipulations" of marketing. In a few words, they claim the necessity to find new ways and forms for brand discourses because of advertising literacy [33, 34]. This is amplified when the audience is under forty. Its affinities with information and communication technologies and its use of "social" networks lead the advertising professionals to conclude that classical advertising is to be avoided, in order to move towards online resources.

Unadvertization refers to a set of communications tactics designed to be different from the most recognizable and classic forms of advertising by switching to forms that are supposed to be more discreet. Advertising is taken in the restricted and professional sense of the term, which is traditional media advertising. Taken in the restricted and professional sense of the term, that is classical media advertising. Unadvertizing mainly uses three sets of ways:

- Entering an already existing media production as in product placement in TV shows, and series, movies, games. Sponsor broadcasted programs also take place here.
- Imitating: 1/existing media products and producing consumer magazines, branded web series as Ikea Easy to Assemble, brand games, 2/existing cultural products as brand movies ("Prada presents A Therapy, by Roman Polanski, starring Ben Kingsley and Helen Bonham Carter), or books as Recipe books about Philadelphia, or Oreos.
- Trying to benefit from new forms of communication that are supposed to redistribute communication parts such as blogs, co-produced content, and social media. The brand conversation takes place in this last.

Hyperadvertization is the counterpart of unadvertization and consists of a hypertrophy of the advertising aspects. In contrast to the processes of masking and erasing of advertising forms specific to unadvertization, hyperadvertization is based on a search for maximizing the advertising presence either qualitatively, by working the message, or quantitatively, by seeking to create new media. In the first case, the aim is semiotic densification of advertising, through creative and/or aesthetic work. In the second case, maximization is characterized by a continuous creation of "media" with spaces still available such as urban furniture, buildings, vehicles, coffee tables.

4.2   Extension of the Advertising Field

Thus advertising, unadvertization, and hyperadvertization messages multiply the presence of brand messages in everyday life, both online and offline. At the same time, these new variations around advertising and its blurring meet the skills developed by audiences to spot, or even discard, advertising messages. For professionals, the definition of advertising is relatively easy and circumscribed: "mass communication made on behalf of a clearly identified transmitter that pays for media (press, TV, radio, display, Internet, cinema) to insert its promotional messages in spaces separate from the editorial content and distribute them to selected media audiences." [35] Things are not so simple on the side of the vast majority of "non-professionals of advertising" who, during their daily lives, encounter numerous occurrences and speeches related to brands and tend to requalify most of these branded communications as "advertising." In doing so, they demonstrate a remarkable literacy that significantly expands the definition of advertising. This helps to fully understand the commonly held view that advertising is misleading and influences people without their knowledge.

This absence of differentiation in the minds of non-professionals explains the relevance of the stickers on many French mailboxes "STOP ADVERTISING," "No advertising, thank you" since, from a strictly professional point of view, there is no advertising in a mailbox other than that contained in magazine subscriptions delivered by postal services. This means that things that professionals qualify as direct-marketing (brochures, catalogs, promotional leaflets, and free papers) are seen and gathered under the name "advertising" by the rest of the population. The definition is broad to the point that any commercial communications enters within the ordinary meaning of the term "advertising," including brand discourses on the internet and in "social" networks (such as Facebook, Pinterest, Twitter, Instagram). It creates, with television sponsorships and other street actions, a kind of global advertising space.

Common advertising literacy enables the general public to be aware of a complex phenomenon. From a semiotic point of view, the advertising discourse is the place of ostentation of the brand, and thus, it is deeply its discourse of existence. Its formal configurations are capable "in a given context, to manifest their intention of communication and a meta-communicational proposal." [36] The mere presence of a brand in a discourse transforms it into advertising; it is then engaged in a semiotic market predilection. In other words, the real definition of advertising is: brand = advertising. When a brand is the source of discourse, it brings it into the order of advertising. Moreover, the extension of advertising to other forms of influence communication is a fact; this makes advertising not only the matrix of the brand and commercial discourses in general, but also of other discourses. We propose to call this matrix aspect *advertisingness*.

5 Conclusion: First Steps in Advertising Digital Literacy

We have collected, described, and analyzed manifestations of advertising literacy since the French nineteenth century, and the question is now to detect and describe forms of digital literacy of advertising. What do digital communications do to the distanciation? A series of individual and group researches, international seminars at Sorbonne University, and a session held as part of HCII2019, now allow us to sketch the first outlines of advertising digital literacy.

First of all, audiences interact with brands on social media, in ways that are informed – they know they are in contact with people working in communications services – and consented, since they need to register. It is quite apparent on the Facebook accounts of the M&ms and Oasis brands, when the participants write: " my favorite is still the one where red takes it all off I miss that commercial, " "The best ever *M&M* commercial is the one with Santa," "the absolute best *M&M* commercial ever!!!!!!", or "you are nuts you advertising people at Oasis." [32] However, they have registered to receive free advertising content and seem to consume much more the brand's signs than its products. It is, therefore, a kind of advertising show essential and much appreciated.

In an irenic way, marketing professionals talk about a digital conversation between brands and consumers. However, it can appear that the conversation is biased, from the outset, by a suspicion of manipulation as developed by Andriuzzi and Michel [34], that leads some people (the lurkers) to stay back, watching the exchanges between the posters and the brand community managers. They also demonstrate that the benevolence or kindness of the exchanges written by the employees of the brand can induce, on the audience side, reverse effects, and make them suspicious: "consumers may think that the brand is trying to manipulate them using flattery." Assuming that advertising literacy is acquired through a cumulative experience with brand advertising communications, it is possible to think that the more a person appreciates a brand, the more familiar she is with its messages and therefore the more she develops a knowledge that allows her to decode better "the brand's social media strategies."

In an agonistic way, the general public understood quickly that the presence of brands on social networks enables to express easily, with a broad audience, criticisms, or complaints about brands. Thus, for some brands, social networks have become a place for a new kind of crisis communication [37], that can be described as "permanent." In addition, it is not always easy for brand representatives to know how to interact in these new situations where digital literacy and advertising literacy meet to create interlocutors sharpened in their actions.

The other significant impact of digital on advertising is linked to algorithms that calculate what people do online and, in an advertising perspective, try to select the more appropriate offer or ad instead of sending the same ad to everybody. This is more than useful when one knows that "traditional" digital ads can be very easily avoided, for free, with efficient adblockers. Algorithms are the newcomers in advertising with actual possibilities and a long tail of imaginary, including surveillance, the promise of objectivity, and even algorithmic truth [38].

Trindade questions the algorithms as mediatic instances of daily life, producing a suggested narrative of consumption which creates a socio-cultural advertising writing. One can even imagine that algorithms come with AI in order to rule consumption; the first "calculate all consumption possibilities" when the last could "define the consumption pattern of humanity." But the tipping point is the persistent feelings linked to brand experience: "algorithm can recognize, describe, indicate, induce, but they cannot experience or feel" and, ultimately, "advertising algorithms are constituents of consumption realities while being co-fabricated by the realities that are inserted."

In another perspective, the analysis of the links between algorithms and advertising allows questioning, retrospectively, the various forms of digital advertising produced during the last twenty years [39]. Eugeni proposes a first period called "Network Capitalism," from the 1990s' to the 2000s, when the web was a new space, a new media for advertising, with the added value of networks. Then came, between 2000s' and 2010s', the "platform/data capitalism" or "sensor-capitalism" with the rise of a platform sociality and branded content, accompanied by the discovery by companies of "the usefulness of the traces left by users in their web browsing as evidence of their habits, tastes, preferences." Data are not only big; they are "sensors" since they show variety, velocity, veracity, and value. The last period started at the beginning of the 2010s; it is the one of "algorithmic capitalism" which allows advertising customization and devices or dispositives such as Alexa (Amazon), which is much more "perfectly integrated into the network of everyday practices" and consumption than other digital personal assistants.

Finally, from all these transformations, advertising digital literacy appears to be deeply rooted in culture, digital culture, popular culture, but also in advertising culture sometimes seen as a global discourse [40].

The Internet certainly gives unprecedented access and visibility to cultural forms that concern advertising. There are the nostalgic PowerPoints, sent by email, showing nineteenth-century advertisements that Internet users can only know as reminiscence of a time they never knew. One can also find some critical evaluations of advertisements, in online discussions about advertising music, favorite claims or commercials. It is a whole world of practices that still has to be discovered, in order to understand fully how digital advertising literacy is developing and evolving.

References

1. https://unesdoc.unesco.org/ark:/48223/pf0000225606
2. Grizzle, A., et al.: Media and information literacy: policy and strategy guidelines, UNESCO (2013)
3. Malmelin, N.: What is Advertising Literacy? Exploring the dimensions of advertising literacy. J. Vis. Lit. **29**(2), 129–142 (2010)
4. Erdem, N.: Argumentative study on digital advertising literacy. In: Taskiran, N.O. (ed.) Handbook of Research on Multidisciplinary Approaches to Literacy in the Digital Age. IGI, Hershey (2019)
5. Berthelot-Guiet, K.: Paroles du pub, Le Havre, Editions Non Standard (2013)
6. Tchakhotine, S.: The Rape of the Masses; the Psychology of Totalitarian Political Propaganda. George Routledge, London (1940/2007)
7. Adorno, T., Horkheimer, M.: Dialectic of Enlightenment. Verso, Milano (1997)
8. Habermas, J.: The Structural Transformation of the Public Sphere: An Inquiry into a Category of Bourgeois Society. MIT Press, Cambridge (1989)
9. Marcuse, H.: One-Dimensional Man. Routledge, London (1964–2006)
10. Galbraith, J.K.: Economic Development in Perspective. Harvard University Press, Cambridge (1962)
11. Packard, V.: The Hidden Persuaders. Longmans, Green and Co, London (1957)
12. Ewen, S.: Captains of Consciousness: Advertising and the Social Roots of the Consumer Culture. McGraw-Hill Professional, New York (1977)
13. Baudrillard, J.: The System of Objects. Verso, Milano (2006)
14. Morin, E.: L'esprit du temps. Essai sur la culture de masse. Grasset, Paris (1962)
15. Herpin, N.: Sociologie de la Consommation. La Découverte, Paris (2001)
16. Katz, E., Liebes, T.: Interacting with "Dallas": cross-cultural readings of American TV. Can. J. Commun. **1**, 41–66 (190)
17. Eco, U.: La Structure Absente: Introduction à la recherche sémiotique. Mercure de France, Paris (1972)
18. Lipovetsky, G.: Le Bonheur paradoxal. Gallimard, Paris (2006)
19. Jensen, K.B., Rosengren, K.E.: Five traditions in search of the audience. Eur. J. Commun. **5**(2), 207–238 (1990)
20. Hoggart, R.: The Uses of Literacy. Aspects of Working-Class Life. Penguin Books, London (1957/1990)

21. Jeanneret, Y.: Critique de la Trivialité. Les Médiations de la Communication, Enjeu de Pouvoir, Le Havre, Editions Non Standard (2014)
22. Goody, J.: Literacy in Traditional Societies. Cambridge University Press, Cambridge (1968)
23. Jeanneret, Y.: Penser la Trivialité. La Vie Triviale des Etres Culturels. Hermès-Lavoisier, Paris (2008)
24. Zmelty, N.-H.: L'Affiche illustrée au temps de l'affichomanie (1889-1905). Mare & Martin, Paris (2014)
25. Amossy, R.: Les idées reçues : sémiologie du stéréotype. Nathan, Paris (1991)
26. Martin, M.: Histoire de la publicité en France. Presses Universtaires de Paris Ouest, Nanterre (2012)
27. Sacriste, V.: Les français et la publicité. Une longue tradition de contestation, La publicité aujourd'hui, La revue du CIRCAV, pp. 13–30. L'Harmattan, Paris (2009)
28. Parasie, S.: Et maintenant une page de pub! Une histoire morale de la publicité à la télévision française (1968-2008). INA, Paris (2010)
29. Klein, N.: No Logo. Taking Aim at the Brand Bullies. Knopf Canada, Toronto (1999)
30. Martin, M.: Trois Siècles de Publicité en France. Odile Jacod, Paris (1992)
31. Berthelot-Guiet, K., Marti de Montety, C., Patrin-Leclère, V.: La Fin de la Publicité? Tours et Contours de la Dépublicitarisation. Bord de l'eau, Lormont (2014)
32. Gruber-Muecke, T., Rau, C.: "Fake it or make it" – selfies in corporate social media campaigns. In: Meiselwitz, G. (ed.) SCSM 2016. LNCS, vol. 9742, pp. 417–427. Springer, Cham (2016). https://doi.org/10.1007/978-3-319-39910-2_39
33. O'Donaohe, S., Tynan, C.: Beyond sophistication: dimensions of advertising literacy. Int. J. Adv. 17(4), 462–482 (1998)
34. Andriuzzi, A., Michel, G.: Social media conversations: when consumers do not react positively to brands' kindness to others. In: Meiselwitz, G. (ed.) HCII 2019. LNCS, vol. 11579, pp. 268–278. Springer, Cham (2019). https://doi.org/10.1007/978-3-030-21905-5_21
35. June 2015. http://www.mercator-publicitor.fr/lexique-publicite-definition-publicite
36. Barthes, R.: Mythologies. The Noonday Press, New York (1991)
37. Halpern, D., Kane, G.C., Montero, C.: When complaining is the advertising: towards a collective efficacy model to understand social network complaints. In: Meiselwitz, G. (ed.) HCII 2019. LNCS, vol. 11579, pp. 330–345. Springer, Cham (2019). https://doi.org/10.1007/978-3-030-21905-5_26
38. Trindade, E.: Algorithms and advertising in consumption mediations: a semio-pragmatic perspective. In: Meiselwitz, G. (ed.) HCII 2019. LNCS, vol. 11579, pp. 514–526. Springer, Cham (2019). https://doi.org/10.1007/978-3-030-21905-5_40
39. Eugeni, R.: The post-advertising condition. a socio-semiotic and semio-pragmatic approach to algorithmic capitalism. In: Meiselwitz, G. (ed.) HCII 2019. LNCS, vol. 11579, pp. 291–302. Springer, Cham (2019). https://doi.org/10.1007/978-3-030-21905-5_23
40. Hellín Ortuño, P.A.: The cultural component in advertising analysis. A non-numerical vision of the programmatic advertising. In: Meiselwitz, G. (ed.) HCII 2019. LNCS, vol. 11579, pp. 346–360. Springer, Cham (2019). https://doi.org/10.1007/978-3-030-21905-5_27

Research on Computational Simulation of Advertising Posters Visual Cognition

Xueni Cao[1], Ying Fang[1], Liyu Zhu[1], Xiaodong Li[2(✉)], and Liqun Zhang[1(✉)]

[1] School of Design, Shanghai Jiao Tong University, Shanghai, China
zhangliqun@gmail.com
[2] China National Gold Group Gold Jewellery Co., Ltd., Beijing, China
lixiaodong@chnau99999.com

Abstract. Vision, as the main channel for humans to obtain external information, has always been a hot area of research. Especially under the current heat of research on artificial intelligence, a large amount of research has been focused on intersecting research results in psychology and neuroscience with computer science to improve simulation capabilities of computers systems. This article briefly reviews the research progress in human visual cognition processes and their simulation methods in the fields of psychology, neuro-science, and computer science. In addition, eye movement experiments were carried out and models were built based on human cognitive processes to explore the influence of factors such as prior knowledge and emotional experience on model accuracy. Furthermore, the limitations and application prospects of the model were discussed.

Keywords: Visual cognition · Perception · Attention · Saliency · Eye-tracking

1 Introduction

Cognition is a high-level psychological process for humans to understand things, including the entire process of obtaining information, understanding and thinking. The cognition process mainly includes several stages including attention, memory, thinking, speech, decision-making and other stages. Perception is part of the cognitive process and is the basis of advanced psychological processes in the entire cognitive process. Visual cognition is the process by which humans respond to visual stimuli, acquire knowledge, and understand and process them.

Many researches have been done on human visual cognition in the fields of psychology and neuroscience. The process of visual perception includes the acquisition and analysis of visual information. The light information falling on the retina is converted into neural impulses and transmitted to the cerebral cortex where the primary visual information is processed and then object recognition and spatial perception is performed. This helped people understand the human visual cognition process and inspired scholars in the computer field to use computing to simulate human visual cognitive processes. With the deepening and expansion of human visual cognition research in psychology and neuroscience, the research on more complex tasks of visual

G. Meiselwitz (Ed.): HCII 2020, LNCS 12195, pp. 295–308, 2020.
https://doi.org/10.1007/978-3-030-49576-3_22

cognition such as recognition, emotion, and aesthetics has become a research hotspot. The simulation of human advanced visual cognition tasks has further improved the effectiveness of computer vision tasks, and has greatly widened the application of computer vision.

Here, in order to explore the application of computational simulation of human visual cognition in the design field, a computational model was trained. In view of the differences in content between poster design works and ordinary photos, in order to better simulate human visual perception of poster stimuli, advanced visual cognition was simulated and its impact was explored.

This paper will be developed from the following aspects:

(A) Human visual cognition process: To better understand human cognition process, knowledge from both biology and psychology is needed. Since vision is the main source of information for human beings, researches on the entire process of human visual cognition will be focused on.

(B) Computational simulation of visual cognition: As far as the current researches are concerned, the simulation of objective visual cognition in the field of computer vision has achieved fruitful results, but research on subjective factors such as experience, aesthetics, and emotion are relatively unabundant. Due to the artificially designed elements in the advertising posters, subjective factors, which may affect the process of visual perception, should be considered.

(C) Experiments on models of advertising poster visual cognition: Elements and features are extracted according to the characteristics of advertising posters, and visual cognition simulation of unnatural scenes is explored based on the data of eye movement experiments.

(D) Application prospects: The possible application of the model in the prediction of advertising performance and the estimation of advertising time is discussed.

(E) Experimental discussion: The limitations of the model and the possible future research is discussed.

2   Related Work

The computational simulation of human visual cognition is an intersection of neuroscience, psychology and computer science.

Neuroscience and psychology have long begun to explore human cognitive mechanisms. Neuroscience research on brain structure and function and psychology on task decomposition of cognitive processes provide a theoretical basis for the study of computer vision. Early research mainly focused on the extraction and processing of primary visual features. However, with the deepening of research and the improvement of accuracy requirements, not only the more detailed analysis of the extraction process of primary visual features, but also the attention of advanced cognitive tasks is needed. Some experimental data show that the speed of human visual cognition is extremely fast, even including some advanced visual cognitive processing, such as the recognition and classification of stimuli with strong socio-psychological significance to humans like faces, speech, etc. The processing can make adjustments to follow-up activities through the top-down mechanism [1]. The rapid response of humans to visual stimuli leads to the interaction of cognitive results and cognitive processes, where the top-down and bottom-up mechanisms work together. Therefore, simulating visual cognition needs to take into account both primary and advanced cognitive tasks and their interactions.

2.1   Visual Perception

Receptive Field. The area of light stimulation that can fire the activity of a nerve cell is defined as the visual receptive field of the cell.

Kuffler first proposed the receptive field of a concentric circle structure [2]. The discharge pattern of the central region and the periphery are the opposite. The two patterns are the "on" center one where the center gives "on" while the surround gives "off" discharges, and the "off" center one where the center gives "off" while the surround gives "on" discharges. This concentric circle structure is the Classic Receptive Field (CRF).

Subsequent research found that there are larger areas outside the CRF that can regulate the response of neurons to stimuli. Mcilwain, [3] Ikeda and Wright [4] found that there is a region surrounding the classical receptive field that has a de-inhibition effect on it, the disinhibitory area outside the CRF. Li Chaoyi conducted research on the size and action mode of the disinhibitory surround. Shou Tiande et al. conducted a large number of studies on the response of the disinhibitory surround to the grating stimulus, and many valuable results were obtained.

Visual System. The vision system mainly includes the retina, the lateral geniculate body (LGN), and the visual cortex. It acquires and processes information in visible light to form vision.

The cone cells and rod cells on the retina convert the received light stimulation into nerve impulses which are then conducted to the brain.

The lateral geniculate nucleus (LGN) is a sensory repeater in the thalamus and also a processing center. It receives mutual input from the cortex and subcortex, and mutual innervation from the visual cortex [5].

The visual information passing through the lateral geniculate body enters the visual cortex from visual area 1 (V1, Brodmann area 17), and is further transmitted to Brodmann area 18, 19, etc. (V2–V5).

Neurons of primary visual cortex (V1) can distinguish small changes in visual orientation, spatial frequency, and color. V1's selectivity of orientation of objects' boundary plays a key role in the perception of shape [6]. Li Chaoping [7, 8] proposed that the primary visual cortex (V1) creates salient maps through the autonomous intracortical mechanisms to guide attention or gaze shift, which has an impact on the top-down selection mechanism. The saliency of a visual location describes the its ability to attract attention without the top-down factor.

The secondary visual cortex (V2) is the second major area in the visual cortex. In the macaque brain, V2 receives strong feedforward connections from V1 and sends strong projections to the other visual cortex areas (V3, V4, and V5) [9, 10]. Neurons of most primate in this area are tuned to visual features such as orientation, spatial frequency, size, color, and shape [11–13].

There still exists some controversy over the exact scope of the V3 region. Some researchers have suggested that the cortex located in front of V2 may include two or three functional subdivisions. For example, David Van Essen et al. proposed the existence of a "dorsal V3" in the upper part of the cerebral hemisphere, which is different from the "ventral V3" (or posterior ventral VP) located in the lower part of the cerebral hemisphere.

V4 has a strong regulating effect on attention. Moran and Desimone [14] found that selective attention had a significant effect on the firing rate of V4.

The middle temporal region (MT or V5) is the area of extrastriate visual cortex. Most neurons in MT are adjusted to the speed and orientation of moving visual stimuli [15, 16]. Born and Bradley suggested that the MT of primates is closely related to the perception of motion, the integration of local motion signals into global percepts, and the guidance of some eye movements [17]. Lesion studies also support the role of MT in motion perception and eye movement [18].

The dorsal region (DM, also V6) is a subdivision of the primate visual cortex which responds to visual stimuli related to self-motor [19] and wide-field stimuli [20].

Ventral-Dorsal Model. Information transmission from V1 has two main channels of ventral stream and dorsal stream. The ventral stream starts at V1, passes through V2 and V4 and finally reaches the inferior temporal cortex. Dorsal stream starts at V1, passes from V2 to V5, V6, and finally reaches the posterior parietal cortex. The ventral stream is related to object recognition which is the reason it is called "what pathway", while the dorsal stream is related to the position and motion representation of the subject and the control of eyes and arms, which is the reason it is called "where pathway".

Deco and Rolls [21] established a two-channel fusion model at the neuron level. Both the dynamic and static sensory interaction mapping mechanism in V1 and V2 was simulated to realize the joint extraction of appearance information and motion information. Chikkerur et al. [22] proposed a Bayesian inference model with dual visual pathways. In view of the ability of human visual system to perceive edge information of the object, according to the receptive fields of LGN and simple cells in V1, a brain-inspired Feedforward LGN-V1 (FLV) model for visual perception is put forward. This proposed model is more effective and has better robustness in edge detection than traditional methods [23].

2.2 Visual Cognition

The research on the primary visual process helps people understand the process of human visual perception, but to complete the visual cognition process requires the integration of perceptual information and internal knowledge. Many scholars have studied how humans combine these two segments for cognition, and they have put forward many hypotheses on the mechanism of human cognition.

Treisman and Gelade [24] proposed the feature integration theory, which believed that in the early stage of visual attention, independent features such as color, brightness, orientation, size, and motion were input and processed in parallel. After that, various features are integrated and finally, an overall representation of the object is formed. The entire integration process requires the participation of visual attention. This theory emphasizes the coexistence and interaction of both top-down and bottom-up mechanisms in the process of visual cognition.

The development of neuroscience and psychology gave birth to early computer vision research, making visual cognitive a more integrated field. Marr's Vision marked computer vision as an independent discipline [25]. He believes that the main task of vision is three-dimensional reconstruction, that is, to recover the visible three-dimensional shape of a spatial object from the two-dimensional image on the retina, and this process can be completed by calculation. In his book, he divided the vision task into at three levels of calculation, algorithm and execution. For the algorithm part, Marr explained in detail that to complete the process of transforming the image to the three-dimensional expression, three levels of calculation are needed. Firstly, get Primal Sketches from the image. Then upgrade the primitives through modules such as stereopsis to 2.5-dimensional expression. Finally, transform it to 3D expression. Although Marr's ideas have been continuously challenged and revised in subsequent studies, they have indeed inspired a lot of research.

Selective Attention. Ullman proposed the concept of visual routine [26, 27] which consists of a series of ordered basic operations of vision system. By adjusting the order of these operations, different vision routines can be composed to complete various shape and spatial analysis which plays an important role on visual cognition. Ullman gave some examples to explain the idea of basic operations. He pointed out that the foundation of applying visual routines is the selection of location for it to take place. It is a must for application of visual routines to find out the "directing mechanism" of the processing focus. Many other scholars have conducted research on what Ullman called the processing focus. Kahneman et al. [28] call it object file, which can store and update the object's information. Pylyshyn's FINST (Finger of Instantiation) can indicate the position of the object [29].

Although there are some differences in the interpretation of this focus location, there is a consensus on the role that the focus point plays in the storage and processing of visual information. Humans have limited capabilities and can only selectively process information. This is also the most classic explanation of attention (Posner, Michael, I. Boies, Stephen, & J., 1971). Since humans can only handle only a few tasks at a time, attention mechanisms are needed to help filter out too much information.

Locations of a series of attention constitute a map, that is, a saliency map, and this map can also reflect the planning of sight when the human is watching. One of the well-known studies is the early saliency model proposed by Itti et al. [30] which applied the feature integration theory. Since then, many scholars have conducted more in-depth research on saliency models from the perspective of perception mechanisms and cognitive styles, so as to constantly improved its accuracy.

Attention and Cognition. A lot of research shows that human's visual cognition speed is extremely fast (Reviewed by [1]). In the experiments of Potter et al. [31], it was shown that people can conceptually understand pictures in only 13 ms. The duration of eye fixation generally exceeds the time needed to perceive the scene, because it include the time to encode the scene into memory and to plan and launch the next saccade. Therefore, the quickly obtained cognitive results will have an impact on subsequent cognitive processes. The processing of visual stimuli in the feedforward computational model of the visual system [32] is arranged in a hierarchy. Neurons in the high-level region receive ordered input from the low-level region to perform increasingly complex analysis. A more accepted visual theory states that perception is performed through a combination of feedforward and feedback connections. The results of the initial feedforward activation are fed back and compared with lower-level processing for confirmation, thus forming a loop [33–35]. Aiming at whether the visual system is a serial mechanism or a parallel mechanism, Wolfe [36] uses carwash to metaphorize a mixed model of both parallel and serial process and describe the relationship between attention, memory, and cognition.

2.3 Visual Aesthetic Experience

Ramanchandran and Hirstein [37] proposed that there is a neural circuit of visual emotion perception in the brain, linking together visual emotion, cognition and neuroscience. Zeki defined neuroaesthetics as a field for studying the physiological mechanisms of aesthetic experience [38]. Since then, domestic and overseas scholars have conducted a lot of research on the brain mechanism of visual aesthetic experience. Jacobsen's team used magnetic resonance imaging (MRI) to study the emotional response of participants' neural circuits when judging geometric shapes and appreciating visual arts [39, 40]. Kirk et al. [41] discovered brain regions related to artistic appreciation through analysis of MRI, pointing out that the perception of emotion in visual art aesthetics is a combination of visual expression, object recognition, emotional mechanism and cognition. A number of other studies have also experimented with brain regions related to art appreciation and emotional experience [42–44].

Based on the emotional response to visual perception, many scientists and scholars have put forward their views on the information processing mechanism of the visual system.

The visual emotion perception model proposed by Redies [45] includes two parallel channels of the top-down channel and the bottom-up one. The model distinguishes between external information and internal representation. Subjects can not only obtain cognitive information by viewing the content and context of the artwork, but also acquire knowledge through communication. In addition, they can retrieve previously obtained context information from their memory and then perform further information processing in the brain. Two different channels of information processing- perceptual processing and cognitive processing can trigger aesthetic experience, and these two channels can arouse emotions and regulate the degree of aesthetic experience (See Fig. 1).

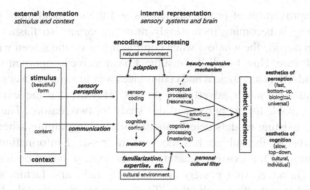

Fig. 1. Redies' model

Chatterjee proposed a visual emotion perception model with hierarchical serial and sibling parallel structure [46], which reflects the interaction between attention, early vision features, processed vision information, and emotional responses. Chatterjee's model emphasizes the importance of visual information processing and visual attention to emotion perception, which also affirms the role of primary visual features, visual information processing, and emotion perception on visual attention (See Fig. 2).

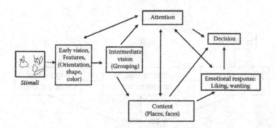

Fig. 2. Chatterjee's visual emotion model

3 Experiments

Due to the rich prior knowledge and experience, human beings can quickly respond to visual information and perform processing such as recognition, thinking, and imagination. Therefore, in the process of human cognition, the process from perception to processing is often instantly done, making it difficult for humans to segment the entire cognitive process. For computers, there are obvious differences in perception and cognition. Because computers cannot automatically complete the cognition process after collecting information, it is difficult to simulate the impact of high-level psychological processes on perception in the cognitive process. Therefore, although the model based on early visual information can efficiently process images in the field of computer vision, the simulation of human visual cognitive process is not satisfactory.

With the improvement of product functions and the assimilation of product properties, advertising is becoming increasingly more important, so flashes of advertisements spring up outside the window when commuting or on the screen when opening a webpage or software. How to tell if the subject has received important information in just a few seconds? It is an efficient and economical way to simulate a cognitive process model when humans watch advertising posters. However, some existing saliency models are not suitable for the purpose of this study for two reasons. The first reason is that most of the existing models detect salient objects, but judging salient objects still cannot judge whether the subject has received the product information. The second reason is that most of the existing datasets and models are based on natural pictures, while elements in advertising posters are relatively rich, and factors such as color, objects, text, and layout affect each other. Traditional saliency models did not include these factors. Therefore, a model suitable for advertising poster research should be built to better serve design purposes.

Through the study of visual cognitive processes in the fields of neuroscience, psychology, and computers, we believe that human visual cognition is an interactive process, and the results of intermediate and advanced visual processes (recognition, association, emotion, etc.) have significant impact on attention In order to more accurately simulate the process of humans watching advertising posters, and to test the impact of intermediate and advanced visual processes on attention, the following experiments were carried out (Fig. 3).

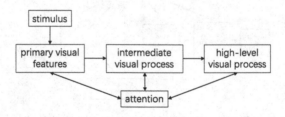

Fig. 3. Visual cognition

3.1   Datasets

To predict human's pattern of watching posters and evaluate the effectiveness of the advertisements, we conducted an eye-tracking experiment on 60 subjects and created a dataset with 1800 pictures of posters from 16 different fields like cars, cosmetics, food, games and toys. Each of the pictures has at least 15 copies of eye-tracking data.

In order to focus on the effects of advanced cognition processes on attention, in this study, a subset of 136 pictures was selected and the objects and their semantic information was analyzed.

3.2   Procedures

Experiment Environment

Experimental equipment: Tobii T60
Screen resolution: 1280 * 1024
Software environment: MATLAB R2018b 9.5.

Experiment Procedures. The experiment was conducted in a quiet office room with moderate light. The subject's sight is aligned to the height of the screen and is 50 cm from the screen. Before the beginning of the experiment, the experiment is explained, and the subjects are required to keep their heads straight and still and watch the stimulus pictures freely. After the calibration, the experiment is officially started and the experimenters leave to avoid interference. There are reminders at the beginning, middle and end of the entire experiment, and each photo is displayed for 3 s.

3.3   Data Analysis

Primary Visual Features Extraction. Here we choose the classic Itti's saliency model [30] for primary visual feature extraction. Saliency maps are first generated respectively based on intensity, color, orientation, and then fused to obtain the overall saliency map of the primary visual features.

Object Features Extraction. Studies [47–49] have shown that objects have a noticeable attraction to attention, so the objects in the stimulus are circled (No object category recognition is performed to avoid the influence of semantic factors). We adopted the experimental method of Juan Xu et al. After the objects are circled, their saliency are measured on five dimensions of size, convexity, solidity, complexity and eccentricity. For the details, please refer to the literature [50].

Semantic Features Extraction. Objects contain rich semantic information in addition to their physical properties, which can trigger associations, emotions, etc. Objects with rich semantic information tend to have greater saliency. Visual attention has a significant preference for faces [51–53], especially facial expressions that show strong emotions [54]. Besides, some objects, such as words and signs, are supposed to attract human attention or guide humans to interact with it. Objects related to the senses of humans also tend to attract attention [55]. In addition, for advertising posters, in order to impress people and have a better publicity effect, some interesting elements like exaggeration and metaphor are used, which have significant impact on saliency as well.

Therefore, after synthesizing various elements, the semantic features are classified into four categories in this experiment, which are text, face, sense, and fun. The text category contains all the elements such as text, logos, and QR codes that are designed to attract attention and interaction. The face category includes not only human faces, but also the faces of animals who has similar facial structural features to humans. The sense category contains objects that are likely to trigger most people's association or empathy with vision, hearing, smell, touch or taste. The fun category includes objects whose original properties are changed by using exaggerations, metaphors, and so on (See Fig. 4).

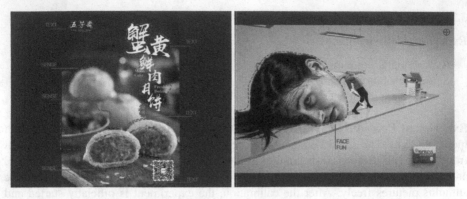

Fig. 4. Semantic features extraction examples

3.4   Results

We obtained three sets of experimental data, the first set of data is "model", which is the final model of this experiment, combing primary features, intermediate vision process and high-level vision. The second set of data is "test 1", in which the objects are circled but the semantic information of the them is not contained. So in "test 1", the effect of advanced visual processes on attention is ignored. The third set of data is "test 2", and only the primary visual features are collected.

The results of the three sets of experimental data comparing with the ground truth on normalized scanpath saliency (NSS), Pearson correlation coefficient (CC), and Kullback-Leibler divergence (KL) and the Precision-Recall (PR) curves prove that our model has the best performance in all indicators, and the performance of test 1 is better than test 2 (See Table 1 and Fig. 5).

Table 1. Comparison of experiment data.

	NSS	CC	KL
Model	1.9382	0.3398	2.4957
Test 1	1.7449	0.3066	2.5491
Test 2	0.9041	0.1348	3.0967

The experiment results show that, in the process of human visual cognition, attention is not only guided by primary visual features, but also influenced by inter-mediate and advanced vision processes. The significant role of guidance that recog-nition of objects and the association with semantic information plays on attention supports the interaction of attention with primary visual features and visual processing results.

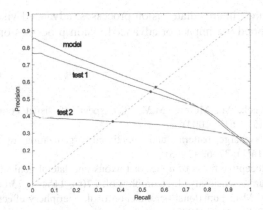

Fig. 5. Precision-Recall curve of three experiments

3.5 Discussion

Limitations. The knowledge, experience, cultural background, and preferences of each individual varies a lot. The association, memory, and emotion triggered by the same object may be significantly different. The model can simulate the general and universal laws but cannot cover the individual's unique personal attributes.

In order to avoid the influence caused by the language of the text, a large number of foreign language advertisements were abandoned in the experiment, resulting in a small sample size containing the element of fun, so there may be some deficiencies in the study of this factor.

Applications. The experimental model is trained through a large amount of real advertising poster viewing data, which can effectively simulate the cognition of humans when watching posters, and has high application value in advertising design evaluation. Through this model, subjects' areas of interest when watching advertising posters can be predicted, so that the effect of ads can be evaluated in advance. To make predictions before ads are distributed can effectively avoid wasting resources. In addition, the model can guide the automatic generation of posters to improve the quality of computer-generated posters.

4   Conclusions

We have studied the analysis and simulation of human visual cognitive mechanisms and processes in the fields of neuroscience, psychology and computer science. The research of saliency models constructed by simulating the processing of primary visual features by the human visual system has already been very deep, and more and more scholars have begun to pay attention to advanced vision processes. According to the characteristics of advertising stimuli, we selected three attributes of primary, object, and semantic features to build a model to simulate human internal visual cognitive mechanism. The analysis results of each set of data verified the interaction between primary visual features, intermediate vision processes, advanced visual cognition, and attention, and supported the impact of advanced vision processes on attention.

References

1. Michel, C.M., Seeck, M., Murray, M.M.: The speed of visual cognition. Suppl. Clin. Neurophysiol. **57**(57), 617 (2004)
2. Kuffler, S.W.: Discharge patterns and functional organization of mammalian retina. J. Neurophysiol. **16**(1), 37–68 (1953)
3. Mcilwain, J.T.: Receptive fields of optic tract axons and lateral geniculate cells: peripheral extent and barbiturate sensitivity. J. Neurophysiol. **27**(6), 1154–1173 (1964)
4. Ikeda, H., Wright, M.J.: Functional organization of the periphery effect in retinal ganglion cells. Vis. Res. **12**(11), 1857 (1972)
5. Tovée, M.J.: An Introduction to the Visual System. Cambridge University Press, Cambridge (2008)
6. Mansfield, R.J.W.: Neural basis of orientation perception in primate vision. Science **186** (4169), 1133–1135 (1974)
7. Li, Z.: A saliency map in primary visual cortex. Trends Cogn. Sci. **6**, 9–16 (2002)
8. Li, Z.: The primary visual cortex creates a bottom-up saliency map. In: Laurent Itti, G.R., Tsotsos, J.K. (ed.) Neurobiology of Attention. Academic Press, pp. 570–575 (2005)
9. Gattas, R., et al.: Cortical projections of area V2 in the macaque. Cereb. Cortex **7**(2), 110–129 (1997)
10. Stepniewska, I., Kaas, J.H.: Topographic patterns of V2 cortical connections in macaque monkeys. J. Comp. Neurol. **371**(1), 129–152 (1996)
11. Hegdé, J., Van Essen, D.C.: Selectivity for complex shapes in primate visual area V2. J. Neurosci. **20**, RC61 (2000)
12. Hegdé, J., Van Essen, D.C.: Temporal dynamics of shape analysis in macaque visual area V2. J. Psychol. **92**(5), 3030–3042 (2004)
13. Anzai, A., Peng, X., Van Essen, D.C.: Neurons in monkey visual area V2 encode combinations of orientations. Nat. Neurosci. **10**(10), 1313–1321 (2007)
14. Moran, J., Desimone, R.: Selective attention gates visual processing in the extrastriate cortex. Science **229**(4715), 782–784 (1985)
15. Dubner, R., Zeki, S.M.: Response properties and receptive fields of cells in an anatomically defined region of the superior temporal sulcus in the monkey. Brain Res. **35**(2), 528–532 (1971)
16. Maunsell, J.H., Van Essen, D.C.: Functional properties of neurons in middle temporal visual area of the macaque monkey. I. Selectivity for stimulus direction, speed, and orientation. J. Neurophysiol. **49**(5), 1127–1147 (1983)
17. Born, R.T., Bradley, D.C.: Structure and function of visual area MT. Annu. Rev. Neurosci. **28**, 157–189 (2005)
18. Dursteler, M.R., Wurtz, R.H., Newsome, W.T.: Directional pursuit deficits following lesions of the foveal representation within the superior temporal sulcus of the macaque monkey. J. Neurophysiol. **57**(5), 1262–1287 (1987)
19. Cardin, V., Smith, A.: Sensitivity of human visual and vestibular cortical regions to stereoscopic depth gradients associated with self-motion. Cereb. Cortex **20**(8), 1964–1973 (2010)
20. Pitzalis, S., et al.: Wide-field retinotopy defines human cortical visual area v6. J. Neurosci. Off. J. Soc. Neurosci. **26**(30), 7962–7973 (2006)

21. Deco, G., Rolls, E.T.: A neurodynamical cortical model of visual attention and invariant object recognition. Vis. Res. **44**(6), 642 (2004)
22. Chikkerur, S., et al.: What and where: a Bayesian inference theory of attention. Vis. Res. **50** (22), 2233–2247 (2010)
23. Chao, L., et al.: Brain-inspired edge detection model. Comput. Eng. Appl. **53**(24), 142–146 (2017)
24. Treisman, A.M., Gelade, G.: A feature-integration theory of attention. Cogn. Psychol. **12**(1), 97–136 (1980)
25. Marr, D.: Vision: A Computational Investigation into the Human Representation and Processing of Visual Information. Henry Holt and Co., Inc., New York (1982)
26. Ullman, S.: Visual routines. Cognition **18**(1–3), 97–159 (1984)
27. Ullman, S.: High-Level Vision: Object Recognition and Visual Cognition, vol. 2. MIT Press, Cambridge (1996)
28. Kahneman, D., Treisman, A., Gibbs, B.J.: The reviewing of object files - object-specific integration of information. Cogn. Psychol. **24**(2), 175–219 (1992)
29. Pylyshyn, Z.: The role of location indexes in spatial perception: a sketch of the FINST spatial-index model. Cognition **32**(1), 97 (1989)
30. Itti, L., Koch, C., Niebur, E.: A model of saliency-based visual attention for rapid scene analysis. IEEE Trans. Pattern Anal. Mach. Intell. **11**, 1254–1259 (1998)
31. Potter, M.C., et al.: Detecting meaning in RSVP at 13 ms per picture. Atten. Percept. Psychophys. **76**(2), 270–279 (2014)
32. Serre, T., Oliva, A., Poggio, T.: A feedforward architecture accounts for rapid categorization. Proc. Natl. Acad. Sci. U.S.A. **104**(15), 6424–6429 (2007)
33. Lollo, V.D., Enns, J.T., Rensink, R.: Competition for consciousness among visual events: the psychophysics of reentrant visual processes. J. Exp. Psychol. Gen. **129**(4), 481 (2000)
34. Enns, J.T., Lollo, V.D.: What's new in visual masking? Trends Cogn. Sci. **4**(9), 345–352 (2000)
35. Hochstein, S., Ahissar, M.: View from the top: hierarchies and reverse hierarchies in the visual system. Neuron **36**(5), 804 (2002)
36. Wolfe, J.M.: Moving towards solutions to some enduring controversies in visual search. Trends Cogn. Sci. **7**(2), 70–76 (2003)
37. Ramachandran, V.S., Hirstein, W.: The science of art: a neurological theory of aesthetic experience. J. Conscious. Stud. **6**, 15–51 (1999)
38. Zeki, S.: Inner Vision: An Exploration of Art and the Brain. Oxford University Press, Oxford (1999)
39. Jacobsen, T.: Beauty and the brain: culture, history and individual differences in aesthetic appreciation. J. Anat. **216**(2), 184–191 (2010)
40. Jacobsen, T., et al.: Brain correlates of aesthetic judgment of beauty. NeuroImage **29**(1), 276–285 (2006)
41. Kirk, U., et al.: Brain correlates of aesthetic expertise: a parametric fMRI study. Brain Cogn. **69**(2), 306–315 (2009)
42. Cattaneo, Z., et al.: The role of the lateral occipital cortex in aesthetic appreciation of representational and abstract paintings: a TMS study. Brain Cogn. **95**, 44–53 (2015)
43. Cattaneo, Z., et al.: The role of prefrontal and parietal cortices in esthetic appreciation of representational and abstract art: a TMS study. NeuroImage **99**, 443–450 (2014)
44. Cela-Conde, C.J., et al.: Dynamics of brain networks in the aesthetic appreciation. Proc. Natl. Acad. Sci. U.S.A. **110**(2), 10454–10461 (2013)
45. Christoph, R.: Combining universal beauty and cultural context in a unifying model of visual aesthetic experience. Front. Hum. Neurosci. **9**, 218 (2015)

46. Chatterjee, A.: Prospects for a cognitive neuroscience of visual aesthetics. Bull. Psychol. Arts **4**(2), 55–60 (2003)
47. Nuthmann, A., Henderson, J.M.: Object-based attentional selection in scene viewing. J. Vis. **10**(8), 20 (2010)
48. Einhäuser, W., Spain, M., Perona, P.: Objects predict fixations better than early saliency. J. Vis. **8**(14), 18 (2008)
49. Foulsham, T., Kingstone, A.: Optimal and preferred eye landing positions in objects and scenes. Q. J. Exp. Psychol. **66**(9), 1707–1728 (2013)
50. Juan, X., et al.: Predicting human gaze beyond pixels. J. Vis. **14**(1), 28 (2014)
51. Bindemann, M., et al.: Faces retain attention. Psychon. Bull. Rev. **12**(6), 1048–1053 (2006)
52. Cerf, M., Frady, E.P., Koch, C.: Faces and text attract gaze independent of the task: experimental data and computer model. J. Vis. **9**(12), 10 (2009)
53. Vuilleumier, P.: Faces call for attention: evidence from patients with visual extinction. Neuropsychologia **38**(5), 693–700 (2000)
54. Adolphs, R.: What does the amygdala contribute to social cognition? Ann. N. Y. Acad. Sci. **1191**(1), 42–61 (2010)
55. Onat, S., Libertus, K., König, P.: Integrating audiovisual information for the control of overt attention. J. Vis. **7**(10), 11–16 (2007)

"Fail, Clickbait, Cringe, Cancel, Woke": Vernacular Criticisms of Digital Advertising in Social Media Platforms

Gustavo Gomez-Mejia(✉) (iD)

PRIM – Université de Tours, 37000 Tours, France
gustavo.gomez-mejia@univ-tours.fr

Abstract. Within the commercial landscape of "social networking sites" turned into "social media platforms", the aim of this paper is to gain insight on the ways in which ordinary users express criticisms towards digital advertising. In order to highlight the existence of a specific digital advertising literacy, we focus on the study of a new generation of vernacular expressions which seem to characterize a critical experience of ads and promotional contents on social media platforms: "fail", "clickbait", "cringe", "cancel", "woke". A corpus of French-speaking Twitter contents documents the use of such terms as criticisms aimed at different digital promotional genres (ads, hashtags, sponsored posts, articles, banners, embedded videos). By conducting a micrological analysis of platformized user reactions, we show that an entire set of digital literacy skills can be conceptualized by observing the vernacular development of a vocabulary for the criticism of promotional contents and everyday ads.

Keywords: Internet culture · Language · Digital literacy

1 From "SNS" to "Platforms": Towards a Vernacular Criticism of Digital Advertising?

During the first decade of the 21st century, "Social networking sites" (SNS) were initially conceptualized as spaces where users could share connections and engage in different types of interaction with other contacts, whether they were to be called "friends", "followers", etc. An entire generation of users, from the years that came before Facebook's breakthrough, may recall Myspace's classic tagline –"*a place for friends*"– as a good example of how once new digital features were thought of mostly in terms of enhancing "ties", "meeting new people" or exploring "community tools". Take, for instance, Boyd & Ellison's [1] seminal definition: "We define social network sites as web-based services that allow individuals to (1) construct a public or semi-public profile within a bounded system, (2) articulate a list of other users with whom they share a connection, and (3) view and traverse their list of connections and those made by others within the system". Within the scope of that 2007 human-centered definition, there is little room left to conceptualize how those very same "Social networking sites" would evolve into highly competitive "Digital Advertising" machineries. At the time, Boyd & Ellison's paper barely foresees those evolutions by

© Springer Nature Switzerland AG 2020
G. Meiselwitz (Ed.): HCII 2020, LNCS 12195, pp. 309–324, 2020.
https://doi.org/10.1007/978-3-030-49576-3_23

stating that "marketing research indicates that SNSs are growing in popularity worldwide" and that "this growth has prompted many corporations to invest time and money in creating, purchasing, promoting, and advertising SNSs" [1].

In hindsight, such initial human-centered and socially-oriented conceptualizations of "SNS" appear to have played a key role in launching a new generation of popular "networking" websites, whilst celebrating the rise of "participatory cultures" [2] as a global digital phenomenon. Nevertheless, one could argue that those conceptualizations were partial and somehow made it difficult for critical points of view to emerge in public discourse, especially given that the explosion of digital advertising did not seem to be the crux of the matter. Beyond the occasional media coverage of "moral panics" surrounding teenagers or data privacy issues, some further conceptualization efforts were necessary for establishing a strain of contrarian thoughts targeting "Social net-working sites" and their subservience to digital advertising. From a French perspective, Bouquillion & Matthews [3] were among those who denounced the "ideological skillfulness" of "social" web companies which kept on "drawing the outlines of per-sonal enrichment and development" in a way that brought them "direct benefits", working as pseudo-"affective" intermediaries for products and brands in need of "communities" and "engagement". Their 2010 conclusions revisited web-services such as Myspace or Facebook in a critical fashion directly inspired by Adorno's most radical criticism: "The culture industry turns into public relations, the manufacturing of "goodwill" *per se*, without regard for particular firms or saleable objects. Brought to bear is a general uncritical consensus, advertisements produced for the world, so that each product of the culture industry becomes its own advertisement" [4].

By the turn of 2010, as "Social networking sites" conquered new markets and eventually ended up going by the generic name "Social media", specialized scholarship finally found its way towards a conceptualization of such "services" through the prism of a "new advertising industry" gathering "social relationship data" in order to sell more, according to Turow's 2011 critical analysis: "For advertisers as well as the agencies and data firms that serve them, the benefits from social media are focused on three linked opportunities: the chance to shape target audiences' visions of their brands through both earned media and owned/paid media; access to information regarding what specific types of people say and do regarding their products; the opportunity to identify likely customers and target them with ads and earned and paid media" [5].

Throughout a couple of decades, theoretical developments along the lines of the aforementioned conceptualizations have progressively paved the way for a broader critical comprehension of the role played by digital advertising in contemporary social media environments (Facebook, Twitter, Youtube, Instagram, etc.). In parallel, within that particular genre of "services", new generations of users have found themselves in charge of developing a particular digital advertising literacy, both by deconstructing the old "sharing connections with friends" narrative and by critically assessing the fully commoditized promotional dynamics of social media (as marketplaces for different types of content producers such as brands, companies, agencies, etc.). In other words, for scholars and users, this progressive development of a digital advertising literacy can be historically understood in the light of what Anne Helmond [6] calls the "plat-formization of the web" –i.e. "the transformation of social network sites into social media platforms"– in order to understand how promotional contents fit the "business model of a "multi-sided market", in which a platform enables everyday interactions between two or more distinct parties" (users, advertisers, developers).

Following that historical and ideological context, the aim of this paper is to gain insight on the part played by users within the ad-fueled "multi-sided markets" of social media platforms. How do users react to the promotional features and advertising contents that pervade "social media"? To which extent the contemporary forms of digital advertising culture may become the target of new generational criticisms? In order to highlight the existence of a specific digital advertising literacy, we will focus on the study of five vernacular expressions which all seem to characterize a critical experience of ads and promotional contents on "social media": *fail, clickbait, cringe, cancel, woke*. In recent years, such expressions have become usual in posts and comments reacting to the everyday experience of ads and promotional contents, both in English and other languages. As such, the study of this vocabulary sheds light on the cultural complexities of our subject: a contemporary digital advertising literacy, which is not just about being "able to perceive and interpret advertising messages mediated in digital media" through "different formats" [7] but also about labelling and expressing critical assessments of promotional contents on social media platforms, by deploying different levels of interpretation, encompassing technical, strategic, aesthetic and ethical considerations.

For each of the following short studies, we will focus on the vernacular uses of the aforementioned terms *(fail, clickbait, cringe, cancel, woke)*, by analyzing a collection of Urbandictionary.com definitions and a corpus of French-speaking Twitter posts[1]. Through a "micrological-philological" [8] approach of emblematic sets of quotations, translations and screenshots, these collected resources document a wide range of user reactions that question both the materiality of "platforms" as "screen writings" [9] and the discursive perceptions of specific genres of promotional contents (e.g. tweets, ads, hashtags, sponsored posts, articles, embedded videos). Our main argument is that the skills of what can be called a "digital advertising literacy" are necessarily related to the ways in which a "vernacular creativity" [10] develops its own vocabulary for the criticism of ads and promotional contents. By engaging in a close reading of tweets in which French-speaking users ordinarily apply terms such as *"fail"*, *"clickbait"*, *"cringe"*, *"cancel"* or *"woke"* to digital advertising, these dedicated microstudies serve the dual purpose of documenting subtle "vernacularization" [11] processes across languages while reflecting on the social significance of a new generation of critical keywords [12].

---

[1] Note: A decade-spanning (2013–2020) collection of 25 tweets containing "fail", "clickbait", "cringe", "cancel" or "woke" as search keywords was retrieved via http://search.twitter.com using the "lang:fr" language filter. Fully anonymized text contents in French (including original emojis) are reproduced throughout this paper without spelling or typographic corrections, followed (in brackets) by English translations and publication dates. For tweets including screenshots, direct links to visual contents are provided in footnotes.

2   "Fail": Reporting Paratextual Inconsistencies and Conflictive Editorial Contexts in Digital Advertising

2.1   Vernacular Definitions of "Fail": Beyond 'Unsuccessful' Ads

"Fail" is a term with negative and evaluative semantic features which has spread across recent decades over the Internet and beyond. According to popular Urbandictionary.com definitions [13]: "Fail is a word that is more than often overused online. Unfortunately, it has spewed into mainstream society and now is being used in everyday life" (24/4/2009). Such vernacular definitions provide us with some insight on how the term gained popularity by the end of last decade, when it became some sort of generational signifier: "A word that used to mean "not succeeding" and was used by normal, literate people. But these days "fail" is mostly used on the internet by no-life teenage losers. (Sometimes even in real life). They say phrases such as "this FAILS", "you FAIL at life" and "FAIL" and "EPIC FAIL"" (26/11/2009). Since "Fail" allows users to concisely express a blunt judgement aimed at diverse situations or contents, it is worth noting that the term has historically been documented "either (as) an interjection used when one disapproves of something, or (as) a verb meaning approximately the same thing as the slang form of suck." (22/7/2003). "Fail" is also the subject of a separate hashtag entry on Urbandictionary.com where the more recent form "#Fail" is equally acknowledged as a widespread term: "Play on the fail that is used when something goes wrong or is bad or not up to standard. The hashtag is common Twitter parlance, so this is predominantly used on Twitter but has broken out into everyday speech" (2/3/2012).

At the intersection of #Fail and digital advertising, the online vernacular use of such term seemingly targets "unsuccessful" promotional contents. Getting to express a very concise opinion about an ad or a campaign by considering it a "fail" is perhaps a basic skill in terms of digital advertising literacy. Nevertheless, once we go beyond the apparently simplistic nature of such rudimentary negative judgment, more complex questions can arise; especially if we try to reassess the ordinary evaluative skills of Internet users: which are the implied criteria that may determine what is a success or a failure for a specific type of content? French-speaking Twitter gives us access to a series of vernacular examples in which the anglicism *"fail"* is applied to different types of promotional contents. While "Fail" generally tends to reject a dysfunctional or counter-productive advertising strategy, a close reading of tweets in French -containing the words *"fail"* and *"pub"* (ad)- suggests two analytical directions in which "fail" can be used on the basis of more particular sets of evaluative criteria.

2.2   #EpicFail. The Accidental Inconsistencies of Promotional Texts

On a first level of analysis, we can observe that "Fail" has been historically used to pinpoint an inconsistency or a contradiction within the actual contents of a promotional message. A rather old 2013 tweet points out, for instance, that a sponsored post promoting Samsung was actually sent from an iPhone: *"Le tennisman David Ferrer faisait la pub de Samsung... depuis son iPhone;) #epicfail"* ("Tennis player David Ferrer was promoting Samsung... from his iPhone;) #epicfail, 2/5/2013). In order to stress the "epic" nature of such "fail", a screenshot documents how @DavidFerrer87's sponsored tweet, in which he redundantly claims to be "so happy with his new #GalaxyS4, setting up the S Health in his new #GalaxyS4, the new app to help during training sessions @SamsungMobile", also bears the caption sent "via Twitter for iPhone" under its publication date, an unfortunate detail which is highlighted by a red square. This emblematic screenshot[2] is linked to a Swiss news article[3] in which journalist Simon Koch accurately refers to "the tweet's paratext" in order to locate the promotional failure. Gérard Genette's definition of a "paratext" [14] can indeed conceptualize in a very precise fashion what happened on-screen with that tweet: both by stressing that there is major cacophony in "thresholds" between two textual zones and by suggesting that there is a literate approach to that tweet-friendly "#epicfail" hashtag. In terms of digital advertising literacy, "epic fail" is perhaps the shortest way to name the accidental inconsistency of a promotional text. In this case, a sponsored tweet that intentionally multiplies Samsung-related passing-signs (two Galaxy hashtags and a corporate account mention) but unintentionally carries an infra-ordinary portion of auto-generated text displaying the name of its "nemesis" Apple product (the iPhone): a contradictory appendix which ends up being read as part of the same screen text and therefore may deceive either brand consistency or influencer loyalty expectations.

A similar use of "fail" is documented by another user sarcastically tweeting about a "genius" level of inconsistencies in an advertisement for Virgin Mobile: *"La définition d'1 fail: 1 Samsung sous iOS avec 1 réseau Free dans 1 pub Virgin Mobile. Des genies!"* ("The definition of a fail: 1 Samsung Phone running under Apple's iOS while connected to rival network Free in an ad for Virgin Mobile. Geniuses!, 4/11/2014). A judgmental tweet that sparked a debate with its author's followers about whether that advertisement was actually an intentional "fail" (or not). In terms of digital literacy, such an assessment involved the exploration of possible "irony" and a multilayered interpretation of the visual portion of the ad[4]. Through an "oversemiotized" approach of the device -examining its connection status icons, its operating system interface, its browser and its loaded page- users' reply-tweets even speculated about hypothetical technical processes which could bridge all these contradictory rival brand gaps and thresholds altogether.

2.3 "Fails" Within Websites. Conflictive Editorial Contexts or Algorithmic Ad-Mismatchings?

On a broader level of analysis, we can observe other uses of "#fail" which also express a negative judgment towards promotional contents but tend do so by "zooming out" from internal message inconsistencies or inherent contradictions, therefore questioning the wider role of contemporary editorial environments. Given that digital advertising coexists with other kinds of content, "Fail" can be alternatively used for describing a conflictive relation towards editorial contexts. Numerous French-speaking tweets document this kind of onscreen situations through a series of screenshots and captions

---

[2] https://pbs.twimg.com/media/BJQAV8VCMAADhP3?format=jpg&name=small.

[3] https://www.24heures.ch/high-tech/web/pub-samsung-iphone/story/21883754.

[4] https://pbs.twimg.com/media/B1oTmt4CYAAanLe?format=jpg&name=900x900.

mostly aimed at online media publishers and promoted brands. On the one hand, Twitter users may directly complain to media websites and promoted brands about page design issues and legibility struggles related to pop-up ads: "*La #pub est si invasive qu'on ne peut même plus lire les articles... @LesEchos #fail #Advertising #DigitalMarketing @CreditMutuel*" ("Advertising is so invasive that one cannot even read the articles anymore", 27/1/2020[5]). On the other hand, users may express their perplexity when the promotional pretentions of a particular ad suddenly happen to be neutralized by its context of appearance or by other neighboring contents: "*Cet incroyable #fail signé @Le_Figaro avec cette pub pour la @Caisse_Epargne !* 😱 *#ongagneparfoisaprendredresrisques #FeteDeLaMusique*" ("This incredible #fail by @Le_Figaro with this ad for @Caisse_Epargne! 😱", 22/6/2017). This tweet refers to an article about a 35 old man who killed himself by jumping off a Parisian bridge. A news piece that ironically happens to be surrounded by a promotional background with clickable banners for the Caisse d'Épargne's life-insurance, which depict summer-themed characters enthusiastically jumping off balneary cliffs under the slogan "sometimes you win by taking risks"[6].

A similar "#fail"-report is documented by another screenshot[7] showing a Le Figaro article on "tax evasion" via HSBC which happens to be surrounded by a promotional background for the bank itself: "*Le placement pub qui tue #fail #HSBC*" ("A killer ad placement #fail #HSBC", 27/1/2014). Since ad campaigns do not necessarily foresee their actual onscreen environments, this type of *conflictive relation towards editorial contexts* inspires a peculiar distancing effect for users who even get to express *a suspicion of algorithmic mismatching* by using the word "fail": "*J'aime beaucoup le travail de @Numerama. À tel point que je désactive mon anti-pub, c'est dire... Mais là pour le coup, la pub affichée est très mal venue vu le sujet. C'est dommage car le papier en question est bon. Petit fail des algos j'imagine ? :-/*" ("I love @Numerama's work so much that I even turn my ad-blocker off... But this time, the ad they are displaying is very unfortunate given the subject. A little fail from the algos, I guess? :-/", 24/11/2019[8]). This tweet refers to an article in which Numerama proudly states that they want no revenues from Google ranking their contents, while simultaneously including a top-of-page promotional banner for Google's Pixel phone. In terms of digital literacy, these "fail"-related screenshots capture an ordinary and partial comprehension of paradoxical editorial results. The skills required for reporting this kind of counter-productive ads also involve taking position in vivid contemporary critical debates: either by questioning the commoditization of visual surfaces in media websites or by highlighting the role played by placement mechanisms and so-called "semantic approaches" to "contextual" matching in ad-networks [15].

---

[5] https://pbs.twimg.com/media/EPSC0mfX0AIv2NG?format=jpg&name=large.

[6] https://pbs.twimg.com/media/DC6jP0lXYAExRfw?format=jpg&name=medium.

[7] https://pbs.twimg.com/media/Be_IbvwCcAAGqDZ?format=png&name=large.

[8] https://pbs.twimg.com/media/EHn8nmyXkAA9V7H?format=jpg&name=large.

3 "Clickbait": Recognizing Sensationalist Hyperlinked Rhetorics and Attention-Trafficking Effects

3.1 On "Clickbait" and *"Putaclic"*: Vernacular Definitions

Through the lens of a usual fishing and promotional metaphor, "Clickbait" describes a particular type of content which has been purportedly designed for attracting one's attention in order to generate traffic between websites. According to Urbandictionary's Top definition [16], "Clickbait" is a self-explanatory portmanteau: "It means what you think it means: bait for clicks. It's a link which entices you to click on it. The "bait" comes in many shapes and sizes, but it is usually intentionally misleading and/or crassly provocative. Clicking will inevitably cause disappointment. Clickbait is usually created for money. One common type is adverts and spam, such as you might find on a random website or in your Facebook feed. Such clickbait usually leads to a site which tries to sell you something or possibly extort you, by withholding the promised "bait"". French-speaking users can also refer to "Clickbait" as *"Putaclic"* (literally "click-whore"), a neologism that is defined by Le Wiktionnaire [17] as a "label for an article or video whose title or lead is deliberately exaggerated in order to attract more and more users or spectators", with especially "lurid and enticing click-provoking headlines". Thus, in terms of digital advertising literacy, "clickbait" is a vernacular term that can be used for describing an established genre of deceptive contents (news, ads, special offers, gossip) but also for addressing particular criticisms towards the machineries of "the attention economy" [18].

3.2 Sensationalist Hyperlinks. The Performative Means of the "Clickbait" Genre

As an established digital genre, French-speaking tweets ascribe "clickbait" ads to specific text formats and web locations: almost 20 tweets mention for instance Taboola's "recommended links" sections which are usually located "under" news articles in well-respected websites (e.g. 20minutes.fr). A "Clickbait ad" (*"pub click-bait"* or *"pub putaclic"*) is used to label promotional content whose onscreen presence has become habitual and provides users with regular amounts of (often deemed laughable) *sensationalist hyperlinked rhetorics*. This inspires, for instance, a tweet commenting an ad's unsurprising 'surprise' effects: *"Nan mais mdr je fais un tour de 2 min sur CCM pour télécharger ganttproject et je tombe sur une pub putaclic x): «Les 5 meilleurs antivirus de 2019 (vous ne devinerez jamais lequel est numéro 1)"* ("Nope, LOL, I spend 2 min on the CCM website for downloading Ganttproject and I stumble upon a clickbait ad: 'The 2019 Top 5 Best Antivirus (you'll never guess which one is n °1'", 15/12/2019[9]). Clickbait ads can also be disregarded as rather memorable lies or as ironically collectible elements: *"C'est quoi votre récurrence de pub clickbait préférée ? Perso j'hésite entre "le galaxy S8 à 1€" ou "la version cachée du jeu naruto a été rendue publique!!"* ("Which is your favorite recurring clickbait ad? I personally swing

---

[9] https://pbs.twimg.com/media/EL1sj2rW4AIaH2X?format=png&name=360x360.

between 'Galaxy S8 for 1€' and 'The hidden version of the Naruto Game is now public!'", 26/3/2018). In terms of digital literacy, such observations not only poke fun at the *clickbait* or *putaclic* ad genre: users actually get to quote and locate their criticisms in the very linguistic or visual materiality of a particular hyperlinked text that pretends to be highly "seductive" [19]. An incomplete heading that challenges a user's curiosity and promises access to a desirable information, branded product or suggestive image, becomes somehow suspicious: under these generic features, the performative means of "Clickbait" rhetorics tend to recognized by newer generations as peripheral clutter desperately asking a user to "click for more".

3.3   Is It "Clickworthy"? The Critical Comprehension of Traffic Cycles

"Clickbait" may also inspire small analytical sequences in which users recontextualize its *sensationalist* features and *attention-trafficking effects* within a more complex digital apparatus. When a digitally literate user posts a diptych with screenshots as "clickbait" evidence, there is an attempt to fully describe an entire promotional circuit. A tweet can, for instance, show the evidence of a paid tweet promoting an article by French magazine OhMyMag, whose title intriguingly announces *"The incredible reaction of a rapist who discovers that his victi..."* and then leads visitors to a site packed with ad-videoplayers and Taboola-like shady contents: *"Clickbait sponsorisé pour arriver sur une page blindée de pub, qui parle d'un sujet qui date de quelques années* ☹" ("Sponsored clickbait[10] to land on an ad-crammed page[11] talking about a subject from a couple of years ago ☹", 31/3/2019).

Similar critical intentions towards "unworthy" contents inspire another tweet (with a screenshot[12] and link) commenting on how a 20minutes.fr headline -*"Spotify will impose advertisements to paid subscribers too"*- slickly triggered all sorts of rejectful comments from readers and Spotify subscribers: *"Toujours puissant le clickbait sur nos boomers (parce qu'en fait, c'est pas vraiment de la pub, c'est des annonces person-nalisées qui seront désactivables)* https://20minutes.fr/high-tech/2640419-20191030-spotify-la-pub-aussi-pour-les-abonnes-payants" ("Clickbait is always powerful over our boomers (because there will be no commercials but rather personalized ads which you will be able to turn off)", 2/11/2019). In terms of digital advertising literacy, it is worth noting how criticisms on "Clickbait" eventually unfold the anticipation of a complete traffic cycle: one that goes from reading a triggering headline to feeling the need of reacting through the comments section. This critical comprehension of "clickbait"-led traffic dynamics can also be interpreted as a stigmatization of both third-party websites (e.g. OhMyMag, 20minutes.fr) and fellow vulnerable readers. In the latter case, the awareness of such attention-trafficking cycles is stereotypically corre-lated to other generational factors: by exposing the result of those clicks quickly turned into indignation comments, the author implies that "boomers" tend to be more naïve (more likely to take the indignation bait) or less literate (uncapable of understanding the

---

[10] https://pbs.twimg.com/media/D2-xJH3XQAEkynv?format=jpg&name=large.

[11] https://pbs.twimg.com/media/D2-xJH2WwAA2QX8?format=jpg&name=large.

[12] https://pbs.twimg.com/media/EIXv4g7WwAIv-sx?format=png&name=900x900.

adaptable settings of how personalized ads work) than younger "visitors" (implicitly viewed as more capable of evaluating what is news-, comment- or click-worthy).

4 "Cringe": Performing Taste-Based Catharsis and Parodic Paranoia

4.1 From "Cringe" to *"Malaisant"*: Preliminary Definitions

"Cringe" refers to matters of taste which may result in experiencing an subjective malaise towards diverse contents, aesthetics or narratives. In top definitions from Urbandictionary [20], "Cringe" is associated to a peculiar palette of situations and feelings: "When someone acts/or is so embarrassing or awkward, it makes you feel extremely ashamed and/or embarrassed" (7/2/2017); "Before the internet trolls changed the meaning of this word, "cringe" was a verb used to express embarrassment or disgust. Now, this word is mostly used to define something that you dislike or do not understand." (15/7/2016). The term appears to be used for describing rather dysphoric states onscreen (from guilty perplexity to open embarrassment) by insisting on the "cringeworthy" nature of some digital content consumption experiences. Both as an adjective and as a verb, *"Cringe"* (sometimes *"cringer"*) has become usual in French social media vernacular expressions, standing next to almost equivalent terms (such as *"malaise"* or *"malaisant"*) which also relate to expressing an occasional feeling of uncomfortable spectatorship. After years of press-fueled linguistic debates [21], 2019's edition of French dictionary Le Petit Robert finally inducted an "official" definition of *"malaisant"*: *"Qui met mal à l'aise, qui crée un malaise, une gêne"* ("What makes one uncomfortable, that creates discomfort, embarrassment.") [22].

4.2 "So Cringe", *"Tellement Cringe"*: A Cathartic Taste-Based Reaction Towards Promotional Contents?

"Cringe" can be found in tweets as a short evaluative term used by French-speaking spectators of digital ads: *"La pub Chanel so cringe mdr"* ("The ad for Chanel is so cringe LOL", 19/11/2019); *"J'ai pas pour habitude de retweeter une pub, mais celle-ci est tellement cringe que je résiste pas* 😭*"* ("*I don't usually retweet an ad but this one is so cringe that I can't resist* 😭", 21/11/2019). From the standpoint of digital literacy, it is worth noting that "cringe" emerges as a somewhat *cathartic reaction* to the aesthetically-doomed or pseudo-empathetic attempts of promotional objects. In the first case, "so cringe" applies to a pretentious campaign for a well-established luxury brand. In the second example, "cringe" relates to a humble corporate tweet from French electronic appliances retailer Boulanger, whose smiling and welcoming staff strikes a pose for a group pic in order to invite users for coffee at the local mall.

4.3   When "Cringy" Ads Go Viral: From Strategic Concerns to Parodic Paranoia?

Promotional contents dubbed as being "cringe" can also foster viral attention movements that show us how ordinary ad-related digital skills are put to work in platforms. This tweet by French youtuber Sylvain mocking a 'cringeworthy' ad for nutritional brand Feed offers a rather complete case study: *"Oh ben Feed a posté une vidéo/pub sur Facebook avec des supers acteurs mais ils ont oublié de la mettre sur Twitter* 😆 *(vous allez voir l'intensité ne fait qu'augmenter au fil des secondes)"* ("Well Feed posted a video/ad on Facebook featuring some super actors but they forgot to post it on Twitter 😆 (you'll see how the intensity grows and second after second)", 21/2/2019). Such a sarcastic take on a badly performed ad invites his followers to see Feed's content by themselves. The collective "cringe" impression is confirmed by a series or quote and reply-tweets that caption the video or directly complain to Feed's community managers: *"L'art de communiquer version Feed (qu'est ce que c'est cringe)"* ("The art of communication à la Feed (how cringe that is)", 21/2/2019); *"@feed à quel moment vous vous êtes dit c'est une bonne pub svp ? j'ai jms rien vu d'aussi cringe"* ("I've never seen something that cringe. You need to fire your marketing director now. This reaches the same level of TV shopping on M6. You are on the Internet and this type of communication won't get through", 22/2/2019). This type of vernacular reactions to "cringy" contents show us how users express diverse strategic concerns about digital communications. Such concerns may be addressed by referring to what is being posted (or not) across platforms, to Internet-related audiovisual aesthetic expectations (vs. TV formats), and to brand executives who should be held accountable.

On a further level of digital literacy, other comments can also develop their own parodically paranoid speculative theories on ad-related "malaise". Funny 'plausible' interpretations can emerge by ironically relating the Feed ad to a popular Twitter account devoted to curating cringeworthy video contents: *"'C'est top le goût'... Franchement, @feed, une production réalisée par Malaise TV?"* ("'Great taste!' Frankly, @feed, is this a Malaise TV production?", 22/2/2019). In more assertive cases, as parodic contents proliferate spreading variations of an ad, other users get to publicly express their own conspiracy-driven second thoughts: *"CONSPIRACY THEORY: Feed a fait exprès de faire cte pub CRINGE pour qu'il y ait des parodies qui popularisent leurs produits..."* ("Conspiracy theory: Feed intentionally made a CRINGE ad in order to inspire parodies making their products more popular...", 23/2/2019). Such reactions point towards a vernacular reinterpretation of the old saying "There is no such thing as bad publicity" as rephrased by another tweet stating that: *"Bad buzz is buzz c'est bien connu* 👏👏🤷" ("We all know a bad buzz is still a buzz", 22/1/2019). The assessment of a "cringeworthy" ad therefore implies establishing possible links with other fashionable ironic post-Internet anti-aesthetics (Malaise TV) and understanding how parody emancipates contemporary digital advertising from its canonic focus on plain "euphoric values" [23].

Critical statements on "cringe" also give us some insight on how contemporary digital literacies tend to develop their own self-referential evaluative scales: *"On a trouvé le nouveau mètre-étalon du malaise. Exit l'échelle de Villejuif, bonjour l'échelle de Feed"* ("We just found a new standard measure for malaise. Goodbye Villejuif scale, hello Feed scale", 21/1/2019). This tweet refers to a vernacular "malaisological" scale originated in the "18-25 yo" section of French forum Jeuxvideo.com. The original 10 point parody of a rating "scale" was inspired by the "traumatic" experience of watching 2016 *malaisant"* footage from a Carrefour store in Villejuif: a video capturing how supermarket employees tried to perform a Disney-like theatrical situation in front of highly indifferent and very uncomfortable customers [24]. Far from being anecdotal generational jokes, this kind of viral "cringe" assessing episodes may eventually stick to a brand's reputation in less parodic fashion: *"Est ce que Queal sont moins insupportable que Feed en terme de marketing ? Parce que Feed avec son ciblage startup nation gamer qui lache pas son clavier, ou genre "pas le temps de manger c'est un truc de la plebe" c'est un peu cringe".* ("Is Queal less unbearable than Feed in terms of marketing? Because Feed, with their focus on targeting start-up nation gamers who never get away from their keyboards or say "no time for eating, it's a plebeian thing", is a bit cringe", 11/3/2019). As a potentially "viral" promotional genre, "cringeworthy" ads foster a literacy that may lead to a critical assessment of strategic positions, parodic intents, generational targets, aesthetic preferences and rivalries within niche markets.

5 "Cancel" or "Woke"? Debating About Brand Risks, Values and Micro-controversies

5.1 "Cancel" and "Woke": Two 'Terms of the Decade' from People to Brands

Vulture's decade-spanning "A–Z of Words That Defined the Internet in the 2010s" [25] included two terms that open new perspectives in terms of digital advertising literacy: "cancel" and "woke".

For the first term, according to Vulture, being "Canceled" currently "describes when someone is shut down or deplatformed, à la a television show being canceled. It's linked to callout culture, a form of public shaming". In that specific sense, "Cancel culture" gets a separate entry on Urbandictionary.com [26]: "A modern internet phenomenon where a person is ejected from influence or fame by questionable actions. It is caused by a critical mass of people who are quick to judge and slow to question. It is commonly caused by an accusation, whether that accusation has merit or not. It is a direct result of the ignorance of people caused communication technologies outpacing the growth in available knowledge of a person.". It is worth noting that although such definitions refer to "a person" (i.e. a celebrity, an influencer) they may also apply nowadays to any company or brand whose reputation can be suddenly hit by a wave of criticism resulting on different types of *sanctions and collective retaliations*.

For the second term, Vulture gives this definition of "Woke": "To be aware of the societal issues that affect marginalized communities. Originated in Black English.". A topic that is further developed by other Urbandictionary contributors [27]: "A word currently used to describe "consciousness" and being aware of the truth behind things "the man" doesn't want you to know i.e. classism, racism, and any other social injustices. The term comes from a genuine place but is becoming overused. People mainly use it to sound like deep thinkers when they are really just following a trend";

"The act of being very pretentious about how much you care about a social issue". Once again, the term "Woke" is defined in terms of personal attitudes but is nowadays also used for describing brands who highlight a *public endorsement of societal issues* through their digital communications – and can even be accused of "woke-washing" [28] if their engagements seem suspicious from the point of view of a critical audience.

5.2   Boycotting or Supporting an Ad? "Cancel" and "Wokeness" as Digital Trends Debated by Critical Audiences

The risk of being "canceled" and the interest of being "woke" are two facets of a contemporary problem that brands seem to be facing across digital platforms: since advertisements and promotional contents happen to be embedded in the feeds of everyday life, their messages are subject to a new type of *permanent public scrutiny* by platform users, which depending on their ideological positions may as well "cancel" a brand (on the basis of a misconduct) or reward it for defending "woke" values. This set of French-speaking tweets is somehow emblematic of how linked these dialectical outcomes are for users: "*Vous allez cancel Apple s'il faisait une campagne de publicité raciste?*" ("Are you going to cancel Apple if they run a racist ad campaign?", 22/4/2019); "*J'espère vraiment que Zara ne va jamais faire quoi que ce soit de problématique, parce que Dieu sait que ce sera au dessus de mes forces de cancel cette marque* ("I truly hope that Zara won't ever do anything problematic, cause God knows I don't have enough strength to cancel that brand", 18/3/2018); "*Tu boycottes aussi h&m et pas zara et compagnie ? de même pour kanye west ? Donc en clair tu es cool avec n'importe quel artiste ou marque, mais à la moindre sauce où le FC woke dit qu'il faut cancel tel individu ou organisation, tu t'exécutes ?*" ("Do you also boycott H&M and Zara & co? And Kanye West? So actually, you are cool with any artist or brand but whenever the Woke F.C. says that you have to cancel this individual or organization, you immediately do so?", 15/9/2019). From the standpoint of digital advertising literacy, the possibility of "cancelling" a brand involves the skills of *assessing a potential ethical or image risk* and the *ability to take part in a boycott operation* through digital means (unfollowing, blocking, hashtags, petitions, comments).

As for the possibility of recognizing that an ad is explicitly "woke" based on how it deals with identity politics, race or gender representations, users seem literate enough so as to spot a discursive trend within platforms and therefore express their own diverse ideological nuances: "*Le fait de faire de la pub sur des sujets de société (aka Gillette et la masculinité toxique, pepsi et le racisme) ça s'appelle le woke capitalism*". ("The fact of making advertising for societal issues (aka Gillette and toxic masculinity, Pepsi and racism) is called woke capitalism", 28/1/2020); "*C'est sans doute mieux d'avoir des pubs woke que racistes ou sexistes mais j'ai quand même pas envie d'entendre parler de pub. La pub c'est de la merde. Parlons d'autre chose, merci*" ("No doubt that it is better to have woke ads rather than racist or sexist ones but yet I don't want to hear conversations about advertising. Advertising is shit. Let's talk about something else, thanks", 16/1/2019). At the intersection of digital literacy and cultural studies in the vein of Stuart Hall, assessing "Wokeness" in ads involves a *semiotic recognition of "differences that matter"* [29] for a particular audience (a representational nuance expressed by a character, a color, a pronoun, a storyline, a symbol, etc.).

Interpreting "woke" promotional contents also requires users to *anticipate conflictual ties between antagonistic audience-"clusters"* [30] and to engage in sub-sequent debates (by replying or quote-tweeting reactions from "anti-woke" individuals). A promotional Netflix post announcing that the initial release date of their *Street Food* documentary series had be postponed "because of the Ramadan" is in that sense polemically quote-tweeted by a user as being emblematic of so-called "woke marketing": «*Si ce tweet n'était pas prévu d'avance...* 🤭 *Nouvel exemple du "woke marketing"* (...) *Les haineux vont hurler, les autres aimer les voir hurler, les 2 feront du buzz et de la pub gratuite.*» ("If this tweet was not scheduled in advance... 🤭 A new "woke marketing" example... Haters gonna yell and the others will love to see them yell, both of them will make some buzz and free advertisement", 15/4/2019). Since online conflict is both lucrative and "mediagenic" [31], this kind of contemporary statements on "cancel" and "woke"-related debates show us that users also tend to criticize the fact that digital advertising on platforms may voluntarily play with the *inflammatory dynamics of micro-controversies* between "haters" and "supporters" as part of ambivalent promotional strategies.

6   Conclusion

As successive generations of Internet users engage with new words for criticizing digital advertising, the study of their mutant vocabularies offers us a standpoint from which to assess the current forms of digital literacy. A digital literacy which necessarily involves ad-related skills. If we follow Milad Doueihi's definition, "Digital literacy" [32] is "not only the knowledge required to access and manipulate the basic tools of the digital environment"; "Instead, digital literacy is the sum of evolving practices that are essentially cultural. They are cultural because they both inform choices and shape perceptions". Such cultural choices and perceptions nowadays involve the many ways in which users relate to tech industries, to "social" interfaces and more specifically to their pervasive promotional features and contents.

Thus, among the multiple expressive facets of "vernacular creativity" [33], we can observe how a digital advertising literacy develops its own vocabulary for the onscreen criticism of promotional contents in everyday life. What can we learn by collecting "scraps of language" and "tatters of speech" [34] in relation to digital ads? Our fragmentary corpus of French-speaking tweets documents the vitality of a new set of words -such as "fail", "clickbait" or "*putaclic*", "cringe" or "*malaisant*", "cancel" or "woke"- that can all be found in contemporary user reactions to online ads across social media platforms. A close reading of those reactions suggests that users have become more literate or more critically aware towards digital advertising, applying such vernacular terms to very specific textual dimensions of the promotional contents they are faced with, and developing a set of discursive and hermeneutic skills that can be summarized as follows (Table 1):

Table 1. Five vernacular criticisms of digital advertising in social media platforms

Term	Literacy skills	Related platform textualities	Criticized third-parties
"Fail"	Reporting paratextual inconsistencies and conflictive editorial contexts	Sponsored tweets, promotional hashtags, brand account mentions, tweet data; Device/system/network/browser details; Pop-up ads, media account mentions, promotional backgrounds and banners, media website interfaces. Article contents, Ad-networks matching algorithms	Samsung mobile, Galaxy S4, David Ferrer (vs iPhone); Virgin mobile (vs. Samsung/iOS/Free); Crédit Mutuel, Les Echos, Caisse d'épargne, Le Figaro, HSBC; Numérama, Google Pixel
"Clickbait" or *Putaclic*	Recognizing sensationalist hyperlinked rhetorics and attention-trafficking effects	Recommended articles sections; Website ads, banners, links; Sponsored tweets, article headlines, video players; News headlines, Comment sections, Personalized ad settings	Taboola/20minutes.fr; Galaxy S8, Naruto Game, CCM site, Top Antivirus; Twitter, OhMyMag; 20minutes.fr, Spotify
"Cringe" or *Malaisant*	Performing taste-based catharsis or parodic paranoia	Commercials; Corporate "staff" tweets; Facebook Video posts; Account mentions; Parodic tweets	Chanel; Boulanger; Feed (brand executives, vs. Queal); Carrefour
"Cancel"	Debating potential brand risks or taking part in boycott operations	Problematic Ad campaigns; Hypothetical tweetstorms	Apple; Zara, H&M. Kanye West
"Woke"	Debating societal issues ("differences that matter") and engaging in micro-controversies	Anti-racist/anti-sexist ads; Release date announcements; Polemical quote-tweets	Pepsi, Gillette; Netflix France

In the light of our findings, the "culturological" study [35] of this vernacular vocabulary reveals the complexities of a digital advertising literacy which deals with multiple platform textualities by deploying different levels of interpretation. Within the scope of ordinary tweets that could be generically and dismissively called "negative reactions", we have a chance to observe how the use of these "new generations" of globalized words allows subjects to elaborate quite critical assessments of the diverse promotional genres that they have to experience and endure through "social" commercial platforms. If reporting a "fail" requires the skills of shifting from an immanentist (content-centered) to a context-oriented literacy, then a term such as "clickbait" reveals another dimension of platform experiences by locating its criticism at the very intersection of hypertextual and economic literacies. When "cringe" addresses matters of taste, users get to exercise an aesthetic or parodic sense of spectatorship, whereas "woke" and "cancel" foray into debating and criticizing advertising from the standpoint of renewed societal and ethical literacies. Such terms can therefore be considered as new cardinal points for a multilayered understanding and critique of digital advertising, in terms of textuality, strategy, style and ideology. Whether in English, in French or in other languages, the cultural "inventiveness" [36] of the aforementioned words reflects the contemporary evolutions of our digital "social" landscape is a rather peculiar way: in the moving landscape of networked "places for friends" turned into "platformized" promotional marketplaces, successive generations of "social media" users have learnt to perform new vernacular tricks in order to express their own brand of criticisms towards the vast spectrum of digital ad campaigns that keep on pervasively targeting them.

References

1. Boyd, D., Ellison, N.: Social network sites: definition, history, and scholarship. J. Comput.-Mediated Commun. **13**, 210–230 (2007)
2. Jenkins, H.: Fans, Bloggers, and Gamers: Exploring Participatory Culture. New York University Press, New York (2006)
3. Bouquillion, P., Matthews, J.T.: Le web collaboratif. Mutations des Industries de la Culture et de la Communication. PUG, Grenoble (2010)
4. Adorno, T.W.: Culture industry reconsidered. New German Critique **6**, 12–19 (1975)
5. Turow, J.: The Daily You: How the New Advertising Industry is Defining Your Identity and Your Worth. Yale University Press, New Haven (2011)
6. Helmond, A.: The platformization of the web: making web data platform ready. Soc. Media + Soc. **1**, 1–11 (2015)
7. Nur Erdem, M.: An argumentative study on digital advertising literacy. In: Taskiran, N. (ed.) Handbook of Research on Multidisciplinary Approaches to Literacy in the Digital Age, pp. 160–178. IGI, Hershey (2019)
8. Bloch, E.: Recollections of Walter Benjamin. In: Smith, G. (ed.) On Walter Benjamin: Critical Essays and Reflections, pp. 338–345. MIT Press, Cambridge (1988)
9. Souchier, E., Candel, E., Gomez-Mejia, G., Jeanne-Perrier, V.: Le numérique comme écriture, Théories et méthodes d'analyse. Armand Colin, Paris (2019)
10. Burgess, J.: Hearing ordinary voices: cultural studies, vernacular creativity and digital storytelling. J. Media Cult. Stud. **20**(2), 201–214 (2006)
11. Appadurai, A.: Modernity at Large: Cultural Dimensions of Globalization. University of Minnesota Press, Minneapolis (1996)
12. Williams, R.: Keywords. A Vocabulary of Culture and Society. Fontana, London (1976)
13. Urban Dictionary: Fail. https://www.urbandictionary.com/define.php?term=Fail. Accessed 30 Jan 2020
14. Genette, G.: Seuils. Seuil, Paris (1987)
15. Broder, A., Fontoura, M., Josifovski, V., Riedel, L.: A semantic approach to contextual advertising. In: 30th SIGIR Proceedings, pp. 559–566. ACM, New York (2007)

16. Urban Dictionary: Clickbait. https://www.urbandictionary.com/define.php?term=clickbait. Accessed 1 Feb 2020
17. Wiktionnaire: «Putaclic». https://fr.wiktionary.org/wiki/putaclic. Accessed 1 Feb 2020
18. Goldhaber, M.: The attention economy and the net. First Monday 2(4) (1997). https://doi.org/10.5210/fm.v2i4.519
19. Saemmer, A.: Rhétorique du texte numérique : figures de la lecture, anticipations de pratiques. Presses de l'Enssib, Lyon (2015)
20. Urban Dictionary: Cringe. https://www.urbandictionary.com/define.php?term=cringe. Accessed 2 Feb 2020
21. 20 Minutes: Le mot «malaisant», ça passe ou ça casse?, 17 March 2017. https://www.20minutes.fr/insolite/2033003-20170317-mot-malaisant-ca-passe-ca-casse. Accessed 3 Feb 2020
22. Le Monde: Malaisant est un adjectif extraordinaire : il suscite chez celui qui l'entend exactement ce qu'il cherche à dire, 18 May 2019. https://www.lemonde.fr/idees/article/2019/05/18/malaisant-est-un-adjectif-extraordinaire-il-suscite-chez-celui-qui-l-entend-exactement-ce-qu-il-cherche-a-dire_5463712_3232.html. Accessed 3 Feb 2020
23. Barthes, R.: Rhétorique de l'image. Communications 4–1, 40–51 (1964)
24. Wiki de Jeuxvideo.com: Malaisologie. https://wiki.jvflux.com/Malaisologie. Accessed 3 Feb 2020
25. Vulture: An A–Z of Words That Defined the Internet in the 2010s, 24 February 2019. https://www.vulture.com/2019/12/online-words-from-the-2010s-defined.html. Accessed 5 Feb 2020
26. Urban Dictionary: Cancel culture. https://www.urbandictionary.com/define.php?term=cancel%20culture. Accessed 5 Feb 2020
27. Urban Dictionary: Woke. https://www.urbandictionary.com/define.php?term=woke. Accessed 5 Feb 2020
28. The Guardian: Woke-washing: how brands are cashing in on the culture wars, 23 May 2019. https://www.theguardian.com/media/2019/may/23/woke-washing-brands-cashing-in-on-culture-wars-owen-jones. Accessed 5 Feb 2020
29. Hall, S.: Une perspective européenne sur l'hybridation: Éléments de réflexion. Hermès 28, 99–102 (2001)
30. Chun, W.H.K.: Queerying homophily. In: Apprich, C.C.W., Cramer, F., Steyer, H. (eds.) Pattern Discrimination, pp. 59–98. Meson, Lüneburg (2018)
31. Marion, Ph.: Médiagénies de la polémique. Les images "contre": de la caricature à la cybercontestation. Recherches en communication 20, 120–154 (2003)
32. Doueihi, M.: Digital Objecthood and Scholarly Publishing (2009). https://ecommons.cornell.edu/bitstream/handle/1813/12020/HumPubForum_Doueihi.pdf. Accessed 6 Feb 2020
33. Burgess, J.: Vernacular Creativity and New Media. Queensland University of Technology, Brisbane (2007)
34. Benjamin, W.: An outsider attracts attention. In: Kracauer, S. (ed.) The Salaried Masses, pp. 109–114. Verso, London (1998)
35. Benveniste, É.: Baudelaire. Lambert-Lucas, Limoges (2011)
36. de Certeau, M.: L'invention du quotidien. 1. arts de faire. Gallimard, Paris (1980)

A Study on the Similarity of Fashion Brands Using Consumer Relationship and Consumer Sense

Yuzuki Kitajima[1]($\boxtimes$), Kohei Otake[2], and Takashi Namatame[3]

[1] Graduate School of Science and Engineering, Chuo University,
1-13-27 Kasuga, Bunkyo-ku, Tokyo 112-8551, Japan
a16.tdsm@g.chuo-u.ac.jp
[2] School of Information and Telecommunication Engineering,
Tokai University, 2-3-23 Takanawa, Minato-ku, Tokyo 108-8619, Japan
otake@tsc.u-tokai.ac.jp
[3] Faculty of Science and Engineering, Chuo University, 1-13-27 Kasuga,
Bunkyo-ku, Tokyo 112-8551, Japan
nama@indsys.chuo-u.ac.jp

Abstract. In recent years, in the apparel industry, the EC market and SNSs have been expanding. Then it is needed a marketing strategy considering the needs of customers. In this study, we aim to identify fashion brands related to similar brands and customer growth (named "key brands") which promote brand transition using a questionnaire data targeting about 30,000 monitors. Specifically, we used questions about consumption values and favorite fashion brands. We conducted the factor analysis using the question items to obtain potential factors of consumption values. Next, we classify monitors based on the result of factor analysis. Then, we aggregate question about favorite fashion brands and reveal key brands at each age and cluster. Finally, we compare to similar brands from questionnaire data with similar brands from tweet data from Twitter.

Keywords: Consumption values · Social Networking Services · Fashion industry

1 Introduction

In recent years, in the apparel industry, consumer needs are increasingly diversified according to the expansion of the EC (Electronic Commerce) market, lifestyle changes and the rise of fast fashion. Such the situation, it is not enough to only merchandise development according to fashion trend such as color and style of the conventional approach. In the marketing field, it is necessary to consider the new campaigns and product planning that take into account consumer values. However, it cannot be easily figured consumer sense of value. This is attributed to the change in values with time series. From the survey by NRI (Japanese company) [1], it is possible to grasp changes in the values of Japanese consumers' consumption behavior by time series.

On the other hand, Social Networking Services (SNSs) are also expanding. SNSs are online services that provide various function to maintain and promote social

© Springer Nature Switzerland AG 2020
G. Meiselwitz (Ed.): HCII 2020, LNCS 12195, pp. 325–335, 2020.
https://doi.org/10.1007/978-3-030-49576-3_24

connection among members. It provides a place to build new relationships through common points and connections, such as hobbies and lifestyle. Especially in the apparel industry, marketing utilizing SNSs are being actively conducted.

Among SNSs users, especially users on Twitter can classify consumer lifestyle using only consumer relationships. Yamashita et al. [2] argues that it is effective to cluster users using only their follow relationship. Moreover, Twitter is one of the most popular SNSs in Japan, about 40% of all ages use Twitter [3]. Therefore, there are a lot of customer relationships data on Twitter based on hobbies and lifestyle.

We can understand and compare these two trends by taking into account the trends of SNSs and understanding consumer preferences based on consumer values. In addition, we consider that companies can be branding with greater awareness of consumer needs.

From this background, this study focuses on consumer values and SNSs.

2   Purpose of This Study

In this study, we aim to identify fashion brands related to customer growth (named "key brands") which promote brand transition using a questionnaire data targeting about 30,000 monitors. In particular, we evaluate similar brands from social data from Twitter. For more detail, we clarify the relationship between consumer values and favorite brands using factor analysis and Multiple Correspondence Analysis. In addition, we tried to find similarity brands using Cosine Similarity. Finally, we tried to understand the relationship between consumer values and SNSs by comparing with the questionnaire data to the social data.

3   Datasets

In this study, we use two datasets. One of the use datasets is questionnaire data and another is social data. In this section, we explain these datasets.

3.1   Questionnaire Data About Consumer Sense of Value

We used questionnaire data in 2015 targeting about 30,000 monitors. This target respondents were men and women 20 to 50 years old (14,527 respondents). Additionally, in this study, 152 items related to lifestyle, the target question items were related to consumer value (14 items, Table 1) and the question items related to priority brands (1 item, 130 brands for women, 103 brands for men). Note that all question items (Table 1) are five scale (1: Strongly agree, 2: Agree, 3: Neither, 4: Disagree, 5: Strongly disagree).

Table 1. Question lists about consumer sense of value

No.	Question sentences
Q1	If you like itself, you can not bother and reputation
Q2	It is often practicing to buy and intuitively
Q3	You often want to get what you have any acquaintance
Q4	It's better to buy new products
Q5	You refer sales ranking
Q6	The price is proportional to the value
Q7	You often continue buying favorite products and brands
Q8	You would like to make good products as much as possible
Q9	You like to have a brand
Q10	You don't want to have anything I like
Q11	You don't want to have same items with surrounding people
Q12	You search until find something I want
Q13	Personality expresses in your way of shopping
Q14	You think shopping is fun

3.2 Social Data from Twitter

We used social data from twitter about 43 fashion brand accounts. There brands were selected based on the result of questionnaire data about consumer sense of value (Table 2). Here, "(Japan)" means the account specifically for Japanese. So almost of

Table 2. Fashion brands using this study

Brand name	
Calvin Klein	DAKS (Japan)
AVIREX (Japan)	dunhill
aquagirl (Japan)	TSUMORI CHISATO (Japan)
aquascutum	DOLCE&GABBANA (Japan)
ANNA SUI (Japan)	nano·universe (Japan)
American Eagle Outfitters (Japan)	NICOLE CLUB (Japan)
A·R·W (Japan)	HEART MARKET (Japan)
UNDERARMOUR (Japan)	PINKY&DIANNE (Japan)
EASTBOY (Japan)	FILA (Japan)
E hyphen world gallery (Japan)	Brooks Brothers (Japan)
Saint Laurent	FRED PERRY (Japan)
ikka (Japan)	Heather (Japan)
Vivienne Westwood (Japan)	UNITED COLORS OF BENETTON (Japan)
WEGO (Japan)	Max Mara
ELLE (Japan)	mystic (Japan)
GALLARDAGALANTE (Japan)	MISCH MASCH (Japan)
GUCCI (Japan)	LIZ LISA (Japan)
COMME des GARÇONS	L'EST ROSE (Japan)
JAYRO (Japan)	Laura Ashley
JILLSTUART NEW YORK (Japan)	one after another NICE CLAUP (Japan)
Stüssy (Japan)	one way (Japan)
SLY (Japan)	

these accounts are written in Japanese. The others are international accounts (written in English). In these data retrieval period was from November 18, 2019 to December 16, 2019.

4 Analysis Procedures and Results

In this section, we explain the analysis procedure using this study and the results.

In Subsect. 4.1, we explain methods that classify users using questionnaire data. In Subsect. 4.2, we explain a method to a method to find similarity brands of each cluster using the results of clusters. Moreover, we found similarity brands on Twitter. This will be detailed in the Subsect. 4.3.

4.1 Typology of Consumers Based on Sense of Values

First, we classify consumers using Factor Analysis (FA) with question items to extract some consumer values. In this method, that aims to observed common factors from the correlation between variables. In this study, we adopt two factors model by formula (1). x_{ik} is the observed variable k of the respondents i, f_{ij} is the factor score of the factor j, a_{ik} is the factor loading, and u_{ik} is the individual factor.

$$x_{ik} = a_{k1}f_{i1} + a_{k2}f_{i2} + u_{ik} \tag{1}$$

Next, we classified monitors with k-means clustering based on factor scores. Specifically, we set the number of clusters to 6, and classified monitors into 6 clusters (named "sense cluster"). We named each sense cluster based on factor scores and question items for consumer sense of value questionnaire [4] (Table 3).

Table 3. Each cluster names

Cluster no.	Cluster name
1	Indifferent for Fashion Cluster
2	Emphasis on Quality and Personal Cluster
3	Collaborative Brand-focused Cluster
4	Following the Crowds Cluster
5	Self-Respect Cluster
6	Spendthrift Cluster

The characteristic of each cluster is as follows.

Indifferent for Fashion Cluster: A cluster that does not have a deep obsession with fashion that does not require a brand or individuality.

Emphasis on Quality and Personal Cluster: A cluster that does not care about the brand's reputation and values the personality that likes one's favorite.

Collaborative Brand-focused Cluster: A cluster that cares about brand reputation and likes longevity without worrying about reputation.

Following the Crowds Cluster: A cluster that love the neighborhood and high brands, likes shopping.

Self-respect Cluster: A cluster that value individuality and love their own If so, the cluster that also makes impulse purchases.

Spendthrift Cluster: A cluster that is not interested in branded goods but likes shopping and likes what the surroundings have.

4.2 Clarifying Similar Brands for Each Sense Cluster

Next, we classified respondents in each cluster based on age. We further analysis to understand the brands that each cluster user likes at the same time. We explain the concrete procedure in below.

First, we extract the top 120 brands supported by respondents for each sense cluster. Then, we delete some brands which appear in all clusters. The number of remaining brands is 43 (Table 2). Moreover, each cluster classify by age.

Second, we aggregated the number of users who supported each brand by age. Then, we did Multiple Correspondence Analysis (MCA) for each sense cluster using aggregated data. MCA [5] is an extended method of conventional Correspondence Analysis which reveals the relationship among multiple qualitative values. Figure 1, 2 and 3 are results of clusters 1–6.

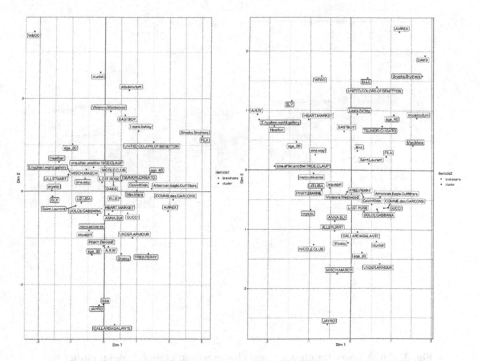

Fig. 1. MCA result for cluster 1 and cluster 2 (left: cluster 1, right: cluster 2)

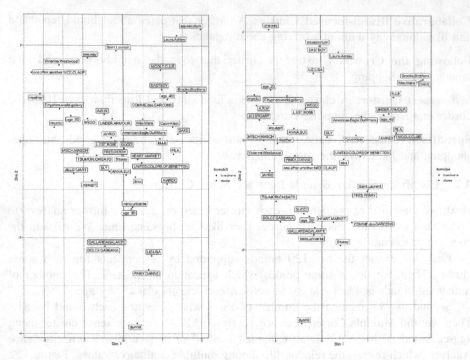

Fig. 2. MCA result for cluster 3 and cluster 4 (left: cluster 3, right: cluster 4)

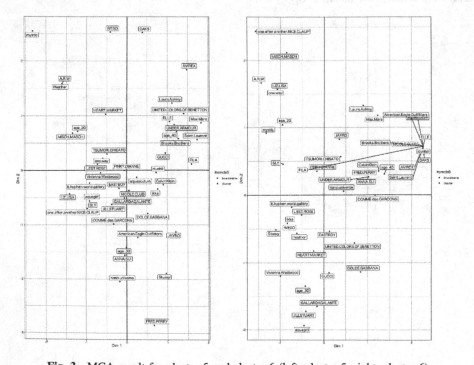

Fig. 3. MCA result for cluster 5 and cluster 6 (left: cluster 5, right: cluster 6)

From these figures, we interpreted that the horizontal axis (Dim 1) represents the change of age and the vertical axis (Dim 2) represents the distance among brands. In other words, it indicates that the brands which re close together are liked at the same time in the cluster, while brands that are far away are not so.

Focusing on the brands, we can see that even with the same brand, each cluster has a different age at which the cluster users prefer that brand. This can find by comparing each cluster. For example, "nano·universe" is most favored in the 30s in cluster 1 (Indifferent for Fashion Cluster). Meanwhile, it is in the middle of the 20s and 30s in cluster 2 (Emphasis on Quality and Personal Cluster).

From the results, we figure that the characteristics are different in each cluster. Tables 4, 5, 6, 7, 8 and 9 are the brands that were close in each cluster.

Table 4. Close brands with short distance in cluster 1

Brand name 1	Brand name 2
JILL STUART	E hyphen world gallery
HEART MARKET	ANNASUI
PINKY DIANNE	A·R·W
ikka	JAYRO
FILA	Brooks Brothers

Table 5. Close brands with short distance in cluster 2

Brand name 1	Brand name 2
COMME des GARÇONS	GUCCI
A·R·W	E hyphen world gallery
LIZ LISA	PINKY DIANNE
DOLCE&GABBANA	Calvin Klein

Table 6. Close brands with short distance in cluster 3

Brand name 1	Brand name 2
FRED PERRY	GUCCI
JAYRO	L'EST ROSE
HEART MARKET	UNITED COLORS OF BENETTON
DOLCE&GABBANA	GALLARDAGALANTE

Table 7. Close brands with short distance in cluster 4

Brand name 1	Brand name 2
GALLARDAGALANTE	nano·universe
FRED PERRY	Saint Laurent
FILA	AVILEX
Brooks Brothers	Max Mara

Table 8. Close brands with short distance in cluster 5

Brand name 1	Brand name 2
Heather	A·R·W
one way	L'EST ROSE
SLY	aquagirl
ikka	Calvin Klein

Table 9. Close brands with short distance in cluster 6

Brand name 1	Brand name 2
LIZ LISA	one way
one way	L'EST ROSE
aquascutum	Brooks Brothers
American Eagle Outfitters	AVILEX

The closeness of brands from Tables 4, 5, 6, 7, 8 and 9 figure from the results of the MCA in Figs. 1, 2 and 3. From the results, we can read that there are differences between brands that appear in many clusters or do not.

4.3   The Distance Between Brands from Each Brand Follower on Twitter

Next, we analyzed fashion brands follower in Twitter. We collected follower information about 43 fashion brand accounts (Table 2) by using Twitter Application Programming Interface (Twitter API). We extract Japanese user of each brand follower. Specifically, among the acquired users, we decided the users whose username or biography include Hiragana or Katakana (full-width or half-width) as Japanese users. Moreover, in this study, we calculate Cosine Similarity of fashion brands using followers who follow more than 4 brands out of 43 brands. Cosine Similarity is method to measure the cosine value of the angle between two vectors. Given two vectors $\vec{a}$ and $\vec{b}$, the Cosine Similarity between them calculates formula (2).

$$\cos\left(\vec{a}, \vec{b}\right) = \frac{\vec{a} \cdot \vec{b}}{|\vec{a}||\vec{b}|} = \frac{\sum_{i=1}^{N} a_i b_i}{\sqrt{\sum_{i=1}^{N} a_i^2} \sqrt{\sum_{i=1}^{N} b_i^2}} \tag{2}$$

Where N is N-dimensional vectors. In this study, in order to calculate the distance among brands, a non-negative number vector uses. Therefore, the angle formed from $0°$ to $90°$. In other words, the Cosine Similarity between any two brands is represented by [0, 1]. The highest similarity value was 0.52, and the lowest similarity value was 0.0.

5   Discussions

First from the results of FA, it was clear the most important values for consumers are "own personality" and "brand reputation". Furthermore, we have concluded that "co-operativeness" and "quality" are considered as a pair of values of "own personality" and "brand reputation". Altogether, the company has to know the appropriate needs for consumers.

Second, we focused on MCA results. From Figs. 1, 2 and 3, it can be seen that some clusters show similar dispersion and some do not.

Cluster 1 (Indifferent for Fashion Cluster) speculated it is no variation a distance for each brand. In addition, from the aspect of brands scattered on figures, this cluster similar to Cluster 3 (Collaborative Brand-focused Cluster). Moreover, brand positions are concentrated in 30s and 40s than 20s. It suggests that their interest in fashion is expected to increase with age. In addition, fashion styles that are close distance between brands on figure are hardly match. For example, the table of Cluster 1 (Table 4), "JAYRO" and "ikka" are close together. "JAYRO" is feminine, "ikka" is natural. This means, cluster 1 does not show any commitment to fashion style, and it is best to recommend clothes with high-cost performance.

Cluster 2 (Emphasis on Quality and Brand Cluster) is similar to Cluster 4 (Following the Crowds Cluster). From the closeness of brands, this cluster suggests that the preferred fashion style changes for each generation. Specifically, they are feminine in their 20s, mode in their 30s and elegant in their 40s. It suggests that individuality comes out as the age increases.

Brands are densely packed from 20s to 40s in Cluster 3. Therefore, it can be considered that the consumer behavior took with emphasis on the brand since 20s.

Users of Cluster 4 tend to follow the crowds. From Fig. 2, it can be seen that the favorite brands change according to their chronological. For this reason, this cluster has few brands that can be expressed as similar in value.

Cluster 5 (Self-Respect Cluster) has extremely few favorite brands preferred in its 20s compared to other Clusters 1 to Cluster 4. This indicates that the degree of support in those in their 30s and 40s is high. In other words, it is thought that users belonging to the self-respect cluster choose their own style from their 30s.

Cluster 6 (Spendthrift Cluster) has the most brand change from generation to generation. Therefore, it suggests that a spendthrift has clearly decide the brand to purchase for each generation.

From these things, it is effective we decide to target consumer and know their detailed needs. Detailed needs are price, lifestyle. Additionally, these facts also reveal that consumer-preferred fashion brands vary by age.

Next, focusing on brand similarity obtained from social data from Twitter.

Tables 10 and 11 are results of brands that have a high similarity overall. From Table 10, "E hyphen world gallery" appeared three times, and the combination of the brand with the highest similarity was the one combined with "E hyphen world gallery". Therefore, we imply that many users who followed a certain brand tend to eventually follow the same brand. The following are the reasons. On twitter, we may recommend an account that is similar to the account you follow (named on twitter "you might like"). By using this, it estimates that the similarity between brands that have the concept of the same fashion style will be higher. From the overall results, "Saint Laurent" from France and "Calvin Klein" from United States, "Vivienne Westwood" from United Kingdom and "ANNA SUI" from United States have a high similarity, it is likely that similar brands will be gathered when brands with different birthplaces deal with the same type of fashion.

Finally, we compare similar brands from questionnaire data with brands from twitter follower data. As a result, we reveal that the decisive difference between two data. This is attributed to purpose for consumers. In the questionnaire, respondents select from choices of favorite fashion brands that they have purchased. Whereas, in the twitter, users tend to select one of the favorite brand accounts and then follow the fashion brand recommended by twitter at the same time.

Table 10. Part of results of cosine similarity (value more than 0.3)

Brand name 1	Brand name 2	Cosine similarity
One after another NICE CLAUP	Heather	0.520
Saint Laurent	Calvin Klein	0.505
One after another NICE CLAUP	E hyphen world gallery	0.412
Heather	E hyphen world gallery	0.382
WEGO	E hyphen world gallery	0.368
LIZ LISA	WEGO	0.326
One after another NICE CLAUP	mystic	0.300

Table 11. Part of results of cosine similarity (value 0.2 to 0.3)

Brand name 1	Brand name 2	Cosine similarity
mystic	E hyphen world gallery	0.285
Saint Laurent	GUCCI	0.279
mystic	Heather	0.272
ANNA SUI	JILL STUART	0.271
American Eagle Outfitters	Brooks Brothers	0.271
WEGO	Heather	0.264
JILL STUART	MISCH MASCH	0.253
One after another NICE CLAUP	WEGO	0.251
Calvin Klein	GUCCI	0.247
FRED PERRY	Brooks Brothers	0.232
nano·universe	FRED PERRY	0.228
DOLCE&GABBANA	GUCCI	0.224
SLY	WEGO	0.214
Heather	MISCH MASCH	0.206
ANNA SUI	Vivienne Westwood	0.205

Therefore, the questionnaire data is suitable to obtain the change of the value with the spread of the EC site. On the other hand, by using Twitter, it is thought that it is possible to recognize fashion brands that are regarded as similar from the viewpoint of customers.

6 Conclusion

In this study, we grasped the differences in fashion brands preference based on consumer values based on a year questionnaire data targeting about 30,000 monitors. Specifically, we determined FA for question items of consumer values. In addition, we classified 6 clusters using the results of factor scores. Next, we output the top 120 fashion brands supported by each cluster and did MCA. Then, we tried to calculate the Cosine Similarity of fashion brands followers on twitter. Finally, we compared between similar points between 2 data.

As a result of FA, we cleared the values consumers values the most. As results of MCA and Cosine Similarity, there was a slight commonality was found. Although, it is thought that the data can be understood differently, so it is unlikely that the closeness of fashion brands from the viewpoint of values matches the closeness of fashion brands calculated from Twitter.

For the future perspective, we would like to more deeply analysis targeting SNS users. In this study, questionnaire data and social data from Twitter differed by user. Therefore, we need to analyze the same user to get a better understanding of their needs. Regarding the data, the questionnaire data was in 2015, but the social data was obtained in 2019, and the acquisition period was different. Although the same brand is used, the analysis results may be different, so it is necessary to use the same year's data.

Acknowledgement. We would like to thank the questionnaire survey companies who provided the data for this research. This work was supported by JSPS KAKENHI Grant Number 19K01945 and 17K13809.

References

1. Nomura Research Institute: Changes in Japanese Consumption Values and Consumption Behavior in 10,000 Consumer Questionnaire Surveys (8th Survey) (2017)
2. Yamashita, T., Sato, H., Koyama, S., Kurihara, M.: Community extraction from Twitter based on following relations. Inf. Process. Soc. Jpn. **75**, 107–108 (2013)
3. Ministry of Internal Affairs and Communications: Survey report on information communication media usage time and information behavior (2018)
4. Kanemitsu, J.: Structure of high fashion brands: examination of a three-partite network model of brands linking consumers with life values/personas. Kyoto Manag. Rev. **20**, 93–109 (2012)
5. MacQueen, J.: Some methods for classification and analysis of multivariate observations. In: Proceedings of the Fifth Berkeley Symposium on Mathematical Statistics and Probability, vol. 1, pp. 281–297. University of California Press (1967)

Analysis of Consumer Community Structure and Characteristic Within Social Media

Shin Miyake[1(✉)], Kohei Otake[2], and Takashi Namatame[3]

[1] Graduate School of Science and Engineering, Chuo University,
Hachiōji, Japan
a15.66cc@g.chuo-u.ac.jp
[2] School of Information and Telecommunication Engineering, Tokai University,
2-3-23, Takanawa, Minato-ku, Tokyo 108-8619, Japan
otake@tsc.u-tokai.ac.jp
[3] Faculty of Science and Engineering, Chuo University,
1-13-27, Kasuga, Bunkyo-ku, Tokyo 112-8551, Japan
nama@indsys.chuo-u.ac.jp

Abstract. The spread of Social Networking Services (SNSs) changes personal communication around the world rapidly in recent years and the impact has affected the business field. Then many companies approach their consumers by using SNS, but those marketing effects are completely different depending on each community structure. Especially, there is a large difference in the cost that diffuses the information transmitted when the community is concentrated or scattered. It is important to perform a marketing approach that considers the community structure of each company. In this study, we use a brand in the fashion market to detect consumer community structure on SNSs. In addition, based on the formed community, we clarify the characteristic of each community by using posted contents posted by consumers and suggest the method of promotion to consumers via SNSs.

Keywords: Network analysis · Social networks service

1 Introduction

With the expansion of internet environment and diffusion of mobile devices such as smartphones, social networking services (SNSs) has been spreading through our life as a way of communication [1]. On SNSs, users can form new connections with other users who have similar interests in SNSs activities. Under these circumstances, marketing activities using SNSs are attracting attention for the purpose of understanding consumers. These are called "Social Media Marketing" (SMM). Particularly, attracting and promoting customers using SNSs in the fashion and apparel business is indispensable.

Companies have an advantage that can advertise the information about new products and events quickly to consumers who connected on SNS and this advantage motivates consumers to follow a specific brand account on SNSs. For this reason, a brand has a community that is spontaneously formed by each consumer on SNSs. The

© Springer Nature Switzerland AG 2020
G. Meiselwitz (Ed.): HCII 2020, LNCS 12195, pp. 336–354, 2020.
https://doi.org/10.1007/978-3-030-49576-3_25

companies approach their consumers by using SNSs, but the consumer community structure formed among consumers is completely different between companies. To consider the effective operation of SMM, it is one of the most important issues to understand the shape of connections between consumers connected to the company, and to consider what kind of advertisements and promotions can be made within the community shape.

In this study, we detect the community in SMM space and evaluate the community structure. Furthermore, we clarified the characteristics of each community using the posted contents posted by consumers belonging to each community. By considering SMM in each community, effective marketing activities can be carried out in diverse consumer values.

2 Purpose of This Study

In this study, we aim to discover the community of consumers on SNSs and analyze their consumer network. Furthermore, we categorize the content posted by consumers belonging to each community and propose the marketing promotions to each community. We target a popular brand in the fashion market. Within the community formed through the specific official fashion brand, consumer thoughts and preferences are expected to be similar. For this reason, it is thought that similarities will appear in the user relationship on SNSs. Moreover, we focus on the official twitter accounts of a fashion brand on Twitter and create a consumer network using the follow-follower relationship of users who follow the official accounts.

3 Datasets

In this section, we describe the details of datasets used in this study.

3.1 Data Extraction

In this study, we target a specific brand in the fashion market. Table 1 shows an overview of the fashion brand.

Table 1. Overview of the fashion brand

MichaelKors @MichaelKorsJP 30,098 followers	MichaelKors is a world-renowned, award-winning designer of luxury accessories and ready-to-wear. His namesake company, established in 1981, currently produces a range of products under his signature MichaelKors Collection, MICHAEL MichaelKors and Michael KorsMens labels. These products include accessories, footwear, watches, jewelry, women's and men's ready-to-wear, wearable technology, eyewear and a full line of fragrance products

The target brand is popular from teens to thirties women and has stores mainly in major department stores. Figure 1 shows the two-stage data extraction flow. First, we extracted information about users who follow the MichaelKors Japan account on Twitter.

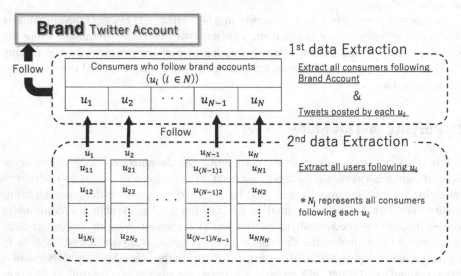

Fig. 1. Data extraction flow

At the 1st data extraction in Fig. 1, we selected 1,000 users in order from the newest users who are following each of the MichaelKors Japan account. The user to follow this brand is represented as u_i and set the value of N to 1000. Here, regarding this u_i, we selected users who were all Japanese users and were not official users. In addition, we extracted the posted contents posted from July 1 to December 1, 2019 by u_i. In the 2nd stage data extraction in Fig. 1, we collected all user information who follow u_i. Additionally, users who follow u_i are represented as u_{ij} and N_i is determined by the total number of consumers who follow u_i. We obtained all these data using Twitter API (Application Programming Interface).

The data is collected from August 1st to December 1st, 2019.

4   Analysis Method

In this section, we describe the analysis methods. Figure 2 shows the flow of analysis methods. In this flow, there are three elements. First of all, we describe the method to create the dataset for consumer network using extracted data. At the second, we create the network by visualizing technique created dataset and method of community detection. Finally, we describe the method to clarify the characteristic of each community using posted contents and results of the detected community.

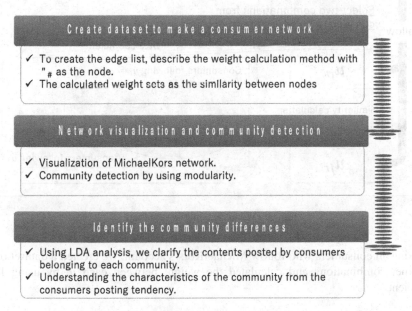

Fig. 2. The flow of the analysis

4.1 Dataset for Community Detection

At first, we describe the creation method of the dataset to create consumer networks using follow-follower relationship information using social network analysis. Social network analysis is an analysis method that considers adjacency from the viewpoint of nodes and edges based on graph theory [2]. This analysis is widely used especially in research targeting SNSs [3, 4]. We create a consumer network using the extracted data. Specifically, from Fig. 1, u_i is a node, more edges are tied when u_i has a follow-follower relationship with another user u_j. Further, the edge is weighted based on the similarity between users. In this study, Dice coefficients were used for weights. (Eq. (1)).

$$Dice(A, B) = \frac{2|A \cap B|}{|A| + |B|} \tag{1}$$

When the value is large, then these two nodes have high similarity. Figure 3 shows an example of the weight calculation process among users.

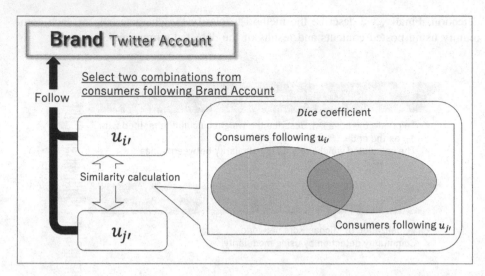

Fig. 3. Weight calculation method

Using all consumers who follow MichaelKors's account, we created a dataset of all consumer combinations and calculated the weight between each u_i by using Dice coefficient.

4.2   Network Visualization and Community Detection

At the second, we describe the network visualization and community detection. Figure 4 shows the constructed network based on the created dataset.

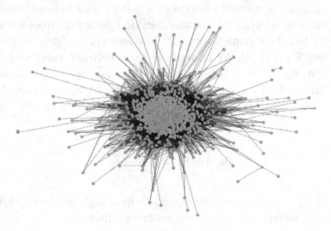

Fig. 4. Consumer network

From the result of the network in Fig. 4 and dataset, it is found that the trend is low density and sparse network. For this reason, we used only edges with weights higher than 0.03 to more express the feature of connection. About the network, the total number of nodes is 309, a total number of edges is 826 and an average of degree is 5.436. We visualized the network using the "Fruchterman Reingold model" [5].

Furthermore, we detect the community from created the network. Community detection extracts a relatively dense part of the network as a subgroup (called "community"). It is possible to know a more detailed network structure by discovering a particularly densely community in the network. We explain the method to perform community detection on the created weighted graph. Recently, various methods and indices for community detection have been developed. One typical method is community division by "Modularity" [8]. Modularity is a community evaluation index becomes higher value when the edges in a community are dense and the edges between communities are sparse. The calculation of modularity is expressed in Eq. (2).

$$Modularity = \frac{1}{2M} \sum_{ij} \left(A_{ij} - \frac{k_i k_j}{2M} \right) \delta \left(C_i, C_j \right) \tag{2}$$

where A_{ij} represents the ij elements of the adjacency matrix of the graph. k_i and k_j represents the respective degree of nodes i and j. δ represent the Kronecker delta, and k_i and k_j becomes 1 if the community C_i and C_j to which nodes i and j belong are the same. When using a weighted graph like this study, it can be expanded like Eq. (3). When we use the weighted graphs, we use the Q values as modularity.

$$Q = \frac{1}{2W} \sum_{ij} \left(W_{ij} - \frac{w_i w_j}{2W} \right) \delta \left(C_i, C_j \right) \tag{3}$$

In Eq. (3), W represents the sum of the weights of all edges, and the degree k_i and k_j of the nodes i and j represent the sum of the weights adjacent to the nodes. For the created brand, we have divided the community so that the Q values of the network to maximized. We apply the above community detection method using Q values to the consumer network.

Furthermore, as a result of community detection, we capture features using the following community indicators. In addition, the community number is a unique value that distinguishes communities.

- **Community Density**: An indication representing the density within each community.
- **PageRank Average**: An indication representing the average value of PageRank [7] values of each user in the same community. Here, the PageRank indicates the importance of a certain user in the network.
- **Average of degree**: An indication representing the average degree of a single node in each community.
- **Number of nodes**: An indication representing the number of nodes in each community.

- **Component Ratio of node**: An indication representing the composition ratio of the number of nodes in each community.

Finally, we clarify the characteristic of each community. By a topic model using posted contents, we are able to understand the characteristic posting tendency of each consumer. In addition, aggregating the posting tendency for each detected community, we clarify the characteristic of each community using correspondence analysis. In the next section, we describe the analysis method of the topic model.

4.3   LDA (Latent Dirichlet Allocation)

In this section, we describe a topic model to estimate what topics exist using the content posted by consumers. The topic model is a method of assuming that words in a document appear depending on the potential meaning (topic) of the document, and estimating the topic from the frequency of words appearing in the document.

As the representative of the topic model, there are some models such as Latent Semantic Analysis (LSA) [9], Probabilistic Latent Semantic Indexing (PLSI) [10], and Latent Dirichlet Allocation (LDA) [11]. LDA can estimate topics more accurately than LSA and PLSI, and it has high calculation efficiency. For this reason, in this study, we select the LDA model as the topic model.

LDA is a model that statistically represents the process of generating a document. To postulate that the document has multiple potential topics, each document has a topic distribution θ that indicates the percentage of topics included in the document. The topic z in the document is selected according to θ. When a topic is selected, words are generated according to the word distribution ϕ corresponding to the topic. θ is generated from the Dirichlet distribution for each document, and the parameter α of the Dirichlet distribution is called a hyperparameter. ϕ for each topic is generated from the Dirichlet distribution $Dir(\theta|\alpha)$, and the hyperparameter is β.

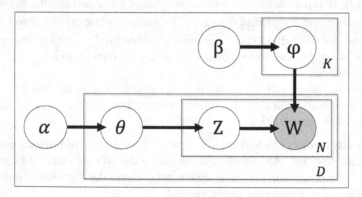

Fig. 5. LDA graphical model

The LDA graphical model is shown in Fig. 5. In Fig. 5, W indicates the words in the observed document. K is the number of topics, D is the number of documents, N is the number of words in the document, Z is the topic, ϕ_k is the word distribution of topic k, and θ_k is the topic distribution of document d. α and β are parameters of the Dirichlet prior to distribution. Posterior distribution about the set W of documents and the set Z of topics in the topic model are represented by Eqs. (4), (5) and (6).

$$P(W, Z | \alpha, \beta) = P(Z | \alpha) P(W, Z | \beta) \tag{4}$$

$$P(Z | \alpha) = \left(\frac{\Gamma(\sum_{k=1}^{K} \alpha_k)}{\prod_{k=1}^{K} \Gamma(\alpha)^K} \right)^D \prod_{d=1}^{D} \frac{\prod_{k=1}^{K} \Gamma(N_{kd} + \alpha_k)}{\Gamma(N_d + \sum_{k=1}^{K} \alpha_k)} \tag{5}$$

$$P(W | Z, \beta) = \left(\frac{\Gamma(\sum_{v=1}^{V} \beta_v)}{\prod_{v=1}^{V} \Gamma(\beta_v)} \right)^K \prod_{k=1}^{K} \frac{\prod_{v=1}^{V} \Gamma(N_{kv} + \beta_v)}{\Gamma(N_k + \sum_{v=1}^{V} \beta_v)} \tag{6}$$

Where $\Gamma(*)$ represents the gamma function, V represents the number of vocabularies, and N_{kd} represents the number of topics k included in document d. $N_d = (\sum_{k=1}^{K} N_{kd})$.

N_{kv} represents the number of vocabularies v assigned to topic k. $N_k = (\sum_{v=1}^{V} N_{kv})$

The topic distribution in document d represents as θ_d, and the word distribution for topic k represents as ϕ_k. Each value estimates by the following Eqs. (7), (8).

$$\hat{\theta}_d = \frac{N_{kd} + \alpha}{N_d + K_\alpha} \tag{7}$$

$$\hat{\phi}_k = \frac{N_{kv} + \beta}{N_k + V_\beta} \tag{8}$$

In addition, we use coherence [12] and perplexity [13] as indices to estimate the optimal number of topics. The coherence is an indication that considers the topic to be more coherent as the frequency of co-occurrence in the external corpus of the top N word pairs with high probability values for each ϕ_k increases. The perplexity is an indication that measures the generalization performance of the model and is given by normalizing the likelihood prediction of the words in the trained model. Using these two indices, we estimated the optimal number of topics.

5   Results

First, we show the results of consumer network and community detection. Figure 6 shows the results of the detected consumer community of MichaelKors's account on SNSs. As described above, this consumer community created by using only the edges with 0.03 or more dice coefficient values. The total Number of nodes is 309, a total number of edges is 826 and an average of degree is 5.436.

Furthermore, the number of communities is 37 in total. The Modularity value is 0.7101.

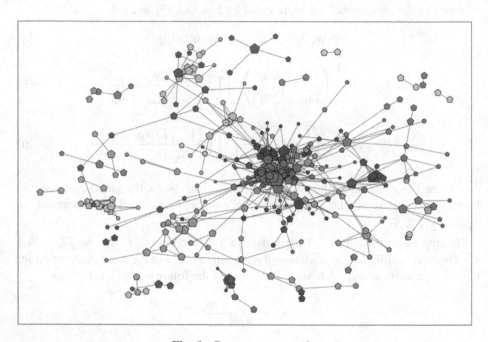

Fig. 6. Consumer community

From the results of community detection, it is found that there is a concentration of communities at the center of the network. In this study, we call this concentration of communities as "core community". From the result, the core community is formed by a small number of communities with a large number of nodes (large-scale community). Around the core community, there are some communities with a medium number of nodes (medium-scale community). Furthermore, it was found that small communities composed of broadly two to six nodes (small-scale community) were scattered outside of the network. Next, we summarize the indices of each community at Table 2.

Table 2 summarizes community indicators of medium-scale and large-scale communities with 6 or more nodes in Fig. 6.

Table 2. Michaelkors's community Indicators (number if nodes > 6)

Community number	Community density	PageRank average	Average of degree	Number of nodes	Component ratio
2	0.231	0.005	0.045	53	0.172
6	0.400	0.003	0.013	11	0.036
13	0.652	0.003	0.023	12	0.039
15	0.667	0.003	0.013	7	0.023
0	0.234	0.003	0.018	22	0.071
5	0.125	0.003	0.011	27	0.087
1	0.138	0.003	0.017	30	0.097
8	0.192	0.003	0.008	13	0.042
4	0.181	0.003	0.017	19	0.061
3	0.176	0.003	0.009	14	0.045
7	0.364	0.003	0.013	11	0.036
11	0.219	0.003	0.012	15	0.049
10	0.140	0.002	0.010	17	0.055

According to the result of summarizing in Table 2, Community 2 have the maximum PageRank Average value (0.005). Furthermore, since Community 2 takes the maximum values in both the Average of degree and the number of nodes. From this result, it can be interpreted that the Community 2 is a community of considerable influence that has many connections with other communities. Additionally, since it can be interpreted that the Community 2 is an influential community that has many connections with other communities, it can be inferred that the Community 2 forms the core community. Moreover, in a medium-scale community, the number of nodes is about 10 to 30 as a whole. In particular, Community 1 and Community 5 are composed of a large number of communities with 30 and 27 nodes.

Referring to the results of the communities at Fig. 6, we can see that these communities also form the part of the core community and play a role in expanding the connection with the other medium-sized communities around the core community.

Many of the medium-scale communities are located separately around the core community and density of individual community are high. Therefore, it can be inferred that medium-scale communities are independent and do not support each other.

Also, small-scale community are spread outside the network, so each community is isolated from others. From the above results, it is found that the consumers have a relatively consistent preference in the core community. On the other hand, medium-scale and small-scale communities tended to be self-contained and organized separately in individual community. Next, using LDA model, we classify what content was posted by consumers belonging to each community. First, we presume the number of topics to classify the posted contents using two values, coherence and perplexity. Figure 7 shows the transition of values about coherence and perplexity in the change of the number of topics.

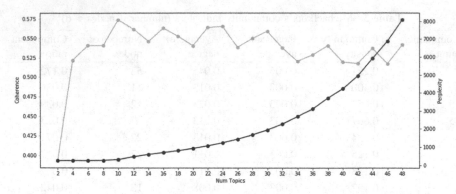

Fig. 7. Transition of coherence and perplexity in the number of topics

As a result of calculating the optimal number of topics by coherence and perplexity, each post content is assigned to 10 topics in Fig. 7. Therefore, we create a model that classifies each posted content into 10 topics. Table 3 shows the top 10 words with the highest probability of word distribution in each topic.

In the result of Topic 1, 4, 7, and 8, words such as "フォロー (Follow)", "キャンペーン (campaign)" and "プレゼント (present)" are calculated as representative words. It is considered that these topics are related to a free gift promotion via Twitter. As a free gift promotion, there is not only the promotion of a company's SMM but also the promotion of general users. Each word consist of each topic is created based on the occurrence and co-occurrence of all words in posted contents. For this reason, there are some differences in nuances and words between similar some topics. In this case, these differences of topics are considered to be classified according to the word of winning products, such as product presents, gift certificates, and products within specific application software.

In the Topic 8 result, the word of the "カード (card)" is more important, while the "券 (ticket)" is important in Topic 1 as the free gift promotion. Further, in Topic 4 result, it is considered the multiple promotions of a gift from words such as "弾 (eachstep)". In the Topic 7 result, the words "名 (Number of people)" and "抽選 (drawinglots)" representing the number of people indicate that there are restrictions due to the number of winners. In the Topic 2 result, from the results of words such as "肌(skin)", "メイク(makeup)" and "色 (color)" are presumed to be topics related to cosmetics. From the result of Topic 3, it is found that topic is related to celebrity from the words of "公開 (release)" and "番組 (TV programs)". In more detail, word of "本田" means actress name that Michaelkors selected as the model of the brand in Japan. The fact that her name selected as one topic from posted content means some consumers support her in the consumer community. The Topic 5 contains words such as "住所 (address)", "全国 (whole country)", "最新 (latest)", and "販売 (sales)". From these results, it is considered these topics are related to product sales on SNS. The product sales on SNS is one of SMM, and these kinds of contents are very common in Japan.

In Topic 6 result, there is no commonality between words, such as "私 (I)", "感想(thoughts)", and "彼氏 (boyfriend)", but all these words are frequently used in

Table 3. Characteristic words in each topic

Topic 1	Topic 2	Topic 3	Topic 4	Topic 5
フォロー Follow	フォロー Follow	日 day	フォロー Follow	住所 address
名 Name	肌 skin	公開 release	10 10	全国 whole country
応募 apply for	名 name	10 10	名 people	事業 business
プレゼント (gift, present)	プレゼント (gift, present)	design design	キャンペーン campaign	販売 sales
10 10	10 10	本田 Actress name	応募 apply for	日本 Japan
キャンペーン campaign	色 color	月 month	日 day	最新 latest
抽選 drawing lots	肉 meat	放送 broadcast	弁当 Lunch box	別 another
方法 method	キャンペーン campaign	番組 TV program	map map	一番 No.1
券 ticket	メイク make up	gt gt	弾 each step(unit)	代表 representative
円 Yen	投稿 posted	配信 delivery	万 ten thousand	用 purpose
Topic 6	**Topic 7**	**Topic 8**	**Topic 9**	**Topic 10**
私 I	フォロー Follow	プレゼント (gift, present)	RWC RWC	人 People
人 people	プレゼント (gift, present)	フォロー Follow	de de	くん Mr.
自分 My	名 Number of people	円 Yen	France France	こと thing
感想 thoughts	応募 apply for	名 name	ans ans	年 year
感じ feel	キャンペーン campaign	10 10	レッド red	僕 My
まとめ to gather	抽選 drawing lots	カード card	今 now	時 timing
評判 reputation	祈願 prayer	応募 apply for	的 like~	好き favorite
彼氏 boyfriend	ツイート Tweet	100 100	先輩 senior	デビュー debut
評価 reputation	日 day	お知らせ notice	2019 2019	そう yes
方 way	amp & (sign)	抽選 drawing lots	猫 cat	中 in

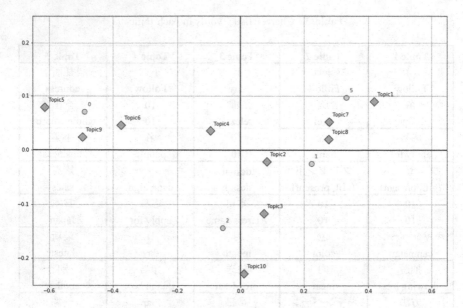

Fig. 8. Positioning of large-scale communities and topics

daily life. It is considered that the contents of daily conversation are assigned to this topic. On the other hand, Topic 9 describes the trend of sports in Japan from the word "RWC". In Topic 10, from the words such as "デビュー (debut)" and "Mr.", we assume the topic to be related to male such as boys idols group or model in Japan. Although there is no gender information in the data, from these results, we recognize that the brand is mainly targeting women. Using the created LDA model, we calculate the allocation ratio of the contents posted by consumers within the duration into each topic. Furthermore, we calculate the average score for each topic in the posted content of each consumer. We use this value as the contribution tendency to the topics of each user. In particular, from the result of community detection, we assign communities with 6 or fewer nodes to a small-scale community, communities with 6 or more and less than 20 to medium-scale community and communities with 20 or more to a large-scale community. In addition, based on this community result, we calculated the community posting tendency by the average consumer tendency of each community. From this result, we clarify the relationship between each topic and each community and clarify the characteristic of each community using correspondence analysis. We use the correspondence analysis to the cross-tabulation results of the community and each topic separately according to the size of the community.

First, we refer to the large-scale community results. Figure 8 shows the results of a correspondence analysis of a large-scale community and each topic.

As the topic results, gift promotion topics (Topic 1, 4, 7 and 8) are located collectively.

Also, there is Topic 4 at the center of the topics. Topic 5 (about product sales) and Topic 10 (about male) are located away from the center. Moreover, from the results of

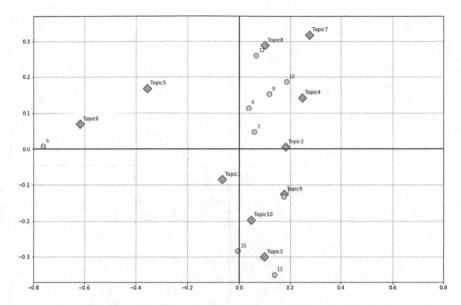

Fig. 9. Positioning of medium-scale communities and topics

each community position, it is clear that each community on a large-scale had a different tendency to post. Because Community 2 has a largest number of nodes, individual differences in posting tendency are not expressed than in other communities. At the around of Community 2, there are Topic 3 (about celebrity) and Topic 10 (about male). From this result, it turned out that Community 2 has the interest in the contents of the talent and celebrity. The fact that the most influential community that Community 2 with the highest PageRank has an interest in the contents about the model of MichaelKors make expand the possibilities of advertisements and promotions about MichaelKors. From the result of Topic 2 (about cosmetics) and Topic 8 (about gift promotion) at the around of Community 1, it turned out that Community 1 has an interest in the contents of the cosmetics and about gift promotion. In addition, at the around on Community 5, gift promotion topics (Topic 1, 7) are located closely. At the viewpoint of interest for gift promotion, Community 1 and Community 5 are similar. However, the differences are whether the community interested in any other topics of gift promotion. When promoting some information, it is very important to understand the interest customers because wide consumers' interest makes an important role when considering a wide approach to consumers. Furthermore, Topics 5, 6 and 9 are located around Community 0. From this result, it is found that Community 0 has an interest in the contents of product sales, the trend of the sports and has the tendency of the post the contents about daily life more than any other the large-scale community. From the above results of large-scale community, each community had different characteristics about posted tendency. In other words, it is clear that each community had a different preference and interest for content.

Next, we refer to the medium-scale community results. Figure 9 shows the results of correspondence analysis of a medium-scale community and each topic.

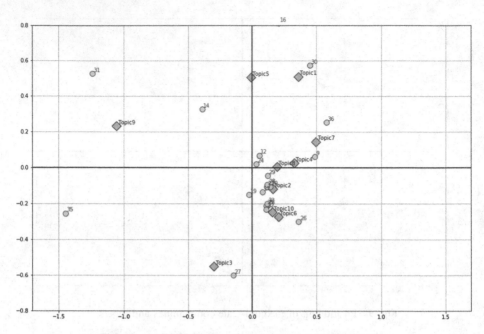

Fig. 10. Positioning of small-scale communities and topics

As the topic results, in spite of the same topics of gift promotion, Topic 1 is positioning aloof from the other topics (Topic 4, 7 and 8). From this result, it is found the difference occurs when considering the tendency of each community although at the between of the same topics. When using the LDA model, it calculated posting tendency by co-occurrence of words in posted contents so therefore, we consider these differences are occurred by the difference of words and nuances in the text of posted contents. Compared to the large-scale community result where the same topics were collective, it becomes clear that the medium-scale community has a more detail tendency and interest for topics. Focusing on the community position, it can be seen that the Community 11 is located near Topic 8, Community 6 located near the Topic 6, Community 7 located near the Topic 9 and Community 13 located near Topic 3. From these results, these communities are interested in only one topic. Whereas, from the results of the location that the Community 3, 4, 8, 10 is near Topic 2 and 4, it is found that these communities have an interest in the contents of cosmetics and gift promotion. Furthermore, Community 15 is located near Topic 3 and 10. From this result, it is found that Community 15 has the interest in the contents of cosmetics and males. The medium-scale community has a total of 9 communities, and the community has an interest in some topics are 5 in total. Compared to the large-scale community result, there are many communities with multiple interests in the medium-scale community.

Finally, we refer to these small-scale community results. Figure 10 shows the results of a correspondence analysis of a small-scale community and each topic.

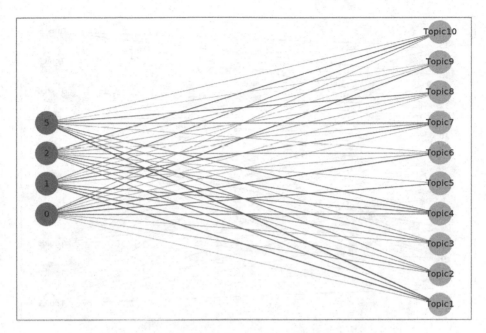

Fig. 11. Large community's bipartite graph (Color figure online)

At Fig. 10, unlike the result of medium-scale community, gift promotion topics (Topic 1, 4, 7, 8) are located collectively.

Here, please note that because the number of consumers that make up each community is smaller than large-scale and medium-scale communities, the result is more influenced by the differences in the individual tendency.

From the results of location about Community 14, 31 and 35, these communities are located around Topic 9. It is clear that these communities mainly posted the contents of daily conversations. In addition, we infer the difference of individual posting tendency affects the reason why each community is not close to Topic 9. From the results of location about Community 30, it is clear that Community 30 mainly posted the contents of gift promotion. At the results of the other communities and Topic 2,4,6,7 and 8, these are concentrated in one location. From these results of large-scale, medium-scale and small-scale, it is found that these communities have more interesting topics than the large-scale community and medium-scale community.

6   Discussions

According to these results, it was turned According to these results, it was turned that there are differences in interest to each topic for each community. From these differences, we consider the actual SMM for each community. In addition, we treat the large-scale community and medium-scale community as the target of SMM. For each scale of community, we create the bi-graph of the communities and topics using the average of the contribution trends of users belonging to each community as weights (Fig. 11

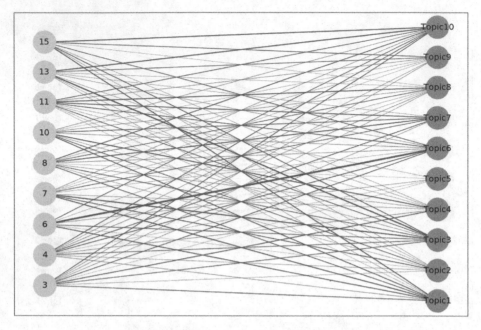

Fig. 12. Medium community's bipartite graph

and 12). Red edges in the graphs represent cases where the probability is higher than 0.1.

Because of the large-scale community composed of a large number of consumers, it supposes that these community interests mainly reflect the interest of consumer network. From the results of the large-scale community in Fig. 8, interest to each topic were divided. It can be seen the Community 2 with the highest number of PageRank Average and Number of nodes interested in Topic 2, 3 and 10 at Fig. 11. These topics are the contents of cosmetics, celebrity, and male. In particular, in this consumer network, the topic of celebrity means the interested in the model of MichaelKors. In such an environment, it is considered that the promotion and advertising using this model is the most effective to Community 2. On the other hand, Community 5 shows a high interest in Topic 1 about the contents of present promotion. For Community 5, it is considered that advertising such as an actual present promotion or distributed the coupons via SNSs is most effective for this community. Moreover, because Community 1 shows the interest in Topic 3 and Topic 1, it is considered these approaches are effective for Community 1 the same. From the result of Community 0 with interest in Topic 6, it is considered the method of approaches for Community 5 effective. In addition, Community 0 also has an interest in Topic 5 about the contents of product sales, it is considered that promotion flowing into the MichaelKors EC sites is effective too.

Considering advertising cost, as the approach for consumers, we just need to narrow down only to the method for the large-scale community. However, it needs to change frequency of each advertising depending on each community interest.

Figure 12 shows the results of the bipartite graph for the medium-scale community.

Compared to the large-scale community result in Fig. 9 and Fig. 11, each interest of communities is more complex. If the community has the interest for only Topic 6 about a daily conversation like Community 6, from the viewpoint of information diffusion, it is considered that is best not approach to Community 6.

From the above results of community detection and topic tendency, we could understand the interesting tendency of each community. By doing advertising and promotion based on these tendencies, we can approach consumers more effectively and reduce the cost of information diffusion.

7 Conclusion

In this study, we detected the core community from the results of network analysis about consumer networks and communities. The core community was seen in the central part by using a force model. In addition, the core community was composed by the large-scale community with a large number of nodes. There were some medium-scale communities with a medium number of nodes around the core community and small-scale communities with a small number of nodes are scattered outside of the consumer network. According to these results, we visualized the follow-follower relationship and community shape on SNSs. Moreover, considering the actual operation of SMM, we used the posted contents posted by consumers to evaluate the difference between each community in more detail. We used the topic model to clarify the existing topics on the consumer network and visualized the relationship between topics and communities by using correspondence analysis. From this result, it turned out there is a difference of posting tendency in each community. In the future, we plan to conduct the information diffusion of each user in the community. Through these analyses, we try to identify influential users within the community. Specifically, we consider the time-series analysis of how the information transmitted by users spreads within the community.

Acknowledgment. This work was supported by JSPS KAKENHI Grant Number 19K01945 and 17K13809.

References

1. Ioanăs, E., Stoica, I.: Social media and its impact on consumers behavior. Int. J. Econ. Pract. Theories **4**(2), 295–303 (2013)
2. Ashley, C., Tute, T.: Creative strategies in social media marketing: an exploratory study of branded social content and consumer engagement. Psychol. Market. **32**(1), 15–27 (2015)
3. Boyd, D., Golder, S., Lotan, G.: Tweet, tweet, retweet: conversational Aspects of retweeting on twitter. In: Proceedings of the 43rd Hawaii International Conference on System Sciences, pp. 1–10 (2010)
4. Kazama, K.: Information diffusion on twitter. J. Jpn. Soc. Artif. Intell. **27**(1), 35–42 (2012). (in Japanese)
5. Fruchterman, T.M.J., Reingold, E.M.: Graph by force-directed Placement. Softw. Pract. Exp. **21**(11), 1129–1164 (1991)

6. Otake, K., Namatame, T.: Analysis of impacts on the purchasing behavior using information on social networking services. In: Proceedings of the 14th Asia Pacific Industrial Engineering and Management Society, p. 6 (2016)
7. Page, L., Brin, S., Motwani, R., Winograd T.: The PageRank Citation Ranking: Bringing order to the web, Technical Report, Stanford Digital Library Technologies Project (1999)
8. Newman, M.E.J.: Fast algorithm for detecting community structure in networks. Phys. Rev. E **69**(066133), 1–5 (2004)
9. Deerwester, S., Dumais, S.T., Furnas, G.W., Landauer, T.K., Harshman, R.: Indexing by latent semantic analysis. J. Am. Soc. Inf. Sci. **41**(6), 391–407 (1990)
10. Hofmann, T.: Probabilistic latent semantic indexing. In: Proceedings of the 22nd annual international ACM SIGIR Conference on Research and Development in Information Retrieval, pp. 50–57 (1999)
11. Blei, D.M., Ng, A.Y., Jordan, M.I.: Latent Dirichlet allocation. J. Mach. Learn. Res. **3**, 993–1022 (2003)
12. Roder, M., Both, A., Hinneburg, A.: Exploring the space of topic coherence measures. In: Proceedings of the Eighth ACM International Conference on Web Search and Data Mining - 2015, pp. 399–408. ACM Press, New York (2015)
13. Azzopardi, L., Girolami, M., Rijsbergen, K.: Investigating the Relationship between language model perplexity and IR precision-recall measures. In: Proceedings of the 26th Annual International ACM SIGIR Conference on Research and Development in Information Retrieval, pp. 369–370, (2003)

Exploring Advertising Literacy Digital Paths: Comparison Between Gender Approaches Among Chilean Students

Claudia Montero-Liberona[✉], Gianluigi Pimentel Varas, and Gregorio Fernández Valdés

Pontificia Universidad Católica de Chile, Alameda 340, Santiago, Chile
{clmonter,gpfernandezv}@uc.cl, gpimentel@puer.to

Abstract. In a world full of signals and messages surrounded by mass medias as well as digital media, advertising literacy is considered a powerful tool for social communication. Based on today's context, this exploratory research compared two advertising approaches: (a) the global phenomenon of femvertising, which empowers women in advertising, and (b) the emergence of the conception of a new man towards a more inclusive society. Drawing from Schema Congruence Theory, both paths were studied considering the importance of ads in the representation of gender roles and stereotypes, as value perceptions of justice, impartiality, traditional acceptance, cultural acceptance, family acceptance, and morality among young people in Chile. Participants were 110 students mainly from communication studies, who were exposed to six advertising messages shown on hybrid type of media, including social media. Quantitative statistical analysis was performed. Overall, findings revealed a favorable tendency of congruence between roles and stereotypes that students expected to be represented in both approaches, as well as with values that they associated with both types of perspectives. However, it is important to consider differences found among gender, student's age and student's school year variables for each approach. This study opens new paths to continue exploring further aspects of digital advertising literacy such as affective components, visual elements, among others.

Keywords: Social media · Advertising · Gender · Congruence theory

1 Introduction

In a world full of signals and messages surrounded by mass medias as well as digital media, advertising is considered a powerful tool for social communication [1]. It is not accidental that advertisement is defined as "the placement of announcements and messages in time or space by business firms, nonprofit organizations, government agencies, and individuals who seek to inform/or persuade members of a particular target market or audience regarding their products, services, organizations or ideas" [2]. Through ads, people are persuaded, molded, or manipulated to shape consumer behaviors.

© Springer Nature Switzerland AG 2020
G. Meiselwitz (Ed.): HCII 2020, LNCS 12195, pp. 355–373, 2020.
https://doi.org/10.1007/978-3-030-49576-3_26

Todays' advertising era is not only limited to public spheres; as traditional conception of advertising has been challenged by the emergence of digital media. This hybrid has resulted in "a complex interplay between the effects of the broader social environment and the new specifics of education and training" [3]. In this intertwined and convoluted environment, reading advertising texts implies that the reader must be,

"selective, active and skeptical during the reading experience … able to make subtle inferential distinctions using a variety of verbal and non-verbal cues simultaneously …. an agile reader, who can change frames and strategies even within the temporal space of a single reading and alter expectations as the textual task seems to suggest … an experienced reader, one with a broad-based interpretative repertoire, including a capacity for highly metaphorical, imaginative thinking" [4].

As a response to the need of individuals', to acquire knowledge and a critical stance to interpret current hybrid advertising formats media literacy surfaces [5]. This requirement fits the consideration made by the European Commission (2007), which postulated that media literacy "is based on the fact that there is a need to build up a better understanding of how the media work in the digital world and that citizens need to understand better the economic and cultural dimension of the media" [5]. Therefore, advertising literacy paths comes up as specific type of literacy, affected by today's convulsions worldviews across nations. In this context, two main gender stereotypes aspects have influenced advertising future agenda: on the one side, "Femvertising" conceived as "the influx of marketing campaigns that feature female empowerment messaging" [6] and, on the other side, portraying of men in advertising has also changed as recent advertising has shown "fewer men in the lead and some suggest that male characters are being portrayed to reflect society's changing view of men and women's roles" [7]. An example of this last conception is how men are portrayed as fathers, or how they can do the same things that women do.

The purpose of this explorative study is to compare two recent advertising approaches: (a) the global phenomenon of femvertising, which empowers women in advertising; and (b) the emergence of the conception of a new man towards a more inclusive society. Specifically, both paths are studied considering the importance of ads in the representation of gender roles and stereotypes, as well as value perceptions of young people, specifically in Chile. Therefore, these two different perspectives are examined under the magnifying glass of advertising literacy, specifically related to its content.

1.1   Digital and Advertising Literacies Paths

In a new 21st century, surrounded of information competitiveness, literacy roles acquire a remarkable society commitment. The conception of literacies fosters new ways for citizens to acquire essential knowledge required for a better life quality for themselves and others. In this context, media literacy constitutes a fundamental challenge to implement across the globe. From a theoretical perspective, media literacy has been described as a wide umbrella [5], fundamental to provide a "critical autonomy relationship to all media" [8]. Besides the expected abilities to read, write or interpret media messages, media literacy stresses the importance of "including citizenship, aesthetic appreciation and expression, social advocacy, self-esteem, and consumer competence" [8]. Thus, media literacy compromises and impacts a long-term responsibility among societies for their own advance.

From a practical perspective, literacies correspond to wide conceptualizations. According to Cordes (2009) comprehensives' review, literacy types considers information literacy, visual literacy, multicultural literacy, and multimodal literacy, among others. In this categorization, media literacy has been defined as "the process of accessing, analyzing, evaluating and creating messages in a wide variety of media modes, genres and forms" [9]. Moreover, under this initial notion, a second level of literacy is compromised which, in turn, anchors other two subtypes of literacy, such as digital literacy and advertising literacy.

Digital literacy embraces the ability to read and comprehend hypertext in a digital environment [5]. This last approach has been conceptualized as,

"the awareness, attitude and ability of individuals to appropriately use digital tools and facilities to access, manage, integrate, evaluate, analyze and synthesize digital resources, construct new knowledge, create media expressions, and communicate with others, in the context of specific life situations, in order to enable constructive social action; and to reflect upon this process" [5].

Although digital literacy is mainly characterized by an online environment, it is also applicable to other technological media. As Bawden [10] adds, digital literacy is further circumscribed to "the presentation of information, without subsuming creative writing and visualization. It encompasses the evaluation of information, without claiming systematic reviewing and meta-analysis as its own" [10]. This last feature makes digital literacy sensitive to be combined with other types of literacy forms and contents.

Linked to digital literacy, advertising literacy has also been established as a fundamental component of media literacy. Hudders, De Pauw, Cauberghe, Panic, Zarouali and Rozendaal [11] have defined advertisement literacy as "an individual's knowledge, abilities, and skills to cope with advertising" [11]. In this sense, the importance of this type of literacy relies in that it works "as a 'filter' or 'radar' enabling consumers to critically evaluate the persuasion attempt" [11]. In consequence, advertising literacy poses a challenge involving knowledge, abilities and skills confronted to the adverting domain. In a deeper point of view, Hudders et al. [11] distinguished three particular elements that belong to advertising literacy: (a) a cognitive perspective, referred as "the ability to recognize advertising, to understand its selling intent and persuasive intent, and to understand its persuasive tactics"; (b) a moral angle, which "reflects individual's ability to develop thoughts about the moral appropriateness of specific advertising formats and compromises general moral evaluations individuals hold toward these formats and towards advertising in general, including its persuasive tactics"; and (c) an affective or attitudinal dimension, that "emphasizes on the importance of emotion regulation to counterbalance the affective reactions evoked by the persuasion messages". Thus, advertising literacy considers several dimensions to be studied, that require to previously be framed.

1.2   Schema Congruence Theory Linked to Advertising Literacy

Based on the persuasion literature, how people interpret and develop personal knowledge has been studied. Friestad and Wright [12] have proposed the Persuasion Knowledge Model (PKM), which stated that:

"people's persuasion knowledge is developmentally contingent (...) as it continues developing throughout lifespan. It is also, to some degree, historically contingent. The culturally supplied folk wisdom on persuasion changes over time, so that each generation's and culture's thinking may differ somewhat from that of past generations and other cultures" [12].

Experts also recognized that the persuasion process compromises several ways: "from firsthand experiences in social interactions with friends, family, and co-workers; from conversations about how people's thoughts, feelings and behaviors can be influenced; from observing marketers and other known persuasion agents; and from commentary on advertising and marketing tactics in the news media" [12]. Therefore, connected to situations above, persuasion knowledge "performs schemalike functions", as it influences individual's attention and frames people's worldviews, known as "schemer schema" [12]. According to Jurca and Madlberger [13], the advertising schema corresponds to "enduring understandings of particular phenomena that usually do not easily change once they are established" [13]. Moreover, each time a novel experience occurs the corresponding schema is activated. As researchers detailed,

"since advertising is incoming information to be processed by consumers, schema theory is applicable to consumers information processing behavior on advertising messages. The advertising schema can help individuals interpret advertisements quickly as persuasive and thus shape their future responses attempts" [13].

Once a congruity is obtained, a feeling of "familiarity" is perceived, and a comfortable sensation emerges.

Today, the traditional notion of gender schema has been challenged. In this direction, advertising literacy education has become a process involved with the study of ads contents as persuasive messages. Among the components that have been proved to affect advertising literacy is age [14], as individuals obtain greater experience and education on advertising literacy as they get older after being more exposed to ads. This is explained as advertising literacy "denotes consumers' ability to understand vocabulary, elements and styles of advertising and decode complex visual elements and make brand inferences from minimal cues" [13]. This expertise is acquired as consumers possess the ability to understand advertising and recognize types of messages and tactics presented and developed.

Besides age, advertising literacy is connected to previous knowledge or advertising literacy to face ads. As Malmelin [15] explained, "understanding consumers literacy skills is a key condition for successful communications. As different audiences take a different attitude towards the media and to advertising, the way in which people receive the messages is crucially important to the planning of communication and its success" [15]. In the case of adolescents, Boush, Friestad and Rose [16] found that "having higher levels of knowledge about advertiser tactics was positively related to being more skeptical of advertising" [16], although this finding was also linked to individual personality variables. This is likewise sustained by Yoon [17], who recognized that "the more knowledgeable a person is on a topic, the more complex the person's knowledge structure will be, making him/her more cognitive flexible in dealing with unexpected information" [17]. Thus, as Jurca and Madlberger [13] described, advertising experts are "acquainted with the tricks of the trade, they can deconstruct advertising campaigns in double-quick time and outmaneuver even the most cunning marketing strategist" [13].

1.3 Gender Roles and Stereotypes

Gender stereotypes in advertising correspond to one of its most influential areas [7] and, in turn, to a subtype of social stereotypes [18]. A gender stereotype is defined as "psychosocial characteristics that are considered prototypical", including gender "features, roles, motivations and behaviors that [culturally] are assigned differentially to women and men" [18]. In this context, advertising plays a fundamental role as it assumes a social responsibility by using gender stereotypes to study and understand the complexity that people perceive from their environments.

For decades, the portrait of women and men in advertising has undergone major changes [7]. In the seventies, the stereotype of women in advertising was limited to being a wife and mother, privileging the internal scope of the home and family; meanwhile, the man was responsible for bringing money home, associating to a more aggressive attitude and willing to adventure [1]. Challenging this traditional perspective, current changes in the world have contributed to the emergence of new approaches linked to gender stereotypes in advertising. This research considers two main viewpoints: a) femvertising, as the empowerment towards the traditional stereotype of women in advertising and, b) a change of men in the inclusion of activities that traditionally were primarily linked to the field of women, such as household chores.

Femvertising: "Empowering" Women in Advertising. Women empowerment has become one of the most recent advertising contents. As Menéndez Menéndez [19] acknowledges, it is an area of fertile study for "multidisciplinary" research that considers the combination of "feminist, cultural, advertising and/or communicational theories" [19]. Although this type of advertising "is still scarce, and in the Spanish language it practically does not exist" [19], it is becoming more popular as feminist movements worldwide have made strong contributions to put on the agenda this issue.

Femvertising is based on the concept of "empowerment" of women coming from feminist ideologies that aspire to achieve gender equality [6]. Åkestam, Rosengren and Dahlen [20] has defined it "as contemporary advertising campaigns that question the traditional female gender stereotypes used in advertising" [20]. As [19] describes, companies choose to portray three types "empowered" women: (1) with traditionally masculine traits "such as ambition or courage, in the context of activities more related to the socialization of men, such as some sports", (2) accentuation of feminine traits, "putting an important emphasis on appearance", and (3) "a woman rather ambivalent: beautiful, but strong, willing, but kind" [19]. This recent approach has broken into the current of global advertising messages, with special strength in young people seduced by overcoming traditional sexist paradigms.

Towards a More Inclusive Society. Today, the emergence of a new male stereotype in advertising has also challenged traditional stereotypes. As Condo and Hurtado [21] described,

> "men have entered worlds that seemed exclusive to women; consumes products previously perceived as exclusively feminine (perfumery, cosmetics, etc.), breaks into spaces that were represented as mostly occupied by women (home, childcare) and assumes roles that a few decades ago were not attributed to him with so easy" [21].

However, the background is not to show a more "feminized" man [22]; the intention is to portray male representations with a tendency were chores are done equally by genders. For instance, after studying stereotypes associated with parents who care for their children, Ilicic, Baxter and Kulczynski [23] proved that, "the representation of men as caregivers is perceived as atypical for the current advertising environment, [as] individuals ... express positive attitudes towards advertisements that challenge traditional gender stereotypes" [23]. Along these lines, it is expected that this approach an advertising approach to be explored.

Based on these previous approaches, this work explores how each of them are connected to advertising literacy. Therefore, based on a cognitive dimension [11], young men and women Chilean university students are asked their perception for both perspectives. Thus, this study posits the following two research questions:

Research Question 1 (RQ1): Do Chilean students with advertising literacy differ in their opinions regarding the congruence of roles presented in the advertising message on the two approaches studied—femvertising and towards a more inclusive society— with what they think about gender stereotypes of men and women in Chilean society? Research Question 2 (RQ2): Do Chilean students with advertising literacy perceived differences in the roles portrayed in each advertising message belonging to the two approaches studied?

1.4   Value Perception Among Young Chileans

The emergence of both previous advertising approaches has not passed unaware in Chile, as advertising approaches are fundamental building blocks on socially shared beliefs and values. Courtney and Whipple [24] suggests the influence of ethical judgments and their possible effects in the field of advertising. Moreover, LaTour and Henthorne [25] studied the dimension of moral equity on advertising. In addition, [25] justify the need to consider the relationship between the ethical evaluation process and the social sphere, as well as the cultural influences on individuals'. As result, variables integrated by "culturally acceptable and traditionally acceptable elements represent influences, patterns and parameters manifested by society", which contribute to knowing the current sexuality parameter in advertising regarding what is currently acceptable [25].

Shaping New Values Among Chileans. Chilean advertising is undergoing a significant evolution concerning current gender stereotypes in advertising. As Vergara and Rodríguez [26] found, "advertising in Chile is aimed at stereotypes of a general [referring to traditional] nature, so this would not produce a direct appropriation and identification with young people" [26]. A recent study by Farías Muñoz and Cuello Riveros [27] established that young Chilean, belonging to a regional university, recognized "the persistence of machismo, as well as the emergence of a new female stereotype that demands a change from man" [27]. Furthermore, after studying advertising messages about the promotion of Chilean universities targeting young people, researchers pointed out that in the advertising materials "a stereotype of an empowered woman emerges, which assumes feminism in an inclusive manner with man. In the same way, men are oriented to an equal relationship of alterity with women" [27]. Therefore, advertising in Chile is changing as the dynamic Chilean reality has already begun to change.

Based on these previous descriptions, this work aims to examine the moral advertising literacy dimension [11]. Thus, men and women Chilean university students are asked their moral perception for both perspectives. Therefore, this research states the following two research questions:

Research Question 3 (RQ3): Are there differences in the opinions of Chilean university students with advertising knowledge on the two approaches studied regarding values of justice, impartiality and levels of traditional, cultural, family and moral acceptance in Chile?

Research Question 4 (RQ4): Are there differences in value perceptions of Chilean university students with knowledge in advertising about each of the advertising messages belonging to each approach studied?

2   Methods

2.1   Sample and Procedure

Participants were in total 110 students (women n = 70), corresponding to: a) Advertising career (n = 69); b) Communications programs (n = 33); and c) Engineering programs (n = 8). All students attended from 1st year to 5th year of studies at the Pontificia Universidad Católica de Chile (UC) in Santiago, Chile. Unfortunately, not all participants answered their career year obtaining 104 responses. This study obtained IRB approval by the Scientific Ethical Committee in Social Sciences, Art and Humanities of the Pontificia Universidad Católica de Chile. Informed consent was previously obtained from each participant.

A total of six advertising messages were selected to be seen by participants. Answers were provided in a pen and paper survey. Firstly, students provided sociodemographic information in the questionnaire. Secondly, participants were exposed to each of the chosen advertising messages; followed by 10 min to answer questions about the advertising message visualized. This dynamic was carefully carried out for the total of six advertising messages chosen in this study.

Response Rate. The total number of possible answers of the survey were N = 660. A total of 512 answers were obtained, corresponding to a response rate of 78%.

2.2 Dependent Variables

Gender Roles and Stereotypes in Advertising Messages Studied. A Likert scale of semantic differential ranging from 1 to 7, previously validated and adapted from the studies of Orth and Holancova [28] and Choi, Yoo, Reichert and LaTour [29] was used. For each advertising message, respondents were asked their perception regarding the congruence of the representation of the content of the advertising message with the gender role that was portrayed in the message, ranging from 1 = totally disagree to 7 = totally agree (M = 5.34; SD = 1.79; Cronbach's α = .74).

Value Perception Among Young Chileans About the Advertising Messages studied. A Likert scale of semantic differential ranging from 1 to 7, previously validated and adapted from the studies of [29] was applied. For each adverting message, respondents were asked: (1) degree of the concept of justice associated with the content of the advertising message, ranging from 1 = unfair to 7 = fair (M = 5.57; SD = 1.76; Cronbach's α = .73); (2) degree of impartiality associated with the content of the advertising message, ranging from 1 = is not impartial to 7 = is impartial (M = 4.29; SD = 2.09; Cronbach's α = .75); (3) degree of traditional acceptance for Chilean society associated with the content of the advertising message, ranging from 1 = is not traditionally acceptable to 7 = is traditionally acceptable (M = 4.20; SD = 2.11; Cronbach's α = .76); (4) degree of cultural acceptance for Chilean society associated with the content of the advertising message, ranging from 1 = is not culturally acceptable to 7 = is culturally acceptable (M = 4.76; SD = 1.95; Cronbach's α = .75); (5) expected degree of family acceptance that your family would have to the content presented in the advertising message, ranging from 1 = is not acceptable to my family to 7 = is acceptable to my family (M = 5.61; SD = 1.74; Cronbach's α = .74); and (6) degree of morality associated to Chilean society regarding the content of the advertising message, ranging from 1 = is not morally correct to 7 = is morally correct (M = 5.70; SD = 1.72; Cronbach's α = .73).

2.3 Independent Variables

Advertising Messages for Femvertising: "Empowering" Women in Advertising Approach. A total of three advertising messages were considered: (1) "Delicious Calm" ("Deliciosa Calma" in Spanish) by Pavofrío, Campofrío, corresponding to a cold ham food item available at: https://www.youtube.com/watch?v=aZSSiYvgxsU. The message portraits a group of desperate women, tired of their daily chores, who order in the first stress-free restaurant recipes such as: "I have not gone to the gym because I have not felt like it", "I have crow's feet, so what?", or "I do not marry because I do not feel like it with turkey taquitos", among others. At the end, the advertising message slogan ends with the line: "A balanced society helps to reduce stress. Pavofrío, feeding another model of woman"; (2) "The Best Work in the World", by Procter & Gamble (P&G), related to consumer goods available at: https://www.youtube.com/watch?v=lnGkW9lFTd4. This advertising message characterizes the story of three mothers who, with their domestic chores' effort and care, help their children to succeed in the sport they each practice. Therefore, the message shows how the strength of mothers' is transmitted to their children, ending with the slogan line: "The most difficult job in the world is the best job in the world. Thanks Mom"; and (3) "My expression, my choice" by Ésika. Belonging to the makeup category, it is available at: https://www.youtube.com/watch?v=GTNwHGC8PZY. The advertising message shows women performing boxing, eating fast food, working professionally in an office and putting on makeup, associating each of these activities with the slogan: "It is my choice, it is my expression", highlighting to option of women to choose whatever activity they want to perform.

Advertising Messages for Towards a More Inclusive Society. A total of three advertising messages were considered: (1) "Billie's Body Hair", belonging to feminine beauty products available at: https://www.youtube.com/watch?v=P4DDpS685iI. The advertising message shows four different young women shaving with the razor Billie, which traditionally has been associated to a male practice. Each of the women presented have different physical structure, which is contrasted with music and images highlight specific objects such as a cactus, nail polish, and others; (2) "Urufarma", belonging to the category of female contraceptives available at: https://www.youtube.com/watch?v=WmEGCN0nNHc. The advertising message was launched on Women's Day, revealing that men and women can do the same things, regardless of men's gender: "Now they can cry, they can spin, they can dress well and have light drinks, (…) they can be with divorced, single mothers or with a woman who doesn't want children, (…) or they can end up dedicating their lives to another man…". The message ends with the slogan: "Our struggle is for everyone"; and (3) "Ariel", belonging to the category of cleaning products available at: https://www.youtube.com/watch?v=J7xcBJ1lCw0. The advertising message characterizes a father who writes a letter to his daughter asking her for forgiveness, as he had never helped with household chores such as washing clothes. In the father's narration, he recognizes the pride he feels for his daughter, and that only "what is seen, is learned", alluding to the fact that he has not set the example with helping. At the end of the advertising message, the father travels back to his home and helps his own wife with the laundry. The closure of the message states: "Why should the laundry just be the work of a mother? Parents # share the load".

Advertising messages (AM) of this study were shown to students in the following order: a) Campofrío (AM1), b) Billie (AM2), c) Urufarma (AM3), d) P&G (AM4), e) Ésika (AM5), and f) Ariel (AM6). In addition, messages are available for students on hybrid type of media, including social media.

2.4   Control Variables

Undergraduate Chilean Students. Considering students with similar level of advertising literacy, we chose a sample of university students that belong to the same university—Pontificia Universidad Católica de Chile (UC)—, and at least have taken one course belonging to the undergraduate career coursework of Advertising at UC.

2.5   Moderator Variables

Students' Gender. In this research, gender approaches among Chilean students constitute a crucial variable to study. Therefore, based on traditional gender categorization we classified students only as women or men.

Students' Age. Research considered students ages connected to their level of advertising literacy. Therefore, ages ranged from 18 to 26 years. Considering that the median age was 20 years old (M = 20); two groups based on intervals were conformed: (a) one younger group with ages ranging from 18 to 20 years old; and (b) one older group with ages fluctuating between 21 to 26 years old.

Students' School Year. In average, undergraduate careers in Chile last a total of 5 school years. Based on the medium of undergraduate careers years, and that school year is also connected to advertising literacy, we divided students in two groups: (a) one group with undergraduate students that belonged to 1st and 2nd years of undergraduate careers; and (b) a second group of undergraduates coursing their 3rd, 4th and 5th year of undergraduate career.

3   Results

To answer our research questions, descriptive and inferential statistics were performed. Data analysis was estimated using software SPSS v.22.

Concerning RQ1, which asked about Chilean students with advertising literacy opinions' regarding the congruence of roles presented in advertising message on both approaches studied with what they think of gender stereotypes of men and women in Chilean society, we found that students perspectives were favorable for both. However, Approach 1 (M = 6.2; SD = 1.39) was perceived as more positive Approach 2 (M = 5.29; SD = 1.77). Considering control variables, as presented in Table 1, the unique statistical difference was for Approach 1—Femvertising "Empowering" women in advertising—by schooling years, being more favorable according to students with less years of study.

RQ2 asked if Chilean students with advertising literacy perceived differences in the roles portrayed in each advertising message belonging to both approaches studied. Results presented in Table 2 revealed that only two differences were statistically significant ($p < 0.05$): a) For Approach 1, roles in advertising message 4 were perceived as more favorable by students with less years of schooling; and, (b) For Approach 2, roles in advertising message 3 were better perceived by males' students.

Concerning RQ3, which asked about differences in opinions of Chilean university students with advertising literacy on the two approaches studied regarding values of justice, impartiality and levels of traditional, cultural, family and moral acceptance, statics were calculated. As presented in Table 3, from eighteen calculations, only seven were statistically significant: (a) Three differences were statistically significant for both approaches by gender, corresponding to males cultural and family acceptance for

Approach 1, and males for cultural acceptance for Approach 2; (b) Two statistically significant differences were found by student's age; corresponding for Approach 1 to morality value for younger students; meanwhile for Approach 2, justice value was more acceptable for older students'; and (c) The last two statistically significant differences were found by students schooling years, corresponding both to Approach 1, for students with more schooling years.

Finally, RQ4 considered differences in value perceptions of Chilean university students with advertising literacy for each of the advertising messages belonging to each approach studied. Findings of Approach 1 are presented in Table 4, revealing five statistical significant differences: (a) By gender, men perceived that advertising message 1 was more fair (justice value); while women conceived it as more familiarly acceptable; (b) By student's age, there were only different responses for advertising message 5, were younger students perceived it as more favorably regarding being morally acceptable; and, (c) By school years, results revealed two significant differences in which, youngest students think advertising message 1 is more impartial, meanwhile advertising message 5 was seen as more culturally acceptable by those with greater schooling years. For approach 2, a total of five statistically significant differences were found, corresponding to: (a) By gender, two significant differences in advertising message 3 were men had a more favorable opinion regarding cultural and family acceptance; and (b) By age, two statistically significant differences raised for advertising message 3 on fair and impartiality values of the message for older students'; as well as one statistically significant difference was found for advertising message 2, as younger students' perceived it as more morally acceptable. No significant differences were found by schooling years in advertising messages about values for this approach (Table 5).

Table 1. Statistics for roles key variables of the study by approaches. Notes. 1 = Students' Gender; 2 = Students' Age; and 3 = Students' Year of Undergraduate Studies; APP1 = Approach 1- Femvertising "Empowering" women in advertising; APP2 = Approach 2- Towards a More Inclusive Society.

	1 Women (N = 57)	1 Men (N = 33)		2 Younger Student's (N = 52)	2 Older Student's (N = 56)		3 1st and 2nd years (N = 52)	3 3rd, 4th and 5th years (N = 53)	
	M (SD)	M (SD)	p	M (SD)	M (SD)	p	M (SD)	M (SD)	p
APP1	5.22 (1.77)	4.83 (1.76)	0.08	5.16 (1.67)	4.95 (1.96)	0.36	5.26 (1.58)	4.81 (1.95)	0.04*
APP2	5.63 (1.87)	5.84 (1.47)	0.25	5.63 (1.75)	5.84 (1.70)	0.18	5.72 (1.78)	5.74 (1.70)	0.90

Note. M = Statistical Mean; SD = Standard Deviation.
*p < 0.05

Table 2. Statistics for roles key variables of the study by advertising messages (AM). Notes. 1 = Students' Gender; 2 = Students' Age; and 3 = Students' Year of Undergraduate Studies.

Approach 1 - Femvertising "Empowering" women in advertising

	1 Women (N = 70)	1 Men (N = 40)	p	2 Younger Student's (N = 52)	2 Older Student's (N = 56)	p	3 1st and 2nd years (N = 52)	3 3rd, 4th and 5th years (N = 53)	p
	M (SD)	M (SD)		M (SD)	M (SD)		M (SD)	M (SD)	
AM1	4.71 (1.79)	4.56 (1.74)	0.69	4.60 (1.58)	4.74 (1.96)	0.72	4.91 (1.47)	4.33 (1.98)	0.12
AM4	4.73 (1.92)	4.12 (1.87)	0.15	4.76 (1.80)	4.25 (2.00)	0.20	4.88 (1.79)	4.00 (1.94)	0.03*
AM5	6.23 (1.04)	5.81 (1.85)	0.09	6.12 (1.15)	6.02 (1.06)	0.68	5.98 (1.20)	6.21 (0.98)	0.35

Approach 2 - Towards a More Inclusive Society

	1 Women (N = 70)	1 Men (N = 40)	p	2 Younger Student's (N = 52)	2 Older Student's (N = 56)	p	3 1st and 2nd years (N = 52)	3 3rd, 4th and 5th years (N = 53)	p
	M (SD)	M (SD)		M (SD)	M (SD)		M (SD)	M (SD)	
AM2	5.86 (1.60)	5.45 (1.60)	0.24	5.80 (1.54)	5.61 (1.67)	0.59	5.86 (1.46)	5.50 (1.77)	0.29
AM3	5.31 (1.99)	6.26 (0.99)	0.01*	5.52 (1.68)	5.84 (1.77)	0.39	5.78 (1.69)	5.58 (1.81)	0.60
AM6	5.70 (1.20)	5.94 (1.66)	0.57	5.57 (2.02)	6.07 (1.66)	0.21	5.51 (2.14)	6.15 (1.46)	0.11

Note. M = Statistical Mean; SD = Standard Deviation.
*p < 0.05

Table 3. Statistics for values key variables of the study by approaches. Notes. APP1 = Approach 1- Femvertising "Empowering" women in advertising; APP2 = Approach 2- Towards a More Inclusive Society.

		Women (N = 57)	Men (N = 33)	p	Younger Student's (N = 52)	Older Student's (N = 56)	p	1st and 2nd years (N = 52)	3rd, 4th, 5th years (N = 53)	p
		M (SD)	M (SD)		M (SD)	M (SD)		M (SD)	M (SD)	
Justice	APP1	5.40 (1.85)	5.07 (1.81)	0.13	5.49 (1.70)	5.13 (1.94)	0.08	5.41 (1.66)	5.14 (2.01)	0.20
	APP2	5.82 (1.80)	6.09 (1.24)	0.17	5.66 (1.73)	6.14 (1.53)	0.01*	5.75 (1.67)	6.02 (1.65)	0.15
Impartiality	APP1	4.28 (1.92)	4.18 (1.90)	0.67	1.79 (1.45)	4.15 (2.02)	0.28	4.46 (1.76)	3.97 (2.02)	0.02*
	APF2	4.30 (2.20)	4.32 (2.28)	0.94	4.06 (2.21)	4.52 (2.25)	0.07	4.11 (2.22)	4.43 (2.27)	0.21
Traditional A	APF1	4.86 (2.05)	5.02 (1.70)	0.50	4.88 (1.95)	4.91 (1.95)	0.89	4.97 (1.92)	4.85 (1.97)	0.59
	APF2	3.53 (2.14)	3.58 (2.03)	0.84	3.59 (2.04)	3.43 (2.16)	0.50	3.38 (2.01)	3.71 (2.19)	0.16
Cultural A	APP1	5.23 (1.79)	5.62 (1.42)	0.05*	5.40 (1.66)	5.30 (1.73)	0.61	5.50 (1.57)	5.19 (1.82)	0.11
	APP2	4.05 (2.11)	4.64 (1.86)	0.01*	4.19 (1.97)	4.24 (2.14)	0.82	4.10 (2.03)	4.29 (2.09)	0.43
Family A	APP1	5.69 (1.80)	6.13 (1.14)	0.02*	5.89 (1.60)	5.81 (1.66)	0.64	5.92 (1.54)	5.79 (1.71)	0.49
	APP2	5.27 (1.98)	5.66 (1.73)	0.08	5.55 (1.75)	5.27 (2.04)	0.20	5.32 (1.93)	5.43 (1.92)	0.62
Morality	APP1	5.48 (1.84)	5.72 (1.62)	0.25	5.81 (1.56)	5.34 (1.92)	0.02*	5.81 (1.54)	5.36 (1.94)	0.02*
	APP2	5.65 (1.86)	6.00 (1.27)	0.08	5.86 (1.57)	5.68 (1.81)	0.35	5.84 (1.61)	5.67 (1.81)	0.40

Note. M = Statistical Mean; SD = Standard Deviation.
*p < 0.05

Table 4. Approach 1- Femvertising "Empowering" women in advertising. Statistics for values by advertising message (AM) of the study.

		Women (N = 57)	Men (N = 33)		Younger Student's (N = 52)	Older Student's (N = 56)		1st, 2nd years (N = 52)	3rd, 4th, 5th years (N = 53)	
		M (SD)	M (SD)	p	M (SD)	M (SD)	p	M (SD)	M (SD)	p
Justice	AM1	4.91 (1.86)	4.78 (1.57)	0.72	4.98 (1.58)	4.79 (1.91)	0.56	5.00 (1.50)	4.79 (2.01)	0.55
	AM4	4.87 (1.90)	4.31 (2.11)	0.17	5.00 (2.02)	4.45 (1.92)	0.15	4.96 (1.96)	4.32 (1.96)	0.10
	AM5	6.42 (1.33)	6.14 (1.15)	0.29	6.48 (0.87)	6.18 (1.54)	0.22	6.25 (1.12)	6.35 (1.44)	0.69
Impartiality	AM1	4.28 (1.72)	3.41 (1.59)	0.01*	4.24 (1.60)	3.76 (1.79)	0.16	4.36 (1.50)	3.60 (1.84)	0.02*
	AM4	4.18 (1.88)	4.54 (2.04)	0.36	4.49 (1.84)	4.18 (2.02)	0.41	4.55 (1.88)	4.00 (1.94)	0.15
	AM5	4.39 (2.16)	4.62 (1.86)	0.58	4.39 (1.94)	4.49 (2.19)	0.81	4.48 (1.90)	4.33 (2.24)	0.71
Traditional A	AM1	4.48 (2.02)	4.26 (1.55)	0.57	4.51 (1.85)	4.24 (1.92)	0.45	4.60 (1.89)	4.26 (1.86)	0.37
	AM4	5.78 (1.81)	6.14 (1.46)	0.31	5.92 (1.76)	5.91 (1.62)	0.97	6.02 (1.63)	5.75 (1.77)	0.43
	AM5	4.33 (2.03)	4.68 (1.51)	0.37	4.25 (1.84)	4.58 (1.91)	0.35	4.33 (1.81)	4.54 (1.97)	0.57
Cultural A	AM1	4.90 (1.64)	5.08 (1.63)	0.59	5.23 (1.53)	4.69 (1.75)	0.09	5.44 (1.33)	4.47 (1.84)	0.00*
	AM4	5.77 (1.79)	6.24 (1.16)	0.15	5.94 (1.74)	5.93 (1.48)	0.97	5.98 (1.63)	5.91 (1.58)	0.81
	AM5	5.01 (1.83)	5.54 (1.19)	0.12	5.04 (1.59)	5.27 (1.74)	0.47	5.08 (1.63)	5.19 (1.75)	0.73
Family A	AM1	4.94 (2.01)	5.92 (1.26)	0.01*	5.48 (1.75)	5.15 (1.90)	0.35	5.42 (1.75)	5.31 (1.86)	0.75
	AM4	6.12 (1.55)	6.27 (1.12)	0.59	6.13 (1.55)	6.13 (1.44)	0.97	6.31 (1.21)	5.92 (1.74)	0.19
	AM5	6.01 (1.61)	6.21 (1.03)	0.49	6.06 (1.45)	6.15 (1.42)	0.75	6.02 (1.50)	6.14 (1.40)	0.69
Morality	AM1	5.09 (2.09)	5.45 (1.64)	0.36	5.49 (1.73)	4.98 (2.11)	0.17	5.56 (1.67)	5.02 (2.12)	0.15
	AM4	5.32 (1.73)	5.43 (1.95)	0.76	5.48 (1.77)	5.20 (1.91)	0.43	5.61 (1.63)	5.01 (1.98)	0.14
	AM5	6.04 (1.53)	6.30 (0.98)	0.35	6.46 (0.94)	5.85 (1.61)	0.02*	6.29 (1.15)	6.00 (1.56)	0.28

Note. M = Statistical Mean; SD = Standard Deviation.
*p < 0.05

Table 5. Approach 2- Towards a more Inclusive Society. Statistics for values by advertising message (AM) of the study.

		Women (N = 57)	Men (N = 33)	p	Younger Student's (N = 52)	Older Student's (N = 56)	p	1st, 2nd years (N = 52)	3rd, 4th, 5th years (N = 53)	p
		M (SD)	M (SD)		M (SD)	M (SD)		M (SD)	M (SD)	
Justice	AM2	5.91 (1.68)	5.87 (1.27)	0.88	5.75 (1.49)	6.05 (1.57)	0.31	5.78 (1.51)	5.96 (1.59)	0.56
	AM3	5.35 (2.11)	6.00 (1.38)	0.09	5.08 (2.05)	5.95 (1.75)	0.02*	5.35 (1.95)	5.60 (1.98)	0.50
	AM6	6.22 (1.47)	6.41 (1.01)	0.50	6.15 (1.42)	6.42 (1.21)	0.30	6.12 (1.42)	6.50 (1.18)	0.14
Impartiality	AM2	4.33 (2.06)	4.03 (2.18)	0.49	4.40 (2.08)	4.05 (2.16)	0.41	4.42 (2.11)	3.98 (2.13)	0.30
	AM3	4.06 (2.17)	3.84 (2.34)	0.63	3.51 (2.14)	4.44 (2.27)	0.03*	3.61 (2.22)	4.33 (2.24)	0.17
	AM6	4.52 (2.37)	5.11 (2.15)	0.21	4.31 (2.35)	5.09 (2.25)	0.09	4.31 (2.29)	4.98 (2.35)	0.15
Traditional A	AM2	2.52 (1.83)	2.00 (1.20)	0.12	2.46 (1.61)	2.18 (1.67)	0.37	2.29 (1.54)	2.40 (1.79)	0.76
	AM3	3.87 (2.13)	4.13 (1.90)	0.53	4.04 (1.92)	3.84 (2.17)	0.62	3.85 (1.94)	4.11 (2.16)	0.51
	AM6	4.20 (2.10)	4.59 (1.88)	0.34	4.27 (2.09)	4.29 (2.04)	0.97	3.98 (2.08)	4.62 (1.98)	0.11
Cultural A	AM2	3.22 (1.94)	3.49 (1.97)	0.50	3.25 (1.76)	3.29 (2.13)	0.93	3.25 (1.84)	3.26 (2.04)	0.98
	AM3	4.25 (2.10)	5.05 (1.58)	0.04*	4.47 (1.97)	4.52 (2.00)	0.90	4.42 (2.00)	4.51 (1.99)	0.83
	AM6	4.70 (2.04)	5.38 (1.46)	0.07	4.85 (1.85)	4.93 (1.97)	0.82	4.63 (1.99)	5.09 (1.84)	0.22
Family A	AM2	4.56 (2.08)	4.41 (1.91)	0.67	4.90 (1.73)	4.23 (2.21)	0.08	4.37 (1.96)	4.59 (2.07)	0.59
	AM3	5.42 (1.96)	6.24 (1.26)	0.02*	5.72 (1.80)	5.61 (1.86)	0.76	5.69 (1.80)	5.64 (1.88)	0.89
	AM6	5.80 (1.71)	6.32 (1.25)	0.10	6.02 (1.54)	5.98 (1.61)	0.90	5.88 (1.70)	6.06 (1.49)	0.58
Morality	AM2	5.44 (1.90)	5.57 (1.46)	0.71	5.90 (1.42)	5.14 (1.95)	0.02*	5.63 (1.65)	5.38 (1.86)	0.47
	AM3	5.39 (2.00)	5.92 (1.24)	0.14	5.38 (1.84)	5.66 (1.81)	0.42	5.62 (1.77)	5.40 (1.91)	0.54
	AM6	6.13 (1.60)	6.51 (0.90)	0.18	6.31 (1.26)	6.25 (1.52)	0.83	6.27 (1.30)	6.25 (1.53)	0.92

Note. M = Statistical Mean; SD = Standard Deviation.

*p < 0.05

4   Discussion

This work presented an explorative study concerning two recent advertising approaches, considering the importance of ads in the representation of gender roles and stereotypes, as well as value perceptions of young people, specifically in Chile. Directly connected to this study, advertising literacy was also compromised as the basic knowledge that Chileans students of this research had, specifically regarding messages content.

4.1   Theoretical Implications

This paper confirmed the reach and importance of digital adverting literacy, as young Chilean university students were aware of the presence of these two advertising approaches, which they distinguished in the advertising messages studied. Consistent with previous research, both approaches were favorably conceived by students' for roles and values socially informed. Based on the Schema Congruence Theory [13], advertising schemas for the two approaches studied were confirmed, as students' had knowledge on the persuasive contents of the ads. This last finding was closely tied to content cognitive schemas, which were reflected by the favorable means obtained for each of the advertising messages, demonstrating how comfortable students felt with the contents shown in the ads.

Regarding the variables studied about gender, student's age, and schooling year; overall, no main differences were obtained for the first two ones. However, for Approach 2, it was more frequent to find in students with older schooling years, less congruence with the ads exposed. In other words, this last group of students' questioned more what they saw on the messages. This last finding can be explained as higher level of school year entails higher level of digital advertising literacy and knowledge, directly impacting on cognitive schemas to interpret reality.

Concerning values, this study confirmed that to develop a critical stance in face of digital advertising literacy, critical knowledge is required to be examined. Our findings related to values of justice, impartiality and levels of traditional, cultural, family and moral acceptance, for both approaches, showed variations according to gender, students' age, and years of schooling. Absolutely, in the same line of experts [12], our work confirmed values as patterns contained in students' opinions' related to their social interactions. Moreover, statistically significant differences found in this exploratory study revealed student's levels of cultural and familiar acceptance of values, in the content of the messages, by gender and age. Nevertheless, we believe and recommended that, in future studies consider, other more detailed components of the advertising messages, such as variations on the approaches studied, affective components, detailed stories, visual elements, or schemas might also be added. This last recommendation will strongly contribute to open new paths to continue exploring further aspects of digital advertising literacy, as well as to other literacies too.

4.2   Practical Implications

Besides the implications presented above, this work also considered practical signifi-cance for digital advertising literacy. This research adds evidence related to cognitive and value aspects regarding two advertising approaches of social relevance. Therefore, we expect that this investigation constitutes a contribution to existing evaluations of persuasive interventions based on advertising approaches and messages. Nevertheless, we share findings of this work warn for an effective practice of advertising, which still needs to be expanded and deepened with much more information of national and international realities upon digital advertising literacy. Thus, future studies linked to effective digital advertising literacy should focus more on information of target pop-ulations' schemas and value positions. There is no doubt that this last recommendation would buttress a more powerful response to individuals' need to acquire knowledge and a critical stance [5].

Interestingly, however the results of our study found that, for each approach studied, there was one advertising messages that most often obtained statistically significant differences. In the case Approach 1, advertising message 1 was the common one. A plausible explanation is based on the type of content of the ad, which claims women to generate a social rupture with social traditional schemas. At the same time, in Approach 2, advertising message 3 was perceived by participants as the closest one to their own schemas, based on the statistical differences obtained. To us as researchers, we explain that both messages contained breaking off messages that are nearer to what student's with advertising knowledge believe advertising should contain.

4.3   Limitations

This study has several limitations that need to be taken in consideration for future study attempts. First, the sample of this study was relatively small. As the advertising career in UC University is relatively new, classes related to this undergraduate career are still at a small-scale. Nevertheless, a study of this type can be opened to other university and schools, in order to find what other target audiences, think about advertising approa-ches. Second, besides quantitative analysis, qualitative analysis may be also considered in future studies. To explore the richness of the target audiences' insights would also provide deeper knowledge on their own digital advertising literacy experiences, related to this and other approaches. Finally, this cross-sectional study may be improved, as it would be interesting to study changes among a same cohort of audience regarding different types of advertising approaches in the future.

Acknowledgements.   The authors of this research would like to gratefully thank all students and professors who contributed with their participation in this study belonging to the undergraduate Adverting Studies Career (Publicidad UC), belonging to Facultad de Comunicaciones, Pontificia Universidad Católica de Chile. Each of your contributions was key to achieve this work. Thank you to all of you!

References

1. Sharma, S., Das, M.: Women empowerment through advertising. Eur. J. Soc. Sci. (2019). https://www.europeanjournalofsocialsciences.co.uk/pdfs/ejss1903.pdf. in Press
2. American Marketing Association (n.d.). Advertising. https://www.ama.org/topics/Adverti sing/
3. Apostolov, G., Milenkova, V.: Mobile learning and digital literacy in the context of University young adults. In: International Association for Development of the Information Society, 14th International Conference Mobile Learning, p. 108 (2018)
4. O'Donohoe, S., Tynan, C.: Beyond sophistication: dimensions of advertising literacy. Int. J. Advert. **17**(4), 467–482 (1998)
5. Koltay, T.: The media and the literacies: media literacy, information literacy, digital literacy. Med. Cult. Soc. **33**(2), 211–221 (2011). p. 212, p. 216
6. Drake, V.E.: The impact of female empowerment in advertising (femvertising). J. Res. Market. **7**(3), 593–599 (2017)
7. Grau, S.L., Zotos, Y.C.: Gender stereotypes in advertising: a review of current research. Int. J. Advert. **35**(5), 761–770 (2016). p. 767
8. Aufderheide, P.: Media Literacy. A Report of the National Leadership Conference on Media Literacy, p. 212 (1993)
9. Cordes, S.: Broad Horizons: The Role of Multimodal Literacy in 21st Century Library Instruction, p. 3 (2009). http://citeseerx.ist.psu.edu/viewdoc/download?doi=10.1.1.150.638 5&rep=rep1&type=pdf
10. Bawden, D.: Origins and concepts of digital literacy. Digit. Literacies: Concepts, Pol. Pract. **30**, 17–32 (2008). p. 26
11. Hudders, L., De Pauw, P., Cauberghe, V., Panic, K., Zarouali, B., Rozendaal, E.: Shedding new light on how advertising literacy can affect children's processing of embedded advertising formats: a future research agenda. J. Advert. **46**(2), 333–349 (2017). p. 334
12. Friestad, M., Wright, P.: The persuasion knowledge model: how people cope with persuasion attempts. J. Consum. Res. **21**(1), 1–31 (1994). p. 1
13. Jurca, M.A., Madlberger, M.: Ambient advertising characteristics and schema incongruity as drivers of advertising effectiveness. J. Market. Commun. **21**(1), 48–64 (2015). p. 52, p. 57
14. Hwang, Y., Yum, J.Y., Jeong, S.H.: What components should be included in advertising literacy education? Effect of component types and the moderating role of age. J. Advert. **47**(4), 347–361 (2018)
15. Malmelin, N.: What is advertising literacy? Exploring the dimensions of advertising literacy. J. Vis. Lit. **29**(2), 129–142 (2010). p. 138
16. Boush, D.M., Friestad, M., Rose, G.M.: Adolescent skepticism toward TV advertising and knowledge of advertiser tactics. J. Consum. Res. **21**(1), 165–175 (1994). p. 172
17. Yoon, H.J.: Understanding schema incongruity as a process in advertising: review and future recommendations. J. Market. Commun. **19**(5), 360–376 (2013). p. 369
18. Gavaldón, B.G.: Los estereotipos como factor de socialización en el género. Comunicar **12**, 79–88 (1999). p. 84
19. Menéndez Menéndez, M.I.: Can Advertising be Feminist? Ambivalence and Gender Interests in "Femvertising" from a Case Study: Campofrio' s "Deliciosa Calma". Revista de Estudios Sociales (68), 88–100 (2019). p. 91
20. Åkestam, N., Rosengren, S., Dahlen, M.: Advertising "like a girl": toward a better understanding of "femvertising" and its effects. Psychol. Market. **34**(8), 795–806 (2017). p. 796

21. Condo, M., Hurtado, M.: La mujer y el hombre en la publicidad televisiva: Imágenes y estereotipos. Zer: Revista de Estudios de Comunicación, **11**(21), 163–177 (2006), p. 121
22. Palacios, M.L.F., Zenizo, M.D.P.S.P., Puente, K.N.T., Villarreal, P.: Estereotipos sexualizados de la mujer y el hombre en la publicidad. Perspectivas de la Comunicación **10**(1), 119–135 (2017). ISSN 0718-4867, p. 122
23. Ilicic, J., Baxter, S.M., Kulczynski, A.: The impact of age on consumer attachment to celebrities and endorsed brand attachment. J. Brand Manage. **23**(3), 273–288 (2016)
24. Courtney, A.E., Whipple, T.W.: Sex Stereotyping in Advertising. Lexington Books, Lexington (1983)
25. LaTour, M.S., Henthorne, T.L.: Ethical judgments of sexual appeals in print advertising. J. Advert. **23**(3), 81–90 (1994). p. 84
26. Vergara Leyton, E. Rodríguez, M.: El impacto social y cultural de la publicidad entre los jóvenes chilenos, p. 113–119 (2010). p. 118
27. Farías Muñoz, L., Cuello Riveros, V.: Percepción y autopercepción de los estereotipos de género en estudiantes universitarios de la región de Valparaíso a través de la publicidad. Revista de Comunicación **17**(1), 155–165 (2018). p. 155, 165, 166
28. Orth, U.R., Holancova, D.: Men's and women's responses to sex role portrayals in advertisements. Int. J. Res. Market. **21**(1), 77–88 (2004)
29. Choi, H., Yoo, K., Reichert, T., LaTour, M.S.: Do feminists still respond negatively to female nudity in advertising? Investigating the influence of feminist attitudes on reactions to sexual appeals. Int. J. Advert. **35**(5), 823–845 (2016)

Comparison of the Purchasing Behavior for Oneself or Other Using Eye Tracking Gaze Data

Mei Nonaka[1]([✉]), Kohei Otake[3], and Takashi Namatame[2]

[1] Graduate School of Science and Engineering, Chuo University,
Hachioji, Japan
a16.kyp4@g.chuo-u.ac.jp
[2] Faculty of Science and Engineering, Chuo University, 1-13-27, Kasuga,
Bunkyo-ku, Tokyo 112-8551, Japan
nama@indsys.chuo-u.ac.jp
[3] School of Information and Telecommunication Engineering, Tokai University,
2-3-23, Takanawa, Minato-ku, Tokyo 108-8619, Japan
otake@tsc.u-tokai.ac.jp

Abstract. In recent years, as the ratio of e-commerce is increasing, in the real store, it is necessary to use the strength of touching products. In order to be seen more products, we need to improve the layout at the real store. Therefore, it is necessary to understand the purchasing behavior of customers. Based on the idea that behavior changes depending on the purpose of purchase, we considered two types of purchasing behaviors: one for oneself and another for others. In this paper, we conducted the experiment of viewpoint observation about two kinds of the purchasing behaviors with the eye tracking device like glasses at an apparel store. In this study, we evaluate the difference of the purchasing behaviors by network analysis using gaze data obtained by experiments. Specifically, we clarify the relationships between showcases by network analysis. We analyzed the clusters between the showcases to use the average data of subjects for each scenario and we compared the two clusters. As a result, we found the differences and the features of two clusters.

Keywords: Purchasing behavior · Eye tracking device · Network analysis

1 Introduction

In recent years, the ratio of e-commerce is increasing. In that situation, in apparel stores, it is necessary to take advantage of the unique strength of real stores such as actually seeing products and having products in our hands. Therefore, improving the layout of apparel stores and the customer service method so that customers pay attention to more products is one of the important issues. To improve the layout, we need to understand customer behavior. When consumers purchase an item, sometimes the influence from others makes changes in purchasing behavior [1]. Similarly, when the purpose of purchase changes, such as the purpose of purchasing presents to others, it is assumed that the purchasing behavior makes changes in product search and

© Springer Nature Switzerland AG 2020
G. Meiselwitz (Ed.): HCII 2020, LNCS 12195, pp. 374–388, 2020.
https://doi.org/10.1007/978-3-030-49576-3_27

selection behavior. Therefore, when analyzing purchasing behavior, it is necessary to consider two types of situations: one for oneself and another for others. As a related study, Saijo etc. [2] shows layout improvement obtained from the identification of the golden zone using the eye tracking device. However, it is not clear about experiment and analysis under the condition such as purchasing products for oneself and for others.

2 Purpose of This Study

As shown in the previous section, we believe that there is the difference of interest by purchasing products for oneself and for others. In this study, we conducted the experiment of viewpoint observations at an apparel store with the glasses-type eye tracking device to compare two kinds of purchasing behaviors: for oneself and for others. The purpose of this study is to determine the differences and characteristics of two kinds of purchasing behaviors. As the analysis, we used t-test and network analysis, modularity.

3 Experiment

This section describes the outline of own experiment.

3.1 Outline of Experiment

We conducted experiment targeted at women at an apparel store in Japan. We did the experiment on 15 and 17 October 2019. We targeted subjects to women in their early twenties. To compare two kinds of purchasing behaviors, we readied for two scenarios. Table 1 shows the contents.

Table 1. Scenario

Number of	Scenario	Situation
12	Finding products for yourself	For oneself
6	Finding birthday presents to the author	For other

In order to unify the experimental conditions of time, subjects looked around all floors in the store for 20 min.

3.2 Eye Tracking Device and Software

We used "Tobii Pro Glasses 2" [3] to record the eye tracking while the experiment. This device can move freely while wearing and record what subjects are looking at. Moreover, when we analyze the recording data, we used "Tobii Pro Lab" [4] to process the recording data.

3.3   Target Store

In this experiment, we conducted at an apparel store located in central Tokyo, Japan. The main target at this bland is women in their twenties and thirties. There are three floors. The main products are bags, clothes, accessories, wristwatches, and shoes. There are men's products at B1 floor, and there are women's products at 1F and 2F floor. Tables 2 and 3 show the list of the showcases in each floor. Figures 1 and 2 show layouts in the store.

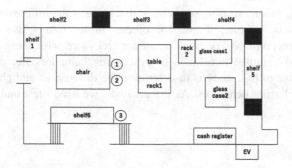

Fig. 1. Layout at 1F

Table 2. Showcase list at 1F

Showcase	Kinds of products
Shelf1	Collaboration products
Shelf2	New arrivals, handbags, tote bags, backpacks
Shelf3	Handbags, tote bags
Shelf4	Pass cases, wallets, handbags, shoulder bags
Shelf5	Shoulder bags, boots, handbags, backpack, body bags
Shelf6	Shoulder bags, backpacks, tote bags, sneakers, for men
Chair	Handbags, sneakers
Table	T-shirts, handbags, wallets
Glass shelf1	Wallets, pass cases, iPhone cases, key cases, pouches, key rings
Glass shelf2	Wristwatch
Rack1	Small shoulder bags
Rack2	Large shoulder bags

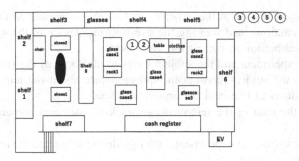

Fig. 2. Layout at 2F

Table 3. Showcase list at 2F

Showcases	Kinds of products
Shelf1	Sneakers, boots
Shelf2	Small handbags, sneakers
Shelf3	Sandals, boots, handbag
Shelf4	Small handbags, tote bags, iPhone cases
Shelf5	Small handbags, shoulder bags, wallets
Shelf6	Medium handbags, shoulder bags, sneakers, backpacks
Shelf7	Handbag, shoulder bags, mini wallets, boots
Shelf8	Boots, pumps
Glasses	Sunglasses
Table	Handbags, backpacks, body bags, sneakers
Clothes	T-shirts, jackets
Glass case1	Pass cases, key cases, wallets, iPhone cases, pouches, key rings, handbags
Glass case2	Wallets, key cases
Glass case3	Wristwatches
Glass case4	Accessories
Glass case5	Wristwatches
Rack1	Small shoulder bags
Rack2	Large shoulder bags
Shoes1	Sneakers
Shoes2	Sandals, pumps

3.4 Experimental Procedure

The flow of the experiment day is shown below.

1. We gather subjects on rental space.
2. The experimental staff explain the documents to be described to a subject. The subject writes consent forms, receipts, and preliminary questionnaires.
3. The experimental staff guide the subject to the experimental store.

4. When the subject arrives at the experimental store, we explained the experiment, scenarios, precautions, and wearing the eye tracking device to the subject.
5. We perform calibration to correct the viewpoint.
6. We start the experiment and the subject looks at all floors of the store for 20 min.
7. After 20 min, the subject answers the questionnaire about the atmosphere in the store, the products to like, and the products to want.
8. We back up the data of the removed eye tracking data and prepare for the next subject.
9. After the experiment, the experimental staff guide the subject to the rental space and the subject receive the reward.

4 Dataset

The subjects analyzed in this experiment were a total of 18 subjects. We ask 12 people to find the best items for oneself and other 6 people to find the birthday present to the author. In the case of gazing at the showcase for four seconds or more, we counted the subject as gazing at the showcase. We made four of the datasets as below.

- Gaze time of the showcases
- Adjacency matrix of time of gazing at the showcases
- Adjacency matrix of number of moves
- Adjacency matrix of the showcase distance.

We normalized gaze time of the showcases for the subjects and normalized adjacency matrixes for each floor except for the adjacency matrix of the showcase distance.

5 Results and Discussion

This section describes result and discussion.

5.1 Statistical Test

In order to compare the differences in the gaze time of showcases between scenarios we used t-test. First, we performed F-test because the method of T-test changes depending on whether the variance is different or not. We set hypothesis null (H_0) and alternative one (H_1) as below.

H_0:   There is no difference in variance of the gaze time of the showcase between the scenarios.

H_1:   There is a difference in variance of the gaze time of the showcase between the scenarios.

When we set significant level as 5%, their p-value is less than 0.05 and the null hypothesis is rejected, we judge that there is the difference between scenarios, and we used Welch's test without assuming equal variances. On the other hand, when p-value is more than 0.05 and the null hypothesis is adopted, we judge that there is no difference between scenarios, and we used independent t-test with assuming equal variances. We hypothesized as below to perform t-test.

H_0:   There is no difference in the average of the gaze time of the showcase between the scenarios.

H_1:   There is a difference in the average of the gaze time of the showcase between the scenarios.

When we set significance level as 5%, p-value is less than 0.05 and the null hypothesis is rejected, we judge that there is a difference between scenarios. When p-value is more than 0.05 and the null hypothesis is adopted, we judge that there is no difference between scenarios.

5.2   Network Analysis

In order to visualize the purchasing behavior of the subjects, we used network analysis. We used an index called degree centrality which appreciates the showcases related to more showcases. The adjacency matrix of a graph is $A = (a_{ij})$, and the indegree and outdegree are defined as $C_{id}(i)$ and $C_{od}(i)$ of node i. The degree centrality $C_d(i)$ is defined as the Eq. (1).

$$C_d(i) = C_{id}(i) + C_{od}(i) = \sum_{j=1}^{n} a_{ji} + \sum_{j=1}^{n} a_{ij} \qquad (1)$$

For the node, we used the showcases in the store. For the size of node, we used the value obtained from the degree centrality. The dataset is an adjacency matrix of time of gazing at the showcases averaged by each scenario. For the weight of edge, the dataset is an adjacency matrix of number of moves at the showcases averaged by each scenario.

5.3   Modularity

We used modularity in order to compare to the clusters between the showcases. Modularity Q proposed by Arenas [5] is defined as the Eq. (2).

$$Q = \frac{1}{2w} \sum_i \sum_j \left(w_{ij} - \frac{w_i w_j}{2w} \right) \delta(C_i, C_j) \qquad (2)$$

Where C_i is the community to which node i is assigned, and the definition of modularity is expressed in terms of the weighted adjacency matrix w_{ij} and the strength is $w_i = \sum_j w_{ij}$. δ is the Kronecker's delta, and the total strength is $2w = \sum_i w_i = \sum_i \sum_j w_{ij}$

In this study, we defined the weighted adjacency matrix w_{ij} as the inner products of three adjacency matrices that are adjacency matrix of time of gazing at the showcase, number of moves and shelf distance. We calculated w_{ij} for each subject, and we used the average for each scenario.

5.4   Analysis Result and Discussion

Tables 4 and 5 show the result of t-test.

Table 4. t-test at first floor

Showcase	p-value
Shelf1	0.292
Shelf2	0.647
Shelf3	0.865
Shelf4	0.777
Shelf5	0.505
Shelf6	0.255
Table	0.831
Chair	0.568
Glass shelf1	0.361
Glass shelf2	0.130
Hanging rack1	0.902
Hanging rack2	0.090

Table 5. t-test at second floor

Showcase	p-value
Shelf1	0.346
Shelf2	0.066
Shelf3	0.010*
Shelf4	0.346
Shelf5	0.874
Shelf6	0.038*
Shelf7	0.476
Shelf8	0.889
Glasses	0.045*
Table	0.213
Clothes	0.125
Glass case1	0.620
Glass case2	0.912

(*continued*)

Table 5. (*continued*)

Showcase	p-value
Glass case3	0.033*
Glass case4	0.816
Glass case5	0.137
Hanging rack1	0.375
Hanging rack2	0.225
Shoes1	0.752
Shoes2	0.128

According to Table 4, there are no differences in t-test on the first floor. In the first floor, there is several kinds of products in one showcase. It is assumed that there were many subjects who looked at each showcase regardless of the scenario, thus it was difficult to make a difference. Therefore, to perform t-test at first floor, we need to analyze not showcases but products. According to Table 5, there are four differences of t-test between the showcases. There are sandals and boots in shelf3, handbags, shoulder bags and backpacks of new arrivals in shelf6, sunglasses in glasses, and wristwatch in glass case3. We considered that the difference of purchasing objectives significantly affected the results of the t-test.

Figures 3, 4, 5 and 6 show result of network analysis.

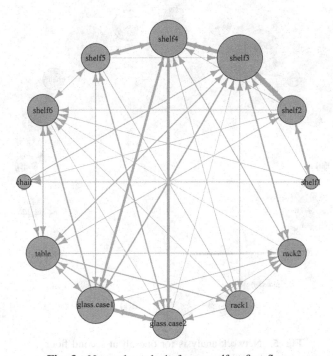

Fig. 3. Network analysis for oneself at first floor

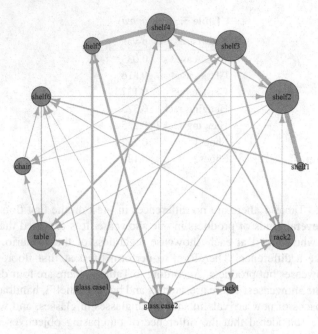

Fig. 4. Network analysis for other at first floor

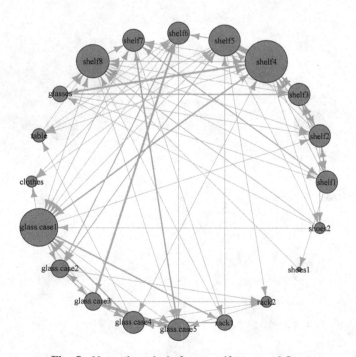

Fig. 5. Network analysis for oneself at second floor

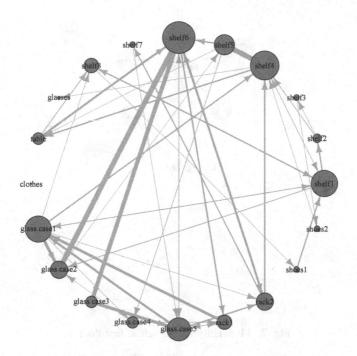

Fig. 6. Network analysis for other at second floor

According to Figs. 3 and 4, when we pay attention to the size of node, the size of shelf1 and chair is small, however the size of rack1 of Fig. 3 is bigger than Fig. 4. There are small shoulder bags in rack1, therefore, small shoulder bags are attracted attention from the scenario for oneself. Focusing on the thickness of the edge, it is different from the shelf that is the center depending on the scenario. It can be seen that shelf3 is seen in the scenario for oneself and glass case1 is seen in the scenario of others. It is easy to be seen bags for purchasing behavior for oneself and it is easy to be seen small items for purchasing behavior for others. According to Figs. 5 and 6, focusing on the size of the node, except for the characteristic showcases, which are shoes, clothes, and sunglasses, the size of the node is a similar size in the scenario for oneself. On the other hand, the difference between the showcases that is often seen and the showcase that is not seen is large in the scenario for others.

Figures 7, 8, 9 and 10 show the result of modularity. To grasp network formation, Figs. 11, 12, 13 and 14 show the result of modularity in layout at the store.

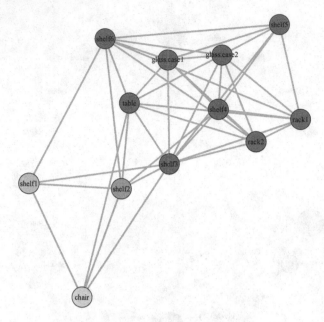

Fig. 7. Modularity for oneself at first floor

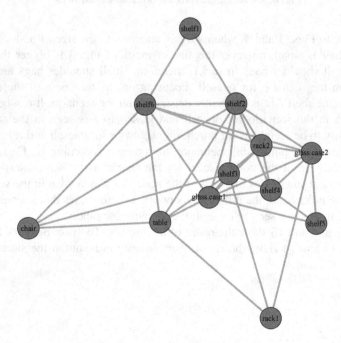

Fig. 8. Modularity for other at first floor

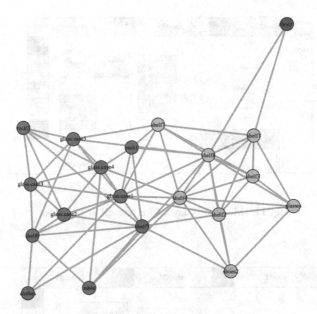

Fig. 9. Modularity for oneself at second floor

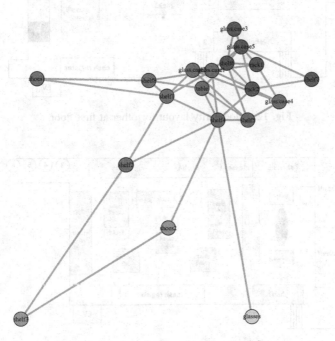

Fig. 10. Modularity for other at second floor

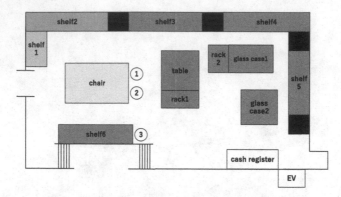

Fig. 11. Modularity layout for oneself at first floor

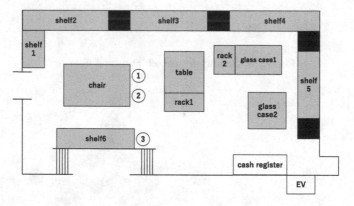

Fig. 12. Modularity layout for other at first floor

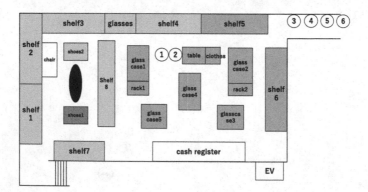

Fig. 13. Modularity layout for oneself at second floor

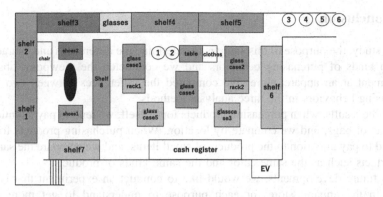

Fig. 14. Modularity layout for other at second floor

According to Figs. 7 and 11, the showcases were divided into several groups, however, the three showcases have separated by themselves. In addition, the showcases about Figs. 8 and 12 were not divided into groups belonging to the same community. As the reason for this, there were several kinds of products in one showcase, thus there were many kinds of elements when the showcases on the first floor were divided. Therefore, we need to divide groups by the products, not by the showcases on the first floor. When we compared Figs. 9 and 10, we understood the differences on how to divide these showcases. According to Figs. 9 and 13, the place of the showcases was the important element to perform clustering because the green group has the showcases on the left side when viewed from stairs and the light blue group has the showcases on the right. According to Figs. 10 and 14, what has the products in the showcase is the important element to perform clustering because the showcases which have sandals and sunglasses were independent. In addition, the green group has wristwatches and shoulder bags and the orange group has small articles, accessories, sneakers and small handbags.

5.5 Layout Improvement Plan

Before the customers see and purchase more products, the impact of the appearance of the products is also important, but the right approach to buying is so important. For that reason, it is necessary to improve the layout of products and the customer service methods in accordance with the guidelines of the store. When considering the actual situation of a store, we suggest the improvement plan at the store from the result of analysis as follows. When purchasing products for oneself, we tend to compare by location. Therefore, it is effective to arrange products so that they can see more types of products. As a method, we place products that are easy to choose by situation for oneself, such as bags, and with the eye-catching products, torrent products, and new products in the same space. When purchasing products for others, we compare by the same kinds of products such as the same color and the same kinds of products. Therefore, to make it easier for customers to compare products, it is better to place small items that are easy to select in the same space.

6   Conclusion

In this study, the purpose of this study is to determine the differences and characteristics of two kinds of purchasing behaviors and we conducted the viewpoint observation experiment at an apparel store. We compared the differences between two kinds of purchasing behaviors in the three analysis methods.

As the results, when purchasing products for oneself, we tend to pay attention to the products of bags, and we compare by location. When purchasing products for others, we tend to pay attention to the products of small items, and we compare the same kinds of products such as the same color and the same kinds of products.

As future developments, we would like to conduct an experiment that is a simulation in the apparel store for each purpose to understand to get more products effectivity.

Acknowledgment. We thank the target store for this study, employees of this store and participants of this experiment for providing experimental opportunity. This work was supported by JSPS KAKENHI Grant Number 19K01945 and 17K13809.

References

1. Miyazawa, K.: Consumer behavior from relationship with others. Jpn. Market. J. **33**(4), 131–142 (2014). (in Japanese)
2. Saijo, N., Tosu, T., Morimura, K., Otake, K., Namatame, T.: Evaluation of store layout using eye tracking data in fashion brand store. In: SCSM 2018: Social Computing and Social Media. User Experience and Behavior, pp. 131–145 (2018)
3. Tobii Pro Glasses 2 wearable eye tracker. https://www.tobiipro.com/product-listing/tobii-pro-glasses-2/
4. Tobii Pro Lab software. https://www.tobiipro.com/product-listing/tobii-pro-lab/
5. Arenas, A., Duch, J., Fernández, A., Gómez, S.: Size reduction of complex networks preserving modularity. New J. Phys. **9**(76), 1–15 (2007)

Analysis of Fashion Market Trend Using Advertising Data of Shopping Information Site

Retsuya Saito[1(✉)], Kohei Otake[2], and Takashi Namatame[3]

[1] Graduate School of Science and Engineering, Chuo University, 1-13-27,
Kasuga, Bunkyo-ku, Tokyo 112-8551, Japan
a16.hd5r@g.chuo-u.ac.jp
[2] Faculty of Science and Engineering, Tokai University, 2-3-23, Takanawa,
Minato-ku, Tokyo 108-8619, Japan
otake@tsc.u-tokai.ac.jp
[3] Faculty of Science and Engineering, Chuo University, 1-13-27, Kasuga,
Bunkyo-ku, Tokyo 112-8551, Japan
nama@indsys.chuo-u.ac.jp

Abstract. In recent years, consumer needs for products have been diversified, and companies need proper site management considering trends. As the needs of consumers diversified, it became difficult to grasp the needs. In this study, we analyzed diversifying customer needs by focusing on internet advertising. We classify it into a company's products by Doc2Vec using each shopping site documents to segment the market using word similarity in the fashion market and verify that a company can accurately identify the needs of consumers in fashion sites. Afterwards, we consider the impression tendency of sites with similar ones by using time-series clustering.

Keywords: Doc2Vec · Time series clustering · Fashion market

1 Introduction

Internet advertising was born around 1995, but at that time it was mainly advertising using mass media such as TV commercials and flyers due to not enough the internet usage environment, etc., and the effect of advertising on the internet reaching consumers was low. However, since around 2000, the use of the broadband internet in Japan has rapidly increased, and the internet usage rate has also rapidly increased. At the same time, internet advertising reaches consumers. At the end of 2002, Google launched the first search-based advertising service in Japan, and the internet advertising market grew significantly. Today, with the spread of PC and smartphone, the size of the internet advertising market is about 1/4 of the total advertising market in Japan. With the expansion of the internet market, customer needs have diversified, and the era has shifted from manufacturers to consumers.

One of the research fields using query logs accumulated in search engines is query clustering. It is possible to find frequent queries and related queries by clustering queries [1, 2]. As for how to determine the similarity between queries when clustering the queries, similarities from various viewpoints such as click-through logs and

© Springer Nature Switzerland AG 2020
G. Meiselwitz (Ed.): HCII 2020, LNCS 12195, pp. 389–400, 2020.
https://doi.org/10.1007/978-3-030-49576-3_28

synonyms have been proposed. However, there are few studies that focus on the temporal change of similarity. We consider that clustering that reflects temporal fluctuations over time will help to recognize trends in the market.

2 Purpose of This Study

As shown in the previous section, advertiser need to do internet advertising using query logs. In this study, we classify the advertisers in shopping information sites by considering the change of temporal trends and search queries. This analysis uses conversion data from internet search sites. The data includes 490 advertisers, from which to select for clustering. In particular, we use the data about fashion. In order to determine the market for a site based on the products being advertised, we use Google Shopping to find the most searched search queries on each site by using Doc2Vec [3] and the search results for analysis by DTW (Dynamic Time Warping) [4].

As own related study, we related previous studies. Motohashi, et al. showed a method for classifying the search query purpose by using the query log of Yahoo! Japan [5]. Comparing this study, we perform clustering based on each advertiser's search query, then clustering based on the impressions of them, and evaluate each cluster.

3 Dataset and Analysis Method

We use conversion data to segment advertisers by market. After that, the advertisers related to fashion are extracted from the conversion data. In addition, we classify the advertisers with similar impression shapes by time-series clustering. First, we summarize the items of data in Table 1.

Table 1. Data description

Data	Conversion data in the internet advertising
Duration of data	April,1, 2018 ~ March 31, 2019
Advertiser	490
Conversion data (total of 11, 126, 050)	Data about conversions per day per word • Advertiser (the name of the site that has been published) • Search query • Date (date searched) • Impression • Click • Conversion

3.1 Doc2Vec

We use Doc2Vec to segment each site's market from search queries. The structure of Doc2Vec consists of two layers, that are a hidden layer and an output layer. This is a simple neural network that obtain a distributed representation of words and finds the vector of the text itself by combining word vectors and paragraph vectors.

Doc2vec has two methods of logical structures, that are PV-DBOW (Distributed Bag-Of-Words) and PV-DM. In this study, we used PV-DBOW. This predicts the probability of words likely to be included in the document, ignoring the word order contained in the document.

We generate data from shopping information sites to categorize search queries. It is the data that all sentences of the merchandise from multiple sites outputted by each advertiser's search query are evaluated as one sentence, and classified by using the similarity between sentences. We narrowed down the results extracted from the search query to 8544 words based on the word frequency and the word count. In addition, we create that result from the 300-dimensional variance matrix.

3.2 Spherical Clustering

We classify multidimensional representations created by Doc2Vec using Spherical k-means [6] that is clustering method. This is used when measuring the distance by the angle between cases, not by Euclidean distance. We obtain similarity by taking a least-squares approximation of a linear subspace spanned by concept vectors as Eq. (1).

$$Q\left(\{\pi_j\}_{j=1}^k\right) = \sum_{j=1}^{K} \sum_{x \in \pi_j} x^T c_j \tag{1}$$

where, π_j is the jth cluster, c_j is the center of the cluster, and the centroid vector is normalized to size 1.

We seek a partitioning of the document vectors $x_1, x_2, \ldots, x_n$ into k disjoint clusters $\pi_1^*, \pi_2^*, \ldots, \pi_k^*$ that maximizes the objective equation in (1), that is, we seek a solution to the following maximization problem:

$$\left\{\pi_j^*\right\}_{j=1}^k = \arg\max Q\left(\{\pi_j\}_{j=1}^k\right) \tag{2}$$

we repeat the following equation in (3) to maximize (2) and determine the center of it.

$$mean\left(\pi_j^{t+1}\right) = \frac{\sum_{x \in \pi_j^{t+1}} x}{\left\|\sum_{x \in \pi_j^{t+1}} x\right\|} \tag{3}$$

In this study, we assumed the example as the site name and measured the similarity between the sites in terms of angles.

3.3 Dynamic Time Warping

In this study, we dealt with the daily sum of the impressions of queries searched on the shopping search site during the advertising period by each advertiser as time-series data. Also, we perform shape clustering based on time variation. We use DTW (Dynamic Time Warping) to classify the results of distance calculation between advertisers using k-means++ for time-series clustering. The DTW equation is shown as Eq. (4) and (5).

$$\delta(i,j) = \left| s_i - t_j \right| \tag{4}$$

where, $S = (s_1, s_2, \ldots, s_n)$ and $T = (t_1, t_2, \ldots, t_m)$ are time series data.

$$DTW(S, T) = \min_W \sum_{k=1}^{p} \delta(w_k) \tag{5}$$

where, $W = (w_1, w_2, \ldots, w_n)$ is a numerical value that is aligned to be the minimum distance between each element of S and T. In this study, we use a five-day moving average in order to use the impression trends due to time fluctuations, and standardized so that the average is 0 and the standard deviation is 1 in consideration of the maximum amount of advertising between the advertiser. Also, we target 81 advertisers about fashion site that has been running for more than three months.

4 Results

In this section, first we show the result of the clustering of the site from data of shopping information site. We further classify the clusters as fashion clusters based on the clustering results. Then, we compare these clustering results.

4.1 Result of Clustering of Site

First, we classify the market by the words that are characteristic words of each advertiser from the search results of shopping information sites. As a result, we classify the advertisers into four clusters and summarize the parameters for each cluster in Table 2.

Table 2. Market clustering

Cluster no.	1	2	3	4
Imps	16,665,395	41,396,643	32,574,015	9,396,603
Click	473,933	1,068,266	10,622,613	277,823
CV	5,032	5,501	7,678	3,862
CTR	5.44%	4.69%	4.60%	5.19%
CVR	0.81%	0.54%	0.68%	1.04%
Period	105 day	94.1 day	107 day	98 day
Adb	98	186	158	48

"Imps" is the total impressions of each cluster, and "Click" and "CV" mean the total number in the same way. "CTR" is the average value of the total clicks per day for each advertiser divided by the total Impression. "CVR" is the average value of the total CV per day for each advertiser divided by the total Click. "Period" is the average advertising period of the advertiser in each cluster. "Adb" is the total number of advertisers in each cluster.

We classify cluster 1 as "food", cluster 2 as "fashion", cluster 3 as "life goods", and cluster 4 as "beauty and health" from the characteristic words of the classified advertisers. Table 2 shows a difference in the number of advertisers. In addition, there is no difference in the advertising period, and it is approximately 100 days. Also, Table 2 cluster 1 has the highest average CTR and cluster 4 has the highest average CVR.

Table 3 shows the number of impressions per advertiser.

Table 3. Impressions per day by advertiser in each market cluster

Cluster no.	1	2	3	4
Ave-imps	1619.6	2365.2	1926.8	1997.6

"Ave-imps" shows impressions per day by the advertiser in each cluster.

Table 3 shows that cluster 2 has the highest number of impressions per advertiser. The results show that the consumers in cluster 2 are active in internet advertising. Therefore, we will further analyze cluster 2 which is the highest penetration rate in internet advertising.

After that, we focus on cluster 2 and perform the analysis. Cluster 2 which is regarded as the fashion site to be focused is further classified because it is considered that there is a difference in conversion and the like depending on the product being handle. As a result of clustering, we classify into 11 clusters in Table 4 and Table 5.

Table 4. Fashion site clustering (1)

Cluster no.	1	2	3	4	5	6
Imps	5,373,254	3,619,093	3,455,824	2,666,903	3,327,619	2,048,011
Click	155608	87189	82412	50173	102113	42122
CV	974	244	356	202	580	337
CTR	6.04%	4.95%	2.88%	5.92%	4.99%	3.09%
CVR	0.44%	0.39%	0.66%	0.39%	0.44%	0.46%
Period	87.2 day	88.4 day	109.1 day	91.1 day	92.1 day	91.9 day
Adb	25	19	15	18	17	13

Table 5. Fashion site clustering (2)

Cluster no.	7	8	9	10	11
Imps	5,555,013	3,239,200	2,825,497	5,113,809	4,163,737
Click	159,931	53,329	81,441	160,836	92,901
CV	638	208	388	770	803
CTR	4.09%	3.41%	3.72%	3.30%	7.10%
CVR	0.67%	0.58%	0.57%	0.57%	0.83%
Period	109 day	93.6 day	82.1 day	120.5 day	75.3 day
Adb	20	16	10	15	18

Tables 4 and 5 show that there is difference in the advertising period and cluster 11 has the highest average CTR and average CVR. Cluster10 has the longest advertising period, and cluster 11 has the shortest advertising period. Since we classify only one search query for each site, the effect of one product greatly affects the clustering results. Therefore, we classify the clustering results into 4 genres and consider them.

Table 6 shows the results of classifying 11 clusters classified by documents vector into 4 genres.

Table 6. Contents of fashion site cluster

Cluster no.	Contents	Genres
1	Clothing	Clothing
2	Coat	Clothing
3	Watches & shoes	Accessory
4	Jewelry (1)	Jewelry
5	Wallets and small articles	Accessory
6	Jewelry (2)	Jewelry
7	Bag	Accessory
8	Tie lower & body clothing	Clothing
9	Tortoiseshell accessories	Accessory
10	Functional items	Outdoor
11	Women's clothing	Clothing

So, we classify the advertisers into 4 genres and summarize the parameters for each cluster in Table 7.

Table 7. Genres clustering

Genre	Clothing	Accessory	Jewelry	Outdoor
Imps	16,395,284	15,163,953	4,714,914	5,113,809
Click	389027	425897	92295	160836
CV	2229	1962	539	770
CTR	5.48%	3.99%	4.73%	3.30%
CVR	0.54%	0.59%	0.42%	0.57%
Period	86.1 day	100.3 day	91.4 day	120.5 day
Adb	78	61	31	15

"Clothing" has the highest impressions followed by "Accessory" and that "Accessory" with fewer impressions than "Clothing" has more clicks than "Clothing". It can be seen that "Clothing" has the highest CTR and "Accessory" has the highest CVR. It can be seen that "Outdoor" has the highest CVR after "Accessory", and the average advertising period is more than 20 days higher than other genres.

We show impressions per advertiser by genre in Table 8.

Table 8. Impression per day by advertiser in each genre

Genres	Clothing	Accessory	Jewelry	Outdoor
Ave-imp	2440.6	2655.6	1655.0	2829.2

Table 8 shows that "Outdoor" has the highest number of impressions per publisher. The results show that the consumers in "Outdoor" are active in internet advertising. On the other hand, the average number of impressions for "Jewelry" is low. It is presumed that this is because jewelry is an expensive item, and generally expensive items are picked up and confirmed before making a purchasing decision.

4.2   Results of Time Series Clustering of Site

In this study, we handle the data obtained by summing the impressions of the terms searched on the shopping search site during the advertising period of each advertiser on a daily basis as time-series data. In addition, in order to perform shape clustering based on temporal fluctuation, we analyzed 81 advertisers whose cluster 2 classified as "fashion" in the previous section had an advertising period of more than 3 months. We use DTW to classify companies with similar impression shapes. We use a five-day moving average to account for small fluctuations in impressions. Also, we standardize the impressions of each advertiser so that the average is 0 and the variance is 1.

Now, we classify the advertiser's impressions into four clusters in Fig. 1.

Figure 1 shows the changes in impressions of companies classified by impression shape and the number of days to be placed on the x-axis and the impression value on the y-axis.

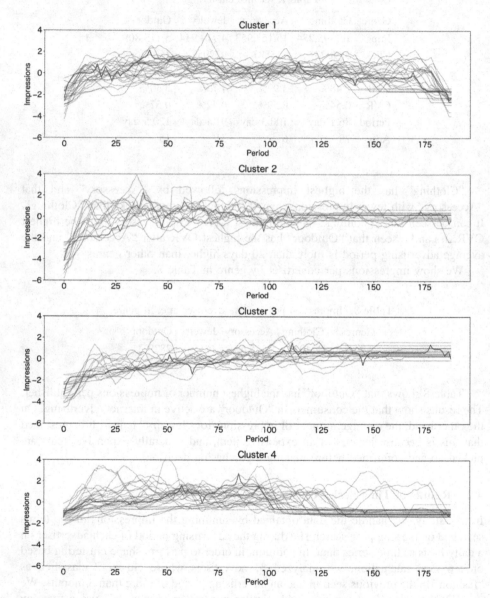

Fig. 1. Time series clustering of impressions

From the results in Fig. 1, we see that cluster 1 is a cluster with constant fluctuations of impressions, clusters 2 and 4 are clusters whose impressions raised in one season, and cluster 3 is that the impressions gradually rise with time. We see that in clusters 2 and 4, which have similar impression trends, cluster 2 has a faster rise in impressions than cluster 4.

Also, we summarize the parameters for each time series cluster in Table 9.

Table 9. Time series clustering

Cluster no.	1	2	3	4
Imps	14,906,022	6,283,388	5,514,259	5,939,732
Click	390,286	181,609	138,972	156,685
CV	1,814	933	908	753
CTR	2.95%	2.92%	3.62%	3.18%
CVR	0.58%	0.68%	0.67%	0.46%
Period	220.3 day	141.5 day	130.4 day	131.5 day
Adb	24	15	16	26

There is a difference of more than 90 days in the average advertising period. Cluster1 has the longest advertising period, and cluster 3 has the shortest advertising period. Also, we see that cluster 3 has the highest average CTR and cluster 2 has the highest average CVR. It is considered that cluster 1 has the highest impression, and the needs of consumers are accurately grasped.

5 Discussion

First, we discuss market clustering. From the results in Table 3, we consider that the fashion cluster is the most popular EC and the food cluster is not. One of the reasons that the EC of food cluster is not popular is that unlike fashion and household goods, there is no renewed trend, so it is difficult to operate on a basis other than the existing market base. From these facts, we analyze fashion clusters where consumers are agile with trends and EC is considered to be the most popular.

From the results in Table 6, we see that the fashion clusters are classified into 11 clusters and 4 genres. From the results in Table 8, we see that outdoor, which we can compare by functionality, not appearance, have the highest number of impressions per advertiser. We consider that expensive items such as jewelry still tend to be decided at the physical store after seeing the physical object.

Second, we consider time-series clustering. As a result of time-series clustering, we classify the advertisers into four clusters. We show the average value of impressions in each cluster in Fig. 2.

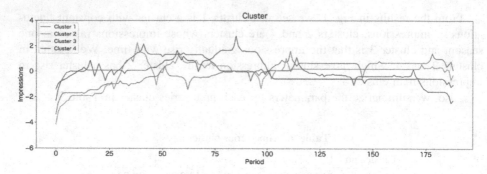

Fig. 2. Average impressions by time series cluster

In cluster 1, the width of the top and bottom of the impression is small, and the advertising period is long. In cluster 2, the impressions increased substantially on the 30th day of publication and remained at a high level. In cluster 3, the impressions gradually increased until the 100th day. In cluster 4, the impressions increased significantly once about the 90th day, but the impressions fluctuate temporarily. As for the tendency of impressions, it is better that the width of the top and bottom is small, and it is considered that this is an advertiser that stably captures consumer needs. We show the impressions per advertiser in Table 10.

Table 10. Impression per day by advertiser in each time series cluster

Cluster no.	1	2	3	4
Ave-imps	2819.27	2960.37	2642.95	1737.27

We see that cluster 2 has the highest number of impressions per publisher, followed by cluster 1. We see that cluster 4 has the lowest number of impressions per day, and cluster 3 has the second-lowest number of impressions, indicating that a cluster with a slower rise in impressions has a lower impression per advertiser.

Finally, we compare whether the genre influences the time-series cluster by comparing the inclusion rate of the fashion cluster for each time-series cluster. We show the inclusion rate of the fashion genre by time-series cluster in Table 11.

Table 11. Inclusion rate of fashion genre by time series cluster

		Time cluster no.			
		1	2	3	4
Fashion site genres	Clothing	29.17%	53.33%	37.50%	38.46%
	Accessory	45.84%	20.01%	50.00%	38.46%
	Jewelry	20.83%	6.67%	6.25%	19.23%
	Outdoor	4.17%	20.00%	6.25%	3.85%

We see that clusters 1 and 3 have the highest inclusion rate of accessory sites, cluster 2 has the highest inclusion rate of clothes, and cluster 4 has the highest rate of inclusion of accessories and clothes from Table 11. We also see that the total inclusion rate of clothes and accessories in all clusters exceeds 70%.

We consider that cluster 2 has a higher outdoor site inclusion rate than other clusters and, as can be seen from Table 8 of Sect. 4.1, outdoor have the highest average impressions, which is probably due to the higher average impression of cluster 2 in Table 10. Also, we compare cluster 1 and cluster 4 with low outdoor. We see from Table 10 that cluster 1 differs from cluster 4 in average impressions by more than 1,000 days, despite almost similar outdoor site inclusion rate. From these facts, we consider that not only the difference in the inclusion rate but also the ability to capture the needs of consumers affects the difference in impressions.

6 Conclusion

We classified the advertisers from the search results of the search queries by using the search queries most frequently searched during the advertising period as the feature words. As a result of clustering, we classified the advertisers into four clusters, one of which was further classified into eleven clusters and genres as fashion clusters.

We classified advertisers not only by search queries, but also by the change in impressions. As a result of the time-series clustering, we classified it into four clusters. There was a difference between the parameters of the time-series clusters and outdoor site inclusion rate was affecting time series clusters. Also, we saw that comparing the time-series clusters with similar inclusion ratios of the fashion clusters affected customer needs.

As for the future prospects, it is desirable to increase the number of advertisers and the advertising period, and to study not only the shape of impressions but also the timing of publication.

Acknowledgment. We thank Feedforce Inc. for permission to use valuable datasets and for useful comments. This work was supported by JSPS KAKENHI Grant Number 19K01945 and 17K13809.

References

1. Kida, T., Toyoda, M., Kitsuregawa, M.: A method for clustering search queries by changes in trends. DBSJ J. **9**(1), 12–17 (2010)
2. Wen, J., Nie, J., Zhang, H.: Clustering user queries of a search engine. In: Proceedings of the 10th International Conference on World Wide Web, pp. 162–168 (2001)
3. Le, Q.V., Mikolov, T.: Distributed representations of sentences and documents. In: Proceedings of the 31st International Conference on Machine Learning, pp. 1188–1196 (2014)
4. Banerjee, A., Dhillon, I.S., Ghosh, J., Sra, S.: Clustering on the unit hypersphere using von mises-fisher distributions. J. Mach. Learn. Res. **6**, 1345–1382 (2005)

5. Motohashi, E., Isozaki, N., Nagao, H., Higuchi, T.: CTR prediction of internet advertising using state space model. Commun. Oper. Res. Soc. Jpn. **57**(10), 574–583 (2012)
6. Berndt, D.J., Clifford, J.: Using dynamic time warping to find patterns in time series. In: AAAI Technical Report WS-94–03, pp. 359–370 (1994)

The Power of Social Media Marketing on Young Consumers' Travel-Related Co-creation Behavior

Farzana Sharmin[✉] and Mohammad Tipu Sultan

Shanghai Jiao Tong University, Shanghai 200240, China
sharminf@sjtu.edu.cn

Abstract. The extensive advancement of information technology, travel-related content creation is largely influenced by the use of social media. Travel-related social media (TSM) users do not only accept products and services but also participate in the operation process and play central roles in strengthening the creating value. Young consumers' have a more dynamic relationship with social media technology, which is tapping into innovative creation behavior. While very few studies have focused on social media marketing activities in terms of co-creation value. With this realization, the aim of this study is to investigate the effects of social media marketing activities to examine the travel-related co-creation intention of young consumers. To empirically test the hypothetical model, this study conducted a paper-based survey on 365 young social media users from China for data analysis. The analytical results of structural equation modeling indicated that social media marketing activities have a positive significant effect on towards travel-related co-creation intention through the mediating effect of perceived satisfaction. Finally, the implications based on the empirical results of this study are provided as references for the improvement of social media marketing activities to promote the co-creation behavior.

Keywords: China · Co-creation · Intention · Perceived satisfaction · Social media marketing activities (SMMA)

1 Introduction

The rapid growth of dimensions in social media (e.g., social networking sites, weblogs, photo & video sharing, and virtual communities), consumers are engaging in interaction and communication. Consumers' have a more dynamic relationship with this platform, which is tapping into innovative travel marketing dimensions and changing consumers' interpersonal message [1]. Social media has been dramatically changing the relationships between individuals, firms, and societies [1, 2]. Adoption of social media applications has been reportedly rapid and impacts on daily life and other emerging industry. In the tourism sector, social media technology reflects individual engagement which may influence travel marketers to better understand consumers interaction behavior. Given the importance of travel-related marketing activity, consumers have focused on co-creation experiences and outcomes [3–5]. Therefore, it is important to take account of social media marketing activities for travel-related

© Springer Nature Switzerland AG 2020
G. Meiselwitz (Ed.): HCII 2020, LNCS 12195, pp. 401–414, 2020.
https://doi.org/10.1007/978-3-030-49576-3_29

co-creation intention. There were few studies analyzed the conditions of facilitating customer cocreation in a computer-mediated environment. To address these research gaps, we have applied the concept of social media marketing activities (SMMA) [6] to identify consumers satisfaction to participate and co-create about travel-related information through social media.

The variety of social media sites include Facebook, LinkedIn, Google + (social networking sites), Twitter (a microblogging site), Youtube (a video site), Instagram and Flickr (photo sharing sites), Wordpress (a blog), Microsoft MSDN (a forum), and WhatsApp (a messaging app) have been popular and emerging for the real-time interaction dimension [6–9]. In China, the top three social media platforms are owned by Tencent: Wechat with 1.15 million monthly active users, QQ with 803 million active users, and Youku with 580 million active users [10]. Similar to other counterparts, Chinese social media users can share their views, comments, photos, and videos with fellow users regarding their experiences with different kinds of services and products, ranging from a bus ride to the purchase of an apartment [8, 11, 12].

This study mostly focused on Chinese social media, which has the advantage of a promotion, advertisements or marketing facilities over traditional tools in terms of speed, flexibility, transaction, reading, and tracking events in real-time. Accordingly, the objectives of the paper are two main focused. First, we examine the most influential attributes (entertainment, interaction, trendiness, customization, word-of-mouth) from social media marketing activities (SMMA) which create young consumers satisfaction towards social media. Finally, we investigate individuals' intention to co-create with Chinese social media for travel purposes. To select young consumers from China (18 to 36 years old), who grew up with the internet and mobile phones, and are therefore referred to as the Net-Wired Generation or Digital Natives [8, 11, 12].

2 Literature Review and Hypotheses Formulation

2.1 Social Media Marketing Activities (SMMA)

Social media marketing activities (SMMA), as a vital part in the process of commercial activities [6], which aim to facilitate interactions, collaborations and the sharing of content [12–14]. The research about travel marketing through any kind of social media pointed out the community marketing campaigns of products or services. The marketing factors (e.g., entertainment, interaction, trendiness, customization and word-of-mouth), produce significant impacts on customers' brand equity [2, 15].

Understanding an individual's perceptions of social media marketing can prime to create a vital role towards involvement. A large part of the global population is now connected to social media to share their ideas, exchange information, interaction with online communities, sharing news, as an overall entertainment [8, 14, 16]. This poses a distinct challenge for online destination managers', because of the most up-to-date news and information thereby making it a tool to search for the most practical products or purchase. Some scholars argued that many destination organizations using social media as a collective of tactics such as by developing social presence, tweeting links, posting videos, and doing few promotions without a proper understanding on consumers behavior [12, 13]. However, there is still a gap between social media marketing features and consumers co-creation behavior.

2.2 Entertainment

Entertainment refers to the way of fun and plays emerging from social media for entertaining and escaping pressure [6]. According to the model proposed by [17], entertainment, measured by receiving and disseminating any kind of message, whether commercial or general information. In particular social networking sites (e.g. Facebook, WeChat), active members receive a product message and attempt to attach their own views and interest to conduct with social affiliation, enjoyment and positive attitude towards it [1, 8]. Consumers actively choose social media to satisfy their specific needs rather than passively obtain information, which creates a gratification and social media-based brand connection [18, 19]. Based on the SMMA, we postulated:

H1. Entertainment has a positive significant effect on consumers' satisfaction towards social media use.

2.3 Interaction

Social interaction through networking sites is fundamentally changing communication between products, services and customers [8]. Users can easily discover information about opening hours, offers and customer communications from their network [20, 21]. The current research focused on interaction to examine individuals interface with social media to create travel-related content as other literature has given priority [15, 19]. Such interaction makes them feel more socially connected, increases the chance that others can weigh in, satisfy their needs and puts more focus on participation and co-creation intention [22, 23]. Therefore we proposed:

H2. Interaction has a positive significant effect on consumers' satisfaction towards social media use.

2.4 Trendiness

In accordance with [19, 24], trendy information on social media covers four sub motivations: surveillance, knowledge, prepurchase information, and inspiration. Surveillance describes observing, and remaining updated about, one's social environment. It has to change consumers trends towards social media acceptance for tourism products and follow the advertisements [2, 18, 25]. Because, social media provide the latest news, hot discussion topics, and are also core product search channels [26–28]. Therefore, this study hypothesizes trendiness as an influential attribute to cope-up with new trends which derived by the customer acceptance behavior. Moreover, individuals follow the most up-to-date information while the purpose of travel product, place and services. Thus we proposed:

H3. Trendiness has a positive significant effect on consumers' satisfaction towards social media use.

2.5   Customization

In accordance with customization, it refers to the degree by which a service is customized and made satisfy the users [29]. According to [30], a customized message targets a specific person or a small audience (e.g. Facebook posts) and a broadcast message target anyone who is interested (e.g. Twitter tweets). Most of the marketer's and service providers, nowadays to connect with the social media community (e.g. Burberry and Gucci) to make significant use of their online presence. To sending any personalized messages to individual customers, enabling them to customize and design their own products [6, 12, 19]. Thus this study proposed the following hypothesis:

H4. Customization has a positive significant effect on consumers' satisfaction towards social media use.

2.6   Word-of-Mouth (WoM)

Social media and word-of-mouth have been recognized as a dominant factor in shaping consumer recommendation behavior [31]. Social media associate electronic word-of-mouth (e-WOM) with online consumer-to-consumer interactions and exchange of product or service evaluations among people who meet, talk, and text each other in the virtual world [2, 32, 33]. Previous literature mostly focused on e-WOM utilization behavior of individuals as it has higher credibility, empathy, and relevance. In contrast, word-of-mouth has a higher satisfaction and significantly influenced by the perceptions of interactional marketing features [6, 34]. Thus we proposed:

H5. e-Word of mouth has a positive significant effect on consumers' satisfaction towards social media use.

2.7   Consumers' Satisfaction and Behavioral Intention

In accordance with the expectation confirmation theory (ECT), satisfaction refers to a customer's expectation for any service to which users pleased these expectations [35]. In the context of social media marketing activities, consumers mostly depend on systems applications and prefer sustainable support [36–38]. On the other side, the more difficulty occurs the less satisfaction and usage intention. Tourism marketers consider managing travel marketing activities through social media to operate and increasing users' intention. In this study, two kinds of intention, participation and co-creation, therefore, represents the individual's subjective probability to follow the social media marketing activities in terms of travel-related attitude toward a given object or behavior [39–42]. In this vein, if users have a high dependency on the marketing information, they are expected to proactively and positively spend more time and energy using social media services to increase feelings of possession [43]. Thus the following hypotheses have formulated:

H6. Consumers' perceived satisfaction towards social media marketing activities has positive significant effects on participation intention.

H7. Consumers' perceived satisfaction towards social media marketing activities has positive significant effects on co-creation intention.

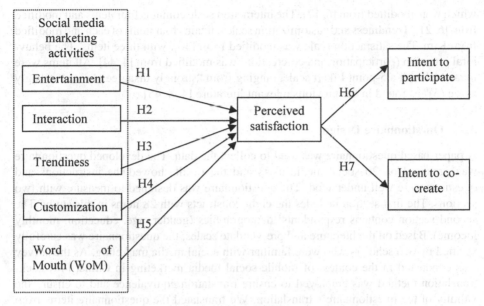

Fig. 1. The conceptual model

3 Research Methods

3.1 Sample and Procedure

The population of this study consists of Chinese young (age 18 to more than 30 years old) consumers, who sent out at least one message at their social media pages or groups during the last month (monthly active users). Moreover, who has been knowledge about travel marketing through social media. This requirement fits with active social media users. Second, this study surveyed only residents of Shanghai, China. Because this city has large commercial and financial centres by which attracts tourists to visit.

In addition, this study also selected young social media users as a sample, which enables us to investigate the users' interaction with social media to co-create their travel information. Moreover, students most likely are active social media applications than others [14, 27]. In light of these observations, we argue that using university students as a sample for data collection is an appropriate approach when the aim is to understand young consumers' participation and co-creation behavior. Previous studies have also shown that it may be reasonable to utilize and employ students as subjects.

3.2 Measures

The current research consists of eight constructs including entertainment, interaction, trendiness, customization, word-of-mouth, consumers' satisfaction, participation intention, and co-creation intention. The measurement of entertainment contains four items which were modified from [6, 17]. The interaction scale contains four items and modified from [6, 21]. Trendiness and customization scale contains four items of each and modified from Kim. The satisfaction scale was modified from [36], with three items. The behavioral intention (participation and co-creation) was modified from [4, 44]. All items were measured with a 5-point Likert scale, ranging from "strongly disagree (1)" to "strongly agree (5)" as found in the previous relevant literature [4, 8, 45].

3.3   Questionnaire Design

A paper-based questionnaire was used to collect the data. The developed questionnaire was pretested on 20 social media users and the result showed the instructions and questions were well understood. The questionnaire was designed to measure with two sections. The first section includes the eight constructs with 28 items in this study. The second section contains respondents' demographics (gender, age, education, monthly income). Based on the literature and pre-validate scales, the questionnaire was carefully verified by two scholars who were familiar with social media marketing. As the survey was conducted in the context of mobile social media marketing in China, [46] back-translation method was employed to ensure translation equivalence and to ensure the validity of the questionnaire's translation. We translated the questionnaire items from English into Chinese and proof examined by two native speakers to ensure the consistency of the content [4, 47, 48]. Then invited another experienced researcher to translate the items from Chinese back into English. This procedure reduces any discrepancies in the questionnaire items.

3.4   Data Collection

The probability multistage cluster sampling technique used. In the first stage, four universities from Shanghai (two Chinese leagues and two normal) were randomly selected using a random number generator from the list of universities available at the Shanghai education website. In the next step, the study program from an undergraduate to a doctoral degree was purposively selected. This program had the probability of providing different age groups as well as different maturity levels of the respondents. In the following stage, two schools were randomly selected from each university.

At first, respondents were asked to answer two screening questions: (1) Are you a monthly active user of social media? (2) Do you follow any travel-related marketing activities on social media? (3) Have you ever participated, posted, and created any travel information on social media? Who ensured these answers we proceed for the rest of the questionnaires. 450 hard copies of the questionnaire distributed. In the end, 400 responses were returned, representing an 89% response rate. Finally, a total of 365 responses was considered during analysis, after removing incomplete responses the valid percentage is 91%. Regarding the sample size, it was suggested that there should be a minimum of 10 cases per parameter or items required in statistical analysis [49].

So, a minimum of 280 responses was required as the study has 28 items (eight constructs). The IBM SPSS V. 23.0 statistical software was used to encode the questionnaire data and carry out descriptive statistics analysis on the collected data.

3.5 Data Analysis

In this study, the two-step procedure (CFA-SEM) suggested by [50] have followed to make the results more significant. At first, confirmatory factor analysis (CFA) was conducted using AMOS V.21 to test a measurement theory based on the overall model fit, construct reliability and validity of the eight constructs (entertainment, interaction, trendiness, customization, word-of-mouth, consumers' satisfaction, participation intention, and co-creation intention). Second, AMOS V.21 was employed to test the structural equation modeling (SEM) and the model fit indices [51].

4 Results

4.1 Demographic Data

Among the 365 respondents, 60.9% of them were males and 39.1% were females. Their ages ranged from 18 to 34 years and above, 36.6% were aged between 18 and 25. The majority of respondents were bachelor or graduate degree (75.1%). 59.8% of the respondents spent more than 1 h on social media daily and 64% of them have been used for more than one year. 56.4% of the respondents' monthly expenditures were less than 2000 RMB and 75% had less than 100 friends on different social media.

4.2 Measurement Model

As shown in Table 1, the values of Cronbach's Alpha (α) exceed the threshold value of 0.7 [52]. Internal consistency was assessed by composite reliability (CR). All the CRs exceed the threshold value of 0.7 [51] indicating good reliability. Convergent validity was accessed by factor loadings, an average of variance extracted (AVE), and squared multiple correlations (SMC) [51, 53]. The factor loadings ranged from 0.72 to 0.96, which is greater than the threshold value of 0.7 [49]. The average variance extracted (AVE) for each construct exceeds 0.5 suggesting adequate convergence. The outcomes indicate that the AVE values of all constructs (diagonal elements in Table 2) exceed the squared correlations between any two constructs (off-diagonal elements in Table 2), which supports the discriminant validity. Furthermore, the square root of AVE for each construct exceeded the correlations between the given construct and other [53]. Hence, the discriminant validity of the instrument was supported.

Table 1. Results of measurement model: reliability and convergent validity test

Constructs	Items	Mean	SD	S.F.L.	S.E.	CR	AVE	Cronbach's alpha (α)
Entertainment (ENT)	ENT1	4.05	0.70	0.89	0.04	0.89	0.73	0.905
	ENT2	4.04	0.69	0.83	0.04			
	ENT3	4.06	0.71	0.85	0.04			
	ENT4	4.12	0.66	0.78	0.03			
Interaction (INT)	INT1	4.35	0.66	0.90	0.0	0.92	0.79	0.920
	INT2	4.34	0.64	0.90	0.03			
	INT4	4.34	0.64	0.88	0.03			
Trendiness (TRE)	TRE1	4.18	0.64	0.83	0.03	0.88	0.72	0.880
	TRE2	4.27	0.64	0.81	0.03			
	TRE4	4.23	0.64	0.91	0.03			
Customization (CUS)	CUS1	3.82	0.81	0.80	0.04	0.87	0.70	0.923
	CUS2	3.86	0.84	0.88	0.04			
	CUS3	3.78	0.81	0.84	0.0			
	CUS4	3.87	0.82	0.86				
Word-of-Mouth (WoM)	WoM1	4.25	0.63	0.89	0.03	0.88	0.72	0.893
	WoM2	4.22	0.65	0.85	0.03			
	WoM3	4.24	0.68	0.81	0.03			
	WoM4	4.18	0.66	0.74	0.03			
Satisfaction (SAT)	SAT1	4.20	0.66	0.75	0.04	0.78	0.74	0.889
	SAT2	4.17	0.63	0.74	0.04			
	SAT3	4.16	0.63	0.72	0.04			
Participate intention (PI)	PI1	4.18	0.67	0.81	0.03	0.89	0.75	0.890
	PI2	4.20	0.65	0.96	0.03			
	PI3	4.14	0.67	0.82	0.03			
Co-creation intention (CoI)	CoI1	4.35	0.61	0.87	0.03	0.90	0.76	0.898
	CoI2	4.24	0.63	0.86	0.03			
	CoI3	4.30	0.62	0.87	0.03			

Note: SD = Standard Deviation; S.F.L. = Standardized Factor Loading; S.E. = Standard Error; CR = Composite Reliability; AVE = Average Variance Extracted.

Table 2. Results of discriminant validity.

	Constructs	1	2	3	4	5	6	7	8
1	Entertainment	***							
2	Interaction	.473**	**.88**						
3	Trendiness	.425**	.495**	**.84**					
4	Customization	.417**	.417**	.444**	**.83**				
5	Word of Mouth	.476**	.451**	.417**	.453**	**.84**			
6	Satisfaction	.505**	.492**	.600**	.475**	.478**	**.73**		
7	Participation intention	.403**	.453**	.379**	.365**	.445**	.355**	**.86**	
8	Co-creation intention	.409**	.478**	.448**	.324**	.412**	.432**	.468**	**.86**

Notes: 1. The square roots of AVE are shown on the diagonal of the matrix.
2. **denotes $p < .01$.

4.3 Structural Model

After all the variables in the measurement model were found to satisfy the specific threshold in the reliability and validity tests, the research hypotheses in the structural model were further examined [49]. AMOS V.21 was employed to test the structural model and the model fit indices ($\chi 2$ = 560.009; degree of freedom = 305; probability level = 0.000). The results showed that goodness of fit statistics of the theoretical framework indicates a good fit, as it lies in the satisfactory edge ($\chi 2$ = 560.009, $\chi 2/df$ = 1.836, Goodness of Fit index (GFI) = .900, Adjusted Goodness of fit index (AGFI) = .876, Tucker-Lewis Index (TLI) = .959, Comparative Fit Index (CFI) = .965, Incremental Fit Index (IFI) = .965, Root Mean Square Error of Approximation (RMSEA) = .048). The observed value of AGFI was .878 that exceeds the cut-off level of .8 [54]. This outcome represents a good data fit the proposed theoretical framework for consumers intention to co-creation (Fig. 1). Then this study evaluated the structural model to examine the hypothesized relationships. The outcomes show the standardized path coefficients are statistically significant supporting the proposed hypotheses.

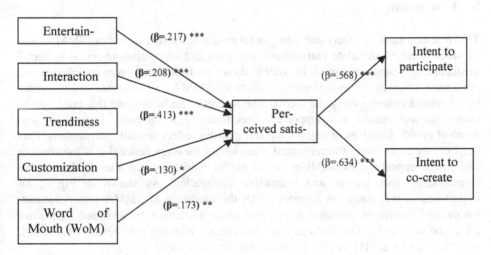

Fig. 2. Model testing results *Notes.* ***$p < 0.001$; **$p < 0.01$; *$p < 0.05$

4.4 Hypotheses' Testing

Figure 2 presents the result of the structural model analysis, including the R2, standardized path coefficients p-values, and t-values for all hypothesized relationships. Entertainment (β = 0.217***, p < 0.001, t = 4.774), interaction (β = 0.208***, p < 0.001, t = 4.774), trendiness (β = 0.413***, p < 0.001, t = 4.774), customization (β = 0.130*, p < 0.001, t = 4.774), and word-of-mouth (β = 0.173**, p < 0.001, t = 4.774) are found to have a significant, positive effect on satisfaction, indicating they are important predictors of satisfaction. Thus, hypotheses 1–5 are statistically validated. Moreover, perceived satisfaction (β = 0.568***, p < 0.001, t = 4.774); significantly influence positive intention towards participation (β = 0.634***, p < 0.001, t = 4.774); and co-creation intention ($\beta = 0.44^{***}$, p < 0.001, t = 4.774). Hence, hypotheses 6 and 7 are statistically supported. Figure 2 and Table 3 show the outcomes of hypotheses testing and path coefficients.

Table 3. Summary of hypotheses' testing results.

Hypothesis	Path	β-value	t-value	Result
H1	Entertainment → perceived satisfaction	.217	4.001	Supported
H2	Interaction → perceived satisfaction	.208	3.823	Supported
H3	Trendiness → perceived satisfaction	.413	7.245	Supported
H4	Customization → perceived satisfaction	.130	2.526	Supported
H5	Word of mouth → perceived satisfaction	.173	3.229	Supported
H6	Perceived satisfaction → intention to participate	.568	9.250	Supported
H7	Perceived satisfaction → intention to co-create	.634	10.485	Supported

5 Discussion

This research aims to understand what social media marketing activities (SMMA) and satisfaction might stimulate participation intention and co-creation intention in social media among young consumers. In order to do so, we formulated seven hypotheses and conducted a survey to understand the effects of SMMA to participate and co-create travel-related contents on social media. The research results indicate that our hypothesized research model was supported. Specifically, entertainment, interaction, and word-of-mouth found most significant and positive effect towards satisfaction. Participants are more likely to understand a marketing message better if it is informative and image appealing. In addition, social media marketing activities facilitated the formation of participation and interactive co-creation. As shown in Fig. 2, all hypotheses of this study are supported. All the attributes of SMMA (entertainment, interaction, trendiness, customization, word-of-mouth), have positive and significant effects on satisfaction. Our findings were consistency with this prior research [2, 4, 12], and the hypotheses (H1 to H7) are supported in this study.

6 Implications

This study makes several contributions to the academic world. First, the concept of SMMA was applied to examine Chinese young consumers' behavioral intention to participate and co-create about travel-related contents. Second, the dimensions of SMMA were mediated by consumers' satisfaction towards the use of social media. Finally, the findings of this study will provide important implications to helps understand consumers' usage intention of social media in different ways. So, travel firms on social media are advised to devote more resources and efforts to promote their products and services in other popular social media sites in China (e.g. Sina Weibo, QQ, QZone). Understanding such behavior is vital to increase the usefulness of this type of communication since online strategies can be adjusted to country-specific situations. In the Chinese context, young consumers' mostly prefer to share travel contents (pictures, videos, repost) within the groups rather than in a public forum [1, 8, 19]. Travel-related community operators are suggested to increase forum content and activities (e.g., rating, ranking, test reports for new products, sharing user experiences, as well as using a motivation system to increase member interaction) before social media marketing activities. Members can be invited to share the reasons they chose this travel services and products so that others are aware of other competitions.

7 Limitations and Future Research

Although this study has produced meaningful results, there are limitations to what can be accomplished in a single study. First, the research model tested in this study has been empirically assessed not only one particular adoption of social media. Thus, the comparison and rationality of the results of this study is not known. Future research should apply and test the research model to compare other social media adoption contexts (e.g., Sina Weibo, Renren, WeChat). Second, China has a culture that emphasizes collectivism, which may affect e-WOM, one of the antecedents of SMMA, more than in other cultures. Future research may examine this research model in other cultures. Third, this study examines consumers' participation by focusing mainly on participation and co-creation intention, which both relate to user's engagement behavior. Future research may be extended to discuss extra-role behaviors such as recommendations. Finally, sample locations (Shanghai), sampling methods (cross-sectional), and sample size ($n = 365$) might be limited. Future studies may include more diversity of the samples (young versus mid-age), in which consumers will have different orientations and group behavior.

8 Conclusions

The current study was based on the concept of social media marketing activities (SMMA) which proposed by [6]. The purpose of this study was to examine the influencing factors of marketing activities through social media for co-creation about travel information. The empirical results of this study make two important conclusions and contributions. First, the effects of social media marketing activities have mostly gone overlooked in most studies on social media. This study confirmed that social media marketing activities have a significant effect on consumers' satisfaction, participation intention and co-creation intention about travel-related information. Thus, this model helps understand users' usage intention for social media and can help to maintain consumers' travel content creation behavior.

In today's world, with its fast-developing information technology, social media marketing is an alternative to paper-based marketing or other types of promotional media. Reading travel information in social media is a part of the participation, engagement and further to co-create. As discussed above, our results provide strong support for the effect of social media marketing on the relationship between technology acceptance towards co-creation intention. However, these results may reflect an individual attitude towards the role of social media marketing, other social media platform (Sina Weibo, Youku, Duokan etc.) in China could be more influential for other emerging markets.

References

1. Chang, Y.P., Zhu, D.H.: Undertanding social networking sites adoption in China: a comparison of pre-adoption and post-adoption. Comput. Hum. Behav. **27**(5), 1840–1848 (2011)
2. Chen, S., Lin, C.: Understanding the effect of social media marketing activities: the mediation of social identification, perceived value, and satisfaction. Technol. Forecast. Soc. Change **140**, 22–32 (2019)
3. Chen, Y.R.: Perceived values of branded mobile media, consumer engagement, business-consumer relationship quality and purchase intention: a study of WeChat in China. Public Relat. Rev. **43**(5), 945–954 (2017)
4. Cheung, M.F.Y., To, W.M.: Service co-creation in social media: an extension of the theory of planned behavior. Comput. Hum. Behav. **65**, 260–266 (2016)
5. Gretzel, U.: Consumer generated content - trends and implications for branding. E-Rev. Tour. Res. **4**(3), 9–11 (2006)
6. Kim, A.J., Ko, E.: Do social media marketing activities enhance customer equity? An empirical study of luxury fashion brand. J. Bus. Res. **65**(10), 1480–1486 (2012)
7. Huang, L., Mou, J., See-to, E.W.K., Kim, J.: Perceived value preferences for mobile marketing in China: a mixed method approach. J. Retail. Consum. Serv. **48**, 70–86 (2019)
8. Lien, C.H., Cao, Y.: Examining WeChat users' motivations, trust, attitudes, and positive word-of-mouth: Evidence from China. Comput. Hum. Behav. **41**, 104–111 (2014)
9. Kaplan, A.M., Haenlein, M.: Users of the world, unite! The challenges and opportunities of social media. Bus. Horiz. **53**(1), 59–68 (2010)
10. chinainternetwatch.com: Chinese social media (2020). https://www.chinainternetwatch.com/tag/social-media/. Accessed 10 Jan 2020
11. Li, Y., Yang, S., Zhang, S., Zhang, W.: Mobile social media use intention in emergencies among Gen Y in China: an integrative framework of gratifications, task-technology fit, and media dependency. Telemat. Inform. **42**, 101244 (2019)
12. Wang, W., Rui, R., Xiaojuan, C., Jifan, S.: Media or message, which is the king in social commerce?: an empirical study of participants' intention to repost marketing messages on social media. Comput. Hum. Behav. **93**, 176–191 (2019)
13. Shareef, M.A., Mukerji, B., Dwivedi, Y.K., Rana, N.P.: Social media marketing: comparative effect of advertisement sources. J. Retail. Consum. Serv. **46**, 58–69 (2019)
14. Lee, C.S., Ma, L.: News sharing in social media: the effect of gratifications and prior experience. Comput. Hum. Behav. **28**(2), 331–339 (2012)
15. Hudson, S., Thal, K.: The impact of social media on the consumer decision process: implications for tourism marketing. J. Travel Tour. Mark **30**, 150–160 (2013)
16. Tsang, M.M., Ho, S., Liang, T.: Consumer attitudes toward mobile advertising: an empirical study. Int. J. Electron. Commer. **8**(3), 65–78 (2004)
17. Ducoff, R.H.: Advertising value and advertising on the web. J. Advert. Res. **36**, 21–32 (1996)
18. Gao, Q., Feng, C.: Branding with social media: user gratifiations, usage patterns, and brand message content strategies. Comput. Hum. Behav. **63**, 868–890 (2016)

19. Godey, B., et al.: Social media marketing efforts of luxury brands: influence on brand equity and consumer behavior. J. Bus. Res. **69**(12), 5833–5841 (2016)
20. Choi, E.C., et al.: Social media marketing: applying the uses and gratifications theory in the hotel industry. J. Hosp. Mark. Manag. **25**(7), 771–796 (2016)
21. Fotiadis, A.K., Stylos, N.: The effects of online social networking on retail consumer dynamics in the attractions industry: the case of 'E-da'theme park, Taiwan. Technol. Forecast. Soc. Change **124**, 283–294 (2017)
22. Syed-ahmad, S.F., Murphy, J.: Social networking as a marketing tool: the case of a small australian company. J. Hosp. Mark. Manag. **19**, 700–716 (2010)
23. Wan, J., Lu, Y., Wang, B., Zhao, L.: How attachment influences users' willingness to donate to content creators in social media: a socio-technical systems perspective. Inf. Manag. **54**(7), 837–850 (2017)
24. Pornsakulvanich, V., Dumrongsiri, N.: Internal and external influences on social networking site usage in Thailand. Comput. Hum. Behav. **29**(6), 2788–2795 (2013)
25. Carlson, J., Rahman, M.M., Taylor, A., Voola, R.: Feel the VIBE: examining value-in-the-brand-page-experience and its impact on satisfaction and customer engagement behaviours in mobile social. J. Retail. Consum. Serv. **46**, 149–162 (2019)
26. Malik, A., Dhir, A., Nieminen, M.: Uses and gratifications of digital photo sharing on Facebook. Telemat. Inform. **33**(1), 129–138 (2016)
27. Phua, J., Venus, S., Jay, J.: Uses and gratifications of social networking sites for bridging and bonding social capital: a comparison of Facebook, Twitter, Instagram, and Snapchat. Comput. Hum. Behav. **72**, 115–122 (2017)
28. Schwemmer, C.: Social media sellout: the increasing role of product promotion on YouTube. Soc. Media + Soc. **4**, 2056305118786720 (2018)
29. Lee, S., Joon, K., Sundar, S.S.: Customization in location-based advertising: effects of tailoring source, locational congruity, and product involvement on ad attitudes. Comput. Hum. Behav. **51**, 336–343 (2015)
30. Agha, L., Teoh, K., Cheng, G., Sambasivan, M., Sidin, S.: Integration of standardization and customization: impact on service quality, customer satisfaction, and loyalty. J. Retail. Consum. Serv. **35**, 91–97 (2017)
31. Fu, J., Ju, P., Hsu, C.: Electronic commerce research and applications understanding why consumers engage in electronic word-of-mouth communication: perspectives from theory of planned behavior and justice theory. Electron. Commer. Res. Appl. **14**(6), 616–630 (2015)
32. Chen, C., Nguyen, B., Klaus, P.P., Wu, M., Chen, C., Klaus, P.P.: Exploring Electronic Word-of-Mouth (eWOM) in the consumer purchase decision-making process: the case of online holidays – evidence from United Kingdom (UK). J. Travel Tour. Mark. **32**(8), 953–970 (2015)
33. Erkan, I., Evans, C.: The influence of eWOM in social media on consumers' purchase intentions: an extended approach to information adoption. Comput. Hum. Behav. **61**, 47–55 (2016)
34. Hernández-méndez, J., Muñoz-leiva, F., Sánchez-fernández, J., Muñoz-leiva, F., Sánchez-fernández, J.: The influence of e-word-of-mouth on travel decision-making: consumer profiles. Curr. Issues Tour. **18**, 1001–1021 (2015)
35. Oliver, R.L.: A congitive model of the antecedents and consequences of satisfaction decisions. J. Mark. Res. **17**, 460 (1980)
36. Bhattacherjee, A.: Understanding information systems continuance: an expectation-confirmation model. MIS Q. **25**(3), 351–370 (2001)
37. Casaló, L.V., Flavián, C., Guinalíu, M.: Determinants of the intention to participate in firm-hosted online travel communities and effects on consumer behavioral intentions. Tour. Manag. **31**(6), 898–911 (2010)

38. Chen, Y., Shang, R., Li, M.: The effects of perceived relevance of travel blogs' content on the behavioral intention to visit a tourist destination. Comput. Hum. Behav. **30**, 787–799 (2014)
39. Kuo, Y., Wu, C., Deng, W.: The relationships among service quality, perceived value, customer satisfaction, and post-purchase intention in mobile value-added services. Comput. Hum. Behav. **25**(4), 887–896 (2009)
40. Prayag, G.: Tourists' evaluation of Destination image, satisfaction, and future behavioral intentions-the case of Mauritius tourists. J. Travel Tour. Mark. **26**, 836–853 (2009)
41. Venkatesh, V., Morris, M.G., Hall, M., Davis, G.B., Davis, F.D., Walton, S.M.: User acceptance of information technology: toward a unified view. MIS **27**(3), 425–478 (2003)
42. Wang, C., Hsu, M.K.: The relationships of destination image, satisfaction, and behavioral intentions: an integrated model. J. Travel Tour. Mark. **27**, 829–843 (2010)
43. Zhao, Q., Chen, C., Wang, J.: The effects of psychological ownership and TAM on social media loyalty: an integrated model. Telemat. Inform. **33**(4), 959–972 (2016)
44. Cheung, C.M., Lee, M.K.O.: The impact of electronic word-of-mouth-the adoption of online opinions in online customer communities. Internet Res. **18**, 229–247 (2008)
45. Lisha, C., Fei, C., Yifan, S., Rasli, A.: Integrating guanxi into technology acceptance: an empirical investigation of WeChat. Telemat. Inform. **34**(7), 1125–1142 (2017)
46. Brislin, R.W.: Back-translation for cross-cultural research. J. Cross Cult. Psychol. **1**(3), 185–216 (1970)
47. Gan, C., Lee, F.L.F., Li, Y.: Social media use, political affect, and participation among university students in urban China. Telemat. Inform. **34**(7), 936–947 (2017)
48. Gan, C., Li, H.: Understanding the effects of gratifications on the continuance intention to use WeChat in China: a perspective on uses and grati fications. Comput. Hum. Behav. **78**, 306–315 (2018)
49. Rex, B.: Kline, Principles and Practice of Structural Equation Modeling, 3rd edn. The Guilford Press, New York, London (2011)
50. Anderson, J.C., Gerbing, D.W.: Structural equation modeling in practice: a review and recommended two-step approach. Psychol. Bull. **103**(3), 411–423 (1988)
51. Hair, J.F., Black, W.C., Babin, B.J., Anderson, R.E.: Multivariate Data Analysis, Seventh. Pearson, Essex (2014)
52. Cronbach, L.J.: Coefficient alpha and the internal structure of tests. Psychometrika **16**(3), 297–334 (1951)
53. Fornell, C., Larcker, D.F.: Evaluating structural equation models with unobservable variables and measurement error. J. Mark. Res. **18**(1), 39–50 (1981)
54. Bagozzi, R.R., Yi, Y.: On the evaluation of structural equation models. J. Acad. Mark. Sci. **16**(1), 074–094 (1988)

An Exploratory Investigation of Facebook Live Marketing by Women Entrepreneurs in Bangladesh

Mohammad Tipu Sultan[✉] and Farzana Sharmin

Shanghai Jiao Tong University, Shanghai 200240, China
tipusultan_ctg@sjtu.edu.cn

Abstract. Social media create enormous opportunity for entrepreneurship towards women in the developing country. Rural educated women are utilizing these opportunities for 24/7 business development through virtual platforms. In this context, this study aims to investigate the in-depth insights into women entrepreneurs' behavioral intention to use Facebook live for entrepreneurship marketing. Extending the Technology Acceptance Model (TAM), this research examined the impact of compatibility, brand awareness, consumer relationship perceived ease of use, perceived usefulness and intention in the context of women entrepreneurs. Data were collected using an online survey from 283 women entrepreneurs in Bangladesh who have an online store on Facebook. Confirmatory factor analysis and structural equation modeling employed to examine the hypothetical relationship the constructs. The results suggested that social media live marketing was influenced by women's compatibility, ease of use and usefulness. Additionally, social media usage influence on brand awareness building, while ease of use had a strong direct influence on intention to use Facebook live marketing. The finding confirmed that social media compatibility, usefulness, brand awareness creation is the most significant factors toward women entrepreneurship success. The theoretical and practical implications of the study are discussed.

Keywords: Bangladesh · Women entrepreneurship · Facebook live · Technology Acceptance Model (TAM)

1 Introduction

Globally women's empowerment awareness got considerable importance. This issue documented the benefits of the empowerment that can be attained through the effective participation of women. In this context, Bangladesh is one of the most uprising successful countries of women empowerment. Bangladeshi women's participation in the workplace increasing as a leader to compare with the ratio of male and female. Women being half of the population, who are emerging the sustainable economic development through empowerment efforts. The concept of women empowerment and efforts in this area to attain steady progress in gender equality, which assisted Bangladesh to achieve first place in gender equality (among South Asian countries) in the Gender Gap Index of 2020 [1]. To sustain this achievement, women's equivalent rights are now distinct to women's

© Springer Nature Switzerland AG 2020
G. Meiselwitz (Ed.): HCII 2020, LNCS 12195, pp. 415–430, 2020.
https://doi.org/10.1007/978-3-030-49576-3_30

economic empowerment. The most successful Bangladeshi women in empowerment came through small entrepreneurship. This emerging platform enhances women's economic freedom. Most importantly, the appearance of women entrepreneurship became a new phenomenon for sustainable development which contribute to the national economy [2]. Their positive association with the workplace and leadership upraising gender equality, and moving Bangladesh towards a middle-income country status [3].

Social media grounded great opportunity for Bangladeshi rural educated women entrepreneurs'. This web-based communication platform bridges people and organizations [4]. Mangold and Faulds [5] identified that social media connect existing and potential customers with entrepreneurs' offers. Moreover, social media as a marketing tool allows companies to associate with new product innovation research, connect with the community to get more business opportunities. Small entrepreneurs' adopted new strategies to utilize these new media channels to communicate with their consumers. Additionally, country-wise information technology implementation by the government also plays an important role in Bangladeshi women entrepreneurs [2, 6]. Easy access to the internet transforming social media as an E-commerce platform, which engages people buying and selling of goods and services through virtual storefronts [2]. Where 93.681 million use mobile internet [7] in Bangladesh. Moreover, 35 million users actively use Facebook for social networking [8]. Thus, the live features of Facebook became an influencing marketing tool for social media base entrepreneurs [9]. Accordingly, this study aims to examine the antecedents of Facebook live towards women entrepreneurs social media virtual store establishment intention.

However, few studies have been examined the usage behavior of social media in the context of small and medium-sized enterprises (SMEs). Most of the current studies so far have examined the consumer side of social media adoption, the entrepreneurs' adoption of social media remained largely under-researched [10–14]. This paper aims to examine the factors which influencing Bangladeshi women to use social media for online business by extending new constructs related to entrepreneurship setup. Furthermore, the technology compatibility, brand awareness, and consumer relationship analyzed towards Perceived Usefulness of social media acceptance for small entrepreneurship. Additionally, how social media ease of use and usefulness contributing to the entrepreneurs' intention also has focused on this study. This paper purposes a new dimension of capability, brand awareness and consumer relationship to fill the research gap through the Technology Acceptance Model (TAM). The remainder of his article is organized as follows: the subsequent section of this paper provides a theoretical background and literature review of entrepreneurship and social media with TAM. Next section followed by the methodology and results. Lastly, it discusses the findings and implications of the study presented.

2 Review of Literature and Hypotheses Development

2.1 Compatibility

Compatibility refers to the extent of users' current values, practices, and needs. [15]. This has been measured as a vital factor for innovation acceptance [16]. A number of investigations evidenced the positive and negative impact of compatibility on technology adoption [17–20]. Ainin et al. [18] found that compatibility of Facebook using by small and medium enterprises has significant influence and they mentioned the adopter's current values, practices, and needs towards the technology. Numerous study verified the compatibility as a significant factor which influences the adoption of social media through consistent relation with small entrepreneurship business [21–23]. Therefore, in order to investigate the relationship of compatibility with perceived usefulness, the following hypothesis is proposed:

H1: Compatibility has a positive significant effect on perceived usefulness towards social media acceptance for live marketing.

2.2 Brand Awareness

Brand awareness defines consumers' ability to identify, recall, and recognize a brand [24]. One of the eldest explanations of Brand awareness is the aptitude to identify the brand under diverse circumstances [25]. Building brand awareness and marketing is the foremost challenge faced by SMEs. Limited financial resources restrict the efforts of SMEs to continue promotional activity to the mass level. Furthermore, they have to compete with large business organizations simultaneously [26]. In these circumstances, social media brand awareness enhances its brand value and equity towards potential consumers. Effective use of social media could give a competitive advantage of brand awareness [27]. Using this platform SMEs can connect with consumers at the right time, can offer lower costs and solve the problem with higher efficiency than other outdated communication tools [28]. A number of studies confirmed the association of social media utilization of brand awareness [27, 29, 30]. Consequently, this study proposed the following hypothesis-

H2: Brand awareness has a positive influence on Perceived Usefulness towards social media acceptance for live marketing.

2.3 Consumer Relationship

The notion of relationships increasingly common in the discussion for brand development between customers and brands in order to clarify consumer behavior [31]. Consumer relationship (CR) is the most frequently analyzed characteristic in the field of interpersonal relationships that creates a link to the brand equity [31]. CR becomes the key indicator of business strategies and tools for improving the right product for the consumer to build a better image of the entrepreneur [32]. This approach provides more opportunities for entrepreneurs to know more about their consumers [33, 34]. Moreover, customers can get an opinion on specific products or services, and they can purchase from online store to reduce time. In line with this discussion, this study formulate the following hypothesis to investigate how Facebook live marketing enhances entrepreneurs relationship with consumers:

H3: Consumer relationship has a positive significant effect on Perceived Usefulness towards social media acceptance for Facebook live marketing.

2.4   Technology Acceptance Model (TAM)

TAM was developed by Davis (1989b) to identify user acceptance behavior. This theory was shaped by the inspiration of the Theory of Reasoned Action [36] from the field of social psychology to explain a person's behavior intentions. TAM used to investigate the factors affecting user behaviors about using information technology or adopting new technology. The intention is determined by two constructs: individual attitudes toward the behavior and social norm of individuals or a specific group would approve or disprove of the behavior. Correspondingly, Davis [38] introduced the constructs in the original TAM as follows: perceived usefulness (PU), perceived ease of use (PEOU), attitude, and behavioral intention and actual to use. TAM specifies links between two key constructs: perceived usefulness (PU) and perceived ease of use (PEOU) towards attitudes, intentions and actual use. These two specific variables (PU and PEOU) have been hypothesized to the fundamental determinants of user acceptance of the technology [38]. The TAM is currently extensively accepted by different study settings [39, 40]. Among the concepts, PU and PEOU form the consumer's beliefs on technology and therefore predict his or her attitude toward the technology, which in turn predicts its acceptance. Within the wider field of information systems investigation, the TAM is proposed as a cognitive context that explains how PEOU and PU impact on individual usage intentions [35]. In this study, we contribute to the discipline by examining the role of individual entrepreneurs' perceptions of different aspects of using social media (Facebook live feature) as the antecedents to TAM's cognitive aspects. Focussing on social media extents of compatibility, consumer relationship, brand awareness to examine entrepreneurship acceptance through the extended TAM.

Perceived Ease of Use
Perceived ease of use (PEOU) refers to a person believes of using a specific technology [41]. The ease of use describes the increase of the performance with less strength and allowing more work done by the same effort [42]. This clarifies the user's awareness of the effort compulsory to use the system. Davis (1989b) defined PEOU as "the degree to which a person believes that using a particular system would be free of effort the word from ease". PEOU is a vital factor in the use of technology along with perceived usefulness in TAM [41]. This construct has been widely used to explain the user's adoption of the system or technology [44]. The user-centric application is one of the

influencing factors to perceived ease. Simple design, service navigation, and user interaction should be intuitive for first-time users for the targeted audience of the small business in the social media site [45]. In the context of social media utilization for small business development, a number of studies found the positive influence of PEOU on PU [46–48]. Consequently, this study suggested the following hypotheses:

H4: Perceived Ease of Use has a positive influence on Perceived Usefulness towards social media live acceptance for entrepreneurship marketing.

H5: Perceived Ease of Use has a positive and significant influence on intention towards social media live acceptance for entrepreneurship marketing.

Perceived Usefulness

Perceived usefulness (PU) is defined as persons believe that using a particular technology will enhance his or her job performance [38]. PU describes the user's sensitivity to the extent that technology will expand the user's workplace performance [35]. This means the consumer has an acuity of the usefulness of the technology for performing a specific activity which confirms decreasing the time for doing the job more accurately. A number of studies showed that PU has an influence on the PEU which, then, leads to the actual usage [35, 45, 48]. Furthermore, the association between the PU and the intention to use in the context of the TAM is statistically supported [49]. This study examines the PU relationship for continuous intention to perform social media-live activities for small entrepreneurship marketing. In the context of entrepreneurs' social media acceptance for SMEs' development, few studies have been found [18, 48, 50]. According to the following discussions, this study considers PU as a construct of the research model and hypothesized as follow:

H6: Perceived usefulness has a positive significant effect on intention towards social media acceptance for live marketing.

Intention

User intention to use social media is the key factor in building technology utilization models [41, 50]. According to Davis [41] intention reflects a decision that the person has made about whether to perform a behavior or not. Intention predicts the actual usage of a particular skill which leads to attitude formation [51]. Adoption signifies an assurance or continued usage of the technology over time. In the context of TAM, behavioral intention to use is the precursor of actual usage of computer technology. Numerous empirical studies confirm the intention-behavior relationship found that intention is a good predictor of behavior [45, 52, 53]. This study operationalizes intention as continuous using social media for entrepreneurship marketing activities [36]. Consequently, intention designates a more stable mental status of entrepreneurs using the behavior of social media. The intention of using social media live feature for entrepreneurship marketing is a cognitive representation of the user's readiness for actual use. Previous studies confirmed the importance of intention for entrepreneurship development [48, 50, 54].

3 Methodology

3.1 Sampling and Data Collection

The participants for this study are SME owners in Bangladesh who use Facebook for their business. Considering the context of the study, it is essential to find the key informants of the decision-makers of SMEs. This stud focused on recruiting actual social media base entrepreneurship business owner participants who ensure accurate and rich information regarding social media adoption among Bangladeshi SMEs. The identified candidates were contacted and provided with detailed information about the study and the participation process through Facebook. From the Facebook search, 400 female entrepreneurs were selected as potential samples. An online survey was conducted to collect data. A total of 293 surveys was collected from the participants, of which 283 were found to be usable in the data analysis. These valid responses were analyzed to assess reliability, validity, and appropriateness for hypotheses testing.

3.2 Measurement

The study constructs were operationalized adopting items from earlier empirical studies. Previous research was reviewed to ensure that a comprehensive list of measures was included. Measurements for perceived ease of use (PEOU), perceived usefulness (PU), intention to use (INT) was developed from the study of Davis [41]. Measurements for compatibility (COM), Brand awareness (BA), Consumer Relationship (CR), were developed from Ainan [18], Sasmita and Suki [55], Langaro, Rita, and Salgueiro [56], Y. Wang and Lo [34], Morgan, Slotegraaf, and Vorhies [57] respectively. Each item was measured on a five-point Likert scale, ranging from "strongly disagree" (1) to "strongly agree" (5).

3.3 Data Analysis

The proposed theoretical framework was analyzed using structural equation modeling (SEM) as suggested by Anderson and Gerbing [58]. SEM methods were employed to analyze the relationships among the constructs within the latent and observed variables using multiple indicators. The validity and reliability of the construct were assessed by using the confirmatory factor analysis (CFA), and, later on, hypothesis and model fit were measured by using the 'covariance-based structural equation modeling' approach by SPSS V.24 & AMOS V.22 respectively (Table 1).

Table 1. Demographics of respondents

Demographic variable	Description	n	(%)
Gender	Female	283	283%
	Total	283	100.0
Age group	<20	4	1.4
	20–30	210	74.2
	31–40	66	23.3
	41–50	3	1.1
	Total	283	100.0
Education	High School	19	6.7
	Diploma degree	10	3.5
	Bachelor degree	149	52.7
	Master degree	105	37.1
	Total	283	100.0
Income	Less than 10000 TK	43	15.2
	10001–20000 TK	138	48.8
	20001–30000 TK	68	24.0
	30001–40000 TK	30	10.6
	50001TK or more	4	1.4
	Total	283	100.0
Entrepreneurship category	Agro & food products	4	1.4
	Textiles & garments products	103	36.4
	Home decors	49	17.3
	Books & stationaries	2	.7
	Bags & shoes	78	27.6
	Jewelleries & accessories	40	14.1
	IT Services-Products	7	2.5
	Total	283	100.0

4   Results

4.1   Measurement Model: Reliability and Validity

At first, Confirmatory Factor Analysis (CFA) was applied to measures the validity and reliability of the constructs. Before CFA, internal consistency measured by using Cronbach's α among the items (Table 2), the score ranges from .71 to .91 which lies between the acceptable limit of .7 and higher (Hair et al. [62]). Construct reliability was measured using composite reliability (C.R). The C.R. values also exceed the acceptable limit of 0.6 which ranges from 0.82 to 0.88, indicating the reliability of multiple indicators [60]. Furthermore, Factor Loadings and Average Variance Extracted (A.V.E) parameters were used for measuring convergent and discriminant validity. The standardized factor loading of all the items was above the threshold limit of 0.6 [61]. The A.V.E values are between 0.60 and 0.70, which achieved an acceptable limit of 0.5

as recommended by Hair, Black, et al. [62]. Table 4 shows evidence of discriminant validity according to the square root of AVE for each latent construct value higher than its correlation with other constructs [63]. Therefore, the measurement model confirmed satisfactory reliability and convergent validity (Table 3).

Table 2. Measurement constructs.

Constructs	Items	S.F.L.	Mean	SD.	CR	Cronbach α	AVE
COM	COM1	.91	4.10	.810	.87	.86	.70
	COM2	.75	4.20	.744			
	COM3	.85	4.11	.731			
BA	BA1	.77	4.18	.748	.83	.82	.62
	BA2	.85	4.30	.737			
	BA3	.75	4.22	.760			
CR	CR1	.86	4.25	.628	.82	.81	.60
	CR2	.73	4.26	.631			
	CR3	.74	4.27	.651			
PEOU	PEOU1	.90	4.24	.751	.88	.88	.71
	PEOU2	.77	4.24	.727			
	PEOU3	.87	4.21	.766			
PU	PU1	.71	4.09	.704	.83	.84	.63
	PU2	.83	4.32	.753			
	PU3	.84	4.29	.739			
INT	INT1	.71	4.21	.764	.85	.84	.66
	INT2	.87	4.26	.735			
	INT3	.85	4.24	.710			

Notes:
S.F.L. = Standard Factor Loading, SD = Standard deviation, CR = Composite Reliability,
AVE = Average Variance Extracted.

Table 3. Discriminant validity of all constructs considered for the model.

	Constructs	1	2	3	4	5	6
1	Compatibility	83					
2	Brand awareness	.618**	.78				
3	Consumer relationship	.140*	.174**	.77			
4	Perceived ease of use	.380**	.448**	.068	.84		
5	Perceived usefulness	.573**	.672**	.188**	.450**	.79	
6	Intention	.494**	.598**	.151*	.540**	.519**	.81

Note:
The diagonal values mentioned in bold represent the square root of AVE

4.2   Structural Model: Goodness of Fit Statistics

According to the recommendations of Anderson and Gerbing [58], Bagozzi and Yi, [60] and Chau and Hu [64], the theoretical framework was tested by using the goodness of fit indices. We have tested the significance of the complete model constructs relationships and variances among the multiple variables in the proposed conceptual model. The model achieved a high significance level ($\chi 2$ = 229.382; degree of freedom = 123; probability level = 0.000). The results showed that goodness of fit statistics of the theoretical framework indicates a good fit, as it lies in the satisfactory edge ($\chi 2$ = 229.382, χ^2/df = 1.865, Goodness of Fit index (GFI) = .922, Adjusted Goodness of fit index (AGFI) = .891, Tucker-Lewis Index (TLI) = .955, Comparative Fit Index (CFI) = .963, Incremental Fit Index (IFI) = .964, Root Mean Square Error of Approximation (RMSEA) = .055). The observed value of AGFI was .891 that exceeds the cut-off level of .8 [60, 64, 65]. This outcome represents a good data fit the proposed theoretical framework for predicting entrepreneurs intention to accept facebook live for marketing.

4.3   Hypothesis Testing

All the variables of TAM; Perceived ease of use towards perceived usefulness (β = 0.123, p < 0.05), and intention (β = 0.388, p < 0.001), Perceived usefulness towards intention (β = 0.429, p < 0.001) were significantly related to the entrepreneurs intention towards social media live feature adoption, which supported the hypothesis H4, H5, and H6 respectively. The additional constructs included in the TAM; Compatibility towards perceived usefulness (β = 0.188, p < 0.05), Brand awareness towards perceived usefulness (β = 0.590, p < 0.001) have a significant positive influence on women entrepreneurs social media adoption for Facebook live store establishment, that supported the hypothesis H1 and H2. Hypothesis 3 consumer relationship towards perceived usefulness was not significantly supported (β = 0.056, p = .256). The proposed theoretical framework along with the β value is stated in Fig. 1.

Table 4. Summary of hypotheses' testing results.

Hypothesis	Path	β-value	t-value	Result
H1	Compatibility → Perceived usefulness	0.188	2.472	Supported
H2	Brand awareness → Perceived usefulness	0.590	6.102	Supported
H3	Consumer relationship → Perceived usefulness	0.056	1.105	Not Supported
H4	Perceived ease of use → Perceived usefulness	0.123	2.086	Supported
H5	Perceived ease of use → Intention	0.388	5.620	Supported
H6	Perceived usefulness → Intention	0.429	5.808	Supported

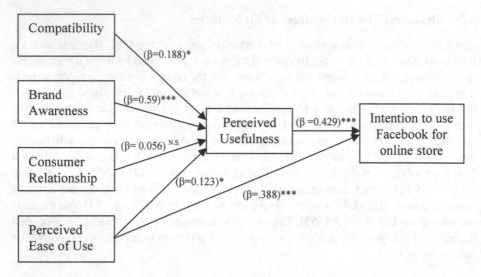

Fig. 1. The causal relationship between study constructs and entrepreneurs' intention towards social media adoption. Notes:*p < .05, ***p < .001.N.S. = Not Supported

5   Discussion

This study endeavored to explore how rural educated unemployed women in Bangladesh are using social media (Facebook) to build small entrepreneurship stores and live marketing factors impact on their intention. The results specify that women are compatible with social media live features to build their marketing activity. More importantly, social media live promotion is very cost-effective for their product or service promotion. They engaged in developing entrepreneurial businesses to sell products directly to the consumer. This approach gives them connectivity to the peer groups, promoting products and services with enjoyment [66]. The ease of use and usefulness of these technologies are positively influencing woman entrepreneur's intention towards accepting Facebook live marketing for online stores. Furthermore, the easy use of social media engagement with a playful mindset for direct selling or promoting the products. This is one of the utmost noteworthy reasons why more than 300,000 of the country's online entrepreneurs selling products through Facebook [67]. Very low start-up investment and an established user base platform Facebook is a recognizable choice for women entrepreneurs in Bangladesh.

Empirical results suggested that compatibility, brand awareness is significantly related to Facebook live usage for entrepreneurship development. The finding proposed that higher levels of Facebook compatibility and brand awareness have a positive relationship with social media use to support online entrepreneurship store marketing. Compatibility (p < .01) and brand awareness (p < .001) on Facebook were found to be the significant factors that influenced women entrepreneurs towards Facebook live using for an online store promotion. Rapid ICT development in Bangladesh with internet connection availability empowered rural women to use Facebook for business

[68–70]. This compatibility of accessible ICT infrastructure in Bangladesh was easily adopted by women entrepreneurs. The findings of this study on compatibility were constant with the earlier research which confirmed the significance of compatibility towards the adoption of technology for entrepreneurship [18, 48].

The result of the association between consumer relationship and perceived usefulness came out surprisingly opposite to the hypothesis. A possible explanation could be the contextual perception of the women entrepreneurs who are more conscious about promotional content development, brand awareness buildup. This study has also inspected the association between perceived ease of use towards perceived usefulness, and intention. As expected, the result specified a significant relationship in the context of online entrepreneurship marketing through Facebook live. A number of similar findings have been found in other studies conducted in different settings [46, 71, 72]. Consequently, the results recommend that women entrepreneurs' are influenced by the user-friendly technological aspects.

To sum up, this study extended the research model (Fig. 1) in the context of social media acceptance for entrepreneurship marketing. Compatibility and brand awareness have an effect on perceived usefulness. Perceived usefulness, Perceived Ease of Use has a strong positive impact on Entrepreneurs' Facebook using aptitude for business. The study results demonstrated the entrepreneur's intention strongly influences constant using Facebook live marketing for future business activity. The result is steady with earlier research findings that found positive associations between technology usage and entrepreneurs attitude to using intention [18, 48, 50]. Social media adoption by women entrepreneurs in the SME context there is very limited studies that have been found in developing country context. This study contributes to the initial investigation approach to find technology adoption by the women entrepreneurs in Bangladesh who are actively marketing their products using Facebook live features to develop their online store.

6 Implications

Numbers of studies have been conducted to investigate the technology acceptance in various contexts [73–78]. But in the context of entrepreneurs' Facebook live feature adoption for online business marketing, few studies investigated the organizational usage of Facebook in an integrated model with TAM [18, 48]. From the theoretical viewpoint, the findings provide a better understanding of the entrepreneurs' Facebook live acceptance intention for online business marketing for economic sustainability. According to the literature search, this study is the initial study that investigating Bangladeshi women entrepreneurs' Facebook acceptance for entrepreneurship development as a SME context.

Bangladesh is going to enter the middle-income country by 2021 [79]. In this perspective, it is most vital to ensure gender equity for the economic stability of the country. The finding of this study is predominantly important for administrators and academics who involved with entrepreneurship development through technology. While the social entrepreneurship consideration in Bangladesh has altered the lives of rural and urban peoples. As a result, strategy and practice could be utilized by low-income countries to develop their economic growth. Social media technology verified its importance by contributing to sustainable socio-economic development through entrepreneurship. This study recommended that women entrepreneurship is one of the effective solutions for a cut of poverty by low-income countries. Empirical results provide a snapshot of how acceptance of Facebook-based entrepreneurship enhances compatibility for business development. From any geological position, interested women's inspired by the context of the study. Facebook, provides numerous opportunities to the women entrepreneurs to create content, share, promote and interact regarding products and services to the targeted audiences [80–82]. Thus, Entrepreneurs should incorporate regular promotional activity through the Facebook page with an opportunity to engage consumers by conversations for long term business relations [83, 84]. Therefore, state policymakers should consider the development and accessibility of information communication technology (ICT) for social media-based small entrepreneurship development. Administrators also may come up with motivational campaigns and training for women for social media base entrepreneurship. Therefore, it would be more functional to involved related industries to engage to develop products and services for the target consumers. This study evidenced the impact of social media acceptance for entrepreneurship development by women in Bangladesh. Consequently, underdeveloped countries and educated unemployed women can consider this opportunity to grow economic freedom through technology.

7   Limitations and Future Studies

There are limitations to this study. First of all, our results are based on a small set of respondents (n = 283), thus, the results cannot be generalized to explore all the online stores with the same factors in the process of adopting and using Facebook live for marketing. Secondly, only one social media platform, Facebook has been selected for the sampling frame. In the future, researchers may consider all kinds of social media platforms user respondents. Third, this study uses a survey approach, some time which is not bias-free from respondents' subjective responses future studies, researchers may use an in-depth face to face interview approach with the target group or focus group discussion (FGD) for more details outcomes. Fourth, this study only focuses on social media base entrepreneurship. There is a plentiful opportunity in this research arena. For example, the researcher may consider economic freedom through sustainable entrepreneurship development and marketing. Researchers may also inspect behavioral theories and issues to improve the prediction of social media utilization for entrepreneurship development. Future studies can help in defining other factors and extending the current research model, such as interactivity, promotion, engagement, etc. Finally, this study was based on Bangladeshi social media base entrepreneurship development. It would be valuable to examine findings if the sample included another entrepreneurship platform in the country as well.

References

1. World Economic Forum: Global Gender Gap Report 2020, Geneva (2020)
2. Afrah, S.H., Fabiha, S.T.: Empowering women entrepreneurs through information and communication technology (ICT): a case study of Bangladesh. Management 7(1), 1–6 (2017)
3. Badruzzaman, M.: Women empowerment through entrepreneurship development: Bangladesh perspective. 2(2) (2007)
4. Tao, Z., Fabiha, S.T.: Understanding online community user participation : a social influence perspective. Internet Res 21(1), 67–81 (2017)
5. Mangold, W.G., Faulds, D.J.: Social media: the new hybrid element of the promotion mix. Bus. Horiz. 52(4), 357–365 (2009)
6. Eng, Z.L.M., Eng, B.: Role of Information and Communication Technology (ICT): Women's Empowerment in Rural Bangladesh (2014)
7. B.T.R. Commission: Internet Subscribers in Bangladesh December, 2019 (2020). http://www.btrc.gov.bd/content/internet-subscribers-bangladesh-december-2019. Accessed 26 Jan 2020
8. napoleoncat: Facebook users in Bangladesh (2020). https://napoleoncat.com/stats/facebook-users-in-bangladesh/2019/10. Accessed 26 Jan 2020
9. Make Influencers More Accessible To Audiences: The impact of live streaming on influencer marketing, pp. 2017–2020 (2019)
10. Jussila, J.J., Kärkkäinen, H., Aramo-Immonen, H.: Social media utilization in business-to-business relationships of technology industry firms. Comput. Hum. Behav. 30, 606–613 (2014)
11. Michaelidou, N.: Institutional repository usage, barriers and measurement of social media marketing : an exploratory investigation of small and medium B2B brands usage, barriers and measurement of social media marketing : an exploratory investigation of small and medium. Ind. Mark. Manag. 0–37 (2011)
12. Marolt, M., Zimmermann, H.D., Žnidaršič, A., Pucihar, A.: Exploring social customer relationship management adoption in micro, small and medium-sized enterprises. J. Theor. Appl. Electron. Commer. Res. 15(2), 38–58 (2020)
13. Cooley, D., Parks-Yancy, R.: The effect of social media on perceived information credibility and decision making. J. Internet Commer. 18(3), 249–269 (2019)
14. Odoom, R., Anning-Dorson, T., Acheampong, G.: Antecedents of social media usage and performance benefits in enterprises (SMEs). J. Enterp. Inf. Manag. 30(3), 383–399 (2017)
15. Ghazizadeh, M., Anning-Dorson, T., Lee, J.D.: Extending the Technology Acceptance Model to assess automation. Cogn. Tech. Work 14, 39–49 (2012). https://doi.org/10.1007/s10111-011-0194-3
16. Cooper, R.B., Zmud, R.W.: Information technology implementation research : a technological diffusion. Manag. Sci. 36(2), 123–139 (1990)
17. Ramdani, B., Kawalek, P., Lorenzo, O.: Predicting SMEs' adoption of enterprise systems. J. Enterpr. Inf. Manag. 22, 10–24 (2011)
18. Ainin, S., Parveen, F., Moghavvemi, S.: Factors influencing the use of social media by SMEs and its performance outcomes. Ind. Manag. Data Syst. 115, 570–578 (2015)
19. Alzubi, M.M.: Using the technology acceptance model in understanding citizens' behavioural intention to use m-marketing among Jordanian citizen. J. Bus. Retail Manag. Res. 12(2), 224–231 (2018)
20. Razak, S.A., Azrin, N., Latip, B.: Factors that influence the usage of social media in marketing. J. Res. Bus. Manag. 4(2), 1–7 (2016)

21. Burgess, S., Sellitto, C., Cox, C., Buultjens, J., Bingley, S.: An innovation diffusion approach to examining the adoption of social media by small businesses : an Australian case study. Pac. Asia J. Assoc. Inf. Syst. **9**(3), 1–23 (2017)

22. Dahnil, M.I., Marzuki, K.M., Langgat, J., Fabeil, N.F.: Factors Influencing SMEs adoption of social media marketing. Procedia - Soc. Behav. Sci. **148**, 119–126 (2014)

23. I. Journal, O. F. Business, and M.: Studies: Business technology adoption and use by small and. **8**(1), 1–19 (2016)

24. Chen, V., Green, R.D.: Brand equity, marketing strategy, and consumer income : a hypermarket study, no. mix. J. Manag. Mark. Res. 1–18 (2011)

25. Keller, K.L.: and measuring, brand managing customer-based equity. **57**(1), pp. 1–22 (1993)

26. Hassan, S., Zaleha, S., Nadzim, A., Shiratuddin, N.: Strategic use of social media for small business based on the AIDA model. Procedia - Soc. Behav. Sci. **172**, 262–269 (2015)

27. Momany, M., Alshboul, A.: Social media marketing: utilizing social media to advance brand awareness and. **9**(1), 33–55 (2016)

28. Kaplan, A.M., Haenlein, M.: Users of the world, unite! The challenges and opportunities of Social Media. Bus. Horiz. **53**(1), 59–68 (2010)

29. Foroudi, P.: International journal of hospitality management in fluence of brand signature, brand awareness, brand attitude, brand reputation on hotel industry' s brand performance. Int. J. Hosp. Manag. **76**, 271–285 (2019)

30. Alhaddad, A.A.: The effect of advertising awareness on brand equity in social media. Int. J. e-Educ. e-Bus. e-Manag. e-Learn. **5**(2), 73–84 (2015)

31. Story, J., Hess, J.: Segmenting customer-brand relations: beyond the personal relationship metaphor. J. Consum. Mark. **23**(7), 406–413 (2006)

32. Saeed, K.A., Grover, V., Hwang, Y.: The relationship of e-commerce competence to customer value and firm performance : an empirical investigation. J. Manag. Inf. Syst. **22**(1), 223–256 (2005)

33. Gefen, D., Karahanna, E., Straub, D.W.: Inexperience and experience with online stores : the importance of TAM and Trust. IEEE Trans. Eng. Manag. **50**(3), 307–321 (2003)

34. Wang, Y., Lo, H.P.: An integrated framework for customer value and management performance: a customer-based perspective from China. Manag. Serv. Qual. **14**(2–3), 169–182 (2004)

35. Davis, F.D.: User acceptance of computer technology : a comparison of two theoretical models. Manag. Sci. **35**(8), 982–1003 (1989)

36. Fishbein, M., Ajzen, I.: Chapter 8: Prediction of Behavior. Belief Attitude Intention Behav. Introduction to Theory Res. (1975)

37. Ajzen, I.: From intentions to actions: a theory of planned behavior. In: Kuhl, J., Beckmann, J. (eds.) Action Control. SSSSP, pp. 11–39. Springer, Heidelberg (1985). https://doi.org/10.1007/978-3-642-69746-3_2

38. Davis, B.F.D.: Perceived usefulness, perceived ease of use, and user acceptance of information technology. MIS Q. **13**, 319–340 (1989)

39. Lai, P.C.: Perceived Risk As An Extension To TAM Model : Consumers' Intention To Use A Single Platform E-Payment Perceived Risk As An Extension To TAM Model : Consumers' Intention To Use A Single Platform E –Payment. Asia-Pac. J. Manag. Res. Innov. (2016)

40. Fathema, N., Shannon, D., Ross, M.: Expanding the technology acceptance model (TAM) to examine faculty use of learning management systems (LMSs) in higher education institutions. J. Online Learn. Teach. **11**(2), 210–232 (2015)

41. Davis, F.D.: Computer and information systems graduate schooi of business administration univeirsity of Michigan. Inf. Syst. J. **3**, 319–340 (1989)

42. Davis, F.D., Bagozzi, R.P., Warshaw, P.R.: Extrinsic and intrinsic motivation to use computers in the workplace 1. J. Appl. Soc. Psychol. **22**(14), 1111–1132 (1992)
43. Davis, F.D.: Perceived usefulness, perceived ease of use, and user acceptance of information technology. MIS Q. **13**(3), 319–340 (1989)
44. Agarwal, R., Prasad, J.: The role of innovation characteristics and perceived voluntariness in the acceptance of information technologies. Decis. Sci. **28**(3), 557–582 (1997)
45. Venkatesh, V., Davis, F.D.: A theoretical extension of the technology acceptance model: four longitudinal field studies. Manag. Sci. **46**(2), 186–204 (2000)
46. Rauniar, R., Rawski, G., Yang, J., Johnson, B.: Technology acceptance model (TAM) and social media usage: an empirical study on Facebook. J. Enterp. Inf. Manag. **27**(1), 6–30 (2014)
47. Zaremohzzabieh, Z., et al.: Information and communications technology acceptance by youth entrepreneurs in rural Malaysian communities: the mediating effects of attitude and entrepreneurial intention. Inf. Technol. Dev. **22**(4), 606–629 (2016)
48. Akgül, Y.: Empirical study on the determinants of social media adoption by Turkish small and medium enterprises. İşletme Araştırmaları Dergisi. **10**, 710–732 (2018)
49. Lee, Y., Kozar, K.A., Larsen, K.R.T.: The technology acceptance model : past, present, and future. Commun. Assoc. Inf. Syst. **12**, 50 (2003)
50. Lorenzo-romero, C., Romero, C.L.: Determinants of use of social media tools in retailing sector. J. Theor. Appl. Electron. Commer. Res. **9**(1), 44–55 (2014)
51. Fishbein, M., Ajzen, I.: Theory-based behavior change interventions: comments on hobbis and sutton. J. Health Psychol. **10**(1), 27–31 (2005)
52. Chen, S.: Using the sustainable modified TAM and TPB to analyze the effects of perceived green value on loyalty to a public bike system. Transp. Res. Part A **88**, 58–72 (2016)
53. Sheppard, B.H., Hartwick, J.P., Warshaw, R., Sheppard, B.H., Warshaw, P.R.: For modifications and future research linked references are available on JSTOR for this article : the theory of reasoned action : a meta-analysis of past research with recommendations for modifications and future research. **15**(3), pp. 325–343 (2019)
54. Chen, L., Gillenson, M.L., Sherrell, D.L.: Consumer acceptance of virtual stores : a theoretical model and critical success factors for virtual stores (2003)
55. Sasmita, J., Suki, N.M.: Young consumers' insights on brand equity: effects of brand association, brand loyalty, brand awareness, and brand image. Int. J. Retail Distrib. Manag. **43**(3), 276–292 (2015)
56. Langaro, D., Rita, P., de Fátima Salgueiro, M.: Do social networking sites contribute for building brands ? Evaluating the impact of users' participation on brand awareness and brand attitude. J. Mark. Commun. **7266**, 1–23 (2018)
57. Morgan, N.A., Slotegraaf, R.J., Vorhies, D.W.: International journal of research in marketing linking marketing capabilities with pro fit growth. Int. J. Res. Mark. **26**(4), 284–293 (2009)
58. Gerbing, D.W., Anderson, J.C.: Structural equation modeling in practice: a review and recommended two-step approach. Psychol. Bull. **103**(3), 411–423 (1988)
59. Hair, J.F., Black, W.C., Babin, B.J., Anderson, R.E.: Multivariate Data Analysis. Pearson Education Limited, London (2014)
60. Bagozzi, R.P., Yi, Y.: On the evaluation of structural equation models. J. Acad. Mark. Sci. **16**(1), 74–94 (1988)
61. Chin, W.W., Gopal, A., Salisbury, W.D.: Advancing the theory of adaptive structuration: the development of a scale to measure faithfulness of appropriation. Inf. Syst. Res. **8**(4), 342–367 (1997)
62. Hair, J.F., Black, W.C., Babin, B.J., Anderson, R.E.: On Multiple Regression Analysis (2014)

63. Fornell, C., Larcker, D.F.: Evaluating structural equation models with unobservable variables and measurement error. J. Mark. Res. **18**(1), 39–50 (1981)
64. Chau, P.Y.K., Hu, P.J.H.: Information technology acceptance by individual professionals: a model comparison approach. Decis. Sci. **32**(4), 699–719 (2001)
65. Kline, R.B.: Principles and Practice of Structural Equation Modeling, 3rd edn. The Guildford Press, New York (2011)
66. Crittenden, V.L., Crittenden, W.F., Ajjan, H.: Empowering women micro-entrepreneurs in emerging economies: the role of information communications technology. J. Bus. Res. **98**, 191–203 (2019)
67. Gilchrist, K.: Facebook and 3 millennials are changing the start-up scene in Bangladesh (2018). https://www.cnbc.com/2018/07/17/shopup-bangladesh-start-up-uses-facebook-to-help-micro-entrepreneurs.html
68. Laizu, Z.: Role of Information and Communication Technology (ICT): Women' s Empowerment in Rural Bangladesh. Murdoch University (2014)
69. Armarego, J., Sudweeks, F.: The role of ICT in women's empowerment in rural Bangladesh (2015)
70. Ahmed, A., Islam, D.: Measuring the impact of ICT on women in Bangladesh. In: CSREA EEE, pp. 180-185 (2006)
71. Rahman, S.A., Taghizadeh, S.K., Ramayah, T., Alam, M.M.D.: Technology acceptance among micro-entrepreneurs in marginalized social strata: the case of social innovation in Bangladesh. Technol. Forecast. Soc. Change **118**, 236–245 (2017)
72. Brandon-jones, A.: Examining the antecedents of the technology acceptance model within e-procurement. Int. J. Oper. Prod. Manag. **38**, 22–42 (2018)
73. Lin, H., Chen, C.: Combining the Technology Acceptance Model and Uses and Gratifications Theory to examine the usage behavior of an Augmented Reality Tour-sharing Application. Symmetry
74. Binti, N., et al.: Acceptance and usage of social media as a platform among student entrepreneurs. J. Small Bus. Enterp. Dev. **24**(2), 375–393 (2017)
75. Venkatesh, V., Speier, C.: User acceptance enablers in individual decision making about technology: toward an integrated model. Decis. Sci. **33**(2), 297–316 (2002)
76. Abebe, M.: Electronic commerce adoption, entrepreneurial orientation and enterprise (SME) performance. J. Small Bus. Enterp. Dev. (2015)
77. Oumlil, R., Juiz, C.: Acceptance of tourism e-entrepreneurship : application to educational Balearic Island context. J. Entrepreneurship Educ. **21**(1), 1–16 (2018)
78. Doha, A., Elnahla, N., Mcshane, L.: Social commerce as social networking. J. Retail. Consum. Serv. **47**, 307–321 (2019)
79. Staff Report; and Statement by the Executive Director for Bangladesh: 2018 Article IV Consultation—Press Release (18) (2018)
80. Burke, L., et al.: Factors affecting home care patients' acceptance of a web-based interactive self-management technology. J. Am. Med. Inform. Assoc. **18**(1), 51–59 (2011)
81. Sashi, C.M.: Customer engagement, buyer-seller relationships, and social media. Manag. Decis. **50**, 253–272 (2012)
82. Greve, A.: Social networks and entrepreneurship. Entrepreneurship Theory Prac. **28**(1), 1–22 (2003)
83. Seock, Y.-K.: Analysis of Clothing Websites for Young Customer Retention based on A Model of Customer Relationship Management via the Internet. The Virginia Polytechnic Institute and State University (2003)
84. Garbarino, E., Johnson, M.S.: The different roles of satisfaction, trust, and commitment in customer relationships. J. Mark. **63**(2), 70–87 (2019)

A Study on Bilingual Superimposed Display Method on Digital Signage

Takumi Uotani[1]($\boxtimes$), Yoshiki Sakamoto[2], Yuki Takashima[2],
Takashi Kurushima[2], Kimi Ueda[2], Hirotake Ishii[2], Hiroshi Shimoda[2],
Rika Mochizuki[3], and Masahiro Watanabe[3]

[1] Faculty of Engineering, Kyoto University, Kyoto, Japan
uotani@ei.kyoto-u.ac.jp
[2] Graduate School of Energy Science, Kyoto University,
Kyoto, Japan
[3] Service Evolution Laboratories, Nippon Telegraph
and Telephone Corp., Tokyo, Japan

Abstract. In order to solve problems of conventional multilingual display method represented by simultaneous multilingual display and language switching display, the authors have proposed a bilingual superimposed display. The purpose of this study is therefore to propose the method and to evaluate it with an experiment by searching optimal bilingual superimposed display and comparing its reading speed with that of language switching display method. In the experiment, two tasks were conducted as follows; (1) Optimal display search task was carried out to optimize reading speed of bilingual superimposed display based on participants' subjective evaluations using interactive genetic algorithm. (2) Silent reading task was carried out to measure reading speed of sentences with monolingual display and optimized bilingual superimposed display. Then, the model of language switching display was created from the result of reading speed of monolingual display, and the expected reading time of the language switching display was compared with the reading time of bilingual superimposed display. As the comparison result, it was found that the reading speed of the bilingual superimposed display is significantly faster ($p < 0.01$).

Keywords: Digital signage · Multilingual · Bilingual superimposed display · Interactive genetic algorithm

1 Introduction

In recent years, Ministry of Internal Affairs and Communications of Japan is working to expand the functions of digital signage for the 2020 Tokyo Olympic and Paralympic Games, aiming for multilingual support and simultaneous information distribution to prepare disasters [1]. When giving some information to plural people who have different native languages, the current multilingual display method are roughly classified into two types: language switching display (LSD) and simultaneous multilingual display (SMD). LSD is the display method

© Springer Nature Switzerland AG 2020
G. Meiselwitz (Ed.): HCII 2020, LNCS 12195, pp. 431–443, 2020.
https://doi.org/10.1007/978-3-030-49576-3_31

in which contents written in a single language are displayed on one screen for a while, and then it is switched over another language. SMD is the display method in which contents written in in plural languages are displayed simultaneously on one screen. In case of LSD, however, the users may wait for displaying the information in their readable language. In case of SMD, the texts may be too small to read because the information in plural languages are displayed at the same time.

There have been a lot of studies on multilingual display on the digital monitor. Ogi et al. proposed the system that exchanges information between digital signage and the user's smartphone and displays his/her native language automatically [2]. Kim et al. designed a digital signage system that supports multilingual display for foreign tourists which can be used without the Internet access [3]. Matsunuma et al. measured the visibility of graphic text written in Japanese, Korean and Chinese on mobile phones using the parameters of visual distance, reading speed, error rate and subjective evaluation of the readability, then implied that graphic text on mobile phones was adequate for practical use [4]. There also have been a lot of studies on characters given animations. Chujo et al. determined the combination of the reading speed of character strings moving from right to left on the monitor and the number of moving characters displayed simultaneously that participants felt the most readable, then indicated the optimal condition of the display method [5]. Minakuchi et al. determined the emotions that participants felt when they looked at the elemental words of emotions given 9 different motions, then they indicated that words and motion patterns can be each categorized into three groups and effects were varied according to a combination of the words and the motions [6]. As described above, a lot of studies on multilingual display and giving animation to characters have been conducted, however there are no proposal of the new multilingual display method using animations suitable for simultaneous information distribution.

In the this study, therefore the authors have proposed a bilingual superimposed display (BSD) to solve problems of conventional multilingual display methods. BSD is a display method in which information written in different languages with different character modifications are displayed at the same time at the same place. The readability of BSD is supposed to be changed depending on the character modifications such as colors and animations. Therefore, the purpose of this study is to evaluate the utility of BSD by searching optimal modification and comparing reading speed of the optimized BSD and LSD to evaluate their readability. Here, optimal BSD means that the distinctiveness of BSD is the highest, the distinctiveness means how both superimposed languages are easy to be distinguished, and readability means how reading speed is fast.

2   Bilingual Superimposed Display and the Optimization Method

2.1   Overview of Bilingual Superimposed Display

As shown in Fig. 1, BSD is the display method in which two sentences written in different languages with effects such as colors and animations are displayed at the same time at same place, thus it aims for the method in which each user whose native language are different can select and read sentences written in their native language when they look at the display at the same time. BSD suppose superimposing any two languages originally. In this study, Japanese and Korean are chosen as superimposed languages, because Korean is the most used language among foreign tourists visiting Japan, and has entirely different script from Japanese [7].

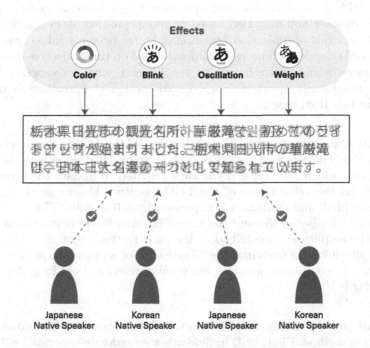

Fig. 1. Concept of bilingual superimposed display. (Color figure online)

2.2   Modification Parameters of Bilingual Superimposed Display

The modification for one language can be expressed with 10 parameters which are classified into one of character color, blink, oscillation and weight (character thickness). Thus, one BSD has a total of 20 parameters in order to apply the effects independently to two languages. The character color is expressed by three parameters of RGB color model. The blink is expressed by three parameters of blink cycle, phase difference and minimum opacity, because it is rendered by changing the opacity of characters following sine wave. The oscillation is expressed by three parameters of oscillation cycle, phase difference and amplitude, because it is rendered by moving characters vertically. Weight which means the thickness of the character is expressed by one parameter.

2.3   Optimization Method of Bilingual Superimposed Display Using Interactive Genetic Algorithm

Overview of Optimization Method. As a method to determine BSD parameters with fast reading speed, optimization based on distinctiveness should be considered. It is however difficult to determine them because there are huge number of combinations of 20 parameters and all of them cannot be evaluated. In this study, an interactive genetic algorithm (IGA) is applied for efficient optimization. IGA is an algorithm that optimizes target individuals by repeating selection, crossover and mutation based on human subjective evaluation. Ordinary IGA performs optimization based on only one person's subjective evaluation. The BSD should be however optimized based on the subjective evaluations of two persons whose native languages are different, since its viewers are both Japanese and Korean speakers. Such a combination of evaluators is called a participant pair from now on.

Details of the Parameters. The each range of the RGB value is expressed from 0 to 255. The range of the cycle of blink and oscillation is expressed from 6 to 60 frame which one frame is the time required to update the screen, and it depends on the refresh rate of the LCD monitor. The range of the phase difference of blink and oscillation is expressed from 0 to 360°. The range of the minimum opacity is 0–50%, and the one of the amplitude is expressed from 0 to 10%. The amplitude is described as the ratio to the height of the imaginary rectangle which covers one character. The range of weight is expressed from 1 to 1000, and this notation, in which big number refers to bold font, depends on web standards [8].

Details of the Optimization Method. Figure 2 shows the procedure of the optimization method. First, BSD individuals are randomly generated within the search range and displayed on the screen. At this time, the number of displayed individuals is set to 12 in order to suppress the fatigue of the evaluators. Next, the evaluators evaluate the distinctiveness of BSD based on five grade Likert scale. A participants pair who are two evaluators with different native languages evaluates each BSD individuals as the same time, so that two evaluation results are obtained for each BSD individual. By taking the product of the pair evaluations, the two evaluation values are integrated into one, and the integrated value is used as the fitness of the BSD individual. After the evaluation, 21 parent individuals are selected with a probability proportional to the fitness allowing duplication. Then, individuals of next generation is generated from parent individuals using simplex crossover (SPX) [9]. SPX is the crossover method that requires 21 parent individuals. The above operation is repeated for 14 times. In the 15th generation, evaluators select the 6 individuals with the highest distinctiveness, and they are the final output of this optimization procedure.

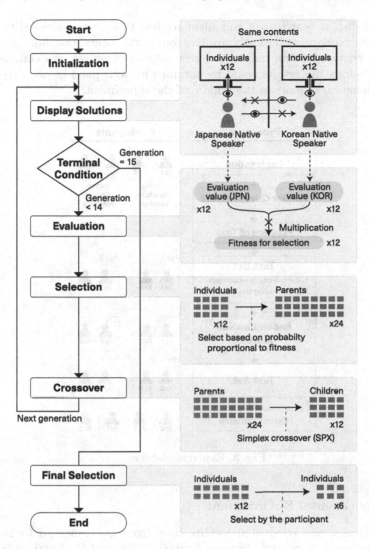

Fig. 2. Flowchart of optimize method and internal process.

3   Experiment of Search and Evaluation of Optimal Display

3.1   Purpose and Overview of the Experiment

The purpose of the experiment is to measure the reading speed on monolingual display (MD) and the optimized BSD to evaluate the proposed BSD. The flow of this experiment is shown in Fig. 3. In this experiment, the task set consisting of optimal display search task and silent reading task was conducted twice per person. One experiment basically involves four participants, two Japanese native speakers and two Korean native speakers, and one task set was conducted by pairs. Therefore, the results could be obtained for four pairs in one experiment by recombination of pairs in the middle of the experiment.

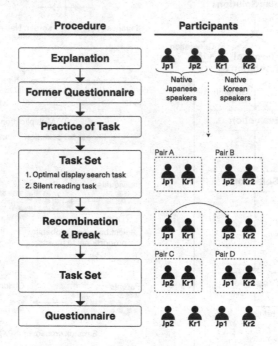

Fig. 3. Experimental flow.

3.2   Experimental Environment

The experiment was conducted for five days from December 16 to 20, 2019. It was conducted in two timeframes: A (9:00–12:00) and B (13:00–16:00). The schedule of the experiment is shown in Table 1. The participants conducted the task displayed on the monitor using the mouse. Figure 4 shows the layout of the experimental environment. Partitions was set up to prohibit participants from seeing the monitor of others. The screen size of the monitor (LG, 43UD79-B) was 42.5 in., the resolution was 3840 × 2160 px, the pixel pitch was 0.2451 × 0.2451 mm, and the refresh rate was 30 fps.

Table 1. Experimental schedule

Contents	Duration (min)
Overview description	10
Former questionnaire	5
Explanation of experiment schedule	5
Instruction of task	5
Practice of task	15
Task set (first time)	60 (maximum)
Pair recombination/Break	5
Task set (second time)	60 (maximum)
Questionnaire	5
Delivery of reward/Finish	10
Total	180 (maximum)

3.3   Experimental Participants

The participants were 20 Japanese native speakers and 16 Korean native speakers gathered by open call and referrals from acquaintances. All participants have normal corrected vision and no color vision deficiencies. The average age of all 36 participants was 21.8 years (S.D. = 4.6).

3.4   Optimal Display Search Task

In this task, the optimal BSD parameters were obtained by the optimization method in Sect. 2.3 based on the evaluation of discrimination. The rendering area of each BSD individual was 1100×300 px, and the background color was always fixed to white. The font was Noto Sans CJK JP/KR with seven weights. The text was drawn in two lines with a font size of 80 px and a line spacing of 70 px. The text was quoted from the corpus and news sites and displayed randomly. The displayed color on the superimposed area of two languages is determined by averaging the RGB value of two alpha-blended colors which is calculated based on two patterns with different combinations of front and back.

3.5   Silent Reading Task

This task was conducted to measure the text reading speed on BSD obtained in the task in Sect. 3.4 and MD. The flow of this task is shown in Fig. 5. When the participant clicked *start* button, a sentence was displayed after a countdown for three seconds. They read the sentence silently, and then they clicked *done* button when they finished reading. They repeated the above operation for 12 sentences.

In this task, the time from displaying the text to clicking the done button was measured. The MD text and the BSD text were displayed alternately. The

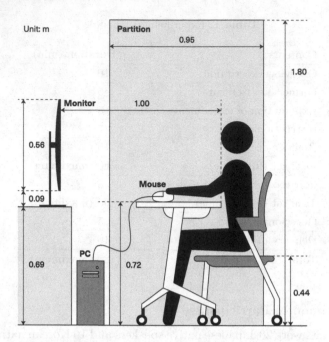

Fig. 4. Position of participants and experimental equipment.

first four sentences were dummy sets to ignore the learning effect. The rendering area was 3300 × 600 px for each sentence, and the background color was always fixed to white. The font was the same as the one in Sect. 3.4. The sentences were displayed in random order from a sentence set containing 12 Japanese sentences and 12 Korean sentences. In the case of MD, only the text in the participant's native language was displayed. The text was displayed in four lines with a font size of 80px and a line spacing of 70px. The number of characters in Japanese sentences was set to 40, and the one in Korean sentences was set to the same amount as Japanese. The text was quoted from news sites.

3.6 Model of Language Switching Display

A model of LSD with two languages was created in order to calculate the switching time in which the expected reading time on LSD is the shortest, and then evaluate the reading time on BSD by comparing to the shortest expected reading time on LSD with the switching time. Assume that the screen switching time of LSD is fixed to t_s, and the total reading time of sentences written in the viewer's native language is expressed as t_r. If the screen is switched before the viewers have read the entire sentence, they can restart reading immediately from where they left off when the native language sentence is displayed again. Figure 6 shows an example of the reading time when maximum number of

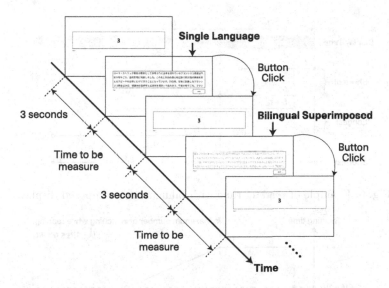

Fig. 5. Overview of silent reading task.

displaying the unreadable page while reading is one, and the maximum number k can be expressed as follows;

$$k = \left\lceil \frac{t_r}{t_s} \right\rceil \tag{1}$$

Therefore, in the case of $(k-1)t_s < t_r \leq kt_s$, the relationship between the reading start time and the required reading time is as shown in Fig. 7, and the expected reading time E can be expressed as follows:

$$E(t_s, t_r) = \frac{3}{2}t_r + \frac{2k-1}{4}t_s \tag{2}$$

3.7   Result

The result of 32 out of 36 participants who successfully completed all tasks were adopted. As the result, 240 data of the reading time on MD and 240 data of the reading time on BSD were obtained. Table 2 shows the results of total reading time for each display method. One-way ANOVA was performed for each display method for the display order of the sentences. As the result, no significant difference was found in the interaction between reading time and displayed order. This means no learning effect was observed in the display order. Figure 8 shows the results of plotting the average of the expected reading times of all participants on a graph with the switching time t_s varied from 1 to 150 seconds with 1-second steps based on the model of Sect. 3.6. According to Fig. 8, the average of the expected reading time is minimum when $t_s = 82$. This means that the shortest reading time can be expected when all the participants are assumed to be the viewers. Therefore, the expected reading time for each participant at $t_s = 82$ was

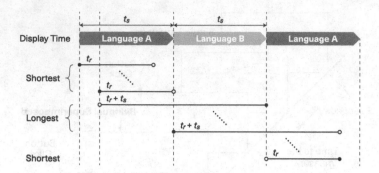

Fig. 6. Example of reading time with bilingual superimposed display.

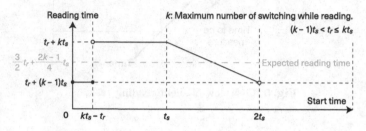

Fig. 7. Model of language switching display.

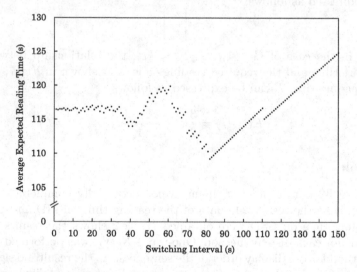

Fig. 8. Average expected reading time with language switching display.

calculated and shown in Table 2. Table 3 shows the results of comparison between the reading time on BSD and the expected reading time on LSD using the paired t-test. According to Table 3, the reading speeds on BSD were significantly faster than those on LSD.

Table 2. Result of silent reading task and comparison of bilingual superimposed display and language switching display

Native language	Monolingual display (s)	Bilingual superimposed display (s)	Expected reading time of switching display (s)	Ratio (BSD/MD)	(BSD/E)
Korean	23.99	39.14	56.49	1.44	0.69
Japanese	69.05	126.70	124.08	0.98	1.02
Korean	45.06	82.70	88.08	1.07	0.94
Korean	57.21	86.84	106.32	1.22	0.82
Japanese	42.69	51.80	84.53	1.63	0.61
Japanese	37.93	45.03	77.39	1.72	0.58
Korean	69.72	103.36	125.08	1.21	0.83
Korean	71.66	85.00	127.99	1.51	0.66
Japanese	61.63	137.67	112.94	0.82	1.22
Japanese	81.30	103.78	142.45	1.37	0.73
Korean	77.76	135.02	137.14	1.02	0.98
Japanese	28.10	48.39	62.65	1.29	0.77
Korean	61.65	118.65	112.97	0.95	1.05
Japanese	76.34	84.61	135.00	1.60	0.63
Korean	58.86	66.10	108.79	1.65	0.61
Korean	74.89	95.82	132.84	1.39	0.72
Japanese	69.99	137.56	125.48	0.91	1.10
Japanese	66.08	71.04	119.63	1.68	0.59
Korean	65.04	165.43	118.06	0.71	1.40
Korean	51.19	74.76	97.28	1.30	0.77
Japanese	36.94	62.30	75.91	1.22	0.82
Japanese	35.95	100.57	74.43	0.74	1.35
Korean	61.66	100.02	112.99	1.13	0.89
Korean	110.04	126.90	226.56	1.79	0.56
Japanese	80.38	153.53	141.07	0.92	1.09
Japanese	63.74	59.71	116.10	1.94	0.51
Korean	62.61	115.79	114.42	0.99	1.01
Korean	25.92	78.05	59.38	0.76	1.31
Japanese	28.21	46.51	62.81	1.35	0.74
Japanese	51.65	70.33	97.98	1.39	0.72

3.8   Discussions

According to Table 2, the maximum ratio of the reading time on BSD to MD was 3.01 while the average ratio was 1.59. However, all of the partners of participants whose ratio of the reading time was more than double had the ratio lower than the average. It is therefore supposed that optimization failed and some BSD individuals with high readability were generated for only one language.

Table 3. t-test for reading time of bilingual superimposed display and language switching display

Bilingual superimposed display		Expected reading time of switching display		t	p	d
M	S.D.	M	S.D.			
92.4	36.0	109.2	40.5	-3.089	0.0044**	0.4917

**Significant at the 0.01 level (2-tailed)
d: Effect size (Cohen's d)

The LSD model assumed in Sect. 3.6 does not include the time of interruption to search the left-off place when the viewers restart reading. Therefore, under the more realistic model, the expected reading time of LSD is extended and it is supposed that the superiority of BSD on reading speed will be further enhanced.

4   Conclusion

In this study, the authors conducted an experiment to evaluate the utility of BSD by comparing the text reading speed between the optimized BSD and the conventional method, LSD. As the result of the experiment, it was found that BSD with the appropriate parameters had a significantly faster sentence reading speed than the expected reading speed of LSD. However, it was also found that the reading speeds of Japanese native speakers and Korean native speakers differed depending on the combination of BSD parameters. In the future study, It is necessary to investigate the contribution of each parameter to reading speed on BSD.

References

1. Ministry of Internal Affairs and Communications, Promotion of ICT in society as a whole toward (2020). https://www.soumu.go.jp/johotsusintokei/whitepaper/ja/h30/html/nd261210.html. Accessed 12 Jan 2020
2. Ogi, T., Ito, K., Konita, S.: Multilingual digital signage using iBeacon communication. In: 2016 19th International Conference on Network-Based Information Systems (NBiS), pp. 387–392, September 2016
3. Kim, S., et al.: Design of on-offline multilingual support digital signage for foreign tourists. In: Proceedings of the International Conference on Research in Adaptive and Convergent Systems (RACS 2016), pp. 247–248. Association for Computing Machinery, New York (2016)
4. Matsunuma, S., Hasegawa, S., Omori, M., Miyao, M.: Usefulness and visibility of graphical characters in mobile phone e-mail. Ergonomics **42**(5), 313–319 (2006)
5. Chujo, K., Notomi, K., Ishida, T.: The effect of the number of characters on the reading rate of character strings moving horizontally on a CRT. J. J. Psychol. **64**(5), 360–368 (1993)

6. Minakuchi, M., Ueda, A., Yamamoto, K., Kuramoto, I., Tsujino, Y.: Preliminary study on influence of motion patterns by kinetic typography on expressed emotion. J. Hum. Interface Soc. **14**(1), 9–20 (2012)
7. Japan National Tourism Organization, Nationality/Monthly The number of Foreign Tourists Visiting Japan (2003–2019). https://www.jnto.go.jp/jpn/statistics/since2003_visitor_arrivals.pdf. Accessed 12 Jan 2020
8. World Wide Web Consortium, CSS Fonts Module Level 4 (2020). https://www.w3.org/TR/css-fonts-4/#font-weight-numeric-values. Accessed 26 Jan 2020
9. Higuchi, T., Tsutsui, S., Yamamura, M.: Simplex crossover for real-coded genetic algorithms. Trans. J. Soc. Artiff. Intell. AI **16**(1), 147–155 (2001)

Social Computing for Well-Being, Learning, and Entertainment

Zika Outbreak of 2016: Insights from Twitter

Wasim Ahmed[1(✉)], Peter A. Bath[2], Laura Sbaffi[2],
and Gianluca Demartini[3]

[1] Newcastle University, Business School, Newcastle, UK
wasim.ahmed@newcastle.ac.uk
[2] University of Sheffield Information School, Sheffield, UK
[3] School of Information Technology and Electrical Engineering, University
of Queensland, Brisbane, Australia

Abstract. An outbreak of the Zika virus in 2016 caused great concern among
the general public and generated a burst of tweets. The aim of this study was to
develop a better understanding of the types of discussions taking place. Tweets
were retrieved from the peak of the Zika outbreak (as identified by Google
Trends). Tweets were then filtered and entered in NVivo to be analysed using
thematic analysis. It was found that tweets on Zika revolved around seven key
themes: pregnancy, travel and the Olympics, mosquitoes and conspiracy, health
organisations, health information, travel and tracking, and general discussions
around Zika. Our results are likely to be of interest to public health organisations
disseminating information related to future outbreaks of Zika and we develop a
set of preliminary recommendations for health authorities.

Keywords: Zika · Twitter · Infectious diseases · Social media · Epidemics ·
Health

1 Introduction

Infectious diseases are among the deadliest threats to human civilization because they
have a very high mortality rate. Moreover, infectious diseases receive a lot of public
attention as demonstrated by the recent coronavirus outbreak which has been reported
intensely since January 2020. Infectious disease outbreaks may cause fear and panic
among the public making it important to study these phenomena. Previous deadly
outbreaks, such as the Black Death for instance, are known to have claimed the lives of
between one-fourth and three-fourths of the world's population across Europe and Asia
and, in Europe only, at least 25 million are estimated to have died from it [1]. The Zika
virus (ZIKV) is a developing arthropod-borne virus (arbovirus) which was first isolated
from a monkey from the Zika forest in Uganda in the late 1940s [2]. Zika sufferers may
exhibit mild symptoms and experience a slight fever or rash, and joint, muscle, or eye
pain. Zika is transmitted from the bite of specific mosquito species carrying the
infection. Zika can also be transmitted through sexual intercourse, and perinatal
transmission has also been reported [3]. There is no cure or anti-viral treatment for the
Zika virus infection, neither is there a vaccine. The Zika virus can spread from the
womb to the child in pregnant women and leads to birth defects such as microcephaly

© Springer Nature Switzerland AG 2020
G. Meiselwitz (Ed.): HCII 2020, LNCS 12195, pp. 447–458, 2020.
https://doi.org/10.1007/978-3-030-49576-3_32

[4]. Zika became a public concern in early 2016, when it first spread outside of Africa and Asia, where the virus had formerly been restricted. This geographical expansion led the World Health Organisation (WHO) to declare the outbreak a public health emergency of international concern (PHEIC) [2]. However, unlike previous infectious disease outbreaks, there appeared to be low public knowledge of the Zika outbreak in the United States, leading to the dissemination of health information such as mosquito-bite prevention notices and recommendations by public health authorities to avoid travelling to Zika-affected areas [4]. Moreover, misinformation on social media platforms has the potential to have adverse consequences if, for example, advice around prevention and transmission are inaccurate.

It is important to understand the types of content shared on Twitter because tweets are viewed widely across the Internet, and a substantive subset of the global human population use the platform on a daily basis [5, 6]. Twitter reports having 328 million monthly active users, with one billion unique monthly visits to sites embedded with tweets [5, 6]. Moreover, it is important to study the types of content shared on Twitter during infectious disease outbreaks because pandemic diseases are ranked as one of the most catastrophic risks facing human civilisation globally [7], and potential misunderstanding and misinformation could have major negative outcomes. Traditionally, printed media have been the main information source for people interested in general health information during a major pandemic. However, during the 2009 swine flu pandemic, it was reported that the Internet overtaken as the most common source of information [8].

Previous research on Twitter has examined correlations between poll data and tweets using sentiment analysis [9]. Twitter has also been utilised for the detection of earthquakes by drawing upon sentiment analysis by examining certain keywords [10]. Twitter was also found to be useful when the Arab Spring was occurring, which were a number of protests that took place in the Middle East and North Africa in 2010 [11]. Henceforth, there has been research conducted on Twitter from a range of disciplines which include health, sociology, business and management.

In the field of marketing, social media provide the ability to rapidly gain insights into how members of the public might response to the release of new products and/or services. There have been a number of 'software as a service' tools that have been created which provide organisations with the ability to monitor conversations that take place on Twitter. This demonstrates the potential of Twitter for social listening, as it is possible to gain insights very rapidly into consumer views, especially from a public health perspective.

Previous research has also examined Twitter across a range of health topics including dementia [12], antibiotics [13], marijuana [14], sexual risk behaviors [15], and vaccination sentiments (i.e., positive or negative views) [16]. There has been empirical research which has analysed Twitter content surrounding swine flu [17–19], and Ebola [20, 21]. However, there is a lack of in-depth qualitative analysis of how Twitter users responded during the Zika outbreak of 2016. This study aimed to address this gap in knowledge by conducting an in-depth thematic analysis of Twitter data relating to the peak of tweets during the 2016 outbreak of the Zika virus.

1.1   Research Aim

The overall research aim of this study was to develop an understanding of the content shared during the Zika outbreak from 2016 in order to develop recommendations for information dissemination during future potential outbreaks of Zika. More specifically, the research question to be addressed was as follows:

- What information were Twitter users sharing related to the Zika virus during a peaks in tweets from 2016?

In order to achieve this research aim, the study retrieved, filtered, and qualitatively analysed tweets on Zika from the peak of tweets from the 2016 outbreak. This is an important topic to study because infectious disease outbreaks are a serious public health threat and potential misinformation on social media platforms such as Twitter could lead to negative public health outcomes. Moreover, infectious disease outbreaks have major impacts on the luxury, lesiure and trade industries.

2   Methods

2.1   Selecting Data

Figure 1 below shows how there was sudden interest in Web Search queries in Zika from March 2015 to July 2016 (note the sudden increase in the Google Trends Score). The keyword 'Zika' was utilised in order to retrieve tweets and only English language tweets were studied.

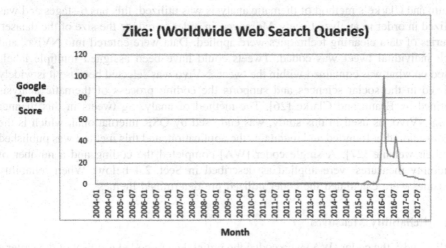

Fig. 1. Zika worldwide Web search queries

The data for tweets on Zika were retrieved using Twitter's Gardenhose API, which is at least 10% of the entire Twitter stream. The BU-TCAT, a product of Boston University, was used to retrieve these tweets [22]. After retrieving data, a total of

749,131 tweets were retrieved from the 2-day period 31st of January to the 1st of February 2016. This falls within the time when there was heightened interest in Zika, as shown above in Fig. 1 above.

2.2   Filtering Data

The data that were retrieved on the Zika outbreak contained 749,131 tweets; however, when near duplicate clusters were removed, the dataset saw a large reduction of duplicate content. Data were filtered using DiscoverText [23, 24]. It appeared that there were a large number of news articles shared, as well as less personal views and opinions which were shared on the Zika outbreak. This aligns with research that has found that there was low knowledge of Zika in the United States [25]. This is summarised in Table 1 below. Exact duplicates included retweets.

Table 1. Research approach for filtering Zika data

Stage	Total
Pre-data cleaning	749,131
Removing Exact duplicates	76,943
Removing Near Duplicate at a 60% threshold	20,421
10% sample included for analysis	2,042

2.3   Data Analysis

Braun and Clarke's method of thematic analysis was utilized; this has 6-stages and was utilized in order to analyze tweets. Moreover, in order to reduce the size of the dataset, a series of data cleaning techniques were applied. Data were entered into NVivo, and each individual tweet was coded. Tweets could have been assigned multiple labels based on what was contained within the tweet. NVivo was selected because it is widely utilised in the social sciences and supports the coding process of thematic analysis outlined by Braun and Clarke [26]. The method of analyzing tweets in this manner using NVivo, as used in this study, was endorsed by QSR international, which is the organisation that founded and maintains the application, and this method was published on their website [27]. A single coder [WA] completed the coding and a number of reliability measures were applied as described in Sect. 2.4 below. When reliability measures were calculated the coder utilized pre-determined themes.

2.4   Reliability Measures

In this study, the coder (WA) who coded the initial data re-coded a subset of data after a period of time had elapsed (three-months) in order to assess test-retest reliability. The percentage agreement was 99.37%. An independent coder also coded a subset of tweets (300) and the inter-coder reliability percentage agreement was 99.24% ($\kappa = 0.56$), which was a moderate level potentially due to the qualitative nature of the study.

3 Results and Discussion

3.1 Results of Tweet Categorization

Table 2 provides the results of the tweet categorization.

Table 2. Overview of themes and sub-themes

Theme (N/%)	Sub-themes (N)
1. Pregnancy (164/8.36%)	1.1 Avoid Pregnancy Narrative (12/0.61%) 1.2 Zika Threat to Pregnant Women (19/0.96%) 1.3 Zika Virus Spreads Fear Among Pregnant Brazilians (22/1.12%) 1.4 Zika Threat to Pregnant Columbians (29/1.47%) 1.5 Abortion Debate (47/2.39%) 1.6 Pregnancy (35/1.78%)
2. Travel and the Olympics (75/3.82%)	2.1 Fear (19/0.96%) 2.2 Olympics Rio 2016 (56/2.85%)
3. Mosquitoes and Conspiracy (259/13.21%)	3.1 Zika Conspiracy (61/3.11%) 3.2 GM Mosquitoes (65/3,31%) 3.3 Mosquitoes (133/6.78%)
4. Health Organisations (365/18.62%)	4.1 Critical of WHO (7/0.35%) 4.2 WHO Related News (358/18.26%)
5. Health Information (160/8.16%)	5.1 Zika Origin (8/0.40%) 5.2 Zika Symptoms (10/0.51%) 5.3 Transmission (19/0.96%) 5.4 Prevention (34/1.73%) 5.6 Zika Vaccine (37/1.88%) 5.7 Microcephaly (52/2.65%)
6. Travel and Tracking (321/16.37%)	6.1 Zika Travel Advice (29/1.47%) 6.2 Zika Spreading Explosively in South and Central America (14/0.71%) 6.3 Zika will Spread Across the Americas (17/0.86%) 6.4 Mentions Brazil and Zika Virus (19/0.96%) 6.5 Geographical Tracking (21/1.07%) 6.6 Geographical Transmission (116/5.91%) 6.7 Travel (45/2.29%)
7. General Discussions (646/32.95%)	7.1 Zika found in Ugandan Forest (15/0.76%) 7.2 Zika and Climate Change or Global Warming (18/0.91%) 7.3 Broadcast Advert (21/1.07%) 7.4 Information Seeking (26/1.32%) 7.5 Politics (26/1.32%) 7.6 Humour and Sarcasm (77/3.92%) 7.7 Name Discussion (124/6.32%) 7.8 Zika Information (General) (363/18.52%)

Overall, tweets contained much more content from news articles shared on Zika than personal views. There were a number of varied discussions taking place around the Zika epidemic based on seven key discussions around pregnancy (164/8.36%), travel and the Olympics (120/6.12%), mosquitoes and conspiracy (259/13.21%), health organisations (365/18.62%), health information (160/8.16%), travel and tracking (246/12.55%), and general discussions around Zika (646/32.95%%). There was discussion surrounding pregnancy because of Zika's known association with microcephaly, which causes complications in children during birth (Mlakar, Korva, Tul, Popović, et al., 2016). For women and couples in Zika-affected areas, it was recommended that pregnancy be avoided. However, Twitter users highlighted the controversial nature of this recommendation in countries where access to contraception can be difficult. Moreover, some users also highlighted the difficulties of requesting an abortion on medical grounds because of tough laws on abortion in some parts of Latin America.

Moreover, general news articles shared on Twitter highlighted similar debates around pregnancy:

'The Zika Virus has sparked a debate around abortion and it is not the first disease to do so [URL]' (1.1)

The tweet (1.1) above was linked to an article that specifies how the mainstream media were aware the Zika outbreak had initiated a debate around abortion, partly because, in certain areas where Zika had spread, laws exist which prohibit abortion [28]. This specific tweet also alludes to previous diseases that have led to similar abortion debates, and it is possible to draw parallels with earlier infectious disease outbreaks. In the 1960s, there were laws that prohibited abortion in the United States and, during this time, there was an outbreak of Rubella, which has the potential to cause complications in foetuses [29]. The debate in the context of Zika centred on whether abortion should be decriminalized in areas such as El Salvador in Central America, where illegal abortions are common place [30, 31]. A number of Twitter users also referred to the practicalities of requesting women to avoid becoming pregnant:

'In Zika affected areas women are being told to not get pregnant, yet, they have no access to contraception' (1.2)

'Wonder if people realise that the narrative of not getting pregnant actually needs rights and resources' (1.3)

'Hopefully not, but if Zika ever gets to Nigeria I wonder if we are going to legalise abortion for affected women?' (1.4)

The series of tweets above highlight some of the debates that were taking place around abortion. In tweet 1.2, the user highlights the controversy of advice to avoid pregnancy when contraception is not readily accessible, which is often the case in the low-income countries affected by Zika [32]. Twitter users, such as the author of Tweet 1.3, suggested that avoiding pregnancy requires certain women's rights, specifically the right to abortion. Tweet 1.4 questioned whether Nigeria, which has strict anti-abortion laws, would legalize abortion [32].

In the context of Zika, it is probable that the perception of benefits would outweigh barriers if travelling was non-essential because of the threat that Zika posed for pregnant women. This argument is further reinforced by the decision of airline companies to offer travel refunds and credits to women travelling in these areas.

Additionally, Twitter users referred to mosquitoes within their tweets, both generally and specifically. These included sharing conspiracy theories that genetically-modified mosquitoes were responsible for the Zika outbreak, and that Zika had been manufactured.

A number of Twitter users shared and discussed conspiracy theories focused around the Zika outbreak:

'Zika – it's a hoax and the cover up related to it continues' (1.5)
'Bill Gates created the Zika virus [URL]' (1.6)
'I wonder who really started the Zika virus' (1.7)
'Why would you invent a virus and not have the antidote?' (1.8)

As the tweets above demonstrate, the Zika outbreak led Twitter users to share and discuss a number of varied conspiracy theories. Some theories purported that Zika had been intentionally spread (as illustrated in tweet 1.5). Other conspiracy theorists suggested that certain prominent figures had intentionally manufactured the Zika virus (as illustrated in tweet 1.6). Tweet illustration 1.6 could also indicate humour because Bill Gates is known for the development of computer software and 'virus' is also a term utilized in the computing industry.

Some Twitter users were also critical towards the WHO, or shared news originating from the WHO during this time period. The WHO may thus be interested to find that they were considered an authoritative information source during the outbreak period. The health information that was shared included information on the transmission of Zika and vaccines. Health authorities could utilise this information to disseminate information around the transmission of Zika and potential vaccines for the virus. When reflecting on the number of general themes, there was a sense that the Zika virus was out of control: news articles would note that the virus was spreading 'explosively' in South and Central America and the Americas. Twitter users expressed an interest in geographically tracking the incidence of Zika. The information derived from tracking Zika could have allowed users to assess their perceived susceptibility of the virus i.e., because their closer proximity may lead to higher potential susceptibility.

A number of Twitter users were concerned about travelling during the Zika outbreak, which coincided with the Olympic Games taking place in Rio de Janeiro:

'Olympic games- because of Zika virus will cancel my trip' (1.9)
'64% of respondents from the USA noted that they will cancel travel to Zika-affected areas' (1.10)

These tweets highlight how the Zika outbreak caused concern to those who were planning to attend the Olympic Games. There were also a number of references to travel credits and refunds for those visiting Zika affected areas:

'Are you worried about Zika and travelling? Some airlines offering refunds [URL]' (1.11)
'Cruise liners are going to waive cancellation fees because of Zika' (1.12)

Citizens who were set to travel to Zika affected areas may have been concerned to do so, because of the dangers associated with the disease. This may be particularly applicable to citizens who may have had a higher perceived risk severity of being infected by the Zika virus, such as pregnant women and couples seeking to start a family.

3.2   Evidence of Themes Across the Outbreak

One of the questions that can be asked of the study is whether the themes identified in the 2-day period are applicable, i.e. scalable to other activity on Twitter. It was not feasible to obtain the complete data on the Zika, outbreak because of the high cost of obtaining historical Twitter data and managing it. However, one method that can be used to search all of Twitter is Twitter's advance search feature. In this study, Twitter's advance search feature was utilized in order to find tweets from across the pandemic, during which Google Trends showed there to be an increased interest in web search queries for the Zika outbreak (from Jan to July 2015). The selection criteria were that the themes that had not been reported in previous literature (i.e., they were specific to this study) and which could be identified by keywords. The themes were selected because they were not specific to the 2-day time period, were not reported in previous literature, and they were searchable by using keywords. Table 3 below maps certain themes to the months from January to July in 2016 and demonstrates how discussion of Zika's name, information seeking and the Olympics occurred throughout the whole of the outbreak period.

Table 3. Finding themes across the outbreak

	Year 2016						
Themes	Jan	Feb	March	April	May	June	July
Name Discussion	x	x	x	x	x	x	x
Information Seeking	x	x	x	x	x	x	x
Olympics Rio 2016	x	x	x	x	x	x	x

3.3   Contribution to Knowledge

Previous research on Zika [33] has found there to exist five key themes: the impact the outbreak was having on society, responses to Zika such as from the general public, government and private sector, pregnancy and microcephaly, the transmission of Zika, and a theme with case reports of Zika. Other research [34] found that people were interested in tracking the Zika virus because it could spread across the world. They also found that tweets frequently mentioned pregnancy and abortion. However, the following themes appear to have not been reported in previous literature:

- Name Discussion
- Information Seeking
- Humour and Sarcasm
- Olympics Rio 2016

Additional themes may have arisen in this present study because of a different method of analysis was utilized, thematic analysis.

3.4 Recommendations

Health authorities may wish to actively monitor Twitter in order to rapidly identify areas in which the public require more information and clarifications on. This information can then be disseminated through social media and/or more traditional means. In the specific case of another Zika virus outbreak, health authorities may wish to focus on providing information highlighting at risk groups, symptoms transmission, prevention, vaccines, and whether it is safe to travel to at risk geographical zones. Health authorities were singled out and criticized for being perceived to be inactive during the outbreak. For future outbreaks, health authorities could disseminate information on the work they have been doing around Zika on Twitter. Furthermore, health authorities can monitor social media Zika for conspiracy theories and disseminate guidance and advice on their legitimacy. For discussions around conspiracy theories, our findings may be of interest to public health organizations that could use this information to monitor further cases of Zika, for these specific conspiracy theories and disseminate guidance and advice on their legitimacy.

3.5 Limitations and Future Work

The data selected was tweeted over a two-day period, and therefore some of the themes that emerged could be specific to this time period. However, Sect. 3.3 identified examples of tweets from across the outbreak of Zika that correspond to the identified themes. Moreover, if different time intervals were examined, it is possible that different themes and sub-themes would emerge. A further limitation is that only English language tweets were examined. This preliminary study has provided insights into the discussions taking place on Twitter during an infectious disease outbreak. Our previous work has analysed data on Ebola [35] reflected on ethical issues for researching social media [36] identified popular health communities on Twitter [37], researched viral health hashtags [38] and explored sociological aspects of infectious disease outbreaks [39]. Future research will seek to consolidate previous research to develop a framework for researching social media for healthcare researchers and organisations. Moreover, a current study is underway which is capturing data on coronavirus which has the potential to be compared to this study [40]. Researchers could also analyse Zika-related content on other social media platforms and/or analyse data on Zika at future time points and compare the results to this study.

4 Conclusions

Overall, it was found that there were many news articles shared on Twitter during this time period, which formed a number of themes. The discussions attracting personal opinions and views centered on conspiracy theories and debates around abortion laws and ethics. It appears that infectious disease outbreaks may lead to a variety of responses from Twitter users which can be general in nature but which can also be specific to the type of disease being discussed. In this study we observed specific discussions directly related to Zika. We also note that, in certain instances, social media may intensify public fears due to the sharing of conspiracy theories and false news.

References

1. Taubenberger, J.K., Morens, D.M.: 1918 influenza: the mother of all pandemics. Emerg. Infect. Dis. **12**, 15–22 (2006). http://wwwnc.cdc.gov/eid/article/12/1/05-0979_article. htm#suggestedcitation
2. Fauci, A.S., Morens, D.M.: Zika virus in the Americas—yet another arbovirus threat. N. Engl. J. Med. **374**(7), 601–604 (2016)
3. Musso, D., Nilles, E.J., Cao-Lormeau, V.M.: Rapid spread of emerging Zika virus in the Pacific area. Clin. Microbiol. Infect. **20**(10), 595–596 (2014)
4. Brasil, P., et al.: Zika virus infection in pregnant women in Rio de Janeiro. N. Engl. J. Med. **2016**(375), 2321–2334 (2016)
5. About Twitter: Twitter Usage/Company Facts (2016). https://about.twitter.com/company. Accessed 19 June 2017
6. Twitter Q1 2017 Company Metrics: Number of monthly active Twitter users worldwide from 1st quarter 2010 to 1st quarter 2017 (in millions). Statista (2017). https://www.statista.com/statistics/282087/number-of-monthly-active-twitter-users/. Accessed 19 June 2017
7. Bostrom, N.: Global Catastrophic Risks. Oxford University Press, Oxford (2008)
8. Jones, J., Salathe, M.: Early assessment of anxiety and behavioural response to novel swine-origin influenza A(H1N1). PLoS ONE **4**, e8032.J (2009)
9. O'Connor, B., Balasubramanyan, R.: From tweets to polls: linking text sentiment to public opinion time series. In: Proceedings of the Fourth International AAAI Conference on Weblogs and Social Media, pp. 122–129. AAAI, Washington, DC (2010)
10. Sakaki, T., Okazaki, M., Matsuo, Y.: Earthquake shakes Twitter users. In: Proceedings of the 19th International Conference on World Wide Web, p. 851. ACM Press, New York (2010)
11. Howard, P.N., Duffy, A., Freelon, D., Hussain, M.M., Mari, W., Maziad, M.: Opening closed regimes: what was the role of social media during the Arab Spring? Project on Information Technology and Political Islam Data Memo 2011.1. University of Washington, Seattle (2011)
12. Robillard, J.M., Johnson, T.W., Hennessey, C., Beattie, B.L., Illes, J.: Aging 20: health information about dementia on Twitter. PLoS ONE **8**(7), e69861 (2013). https://doi.org/10.1371/journal.pone.0069861
13. Scanfeld, D., Scanfeld, V., Larson, E.L.: Dissemination of health information through social networks: Twitter and antibiotics. Am. J. Infect. Control **38**(3), 182–188 (2010). https://doi.org/10.1016/j.ajic.2009.11.004
14. Cavazos-Rehg, P.A., Krauss, M., Fisher, S.L., Salyer, P., Grucza, R.A., Bierut, L.J.: Twitter chatter about marijuana. J. Adolesc. Health Official Publ. Soc Adolesc. Med. **56**(2), 139–145 (2015). https://doi.org/10.1016/j.jadohealth.2014.10.270
15. Young, S.D., Rivers, C., Lewis, B.: Methods of using real-time social media technologies for detection and remote monitoring of HIV outcomes. Prev. Med. **63**, 112–115 (2014). https://doi.org/10.1016/j.ypmed.2014.01.024
16. Salathé, M., Khandelwal, S.: Assessing vaccination sentiments with online social media: implications for infectious disease dynamics and control. PLoS Comput. Biol. **7**(10), e1002199 (2011). https://doi.org/10.1371/journal.pcbi.1002199

17. Signorini, A., Segre, A.M., Polgreen, P.M.: The use of Twitter to track levels of disease activity and public concern in the U.S. during the influenza A H1N1 Pandemic. PLoS ONE **6** (5), e19467 (2011). https://doi.org/10.1371/journal.pone.0019467
18. Szomszor, M., Kostkova, P., St Louis, C.: Twitter informatics: tracking and understanding public reaction during the 2009 Swine Flu pandemic. In: Proceedings of the 2011 IEEE/WIC/ACM International Conference on Web Intelligence (WI 2011), vol. 1, pp. 320–323. ACM Press, New York (2011). https://doi.org/10.1109/wi-iat.2011.311
19. Chew, C., Eysenbach, G.: Pandemics in the age of Twitter: content analysis of Tweets during the 2009 H1N1 outbreak. PLoS ONE **5**(11), e14118 (2010)
20. Jin, F., et al.: Misinformation propagation in the age of Twitter. Computer **47**(12), 90–94 (2014)
21. Odlum, M., Yoon, S.: What can we learn about the Ebola outbreak from tweets? Am. J. Infect. Control **43**(6), 563–571 (2015). https://doi.org/10.1016/j.ajic.2015.02.023
22. Groshek, J.: Twitter Collection and Analysis Toolkit (TCAT) at Boston University (2014). http://www.bu.edu/com/bu-tcat/. Accessed 28 Jan 2018
23. Ahmed, W.: Using Twitter as a data source: an overview of social media research tools (updated for 2017). Impact Soc. Sci. Blog (2017)
24. DiscoverText.com, (n.d.). http://discovertext.com/. Accessed 28 Jan 2018
25. Rasmussen, S.A., Jamieson, D.J., Honein, M.A., Petersen, L.R.: Zika virus and birth defects —reviewing the evidence for causality. N. Engl. J. Med. **374**(20), 1981–1987 (2016)
26. Braun, V., Clarke, V.: Successful Qualitative Research: A Practical Guide for Beginners. Sage, Thousand Oaks (2013)
27. QSR Internation. Qsrinternational.com (2016). http://www.qsrinternational.com/nvivo/nvivo-community/blog/analyzing-tweets-about-infectious-disease-outbreak. Accessed 28 Jan 2018
28. Aiken, A.R., Scott, J.G., Gomperts, R., Trussell, J., Worrell, M., Aiken, C.E.: Requests for abortion in Latin America related to concern about Zika virus exposure. N. Engl. J. Med. **375** (4), 396–398 (2016)
29. Niswander, K.R.: Medical abortion practices in the United States. W. Res. L. Rev. **17**, 403 (1965)
30. Roa, M.: Zika virus outbreak: reproductive health and rights in Latin America. The Lancet **387**(10021), 843 (2016)
31. Williamson, L.M., Parkes, A., Wight, D., Petticrew, M., Hart, G.J.: Limits to modern contraceptive use among young women in developing countries: a systematic review of qualitative research. Reprod. Health **6**(1), 3 (2009)
32. Iyioha, I.O., Nwabueze, R.N.: Comparative Health Law and Policy: Critical Perspectives on Nigerian and Global Health Law. Routledge, Abingdon (2016)
33. Fu, K.W., Liang, H., Saroha, N., Tse, Z.T.H., Ip, P., Fung, I.C.H.: How people react to Zika virus outbreaks on Twitter? A computational content analysis. Am. J. Infect. Control **44**(12), 1700–1702 (2016)
34. Stefanidis, A., et al.: Zika in Twitter: temporal variations of locations, actors, and concepts. JMIR public health and surveillance **3**(2), e22 (2017)
35. Ahmed, W., Demartini, G., Bath, PA.: Topics discussed on Twitter at the beginning of the 2014 Ebola epidemic in United States. In: iConference 2017, Wuhan, China, March 2017
36. Ahmed, W., Bath, P.A., Demartini, G.: Using Twitter as a data source: an overview of ethical, legal, and methodological challenges. In: The Ethics of Online Research, pp. 79–107. Emerald Publishing Limited (2017)

37. Zhang, Z., Ahmed, W.: A comparison of information sharing behaviours across 379 health conditions on Twitter. Int. J. Public Health **64**(3), 431–440 (2019)
38. Ahmed, W.: Public health implications of# ShoutYourAbortion. Public Health **163**, 35–41 (2018)
39. Ahmed, W.: Using Twitter data to provide qualitative insights into pandemics and epidemics. Doctoral dissertation, University of Sheffield (2018)
40. Ahmed, W., Vidal-Alaball, J., Downing, J., López Seguí, F.: COVID-19 and the 5G conspiracy theory: social network analysis of twitter data. J. Med. Internet Res. **22**(5), e19458 (2020). https://doi.org/10.2196/19458. https://www.jmir.org/2020/5/e19458

An Analysis of the Current Policies for Social Media Use in Saudi Higher Education

Faowzia Alharthy[✉], Yuanqiong Wang, and Alfreda Dudley

Computer and Information Sciences Department, Towson University,
Towson, MD 21252, USA
{falharthy, ywang, adudley}@towson.edu

Abstract. This paper presents a research study that investigated and analyzed the status of social media policies at Saudi Arabian higher education institutions (HEIs). This study is the first attempt to review social media policies in 68 Saudi universities and colleges. Social media policies published on the institutions websites were collected. This study focuses on the readability, accessibility, and content coverage of these policies. In addition, the study identified potential gaps concerning learning and teaching with social media policies, as well as how well these policies meet student and faculty needs. A summary of the current status of social media policies at Saudi HEIs and recommendations for improving the current status were presented as the result of this study.

Keywords: Social media policies · Higher education · Policy content coverage

1 Introduction

The Saudi Arabian government is in the process of developing and reforming many of its social services, such as health and education. For higher education specifically, some higher education institutions (HEIs) have started to utilize and analyze social media as a tool for professional and personal communication within academics [1]. This is a logical tool for HEIs because of the rising use of social media in Saudi Arabia [47]. The use of social media has been helpful in education as a method for enhancing learning and empowering social relationships between students themselves and with their instructors.

Social media integration in an educational setting offers many advantages to HEIs. However, researchers have adopted divided opinions about social media integration in higher education due to associated challenges and possible negative outcomes [2]. Various court cases, such as [3] and [4], exemplify how social media integration without effective policy support can cause major issues for HEIs. To minimize the possible negative outcomes of social media integration, educational institutions have started developing social media policies aimed to develop awareness of productive social media usage among potential users [2]. Researchers recommend that HEIs develop social media policies with rules and guidelines that address the unique challenges faced by that institution instead of relying on governmental policies that are too broad for adequate use in higher education [5].

© Springer Nature Switzerland AG 2020
G. Meiselwitz (Ed.): HCII 2020, LNCS 12195, pp. 459–470, 2020.
https://doi.org/10.1007/978-3-030-49576-3_33

The Ministry of Educations of Saudi Arabia webpage [6] lists 78 public and private universities and colleges in the kingdom, while 68 of them have an official website. A review of websites from these institutions show that the majority of HEIs have no policies related to social media usage in place. One possible reason for the lack of social media policies in Saudi Arabian HEIs might be that social media is relatively new to these institutions. Social media was not expected to have such a massive presence in Saudi Arabia in such a short period of time. As a result, Saudi HEIs are ill prepared to regulate social media integration into educational settings [1]. Moreover, ethical and security awareness is a significant consideration in creating social media policies in Saudi HEIs. This research study evaluates policies for social media use in higher education of 68 colleges and universities in Saudi Arabia. Policies published online were evaluated regarding their ease of access, readability and policy content coverage.

2 Related Literature

Social media plays a significant role in students' lives, as around 90% of students actively use social networking sites [7]. Convenient access to social media through personal electronic devices contributes to the greater availability of information, quicker communication, and faster knowledge exchange [8]. Higher education institutions use social media mainly to facilitate student-to-student communication, as well as student-to-teacher communication [9]. Many studies reveal various positive effects, such as enhancing motivation, communication, restudying, resources, and self-evaluation [7, 8, 10–12]. Social media platforms can be used successfully as learning tools in higher education, but they have unintended negative effects as well. Multiple researchers such as [8, 10] and [11] have presented negative effects of social networking within academic settings such as time wasting, the misuse of social media sites, distractions, disturbing content, privacy and security concerns, and addiction.

Many teachers and students emphasize the privacy and security concerns that prevent the active use of social networking sites for academic purposes [9]. Gikas and Grant [13] proposed that many teachers avoid using social media, not due to low perceived usefulness, but due to high-perceived risks. Further exploration suggests that teachers lack policy and administrative support that help to define the limitations of social media usage. Without enough institutional support, it is difficult for teachers to integrate social media into their existing teaching methodologies [14]. Researchers highlight that while considering the perceptions and readiness of students and teachers, institutions must define social media usage policies to avoid possible negative impact and enhance the confidence of the users, primarily students, faculty members, and administrators [15].

Different studies have explored the factors that influence HEIs' formulation of effective social media policies. Some of these factors are a lack of administrative support, resource unavailability, lack of policies that define the social media usage, high privacy risks, and an absence of guidelines and regulations that respond effectively to student and faculty needs in an efficient way as per Al-Khalifa & Garcia [16], Alsufyan, Aloud [17],

Castagnera & Lanza [18], Kim, Sohn & Choi [19], Pookulangara & Koesler [20], Sánchez, Cortijo & Javed [21], Yuan, Powell & Cetis [22] and Viberg & Grönlund [23].

These findings suggest that educational institutions can ensure the successful integration of social media to enhance and encourage collaborative learning by adopting effective and clear social media policies, ensuring adequate administrative support, training faculty to make the best use of social media, and encouraging creative ways of learning. However, Alsufyan and Aloud [17] proposed that the formulation of effective social media policies in educational settings is difficult due to a lack of theoretical support. Hence, there is a need to discuss and understand the challenges that HEIs face while formulating an institution-specific social media policy that minimizes the barriers associated with its academic use and maximizes students' learning experiences. This is not only a problem in Saudi Arabia; in fact, many countries, including the United States of America, suffer from the lack of social media policies with regards to teaching and learning [24–26].

3   Methodology

This study is a first attempt to review social media policies in 68 Saudi universities and colleges. All the universities and colleges were approved based upon the ministry of education in Saudi Arabia [6]. The data was collected by visiting the official websites of each university, and conducting an online search using the following research terms: media guideline, media policies, networking policies, networking handbook, networking guidelines, and media handbook. The initial analysis process used a "yes" and "no" screening measure approach regarding whether the site provided a social media policy. After completing the first round of screening measures for all 68 institutions websites, a detailed analysis of the ease of access, readability and policy content was made regarding the resulting policies of each sites. Details of the research methods that were used to extract and analyze the current social media policies of each site are discussed below.

3.1   Social Media Policy Ease of Access

Ease of access is an important element that is used to determine the level of accessibility of a social media policy [27]. The policy should be easy to locate and reach, so users should not have difficulty finding and accessing the policy [28]. Improving ease of access starts with making the policy easily accessible directly from the sites within three clicks (three- click rule) or through a search function, which is a quicker and easier way to find content on large sites [29]. Therefore, ease of access in this study is evaluated by counting number of clicks to find the policy content on the site, checking availability of the policy through search function, verifying if the policy is a part of another policy or is it a separate social media policy, checking the file formats used for displaying the policy (pdf, html, or word), and reviewing which one would be the more accessible format for the user. Those results will be explained in further detail in the findings section.

3.2   Social Media Policy Readability

The study of readability began in education with the evaluation of books by focusing on the vocabulary and the average word and sentence length [30]. The readability of a policy is important to determine whether the reader can read and understand the policy. The readability measurements that have been used to evaluate the policy are total number of sentences, total number of words, and average words per sentence. The Flesch Reading Ease formula (FRE) gives an approximate score for the policy's difficulty, and Flesch-Kincaid Grade Level (FGL) scores are used to determine the grade level of the policy. Previous research has examined the impact of readability by using the FGL scores [31]. This formula is one of the most popular readability tests that is used to estimate the education level needed to read a text in U.S school grade level [32] Therefore, a score of 7.4 indicates that an average student in 7th grade would understand the text. The Flesch Reading Ease formula (FRE) will output a number from 0 to 100; the range between 100 to 90 is a higher score that can easily be read and understood by an average 11-year old student, while the range between 60 to 70 should be understood by 13 to 15-year old students. College graduates should be able to read and understand text with a score of 0 to 30 [33]. A score between 60 to 70 and an average educational level of 8th and 9th grade were needed to read the policies [34]. All readability tools mentioned above were used to analyze the policies and output the results based on these readability formulas. The website www.webfx.com was used for this study to test the readability of the social media policy by testing the only English version of the policies [35]. The readability results from www.webfx.com and a complete description of findings can be found in the findings section.

3.3   Social Media Policy Content Coverage

In addition, the content analysis was conducted to give a clear picture of the current state of social media policies at Saudi Arabia universities and colleges regarding teaching and learning. This data was analyzed using manual and electronic methods to evaluate the needs within the policy document data in order to achieve the best results [36]. Using software in the data analysis process added accuracy to qualitative research, as well as to the reliability and quality of the analysis [37, 38]. Nvivo is a useful qualitative data analysis tool produced by QSR International for mapping out how themes relate to each other and for viewing the inter-relationships of the codes within a particular context [39].

For this purpose, before using the NVivo software, the researcher fully read all the existing Saudi higher education social media policies collected to generate themes that are common across social media policies at different institutions [26, 40, 41] and [42]. The researcher conducted an inductive coding approach where codes generated while examining the collected policies. Two main codes (security and ethical) were added in the process and two sub-nodes (privacy and limit access) were combined with 'security' node. Two sub-nodes (misuse and copyright) were also combined with 'ethical' node. These codes were used to categorize and develop an understanding of what the social media policy documents and helped to manage the data and remove the irrelevant data [20]. Clarity and a better understanding of these themes are important to conduct an effective policy analysis.

Additionally, the researcher coded the themes by highlighting all places where there is information related to each code to see how the themes have manifested across the policy content. Nvivo was useful at this point for identifying these words in the policy content, so it was easily explored how these words are being used, as well as the context and meaning of words [43]. When this was complete, it was necessary to create a visualization of the data to communicate the findings to others; therefore, reports, queries, charts were created.

4   Findings

This section discusses the findings of this study A review of 68 public and private universities and colleges' websites was conducted to find existing social media policies by visiting each university's official website and using the keywords mentioned previously in methodology section. The chart below shows the number of universities in Saudi Arabia with social media policies on their websites.

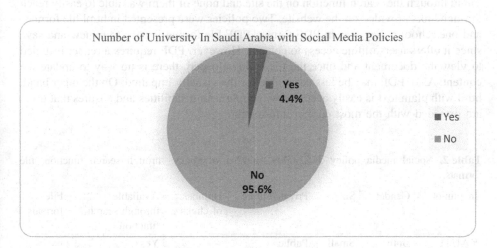

Fig. 1. Number and percentage of institutions with social media policies.

According to the chart shown in Fig. 1, the majority of Saudi universities (65 out of 68, 95.6%) have no policies related to social media usage, with the exception of a few (3 out of 68, 4.4%) such as King Abdullah University of Science and Technology (KAUST), Prince Mohammad Bin Fahd University (PMU) and Umm Al-Qura University (UQU). The webpages/URLs on which the social media content policies were found are listed below in Table 1.

Table 1. Websites researched.

Institution	University social media policy website
King Abdullah University of Science and Technology	https://www.kaust.edu.sa/Documents/downloads/student_handbook.pdf
Prince Mohammad Bin Fahd University	https://www.pmu.edu.sa/policy/policy?ID=224
Umm Al-Qura University	https://uqu.edu.sa/en/it/3953

4.1   Social Media Policy Ease of Access

Table 2 shows the results of only three Saudi universities that have provided social media policies and all of them published in both Arabic and English version where only English version of the policies were analyzed on this study. All three schools accepted both genders. Two universities were small, and one was of larger size. One school is private PMU, while KAUST and UQU are public schools. Only PMU had a comprehensive social media policy, it is a separate policy, while the policies of KAUST and UQU were integrated into other policies in a very general way. All policies were found through the search function on the site and none of them was able to easily reach through links provided on the website. Two policies were presented in html file formats and one school policy was in PDF format. PDF file format is easy to review and save since it offers users offline access to content. However, PDF requires a reader installed to view the document and once the file is downloaded, there is no way to update the content. Also, PDF may be less accessible for the visually impaired. On the other hand, html with plain text is easily accessed by people with disabilities and ensures that users are provided with the most current information.

Table 2. Social media policy availability, number of clicks, through search function, file formats.

Institution	Gender	Size	Private/Public	Number of clicks	Available through search function	File formats
KAUST	Both	Small	Public	–	Yes	pdf
PMU	Both	Small	Private	–	Yes	html
UQU	Both	Large	Public	–	Yes	html

4.2   Social Media Policy Readability

Table 3 shows the summary of the readability scores for the three policies including total number of sentences, number of words, average words per sentence, the Flesch Reading Ease formula (FRE), and Flesch-Kincaid Grade Level (FGL) scores, which shows what level of education the target audience must have to read and comprehend the content of the policy easily. The average total number of sentences is 303.33, while the range was 236 to 387 sentences. PMU had the shortest policy with 236 sentences, while UQU's policy is the longest with 387 sentences. The average number of words for the three universities was 1662, with a range of 1084 to 2719 words. However, the length of policies do not necessarily represent the reading level difficulty.

Table 3. Social media readability of three universities in Saudi Arabia including total of sentence, words, Avg word per sentence, FRE, FGL

Institution	Total sentence	Word	Avg word per sentence	FRE	FGL
KAUST	287	1184	4.12	92.7	1.4
PMU	236	1084	4.59	35.8	9.6
UQU	387	2719	7.02	53.5	7.9
Average	303.33	1662.33	5.24	60.67	6.30

Flesch-Kincaid Grade Level (FGL) scores were obtained for each policy and indicated that the average student in the specified grade level can read the policy. PMU scored the highest level of FGL at 9.6, whereas the lowest FGL score is associated with KAUST at 1.4. The average reading grade level of all policies was 6.30, representing the reading ability of a 6th grade reading level. Once the readability scores are known, the education policy makers can then make necessary improvements in social media policy content so that it is easy for the students, faculty, or staff to read and understand the policy.

4.3   Social Media Policy Content Coverage

The data were analyzed using a qualitative data analysis program to extract different themes regarding the social media policy. In order to process the policy content as NVivo text and to use NVivo's query, analysis started with the creation of a new project, which was named "Saudi Social Media Policy Project". Three source folders were imported into NVivo 12 as a dataset source. In the Tables 4 and 5 below, there are two columns. The first column contains the Nvivo file name and the second column contains the coverage percentage that indicates how much of the policy content is coded at the ethical and security nodes.

Table 4. "Security" code coverage

Item	Percentage coverage
Files\\King Abdullah University of Science and Technology	28.89%
Files\\Prince Mohammad Bin Fahd University	39.45%
Files\\Umm Al-Qura University	0.00%

Table 5. "Ethical" code coverage

Institution	Percentage coverage
Files\\King Abdullah University of Science and Technology	43.39%
Files\\Prince Mohammad Bin Fahd University	10.54%
Files\\Umm Al-Qura University	0.00%

Table 4 above shows the results of the security coding of the three Saudi universities in which the PMU had highest percentage covered with 39.45% of their policy; meanwhile, the KAUST had 28.89% of the ethical rules. Thus, it appears that PMU is more likely than KAUST to focus on the security on their websites.

Table 5 above shows the results of the ethical coding of the three Saudi universities in which the KAUST had highest percentage covered with 43.39% of their policy. On the other hand, UQU had 0.00% of the ethical principles while the PMU had 10.54% of the ethical rules. Thus, it appears that KAUST is more likely than PMU to focus on ethical perspective of social media policies on their websites. Details of the policy analysis results, as well as the data findings from the Nvivo12 software packet, were reported alphabetically by institution's name.

KAUST. The policy of KAUST targets both security and ethical issues with the general standards but focuses more on ethical issues. KAUST had the ethical principles of social media use including communicating legal ramification of social media policy violation. The policy puts emphasis on the privacy of the user, including what you can post and what you cannot post, any content that may create a privacy or security risk, and how to use privacy setting on social media website to protect the user privacy. The policy is clear and straightforward at educating students and faculty in the best practice of social media by providing the most informative policy starting from how to open an account, what email address to use, and ending with how to maintain the account according to the ethical and security principles of use.

PMU. The policy of PMU is comprehensive, and it contains clear guidance for general use of social media, with details on how to behave when using professional or personal social media accounts and how to manage content and posts to be consistent with the University's mission. The policy also includes the risk of reputational damage arising from misuse by faculty, students or employees by inappropriate social media usage such as defamatory comments or posting images about individuals or other organizations.

In addition, it defines information and guidelines that PMU community members must know about privacy and the security risks of managing social media platforms such as using offensive language, bringing up disputes, sharing confidential information, breaching copyright, and making defamatory comments about individuals or other organizations. The main audience is students, but it covers faculty and staff as well.

UQU. UQU does not have a clear policy for academic or general use of social media, as it is only aimed at organizing publishing process such as what kind of news social media can be used for. However, it has a clear policy that is aimed at teaching employees how to deal with crisis, breaking news, and undesirable actions targeted toward the university through the official university account on social media websites. The intended audiences are employees and staff who are responsible for publishing. Overall, nothing has been written for the students or the faculty regarding social media practices and usage.

5 Conclusion

This study evaluated the social media policies of 68 public and private institutions in Saudi Arabia. Three policies were evaluated regarding their ease of access, readability, and content coverage. The results of the evaluated polices were somewhat disappointing. The majority of Saudi HEIs do not have clear policies regarding social media usage on their websites, as 65 of the universities do not have a social media policy and just three of the universities have policies.

In this study, only PMU offered the social media use policy as a separate policy, while UQU and KAUST's policies were integrated into other policies. PMU and UQU presented social media policies as html file formats and KAUST's social media policy was presented in PDF format. None of the universities' social media policies were reachable within three clicks from home page, but all policies were available through the search function. Readability of the policies was evaluated; all three university policies have a readability level equivalent to a 1st and 9th grader who is 7 to 15-years of age. This level is taken as a standard for writing guidelines regarding the social media policy.

Regarding the content coverage, KAUST and PMU policies addressed general guidelines for students and faculty when using social media sites. KAUST provided the most informative policy by providing the best practices of social media use meant to maintain the users account according to the ethical and secure principles of use. PMU's policy was clear and straightforward, providing general rules for all PMU Community members (students, faculty and employees) in a way that mainly focuses on protecting the qualifications and reputation of the University. It specifies guidelines for ethically and securely using the PMU official account, as well as professional, personal, and private accounts. UQU did not have a clear policy because nothing has been written regarding the implementation of social networks for general use or into the classroom for teaching and learning. The policy is unclear regarding ethical and security related issues.

Overall, current Saudi higher education social media policies are not aimed at social media usage for teaching and learning but towards how the universities and colleges would like to be represented publicly. In addition, investigation of the social media policies at Saudi higher education institutions in this study supports previous research that found that Saudi teachers lack the willingness to use social media due to poor guidance from institutional policies [16]. Moreover, faculty fear losing their jobs because of their personal social media, blogging, or other online activities that may be deemed inappropriate [44]. Therefore, SA higher education institutions should have policies that encourage faculty to adapt and use social media sites as learning tools.

Additionally, the rights of the students and faculty must be considered. They have the right to be safe and protected in the online environment [45]. The higher education institutions must have a policy not just for students and faculty members, but also for administrators to direct their actions once the misuse has been reported [45].

To date, no previous research has examined the state of social media policies in Saudi HEIs. There are few studies in the field regarding social networking site usage by Saudi universities; therefore, the adoption of social media as a teaching tool in Saudi Arabian HEIs is unclear [46]. Most of these studies focus on how social media can be used in higher education as a marketing tool. Therefore, the utilization of social media should be encouraged by the Saudi higher education policymakers and administrators by informing students and faculty members about the ethical and security issues involved in using social media sites as learning tools. Additionally, these policymakers and administrators should be establishing polices and guidelines that describe acceptable and unacceptable behaviors on social networking sites. It is planned to continue research on this study by investigating the challenges and policy issues faced by Saudi HEIs when adopting social media into their infrastructure, as well as investigating which factors affect the Saudi policymakers' adoption and formulation of social media policies.

References

1. Abdullatif, A.M., Shahzad, B., Hussain, A.: Evolution of social media in scientific: a case of technology and healthcare professionals in Saudi universities. J. Med. Imaging Health Inf. **7**(6), 1461–1468 (2017)
2. Straumsheim, C., Jaschik, S., Lederman, D.: Faculty Attitudes on Technology. Inside, Washington, DC (2015)
3. Kerr, E.: Professional standards on social media: how colleges and universities have denied students' constitutional rights and courts refused to intervene. JC & UL **41**, 601 (2015)
4. Patrut, M., Patrut, B.: Social Media in Higher Education: Teaching in Web 2.0. IGI Global, Pennsylvania (2013)
5. Kaplan, A.M., Haenlein, M.: Higher education and the digital revolution: about MOOCs, SPOCs, social media, and the Cookie Monster. Bus. Horiz. **59**(4), 441–450 (2016)
6. The Ministry of Education - University Education: Public and private universities and colleges (2019). https://www.moe.gov.sa/en/HigherEducation/governmenthighereducation/StateUniversities/Pages/default.aspx. Accessed Aug 2019
7. Holotescu, C., Grosseck, G.: An empirical analysis of the educational effects of social media in universities and colleges. Internet Learn. **2**(1), 5 (2013)
8. Al-Sharqi, L., Hashim, K., Kutbi, I.: Perceptions of social media impact on students' social behavior: a comparison between Arts and Science students. Int. J. Educ. Soc. Sci. **2**(4), 122–131 (2015)
9. Dunn, L.: Teaching in higher education: can social media enhance the learning experience? (2013)
10. Siddiqui, S., Singh, T.: Social media its impact with positive and negative aspects. Int. J. Comput. Appl. Technol. Res. **5**(2), 71–75 (2016)
11. Vural, Ö.F.: Positive and negative aspects of using social networks in higher education: a focus group study. Educ. Res. Rev. **10**(8), 1147 (2015)

12. Wang, Q., Chen, W., Liang, Y.: The Effects of Social Media on College Students (MBA Scholarship Research). Johnson & Wales University, Providence (2011)
13. Gikas, J., Grant, M.M.: Mobile computing devices in higher education: student perspectives on learning with cellphones, smartphones & social media. Internet High. Educ. **19**, 18–26 (2013)
14. Poore, M.: Using Social Media in the Classroom: A Best Practice Guide. Sage, Thousand Oaks (2015)
15. Manca, S., Ranieri, M.: Facebook and the others. Potentials and obstacles of social media for teaching in higher education. Comput. Educ. **95**, 216–230 (2016)
16. Al-Khalifa, H.S., Garcia, R.A.: The state of social media in Saudi Arabia's higher education. Int. J. Technol. Educ. Mark. **3**(1), 65–76 (2013)
17. Alsufyan, N.K., Aloud, M.: The state of social media engagement in Saudi universities. J. Appl. Res. High. Educ. **9**(2), 267–303 (2017)
18. Castagnera, J.O., Lanza, I.V.: Social networking and faculty discipline: a Pennsylvania case points toward confrontational times, requiring collective bargaining attention. J. Collect. Bargain. Acad. **2**(1), 5 (2010)
19. Kim, Y., Sohn, D., Choi, S.M.: Cultural difference in motivations for using social network sites: a comparative study of American and Korean college students. Comput. Hum. Behav. **27**(1), 365–372 (2011)
20. Pookulangara, S., Koesler, K.: Cultural influence on consumers' usage of social networks and its' impact on online purchase intentions. J. Retail. Consum. Serv. **18**(4), 348–354 (2011)
21. Sánchez, R.A., Cortijo, V., Javed, U.: Students' perceptions of Facebook for academic purposes. Comput. Educ. **70**, 138–149 (2014)
22. Yuan, L., Powell, S.J.: MOOCs and open education: implications for higher education (2013)
23. Viberg, O., Grönlund, Å.: Cross-cultural analysis of users' attitudes toward the use of mobile devices in second and foreign language learning in higher education: a case from Sweden and China. Comput. Educ. **69**, 169–180 (2013)
24. Hurst, T.R.: Give Me Your Password: the intrusive social media policies in our schools. CommLaw Conspec. **22**, 196 (2013)
25. de Zwart, M., Lindsay, D., Henderson, M., Phillips, M.: Teenagers, Legal Risks and Social Networking Sites. Faculty of Education, Monash University, Clayton (2011)
26. Chen, B., Bryer, T.: Investigating instructional strategies for using social media in formal and informal learning. Int. Rev. Res. Open Distrib. Learn. **13**(1), 87–104 (2012)
27. Jothi, P.S., Neelamalar, M., Prasad, R.S.: Analysis of social networking sites: a study on effective communication strategy in developing brand communication. J. Media Commun. Stud. **3**(7), 234–242 (2011)
28. Lazar, J., Feng, J.H., Hochheiser, H.: Research Methods in Human-Computer Interaction. Morgan Kaufmann, Burlington (2017)
29. Meiselwitz, G., Wang, Y.: Evaluations of policies for social networking use in higher education. In: InEdMedia + Innovate Learning, pp. 424–429. Association for the Advancement of Computing in Education (AACE) (2016)
30. Zakaluk, B.L., Samuels, S.J.: Readability: Its Past, Present, and Future. International Reading Association, Newark (1988)
31. Flesch, R.: A dissenting opinion on readability. Elem. Engl. **26**(6), 332–340 (1949)
32. Flesch, R., Gould, A.J.: The Art of Readable Writing. Harper, New York (1949)
33. Kincaid, J.P., Fishburne Jr., R.P., Rogers, R.L., Chissom, B.S.: Derivation of new readability formulas (automated readability index, fog count and flesch reading ease formula) for navy enlisted personnel (1975)

34. D'Alessandro, D.M., Kingsley, P., Johnson-West, J.: The readability of pediatric patient education materials on the World Wide Web. Arch. Pediatr. Adolesc. Med. **155**(7), 807–812 (2001)
35. Web FX: Digital marketing that drives results: readability test tool (2019). https://www.webfx.com. Accessed Oct 2019
36. Welsh, E.: Dealing with data: using NVivo in the qualitative data analysis process. In: Forum Qualitative Sozialforschung/Forum: Qualitative Social Research, 31 May 2002, vol. 3, no. 2 (2002)
37. Hilal, A.H., Alabri, S.S.: Using NVivo for data analysis in qualitative research. Int. Interdiscip. J. Educ. **2**(2), 181–186 (2013)
38. Ozkan, B.C.: Using NVivo to analyze qualitative classroom data on constructivist learning environments. Qual. Rep. **9**(4), 589–603 (2004)
39. Corbin, J.M., Strauss, A.: Grounded theory methodology. Handb. Qual. Res. **17**, 273–285 (2011)
40. Norris, C.: The current state of US higher education social media policies with regard to teaching and learning: a document review needs assessment. University of North Texas (2013)
41. Dyer, M.M., Carver, M., Miller, J.K.: An analysis of states' policies regarding social media use in education. Dissertation, Saint Louis University (2016)
42. Bon, S.C., Bathon, J., Balzano, A.-M.: Social media use—and misuse—by teachers: looking to the courts for human resource policy guidance. J. Sch. Public Relat. **34**(2), 193–217 (2013)
43. Maher, C., Hadfield, M., Hutchings, M., de Adam, E.: Ensuring rigor in qualitative data analysis: a design research approach to coding combining NVivo with traditional material methods. Int. J. Qual. Methods **17**, 1–13 (2018). https://doi.org/10.1177/1609406918786362
44. Stoessel, J.W.: Social Media Policy Implications in Higher Education: Do Faculty, Administration, and Staff have a Place in the "Social Network"? (2016)
45. Jacobsen, W.C., Forste, R.: The wired generation: academic and social outcomes of electronic media use among university students. Cyberpsychol. Behav. Soc. Netw. **14**(5), 275–280 (2011)
46. Abdulaziz, A.K.: Social media adoption among university instructors in Saudi Arabia (2016)
47. Arab Social Media Report (2017). https://www.arabsocialmediareport.com. Accessed Oct 2019

AMISA: A Pilot Study of an Emotional Supporting Device Between Friends Over Long-Distance

Yuanyuan Bian[1] and Teng-Wen Chang[2(✉)]

[1] Beijing Institute of Technology, Beijing, China
bianbian. y@gmail. com
[2] National Yunlin University of Science and Technology, Yunlin, Taiwan
tengwen@yuntech. edu. tw

Abstract. Under the rigid regulation of Chinese 985-Project sponsored university entrance exam for 2.09% in 2018, the new generation of Chinese teenagers usually have to leave their province to another city which is thousand miles away from home. This means that these young adults have to leave familiar family support network and deal with homesickness earlier than other countries. Such lonely experience will affect these young adults who usually grew up as the middle class in the modern Chinese society. Friendship is the only support these young adults will get. And the hug from friends are their most missed interactions. Our research intends to develop an interactive device that can transfer their experience into a supporting comfort system that can provide warm awareness and inter-personal relationship. This paper reports our pilot study: an eMotional Supporting Awareness system (AMISA) as a haptic affect support system that supports affective communication with friends over long-distance. The approach of this study is user centered design, through user interviews and literature reviews, we defined the user requirements and found corresponding technology in HCI to prototype the conceptual design. We developed AMISA from three dimensions: (1) affective analysis; (2) mediated social touch; (3) user experience. Subsequently, we conducted a user evaluation of the prototype, AMISA is used as a data collector to observe user interactions for iterating subsequent design outcomes.

Keywords: Homesickness · Mediated social touch · Friendship connection

1 Introduction

Homesickness is a mixture of emotions in the above-mentioned cultural context, and the interaction design for comforting homesickness with computer is a difficult problem, especially with social implication like the young Chinese middle class. It is an important feature of Chinese society that young people have to migrate to a new environment for higher education and job opportunities. Most of these young people have left their family alone for the first time. Due to the cultural influence of Chinese society, their most typical emotion is homesickness. These young adults as the future Chinese middle class, aged 18−25, are at a critical transition stage in their lives. In the

© Springer Nature Switzerland AG 2020
G. Meiselwitz (Ed.): HCII 2020, LNCS 12195, pp. 471–482, 2020.
https://doi.org/10.1007/978-3-030-49576-3_34

adaptation process, friends are the only support. Our research focuses on the long-distance emotional communication between these young adults and their friends when homesickness appears. And further exploration is conducted with the affective interaction patterns.

The results of our pilot study, based on our findings, answers the following two questions: (1) Why do these Chinese young adults who are far away from their parents communicate with close friends when they feel homesick? (2) What are the requirements in their long-distance emotional communication with close friends? In our user interviews, we found that these young Chinese people are more willing to communicate with friends than to contact their parents when they are homesick. We analyze the culture of Chinese society and further explore the homesickness. Based on the above two issues, we propose and design a system (AMISA) to support long-distance emotional communication that simulates a real hug, to promote the emotional communication between these young people and friends. We developed AMISA from three dimensions: (1) analysis emotional interaction characteristics; (2) explore communication over long-distance; (3) combining interactive mode and technology.

1.1 Cultural Context

Actually, the homesickness in this paper is not only missing parents which often includes a series of negative emotions, such as loneliness, anxiety, confusion and stress [1].These young people are still in the transitional stage of adulthood, and it is difficult to handle such homesick emotions. They often ignore the emotions, caused a backlog of emotions and affected the well-being. Chinese collectivist culture makes individual and their family have a strong connection, but it is different from contacting parents when they are homesick. The relationship between Chinese parents and children is very complicated [2]. In traditional Chinese culture, filial piety is considered to be one of the most important qualities, which means, they should not worry their parents about themselves. Therefore, they will not share their difficulties or bad feelings with their parents, but only communicate good experiences with their parents. On the other hand, they cannot get enough support from their parents when they are encountering difficulties, such as unsatisfactory test scores. In fact, our interviewees' data shows that respondents often contacted their close friends to communicate when they were homesick. Octavia, J.R. et al. showed that it is very important to share difficulties and feelings with close friends over long-distance [3]. Especially in difficult times, friends will support each other by establishing connections. However, the long distance between them has made communication more difficult. Therefore, we aimed at build an emotional support awareness system for emotional communication between friends and promote affective transmission between them over long-distance.

1.2 Awareness System

These young people often find it difficult to show friends their homesickness in communication, or it will be ignored because they are too euphemistic. Since homesickness is not one-off, the emotions that are ignored will continue to accumulate. Therefore, it is important to be aware of the emergence of homesick emotions. Due to the indirect emotional expression of the Chinese, they often express some metaphors words in communication, hoping that other people could understand his intention without showing directly. Technically speaking, the transmission of these implied information needs to be showed by more media. With the development of technology, objects in people's living environment have been able to sense. The study of awareness system, the surrounding environment is often used to create a communication environment to support the user's emotional interaction. The surrounding environment has a great impact on the user over long-distance communication. And we focus on using daily necessities to build awareness systems.

1.3   Emotional and Touch Interface

Touch could transmit positive or negative emotions, and different touch gestures also affect the different emotional transmission. Although there have been many researches on the relationship between couples or family members in long-distance intimate communication, little attention has been paid to intimate communication between friends. Applying haptic technology to long-distance social communication, this field is called intermediary social touch. Mediated social touch is defined as "the ability of one actor to touch another actor over a distance by means of tactile or kinesthetic feedback technology" [4]. Generally, the construction of the mediated haptic prototype should have input-output interactive features. It should be noted that, people should have a common understanding of the intent of the interaction, and based on this common knowledge, emotions can be transmitted more effectively through touch. In face-to-face communication, people could understand the intentions of other's behaviors by observing their expressions, while the mediated social touch loss the channel. Visual display for touch could make people feel real, and it is also a multi-modal interaction. Therefore, visual feedback on haptic interaction is a very important part of our emotional system.

2   Related Studies

There are three main parts in AMISA: (1) awareness system; (2) emotional interface; (3) touch interface. Therefore, the discussion of these three parts is important. It should be noted that due to the complexity of homesickness and the negative emotions usually implied, we will discuss the emotional interface and touch interface separately. One of the goals of our research is to analyze some of the negative emotions implied by homesickness through the analysis of emotions. And a subtle interaction system is essential based on the Chinese indirect emotional expression. Emotional awareness system allows users to establish connections without expressing words. Touch is the most emotional way to express emotions in social interaction, and there are many mediated social touch studies for long-distance communication, we will build an awareness system based on touch.

2.1   Awareness System

One line of the research is to create indirect and subtle interactive environments for users. Hassib, M. et al. Studied the provision of additional communication channels for chat by providing physiological data [5]. They designed and developed a chat application, HeartChat, to support close partners to understand each other's situation and emotional state by sharing heart rate in real time during chat. They designed three views: Heart-Bubbles, Heart-Light, and Heart-Button to support user interaction. In addition, they have implemented implicit and explicit heart rate sharing modes. In their assessment, users will explicitly share with people farther away and implicitly with people who are more closely connected with them. In the final results of their research, it was found that chat with increased heart rate not only enhances people's understanding of each other's state, but also increases people's understanding of their state. Integrating physiological signals such as heart rate with ubiquitous activities in life can effectively promote the development of self-awareness and happiness. In our previous research, SAM constructed two perceptible home spaces by establishing walls formed by plant interfaces, and explored indirect interaction methods and possible intentions of interactive behaviors [6]. It uses the characteristics of light growth of plants to transfer emotions, and achieves the purpose of indirect interaction through light. Lover's Cups uses drinking as an implied communication method and creates multi-modal interactions [7]. When two people are holding a pair of cups at the same time, the cups slowly glow to make the two people realize each other. When two people drink at the same time, the brightness of the light reaches the maximum, indicating the closeness and connection of the two people. This project extends the form of communication from audio and video to other daily life behaviors, which brings new thinking to us to create a long-distance communication system.

2.2   Emotional Interface

Homesickness is a mixture of emotions in the above-mentioned cultural context, and it is complicated to analysis homesickness. Moodsense can infer the user's mood from the information already in the mobile smartphone, and occasionally ask the user to input their mood [8]. Our smartphone already has enough user information, such as location, calendar, phone, etc. In this research, a continuously running recorder was used to record iPhone usage and let users manually input emotions through iPhone. They correlate user-entered emotions with events that occur to figure out which metrics can infer emotions. They reported that emotion classification is very personal, and when based on the data of the same participant, the accuracy of emotion classification improves on average by 91%.

2.3   Touch Interface

Different touch gestures have different effects on the research. Hug is the most emotional gesture among many touch gestures, which can convey love and warmth. "Hug over distance" is a kind of inflatable vest that can simulate the feeling of hugging remotely. It is used to support remote intimate communication between couples in different places [9]. Touch and undisturbed are the focus of the project. The inflatable vest is designed to be a kind of Make intimate contact over long distances without disturbing it. HaptiHug expresses embracing distant hugs via an online communication system that supports haptic feedback [10]. Based on the pressure and duration of the actual hug, the haptihug control system generates a signal that produces a feeling similar to a real hug, will make users have a higher sense of immersion. Block, A.E. and others explored human responses to different robot physical characteristics and hug behaviors [11]. Their goal is to test soft, warm, touch-sensitive PR2 humanoid robots by matching their hugs Stress and hug duration to provide humans with a satisfying hug. Its findings show that people prefer soft, warm hugs to hard, cold hugs. Ugur Yavuz, S. et al. and others designed an EMbody system composed of three prototypes to explore the intimate communication mode in long-distance communication from the aspects of haptic, vision and audio [12]. Their practice did not use a single sensory channel Instead, it combines visual, haptic, and auditory signals, and provides a reference for how to conduct emotional communication through multi-modal sensory interactions. In real life, accepting a hug can be accomplished by sensing temperature, pressure, and touching. As a kind of interface that can show tactile parameters well, haptic devices are used to simulate real hugs.

3 How Do We Approach

3.1 The Problems and the Approach

The focus of this study is on affective communication when migrant young people experience homesickness. There are three reasons for this problem: one is the influence of Chinese cultural atmosphere and cultural normative on the behavior of these young people in life; the other is the indirect emotional interaction of Chinese people, which makes users hidden the emotions and not expressed or ignored because they are too euphemistic, so they cannot be supported. The last reason is that there are restrictions on the interaction in long-distance communication, which hinders the indirect emotional transmission. The approach of this study is user centered design, and we define user requirements through two interviews. Then we review the related literatures to find corresponding technology that can support user requirements. Finally, we developed an emotional support awareness system to help them deal with homesickness and promote emotional transmission in long-distance communication. And by designing and developing a prototype, we finally performing user test and evaluation to iterate the system.

3.2 User Interview

We recruited 10 users whose information are suitable for demands to participate in the interview. The interview sample consisted of 3 male and 7 females. Two of these females have transnational migration experiences, and the remaining interviewees have migrated across provinces. Two male and four females had two migration experience. It was found in our interviews that one of the male participants did not have the typical user characteristics we needed, so the content of his interview was not included in the results. Additionally, we explored user requirements through two phases of interview. In the first interview, initial understanding of the long-distance communication between young people and relatives and friends and the needs of homesickness is focused. The second interview gave a deeper understanding of the user's emotional interaction.

Furthermore, the findings are: (1) Female interviewees have a higher level of homesickness than male, and women have stronger communication needs with friends. Therefore, women are our target group. (2) Most of the homesickness emotions occur when a person is alone, and they are all in the home. And some things have a strong impact on homesickness, such as spending traditional festivals alone and failing the exam. (3) When they miss home, they will not contact their parents first, but communicate with friends to share their difficulties. And they miss the hug from their friends. (4) They usually feeling homesick for a while, but usually not very strong. (5) More than half of the respondents had the habit of turning over old photos when they were homesick. Female respondents would lie on the bed and hold their fluffy pillows. For female respondents, the pillow is the most familiar object when they are homesick, and each female respondent has no less than one pillow on the bed. (6) In most cases, it becomes difficult to take the initiative to share a mood with the previously trusted friend. And if their friends do not respond in time, the sense of loss will increase.

3.3   Requirements

Analysis of interviews with two results: First point is that established a connection between two friends in an indirect, subtle way to express their emotional status. The second point is that the response between friends should be warm and comfortable, which will helpful to communicate the emotion between them. The prediction of homesickness is also an important part. It is found from the interview that the appearance of homesickness is usually related to some troubles in the near future. By breaking down homesick emotions and connecting the corresponding events, there is an opportunity to be able to predict the homesickness.

The emotional support awareness system is developed with three steps: (1) Analyzing the emotional interaction characteristics of target users, and develop interactive modes; (2) Learning about the long-distance communication methods and contents in their daily lives, and look for technologies for the computational support; (3) Combining interactive mode and interactive technology, providing user information through prototype and user testing, and iterative design of the system based on user experience.

4   The AMISA

4.1   Developing Awareness System

We support emotional communication among friends by introducing an awareness system. AMISA is an emotional support awareness system based on touch. On the one hand, touch is used in AMISA as an interactive way to convey emotions. Touch can support the transmission of implied messages among friends, which is also a system of awareness that allows users to make less effort. And we designed a hug device to satisfy the interviewee's hug requirement. The familiar daily objects such as pillow serve as an interactive interface which also provides a familiar environment for the user's emotional interaction.

According to the interaction in the system, we set the pillow mode to three states: (1) Awake status. When the user is holding the pillow, a low-frequency breathing lamp will light up to convey the status of the pillow to the user. (2) Hug status. After receiving the hug signal, the pillow will simultaneously perform three parameters: vibration, temperature, and breathing light. The longer the partner conveys the hug, the temperature will increase over time, but the temperature is always controlled within a safe range. The breathing light will gradually change from the low-frequency cold light in the original awake state to the long and warm light. (3) Response status. After receiving the hug, the receiver can respond to the sender's hug by touching his pillow. When the receiver touches his or her pillow, the pillow of the other part starts to execute the response command, making short vibrations and fast warm light flashes to convey the response to the user who sent the hug.

4.2 Emotional Interface and Information Visualization

Emotional Interface. Since homesickness usually implied negative emotions, in order to enable the system to further decompose homesickness, we have designed an emotional interface to create emotional tags. This interface has three functions: provide more specific emotion categories or feeling options for users to choose; ask users to select the events that occurred during the day when using the emotional interface; record and analysis user data and present them as visual icons. The emotions selected by the users are designed as corresponding emoticons, and text descriptions are added at the same time. Different emotion icons will correspond to different colors, such as orange for happiness and blue for sadness. The emotional interface will record the user's current mood by selecting the emotion icon in the interface (see Fig. 1). After selecting the emotion icon, the interface will let user further choose the activities he has participated in, such as exams, parties, contacting parents, traveling, etc.

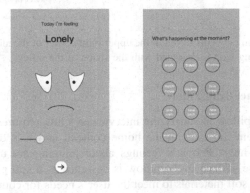

Fig. 1. The emotional interface is designed as an emoticon for users to choose.

In addition, we also designed an album in the emotional interface. In the interview, we found that when there was a feeling of homesickness, most respondents had the habit of turning over old photos. An important feature of photo albums is to allow users to add emotion tags to photos (see Fig. 2). If user wants to see photos, emotional tags allows users to quickly retrieve their goals, and can add detailed descriptions or share them with friends. And the operation will be recognized by the system to record the category of the emotional tag and the time of the operation.

Visualization of Interactive Information. Another important aspect of the emotional interface is to visualize interactive information. Visual feedback on interactive actions is a very important part of the emotional awareness system we create. First, the effectiveness of haptic transmission is greatly increased by the assistance of visual feedback. In face-to-face communication, people will obtain a lot of hidden information by observing each other's expressions and body movements, which will help them better understand the information. For mediated social touch, people cannot see each other due to long-distance online communication, so we use a more direct visual display to remind the interactive action that is taking place in the system. We have designed a small icon that represents hug. When the user receives a hug signal, the pillow will simulate the hug while the hug icon will reminder user by the mobile phone, and it will continue to be displayed until the end of the hug. After receiving the response, the user could also react to the friend. At this time, the friend who received the response will display the same hug icon (see Fig. 2).

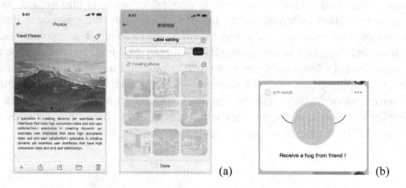

Fig. 2. (a) The emotion tag is displayed in the upper right corner of the album, and you can edit it by clicking it. (b) Hug icon is designed with the shape of the pillow.

4.3   Touch Interface-Hug Pillow

We designed a hug pillow to satisfy the interviewee's hug requirement. The pillow is the most familiar item for users in the home context, and it is designed as a touch interface to convey hugs. People's feelings about hugging are usually warm, comfortable and soft. The surface of the pillow is designed as a soft plush fabric, and the interior is filled with soft materials to meet the user's needs for comfort. The surface of the pillow is sewn with an m-shaped conductive wire. When people hold the pillow, they will touch the conductive wire to send the hug to each other (see Fig. 3). Hugs in real life can be decomposed into many complex physical parameters. We choose to construct the hug interface by embedding three parameters: temperature, vibration, and light in the pillow, and simulate the real hug through the interaction between them.

When user holds the pillow, his hands will come into contact with the surface of the pillow, and the surface of the pillow is sewn with an "m" type conductive wire. When the human body comes into contact with the conductive wire, its original resistance value will be changed, thereby determining whether the user is holding the pillow. Although the pillow is the most familiar interface when the user feels homesick, it is not that the user will hold the pillow when there is a homesick emotion, there will be other situations.

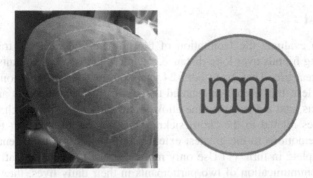

Fig. 3. The pillow is designed with a plush surface, the LED strip is on the side of the pillow. The m-type conductive wire is sewn on the surface to ensure that it can be easily touched.

4.4   User Scenario

We take the event of having the pillow as the trigger point of the AMISA system wake-up. When the user holds the pillow, it connects to the emotional interface via Bluetooth, and the interface further collects the user's current emotional status. When the pillow detects that it has been take up by the user, it will immediately enter the awake status. At this time, the pillow will light up a low-frequency breathing light to remind the user. After receiving the signal transmitted by the pillow, the emotional interface will send an inquiry message to the user's mobile phone to guide the user to enter the interface for determining the emotion. The emotional interface will record the user's current mood by selecting the emotion icon in the interface. After selecting the emotion icon, the interface will let user further choose the activities he has participated in, such as exams, parties, contacting parents, traveling, etc. After inquiring the user by the emotional interface, the system will send a reminder signal to the friend's pillow with the user's consent. When the friend's pillow receives a signal, it will flash a blue breathing light to remind the owner that her friend is in a bad mood. Considering that the user may not be next to the pillow, the user's mobile phone will also receive a reminder message. When the friend saw the blue light flashing on the pillow, she understood that the other person was in a bad mood and needed her comfort. She will send a message to she's friend, and at the same time hold the pillow to send a hug to the friend. After the hug signal is sent, the mobile phone will pop up a prompt. After confirming, the actuator module on the other party's pillow will enter the hug status and start the hugging. The breathing light is to more directly indicate the current status of the system to user through different colors and flashing frequencies, which is convenient for the user to understand.

5 User Test

The approach of this study is user centered design, and we iterate the system by developed prototypes and user tests.

5.1 User Test

Our goal is to evaluate the facilitation of the hug interface on the transmission of emotions among friends over long-distance. We recruited two participants who are real friends in the real life. They were both 24 years old and have migration experiences.

Before the test, the researchers shared the stories of homesickness and wandering with the subjects, and at the same time allowed the participants to watch relevant short films and stories related to the "homesickness" emotions, in an effort to evoke their homesickness emotions to the greatest extent. We provide two test scenarios for each subject to complete in turn. (1) Use only mobile phone to communication. This condition is the communication of two participants in their daily lives, they can use text, video, voice, etc. to communicate. (2) Use mobile phone and the pillow to communicate at the same time.

During the test, the subject was asked to communicate about homesickness related sad topics. It can be a moment of homesickness during the migration process, or some negative emotions arising from it, such as the pressure you feel or the confusion about future things. Talking homesickness to user B from user A, this process lasts about 5 min. User B then expressed support and comfort to user A, transmitting positive emotions. In Scenario 1, only mobile phone communication is used. In Scenario 2, the pillow is used for interaction. The test scenario is shown in the following figure (see Fig. 4).

Fig. 4. Two participants are communication through the pillow.

5.2 Data Collection and Results

Because the emotional state of an individual affects the physiological signals of the body, we use GSR to monitor the physiological signals during the test. GSR is a physiological sensor that monitors the emotional state through changes in skin resistance [13]. The tester's biological signals were collected, and the data is shown below (see Fig. 5).

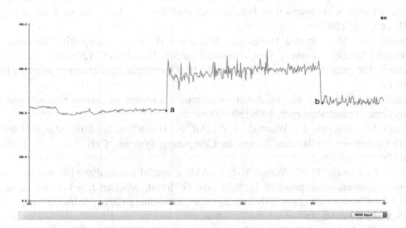

Fig. 5. The two points a and b in the figure are the starting point and the ending point of the hug. We can see that the data has changed greatly from the initial baseline state.

Although such data indicate that the hug pillow has successfully changed the emotional state from the baseline at the beginning, the values collected are rough. And emotions are very subjective, and the degree of emotion caused by each person is different, which needs to be further verified in subsequent studies.

After the test, we interviewed two participants and have the results. Through send hug with pillow could make them feel stronger emotion expression in the communication with friends. And the feel about physical distance from the friend is getting closer. The two participants agreed that the form of a touch interface such as a pillow is very kind, and that a hug system such as AMISA is very useful and necessary.

6 Conclusion

The approach of this study is user centered design, through user interviews and literature reviews, we defined the user requirements and found corresponding technology in HCI to prototype the conceptual design. Finally, we conducted the user evaluation, we tested the prototype on "whether the hug interface promotes the transfer of emotions between friends". We divided the test into two different phases and let the participants complete the corresponding tasks. We evaluated the prototype by using GSR sensors to monitor the biological signals of the participants and interviewing the participants after the test. The results showed that AMISA is successful in promoting the transfer of emotions among friends. We collected the user information for the iterative design, and made suggestions and directions for the next stage of research.

References

1. Poyrazli, S., Lopez, M.D.: An exploratory study of perceived discrimination and homesickness: a comparison of international students and American students. J. Psychol. **141**, 263–280 (2007)
2. ten Bhömer, M., van den Hoven, E.: Interaction design for supporting communication between Chinese sojourners. Pers. Ubiquit. Comput. **17**, 145–157 (2011)
3. Octavia, J.R., van den Hoven, E., De Mondt, H.: Overcoming the Distance between Friends (2007)
4. Haans, A., Ijsselsteijn, W.: Mediated social touch: a review of current research and future directions. Virtual Reality **9**, 149–159 (2005)
5. Hassib, M., Buschek, D., Wozniak, P.W., Alt, F.: HeartChat. In: Proceedings of the 2017 CHI Conference on Human Factors in Computing Systems, CHI 2017, pp. 2239–2251 (2017)
6. Yu, G.-J., Chang, T.-W., Wang, Y.-C.: SAM: a spatial interactive platform for studying family communication problem. In: Salvendy, G., Smith, Michael J. (eds.) Human Interface 2011. LNCS, vol. 6772, pp. 207–216. Springer, Heidelberg (2011). https://doi.org/10.1007/978-3-642-21669-5_25
7. Chung, H., Lee, C.-H.J., Selker, T.: Lover's cups. In: CHI 2006 Extended Abstracts on Human Factors in Computing Systems, CHI EA 2006 (2006)
8. Rebughini, P.: Friendship dynamics between emotions and trials. Soc. Res. Online **16**, 119–127 (2011)
9. Mueller, F.F., Vetere, F., Gibbs, M.R., Kjeldskov, J., Pedell, S., Howard, S.: Hug over a distance. In: CHI 2005 Extended Abstracts on Human Factors in Computing Systems, CHI 2005 (2005)
10. Tsetserukou, D.: HaptiHug: a novel haptic display for communication of hug over a distance. In: Kappers, A.M.L., van Erp, J.B.F., Bergmann Tiest, W.M., van der Helm, F.C.T. (eds.) EuroHaptics 2010. LNCS, vol. 6191, pp. 340–347. Springer, Heidelberg (2010). https://doi.org/10.1007/978-3-642-14064-8_49
11. Block, A.E., Kuchenbecker, K.J.: Softness, warmth, and responsiveness improve robot hugs. Int. J. Social Robot. **11**, 49–64 (2018)
12. Ugur Yavuz, S., Bordegoni, M., Carulli, M.: A design practice on communicating emotions through sensory signals. Concurr. Eng. **26**, 147–156 (2016)
13. Setyohadi, D.B., Kusrohmaniah, S., Gunawan, S.B., Pranowo, P., Prabuwono, A.S.: Galvanic skin response data classification for emotion detection. Int. J. Electr. Comput. Eng. (IJECE) **8** (2018)

An Agile Product Design in a Smart City Context: A Use Case for Air Pollution Awareness

Jaime Díaz[✉][iD] and Oscar Ancán[iD]

Depto. Cs. de la Computación e Informática, Universidad de la Frontera,
Temuco, Chile
jaimeignacio.diaz@ufrontera.cl

Abstract. The rise of systems for smart cities has led to an increase in the incorporation of air quality monitoring and alert systems. However, evidence on the real impact of these initiatives on city-dwellers is still far from conclusive. Recent investigations stress the importance of early user involvement in the appropriation of proposed solutions; this article shows how an approach through product design can support the development and successful implementation of the mobile application AIRE implemented in the context of the SmartArucanía smart city project, from the perspective of iterative design and exploration focusing on citizen participation. The product design process involved three interventions: (i) a market benchmark − presenting the basic principles of functionality and aesthetics adopted by the market; (ii) a heuristic evaluation − evaluating the initial development proposal and identifying preliminary problems with the application; (iii) a user test with citizens − collecting information on the problems identified and general feelings about the use of the application. Through active participation of users in the early stages of product design, we ensured that the AIRE mobile application could inform citizens about complex concepts related with particulate matter which have a direct impact on their health and quality of life. This will improve decision-making in critical pollution episodes.

Keywords: Human-Computer Interaction · Smart cities · Service design · User experience · User-centered design

1 Introduction

It is estimated that around 93% of the polluting emissions in the city of *Temuco, Chile,* come from domestic firewood combustion. These emissions contain high concentrations of ultrafine material which is harmful to health [16]. This situation has continued over the last 10 years without a clear solution for residents.

The *SmartAraucania* project grew out of various initiatives intended to modernise the city, improving the residents' quality of life in traditional areas of smart city development such as security, transport, health, urban infrastructure and

© Springer Nature Switzerland AG 2020
G. Meiselwitz (Ed.): HCII 2020, LNCS 12195, pp. 483–500, 2020.
https://doi.org/10.1007/978-3-030-49576-3_35

the environment. One of the critical issues associated with rapid urbanisation is air quality monitoring, together with smart infrastructures for visualisation and follow-up.

The AIRE mobile application was conceived in this context. It is designed to provide real time information on changes in the levels of $PM_{2.5}$ (particulate matter of diameter smaller than $2.5\mu m$) in different areas of *Temuco*. The application obtains data from a network of monitoring devices containing sensors which capture environmental data every 10 min, 24 h a day. This application forms part of an ecosystem of (mainly open-source) technological solutions, the purpose of which is to offer complete display infrastructure to allow other devices to publish monitoring data.

One of the motivations of the present document is to describe our experience in the integration of iterative software; it was developed under the concept of User-Centred Design, basing all the requirements, times, users and development teams on the reports and demands of a real citizens' initiative.

The present article describes some technical aspects of the architecture and the display. We also describe the interventions carried out to obtain the final product: (i) a User-Centred Design perspective to establish initial expectations; (ii) market analysis; (iii) a usability evaluation test; (iv) final validation by a user test.

As a result, all the experiences, feedback and software iterations enabled the technological team not only to develop a technically robust application, but also to generate social impact and awareness of the problem by providing information to final users in a simple format.

2 Background

2.1 Smart Cities

Although the concept of a *smart city* has become widely used in the last 5 years, the term was first introduced in the late 1990s [8]. It was subsequently adopted by companies such as *IBM* and *CISCO* as a way of representing complex software systems that interact in areas like energy, the environment, education, security and infrastructure [19].

A smart city can therefore be defined as any form of technological innovation that affects urban planning and the development and operation of cities. Nevertheless, important social aspects must also be incorporated which place people at the centre of development, building in collaborative planning and citizen participation to promote integrated, sustainable development [9].

Thus, the essential object of a smart city is to provide a single technological platform, integrating all its services, devices, interfaces and infrastructures, to allow smart functioning of the city; it can then both support society and be improved by user experience.

From the perspective of cyberphysical systems, a smart city must have the following characteristics [11]:

a) **Connectability:** devices connected to networks deliver the information detected to the Web.
b) **Sensitivity:** the characteristics of the environment can be detected by sensors.
c) **Accessibility:** information on the environment is published and accessible to users in the Web.
d) **Ubiquitousness:** users can access the information anywhere, at any time.
e) **Sociability:** users who acquire information can publish it on social media.
f) **Sharing:** not only data can be shared, but also physical objects which can be used when they are unoccupied; cars, houses/flats, etc.
g) **Visibility:** the information is seen not only by individuals on mobile devices but also in physical spaces, e.g. at traffic lights.

All the above elements must interact under a basic, consistent organisation with four levels of development [9]:

a) **Infrastructure and Connectivity:** these are the minimum channels for wired and wireless connectivity for sending and receiving data;
b) **Connected sensors and devices:** allow signals to be captured from the environment and transmitted to the control centre by wired or wireless infrastructure;
c) **Integrated operation and control centres:** software applications offer monitoring and visualization panels, manage devices remotely and distribute information according to different subject areas;
d) **Communication and control interfaces:** allow the population to send and receive information through services, web portals and mobile applications associated with open data platforms.

Smart city initiatives have increased substantially in recent years, due to the falling cost of electronic sensors and circuit boards, the increased potential for processing large volumes of data and the supply of display platforms for cloud-based solutions [21].

The literature reports numerous cases of cities classified as "smart", the most recent being: Italy in 2019 [10], China in 2019 [34], Ruanda in 2019 [18] and Mexico in 2019 [23]. At the same time, the need has been recognised for technological ecosystems which prioritise monitoring of the environment; one of the principal aspects developed has been monitoring critical air quality episodes and issuing alerts.

GreenIot is a technological ecosystem developed in Sweden using an integrated system of environmental sensors and open data, it supports urban planning and sustainable transport [3]. Another example is *PortoLivingLab* in Portugal, which is based on an infrastructure of environmental sensors. Data processing is used in a software ecosystem to manage environmental phenomena, public transport and person flows [30]. Systems with similar characteristics have been applied in Spain in 2019 [29] and New Zealand in 2018 [17].

2.2   Citizen Participation in Design

Citizen participation in the design of user interfaces for mobile applications and webs in the early stages of development is one of the essential characteristics of the implementation of software solutions for smart cities [15]. In this context, avoiding the creation of inefficient interfaces which might result in unsuccessful user experiences or rejection of the interface by users has given rise to design strategies taken from other contexts and applied successfully in the domain of smart cities [2].

Cases like the design of mobile applications for tourism [33], or applications designed for time spent travelling [13] reflect this. Thus studying user experience, in contexts of intelligent cities, does not refer only to web and mobile systems; we have also identified cases of citizen participation in the early design stages of more complex infrastructures that have to deal with specific hardware, such as the management of traffic lights for adjustment to match demand, as discussed by Alnanih et al. [4].

One of these strategies, called *Adaptive Interface Ecosystems (AIE)*, can be applied to the existing interfaces in smart city systems. These do not have to be redesigned, but incorporate progressive adjustment and adaptation mechanisms based on user interaction [32].

2.3   Agile Product Design

In project administration, Agile Software Design and Development is preferred to a predefined sequence of steps [7]. In general terms, this methodology seeks: (i) involvement of human aspects in software development, rather than processes and tools; (ii) early testing and feedback; (iii) cooperation between the developers and final users [1].

The integration of quality practices, and processes which quantify benefits, can improve and increase the speed of software development activities, and therefore increase the satisfaction of final users [5,14].

For this reason, an Agile Software Design and Development application allows the team to obtain rapid responses to the constant changes occurring in the business world [6], focusing on adaptability in the face of uncertainty and frequent changes [22].

Agility in a software development project can be defined as: (i) the performance of the project team; (ii) the influence on their agility of the organisation's capacity to manage change; (iii) the organisation's capacity to deal with the impacts caused by internal and external factors [12].

The characteristics of this approach mean that it is defined by activities which include iterations, continuous tests, self-managing teams, constant collaboration and frequent re-planning based on reality as it is experienced instead of following potentially obsolete plans [20].

In view of the above benefits, the IT development team opted for this approach. Correct application not only brings benefits to the organisation; it also provides for an interchange of knowledge and learning between team members

[31]. For the user, the most visible and significant benefits are the value of the product, better relations with the company and better product quality [28,31].

2.4 Mobile Application Features

Requirements. In Fig. 1, we present the requirements of the AIRE mobile application for particulate matter monitoring and alerts.

- **ACT-01: Citizen.** Resident of the city who wants to be informed of the air and weather situation in his/her own or other areas.
- **ACT-02: API.** System which interacts with the application. Responsible for updating the system and receiving user location data to provide information visualization according to the context of use.

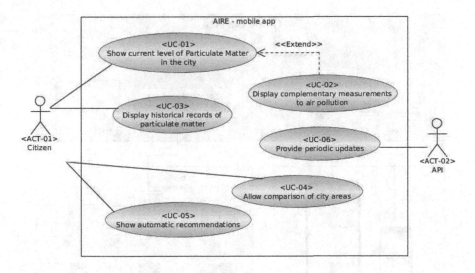

Fig. 1. AIRE mobile application requirements

- **UC-01: Show current level of particulate matter in an area of the city.** Based on data compiling and processing, the system must provide visualization to show the citizen the current measurement and its classification in a range of colours;
- **UC-02: Display complementary measurements to air pollution.** Each of the 10 areas of the city has temperature and humidity sensors which update the measurements periodically. These measurements must be displayed together with the particulate matter but with less emphasis, allowing the user to contextualise variables complementary to particulate matter;
- **UC-03: Display historical records of particulate matter.** The application must provide a display which allows the user to review the progression of particulate matter measurements over 24 h and over a whole month;

- **UC-04: Allow comparison of city areas.** The user must be able to visualize all the areas of the city and compare the different levels of pollution simply;
- **UC-05: Show recommendations.** Based on a specific area of the city and its measurement, the system should offer a set of actions for the user to follow;
- **UC-06: Provide periodic updates.** The application must receive periodic updates previously established by the user. Updates of the atmospheric conditions should be linked with notifications to the user indicating the state of atmospheric conditions.

General Scheme of Operation. The processing units of the AIRE mobile application fall into three blocks (see Fig. 2):

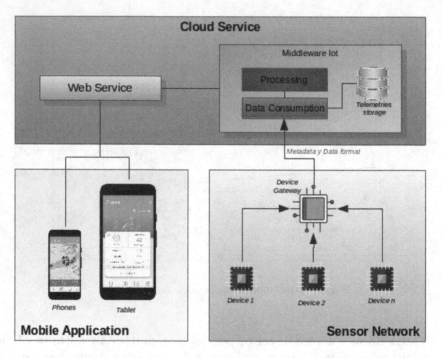

Fig. 2. General scheme of operation: sensor network, cloud services mobile application

a) **Sensor Network:** a network of sensors distributed throughout the city collects atmospheric measurements that are then stored and processed.
b) **Cloud Services:** each device sends data to a service responsible for receiving and validating the measurements (data consumption); this software module interacts with a pre-processing module which orders and filters the data and carries out the calculations for the visualizations generated in the mobile application.

c) **Mobile Application:** the information display seen by the final user contains three display screens constructed from three services. Each web service provides the information needed to construct the principal display of the current state of an area of the city, a comparative map and a history of measurements recorded.

Logical Structure of the Mobile Application. Internally, the AIRE mobile application (a) contains three software artefacts for correct display of the data obtained from the web services. These software artefacts include the computer data model representing the monitoring stations and the remotely recorded measurements which then feed the Principal, Location and History display screens. The *model* artefact interacts with the *pages* artefact to organise the visual elements coherently and to structure all the information seen by the user. Finally, the *network* artefact organises information requests sent to the various web services which can be contacted via the API node. These artefacts are mounted on *Google's Flutter* development framework for mobile applications, providing display in the *Android* and *IOS* platforms (see Fig. 3).

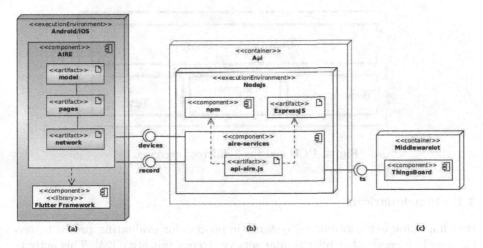

Fig. 3. General deployment of the mobile application.

Taking into account the web services that feed the mobile application, the *API* node (b) contains an execution environment based on *NodeJs*, specifically through the *Expressjs* web services creation framework. Finally, all the information is extracted from the node called *Middleware Iot* (c), responsible for facilitating data requests and for downloading from the devices which make up the IoT network. These three elements interact to deliver location and historical data to the application through web services in the *JSON* format. These services are:

a) **Devices:** responsible for obtaining a list with all the air quality monitoring devices around the city;

b) **Record:** depending on specific parameters, such as location or date ranges, information can be obtained for all the devices, a specific device or a range of remote measurements over a period of time.

3   Validation Methods

The technology team proposed a functional prototype, based on the above definitions and on the needs collected in the recommendations of User-Centred Design.

This section describes the testing and validation methods for this initiative. Three different activities were carried out: (i) market benchmarking, to identify key trends and functionalities; (ii) heuristic evaluation for problem identification; (iii) a user test. In Fig. 4 we show the relation between the exercises described above: the User-Centred Design approach to project development, with the 3 exercises proposed.

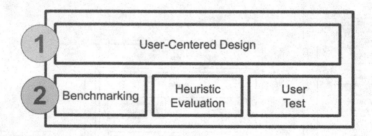

Fig. 4. UCD and the 3 different exercises

3.1   Benchmarking

Benchmarking is a continuous, systematic process for evaluating products, services and processes that offer similar services to our initiative [24]. This activity seeks to create a frame of reference for evaluating the performance, quality and functionality of other applications that offer air quality monitoring and alert systems. The investigation is based on the experiences of the evaluators and the services provided to the final users.

Methodology. Based on criteria of experience and importance, each evaluator selected different proposed information systems, software applications or community services related with air quality. Then a single list was drawn up of the relevant proposals, identifying their basic functionalities.

Participants. Three individuals, all male, aged between 25 and 40 years; all specialists in information systems, software development and technology.

3.2 Heuristic Evaluation

A heuristic evaluation is a method of examining the usability of software systems; it helps to identify usability problems in user interfaces (UI). It involves specialists who examine the interfaces and their interactions, and evaluate compliance with certain principles of usability ("heuristics") [25,27]. The object of this experiment was to analyse the proposal developed and possible problems that might appear. Nielsen's heuristic principles were used [25].

Methodology. Each evaluator identified usability problems independently; then a single list was drawn up, eliminating duplicates. The problems were scored (on a scale of 0 to 4) for "severity" and "frequency". The problems were associated with Nielsen's heuristics. The evaluations were carried out remotely, with each evaluator using an independent calculation document produced by *Google*.

Participants. A team of 3 specialists in Human-Computer Interaction, with more than five years' experience in usability analysis for companies and academic settings. All male, aged between 30 and 40 years. This number of participants follows the proposal of Nielsen and Landauer on cost-benefit in heuristic evaluations [26].

3.3 User Test

The user test was a usability test based on observation and analysis of how a group of final users used the application, noting the problems encountered in order to solve them [24].

The test was carried out "in the laboratory", i.e. in an environment with controlled planning, participation, recruitment and observation.

Methodology. During the test the users were asked to carry out a series of tasks to interact with the product, allowing us to discover navigability and interface problems, positive actions and future functionalities. The objectives to be evaluated included: (i) use of suitable technical terms, and (ii) health precautions and dangers. Both these objectives arise from inconsistencies found in the heuristic evaluation.

Participants. 30 users. Aged between 24 and 84 years (17% under 30 years, 50% 30–60 years, 33% over 60 years). 83% were female. 30% had completed primary education, 30% had completed secondary education and 20% had completed university education. 27% use the internet for 1 to 3 h per day, and 33% for 4 to 7 h. They were all users of the *Android* operating system. Only one had previous experience with the application.

4 Resultados

This section reports the results of the experiments: first the benchmarking process, then the problems identified in the heuristic evaluation, and finally the observations of the user test which reinforced the initiatives.

4.1 Benchmarking

In total, 7 different proposals were identified which address air quality monitoring and control. In Table 1, we show all the proposals, and some important attributes of each one. Keywords were used in the comparison between them.

Table 1. Benchmark results

ID	Proposal	Url	Attributes
B1	DATA Chile (DataWheel)	datachile.io	Free search bar Predefined stories Open data Data VIZ approach
B2	McCann's Toxic Toby	breezometer.com	Ciber-physic approach Social-network integration
B3	Breezometer	breezometer.com	Heat maps Pollution Index Recommendations Technical Explanations Forecast Weather
B4	aqicn	aqicn.org	Pollution Index Forecast Weather
B5	Global Ambient (WHO)	maps.who.int/airpollution	Free Search Bar Heat Maps Pollution Index
B6	Air Index Europa	airindex.eea.europa.eu	Country Filter (EU) Station Filter Technical Explanations Past Measures
B7	AirNow	airnow.gov	Pollution Index Forecast Weather Technical Explanations Summary Table

The first initiative (B1) is DATA CHILE. It is the only initiative that does not deal with air quality, however it is included as a reference in data visualization. It has a simple interface, with predefined stories on the Chilean government, and an open data initiative. The main focus of the "Breezometer" initiatives (B2, B3) is the impact on city residents, by use of an animated *teddy bear* which reacts to air quality, as well a (paid) API which offers tips and specific recommendations to the community.

The other 4 initiatives (B4, B5, B6, B7), work in a similar way: They use a navigable map and colour indicators, and draw on historical and statistical information about air quality conditions.

Aqicn (B4) and Global Ambient Air Pollution (B5), use a worldwide public network of monitoring sensors, whereas Air Index Europa (B6) and AirNow (B7) use sensors specific to their regions.

Fig. 5. A direct and clear message from Breezometer

To summarise, the market proposals are focused mainly on delivering data and statistics to citizens. Their main characteristics include: (i) heat maps, and (ii) explanations and recommendations based on air quality. However the latter function varies depending on the web site, as they are very detailed and complex for the target public.

Finally, considering the importance of providing information on the problem of air quality to the public and raising their awareness, how the message is delivered is critical. The only option of all these that really addresses this aspect is that proposed by Breezometer. In Fig. 5, Sect. 1, we show specific air quality indicators, differentiated by colour. They provide means of similar states, prognoses and recommendations.

4.2 Evaluation of Usability – Heuristic Test

Of a total of 22 problems identified in the application, in Table 2, we show the most "severe" based on the mean scores awarded by the evaluators. Early solutions were sought to these problems, to be validated subsequently in the user test. The first column of Table 2 shows the problem identifier, and the second gives a description. The remaining columns detail "Average Severity" (AVG SEV), "Severity Standard Deviation" (STD SEV), "Average Frequency" (AVG FRE) and "Severity Standard Frequency" (STD FRE).

Table 2. Top 5 several problems.

ID	Description	AVG SEV	STD SEV	AVG FRE	STD FRE
P1	The system marks health-threatening situations in "green"	3.667	0.577	2.333	0.577
P8	The "24 h moving average" is not an important parameter for city residents	3.333	0.577	1.667	0.577
P3	The graph does not show pollution levels by established colours	2.333	0.577	2.000	0.000
P4	The graph detail does not represent pollution levels (by colours)	2.333	0.577	1.333	0.577
P5	The time of the graph (hours) follows advancing time	2.333	0.577	2.000	0.000

The heuristic with the most unmet incidences is H5: "Error Prevention". This rule says *"It is more important to prevent the appearance of errors than to generate good error messages. Actions which may produce errors must be eliminated, or at least located and a question brought up for the user whether it is safe to use them"*. On some occasions, the omission of warnings or messages, or incorrect system functioning, can lead to unforced errors by users of the application. In Table 3, we show all problems and their association with each of the heuristics, as well as their mean severity and frequency.

Table 3. Analysis of unmet heuristics.

	H1	H2	H3	H4	H5	H6	H7	H8	H9	H10
Total	0.00	0.00	2.00	1.00	12.00	0.00	1.00	5.00	0.00	1.00
AVG SEV	0.00	0.00	1.33	2.00	2.00	0.00	1.67	1.33	0.00	1.00
AVG FRE	0.00	0.00	1.00	1.67	1.50	0.00	1.33	1.00	0.00	1.00

To summarise, the proposed application (AIRE), works well. There was never any disconnection or intermittence in the service. The pollution sensors work well, and appear to synchronise without major problems. In general terms, it fulfils the function proposed initially: to make the final user aware of pollution levels.

Although some easily-corrected problems exist (logos, error messages, use of space), certain political problems were detected: how to present the information to the community, based on user needs and not necessarily onbusiness rules. The user test experiment was applied to solve this situation.

4.3 User Test: Validating the Problems

The focus of the user test was to solve and validate the importance of the errors found in the heuristic evaluation test. Only the most severe problems were included. Of the 5 problems identified, two were selected for solution: (i) the appropriate use of colours in the interface, and (ii) simplifying technicisms in the presentation of the information (see Table 4).

Table 4. Problems, Heuristics and Keyword related.

ID	Heuristic	Keywords related
P1	H5	Appropriate use of colours
P2	H5	Technical nomenclature
P3	H5	Appropiate use of colours
P4	H5	Appropiate use of colours
P5	H5	Technical nomenclature

The object of the first task was to identify the problems associated with the technicisms used by the application. The concept of *"24 h moving average"* (see point 1, Fig. 6) represents the mean pollution at the moment of a user enquiry and over the previous 24 h. Although this is considered a standard, it does not represent the real air quality at that moment.

When the user enquires whether the conditions are suitable to go out for a walk, the answer given is right in only 38% of cases. In other words the user may take a decision which is dangerous for his health based on the data supplied by the application (see point 1, Fig. 6).

In response to a repetition of the same enquiry, the application is asked to display additional information (see point 2, Fig. 6): this shows that the $PM_{2.5}$ values are "dangerous", the highest level of care in the system. The "Temperature" and "Humidity" values (see point 3, Fig. 6) also tend to produce errors, as they are not relevant for decision-making on air quality.

In conclusion, the term *"24 h moving average"* tends to produce errors by the user. The terminology and its use in the AIRE application should be modified.

The object of the second task evaluated was to understand the problems associated with the use of colours in graphs in the application. The errors found

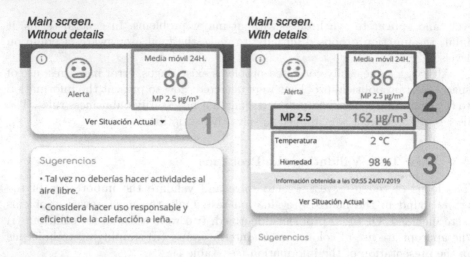

Fig. 6. Technicalities: Use of media mobile

(P3 and P4) arise from the fact that the historical graphs do not use colours; this makes it difficult to obtain important information from them. Two questions were asked about "unhealthy" and "dangerous" episodes. Of all the participants (28 respondents), only 54% correctly identified unhealthy episodes in the month. Of the same participants, only 15% correctly identified dangerous episodes in the month (see point 1, Fig. 8). In conclusion, the bar graphs are only useful for a limited percentage of users. Their usefulness and their presentation need to be reconsidered.

Finally, the object of the third task was to identify whether the iconography, the colours used (green, yellow, red) and the information delivered are "simple" to understand. Of the answers received (27), 56% (15 respondents), were able to order the colours correctly, associating them with air quality levels (green-clean, yellow-alert, red-critical). 44% gave inconsistent answers (see point 2, Fig. 8).

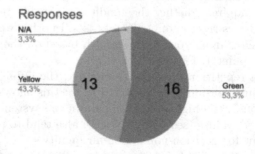

Fig. 7. Test. In what situation you would go for a walk with a 2-year-old child?

The respondents were asked in what situation they would go out for a walk with a 2-year-old child (see point 1, Fig. 6). 53% replied that they would only go out with a "green" situation, while 43% said they would go out with "yellow". Two respondents (13%) who gave CORRECT answers to the order of colours considered yellow to be a healthy option. Ten respondents (83%) who gave INCORRECT answers to the order of colours considered yellow to be a healthy option (see Fig. 7).

This is explained mainly by the fact that pollution events in the city are frequent in winter (when the experiments were carried out), and people had to go on with their "normal" lives independent of "alert" periods.

Finally, an exercise was carried out on the use of iconography to represent the state of the air quality. Of 28 respondents, 11% understood the icons correctly while 89% made one or more mistakes (see point 2, Fig. 8). Of this total, 29% (8 respondents) chose the icon representing clean air quality correctly. 11% (3 respondents) chose the icon representing intermediate air quality correctly. 14% (4 respondents) chose the icon representing bad air quality correctly.

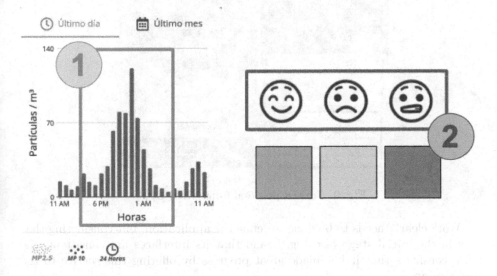

Fig. 8. Bar charts, colours and emoticons (Color figure online)

5   Discussion and Future Work

In general terms (on a 5-point scale), 41% indicated that they could complete the tasks "easily". 59% said that the AIRE application was "easy" to use. 75% said that they needed help in carrying out the tasks at some moment. 41% said that the information provided by the application is easy to understand. Finally, 85% of the respondents said that the performance and functioning of the application were "Average-Good". Some positive aspects of the proposal (obtained by open questions) were: (i) pollution levels are reported in real time, and (ii) it is an education and prevention mechanism.

Negative aspects of the proposal: (i) certain technical terms ($PM_{2.5}$ and PM_{10}) are hard to differentiate, and (ii) the usefulness of the bar graphs is not positively perceived as users cannot interpret them correctly. Suggestions and future works: (i) incorporation of times and prognoses, and (ii) creation of a widget to display the air quality constantly.

The virtue of this proposal is that it complies with one of the main objectives: to provide information and raise awareness in city residents about an extremely important subject. When the users were asked (in the context of the experiment): What is particulate matter? 63% were found to understand the concept of "particulate matter" and associate it with the terms "Pollution/Air Quality". 33% did not understand or did not answer the question. 3% made an inappropriate answer to the question.

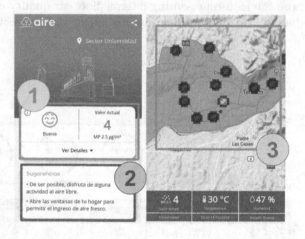

Fig. 9. Current proposal from AIRE APP

Work clearly needs to be done to refine the application, but considering that it is in the initial stage (see Fig. 9) and that its interfaces are consistent, the team considers that it has made great progress by offering this service to the community.

One pending issue is to develop a dashboard for advanced users in order to provide a platform providing not only information but also access to all the data collected by the *SmartAraucanía* sensor network.

References

1. Abrahamsson, P., Salo, O., Ronkainen, J., Warsta, J.: Agile software development methods: review and analysis. arXiv preprint arXiv:1709.08439 (2017)
2. Aceves Gutierrez, L.C., Martin Gutierrez, J., Del-Rio-Guerra, M.S.: Having a smarter city through digital urban interfaces: an evaluation method. Appl. Sci. **9**(17), 3498 (2019)

3. Ahlgren, B., Hidell, M., Ngai, E.C.: Internet of things for smart cities: interoperability and open data. IEEE Internet Comput. **20**(6), 52–56 (2016). https://doi.org/10.1109/MIC.2016.124
4. Alnanih, R.: Characterizing traffic context-based user experience for public safety. Int. J. Innov. Technol. Explor. Eng. **9**(1), 2335–2343 (2019). https://doi.org/10.35940/ijitee.A5241.119119
5. Baseer, K., Reddy, A.R.M., Bindu, C.S.: A systematic survey on waterfall vs. agile vs. lean process paradigms. i-Manager's J. Softw. Eng. **9**(3), 34 (2015)
6. Baweja, S., Venugopalan, N.: Agility in project management. PM World J. Agil. Proj. Manag. **4**, 1–14 (2015)
7. Bogdan, C., et al.: Human-Centered and Error-Resilient Systems Development. Springer, Heidelberg (2016). https://doi.org/10.1007/978-3-319-44902-9
8. Bollier, D.: How Smart Growth Can Stop Sprawl: A Fledgling Citizen Movement Expands. Essential Books, Washington, DC (1998)
9. Bouskela, M., Casseb, M., Bassi, S., Facchina, M.: The Road toward Smart Cities: Migrating from traditional city management to the smart city. Inter-American Development Bank (2016). https://publications.iadb.org/publications/english/document/The-Road-toward-Smart-Cities-Migrating-from-Traditional-City-Management-to-the-Smart-City.pdf
10. Bruneo, D., et al.: An IoT service ecosystem for smart cities: The #smartme project. Internet Things **5**, 12–33 (2019)
11. Cassandras, C.G.: Smart cities as cyber-physical social systems. Engineering **2**(2), 156–158 (2016)
12. Conforto, E.C., Amaral, D.C., da Silva, S.L., Di Felippo, A., Kamikawachi, D.S.L.: The agility construct on project management theory. Int. J. Project Manage. **34**(4), 660–674 (2016)
13. Cornet, Y., Barradale, M.J., Bernardino, J., Lugano, G.: Worthwhile travel time: design challenges of capturing the user experience by smartphone. In: 2019 Smart City Symposium Prague (SCSP), pp. 1–9, May 2019. https://doi.org/10.1109/SCSP.2019.8805706
14. Díaz, J., et al.: Website transformation of a Latin American airline: effects of cultural aspects and user experience on business performance. IEEE Latin Am. Trans. **17**(05), 766–774 (2019)
15. Dupont, L., Guidat, C., Morel, L., Skiba, N.: The role of mock-ups in the anticipation of the user experience within a living lab: an empirical study. In: 2015 IEEE International Conference on Engineering, Technology and Innovation/ International Technology Management Conference (ICE/ITMC), pp. 1–8, June 2015. https://doi.org/10.1109/ICE.2015.7438669
16. Díaz-Robles, L.A., et al.: Health risks caused by short term exposure to ultrafine particles generated by residential wood combustion: a case study of Temuco, Chile. Environ. Int. **66**, 174–181 (2014). https://doi.org/10.1016/j.envint.2014.01.017. http://www.sciencedirect.com/science/article/pii/S0160412014000221
17. Garzon, S.R., Walther, S., Pang, S., Deva, B., Küpper, A.: Urban air pollution alert service for smart cities. In: Proceedings of the 8th International Conference on the Internet of Things, IOT 2018, pp. 9:1–9:8. ACM, New York (2018). https://doi.org/10.1145/3277593.3277599, event-place: Santa Barbara, California, USA
18. Hanyurwimfura, D., Nizeyimana, E., Ndikumana, F., Mukanyiligira, D., Diwani, A.B., Mukamanzi, F.: Monitoring system to strive against fall armyworm in crops case study: maize in Rwanda. In: 2018 IEEE SmartWorld, Ubiquitous Intelligence Computing, Advanced Trusted Computing, Scalable Computing Commu-

nications, Cloud Big Data Computing, Internet of People and Smart City Innovation (SmartWorld/SCALCOM/UIC/ATC/CBDCom/IOP/SCI), pp. 66–71, October 2018. https://doi.org/10.1109/SmartWorld.2018.00046

19. Harrison, C., Donnelly, I.A.: A theory of smart cities. In: Proceedings of the 55th Annual Meeting of the ISSS-2011, Hull, UK, vol. 55 (2011)
20. Highsmith, J.: What is agile software development? Crosstalk **15**(10), 4–10 (2002)
21. Lewis, A., Peltier, W.R., von Schneidemesser, E.: Low-cost sensors for the measurement of atmospheric composition: overview of topic and future applications. World Meteorological Organization, Geneva, Switzerland (2018)
22. Mishra, D., Mishra, A.: Complex software project development: agile methods adoption. J. Softw. Maint. Evol. Res. Pract. **23**(8), 549–564 (2011)
23. Mora, C.J.M.C., Ruiz, G.O., Lobo, L.M.A.: IoT-based panel for real time traffic data monitoring in Smart Cities: a case study in the Guadalajara Metropolitan Zone. In: 2019 International Conference on Electronics, Communications and Computers (CONIELECOMP), pp. 104–111, February 2019. https://doi.org/10.1109/CONIELECOMP.2019.8673236
24. Nielsen, J.: Guerrilla HCI: using discount usability engineering to penetrate the intimidation barrier. Cost-Justifying Usability, pp. 245–272 (1994)
25. Nielsen, J.: Usability Engineering. Elsevier, Boston (1994)
26. Nielsen, J., Landauer, T.K.: A mathematical model of the finding of usability problems. In: Proceedings of the INTERACT 1993 and CHI 1993 Conference on Human Factors in Computing Systems, pp. 206–213. ACM (1993)
27. Nielsen, J., Mack, R.L., et al.: Usability Inspection Methods, vol. 1. Wiley, New York (1994)
28. Pereira, J.C., de FSM Russo, R.: Design thinking integrated in agile software development: a systematic literature review. Proc. Comput. Sci. **138**, 775–782 (2018)
29. Santos, C., Jiménez, J.A., Espinosa, F.: Effect of event-based sensing on IoT node power efficiency. Case study: air quality monitoring in smart cities. IEEE Access **7**, 132577–132586 (2019). https://doi.org/10.1109/ACCESS.2019.2941371
30. Santos, P.M., et al.: PortoLivingLab: an IoT-based sensing platform for smart cities. IEEE Internet Things J. **5**(2), 523–532 (2018). https://doi.org/10.1109/JIOT.2018.2791522
31. Solinski, A., Petersen, K.: Prioritizing agile benefits and limitations in relation to practice usage. Softw. Qual. J. **24**(2), 447–482 (2014). https://doi.org/10.1007/s11219-014-9253-3
32. Sánchez, A.J., Rodríguez, S., de la Prieta, F., González, A.: Adaptive interface ecosystems in smart cities control systems. Future Gener. Comput. Syst. **101**, 605–620 (2019). https://doi.org/10.1016/j.future.2019.06.029. http://www.sciencedirect.com/science/article/pii/S0167739X19302808
33. Zhang, L., Shen, P.: User experience based urban tourism app interface design. In: 2018 IEEE 20th International Conference on High Performance Computing and Communications; IEEE 16th International Conference on Smart City; IEEE 4th International Conference on Data Science and Systems (HPCC/SmartCity/DSS), pp. 1121–1124, June 2018. https://doi.org/10.1109/HPCC/SmartCity/DSS.2018.00187
34. Zhu, S., Li, D., Feng, H.: Is smart city resilient? Evidence from China. Sustain. Cities Soc. **50**, 101636 (2019). https://doi.org/10.1016/j.scs.2019.101636. http://www.sciencedirect.com/science/article/pii/S2210670718325794

Instagram Stories

Cristóbal Fernández-Robin[1]([⊠]), Scott McCoy[2], Diego Yáñez[1],
and Luis Cardenas[1]

[1] Universidad Técnica Federico Santa María, Valparaiso, Chile
{cristobal.fernandez,diego.yanez}@usm.cl,
luis.cardenas.13@sansano.usm.cl
[2] Mason School of Business, Williamsburg, VA, USA
scott.mccoy@mason.wm.edu

Abstract. Instagram is one of the most influential social networks nowadays. This application experienced its largest growth after the implementation of the "Stories" tool, which consists of posts that vanish in 24 h. This study analyzes the factors that influence the intention to use this tool employing the Technology Acceptance Model (TAM) as a basis and complementing it with the variables of perceived enjoyment, social presence, benign envy and malicious envy. A questionnaire was developed on SurveyMonkey, which was responded by 401 people sampled by convenience. The analysis of the results was conducted through a structural equation model (SEM) using SPSS AMOS. Ten hypotheses were proposed, and out of them, eight were accepted and two rejected. Finally, the attitude towards using is the most influential variable over the intention to use Instagram Stories, with a standardized coefficient of .539. This coefficient is mostly explained by perceived enjoyment (.849), which in turn, is explained by social presence (.743). Regarding the envy variables, only benign envy exhibits a relationship with perceived enjoyment, albeit a weak one.

Keywords: Instagram Stories · Technology Acceptance Model · Social media

1 Introduction

Instagram is a social network that is based on the exchange of images and short clips between users. In fact, this platform is defined as a quick and specific way of sharing life events with friends through a series of images [1]. Instagram was launched on October 6, 2010. In its first year, it reached 12 million users and was purchased by Facebook on April 9, 2012 for 1 billion dollars [2]. Currently, Instagram is the fourth largest social network in active users, with 800 million users per month, being surpassed by Facebook (2.167 million), YouTube (1.500 million) and WhatsApp (1.300 million). However, it presents the largest growth and has doubled its number of users in only two years.

Among the features and functions of Instagram, one of the most used and eye-catching is Instagram Stories, which falls within the "ephemeral" category. Ephemeral messaging is a characteristic that allows shared posts or content to disappear automatically within a certain time [3], which in the case of Instagram Stories is 24 h.

© Springer Nature Switzerland AG 2020
G. Meiselwitz (Ed.): HCII 2020, LNCS 12195, pp. 501–510, 2020.
https://doi.org/10.1007/978-3-030-49576-3_36

Such is the relevance reached by Instagram Stories that more than 250 million active users use this tool daily. This has led major brands to focus their advertisement on this tool, paying for having stories linked to the offer of a product or service appearing in the stories of their followers. Furthermore, more than 80% of Instagram users follows at least one company or business profile, which makes Instagram an attractive platform for major brands.

In this case, it is relevant to address generation Z, which is the generation most exposed to technology, even since birth. Some researchers have found that people from this generation prefer communication via ephemeral messaging [3].

This study analyzes several factors that may affect the intention to use Instagram Stories using structural equation modelling (SEM), in addition to a conceptual basis from the technology acceptance model (TAM). Exogenous variables external to TAM were used, namely perceived enjoyment and social presence, which were described by Coa and Setiawan in the study titled "Analyzing Factors Influencing Behavior Intention to Use Snapchat and Instagram Stories". Additionally, two variables were added related to narcissism from the perspective of envy were derived from watching an Instagram story. These two variables are benign envy and malicious envy [4].

Regarding the above, it must be noted that the visual content shared on Instagram can reduce people's well-being, especially because it may facilitate social comparison and cause negative emotions like envy [4]. Based on this point of view, the variables benign envy and malicious envy are incorporated into the model as a way to explore their effect on the intention to use Instagram stories and on the other variables from TAM.

To analyze the user behavior in terms of adoption of innovative technologies, scientific literature has created a number of behavior theories and intention models over the last four decades [5]. The development of these theories emerges from the technology acceptance model (TAM), which has been considered the most robust, parsimonious and influencing on innovation acceptance behavior [6, 7]. TAM departs from the theory of reasoned action (TRA) [8], which was designed to explain virtual behavior, and adapts it to model the user acceptance of information systems [6]. This model has been modified several times and one of its most used variations integrates perceived enjoyment and social presence as variables in studies that explain user behavior toward information technologies.

In this sense, the application of this model to social networks is relevant, as they are one of the most effective means of communication nowadays. In this particular case, Instagram is the popular application or social network, whose Stories tool enjoys considerable use since ephemeral content is one of the most effective tools currently. Thus, it is necessary to study the variables that affect the intention to use this tool in order to produce knowledge useful for future enterprises, as well as new alternatives to direct advertisement in this medium, contributing with ideas for the marketing of interested companies.

2 Literature Review

2.1 Perceived Enjoyment

Perceived enjoyment (PE) is defined as a subjective psychological experience that indicates how pleasant a specific experience is. PE has an exploratory nature in information technologies and computer-mediated environments fields. High enjoyment can lead to the adoption of a technology, even if such a technology does not imply an increase in the productivity of the person adopting it. Some studies often use perceived enjoyment as a variable because entertainment, which is related to enjoyment, is an aspect that plays a key role in the acceptance of a technology. Many systems or technologies more oriented to pleasure than productivity have been designed (hedonic information systems), and social networks are one of them. Therefore, the use of perceived enjoyment could be more suitable for analyzing user acceptance of social networks [3].

In the current context, we consider social networks from both a utilitarian and a hedonic perspective. The original TAM model, its related models and the unified theory of acceptance and use of technology (UTAUT) were only developed and validated in the context of utilitarian systems within a professional setting [9]. Although current information technologies reflected in social networks are mostly employed for leisure and fun, the literature shows that perceived enjoyment is positively related to the constant intention of using social networks [9, 10]. In a study, attitude toward using is a mediating factor between perceived enjoyment and intention to use [3].

2.2 Social Presence

Social presence (SP) is defined as a means that allows a user to feel that everyone is psychologically present. Social presence occurs if there is an interaction between user and technology that makes the user feel the presence of others as well as human warmth [3], that is to say, a feeling closeness with someone who is physically far. A technology can transmit human warmth when it is capable of delivering communication, socialization and sensitivity of human feelings.

The achievement of the above can be enhanced through emoji, images, and videos, as well as effects used today that mostly belong to Instagram. In other words, adding visual content enrichens the message and thereby social presence is increased.

2.3 Benign Envy

Benign envy, a non-malicious form of envy, has the purpose of improving one's situation. When comparing benign and malicious envy, they are different in terms of feelings, thoughts, action tendencies, motivational objectives and motivational experiences [11]. Benign envy promotes a strength that encourages people to work harder to achieve what others have done [12]. It is a positive and motivating force experienced by people who admire others [9, 13]. In the current context, benign envy is closer to a comparison with famous people, for example, athletes, actors, music artists, etc. This comparison leads us to follow their trends, clothes and articles, as well as gestures, websites they visit and places they go to, to narrow the gap that separates us from them. In this way, people adopt the superiority of the person they envy, since it is not in their hands to perform actions to make these people lose their superiority and therefore the only solution is to become closer to them.

2.4 Malicious Envy

Malicious envy is simply called "envy" [14] and is a destructive form of envy that aims at overriding someone. It describes a situation in which a person makes an upward comparison with advantaged people and experiences a feeling of inferiority. This could generate malicious thoughts about others failing or even make people hurt the person they envy [9].

Malicious envy is associated with a series of complex negative feelings of injustice, deprivation, frustration and depression [9]. In this sense, referring to the Chilean context, malicious envy is an upward comparison with a close person, which consists of trying to make that person equal to myself by eliminating their superiority. To this end, people would use all the resources available to eradicate this superiority, such as malicious comments or actions that are morally reprehensible.

2.5 Technology Acceptance Model

The first technology acceptance theory, developed 1989, was termed TAM (Technology Acceptance Model). This theory is an adaptation of the Theory of Reasoned Action (TRA) for information technologies [15] that is used to represent how users accept and use a new technological tool.

TAM postulates two main factors relevant to technology acceptance, namely perceived usefulness and perceived ease of use. The model contains four variables, which are explained below (see Fig. 1):

Perceived Usefulness (U): extent to which one person believes that using a specific system will improve his work performance.

Behavioral Intention (BI): extent to which one person has made conscious plans for developing, or not, some future behavior.

Perceived ease of use (E): extent to which future users believe that using a particular system is effortless.

Attitude toward using (A): Positive or negative feeling related to a behavior.

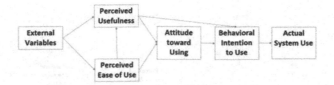

Fig. 1. Technology acceptance model [6].

3   Methodology

This study is divided into two stages: exploratory and conclusive. The exploratory stage comprises a review on the literature about Instagram, Instagram Stories, Snapchat and social networks in general. This will be linked to the models currently known for determining the factors influencing the intention to use a technology (TAM, UTAUT and derived model) in order to find out the main variables involved in the intention to use Instagram Stories. A questionnaire was created based on this review. This quantitative tool contained 29 observable variables aimed at defining the eight latent variables. A 5-point Likert scale was used, ranging from (1) totally disagree and (5) totally agree. The model used is an extension of TAM [3], to which, as mentioned above, the social presence and perceived enjoyment variables are added. Now, since this last variable is extremely important for technology acceptance models, especially for the intention to use social networks, two more variables related to perceived enjoyment arc added [9]. These variables are benign envy and malicious envy.

The final model for analysis is presented in Fig. 2 and is based on the following research hypotheses.

H1: High social presence will result in high perceived enjoyment.

H2: High social presence will result in high perceived usefulness.

H3: High ease of use will result in high perceived usefulness.

H4: High ease of use will result in a favorable attitude toward using.

H5: High perceived usefulness will result in a favorable attitude toward using.

H6: High perceived enjoyment will result in a favorable attitude toward using.

H7: A favorable attitude toward using will result in high intention to use.

H8: High perceived usefulness will result in high intention to use.

H9: High benign envy will result in high perceived enjoyment.

H10: High malicious envy will result in low perceived enjoyment.

The analysis conducted is quantitative and has a confirmatory approach. The nonprobabilistic method called sampling by convenience was used. In other words, only Instagram users responded the questionnaire, which also implies that they use Instagram Stories. The survey was conducted online through the SurveyMonkey platform. Four hundred and one questionnaires were completed. The majority of respondents were university students across Chile, mainly from the Metropolitan and Valparaíso regions, because the survey was disseminated in a university context. Answers were analyzed through structural equation modelling (SEM) using SPSS AMOS, while construct reliability was assessed with IBM SPSS Statistics.

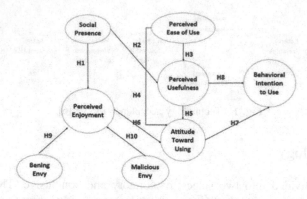

Fig. 2. Instagram stories proposed model

4   Results

4.1   Construct Reliability

Cronbach's alpha was used to assess construct reliability (see Table 1).

Table 1. Cronbach's alpha (Source: Created by the authors).

Perceived Ease of Use	.616
Perceived Usefulness	.712
Attitude Toward Using	.869
Behavioral Intention to Use	.706
Perceived Enjoyment	.795
Social Presence	.644
Benign Envy	.872
Malicious Envy	.866

The limit value of this indicator is .6. This is because the constructs have less than 10 items. In addition, all constructs exhibit a Cronbach's alpha higher than that limit.

4.2   Model Adjustment

Table 2 shows the goodness of fit indicators for the models described. For the Cmin/DF ratio, values between 1 and 3 indicate a good fit and values from 3 to 5 point an acceptable fit that needs to be confirmed by other indicators. In this case, it is clearly observed that in the original model (initial), the Cmin/DF value was between 3 and 5. Then, if the model without PS3 falls within the range between 1 and 3, it has a good adjustment. Nevertheless, the other indicators also need to be revised. First, the Cmin probability level does not change significantly and remains below .05; therefore, the model is acceptable according to these criteria. Additionally, GFI statistics improved from .832 to .851, approaching .9. RMSEA also showed a slightly improve, going from .071 to .069. The above indicates an acceptable absolute fit. NFI also improved notoriously from .804 to .820, while CFI reached a value very close to .9, increasing from .858 to .874, which is an acceptable incremental fit. Finally, the parsimony fit of PNFI also slightly improved, with values increasing from .726 to .738.

Table 2. Goodness-of-fit statistics (Source: Created by the authors).

Cmin	985.236
Cmin/DF	2.898
Probability level Cmin	.000
GFI	.851
NFI	.820
CFI	.874
RMSEA	.069
PNFI	.738

From this section, we can conclude that deleting PS3 improves the model in such a way that this presents an acceptable adjustment. Thus, the following step is to analyze the model without PS3 as our "main model".

4.3   Hypotheses and Regression Estimators of the Model Without PS3

The Table 3 presents the regression estimators and significance of each relationship:

Table 3. Regression estimators and significance of each latent variable in the model (Source: Created by the authors).

Relation	Standarized estimate	p-value
DP <– PS	.743	***
UP <– PS	.859	***
UP <– FU	.359	***
AU <– DP	.849	***
AU <– FU	.280	***
AU <– UP	−.006	.940
IU <– UP	.228	.005
IU <– AU	.539	***
DP <– BE	.167	***
DP <– ME	−.052	.256

When analyzing the P-Value, it must be noted that both attitude toward using (AU) and perceived utility (PU) are significant for predicting the behavioral intention to use (IU) of Instagram Stories, as their P-value is lower than .05. Likewise, both social presence (SP) and ease of use (EU) are significant to predict perceived usefulness (PU). Additionally, social presence (SP) and benign envy (BE) significantly predict perceived enjoyment (PE), as opposed to malicious envy (ME), which is not significant to predict perceived enjoyment as shown by a P-value of .256 > .05. It is noteworthy that perceived enjoyment (PE) and ease of use (EU) predict attitude toward using (AU) in a significant way, whereas perceived usefulness (PU) is not significant in this relationship, as its P-value is .940 > .05.

These results show that exogenous latent variables are the variables that best explain endogenous latent variables, that is, with an acceptable significance. Thus, hypotheses H1, H2, H3, H4, H6, H7, H8 and H9 are accepted. On the contrary, hypotheses H5 and H10 are rejected.

It must be noted that the R2 value of behavioral intention to use (IU) is .499, that is to say, the predictors (exogenous latent variables) of IU (endogenous latent variable) are estimated to explain 49.9% of its variance. In other words, the error variance of IU is approximately 5.1% of IU variance. In addition, the predictors of perceived enjoyment (PE) explain 58.3% of its variance. Predictors of attitude toward using (AU) explain 79.2% of variance. Finally, predictors of perceived usefulness (PU) explain 86.8% of variance.

5 Conclusions

The main objective of this study was to know the factors that influence the intention to use the tool Instagram Stories. The most influencing factor was attitude to use (.539), which means that the more positively the use of Instagram stories is perceived, the more the intention to use it. Perceived usefulness, another factor influencing intention to use in this study, presented a weaker relationship with the construct (.228), in other words, the fact that people feel that Instagram Stories improves their work performance also influences intention to use, but in a more subtle way when compared with the attitude toward using it. From a psychological perspective, a social network needs to generate a positive feeling of be useful for work, so workers do not feel a guilty conscience for spending time on the phone. In addition, psychologists and psychiatrists are often interviewed on TV about the problems that an addiction to social networks may cause, such as on the ego of when working on a profile showing a happy life that may be not true in real life. In summary, social networks need to be perceived as something that brings positive emotions, harmless to mental health and useful for work. The last point can be exemplified by the fact that many people offer products or services through their Instagram profile, particularly by means of stories. In this way, they are giving use to their account and often this mechanism is so successful that it becomes their occupation. This is one of the modern uses of Instagram and features like Stories.

Other latent variables worth analyzing, like perceived enjoyment, should be mentioned. However, in this context, social presence (.743) is the most influencing factor for intention to use. This indicates that feeling human presence on Instagram Stories is strongly related with possible enjoyment while using this application. Since family and friends are usually followers on this social network, feeling their presence and keeping up with their lives is always pleasant, especially if they are physically apart. Therefore, calling upon the emotions of Instagram Stories users is also a good strategy for increasing the daily enjoyment of the application. Benign envy also slightly influences perceived enjoyment (.167), because this type of envy is usually directed to famous people or to people who, at least, are perceived as famous. From this perspective, users try to reach an image of this person by their own means. The above is often observed in ad campaigns, in which a famous person wears or states that use a product to make their followers automatically want to purchase it. The model in this study indicates that this type of envy or upward relationship increases the enjoyment of users when using Instagram Stories, as watching the stories of someone perceived as superior and, in turn, the items or services they use or consume, may lead users to adopt some aspects of their lifestyle. Nevertheless, the influence of malicious envy on perceived enjoyment is close to zero (.052) and thus it has no significant effect on perceived enjoyment, which is proved by the rejection of the hypothesis that both types of envy are related through a p-value equal to .256 > .05. This is in disagreement with the assumptions made prior to this study, since this type of envy generates frustration and hatred, and this is negatively related to perceived enjoyment, that is, an increase in malicious envy reduces perceived enjoyment. As mentioned above, people tend to answer questions about malicious envy incorrectly on purpose, in other words, if they have this feeling, they will hide it even if the questionnaire is anonymous. This is related to a trend to respond to sentences on this topic assertively, because accepting envy is not good in the eyes of society in general. Therefore, people would conceal or deny this feeling, but it is clear that malicious envy exist, and the literature already confirms this.

In another vein, perceived usefulness also operates as a latent variable and social presence is the most influencing factor in this relationship (.859). In other words, feeling the presence of other close people would improve performance at work. This is associated with the psychological fact that feeling the presence of close people supports work performance. Ease of use also affects perceived usefulness, albeit to a lesser extent tan social presence (.359). This is explained by the fact that if an application is easy to use, users will not waste time learning how to use it and can devote time to work.

Finally, the last latent variable of the model is attitude toward using, which is mostly influenced by perceived enjoyment (.849). The amusement we feel when using Instagram Stories strongly influences attitude toward using, that is to say, it brings positive feelings toward the use of the application. Moreover, ease of use also affects this variable less than perceived enjoyment (.280), which entails that the easier to use an application like Instagram Stories, the more positive the feelings toward its use, as comfort increases. The role of perceived usefulness as a predictor of attitude toward using was also analyzed, yielding a .006 coefficient. Since the coefficient is very close to zero, we presume that there is no relationship between the two variables, which is also proved by a p-value equal to .940 > .05; therefore, this hypothesis is rejected. This may be explained by the fact that respondents use Instagram Stories for leisure more than usefulness. In this sense, we may see that most people do not see Instagram as a source of income, which has been gradually changing due to the success of several enterprises that share their profile in this social network and all the factors this involves.

From the above, a chain reaction may be assumed regarding Instagram Stories. A high social presence clearly increases perceived enjoyment, which notoriously influences the attitude toward using this application, and this is the most relevant factor in the intention to use this tool. Thus, social presence is a key factor in the model, as it strongly affects the variables with which it is related.

References

1. Instagram. https://www.instagram.com/about/faq/. Accessed 11 Dec 2019
2. Torres, A.: Instagram y su uso como una herramienta de marketing digital en Chile. Universidad de Chile. (2017)
3. Coa, V.V., Setiawan, J.: Analyzing factors influencing behavior intention to use Snapchat and Instagram Stories. IJNMT (Int. J. New Media Technol.) 4(2), 75–81 (2017)
4. Meier, A., Schafer, S.: The positive side of social comparison on social network sites: how envy can drive inspiration on Instagram. Cyberpsychol. Behav. Soc. Netw. 21(7), 411–417 (2018)
5. Munoz-Leiva, F., Climent-Climent, S., Liébana-Cabanillas, F.: Determinants of intention to use the mobile banking apps: an extension of the classic TAM model. Spanish J. Mark.-ESIC 21(1), 25–38 (2017)
6. Davis, F., Bagozzi, R., Warshaw, P.: User acceptance of computer technology: a comparison of two theoretical models. Manag. Sci. 35(8), 982–1003 (1989)
7. Pavlou, P.A.: Consumer acceptance of electronic commerce: integrating trust and risk with the technology acceptance model. Int. J. Electron. Commer. 7(3), 101–134 (2003)
8. Azjen, I., Fishbein, M.: Understanding Attitudes and Predicting social Behavior. Prentice-Hall, Englewood Cliffs (1980)
9. Wu, J.: Three Research Essays on Human Behaviors in Social Media. University of Wisconsin Milwaukee, UWM Digital Commons Theses and Dissertations (2015)
10. Kim, B.: Understanding antecedents of continuance intention in social networking services. Cyberpsychol. Behav. Soc. Netw. 14(4), 199–205 (2011)
11. van de Ven, N., Zeelenberg, M., Pieters, R.: Why envy outperforms admiration. Pers. Soc. Psychol. Bull. 37(6), 784–795 (2011)
12. Foster, G.M., et al.: The anatomy of envy: a study in symbolic behavior. Curr. Anthropol. 13(2), 165–202 (1972)
13. Polman, E., Ruttan, R.L.: Effects of anger, guilt, and envy on moral hypocrisy. Pers. Soc. Psychol. Bull. 388(1), 129–139 (2012)
14. Smith, R.H., Kim, S.H.: Comprehending envy. Psychol. Bull. 133(1), 46–64 (2007)
15. Davis, F.: Perceived usefulness, perceived ease of use, and user acceptance of information technology. MIS Q. 13(3), 319–340 (1989)

Proposal to Enhance University Students' Motivation to Switch to a Morning-Oriented Lifestyle with a Community Approach

Hidenori Fujino[✉], Taiga Okunari, Yuko Kato, Honoka Kobashi,
Tomoya Tarutani, Nao Miyano, and Soyoka Yagi

Faculty of Ecnomics, Fukui Prefectural University,
4-1-1 Matstuoka-kenjojima, Eiheiji-cho, Fukui 910-1195, Japan
fujino@fpu.ac.jp
http://www.s.fpu.ac.jp/fujino/

Abstract. Most of the university students in Japan think that a morning-oriented lifestyle will be better for their health and studies. However, some of them do not have the custom to wake up before 9 am and have breakfast. Especially skipping breakfast is considered to influence badly to their stats of absence and concentration to their classes before noon. Therefore, our study's purpose is to develop the method to promote them to switch their lifestyle to a morning-oriented lifestyle. Our proposal method consists of following 2 activities; 1) logging time of their waking up and going bed and 2) engaging an online community activity including reporting having breakfast every morning and so on. In order to examine the effectiveness of our proposal, experiment was conducted with university students not having a morning-oriented lifestyle. As a result, our method appears to be effective to let participant have a morning-oriented lifestyle. Furthermore, it seems that the settings that a member who have had such a lifestyle already is in the community as a normal member who standing same place with other members, meaning not a leader, will be more effective.

Keywords: An online community · A morning oriented lifestyle · Breakfast

1 Introduction

1.1 Relationship Between Students' Lifestyle and Their Academic Ability

It is claimed that students academic ability is related to their lifestyle, especially whether they get breakfast every morning. Figure 1 shows the relationship between scores of Japanese and Mathematics the National Assessment of Academic Ability for senior grade students of junior high school in 2017 and their

© Springer Nature Switzerland AG 2020
G. Meiselwitz (Ed.): HCII 2020, LNCS 12195, pp. 511–525, 2020.
https://doi.org/10.1007/978-3-030-49576-3_37

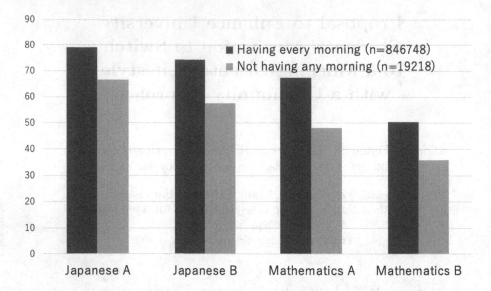

Fig. 1. The differences of the scores of Japanese and Mathematics between students having breakfast every morning and having no breakfast in usual. These scores were captured from the National Assessment of Academic Ability for senior grade students of junior high school in 2017 [1].

custom of having breakfast. This shows students having breakfast every morning get higher scores on all subjects than students not having breakfast any morning.

It is considered that if they do not have breakfast, they cannot supply glucose to their brain and concentrate to classes before noon. Therefore, efficiency of learning of them become less than students having breakfast regularly.

1.2   Universality Students' Lifestyle

On the other hand, there are many Japanese university students who do not have breakfast every morning. Nakai and her colleagues investigated Japanese female students living around Tokyo lifestyle and revealed that 21% of respondents have one or more days they don't have breakfast in a week [2]. Ito and her colleagues also investigated the ratio of people who do not have breakfast regularly in Japan and found that 19.7% of young people from 18 years old to 29 years including not only university students but also workers old don't have custom to have breakfast [3]. Nagahata and her colleagues investigated Japanese university students custom of having breakfast from the view point of difference between students living with their families and those living alone [4]. As a result, 52% of investigated students living with families did not have breakfast everyday and 76% of them living alone did not have breakfast everyday.

1.3   Objective

Based on these results, the purpose of this study is to develop a method to promote university students who don't have breakfast everyday to switch their lifestyle to a morning-oriented lifestyle and get custom of having breakfast regularly.

2   Survey About University Students' Lifestyle

Before developing, we also investigated university students lifestyle and relationship between students lifestyle and their learning performance.

2.1   Method

Investigation was conducted to 1245 students belonging 1st to 3rd grade in a university by sending the link of google form in e-mail that was given by the university to each student.

Questionnaire consisted of 7 questions mainly. First question asked how many times they had breakfast in a usual week. Second one asked why they had such custom to have breakfast as answers to 1st question by choosing from prepared choices. Third one was the question asking whether they had classes in the 1st and 2nd period in any day in a week. Forth and fifth one asked about attendance and concentration in the 1st period and sixth and seventh asked about those in the 2nd period. Of course, forth to seventh questions were only for the students having these classes.

2.2   Result

Ratio of Morning Students and Night Students. Figure 2 shows he ration of investigated university students having breakfast every morning and students having one or more days not having breakfast in a week. On the one hand, 48% of students had breakfast everyday. On the other hand, 52% did not have breakfast one or more days in a week.

Relationship Between Their Lifestyle and Study Performance. Figure 3 shows the result of comparing students having breakfast everyday to student not having on attendance and concentration of the class in the 1st and 2nd period. Performance of students having breakfast was significantly better than students not having on all comparison points.

Reason for Not Having Breakfast. Figure 4 shows result of survey of reason why they did have one or more days not to have breakfast who answering 3 or 4 days they didn't have breakfast in a usual week. The top reason was "Because time to wake up is not regular in each day" and second reason was because they felt bothersome to prepare and have breakfast in some morning.

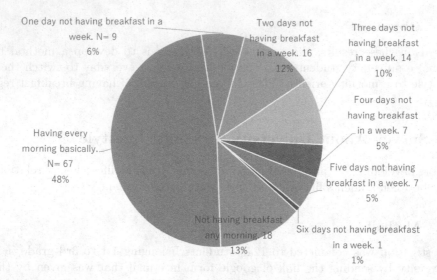

Fig. 2. The proportions of investigated university students having breakfast every morning and students having one or more days not having breakfast in a week.

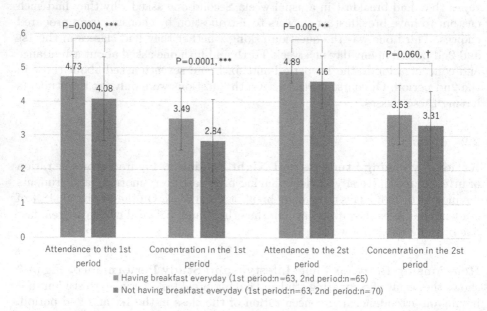

Fig. 3. Differences of attendance to and concentration in the 1st and 2nd period between students having breakfast everyday and not having everyday.

On the other hand, Fig. 5 shows reasons whey they did not have breakfast most days, that is 5 or more days, in a usual week. Top reason was because they did not have enough time to have breakfast in the morning. Second reason

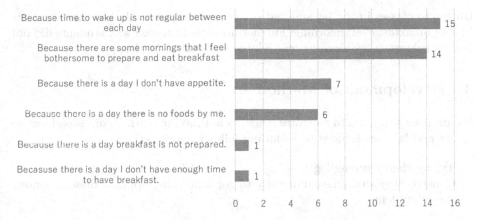

Fig. 4. Reasons for not always having breakfast.

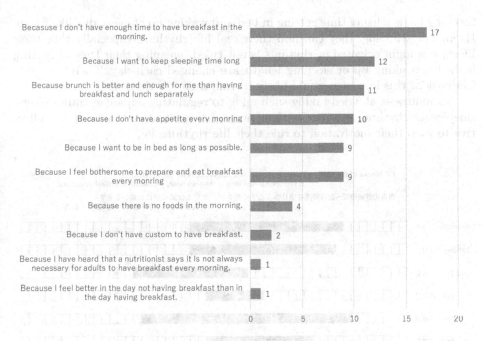

Fig. 5. Reasons for having no breakfast every morning.

was because they wanted to keep a sleep more longer than to wake up and have breakfast.

2.3   Summary

As a result of this investigation, it was revealed that more of students had one or more days not having breakfast and of such students' attendance and concentration to classes in the 1st and 2nd period were significantly less than students having breakfast every morning. Furthermore, main reason why students did not have breakfast every morning was related to their night sleep.

3 Development of Method

We propose a method to motivate students not having morning oriented lifestyle to get and keep such life style including following two activity.

- Taking their sleeping log.
- Constructing an online community to get a morning oriented lifestyle among target students.

3.1 Taking Sleeping Log

Sleeping log is a log of time getting in bed and waking up of every day like Fig. 6. By making this log, they can find their real life rhythms, especially that their lifestyle is night oriented or rhythms is not ruled, meaning their time of getting in bed or waking up or sleeping length are changed each day. Therefore, as a feedback of this log, they would likely to rule their life rhythms.

Nakamura et al. tried taking such a log to regulating Japanese train drivers' sleep–wake rhythms as a part of their proposing method and found it was effective to keep their motivation to rule their life rhythms [5].

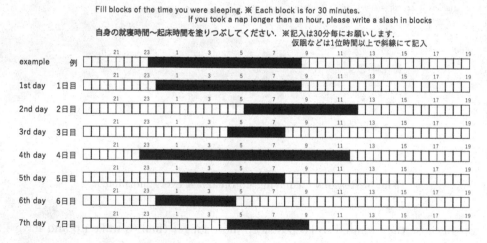

Fig. 6. Example of a sleeping log.

3.2   Online Community of Practice to Get a Morning Oriented Lifestyle

Aoyagi and his colleagues proposed a method with an online community to enhance pro-environmental behaviors. In their proposal, some people will be distributed into an group with an online bulletin board system and be expected to report their pro-environmental behavior that actually they do to the BBS. Theoretically, this method is standing on a group dynamics. Because human has a need of relatedness, they will be forced to practice behavior which group members are recommended to do, if they want to keep a membership to the group. Standing this theory, they will be motivated to pro-environmental behavior gradually by knowing other members' actually doing such behavior through a BBS As a result of their experiment, it was appeared that their proposal was effective to enhance participants' pro-environmental behavior.

Standing on their work, we also apply this online community approach. In our proposing online community, members are expected to engage following activities:

Reporting Having Breakfast. The first one of expected activities is to report it to other members of the community through a prepared bulletin board system or a group chat system of social media like a LINE Group or a Group of Facebook Messenger every morning that they certainly have had breakfast at that day. An example of members report is shown in Fig. 7. As shown, they are requested to report their breakfast with its photograph.

Good morning! This morning I woke up about 8:20 and went to submit a report of micro economics with making up only a little. After coming back my room, I thought of have asleep again first but I remember I have a lot of washing to do. So, I did that with feeling sleepy and after, I had breakfast. Today I have no class in the 2nd period, so I will go to the university afternoon.

My breakfast is saute chicken and Enoki mushrooms with miso, tofu and a drink including protein. Chees for protein!

Fig. 7. Example of reporting having a breakfast to the online community.

Introducing Another Country's Breakfast. The second of the activities is to introduce another country's breakfast with its photograph like Fig. 8. This activity is practiced by one of the members in each day and the member requested to introduce is changed everyday.

スイスの朝ごはんです。🔲
まさにハイジに出てくるよう
な朝ごはんです。干し肉やチ
ーズなどを食べるそうです。
真ん中のパリパリしてそうな
のはじゃがいもを焼いた「ロ
スティ」というスイスの伝統
料理だそうです。

This is a breakfast in Switzerland. This is just like a breakfast in "Heidi, girl of Alps"*. It is said that they eat dry meats and cheeses. The thing looked crispy on the center of the dish in this photo, is Swiss traditional cuisine named "Rosti" grilled of potato.

* One of most famous Japanese animated TV program

Fig. 8. Example of introducing another country's breakfast to the online community.

Commenting to Members' Writing Each Other. As the third activity, they are requested to comment to each other members' breakfast report and the member's article of another country's breakfast with a sentence which can call positive feelings or at least not call negative feelings into members receiving it. The examples of comment submitted to the system is shown in Fig. 9.

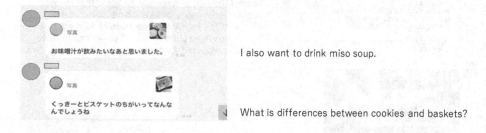

I also want to drink miso soup.

What is differences between cookies and baskets?

Fig. 9. Examples of commenting members' writing.

3.3 Theoretical Framework

The theoretical framework of our proposal is described in Fig. 10. Basic frame of our proposal is relying on the theory of planned behavior [6]. This theory explains people's intentional behavior is induced by subjective norm, perceived control and attitude via intention.

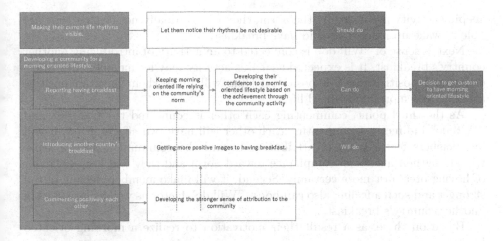

Fig. 10. Theoretical framework of our proposed set of methods.

In our study, subjective norm is considered as "Should do" factor. Namely, they feel they should do the behavior as an norm of the community they belong. Perceived control is considered as "Can do" factor, that is they feel they can do the behavior actually. Attitude is considered as "Will do" factor. It means that they have willingness to do so. All of these three factors should promote his/her intention to do the behavior and he/she will decide to do so. In order to let university students have a morning oriented lifestyle, we have to call these three factors related to a morning oriented lifestyle, concretely, waking up at a suitable time in the morning, having breakfast regularly everyday and going to bed as early as possible in the night.

Then, logging their sleeping time is considered connected to "Should do" factor. By logging it, they can see their current life rhythms is ruled less or placed later than desirable life rhythms. As a result of seeing such a state, it is expected that they feel they should rule their life to get a morning oriented life style. of course, this flow will work only when they accept a common norm that a morning oriented life style is more desirable than night oriented one.

On the other hand, the community approach is connected to "Can do" and "Will do" factors. Respecting "Can do", it is believed it will be necessary to have his/her own experience of accomplishment for the behavior in order to have a sense of control of the behavior. In other word, if they actually accomplish a behavior continually, they will become gradually to consider they can do that behavior. Based on this idea, it is required to practice the behavior even if they do not have a confidence to do it well or even if they don't have enough motivation to do. Therefore, in our proposal, having breakfast is tied to the community activity as stated above. In our method, it is expected they feel there is a community's norm to have breakfast through seeing each other member's breakfast and each of them will engage our breakfast activity by obeying such a norm. Through keeping activity promoted by the norm, they will gradually notice that they are able to wake up more early and have breakfast.

Next, a sense of "Will do" is connected to an activity of introducing another country's breakfast. It is expected that this activity may let members feel interesting and positive. Such a positive feeling will make them have an positive attitude to a morning oriented life.

As the third point, commenting each other is connected to "Can do" and "Will do" indirectly. Commenting each other will have two effects. First, it will let members feel a sense of attribution toward the community. such a sense will strengthen members' compliance toward norm and they will keep behavior of having breakfast more certainly. Second, it will make members feeling of fun stronger and such a feeling also can boost "Will do" factor as well as introducing another country's breakfast.

Based on these, as a result their motivation to realize a morning oriented lifestyle.

4   Experiment

Experiments was conducted for the purpose of examining effectiveness of our proposed method.

4.1   Method

20 university students participated in our experiment and they were grouped into 6 groups as described in Fig. 11. Two experimenters were joined into 2 groups as a group member. They were expected to lead group members' community activities. These two group were in the condition of visible intervention. Other four experiments were also into the other groups. However these experimenters did nothing without watching participants' activities. Furthermore, participants who have had a morning oriented lifestyle already were placed into two group. they were expected to behave a leader of each community while they were not explained these expectation. Moreover, other members of each group did not know there was such a member in their group. Additionally, 3 of 6 groups were formed by members knowing each other and the others were by members having never met each other.

Experiment term was 4 weeks. First week was for getting participants' usual life style. In this term, participants individually reported their time of waking up and going bed and whether they have breakfast or not to experimenters everyday. Therefore, in this week, they had not joined in any group yet. Next two weeks were the term of practicing our proposed method. And last one week was for getting participants life rhythms after practicing our proposal in order to examine effectiveness of our method. Note that all of participants informed experimental term should be just 3 weeks and received no announcement about the forth week. Therefor they requested to report their life log one week without any expectation in them. This operation is because they might make their best for the last week in order to meet our expectation, if they would know that forth week would be also in experimental term.

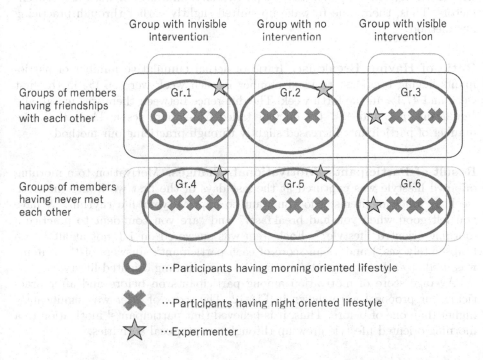

Fig. 11. Settings of experimental groups

4.2   Result

One participant in Gr.4 dropped out in the first week because of this participant's private situation. Furthermore, all of Gr.2 were also withdrawn from data because they could not keep to practice our method for the second and third weeks. Moreover, two participants who have had a morning oriented lifestyle already as mentioned above were also excluded from data. Therefore, following results were derived from data without these six participants.

Time to Go to Bed. The averages of time to go to bed among participants were 25:45 (sd:1 h46 min) in the first week and 24:39 (sd:1 h52 min) in the forth week. The difference between them was definitely significant ($p = 0.00055 < 0.001$ on One-tailed Within-subject T-test by participants and days of week as between-factors. Thus, their time to go to bed shifted earlier through practicing our method.

Time to Wake up. The averages of time to wake up among participants were 9:14 (sd:1 h47 min) in the first week and 8:49 (sd:1 h31 min) in the forth week. The difference between them was marginally significant ($p = 0.086 < 0.1$ on One-tailed Within-subject T-test by participants and days of week as between-factors. Thus, their time to wake up shifted slightly earlier through practicing our method.

Ratio of Having Breakfast. Ratio of actual cumulative number of participants having breakfast to ideal number in each week were 36.1% in the first week and 47.1% in the forth week. The difference between them was marginally significant ($p = 0.064 < 0.1$ on One-tailed Chi-square test). Thus, the more number of participants increased slightly through practicing our method.

Result of Participants' Motivational Changes. Motivation to a morning oriented lifestyle was captured at the last days of the first week and the forth week by following items; "do you want to improve your life rhythm?", "have you felt good when you had breakfast?" and "are you confident to practice a morning oriented lifestyle?". Each item was answered on 1 ("not at all") to 5 ("absolutely yes") and mean score of each participant's answers of these items was used as each participant's motivation to a morning oriented lifestyle.

Average score of motivation among participants on before and after practicing our proposal were shown in Fig. 12. The score of after was significantly higher than one of before. Thus, it is believed that participants' motivation to a morning oriented lifestyle grew up through our proposal activities.

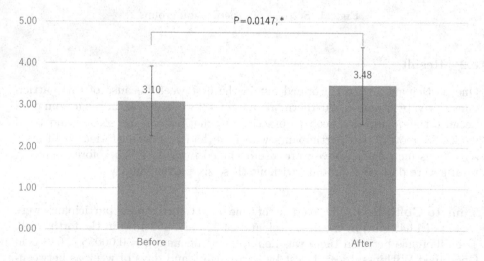

Fig. 12. Difference of motivation to have a morning oriented lifestyle between before and after the experiment.

Influence of Familiarity Among Communities Members. Results analyzed from the view point of familiarity among communities members is shown in Table 1 and Fig. 13.

While respondents numbers of both groups were not enough to examine based on a statistical test, effects of our method is more clearly appeared on groups with members not familiar each other than the other groups.

Table 1. Results by familiarity among communities members of groups

	Going bed time		Waking up time		Ratio of having breakfast	
	Before	After	Before	After	Before	After
Familiar each other (Gr.1–Gr.3, N = 6)	25:28 (sd:1:35)	24:48 (sd:1:28)	8:30 (sd:1:15)	8:52 (sd:1:22)	0.50	0.51
Not Familiar each other (Gr.4–Gr.6, N = 8)	25:59 (sd:1:36)	24:32 (sd:2:10)	9:49 (sd:1:56)	8:47 (sd:1:38)	0.25	0.43

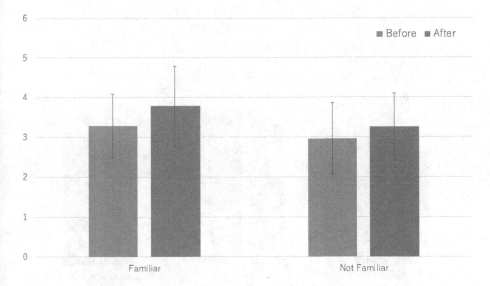

Fig. 13. Difference of motivation to have a morning oriented lifestyle between before and after the experiment by familiarity among communities members of groups.

Influence of Visibility of Intervention. Results analyzed from the view point of visibility of intervention is shown in Table 2 and Fig. 14. While going bed time after practice is 30 min earlier than before on all conditions of interventions, improvement of waking up time is partially. On the conditions of visible intervention and no intervention, waking up time is improved over 30 min. On the other hand, it is improved only around 10 min on visible intervention condition.

Moreover, ration of having breakfast is also improved on invisible and no intervention conditions, while ratio on visible intervention condition is almost not improved. Additionally, improvement of motivation on visible condition appear less than other conditions although they are not tested statistically because of small number of participants in each conditions.

Table 2. Results by visibility of intervention

	Going bed time		Waking up time		Ratio of having breakfast	
	Before	After	Before	After	Before	After
Invisible intervention (Gr.1 and Gr.4, N = 5)	25:57 (sd:1:46)	24:30 (sd:2:08)	9:29 (sd:2:02)	8:50 (sd:1:14)	0.35	0.54
No intervention (Gr.5, N = 3)	25:30 (sd:1:23)	24:30 (sd:1:13)	9:00 (sd:1:18)	8:29 (sd:0:52)	0.33	0.50
Visible intervention (Gr.3 and Gr.6, N = 6)	25:44 (sd:1:35)	24:51 (sd:1:53)	9:10 (sd:1:56)	8:59 (sd:1:38)	0.38	0.39

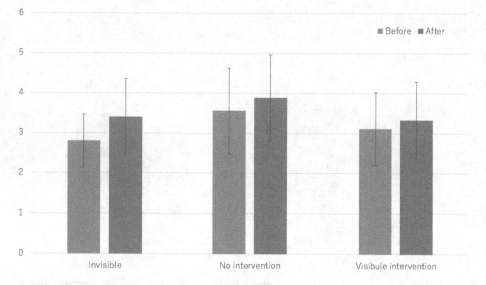

Fig. 14. Difference of motivation to have a morning oriented lifestyle between before and after the experiment by visibility of intervention.

4.3   Summary

In this section, we explained our experiment to examine the effectiveness of our proposal. The experiment was conducted with 20 university students including 2 students who have had a morning oriented lifestyle already. They were distributed into 6 groups with controlling the conditions of familiarity each other and intervention visibility. As a result, it was found that our proposal would be effective over participants and also that it would be more effective on communities with members not familiar each other than communities with members familiar each other. Further, it appeared that intervention visibility would affect the effectiveness of our proposal and invisible intervention or no intervention would be likely to more effective than visible intervention. However it was also considered that no intervention would have a risk that a community itself would be away and members would give up practicing such activities.

5 Conclusion

In this study, we focused on the problem of university students lifestyle. Firstly we investigated the actual situation of university students' lifestyle and found out that lot of students don't have breakfast regularly every morning and also that the main reason of such a situation will be on their sleeping habits. Therefore in the second step of this study, we tried to develop a method to make them have a morning oriented lifestyle. Our developed method consists of two key elements; sleeping log and community of practicing a morning oriented lifestyle. As a result of the experiment, it is observed our developed method will be effective and especially effect will be strong in the community with anyone who's lifestyle have been a morning oriented already. The limited of this study is that the effect was observed only in the experiment. That is, there is a monetary reward to participate in the experiment and such a reward would give any biases to the result. Therefore, the observed effect should be looked carefully and further investigation, if possible without any reward, will be required as a future work.

References

1. https://www.nier.go.jp/17chousakekkahoukoku/factsheet/17middle/. Accessed 19 Feb 2020
2. Nakai, A., et al.: The association between skipping breakfast and healthy lifestyle behaviour of Japanese female students in the metropolitan area. J. Jpn. Soc. Shokuiku 9(1), 41–51 (2015)
3. Ito, C., Nakai, K., Sugiura, S.: Studies on the relationship between breakfast intake behavior and sleeping status. J. Mie Prefectural College Nurs. 2, 95–98 (1998)
4. Nagahata, T., Nakade, M., Hasegawa, J., Kanehira, N., Nishibori, S.: The relationship between skipping breakfast and the living arrangements of university students. Jpn. J. Nutr. Diet. 72(4), 212–219 (2014)
5. Nakamura, S., Fukuma, K., Wada, K., MUeda, M., Hayashi, M.: Intervention for regulating sleep-wake rhythms to prevent sleepiness in Japanese train drivers. Sleep Biol. Rhythms 16(3), 351–356 (2018)
6. Ajzen, I.: The theory of planned behavior. Org. Behav. Hum. Decis. Processes 50(2), 179–211 (1991)

An Exploration of a Social Media Community: The Case of #AcademicTwitter

Lina Gomez-Vasquez[✉] and Enilda Romero-Hall

University of Tampa, 401 W Kennedy Blvd, Tampa, FL 33606, USA
{lgomezvasquez, eromerohall}@ut.edu

Abstract. Online professional communities on Twitter are increasingly gaining attention among users due to benefits such as knowledge sharing, professional development, and relationship building. Millions of hashtags are used every day in different disciplines (e.g., #educhat) or everyday situations (e.g. #MondayMotivation). Hashtags have led to the creation of conversations about topics (e.g., #highered), serving as a point of connection among different types of users. In the academic world, the hashtag #AcademicTwitter has evolved into an online community of educators, graduate students, organizations, and others engaged in the discussion of topics and issues related to academic life, funny moments, and survival stories. This paper examines participants and communication patterns in the #AcademicTwitter community. Using content analysis and social network analysis techniques, the researchers examined tweets including the #AcademicTwitter hashtag to discover the community's network properties, roles of the participants, sentiment, and conversational themes. Findings indicated that the conversation was not centered on one topic, instead several micro-communities were found. Top participants in the #AcademicTwitter community were educators, media platforms, and other professionals which centered on conversations related to topics such as accessibility, academic life experiences, and teaching and research support. The study of social media in academic professional settings is still new. Our work contributes to the literature of social networks in academia, helping better understand how users connect and the network that supports the #AcademicTwitter community.

Keywords: AcademicTwitter · Online professional communities · Teaching · Education · Social media

1 Introduction

The use of social media platforms in the education field are on the rise [1], encouraging scholars to participate in online professional communities to enhance learning [2]. Twitter is used among academics, at all educational levels, as a teaching, learning, and professional development tool [3]. Students, teachers, professors, and other professionals use Twitter as a pedagogical tool for enhancing learning environments that promote engagement among users [1, 4]. It also provides participants with opportunities to collaborate, gather evidence, and reflect on their practice, with other professors and professionals outside their institutions and fields [5].

© Springer Nature Switzerland AG 2020
G. Meiselwitz (Ed.): HCII 2020, LNCS 12195, pp. 526–537, 2020.
https://doi.org/10.1007/978-3-030-49576-3_38

About 1 in 40 scholars are using Twitter for scholarly chat and self-promotion, but also for community building [6]. Educator-driven professional communities on Twitter, such as #AcademicTwitter, #PhDchat, #AcWri, and #AcademicChatter are gaining popularity among academics and students. Particularly, the hashtag #AcademicTwitter has emerged in the past years as a prominent indexing tool where thousands of tweets are sent every month. The hashtag #AcademicTwitter is used to share information, provide support, and engage in conversations regarding the world of academia. Despite the popularity of these social spaces, there is a lack of understanding of how users interact with one another [7]. And while studies have addressed the importance of professional communities and relationships for educators [8, 9], it is yet unclear how online professional communities shape these connections and relationships between educators [10].

Our study contributes to the online professional communities' literature, by gaining insights into the patterns of interactions in the #AcademicTwitter hashtag. The aim of this investigation is to better understand the patterns of interactions of those using the #AcademicTwitter hashtag professional community. The following research questions guided this investigation:

RQ1: What are the demographics of the #AcademicTwitter users (i.e., gender, role, and field)?
RQ2: What sentiments were expressed in the tweets tag with the #AcademicTwitter hashtag?
RQ3: Who are the central participants in the #AcademicTwitter hashtag?

2   Literature Review

There is no denial that social media is now part of our daily lives. There is a range of different social media platforms (i.e., Facebook, Instagram, Snapchat, YouTube, LinkedIn, TikTok) and users are often actively participating in more than one particular social media outlet. One of these social media platforms is Twitter. According to the Pew Research Center [11], Twitter is used by 22% of adults in the United States. In addition to linking with accounts that they wish to follow; Twitter users tend to connect using hashtags. In Twitter, individuals use hashtags to reach a broader audience of individuals who share a similar domain of interest. This is particularly the case of users who seek to connect with a professional network of individuals. According to Romero-Hall [12], professional growth via social media is generated through the social sharing and refining of ideas in a network or community with a common domain.

Various researchers have explored the use of hashtags by different professional communities in Twitter to better understand the social nature of interactions, types of users, and content shared [13–16]. For example, Greenhalgh and Koehler [13] examined targeted and timely professional development after the terrorist attacks in Paris in November 2015 by analyzing tweets with the hashtag #educattentats. This hashtag served as a temporary affinity space to provide support for teachers preparing to address the incident with their students. However, unlike other hashtags use for professional communities in Twitter, this was a temporary space that was only used for 28 days.

Rashid, McKechnnie and Gill [14] investigated advice that is given to newly qualified doctors as they start their career via the hashtag #TipsForNewDocs. The results showed that most tweets focused on professional development as well as knowledge sharing, of both tacit and know-how knowledge. There were also humorous tweets related to socialization. Gomez and Waters [17] explored a Twitter hashtag created by professionals in the Public Relations fields that served as a point of connection among educators, practitioners, students, and various other organizations. An analysis of the network properties and actor roles of the hashtag #PRProfs showed that conversations in this Twitter community are predominantly about sharing knowledge, teaching tips, and trends in the PR industry [17].

Another example of the exploration of hashtags to better understand a Twitter professional community is the research conducted by Kimmons and Veletsianos [18] in which the researchers collected tweets related the American of Educational Research Association (AERA) Annual Meeting to better understand academic Twitter use during, around, and between the annual conference both as a backchannel and general means of participation. Tweets with the hashtags #AERA14 and #AERA15 were collected and analyzed. The results served to compare participation patterns between two years of the conferences. One major finding by Kimmons and Veletsianos [18] was the difference in participation norms by students and professors.

There have been several investigations focused specifically on the use of the #edchat hashtag and its users. For example, Coleman, Rice, and Wright [19] collected post and survey teachers who used the #edchat hashtag to determine if the exchanges between teachers served as continuing education and merited credit. The results indicated that conversations between teachers using the #edchat hashtag were found to generate social capital and bind a professional community. Staudt Willet [15] also conducted an investigation focused on the #edchat hashtag. This author explored the types of tweets that users contributed to #edchat and the purposes observable in the tweets. The results indicated that based on the analysis of the #edchat tweets, posts were mostly on topic related to education and the practice of teaching. Yet, Staudt Willet [15] added that teachers were not using #edchat to its full potential, as tweets were missing important emotional elements that tend to shape relationships and too many times the hashtag was use more for self-promotion.

Researchers have address that the effective use of hashtags is determined by factors other than its affordances and design such as the users' needs and desire, as well as social, cultural, economic, and political environments [16]. In an investigation comparing three hashtags (#NutricionMOOC, #EdTechMOOC, and #PhDChat), Veletsianos [16] observed general participation patterns on these hashtags, the types of user who contributed to the hashtags, and the content tags in the tweets with these hashtags. The results of this particular study showed that there are a variety of outcomes on the potential benefits of hashtags pending the contexts. Two of the hashtags in this investigation (#NutricionMOOC and #EdTechMOOC) primarily served as mediums for announcements and promotion rather than professional development and social connection. Although hashtags offer significant opportunities for professional development, teaching, and learning, they may or may not fulfill the need as expected [16].

The review of the literature gives some insights on how different hashtags in Twitter, related to professional communities, have at times served to create networks, ignite conversations, increase knowledge, and foster relationships. However, it is also clear from the literature that at times hashtags for professional online communities serve for shallow networks [16] or may provide temporary connections in a "just-in-time" format [13]. The creation of quality interactions in any kind of setting requires the investment of time, commitment, and the willingness to engage. Socialization, networking, and the creation of connections are complex processes [14].

As stated by Coleman, Rice, and Wright [19]: "social capital brings members of a group together in solidarity and coalesces a group with string bonds within a community." Given the proper nurturing and attention, professional communities using hashtags in Twitter can provide social capital to those engage. For academics, evidence show that Twitter provides immediacy, reach, and scholarly engagement that is relax, professional, and at time humorous [20, 21]. In addition to the casual chatter, social media used by academics has shown to provide a sense of belonging to a community, cross country interactions, and additional learning resources and research collaborations [22]. Due to the value that Twitter communities provide to academic discourse and socialization, it is important to investigate different elements of this social media network.

3 Methodology

3.1 Data Collection and Cleaning

This study uses quantitative content analysis and social network analysis techniques to examine communication patterns and network properties of the #AcademicTwitter community on Twitter. Netlytic [23], a free cloud-based text and social networks analyzer developed by the Social Media Lab at Ryerson University in Toronto, was used to recollect tweets that have the hashtag #AcademicTwitter. We ran Netlytic software from March 1st to April 1st, 2019, to collect and analyze tweets. The raw dataset has 26,287 unique tweets and 15700 unique users that participated in the discussions.

3.2 Variables

For this investigation, we selected a random sample of 500 users to manually analyze their Twitter bio profiles, following three variables:

1. Gender (individual, organization, or other). "Other" refers to a user who did not provide a clear name, bio, or a photo that makes it harder to categorize as individual or organization.
2. Field: STEM, Social Sciences, Arts & Humanities, Business, Education, Professional Studies, and others.

3. Actor role: Originally 16 categories were identified: 1. Assistant Professor, 2. Associate Professor, 3. Professor, 4. Other professors, 5. Researchers, 6. Teachers, 7. Graduate students, 8. Undergraduate students, 9. Professionals in education, 10. Other professionals, 11. Individuals interested in education, 12. Universities/colleges, 13. Nonprofits, 14. Journalists, 15. Media, 16. Others (do not disclose their profession or job role; usually disclose hobbies or random quotes). After collecting and examining the results, we merged some categories as shown in the findings section.

The categorization was derived inductively, guided by grouping Twitter users by their profession, position, and field. The actor role categories are mutually exclusive. We selected the first role each participant disclosed in the bio for codification. Sometimes users can indicate multiple roles, but researchers always coded the first role or job they disclose. Two coders coded jointly the profiles and discussed to solve coding discrepancies to assure reliability. Sentimental and textual analysis of 26,287 unique tweets were performed as well.

3.3 Social Network Analysis (SNA)

The name network (who mentions whom) was considered for analysis, which revealed 15,052 directional ties among 5560 nodes (posters with ties). We used two centrality measures: in-degree and out-degree. In-degree centrality indicates the number of ties (e.g., messages) a node (user) receives from others. A high in-degree centrality shows the popularity of a user, which is actively mentioned by others. In contrast, a high out-degree indicates an active participant who has the purpose to disseminate information to the network. We used Netlytic software to calculate macro level measurements such as density, diameter, reciprocity, centralization, and modularity to reveal network structure.

4 Findings and Discussion

Researchers were interested in learning about the communication and network structure of the #AcademicTwitter community by identifying influential actors. Descriptive results are presented as follows: 82% of users were individuals, 11% organizations, and 7% others (i.e., researchers could not identify a categorization base on the bio). Figure 1 indicates the most recurrent users, showing the involvement of professionals (professionals working in education or professionals interested in education), graduate students, educators (Assistant, Associate, Professors, Lecturers), and researchers. Most of the actors belonged to the STEM (31%), Social Sciences (23%), and Arts and Humanities (13%) fields. Fourteen percent of the users did not disclose their field.

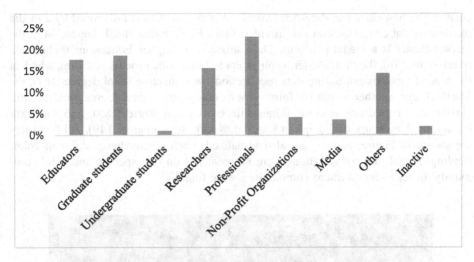

Fig. 1. Most predominant roles of the participants in #AcademicTwitter.

We found that most of the tweets were positive. A total of 4240 posts addressed positive feelings such as great (1256), good (805), love (599), excited (384), and happy (360). Only 584 tweets were negative, conveying feelings such bad (162), lonely (44), tired (44), dull (38), and nervous (37). Figure 2 shows the salient themes in the #AcademicTwitter community indicating discussion topics concerned to graduate students' life and overall success of professionals in academia. We also discovered a call-to-action language that dominated the conversations such as give, make, check, learn, and find.

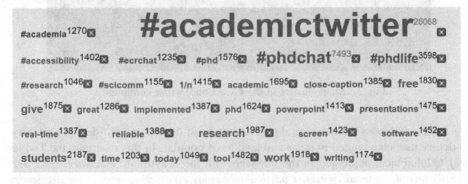

Fig. 2. Salient themes on #AcademicTwitter.

The #AcademicTwitter community consisted of six main clusters with central actors that influenced the way information traveled through the network, as shown in Fig. 3. Clusters are a group of connected people which tend to communicate frequently with others in the group and typically do not communicate with users outside of the cluster. The first cluster in the #AcademicTwitter community is influenced by a media platform-social education content provider: @academicchatter (total degree: 447), the second cluster is a media platform, The Chronicle of Higher Education: @chronicle (total degree: 78), the third cluster, @ph_d_epression, another media platform, which at the time of analysis-not during data recollection-, was inactive (total degree: 167), the fourth cluster, another media platform: @humanbiojournal (total degree: 46), the fifth cluster was a graduate student: @hannahlebovits (total degree: 85), and the sixth cluster, the University of Guelph in Canada: @uofg (total degree: 149). All 6 clusters are shown in Figure; isolates are also visualized. Each cluster has a different color. Findings reveal that conversations were not centered on one specific and solid community, instead several micro communities were found.

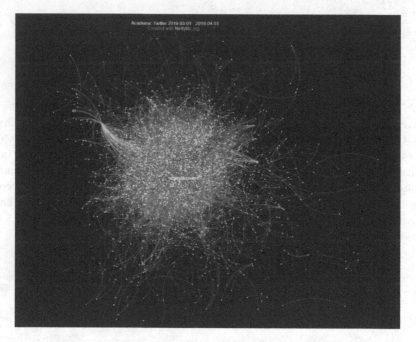

Fig. 3. Main clusters in the #AcademicTwitter community.

Table 1 indicates the top central participants by in-degree and out-degree centrality. In-degree users are tagged in posts and tend to be popular. In this example, the Twitter user @JuliaFtacek is tagged in the message with the @symbol: @*JuliaFtacek I personally love #AcademicTwitter. I particularly enjoy connecting with other academics inside and outside my field. I've had many a good discussion about methodology for research and pedagogical methods for my classroom*). Out-degree users post frequently (either tweeting, retweeting or tagging users) and show good awareness of others. For instance, *RT @zra_research: Staying organized and time management are half the battle in pushing research projects forward. This is a great example.* An interesting finding in the results is the active presence of @AcademicChatter as both an in-degree and out-degree user as shown in Table 1. @AcademicChatter is a social media education content provider for graduate students and academics.

Table 1. Central participants by different centrality measures.

Twitter handle	Actor role	In-degree	Twitter handle	Actor role	In-degree
@uofg	Nonprofit	149	@AcademicChatter	Media	353
@Phdforum	Media	136	@Carlymdunn_mph	Educators	8
@AcademicChatter	Media	94	@HigherEDPR	Professionals	7

The most recurrent posters (out-degree) were media outlets (e.g. @AcademicChatter and @ThePhdStory), other professionals (@HigherEDPR, user is a communication strategist for faculty and researchers), and professors in STEM disciplines (e.g. @Carlymdunn_mph). In-degree users (users mentioned in tweets) were mainly media outlets (@Phdforum, @AcademicChatter) and educational organizations such as @TutorsIndia. It is also worth noting the minimal presence of Twitter accounts of universities and colleges (only 15 profile users were found) in the conversations.

During the one-month period analyzed (March 1–April 1st, 2019), there was a peak of tweets sent during March 21st as illustrated in Fig. 4. This was because several out-degree users retweeted this tweet by *RT @elizabethsiber: "#AcademicTwitter - did you know that there's free, reliable software that will close caption your powerpoint presentation?"* Academics like to learn about free resources to improve our work, especially during times of creating material that are more accessible for students. Figure 4 includes the number of posts over time ranging from as low as 480 tweets per day to more than 1,500 tweets per day in the #AcademicTwitter community. An average of 600–700 tweets were posted per day, making #AcademicTwitter an important resource for academics.

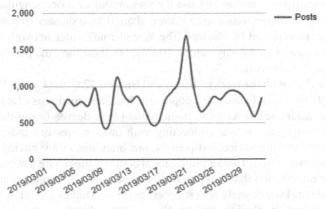

Fig. 4. Number of posts over time.

The #AcademicTwitter network primarily specializes in information and resource sharing but also users are constantly seeking for advice (e.g. *Okay #academictwitter How do I write a paper for a collected volume without sounding like it's my first ever undergraduate essay? For some reason, I seem to have totally lost my ability to, like, use words that make me sound, like, super smart*). The #AcademicTwitter community involves users from a diverse set of professional backgrounds and fields, sharing interesting resources information.

Social network analysis is a useful technique that reveals how information and resources move through the network [24], identifying prominent actors in the network [24, 25]. The social network analysis performed to the #AcademicTwitter community indicated the following measurements: Diameter (44), Density (0.000180), Reciprocity (0.025680), Centralization (0.026280), and Modularity (0.923500). The #AcademicTwitter community is a wide network with a few central participants dominating the information flow, indicating a centralized network. Most users were disseminating or retweeting information, but engagement was not always predominant between network participants. Central actors in networked online communities are opinion leaders who affect others and control the information flow [26], which usually is led by a small group of dominant and engaged actors [27].

The first measurement examined was centralization (0.026280) which indicated that there were few influencers in the network. If values are closer to 1 than 0, indicates that a few central participants dominated the flow of information in the network. In addition, only 40% of the users tweeted more than one time, reaffirming a centralized network. Density is another network measurement which examines how close participants are within a network. The #AcademicTwitter network had a density of 0.000180, which indicates that mostly no one was connected to others in the network (values closer to 1 are evidence of a close-knit community). Diameter calculates the longest distance between two actors in a network, which in the #AcademicTwitter community was 44, showing some actors with higher degrees of separation or connection and presenting a wide network. Reciprocity (0.025680) indicates if users engaged in two-way communication. Results showed that only 0.25% of the users participated in conversations, showing a predominant one-way information network. Lastly, modularity, determines if there are several small communities or a one singular community in the network. A higher modularity (more than 0.5) indicates divisions between communities as represented by clusters. The #AcademicTwitter network presented six different clusters and a modularity value of 0.923500, indicating the presence of micro-communities in this network.

Our results align with the work of Bruns and Burgess [28] and Gruzd, Wellman, and Takhteyev [29] which indicate that people use hashtags to discuss topics of shared interest. The #AcademicTwitter users participated (as in-degree or out-degree) by different reasons which can include connecting with other professors and professionals, sharing resources, seeking advice, self-professional branding, or just having a break from work. All actors involved in Twitter professional communities share a mutual aim which is to distribute information that will potentially impact the communications flow [30].

Our #AcademicTwitter study also supports previous studies (Xu et al. 2015) which found that information sharing and building relationships are the most important aspects of Twitter conversations in online communities. #AcademicTwitter has emerged during the past decade, building a community of educators interested in making connections and relationships, providing support, and sharing resources about teaching, research, service, and overall the academic life. However, there is still participation inequality in social media where 90% of social media users are "lurkers" who do not contribute to the communities [31]. Future studies could examine lurkers in professional communities such as #AcademicTwitter, which could help understand the motivations of their passiveness on social media platforms. In the same line, further studies could answer what motivates academics to engage in learning and professional communities and the benefits they receive. Previous studies [5] have found that online professional communities are a source of continuous professional development for academics, providing authentic and personalized opportunities for learning and support.

5 Conclusions

Our study used Twitter to analyze online professional communities related to academia and how participants were using Twitter and specifically #AcademicTwitter to support their professional development and learning. Our paper also examined communication patterns and user influence in the #AcademicTwitter community.

Social media platforms and online professional communities provide great opportunities for learning, guidance, and academic support. People from diverse backgrounds are turning to social interactions (e.g. online chat groups, discussion lists) to satisfy their needs no matter if they are personal or professional [5]. Our paper contributes to the literature of social media and education, providing insights in the user role and influence in the #AcademicTwitter professional online community. #AcademicTwitter is a growing and popular educational-driven community on Twitter that could attract other active users in the discussion (e.g. nonprofits or industries), to provide helpful information and opportunities to connect with scholars.

This study has some limitations that suggest avenues for further work. This is an exploratory study in the use of Twitter among educational communities. Future studies can take a more in-depth analysis to understand specific topics and content shared among academics in online professional communities. The current study does not involve the codification and further examinations of tweets (messages). Having few influential participants and a network characterized by low two-way conversations, does not mean that real collaboration wasn't involved. In other words, further studies could analyze the collaborative nature of the conversations, and even message purpose (e.g. informative, educative, engagement, mobilization). This work has implications in the education field as it identifies the prominent users in the discussion of educational topics and issues on Twitter. Identifying these influential actors helps to provides opportunities for academics to engage with these prominent users for networking, support and collaborative opportunities.

References

1. Malik, A., Heyman-Schrum, C., Johri, A.: Use of Twitter across educational settings: a review of the literature. Int. J. Educ. Technol. High. Educ. **16**(36) (2019). https://doi.org/10.1186/s41239-019-0166-x
2. Xing, W., Gao, F.: Exploring the relationship between online discourse and commitment in Twitter professional learning communities. Vis. Commun. Technol. Educ. Fac. Publ. **47** (2018). https://doi.org/10.1016/j.compedu.2018.08.010
3. Rosell-Aguilar, F.: Twitter: a professional development and community of practice tool for teachers. J. Interact. Media Educ. **6**(1), 1–12 (2018). http://doi.org/10.5334/jime.452, http://www.springer.com/lncs. Accessed 21 Nov 2016
4. Gruzd, A., Haythornthwaite, C., Paulin, D., Gilbert, S., Esteve Del Valle, M.: Uses and Gratifications factors for social media use in teaching: instructors' perspectives. New Media Soc. **20**(2), 475–494 (2018). https://doi.org/10.1177/1461444816662933
5. Duncan-Howell, J.: Teachers making connections: online communities as a source of professional learning. Br. J. Edu. Technol. **41**(2), 324–340 (2010). https://doi.org/10.1111/j.1467-8535.2009.00953.x
6. Wright, G.: The weird and wonderful world of academic Twitter (2015). https://www.timeshighereducation.com/blog/weird-and-wonderful-world-academic-twitter. Accessed 15 Aug 2019
7. Koehler, M.J., Rosenberg, J.M.: What factors matter for engaging others in an educational conversation about Twitter? In: Proceedings of the 29th Annual Society for Information Technology and Teacher Education Conference, Washington, D.C. (2018)
8. Fullan, M.: The role of leadership in the promotion of knowledge management in schools. Teach. Teach. Theory Pract. **8**(3/4), 409–419 (2002). https://doi.org/10.1080/135406002100000530
9. Talbert, J.E.: Professional learning communities at the crossroads: how systems hinder or engender change. In: Hargreaves, A., Lieberman, A., Fullan, M., Hopkins, D. (eds.) Second International Handbook of Educational Change, pp. 555–571. Springer, Dordrecht (2010). https://doi.org/10.1007/978-90-481-2660-6
10. Cho, V., Ro, J., Littenberg-Tobias, J.: What Twitter will and will not do: theorizing about teachers' online professional communities. LEARNing Landscapes **6**(2), 45–62 (2013)
11. Pew Research Center, Social Media Fact Sheet. Demographics of social media users and adoptions in the United States. Pew Research Center. http://www.pewinternet.org/fact-sheet/social-media/. Accessed 15 Jan 2020
12. Romero-Hall, E.: Social Media in higher education: enriching graduate students' professional growth outside the classroom. In: Şad, S.N., Ebner, M. (eds.) Handbook of Research on Digital Tools for Seamless Learning. IGI Global, Hershey (2017)
13. Greenhalgh, S., Koehler, M.: 28 Days later: Twitter hashtags as 'Just in Time' teacher professional development. TechTrends Link. Res. Pract. Improve Learn. **61**(3), 273–281 (2017)
14. Rashid, M.A., McKechnie, D., Gill, D.: What advice is given to newly qualified doctors on Twitter? An analysis of #TipsForNewDocs tweets. Med. Educ. **52**(7), 747–756 (2018). https://doi.org/10.1111/medu.13589
15. Staudt Willet, K.B.: Revisiting how and why educators use Twitter: tweet types and purposes in #Edchat. J. Res. Technol. Educ. **51**(3), 273–289 (2019). https://doi.org/10.1080/15391523.2019.1611507
16. Veletsianos, G.: Three cases of hashtags used as learning and professional development environments. TechTrends Link. Res. Pract. Improve Learn. **61**(3), 284–292 (2017)

17. Gomez, L., Waters, R.: #PRProfs Twitter community: a social network approach. In: Yook, B., Fay Chen, Z. (eds.) Proceedings 22nd International Public Relations Research, Orlando, Florida, pp. 130–141 (2019)
18. Veletsianos, G., Kimmons, R.: Scholars in an increasingly open and digital world: how do education professors and students use Twitter? Internet High. Educ. **30**, 1–10 (2016). https://doi.org/10.1016/j.iheduc.2016.02.002
19. Coleman, J.M., Rice, M.L., Wright, V.H.: Educator communities of practice on Twitter. J. Interact. Online Learn. **16**(1), 80–96 (2018)
20. Donelan, H.: Social media for professional development and networking opportunities in academia. J. Furth. High. Educ. **40**(5), 706–729 (2016). https://doi.org/10.1080/0309877X.2015.1014321
21. Tattersall, A.: Many a true word is spoken in jest: Twitter accounts that mock, self-ridicule and bring a smile to academia (2016). https://blogs.lse.ac.uk/impactofsocialsciences/2016/04/13/the-weird-and-wonderful-world-of-academic-twitter/. Accessed 14 Jan 2020
22. Romero-Hall, E.: Posting, sharing, networking, and connecting: use of social media content by graduate students. TechTrends **61**(6), 580–588 (2017). https://doi.org/10.1007/s11528-017-0173-5
23. Netlytic Homepage. https://netlytic.org/. Accessed 24 Jan 2020
24. Gruzd, A., Haythornthwaite, C.: Enabling community through social media. J. Med. Res. **15** (10) (2013). https://doi.org/10.2196/jmir.2796
25. Hawe, P., Webster, C., Shiell, A.: A glossary of terms for navigating the field of social network analysis. J. Epidemial Community Health **58**, 971–975 (2004)
26. Rogers, E.M.: Diffusion of Innovations, 5th edn. Free Press, New York (2003)
27. Ahn, Y.Y., Han, S., Kwak, H., Moon, S., Jeong, H.: Analysis of topological characteristics of huge online social networking services. In: Proceedings of the 16th International Conference on World Wide Web, Banff, Canada, pp. 835–844 (2007)
28. Bruns, A., Burgess, J.: The use of Twitter hashtags in the formation of ad hoc publics. In: Proceedings 6th European Consortium for Political Research General Conference, Reykjavik, Iceland (2011)
29. Gruzd, A., Wellman, B., Takhteyev, Y.: Imagining Twitter as an imagined community. Am. Behav. Sci. **55**(10), 1294–1318 (2011). https://doi.org/10.1177/0002764211409378
30. Xu, W.W., Chiu, I.-H., Chen, Y., Mukherjee, T.: Twitter hashtags for health: applying network and content analyses to understand the health knowledge sharing in a Twitter-based community of practice. Qual. Quant. **49**(4), 1361–1380 (2015). https://doi.org/10.1007/s11135-014-0051-6
31. Graham Mackenzie, D.: Improving the quality and impact of public health social media activity in Scotland during 2016: #ScotPublicHealth. J. Public Health, 1–6 (2017). https://doi.org/10.1093/pubmed/fdx066

Does Delivery Method Matter for Multicultural Undergraduate Students? A Case Study of an Australian University in the United Arab Emirates

Ajrina Hysaj[1]([⊠]) [iD] and Doaa Hamam[2] [iD]

[1] UOWD College, University of Wollongong in Dubai, Dubai, UAE
Ajrinahysaj@uowdubai.ac.ae
[2] Higher Colleges of Technology, Dubai, UAE
dhamam@hct.ac.ae

Abstract. For over two decades, higher education has been facing the dilemma of what method of study is better for students. For example, is it face-to-face, online learning, or blended learning? The three mentioned methods are increasingly considered and reconsidered as to which one offers a better alternative to students. Over the last period of time, it has been acknowledged that students from different backgrounds have different learning styles and that alternating teaching methodologies and styles can aid the learning process. The fluid and diverse demographic population of the UAE requires careful consideration when considering the most adequate system/systems of higher education. The chosen method of instruction offered within educational institutions in the United Arab Emirates raises a challenge for educators as to provide active learning set up to maximise individual student satisfaction and performance while enabling students to recognise their own cognitive skillset. The objective of this study was to analyse the preference of undergraduate students' delivery method of their courses. The study involved collection of relevant data through using a survey. A sample size of 37 undergraduate students was used to collect data. The data from the survey was analysed, and the results indicated students' preference of the delivery method. Finally, recommendations for future research were presented.

1 Introduction

The UAE is home to a total population of over 8.2 million, in which the expatriate population accounts for 90% of the entire population, making the UAE's ethnic diversity by far one of the world's highest [5]. Although the majority of the expatriate population of the UAE hails from India, Pakistan, China and Philippines, recently, the diversification of the population has been enriched with people from all around the world, for example; Africa, Europe, Australia and many other countries. The majority of the student population of international branch campuses like the university under study

© Springer Nature Switzerland AG 2020
G. Meiselwitz (Ed.): HCII 2020, LNCS 12195, pp. 538–548, 2020.
https://doi.org/10.1007/978-3-030-49576-3_39

is comprised of foreign students, who may have passed a considerable period of their development years in the UAE and are considered "third culture kids' (TCK's) [42]. The rest of international students belong mainly to South Asia with a smaller percentage from other countries worldwide. It is worth mentioning that institutions of higher education are in a continuous race for understanding students' needs, expectations and they aim for students' retention, students' satisfaction and students' readiness to join the UAE's workforce. Studies by Hysaj et al. [23], Hysaj et al. [24] and Lehtomäki, Moate and Posti-Ahokas [27] concluded that a cross-cultural dialogue creates a sense of connection through diversity, nurtures a fruitful dialogue, and subsequently creates a meaningful learning experience. The three above studies pointed out that although the diversity of students' body is an added advantage to students' experience in higher education, it is vital to design integrated learning approaches that can lead to deeper learning and that can facilitate the development of multicultural knowledge. These are both very valuable for the development of students' new global perspectives. Adaptation of teaching material used for clarification of concepts in a variety of contexts makes learning fun, enjoyable and memorable. If multicultural students learning style preferences are taken into consideration by the lecturers, tutors and course designers while preparing activities or assessment tasks in a face-face, online or blended learning platform, the level of students' interest can be much higher than in the case of the learning preferences not taken into consideration Hysaj et al. [23, 28].

Furthermore, for over two decades, the UAE has experienced an unprecedented increase in the number of universities opening in the country [22]. Due to the large number of universities and the variety of majors offered [50], federal and foreign universities are facing constant challenges to increase the intake of students, retain their students' body, provide students with a good amount of information, support and create opportunities to facilitate their academic growth personally and professionally. Students' learning styles, mobility of the students' body and fulfilment of workforce requirements are factors that need consideration when deciding on blended, online or face-to-face forms of higher education.

Fluidity and continuous growth of the population of the UAE, as well as the ever-increasing number of universities in the country, has increased the competition in the higher education sector [22]. The level of studies offered at undergraduate or post-graduate majors of federal and foreign universities is equally important to the UAE's economy as both types of universities are major stakeholders who are in charge of the provision of the intellectual workforce needed to fulfil the ever-growing needs of the UAE's economy. Therefore, choosing the best and the most appropriate delivery method for university courses is an important and essential process. In addition, many factors should be put into consideration when choosing the correct method like students' preference, background, the context, the learning objectives, the facilities of the university, and many other important factors to ensure the efficiency of the chosen delivery method and to ensure high quality education.

According to Nye [38], multiculturalism which is currently present in the UAE needs not only to be taken into consideration when discussing the demographics of the country, but also most importantly it should be explored and understood. Keeping individual identity intact while coexisting with others within a multicultural society according to (Hall 2000, p. 209) as cited in Nye [38] is particularly challenging in the

UAE, not only due to its enormous diversification of cultures but also due to the fluid nature of its demographics. Recognition of differences amongst cultures and the ways cultures are perceived within the community can serve as a starting point when considering online, face-to-face or blended forms of course delivery. Gaining knowledge on culture and multiculturalism is a two-way street that brings along the need to explore multicultural diversity and especially explore and understand its correlation with the different delivery methods offered in the higher education in the UAE.

2 Literature Review

2.1 Improving Multicultural Students' Writing Skills Through Online Discussions

Cultural perspectives and its correlation with the values instilled by institutions of higher education can impact students' experiences in the academic settings [1, 40]. As Nolan [36] mentions 'being anchored by keeping our cultural identities is necessary for us as people', so it is crucially vital that educators and policymakers create a nurturing environment for students in the ways teaching and learning take place. Students' engagement levels in face-to-face, online or blended platforms are highly correlated with their motivation levels in the same platforms. Shute [44] emphasises that skills acquisition occurs when making mistakes. Consequently, participating in online discussions and receiving clear formative feedback from teachers and comments from their peers through audio/video platforms, has the potential of making teaching and learning less stressful for students and teachers alike.

Moreover, online discussions can facilitate understanding the idea of the place where students are and where they want to be [35, 44]. Therefore, they will be able to fill in the gaps [20] based on the information they have about their online tasks and activities [9]. Therefore, Chinese students, and Arabic speaking females who generally tend to be very timid or even introverts would benefit from participating in online discussion through the online platforms by using words, pictures or graphs when explaining concepts or viewpoints [12, 18, 19, 39]. Arabic, Russian or Hindi-speaking students prefer a micromanaged formative approach, and they benefit enormously from presenting their efforts through online discussions while not being concerned about requiring extensive attention from teacher or peers. In general, online discussions provide a good opportunity for students to express themselves and engage in virtual learning activities more than the normal classroom situation where they can be shy or do not want to speak so as not to make mistakes, or find difficulty working with others from.

On the other hand, not only the students' engagement level should increase in using online platforms, but also their level of satisfaction. McLean [31] and Soltanpour and Valizadeh [45] affirm that students' satisfaction level when using online platforms is higher than when they are present in the traditional classroom. Active online engagement is all around relationships between fellow students, tutors and students. In addition, motivation levels of all parties are involved, as well to the sense of self-belonging and finally the worth of learning. Online discussions if organised appropriately, can facilitate students' understanding of subjects and improve their self-confidence in a relatively more comfortable environment than the traditional classroom. Moreover, the development of adequate academic skills [3, 11, 25, 49] and research skills [10] leads the online presence to be a fun and fruitful experience for multicultural undergraduate students.

Besides, online discussions increase the desire to get engaged with the subject in the virtual world. This is because they inspire the thought development process through virtual conversations that branch into an array of possibilities and offer an excellent platform for knowledge sharing and active and fruitful online presence. Nugent et al. [37] mentioned that the development of effective thinking can occur as a result of understanding and engaging with the topic under study. Therefore, online forums can facilitate the transfer of knowledge resulting in a deep and meaningful thought process. Moreover, challenges influence the co-creation of knowledge positively. They foster innovation and help in finding solutions to complex learning problems. According to McCarthy et al. [29]; discussion forums may serve as a constant source of knowledge acquisition outside the classroom (p. 95). Experts point out the social, cognitive and technological aspects of online learning and refer to it as a very fruitful and beneficial form of education delivery. This is because online interactions through online forums give both instructors and learners the opportunity of utilising a whole range of tools e.g. texts, videos, audios and others, aiming at the development of students' critical and analytical thinking patterns.

Online forums are usually structured through specific tasks, and they typically contribute to assessment through the utilisation of communicative learning tasks and online tools provided by the blended learning platform. Synchronous online forums offer first-year students the possibility of developing digital and academic writing skills in a relatively controlled environment through web-conferencing facilitated by the instructor but empowered by the students' thoughts and perspectives. Synchronous online forums and asynchronous online discussions fulfil the requirements of offering help and support similar to the face to face platforms, but they encourage the reflection process as well and contribute in increased students' interest in the online platform. The asynchronous online discussions may be preceded by the synchronous ones to pave the way to the brainstorming of ideas in a semi-controlled mode before developing into the asynchronous discussions that offer students the ability to reflect and grow academically and personally. The synchronous and asynchronous forums are expected to generate interest in the online platform and provide various options for knowledge sharing, deep learning and self-directed learning.

2.2   Improving Multicultural Students' Writing Skills Through Formative Feedback

Shute [44] and Ebata [16] emphasise that the individualised approach of providing formative feedback can facilitate the development of complex cognitive abilities in students. According to Black and Wiliam [7] as cited in Hattie and Timperley [20], extensive, meaningful and clear feedback leads to the successful completion of existing tasks and a greater understanding of their cognitive applications for more complex topics in the future. Moreover, all students irrespective of their native language tend to have improved understanding when given formative verbal feedback with the focus on the writing structure and when provided with extra comments and practice opportunities for the related linguistic errors. Furthermore, the provision of constant formative feedback through audio/video or written forms from the teacher will cater to students' individual learning preferences and enable deep reflection [19, 28]. Although all-inclusive feedback through the online platform could provide a certain degree of information, it cannot substitute the individualised formative feedback that takes into consideration students' learning preferences.

Furthermore, providing individualised formative feedback through Google Docs supports the teachers' ultimate goal of discussing common errors before providing summative feedback, aiming at active and purposeful participation of students in the online platform. Clawson [13] focuses on the notion of self-concept when addressing students' needs and when providing them with formative feedback. Students learn better if treated as intellectual and moral humans [15, 20, 25]. Hattie and Timperley [20] state; "Feedback may be sought by the students rather than given by the teachers, peers or parents" (p. 86). This concept places learners in the position of influencers, and it empowers them to change, modify, improve and complete their work [44].

In connection with the feedback process, Hofstede (1986) as cited in Sondergaard [46], points out that in collectivist society's individual students will only speak up in class when asked personally by the teacher; harmony is maintained in all situations; neither the teacher nor the students should lose face; students desire to learn how to "do". In individualistic societies, students want to learn how to learn; students will speak in class in response to a general invitation; conflicts and confrontation are accepted; there is no focus on saving face according to Hofstede 1986 p. 312 as cited in Søndergaard [46]. Sully De Luque and Sommer [47] note that collectivist cultures may not seek individual feedback directly and may engage in 'indirect inquiry and monitoring' and ask publically in the behalf of the group (p. 840).

2.3   Improving Multicultural Students' Writing Skills Through Reflection

The continuous use of online discussions can facilitate students' critical and analytical understanding of concepts, and develop their academic and research writing skills. Completion of work through Google Docs and reflective journals introduced after the completion of major tasks through Google Docs can give the students the possibility of reflecting on their learning or on their peers' learning by expressing their views through audios, videos or written comments. Nicol and Macfarlane [35] list "peer dialogue around learning" as one of the seven principles of proper feedback methods. Peer feedback encourages dialogue between learners and helps in creating a positive online environment if received well from students.

To ensure students' collaboration in Google Docs, online discussions online tasks about research, these tools should be introduced, as well as writing and referencing tasks with the focus on the similarities between real-life scenarios and academic writing/referencing. This can encourage the students to accept and offer constructive criticism and correlate their online learning with real-life experiences. Furthermore, the provision of personalised online-formative feedback to students, through videos/audios or written comments aiming at the development of critical/analytical thinking, revising inner speech" [32] and development of proper writing skills [41] are also essential. Continuous online bonding with the course, topic and the teacher can nurture identity, responsibility and accountability [9]. Likewise, the development of referencing skills, according to Pecorari [41] can encourage a reduction in plagiarism' instances.

3 Methodology

The study utilised quantitative methods to explore the students' opinions about the delivery method that they prefer in their undergraduate courses during their time in their university. A survey was chosen as the instrument to collect data because according to Creswell [14], surveys are considered one of the best quantitative research methods to explore opinions in educational research. Therefore, a survey was designed by the researchers, and it included ten multiple-choice questions with the aim of exploring students' opinions about their preferred method of course delivery. The sample chosen was a random sample extracted from students, and it was comprised of 37 students who were enrolled in the undergraduate program. The setting was an Australian university in the Middle East. The study was conducted after obtaining the necessary approvals, and the students came from different nationalities and different backgrounds. The students were informed with the purpose of the study, and they were informed that their participation is voluntary and that it will not have any effect on their current status at the university. After that, the students were asked to fill in the survey. The timeframe for the study was around three weeks after arrangements were made with the university management to collect the required data.

4 Results

The results illustrated the students' preference for the delivery method in their classes. The majority of the participants preferred to have individual feedback from their teachers in class, with a percentage of 81.1%. For the second survey question, only 40% of the students preferred to receive feedback via Moodle; however, a similar percentage did not prefer to use that platform. Only 18.9% of the participants were not sure. For the next question about the method preferred to explain mistakes, and from a choice of audio, video or written feedback, the majority of the participants with the percentage of 62.2% chose the written feedback. About participating in debates in class, the majority of the participants, 62.2% responded yes, so they expressed their preference of having debates in class.

On the other hand, not all students liked the idea of participating in online discussions, 37.8% of the participants liked the idea, but 29.7% of them did not, while almost a near percentage 32.4% were not sure. For the question about writing projects in pairs, 67.6 of the participants expressed that they liked the idea, while 21.6% did not, and 10.8% were not sure. Almost have of the participants expressed that they are fine with working on projects online, while 21.6% mentioned they do not like working online, and 32.4% were not sure. Most of the participants, 54.1% indicated that they prefer to collect their data in class, while a near percentage of 45.9% mentioned that they prefer to collect their date online. For analysing the data, a percentage of 54.1% of the participants indicated that they prefer to analyse their data in class, while 45.9% mentioned that they prefer to analyse data online. Finally, for the majority of the participants 62.2%, what's app was the preferred mode of communication for students to discuss their projects. Only 37% preferred to present their projects in person, and no one preferred to present it on the phone or via emails.

5 Discussion and Recommendations

The findings of the study reflected variations in the students' preferences of the courses' delivery methods. A high percentage of students preferred online methods, but a fair percentage also preferred the traditional methods like meeting in person, analysing and collecting data in class, and discussing feedback with their teachers in person. The finding of the study which reflects the high percentage of students' preference in using technology concurs with the findings of Myers [34] who also stated that a large percentage of undergraduates preferred and relied on the online study methods for their learning and interactions at the university. This finding also concurs with the findings of Vnoučková and Urbancová [48] who also stated that undergraduates preferred the online methods in a business university. According to the authors, students revealed that online methods provide more flexibility and availability of online material. The students also revealed that mobile applications were beneficial and that it was possible to consult teachers through online platforms. Moreover, in a study by Murphy, et al. [33], the authors revealed the importance of "faculty tailoring and adjusting their instruction to accommodate the needs of their students to increase students' achievement, motivation, and engagement in their classroom (p. 100)". This result means that teachers should be aware of their students' learning styles and preferences while designing their courses and planning their lessons and instruction, and this is reflected in the findings of the current study as the students preferred different delivery methods. Therefore, teachers should be aware of their students' needs to fulfil them.

Although many would think that it is easy for professional teachers to use online technology tools in their instruction, this is not always the case. Many teachers did not receive technology training in their formal education, as using technology in teaching can be considered a recent trend to some extent. According to previous research, it is essential to train teachers on teaching with the technology tools. Hewett and Bourelle [21] stated that the teacher trainers should enforce several skill sets like how to create assignments, use technology and incorporate it into the course design and check the students' progress during the course through reflections. When teachers understand more about teaching with technology, it is assumed that they can successfully guide their students to use technology and achieve their learning objectives.

6 Pedagogical Implications

The study paves the road to understanding undergraduates' attitudes towards the delivery methods utilised in their courses. It seems that students are open to the online and blended learning methods to a great extent, according to Kohli, Lancellotti, and Thomas [26]. However, there is quite a good percentage of students who still prefer traditional delivery methods. It also seems that some students might have a slightly negative idea about online methods and that they think these online methods might be ineffective. However, the theoretical background of online methods offers a solid basis for online delivery methods in terms of teaching and learning. After realising that these methods are pedagogically effective for learners based on the literature, for example, the work of Anderson [6], Callister, Love, [8], Wingo, Ivankova, and Moss [51]. The next step is to offer the appropriate delivery method depending on the context, course objective, students' status and background, and other relevant factors to avoid issues during the actual course delivery.

In general, based on the study's findings, it is clear that customising the delivery method for students will guarantee the best results in terms of teaching and learning. Also, the transition from traditional approaches to online learning or blended learning should take time and be gradual to make sure that students accept and adapt to the new delivery methods when it is introduced, and later to engage successfully with the subject matter to achieve their learning objectives. Another issue to be considered according to Altınay [4] when choosing the delivery method is the nature of assessment and the implementation of the assessment during the courses. In choosing online or blended learning methods, assessments should be secured in a way that does not allow cheating or causes other concerns. Besides, since the study was done in an international university which is the home of many nationalities and cultures, it is essential to put culture into consideration when designing and delivering an online or a blended learning course according to McDermott [30].

It is also recommended that the role of teacher education is to be considered when choosing delivery methods. According to Adnan [2], the voice of teachers transitioning from traditional methods to online methods should be heard. Teachers need to be well-prepared and well-acquainted with the learning management systems and the tools they use for delivery to ensure the efficiency of the chosen delivery method. Not only that, but teachers should also put the cultural aspect into their consideration when handling non-traditional delivery methods as culture plays an important role in the process of teaching and learning.

7 Conclusion

In conclusion, it is obvious that instruction can be provided efficiently through the blended learning model and online tools and accepted or recommended by the students. The findings of the current study revealed that the students are tech-savvy and that they prefer to use technology in their learning which is similar to one of the finding of Hamam's [17] study. Therefore, it is a recommendation for curriculum designers and policymakers to use more online tools and blended learning methods in their instruction. "Through the blended learning model, students can save travel time and can work at their pace from any place and at any time. Lecturers can provide recorded video lectures and interactive activities for their students, and they can make them available online for easy access. Through the LMS and other technology tools, interactive chats and discussions can be initiated by students or their lecturers about writing topics, strategies, and other aspects" (p. 200).

Technology can be used in every aspect in the teaching and the learning process like instruction, assessment, peer work, discussions, debates, data collection and many others. That is not all, also applications like what's app and Facebook are preferred among the young generations especially in communication; therefore it is a good idea to include such application to maximise the teaching and learning potentials. For example, there is the study of Rosa and Vital [43] that described many benefits of Facebook in teaching writing, and many other studies that discuss the use of applications and social media and their beneficial role in teaching and learning. A recommendation for future studies can be also looking at gamification in education and its effect on the process of teaching and learning.

To sum up, while the role of technology and the online tools in education cannot be ignored, especially nowadays where almost all institutions rely heavily on technology and online teaching methods, some students still prefer to use the traditional ways to interact with their peers and to discuss the subject matter in person with their teachers. However, the majority of students, especially undergraduates, react very well to online methods and consider them useful and flexible. Therefore, it is concluded that the delivery method does matter for students because if they are satisfied, they become more comfortable, and benefit from saving their time and from having easy access to the information at any time, from any place and on their own pace. Delivering the courses through blended learning or through the technology tools for students who are very much dependent on technology creates a successful teaching and learning environment within their comfort zone. To ensure the success of the online delivery methods, we conclude that teachers also should be more technology-educated, and they should tailor their instruction and delivery methods to accommodate their students' needs. Finally, several factors should be taken into consideration when choosing a certain method such as the context, the students' preference, and the culture to ensure the success of the online delivery method.

References

1. Adams, M.: Cultural inclusion in the American college classroom. New Directions Teach. Learn. **49**, 5–15 (1992)
2. Adnan, M.: Professional development in the transition to online teaching: the voice of entrant online instructors. ReCALL **30**(1), 88–111 (2018)
3. Alavi, S.M., Kaivanpanah, S.: Feedback expectancy and EFL learners' achievement in English. Online Submiss. **3**(2), 181–196 (2007)
4. Altınay, Z.: Evaluating peer learning and assessment in online collaborative learning environments. Behav. Inf. Technol. **36**(3), 312–320 (2017)

5. Al-Jenaibi, B.: The scope and impact of workplace diversity in the United Arab Emirates–a preliminary study. Geogr.-Malays. J. Soc. Space **8**(1) (2017)
6. Anderson, T.: The Theory and Practice of Online Learning. Athabasca University Press, Edmonton (2008)
7. Black, P., Wiliam, D.: Assessment and classroom learning. Assess. Educ.: Princ. pol. Pract. **5**(1), 7–74 (1998)
8. Callister, R.R., Love, M.S.: A comparison of learning outcomes in skills-based courses: Online versus face-to-face formats. Decision Sciences Journal of Innovative Education **14** (2), 243–256 (2016)
9. Castañeda, L., Selwyn, N.: More than tools? Making sense of the ongoing digitizations of higher education. Int. J. Educ. Technol. High. Educ. **15**(1), 1–10 (2018). https://doi.org/10. 1186/s41239-018-0109-y
10. Chatterjee-Padmanabhan, M.: Generic support for English as an additional language (EAL) students. In: Developing Generic Support for Doctoral Students. Routledge (2014)
11. Cheng, L., Wang, H.: Understanding professional challenges faced by Chinese teachers of English. TESL-EJ **7**(4), 4–8 (2004)
12. Choosri, B.: Enhancing students' language skills through blended learning. Electron. J. e-Learn. **14**(3), 220–229 (2016)
13. Clawson, J.G.: Level Three Leadership. Prentice Hall, Upper Saddle River (2002)
14. Creswell, J.W.: Educational Research: Planning, Conducting, and Evaluating Quantitative. Prentice Hall, Upper Saddle River (2002)
15. Crooks, T.J.: The impact of classroom evaluation practices on students. Rev. Educ. Res. **58** (4), 438–481 (1988)
16. Ebata, M.: Awakening Opportunity: Three Elements to Foster Learners' Autonomy, Online Submission (2010)
17. Hamam, D.: A study of the rhetorical features and the argument structure of EAP essays by L1 & L2 students (Doctoral dissertation, The British University in Dubai (BUiD)) (2019)
18. Hanover Research Group: Blended Learning Programs. Hanover Research, Washington (2011)
19. Harrington, A.M.: Problematiznig the hybrid classroom. TESOL EG **14**(3) (2010)
20. Hattie, J., Timperley, H.: The power of feedback. Rev. Educ. Res. **77**(1), 81–112 (2007)
21. Hewett, B.L., Bourelle, T.: Online Teaching and Learning in Technical Communication: Continuing the Conversation (2017)
22. Hijazi, R., Zoubeidi, T., Abdalla, I., Al-Waqfi, M., Harb, N.: A study of the UAE higher education sector in light of Dubai's strategic objectives. J. Econ. Adm. Sci. **24**(1), 68–81 (2008)
23. Hysaj, A., Elkhouly, A., Qureshi, A.W., Abdulaziz, N.A.: Study of the impact of tutor's support and undergraduate student's academic satisfaction. Am. J. Hum. Soc. Sci. Res. **3** (12), 70–77 (2019)
24. Hysaj, A., Elkhouly, A., Qureshi, A.W., Abdulaziz, N.: Analysis of engineering students' academic satisfaction in a culturally diverse university. In: 2018 IEEE International Conference on Teaching, Assessment, and Learning for Engineering (TALE), pp. 755–760. IEEE (2018)
25. Kiely, R.: Classroom evaluation-values, interests and teacher development. Lang. Teach. Res. **5**(3), 241–261 (2001)
26. Kohli, C., Lancellotti, M.P., Thomas, S.: Student attitudes towards hybrid business classes: lessons for implementation. J. Acad. Bus. Educ. **18**, 387–395 (2017)
27. Lehtomäki, E., Moate, J., Posti-Ahokas, H.: Global connectedness in higher education: student voices on the value of cross-cultural learning dialogue. Stud. High. Educ. **41**(11), 2011–2027 (2016)

28. Matters, Q.: Specific review standards from the QM higher education rubric (2018)
29. McCarthy, J.W., Smith, J.L., DeLuca, D.: Using online discussion boards with large and small groups to enhance learning of assistive technology. J. Comput. High. Educ. **22**(2), 95–113 (2010)
30. McDermott, G.: Towards a culturally responsive pedagogy in online teaching: an Irish perspective. Irel. J. Teach. Learn. High. Educ. (2017)
31. McLean, I.: How to make things visible in your English classroom and encourage deep learning. Metaphor **1**, 15–19 (2017)
32. Moffett, J.: Integrity in the teaching of writing. Phi Delta Kappan **61**(4), 276–279 (1979)
33. Murphy, L., Eduljee, N.B., Croteau, K., Parkman, S.: Relationship between personality type and preferred teaching methods for undergraduate college students. Int. J. Res. Educ. Sci. **6**(1), 100–109 (2020)
34. Myers, S.: Student technology use for undergraduate education. Report (2016)
35. Nicol, D.J., Macfarlane-Dick, D.: Formative assessment and self-regulated learning: a model and seven principles of good feedback practice. Stud. High. Educ. **31**(2), 199–218 (2006)
36. Nolan, R.: Communicating and Adapting Across Cultures: Living and Working in the Global Village. ABC-CLIO, Santa Barbara (1999)
37. Nugent, A.: Higher education learning framework: an evidence informed model for university learning (2018)
38. Nye, M.: The challenges of multiculturalism (2007)
39. Palloff, R.M., Pratt, K.: The excellent online instructor: strategies for professional development (2011)
40. Papi, M.: The L2 motivational self-system, L2 anxiety, and motivated behavior: a structural equation modeling approach. System **38**(3), 467–479 (2010)
41. Pecorari, D.: Teaching to Avoid Plagiarism: How to Promote Good Source Use. McGraw-Hill Education, London (2013)
42. Pollock, D.C., Van Reken, R.E., Pollock, M.V.: Third Culture Kids: The Experience of Growing Up Among Worlds: The Original, Classic Book on TCKs. Hachette, London (2010)
43. Rosa, J.P.O.D., Vital, R.A.D.: The use of facebook in argumentative writing: towards an instructional design model. Asten J. Teach. Educ. **1**(2) (2017)
44. Shute, V.J.: Focus on formative feedback. Rev. Educ. Res. **78**(1), 153–189 (2008)
45. Soltanpour, F., Valizadeh, M.: A flipped writing classroom: effects on EFL learners' argumentative essays. Adv. Lang. Lit. Stud. **9**(1), 5–13 (2018)
46. Sondergaard, M.: Research note: Hofstede's consequences: a study of reviews, citations and replications. Organ. Stud. **15**(3), 447–456 (1994)
47. Sully De Luque, M.F., Sommer, S.M.: The impact of culture on feedback-seeking behavior: an integrated model and propositions. Acad. Manage. Rev. **25**(4), 829–849 (2000)
48. Vnoučková, L., Urbancová, H.: Preferable course of study and learning support by business university students. Acta Universitatis Agriculturae et Silviculturae Mendelianae Brunensis **67**(2), 609–620 (2019)
49. Weaver, M.R.: Do students value feedback? Student perceptions of tutors' written responses. Assess. Eval. High. Educ. **31**(3), 379–394 (2006)
50. Wilkins, S.: Higher education in the United Arab Emirates: an analysis of the outcomes of significant increases in supply and competition. J. High. Educ. Pol. Manage. **32**(4), 389–400 (2010)
51. Wingo, N.P., Ivankova, N.V., Moss, J.A.: Faculty perceptions about teaching online: Exploring the literature using the technology acceptance model as an organising framework. Online Learn. **21**(1), 15–35 (2017)

Proposal of the Elderly Supporting System Based on the Perspective of Local Community in Japan

Ayaka Ito[1](✉), Masaya Ando[2], Hitoshi Uchida[3], Muneo Takemoto[3], and Yuichi Murai[1]

[1] Den-en Chofu University, Kawasaki, Japan
a-ito@dcu.ac.jp
[2] Chiba Institute of Technology, Chiba, Japan
[3] Ideafront, Inc., Tokyo, Japan

Abstract. Because of the ageing society, the number of elderly deaths in isolation is increasing and becoming a major problem in Japan. We conducted a quantitative survey in the neighborhood associations to see the likelihood of ICT service introduction in the context of neighborhood monitoring to support the elderly who is living alone. Two local communities in Kawasaki city were selected and the questionnaire was distributed in every household of the associations (250~400 households). The result illustrated that there is a great interest of neighborhood monitoring in urban area contrary to our expectations. Both associations showed that the communities are ageing, however certain amount of residents are using smartphones even if they are categorized as the elderly. Therefore, we concluded the introduction of ICT for neighborhood monitoring in the area is possible.

Keywords: Social welfare · Elderly care · Local community · Digital neighborhood · Questionnaire

1 Introduction

The increasing number of the elderly who live alone is becoming a nationwide trend in Japan, and this tendency is noticeable especially in the large-scale houses and apartments built in 1960s, during the time of the Japanese economic miracle [1].

Recently, the problems senior that citizens encounter in their daily lives are becoming more serious due to a variety of reasons: shrinking family units such as nuclear families, social structural vulnerability, lessening of interaction between local residents in the communities and so forth. Eventually, these factors can become the leading cause for the rise in the number of elderly deaths in isolation, a major contemporary issue in Japan [2].

To prevent these elderly deaths, neighborhood monitoring can be the foundation of a solid local community, and boosts safety by being able to notice unusual behavior in the daily lives of the elderly. Furthermore, as technology develops, ICT handsets have begun to play a major role in elderly care and monitoring activities [3].

© Springer Nature Switzerland AG 2020
G. Meiselwitz (Ed.): HCII 2020, LNCS 12195, pp. 549–558, 2020.
https://doi.org/10.1007/978-3-030-49576-3_40

2 Objective of the Paper

2.1 Related Works

Historically, in Japanese rural area neighborhood monitoring has been one of the key functions of communities based on the interaction of local residents. On the other hand, as the mobility of people has drastically developed in urban area, the trend of using ICT in neighborhood monitoring has emerged in cosmopolitan city since 1970s [4].

Nowadays civil society in Japan is in the midst of a great transformation at a time when "publicness", which used to belong to the authorities, should now involve those whom are concerned with administrative and fiscal reforms. Consequently, people in local communities have growing commitments to participate in policymaking directly in partnership [5]. Furthermore, there is a growing interest in how the authorities should reform their environmental, welfare, and urban development policies at the regional level. It is certain that decision-making should depend on how well the residents of the local district facilitate consensus-building efforts among themselves. Prior to accomplishing agreement, mutual understanding is called for by means of communication in the local community [6].

Based on these arguments, discussing the theoretical possibilities of neighborhood association or resident groups (in Japan these groups are called either "Jichikai" or Chonaikai) within the framework of "civil public sphere [7] " is undoubtedly important, which is described as a communication space in order to present an ideal model of the groups. The model should be considered as a voluntary association, in which the people establish agendas relevant to self-evident "living" in civil society by means of inter-subjective communication [8].

2.2 Accumulating the Perspective of Local Community

Even though the holistic social welfare policy by the government is still playing a big role in the elderly care, knowing their neighbors and helping each other is regarded as a crucial matter to enhance the community bond among local residents [9]. Nowadays, from the perspective of disaster prevention such as earthquake and tsunami, neighborhood monitoring has a certain possibility for building social neighborhood in Japan. In such cases, to what extent the monitoring doers should share the information of individuals always may be the problem to be discussed.

As the boundary between social and digital neighborhoods is blurred in modern times, ICT is expected to help residents from monitoring the elderly both technologically and ethically, ever since Act on the Protection of Personal Information was enacted in 2003 in Japan based on legislation such as Guidelines on the Protection of Privacy and Transborder Flows of Personal Data [10]. However, the possible reaction of the local community for introducing ICT is not well presented in the context of privacy protection. In addition, as for neighborhood monitoring, not only the person who is monitored but also monitoring doers are the elderly in general. In such cases, we need to pay a close attention whether these elderly people can use ICT effectively or not. Therefore, we conducted a quantitative survey in the neighborhood associations to see the likelihood of ICT service introduction.

3 Methodology

In order to conduct a quantitative survey, two local communities in Kawasaki city were selected and the questionnaires were distributed in every household of the neighborhood associations (250 ~ 400 households). Both associations have already launched the organizing committee of neighborhood monitoring in the area and they are holding monthly meeting.

In the meeting, both associations have agreed that grasping the attributions of the area is essential for the smooth introduction of neighborhood monitoring. They are also aware that this actualization contributes to strengthen the community's bond and characterizing of the area. The general architecture of the survey (data collection period, how to distribute and collect the questionnaire) was actively determined by associations. We advised them on the effective PR to gain the higher response rate.

Table 1 is the overview of the survey.

Table 1. Overview of the survey.

	Association A	Association B
Data collection period	January 1st 2019 ~January 20th 2019	December 5th 2019 ~December 31st 2019
Number of distribution	281 households (all member of the association)	351 households (all members of the association)
Number of collection	199 households (71%)	298 households (85%)

Conventionally, in association A the organizing committee holds a strong initiative in decision-making and has been conducting various types of survey about the local community. In other words, association A is accustomed to doing the survey under the leadership of the key person in the area.

To the contrary, association B makes decision by reaching a consensus among group members such as a welfare commissioner, association chair and the local residents. Although the land was developed and sold for households few decades ago, there has not been any general survey conducted by association B so far. In a way the organization committee of the association eager to know the real situation of the area both macro and micro level, namely, there is a big prospect for them to conduct this survey.

The questions were designed based on the general survey about local community and from the request of the associations. Excerpts of questions of the questionnaire are below (Table 2).

Table 2. Excerpts of questions of the questionnaire.

Number	Question	Answer Type
Q 1–4	Basic information of participants (sex, age, household structure, number of family, affiliation, years of living)	SA (Single Answer)
Q 5	Cellphone usage (Smartphone/Other types of Cellphone)	MA (Multiple Answer)
Q 6	Concern about the region	MA
Q 7	Whether you have a good relationship with neighbors (or not)	SA
Q 8	Person to ask your advice	MA
Q 9	Concern about the future life	MA
Q 10	Regional activity you want for the area	MA
Q 11	Whether you want to continue to live in the area (or not)	Yes/No (Y/N)
Q 12	Neighborhood monitoring you are aware of in the area	MA
Q 13	If there is someone needs to be monitored in the neighborhood	Y/N
Q 14	If yes in Q13, the number of the person	SA
Q 15	If yes in Q13, the state of the person	MA
Q 16	Concern about the neighborhood monitoring	MA
Q 17	If there is someone who refuses external support	Y/N
Q 18	How do you want to get involved in the neighborhood monitoring in the future?	MA
Q 19	Requests and comments for promoting neighborhood monitoring	FD (Free Description)
Q 20	What do you think is important to make the area better?	FD

4 Findings

4.1 Cellphone Usage – Association A

To see the likelihood of ICT service introduction in the neighborhood associations A, a cross-tabulation analysis was done to see the phone (smartphones and other types of cellphones) usage among the residents and their age (Fig. 1). The number on the bar graph is not the percentage but the actual number of the households.

In association A, there is a big portion of (not smartphone) cellphone usage among the elderly over 75 years old, which is regarded as the target range of neighborhood monitoring. Especially in the elderly over 80 years old (41 households out of 199), 38 households use these types of cellphones.

As for smartphone usage, mainly 50s and 60s (the child generation of over 75 years old) are the dominant range. Potentially these generations are to be the target users of ICT service in neighborhood monitoring. Overall, in association A cellphones including smartphones are widely used in the elderly contrary to our expectations.

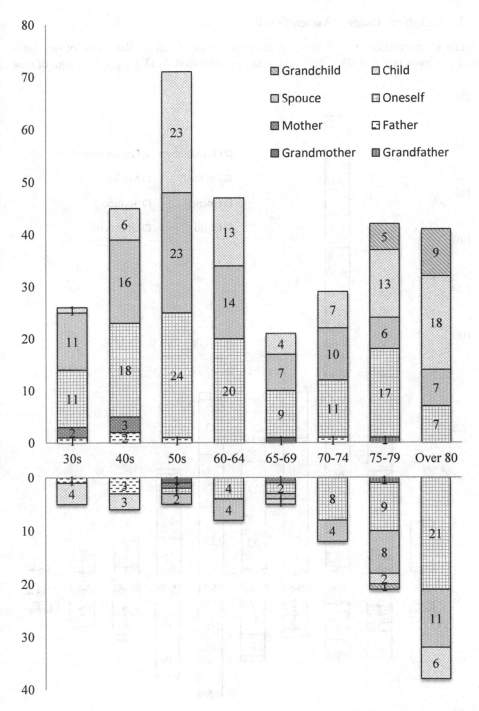

Fig. 1. Age/phone usage. Top: smartphone. Bottom: other types of cellphone. (Association A)

4.2   Cellphone Usage – Association B

Same as association A, a cross-tabulation was made based on the result of question-naire in association B (Fig. 2). Compared to association A, although the usage of (not

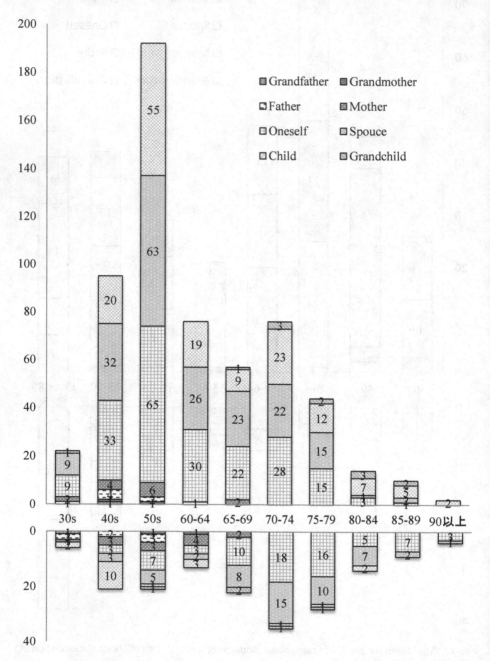

Fig. 2. Age/phone usage. Top: smartphone. Bottom: other types of cellphone. (Association B)

smartphone) cellphone is relatively low, still approximately 65 households of 70s are using them. Additionally, smartphones are widely used in 50s and we can conclude that potential target users are mostly familiar with ICT handsets.

5 Discussion

5.1 Association A

According to the basic information of the questions from 1 to 4, residents in association A tend to live with spouse or child generation; therefore it is possible for the family to monitor the elderly inside the households. However, in most cases they live in only two (old mother/father and a child) and a parent is left alone in the house during the daytime as the child is working until night.

On the other hand, many residents have bought the estate in the same period when the land was initially developed. Reaching consensus is relatively easy because of equal power distribution among residents. This tendency also matches the fact that association A has conducted many surveys about the area smoothly.

Question 7 and 8 revealed that many residents have information anchor to get an advice like a welfare commissioner and have been building a good relationship with neighbors. Question 10 and 18 illustrated they need opportunities to know each other more and wish to make a small community in which has a strong emotional bond within the neighborhood. In free description questions (19 and 20) there was a comment from a resident that neighborhood monitoring might be a trigger to make the "local culture," such as welcoming atmosphere of the area that residents can help each other.

5.2 Association B

Household structure in association B is not so different from association A (married old couple and two generations family are dominant), except that the land was initially developed approximately 10 years later. The average living period among the residents is from 20 to 30 years whereas 30 to 40 years in association A.

As for the age range of the residents, 50 s is the biggest population compared to 70 s and 80 s in association A (question 2 and 4), hence association B is younger even though both areas are ageing. In addition, how to decide organizing committee of the association is annual mandatory member rotation based on the group allocated for residential block. Because of these features, compared to association A association B has weaker neighborhood bond.

This background makes residents aware of the importance of effective countermeasure to the natural disaster such as earthquake (question 6). In question 7 to 9 there were requests for creating a place for the gathering of hobby so they can start to build good relationship within neighbors. There were also comments about motivation to start a small volunteer group for helping others for domestic chores.

5.3   Architecture of the Questionnaire for Higher Response Rate

After the collection period has ended, totaling questionnaire result was conducted in the cooperation with association organizing committee (Fig. 3). The strategy was to motivate local residents to grasp the real situation of the area actively by inputting data into computers and reading opinions. After the totaling, committee member commented "it was a good experience for us to total questionnaire which we designed by ourselves."

This is one way to empower the local community to build a solid foundation of neighborhood monitoring in the area. It is also regarded as one process of human-centered approach [11] to create the prototype of the elderly supporting system, since it is necessary to build a good rapport with the local community for the successful launch of the system.

Fig. 3. Totaling questionnaire with local residents in the associations

6   Conclusion

We conducted a quantitative survey in the neighborhood associations A and B to see the likelihood of ICT service introduction in the neighborhood monitoring. The result illustrated that there is a great interest of monitoring in urban area contrary to our expectations. Both associations showed that the communities are ageing, however certain number of residents are using smartphones and other types of cellphones even if they are categorized as the elderly.

The example of using ICT service into the neighborhood monitoring is proposed in rural area, which has a physical distance between houses [12]. However, this questionnaire has revealed that introducing ICT service in urban city such as Kawasaki is also possible as far as the percentage of cellphone usage is high enough. In this case we need to pay attention that the target users of the monitoring service can also be the elderly (over 60s in general) and the opportunity for the users to familiarize with the service should be provided effectively.

Based on the result of the survey and discussion with local residents, we started to design the supporting system of the elderly for neighborhood monitoring. The system enables monitoring doers to report the information about the elderly they acquired during the local activity via smartphone by user-friendly interface. The system is already launched in the neighborhood association and we are trying to improve the user experience based on the human-centered approach, especially focusing on the feedback from the local users (Fig. 4). We aim that the implementation of the system may contribute the formation of digital neighborhood in the ageing resident groups, and we expect the introduction model of ICT can be applicable to other ageing community in Japan as well.

Fig. 4. Revising the elderly supporting system by feedback of a user

Acknowledgments. JST RISTEX Grant Number JPMJRX17G5 supported this work.

References

1. Masuda, Y., Takada, E., Dai, Y., Itoi, W., Taguchi, R., Kawahara, C.: Study on dilemma and strategy of community support network by community organization for prevention of isolated death in an urban area. Japan. J. Public Health **58**(12), 1040–1048 (2011). (in Japanese)
2. Tamaki, T.: Live and die in solitude away from the family: issues relating to unattended death Kodokushi in Japan. Housei Riron **46**(4), 203–218 (2014)
3. Kumura, D., Kurisu, S., Yamamoto, R., Utatani, M., Nagata, T.: Development of elderly monitoring system by use of ICT. IEEJ Trans. Electron. Inf. Syst. **136**(10), 1460–1465 (2016). (in Japanese)
4. Kutomi, S., Mizuno, Y., Nimura, Y., Takizawa, R., Miyake, A., Saeki, K.: The awareness of older residents and adult residents on monitoring older residents in the community of a metropolitan city. Japan. J. Public Health Nurs. **5**(3), 230–238 (2016). (in Japanese)
5. Sato, Y.: Associative democracy. Yuhikaku Publishing, Tokyo (2007). (in Japanese)
6. Delanty, G.: Community. Routledge, London (2002)
7. Habermas, J.: The Structural Transformation of the Public Sphere: An Inquiry into a Category of Bourgeois Society. MIT Press, Massachusetts (1962)
8. Takahashi, M.: A study of communities, associations, and communication in civil society: civil public sphere interpreted by the ideal model of the Chonaikai. J. Int. Media Commun. Tour. Stud. **6**, 113–134 (2008)

9. Matthews, S.A., Yang, T.: Exploring the role of the built and social neighborhood environment in moderating stress and health. Ann. Behav. Med. **39**(2), 170–183 (2010)

10. OECD Guidelines governing the protection of privacy and transborder flows of personal data. https://www.oecd.org/sti/ieconomy/2013-oecd-privacy-guidelines.pdf. Accessed 31 Jan 2020

11. Buxton, B.: Sketching user experiences: getting the design right and the right design. Morgan Kaufmann Publishers, Massachusetts (2007)

12. Ogawa, A., et al.: A practical report on project of "Aging in place with ICT". Bull. Fac. Soc. Welfare Iwate Prefectural Univ. **13**(3), 65–69 (2011). (in Japanese)

Proposal of the Onion Watch Application for Enjoying a Stroll

Takayoshi Kitamura[1($\boxtimes$)], Yu Gang[1], Tomoko Izumi[1], and Yoshio Nakatani[2]

[1] College of Information Science and Engineering, Ritsumeikan University, Kyoto, Japan
ktmr@fc.ritsumei.ac.jp
[2] Ritsumeikan Trust, Kyoto, Japan

Abstract. In this study, to encourage tourists to visit numerous sightseeing spots, we examine a method of presenting information for sightseeing spots without using a map display and propose the Onion Watch application. It runs on a smartwatch and shows only the distance and direction to registered sightseeing spots and their categories, such as temples, shrines, or monuments. We also test four different methods for presenting the estimated distance remaining to the tourist spot and carry out experiments to verify whether the user is able to predict the distance remaining. The results showed that the logarithmic distance presentation system achieved good results in relation to the user's sense of approach and sense of distance. Therefore, we carried out a case study using this logarithmic distance presentation system in three sightseeing areas. The results showed that the participants enjoyed using the Onion Watch application. We also found that the characteristics of the sightseeing spots influenced their usability impressions of the Onion Watch application.

Keywords: Sightseeing · Smartwatch · Sense of distance

1 Introduction

Tourists visit sightseeing spots in a variety of ways, including being led by a tour guide, visiting famous places described in a guidebook, and gathering information in the field. However, regardless of the type of sightseeing visit, tourists may lose interest in visiting a location if they obtain too much information in advance. This is especially true for tourists whose motivation is to discover the unknown.

Therefore, we propose a smartwatch application that shows only the distance and direction to sightseeing spots and their categories, such as temples, shrines, or monuments. This application aims to support a user who wants to enjoy a leisurely sightseeing stroll. The application specifies that "the specific sightseeing spot is unknown, but the approximate direction and distance to the spot are known." Figure 1 shows the proposed application, which we call the Onion Watch. The missing segments in the yellow and green circles indicate the direction to various sightseeing spots within specified ranges. The size of a circle indicates the distance to a sightseeing spot, and thus reduces as the user approaches the sightseeing spot. The missing segments in the

© Springer Nature Switzerland AG 2020
G. Meiselwitz (Ed.): HCII 2020, LNCS 12195, pp. 559–568, 2020.
https://doi.org/10.1007/978-3-030-49576-3_41

white circle indicate the direction of sightseeing spots outside the specified ranges. The category of a sightseeing spot is indicated by a color (i.e., yellow, green, purple, or red). The watch vibrates and the screen blinks when the user approaches a sightseeing spot.

Fig. 1. Screenshot of the Onion Watch application. (Color figure online)

There were several issues in relation to the Onion Watch application that needed to be resolved. Smartwatches have small displays compared with smartphones, and thus the graphics are concentrated and can be difficult to read if there are numerous sightseeing spots nearby. Meanwhile, the user cannot grasp the sense of distance if the circle does not contract as the user approaches the sightseeing spot.

Thus, in this study, we examined the relationship between the size of the circle displayed on the screen and the distance to a sightseeing spot. Furthermore, we conducted a user test of the Onion Watch application in three sightseeing areas.

2   Related Works

Nakatani et al. [1] noted that when tourists are provided with information maps, they focus their eyes in the vicinity of their hands while reading the information. Therefore, they proposed an interface that facilitated the provision of supplementary information from the surrounding environment by not providing map-based information, and thus the discovery of tourist spots by accident [1].

Kinoshita et al. [2] proposed a strolling support system that used street atmosphere visualization. Their system runs on a smartphone and alerts users to the existence of attractive nearby streets and areas through vibration and visualized characterization [2].

Izumi et al. [3] investigated methods of providing information about tourist spots on a map in such a way that tourists would feel like they were freely choosing a direction in which to explore. As a result of their experiment, the descriptive information regarding the tourist spots and the area or direction suggested for location information achieved a good balance between recommendations from the system and activities chosen by the evaluators [3].

Kurata [4] developed "potentially-of-interest" maps using photographic data from Flickr, and also developed a prototype of a mobile tourist information tool featuring these "potentially-of-interest" maps. Nine of the 12 users in their test expressed an intention to use the tool again for other destinations [4].

All of these studies assume the use of mobile devices such as smartphones, which incorporate a reasonable screen size, but they have not considered the use of smaller screens incorporated in technology such as smartwatches. Furthermore, there have been few studies on the design and presentation of sightseeing information.

3   Usability Test of Methods of Determining the Circle Reduction Rate

The yellow and green circles on the Onion Watch application reduce in size as the user approaches a sightseeing spot. This section compares four methods of determining the circle reduction rate, namely, logarithmic, square root, linear, and exponential methods, as shown in Fig. 2.

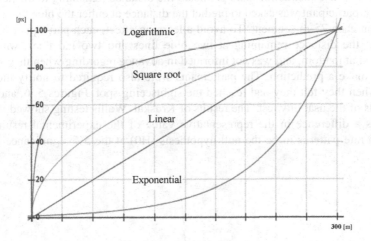

Fig. 2. Four methods of determining the circle reduction rate. (Color figure online)

In this experiment, we obtained the difference between the measured distance and the sense of distance for eight participants. We also measured the distance between the point where the participant felt they had reached the tourist spot and the actual location of the tourist spot. Figure 3 shows the experimental space at the Ritsumeikan University campus in Japan.

Fig. 3. Experimental space.

Figure 4 shows the locations at which each participant predicted the distance remaining to the next spot. A blue line represents a location one-third of the way to the next spot, while a red line represents a location two-thirds of the way to the next spot. The participant checked the Onion Watch application at each blue and red line based on the experimenter's instructions and predicted the distance remaining to the next tourist spot. Each participant was asked to predict the distance at either the blue line or the red line within each 75-m segment. To avoid a learning effect, each participant was asked to predict the distance remaining at two blue lines and two red lines, which were determined at random, and was not informed in advance regarding when they would be asked to make a prediction. The participants were also required to notify the experimenter when they felt they had reached the sightseeing spot. Figures 5, 6, and 7 show the results of the usability test. The results of Kruskal–Wallis testing showed that all of there was a difference in the representative value of the experimental result of four reduction rate patterns to be the null hypothesis (H0) at the 5% significance level.

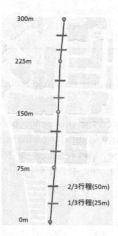

Fig. 4. Locations at which the participants made predictions regarding the distance remaining to spots. (Color figure online)

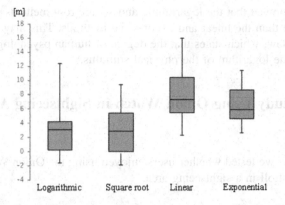

Fig. 5. Box-and-whisker plot of arrival the gap (n = 32).

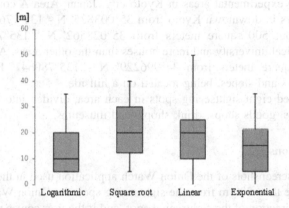

Fig. 6. Box-and-whisker plot of the distance gap (actual distance of 50 m, n = 16).

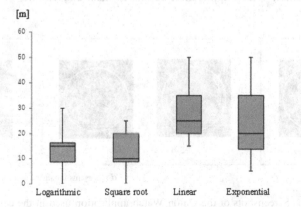

Fig. 7. Box-and-whisker plot of the distance gap (actual distance of 25 m, n = 16).

The results showed that the logarithmic and square root methods provided easy to grasp of distance than the linear and exponential methods. This may be related to the Weber–Fechner law, which states that the degree of human psychological sensation is proportional to the logarithm of the physical stimulus.

4   A Case Study Using Onion Watch in Sightseeing Areas

4.1   Purpose

In this case study, we tested whether users enjoyed using the Onion Watch application during a casual stroll in a sightseeing area.

4.2   Areas

There were three experimental areas in Kyoto city, Japan. Area A consisted of about 500 square meters in downtown Kyoto from 35°003825′ N - 135°776778′ E. Area B consisted of about 500 square meters from 35°028562′ N - 135°782604′ E, and included a historical university and more houses than the other areas. Area C consisted of about 500 square meters from 34°996229′ N - 135°780642′ E and included numerous temples and slopes, being located on a hillside.

We determined eight sightseeing spots in each area, divided into four categories: religious facilities, goods shops, drink shops, and museums.

4.3   Specifications

Figure 8 shows screenshots of the Onion Watch application used in the case study. At distances of more than 500 m from the sightseeing spot, the Onion Watch application only shows the direction of the sightseeing spot, and if the user comes within 500 m of the spot, the inner circle begins to reduce in size. When the user moves within 100 m of the spot, the Onion Watch application begins to flash and vibrate.

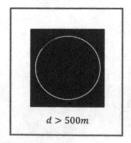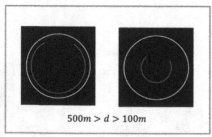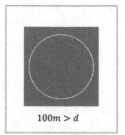

$d > 500m$ $500m > d > 100m$ $100m > d$

※ d represents the distance from the sightseeing spot.

Fig. 8. Screenshots of the Onion Watch application used in the case study.

4.4   Evaluation Procedure

First, we explained the purpose and flow of the experiment to the participants and obtained their consent. Next, we showed them how to use the system. The participants wore a 44 mm Apple Watch with an Onion Watch application installed and strolled around the designated area. They were instructed not to use any other information sources during the experiment. After their stroll, we asked them to answer the following five questions:

1. Did you enjoy your stroll?
2. Did you enjoy using Onion Watch more than using the general map application?
3. Did you think you had arrived at the spot indicated by Onion Watch?
4. Did you find any places you were interested in visiting other than the sightseeing spots presented by Onion Watch?
5. Do you want to keep using Onion Watch?

To record the participants' answers, we prepared a visual analog scale, as shown in Fig. 9.

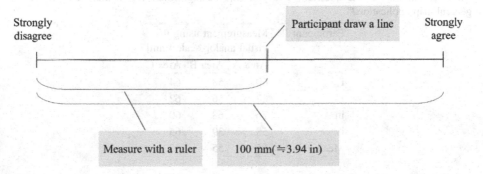

Fig. 9. Visual analog scale.

4.5   Results

Four university students participated in the experiment. Each participant was assigned a random area in which to stroll.

Table 1 shows the results of the answers to the question "Did you enjoy your stroll?" It can be seen that the mean response was at least 80 in all areas, with all participants recording values of at least 88 in Area B, which had a mean value of 93.

Table 1. Answers to the question "Did you enjoy your stroll?"

Participant ID	Measurement using the visual analog scale [mm]		
	Area A	Area B	Area C
i	83	88	85
ii	75	93	85
iii	73	96	83
iv	90	94	73
Mean value	80	93	82

Table 2 shows the results of the answer to the question "Did you enjoy using Onion Watch more than using the general map application?" It can be seen that the mean value of the responses in relation to Area B was relatively low, with participant iv reporting a particularly low value. We interviewed participant iv after the experiment and learned that he had visited Area B before, which would explain his low score.

Table 2. Answers to the question "Did you enjoy using Onion Watch more than using the general map application?"

Participant ID	Measurement using the visual analog scale [mm]		
	Area A	Area B	Area C
i	60	58	64
ii	67	56	62
iii	76	68	60
iv	58	39	65
Mean value	65	55	63

Table 3 shows the results of the answers to the question "Did you think you had arrived at the spot indicated by Onion Watch?" It can be seen that the mean value of scores in relation to Area B was particularly low.

Table 3. Answers to the question "Did you think you had arrived at the spot indicated by Onion Watch?"

Participant ID	Measurement using the visual analog scale [mm]		
	Area A	Area B	Area C
i	58	37	70
ii	71	35	61
iii	56	50	74
iv	56	29	56
Mean value	60	38	65

Table 4 shows the results of the answers to the question "Did you find any places you were interested in visiting other than the sightseeing spots presented by Onion Watch?" It can be seen that the mean values in relation to Areas A and C were lower than that in relation to Area B, with participant iv's score below the midpoint in Areas A and C.

Table 4. Answers to the question "Did you find any places you were interested in visiting other than the sightseeing spots presented by Onion Watch?"

Participant ID	Measurement using the visual analog scale [mm]		
	Area A	Area B	Area C
i	58	85	59
ii	52	73	55
iii	54	79	59
iv	48	64	48
Mean value	53	75	55

Table 5 shows the results of the answers to the question "Do you want to keep using Onion Watch?" It can be seen that the mean values in relation to each area were all at least 73.

Table 5. Answers to the question "Do you want to keep using Onion Watch?"

Participant ID	Measurement using the visual analog scale [mm]		
	Area A	Area B	Area C
i	75	85	75
ii	75	90	65
iii	80	80	73
iv	80	95	78
Mean value	78	88	73

4.6   Discussion

The results showed that using Onion Watch made the trip more enjoyable, and that the testers wanted to use Onion Watch again. Thus, Onion Watch seems to be effective from the viewpoint of creating an enjoyable experience.

However, Area B was relatively low (below the midpoint) scores in Table 3. On the other hand, Table 4 shows Area B had got high scores. One possibility is that participants were influenced by the absence of signage in the field because area B has fewer signboards than other areas. Therefore, it is necessary to promote behavioral observation analysis in the future.

5 Conclusion

In this study, to encourage tourists to visit numerous sightseeing spots, we developed a method of presenting information on sightseeing spots without using a map display and proposed the Onion Watch application, which runs on a smartwatch and shows only the distance and direction to various categories of registered sightseeing spots including temples, shrines, and monuments. We tested four different methods of estimating the distance remaining to the sightseeing spot and carried out an experiment in an attempt to verify whether users were able to accurately sense the distance remaining to the sightseeing spot. The logarithmic distance presentation system showed the best results in terms of the users' sense of approach and sense of distance. Therefore, we carried out a case study using this logarithmic distance presentation system in three sightseeing areas. The results showed that the participants enjoyed using Onion Watch, although we found that the characteristics of the sightseeing spots influenced their impressions of Onion Watch.

Acknowledgment. This work was supported by JSPS KAKENHI Grant Number JP18H03483.

References

1. Nakatani, Y., Tanaka, K., Ichikawa, K.: A tourist navigation system that does not provide route maps. Proc. World Congr. Eng. Comput. Sci. **2**, 1264–1269 (2009)
2. Kinoshita, Y., Tsukanaka, S., Go, K.: Strolling with street atmosphere visualization: development of a tourist support system. In: CHI 2013 Extended Abstracts on Human Factors in Computing Systems, pp. 553–558 (2013)
3. Izumi, T., Kitamura, T., Nakatani, Y.: A Suggestive recommendation method to make tourists "feel like going". IFAC-PapersOnLine **49**(19), 573–578 (2016)
4. Kurata, Y.: Potential-of-interest maps for mobile tourist information services. In: Fuchs, M., Ricci, F., Cantoni, L. (eds.) Information and Communication Technologies in Tourism 2012. Springer, Vienna (2012). https://doi.org/10.1007/978-3-7091-1142-0_21

Online Gambling Activity in Finland 2006–2016

Aki Koivula[1,2(✉)], Pekka Räsänen[2], Ilkka Koiranen[2], and Teo Keipi[3]

[1] Social Psychology, Faculty of Social Science,
Tampere University, Tampere, Finland
akjeko@utu.fi
[2] Economic Sociology, Faculty of Social Science,
University of Turku, Turku, Finland
[3] Design Factory, Aalto University, Espoo, Finland

Abstract. The article examines the recent trends in online gambling in Finland from 2006 to 2016. The data are derived from the "Use of Information and Communication Technology Statistics by Individuals and Household Survey" collected by Statistics Finland (N = 29,214). The analysis focuses on the frequencies of online gambling and the amounts of money spent on gambling applications in different population groups. The findings suggest that while online gambling has become more common in Finland, the amounts of money spent have decreased. Certain persisting differences by economic and socio-demographic characteristics are also detected. In particular, males, employed and under 40-year-old citizens are more likely than others to gamble. However, older people tend to spend higher amounts of money online. In addition, the probabilities of being a gambler are higher among less educated Finns. What is also noteworthy is that online gambling is clearly associated with the overall internet use frequencies and internet use purposes of the respondents. However, the internet use patterns do not associate as clearly with the amounts of money spent on the gaming applications.

Keywords: Online gambling · Gambling expenditure · Survey research · Digitalization

1 Background

1.1 Introduction

The digitalisation of gambling has had a particularly strong impact on schedule and location based limitations of traditional gambling, thus making the activity far more accessible to a wider pool of potential participants [1]. However, while digitalisation has continued in accelerating pace, there are still high inequalities who are able to join digital gambling. In this article, we assess changes in online gambling in Finland during the years 2006–2016 and examine the questions associating with population level disparities.

© Springer Nature Switzerland AG 2020
G. Meiselwitz (Ed.): HCII 2020, LNCS 12195, pp. 569–583, 2020.
https://doi.org/10.1007/978-3-030-49576-3_42

In Finland, gambling is mostly controlled by the state being also an essential part of the Finnish welfare society's financial system [2]. Gambling is an important activity by which Finnish state collect public funds from the citizens. Finns spend an average of 400 euros per year on domestic gambling alone, which has grown the domestic gambling industry to yearly revenue of over 1.5 billion euros [3]. In Finland the one reason for gambling maintaining its popularity is probably in digitalization [4]. In 2014, over 30% of Finns gambled online at least once a year [5], which is larger than an average share in the Western countries [6].

Recent studies have shown that digital gambling assessment cannot done using the same criteria that have been used for studying traditional gambling. Where traditional gambling has been analysed as an isolated problem among a small group of a population [7, 8] or as a general routine activity [9], online gambling can be considered one of the purposes of the Internet for many users.

Digitalisation and the removal of limitations in terms of access through time and location has resulted in problematic issues involved with online gambling to go unnoticed [10, 11]. Many studies have shown relationships between online gambling and unhealthy behaviours [7, 11–13]. For example, gambling age restrictions can be easily overcome in the online setting [13, 14]. It has also been put forth that the transfer of money electronically encourages risk and gambling addiction beyond that taken in the traditional offline setting where money is also handled physically [11]. Furthermore, online gambling leverages increasing amounts of online gaming strategies used to make the activity more attractive, including through graphics, animation and playability [15]. Adding these characteristics is assumed to increase the popularity of online gambling, especially among younger participants for whom using technology and digital services is already part of daily life in other ways.

However, the emergence of online gambling is recent enough that major part of these studies are based on data from offline gambling activity and are not representative on a population level [11, 13]. Using nationally representative time-series data, we fill this gap and assess how common is online gambling among various population groups. We also assess whether online gambling is simply an additional Internet activity, which is affected by similar factors relevant to assessing other Internet behaviours. We propose the following research questions:

1. How did online gambling change among different population groups during the years 2006–2016?
2. Did different population groups spend as much on online gambling during the years 2009–2016?
3. What effect did the diverse Internet use have on online gambling during the years 2006–2016?

The analysis is based on Statistics Finland's "Use of information and communications technology by individuals" data (n = 29,214), which serves as the official Finnish time series data [16]. Before moving on to empirical analysis, we present a short literature review concerning how online gambling can be approached through the perspective of digital divides and the Internet use habits therein.

1.2 Digital Divides and Online Gambling

In general variance in technology use among different population groups has been illustrated by the concept of *digital divides*. Digital divides illustrate how technology and Internet use, use purposes, use potential, motivations and necessary skills are unevenly distributed according to various sociodemographic characteristics. [17–19]. The theoretical basis for digital divides is the concept that all societal inequalities are also reflected in technology use of that same population.

However, in the case of online gambling it is more complicated to utilize the concept of digital divides. For example, who are those in marginalized and weak position when assessing online gambling? Those who are not able utilize online gambling sites due the lack of access, motivation or skills? Or those who are gambling way too much and suffer the consequences? In this respect, online gambling forms sort of double-edged sword type of situation: those in the weakest position are placed both ends of the spectrum. Due to this, we assess online gambling with two different measures, namely online gambling in general and money spending in online gambling.

The analysis of online gambling is often linked to a dimension involving access and gambling enforcement, which are affecting both users and the providers of the activity. First, digitalisation has made it possible for consumers to engage in gambling any time when accessing the Internet. In practice, individuals can choose from a wide range of gambling options online and log on regardless of time or place.

Simultaneously, digital services add new dimensions to gambling experience and in this sense may increase risky behaviour on population level [10]. Similarly, awareness of problematic gambling habits has become more difficult, as Finnish gambling monopolies are forced to compete with international websites, which makes it harder to supervise online gamblers actions for domestic monopolies and also does not encourage them to restrict their costumers' spending. In this sense, it is likely that online gambling will continue to have a significant impact on the domestic online market for similar services. Part of these effects is certainly already visible.

The first wave of research on online gambling was especially concerned with the impressions of Internet dangers, which have become apparent in research on Internet behaviour in other forms as digitalisation has become increasingly common [13, 20–22]. Studies have shown that online gambling brings higher risk taking and negative effects compared to traditional gambling. These conclusions can be made in studies concerned with participants with a high level of gambling activity [12, 13, 23, 24]. On the other hand, past research also opens the door to questioning the Internet's assumed effect on gambling in terms of problems and addiction formation. For example, part of past research on online gambling and problems associated with the activity has been unable to establish any meaningful relationship between the two (Philander & MacKay [25]) or was established using other contextual factors [26].

In terms of a societal assessment of online gambling, the effects of the developments of gambling and Internet use are relevant frames of reference. Past research has shown that demographic and socio-economic factors are related to the quantity of gambling and Internet use habits. In Finland, as well as all over western countries, gambling has generally been more popular among men, young adults, people living alone, the less educated, the wealthier and the employed [9]. On the other hand, relative to income, men, young people, the less wealthy and the unemployed spend most on gambling and have more likely to problems in terms of gambling [27]. The initial users of the Internet and new digital technologies tend to be younger, men, highly educated, more wealthy, live in a city and native to the country in question [28–30].

As such, the same sociodemographic factors can been seen as affecting both general gambling behaviour and Internet use. Various factors in these two areas, including age, education level and income, have been shown in past research to be inversely related. For example, the highly educated have been shown to use the Internet in more diverse ways [28], yet gamble less [9, 31, 32], which also indicates multidimensional inequalities related to gambling. Here, it is clear that relationships between sociodemographic factors and online gambling are complex.

1.3 Hypotheses

Earlier research shows that gambling and Internet use are tied to various contextual social factors. We expect that younger age groups and a significant percentage of men practice online gambling. Notable differences in Internet use behaviour continue to be apparent between high income and high education and low education and low income groups [33, 34]. It is likely that socioeconomic factors linked to Internet use are also reflected in online gambling. Therefore, we expect that (H1) *gambling popularity has grown among population groups, but men, younger people, and those with higher income are more likely than others to have gambled online*.

Although the habits of Internet use continue to differ strongly according to sociodemographic factors [28, 33], it is not obvious that online gambling and money spent would differ in similar ways among population groups. We expect that (H2) *the amount of money spend on online gambling will be distributed differently among different gambling participants when compared to the gambling habits of the population as a whole*. This assumption is based on the perspective that transferring routine activities online does not necessarily increase the quantity of the activity or the level of division of the activity among population groups [30, 34].

Additionally, we can expect that habits and activity level having to do with technology use and Internet use will be central to any inequality in digital technology use. The activity habits of various Internet platforms will be linked to activity frequency, repetition, duration and quantity, scope of activities carried out, types of platforms used and purpose of use, among others [28, 33]. It is likely that (H3) *online gambling is linked to online activity that involves diverse purposes.* It is also likely that those using the Internet for diverse purposes have also tried online gambling at some point. On the other hand, amount of money spent on online gambling is likely not linked to diverse online behaviour.

2 Data, Methods and Measures

2.1 Data

Our analysis is based on the "Use of information and communications technology by individuals" data for the years 2006–2016, which are official Finnish statistics. The national bureau of statistics, Statistics Finland yearly cross-sectional survey assesses the commonality of technology and online platform use, frequency of use, diversity, use purposes, use locations and online shopping [16]. Our total data consist of 29,214 observations. Throughout the analysis, we will take advantage of Statistics Finland's weight factor variables [16].

2.2 Measures

In the empirical part of our article, we first illustrate how online gambling has changed in different years and how money spent have varied. In the original question, participants were asked whether he or she had participated in online gambling during the past 12 months. A binary variable was developed from the question where a value of 0 represented those participants who had not gambled online and 1 represented those who had carried out such activity during the past 12 months.

We also analysed those who had spent money on online gambling during the past 12 months. We separated those who spent 1) less than 49 €, 2) 50 to 99 €, 3) 100 to 199 €, and 4) over 200 € during the past 3 months. Amounts spent are adjusted for inflation (all sums correspond to 2016 prices). Considering inflation allows us to analyse temporal changes in gambling expenditure.

Our independent variables are, for the most part, from respondents' register information. We assess age as a four-class variable, where 16–30, 31–44-, 45–64- and 65–74-year olds each form their own category. The goal of this classification was that age groups would remain well represented regardless of whether the analysis is focused on the entire population or online gamblers alone. Respondent education was categorised according to whether he or she had completed primary, secondary, tertiary or master level education. Finally, in terms of income, we categorised respondents according to the data distribution and separated those who earnt 0 to 1599 €, 1600 € to 2599 €, 2600 to 4099 €, and at least 4100 € per month.

The descriptive statistics for the applied variables are shown in Table 1.

Table 1. Descriptive statistics of the variables

Variable and *categories*	Obs.	Proportion	Min	Max
Online gambling	29,214		0	1
No, during past 12 months		.79		
Yes, during past 12 months		.21		
Online gambling spending (if gambled during past 12 months)	4,396		1	4
0–49 €		.47		
50–99€		.21		
100–199€		.18		
200€-		.13		
Internet use diversity	29,214		1	3
Low (0–3 activities)		.39		
Medium (4 activities)		.30		
High (5 activities)		.31		
Gender	29,214		0	1
Male		.49		
Female		.51		
Age	28,921		16	75
16–30		.22		
31–44		.21		
45–59		.29		
60–75		.28		
Education	29,214		1	4
Primary		.17		
Secondary		.41		
Tertiary		.22		
Master		.10		
Income	25,513		1	4
0–1599 €		.16		
1600–2599 €		.23		
2600–4099 €		.31		
4100-€		.30		

2.3 Methods

In addition to descriptive comparisons, we run logistic regression analysis allowed us to assess the likelihood of online gambling among different population groups when other factors are controlled for. We present both logistic regression results as unstandardized and standardised predictive margins expressed as hundredths in order to reflect a percentage-based likelihood of value 1 occurring in the various variable categories [35].

Models are presented as figures that show 95% confidence intervals (95% CIs), on whose basis we have evaluated the statistical differences between various variables and years. For the sake of clarity, population-based analysis for 2006–2016 is presented in five-year increments. In terms of money spent, however, our data covers the years from 2009 to 2016. Here, we report the estimated effects for 2009, 2013 and 2016. Due to text length limitations, we are not presenting full models. Tables and syntaxes including the full models are provided by the authors via email if needed.

3 Results

3.1 Trends Over Time

The yearly distributions of dependent variables are presented in Figs. 1 and 2. Figure 1 shows that online gambling participation as a portion of the population increased from 10% to approximately 30% during the years 2006–2014. The rise in popularity was particularly strong until 2011, after which growth slowed, and eventually stopped between 2013 and 2016. Money spent has been measure since 2009, which prevents a longer-term time comparison. However, Fig. 2 shows that the population-level patterns in online gambling spending have remained similar during the observation period.

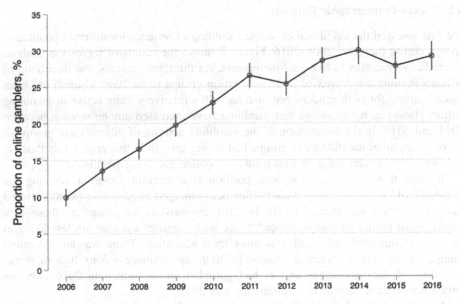

Fig. 1. Proportion of online gamblers in Finnish adult population with 95% CIs, 2006–2016.

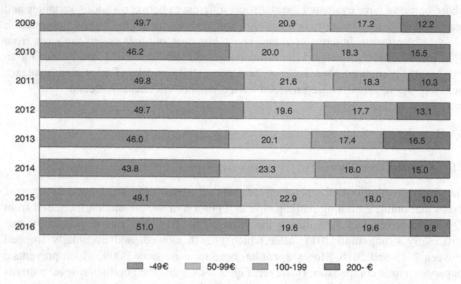

Fig. 2. Money spending in online gambling within past three months, 2009–2016.

3.2   Socio-Demographic Patterns

We first assessed the likelihood of online gambling experience for different population groups during the years 2006–2016. Figure 3 shows the results of regression analysis as predictive margins in five-year increments. As the figure reveals, the likelihood of online gambling has increased in all population groups since 2006. Growth has been equally strong for both genders, but men are still a relatively more active in gambling online. However, figure shows that gambling have increased among women between 2011 and 2016. In the comparison of the gambling activity of different age groups, it becomes apparent the oldest age groups had strong growth in this area, while those at the age of 16–30 showed a slowest growth in online gambling likelihood.

It seem that respondents' societal position is a relevant factor in affecting the likelihood of online gambling. Major differences emerged in gambling trends between various education and income levels. In 2016, the most active groups are those with secondary or higher education. Instead, those with a master's degree are less likely to play when compared those with a primary level education. There was an equivalent change among different income groups. In 2006, approximately 5 to 10% of representatives of various income classes had gambled online, which in 2016 only the lowest and highest income class difference was 20%.

Next, we analysed the likelihood of online gambling spending above the gambler group median level. Analyses were focused on those respondents who had gambled online during the past 3 months from the interview. The results of the logistic regression analysis are presented in Fig. 4. Here, we see that spending has been relatively uniform among all population groups during the time scale assessed. Differences between genders has reduced somewhat during the time scale used, but men are still spending more in online gambling. It also seems that younger gamblers do not spend as much on the activity as do older participants. It seems that online gamblers' education and income levels do not remarkable effects on spending habits on the activity.

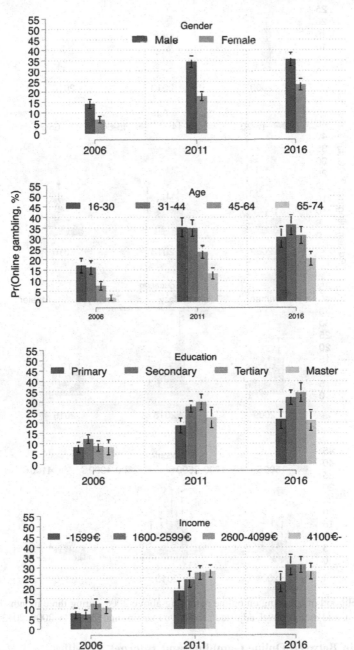

Fig. 3. Likelihood of online gambling at the population level during the years 2006–2016, adjusted predictive margins and 95% CIs.

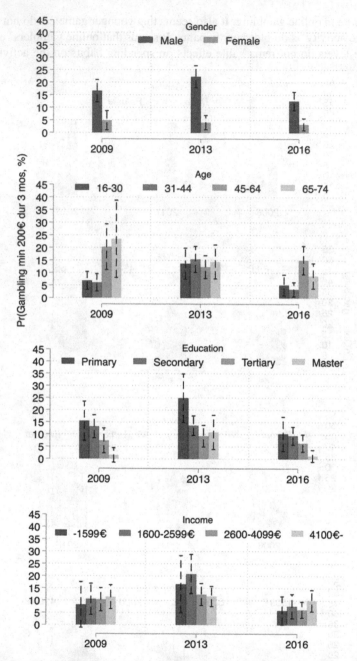

Fig. 4. Likelihood of spending on online gambling above 200€ during three months by gender, age, education, and income level, adjusted predictive margins and 95% CIs, 2009, 2013 and 2016.

Relationship Between Online Gambling and Internet Activities

Finally, we assessed how online gambling associates with other Internet activities. We formed sum variables from various Internet activities through which respondents' diverse internet use was categorised as low diversity, medium diversity or high diversity (see Table 1). The used Internet activities were banking, using email, reading webzines, gaming (no gambling), listening to music, and searching for information. In the analysis, three categories were formed based on whether respondents had under four, four, or five primary Internet activity habits.

We have added the aforementioned sum variable to the baseline models and carried out regression analyses. Complete results of analyses are shown in the appendix, and the effects of internet use diversity are shown in Fig. 4. The left side of the graph shows how gambling likelihood fluctuates on the population level according to diverse Internet use over the years examined. The variables share a relatively strong association. The likelihood of gambling grows as the diversity of online activity grows.

The right side of the table shows the likelihood of varied user activity habits spending money over the median rate on online gambling during the years 2009–2016. The assessment of money spent was targeted at those participants who have gambled online in the past three months from the time of the interview. The diversity of Internet activity habits had such a strong association with online gambling that the margin of error for online gambler respondents grew quite large in the case of users with one-sided Internet activity. The figure makes it clear that diverse Internet activity is not associated with how much one spends on online gambling. No changes between the variables over the years included were detected (Fig. 5).

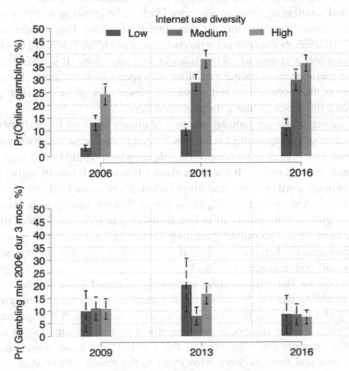

Fig. 5. Likelihoods of online gambling and spending on online gambling above 200€ during three months by internet use diversity, adjusted predictive margins and 95% CIs.

4 Discussion

In this article, we assessed the growth of online gambling in 2006–2016, and in addition the trends in spending in 2009–2016. The results show that online gambling has indeed increased quite unequally among various population groups. Wealthier, younger people and males are more likely to gamble online regularly. On the other hand, males, older age groups, those with less education and one-sided Internet users tend to spend more money on online gambling. The various background variables differ in their effects according to whether they are linked to online gambling or money spent on the activity. Only gender showed a statistically significant difference that remained for both online gambling and amount spent on gambling online. Results are in line with previous studies conducted in the United Kingdom [36] and Australia [37].

The results of the analyses reinforce past research, as we look at differences in digital technology use and online gambling among various population groups. Gambling occurs online and offline in similar ways within specific population groups. On the other hand, online gambling activity varies according to Internet habits and level of online competence, which also are not easily separated from sociodemographic factors themselves. Notably, the amount of time spent online and the diversity of online activity do not have a strong association with amount of money spent on online gambling.

On a related note, we put forth that highly active Internet users with diverse habits, high income and younger age groups are more likely to be involved in trying out online gambling in a conservative fashion. At the same time, older, less socioeconomically secure, one-sided users of the Internet who participate in online gambling can be said to be less careful when it comes to taking risks in such activities. It is also important to note that those participants in online gambling who spend high amounts of money are a small minority of the population, and as such a closer look at problematic gambling habits is beyond the scope of the data presented here.

The diminishing of the per gambler quantity of money spent on the activity may well be linked to online gambling being a relatively benign phenomena that does not increase problematic behaviours such as increased risk-taking, which would be apparent in higher amounts of money spent online. It has been shown that a small part of active gamblers produce a significant portion of the gambling industry's revenue [38].

Many of the findings reflect the digitalisation of Finnish society as a whole, which is shown in the growing popularity of online forms of gambling. In light of the results, the transition from offline to online gambling cannot be said to result in any notable increase in problematic behaviours related to gambling, despite increased ease of access and overall convenience [12, 24, 25, 36].

This study shows that various risks previously assumed to be linked to the digitalisation of gambling can be dismissed for the most part. Online gambling platforms are developing at a faster pace than ever before. Because of this, it is important to note that digital divides do not disappear permanently with the introduction of new technological outlets, despite the narrowing of the gap between those population groups with online access and those without. However, as the results of this study underline, digital divides are increasingly reflected in outcomes of Internet activities [39]. Diverse use of Internet activities is not related to problematic use of gambling sites. In this sense, we can argue that digital divides are also accumulating from one to another level.

The data used in this study and the chosen methods of analysis have some limitations that should be mentioned. First, data on gambling and amount of money spent have been self-reported by participants and as such both dependent variables are estimates. Furthermore, it is important to note that through the survey used performs well as Finland's official statistical basis on a population level, the data does have problems related to respondent distribution. The interpretations presented are based on Finnish respondents and as such broader conclusions requires data from a cross-national perspective.

5 Conclusions

Our findings indicate that the Internet is not its own separate world in terms of gambling. Rather, online gambling reflects the same socioeconomic and demographic factors relevant to traditional gambling. As digitalisation has progressed, so have its possibilities provided in terms of services and platforms. Indeed, the same is true of gambling as few remain without access to online methods for carrying out the activity. The direction of development is also apparent in the findings of this study.

In the assessment of online gambling patterns it is important to note that the increased diversity of gambling possibilities are not relevant to all. In every country, there are consumers who do not have the necessary monetary, technological, skill-based, or motivation resources to participate in online substitutes. Those in the high income and highly educated groups have an advantageous point of departure toward accepting new practical changes to information and communication technologies. As in the case of other resources, skills and knowledge of online gambling platforms are unequally distributed on a societal level among various population groups. Finally, although online gambling does not seem to significantly increase harmful effects of gambling on the population level, it is possible that its growing popularity will increase harm to specific high-risk sub-groups.

References

1. Torres, C., Goggin, G.: Mobile social gambling: Poker's next frontier. Mob. Media Commun. **2**, 94–109 (2014)
2. Roukka, T., Salonen, A.: The winners and the losers: tax incidence of gambling in Finland J. Gambl. Stud. (2019). https://doi.org/10.1007/s10899-019-09899-0
3. Salonen, A., et al.: Rahapelaamine, rahaplihaitat ja rahapelien markkinointiin liittyvät mielipiteet kolmessa maakunnassa. Rahapelikyselyn 2016–2017 perustulokset yksinoikeusjärjestelmän uudistuksessa. THL, Helsinki (2019)
4. Castrén, S., Heiskanen, M., Salonen, A.: Trends in gambling participation and gambling severity among Finnish men and women. BMJ Open **8**(8), e022129 (2018)
5. Koivula, A., Koiranen, I., Räsänen, P.: Digitalisaatio ja verkkorahapelaamisen väestöryhmittäiset muutokset 2006–2014. Yhteiskuntapolitiikka **2016**(4), 371–383 (2016)

6. Gainsbury, S.: Exploring the opportunities and impacts of Internet gambling. Int. Gambl. Stud. **11**(3), 267–272 (2011)

7. Binde, P.: Gambling in Sweden: the cultural and socio-political context. Addiction **109**(2), 193–198 (2014)

8. Hing, N., Cherney, L., Blaszczynski, A., Gainsbury, S., Lubman, D.: Do advertising and promotions for online gambling increase gambling consumption? An exploratory study. Int. Gambl. Sutd. **14**(3), 394–409 (2014)

9. Heiskanen, M., Toikka, A.: Clustering finnish gambler profiles based on the money and time consumed in gambling activities. J. Gambl. Stud. **32**(2), 363–377 (2015). https://doi.org/10.1007/s10899-015-9556-8

10. Griffiths, M.: Gambling technologies: prospects for problem gambling. J. Gambl. Stud. **15**(3), 265–283 (1999). https://doi.org/10.1023/A:1023053630588

11. Griffiths, M., Parke, J.: The social impact of internet gambling. Soc. Sci. Comput. Rev. **20**(3), 312–320 (2002)

12. Griffiths, M., Barnes, A.: Internet gambling: an online empirical study among student gamblers. Int. J. Ment. Health Addiction **6**, 194–204 (2008). https://doi.org/10.1007/s11469-007-9083-7

13. Griffiths, M., Parke, J.: Adolescent gambling on the Internet. Int. J. Adolesc. Med. Health **22**(1), 59–75 (2010)

14. King, D., Delfabbro, P., Griffiths, M.: The convergence of gambling and digital media: implications for gambling in young people. J. Gambl. Stud. **26**(2), 175–187 (2010). https://doi.org/10.1007/s10899-009-9153-9

15. Deterding, S.: Gamification: designing for motivation. Interactions **19**(4), 14–17 (2012)

16. Finland, Statistics: Väestön tieto- ja viestintätekniikan käyttö, Internetin käytön muutoksia. Tilastokeskus, Helsinki (2015)

17. Hargittai, E.: Digital na (t) ives? Variation in internet skills and uses among members of the "net generation". Sociol. Inq. **80**(1), 92–113 (2010)

18. DiMaggio, P., Cohen, J.: Information inequality and network externalities: a comparative study of the diffusion of television and the internet. In: The Economic Sociology of Capitalism, pp. 227–267 (2005)

19. Norris, P.: Digital Divide: Civic Engagement, Information Poverty, and the Internet worldwide. Cambridge University Press, Cambridge (2001)

20. Wellman, B., et al.: The road to utopia and dystopia on the information highway. Contemp. Sociol. **26**, 445–449 (1997)

21. Fisher, D.R., Wright, L.M.: On utopias and dystopias: toward an understanding of the discourse surrounding the Internet. J. Comput.-Mediated Commun. **6**(2), JCMC624 (2001)

22. Katz, J.E., Rice, R.E.: Social Consequences of Internet Use: Access, Involvement, and Interaction. MIT Press, Cambridge (2002)

23. Wood, R.T., Williams, R.J.: A comparative profile of the Internet gambler: demographic characteristics, game-play patterns, and problem gambling status. New Media Soc. **13**(7), 1123–1141 (2011)

24. Kairouz, S., Paradis, C., Nadeau, L.: Are online gamblers more at risk than offline gamblers? Cyberpsychol. Behav. Soc. Netw. **15**(3), 175–180 (2012)

25. Philander, K.S., MacKay, T.L.: Online gambling participation and problem gambling severity: is there a causal relationship?. Int. Gambl. Stud. **14**(2), 214–227 (2014)

26. Gainsbury, S.M., Russell, A.H.N., Wood, R., Blaszczynski, A.: The impact of internet gambling on gambling problems: a comparison of moderate-risk and problem Internet and non-internet gamblers. Psychol. Addict. Behav. **27**(4), 1092–1101 (2013)

27. Turja, T., Halme, J., Mervola, M., Järvinen-Tassopoulos, J., Ronkainen, J.: Finnish gambling 2011. National Institute for Health and Welfare, Helsinki (2012)

28. Koiranen, I., Keipi, T., Koivula, A., Räsänen, P.: Changing patterns of social media use? A population-level study of Finland. Univ. Access Inf. Soc., 1–15 (2019). https://doi.org/10.1007/s10209-019-00654-1

29. Van Dijk, J.A.: The Deepening Divide: Inequality in the Information Society. Sage Publications, Thousand Oaks (2005)

30. Räsänen, P.: Information society for all? Structural characteristics of internet use in 15 European countries. Eur. Soc. 8(1), 59–81 (2006)

31. Raisamo, S., Salonen, A.H.: Muutokset 15–64-vuotiaiden suomalaisten rahapelaamisessa vuosina 2003–2011. Yhteiskuntapolitiikka 78(5), 544–553 (2013)

32. Reith, G.: Gambling: Who Wins? Who Loses?. Prometheus Books, New York (2003)

33. van Deursen, A.J., van Dijk, J.A.: Digital Skills: Unlocking the Information Society. Springer, Heidelberg (2014)

34. Näsi, M.: ICT disparities in Finland-access and implications. Turku: Annales Universitatis Turkuensis B 366 (2013)

35. Buis, M.L.: Predict and adjust with logistic regression. Stata J. 7(2), 221–226 (2007)

36. Griffiths, M., Wardle, H., Orford, J., Sproston, K., Erens, B.: Sociodemographic correlates of internet gambling: Findings from the 2007 British gambling prevalence survey. CyberPsychol. Behav. 12(2), 199–202 (2009)

37. Gainsbury, S., Wood, R., Russell, A., Hing, N., Blaszczynski, A.: A digital revolution: comparison of demographic profiles, attitudes and gambling behavior of Internet and non-Internet gamblers. Comput. Hum. Behav. 28(4), 1388–1398 (2012)

38. Salonen, A.H., Alho, H., Castrén, S.: The extent and type of gambling harms for concerned significant others: a cross-sectional population study in Finland. Scand. J. Public Health 44, 799–804 (2016)

39. Scheerder, A., van Deursen, A., van Dijk, J.: Determinants of inter-net skills, uses and outcomes. A systematic review of the second-and third-level digital divide. Telematics Inform. 34(8), 1607–1624 (2017)

Being Together Apart: Does Communication via Social Media Help or Harm Romantic Relationships?

Mark Turner[✉] [iD] and Emma Prince

Department of Psychology, University of Portsmouth, Portsmouth, UK
Mark.Turner@port.ac.uk, Emma.Prince1@myport.ac.uk

Abstract. Social media has become central to how people form and maintain friendships and romantic relationships, although its effects are not always positive. The current study investigates how social media use impacts satisfaction in three different types of romantic relationships: (i) long-distance relationships, (ii) geographically close relationships, and (ii) couples living together. How young adults communicate with their partner via social media, the shared behaviors they exhibit and their association with the support, conflict, and relationship depth they experience are explored. Responses from 236 participants aged between 18–25 years (M = 20.68, SD = 1.83) were obtained. Complex associations were found between perceived relationship quality and different indices of shared social media behaviors. Findings provide partial support for the idea that social media platforms may provide an effective mechanism to support and maintain long-distance romantic relationships. However, the overall frequency of social media use was not an important factor in maintaining a satisfying relationship, whether couples were long-distance, geographically close or living together. In addition, greater social media use was not predictive of reduced relationship conflict in any form of relationship. Paradoxically, engaging in social media based surveillance behaviors was related to a higher sense of relationship depth. Those in long distance relationships used social media more for direct communication with a partner, but this also correlated with greater levels of relationship conflict.

Keywords: Social media · Romantic relationships · Conflict · Support · Surveillance

1 Introduction

1.1 Background and Aims

Social media use has grown rapidly in popularity, with young adults becoming particularly dependent on its use [16]. One of the primary justifications for using social media is to keep in contact with those whom we already share relationships with [6] although the influence of communication via social media on friendships and romantic relationships may not always be positive [e.g. 27]. The development of romantic relationships plays a significant part in many young adults' lives, and it is common for

© Springer Nature Switzerland AG 2020
G. Meiselwitz (Ed.): HCII 2020, LNCS 12195, pp. 584–597, 2020.
https://doi.org/10.1007/978-3-030-49576-3_43

such relationships to often involve some form of geographical separation [23]. It has been suggested that couples in long-distance relationships experience more stress compared to those who live geographically closer together [11]. It is therefore, important to understand the factors that may contribute to the maintenance of successful distance relationships in young adults and how social media in particular, may facilitate to this.

The potential value of the Internet to relationship formation and development has long been recognized [9]. More recently, the easy and ubiquitous access afforded by mobile devices to multiple, different social media platforms has set new expectations regarding communication patterns between romantic partners [15]. Whilst the prevalence of distance relationships has become increasingly common in modern society as individuals seek employment or educational opportunities in different locations, the use of technology by romantic partners may provide an important means by which behaviors that help maintain relationships can be conveyed [2].

Being in a long-distance relationship *per se* may not necessarily lead to great relationship dissatisfaction [10, 20, 24]. However, Holt and Stone [14] report that couples who spend longer periods of time apart and share lower quality verbal communication were found to experience poorer levels of relationship satisfaction. Whether the increased opportunities for domestic contact afforded by social media technology might offset this effect for geographically distance couples is however, not clear. Hampton, Rawlings, Treger and Sprecher [13] acknowledge a lack of research investigating how technology can help maintain satisfying romantic relationships. In their study of purely long-distance relationships, they found that individuals who used a greater variety of different computer-mediated communication channels experienced greater communication satisfaction, with the use of video-based chat applications being the strongest predictor of overall relationship satisfaction. Turner, Love and Howell [28] demonstrated that voice-based rather than text-based forms of communication were more important in reducing the discrepancy between desired and actual levels of emotional support in close relationships. It follows that relationship satisfaction is not simply a function of geographical distance but will also be dependent on the quality of mediated interaction within a relationship. The specific functionality supported by different social media platforms, and how couples choose to use these platforms may therefore, be important in determining the level of support and relationship depth that couples perceive.

Traditional media choice theories, assume that people choose a medium which best fits with their intended communication purpose, and that richer communication media should be preferred in the case of the maintenance of long-distance friendships where these make it easier to express and perceive emotions and provide feedback [29]. However, many aspects of social media-based communication between partners can also take place publically rather than through direct personal contact such that other social dimensions need to be taken into consideration. For example, Stewart, Dainton, and Goodboy [25] have demonstrated that where partners perceived a greater sense of relationship security they were more likely to engage in online reassurance behaviors, such as posting or commenting on their partner's social media profile. But, where partners perceived greater relationship uncertainty, they were more likely to engage in online monitoring of their partners. Greater partner surveillance behaviors were also linked to increased relational jealousy. This effect has been explained by the observation that social media sites sometimes expose people to potentially ambiguous information about their partner which they would not otherwise have access to, which motivates further social media use and partner surveillance [18]. Since social media makes the surveillance of a romantic partner relatively easy and anonymous [26], it exposes individuals to aspects of their partner's communication with others that arouses feelings of protectiveness or suspicion over their shared relationship, which in the absence of other cues, may be particularly relevant to the feelings experienced in long-distance relationships [3].

Further evidence suggests that where online displays of affection are valued by a partner, these can strengthen a romantic relationship [8]. Several methods through which affection can be displayed via social media have been identified [17] including through the use of features such as relationship status updates, displaying pictures showing shared experiences with a partner, and public commenting on a partner's activities which allow the nature of one's relationship to be declared and vicariously communicated to others. Such mechanisms can be used to emphasize possession and territory, as well as to validate the status of a relationship [4].

Given the complex and still developing channels by which social media may impact on relationships, the current study set out to explore and compare social media use and its links to relationship satisfaction in three different types of partnerships: (i) long-distance relationships (LDR), (ii) couples living apart but with geographically close relationships (GCR) and (iii) cohabiting couples (CC). The study focuses particularly on comparing the shared behaviors used by young adults when communicating with their partners and how they perceive the importance of social media within relationships of different types. Two specific research questions are explored:

Research Question 1: How does the specific nature of social media use in romantic relationships at different geographical distances differ, and what are the consequences of these differences for the relationship support and depth, and conflict experienced?
Research Question 2: How does the perceived importance of social media as facilitating relationship quality vary in relationships at different geographical distances?

2   Method

2.1   Participants and Design

A total of 273 participants were purposively recruited by means of an online survey; all participants were required to be currently in a relationship and actively using social media to communicate with their partner. Participants aged over 25 years, participants who were married, or those who gave incomplete survey responses were screened out, leaving a final sample size of 236 participants.

The study used a quasi-experimental design, whereby participants were naturally separated into three groups: (i) long-distance relationships (LDR, n = 66), (ii) geographically close relationships (GCR, n = 123) and (iii) cohabiting couples (CC, n = 47). Relationship distance was determined based upon the self-categorization approach used in previous research [9]. The geographical distance between the permanent home addresses of the participant and their partner was also recorded, which confirmed LDR participants lived on average 154.9 miles from their partner, and GCR participants lived on average 10.7 miles from their partner ($t(176) = 10.49$, $p < .001$; $d = 1.58$).

The final sample included 180 females and 56 males, with a mean age of 20.68 years (SD = 1.83). Participants' mean self-rated level of social media use for communicating with their partner (on a 10-point scale, where 10 indicated greater use) was 7.97 (SD = 2.45), and the mean length of their relationship with their partner was 2.30 years (SD = 2.08).

2.2 Measures

Social Media Use and Behaviors. Participants were asked a series of questions about the frequency and variety of social media platforms they used to communicate with their partner, and completed assessments of the specific online behaviors they engaged in with their partner and their views of its importance to their relationship.

Shared Social Media Behaviors. A total of 20 different shared online behaviors were identified from existing literature which were used to provide a profile of how each participant communicated with their partner online. Participants were asked to rate how regularly they adopted each behavior (e.g. *Tag them in a picture*) or used embedded social media tools or features to engage their partner (e.g. *Send a voice note to each other*). Each item was rated on a 4-point frequency scale from 'Not At All' to 'Very Much'.

Importance of Social Media. A further 14 questionnaire items were created to assess how each individual felt about the use and importance of social media within their relationship to communicate with their partner. Each statement (e.g. I believe social media helps my partner and I to share common interests) was rated using the same 4-point scale from 'Not At All' to 'Very Much'.

Relationship Quality. The 25-item Quality of Relationships Inventory [19] was used to assess how satisfied participants were in their current relationship. Questions such as, *'How significant is this person in your life?'* and *'To what extent can you turn to this person for advice about problems?'* are rated on a 4-point scale from 'Not At All' to 'Very Much'. The QRI specifically measures three aspects of relationship quality: Perceived Social Support (PSS, 7 items), Relationship Conflict (RC, 12 items), and Relationship Depth (RD, 6 items). Pierce et al. [19] report Cronbach's alpha coefficients for the three subscales to range between 0.83 and 0.91. In addition to their relationship duration, participants were also asked how many days per week they typically met their partner face-to-face.

2.3   Procedure

Participants were informed that the research would investigate social media use within romantic relationships but were not told the study was focused on relationship distance specifically. The survey took between 15–20 min to complete. Question sections were presented in the same order to all participants, with questions about social media use and behavior being presented before questions about relationship quality. The study was conducted in accordance with the appropriate ethical guidelines and approval process of our institution.

3   Results

3.1   Shared Social Media Behaviors

The extent to which romantic partners engaged in different social media behaviors varied considerably across the 20 activities examined (Table 1). Sending messages and pictures directly to each other and also showing each other social media posts when being physically together appeared to be the most universally experienced activities. Liking a partner's picture or tagging them in a picture were also common amongst respondents.

A Factor Analysis using oblique rotation was performed on the 20 social media behaviors to explore latent patterns in participants' responses. A three factor solution was extracted using PCA which was confirmed by parallel analysis as being the most appropriate solution for the data (Minimum random Eigenvalue = 1.55, KMO = .76). Factor I consisted of questions related to the monitoring of a partner's online behavior without their knowledge. The factor, which accounted for 22.5% of the variance in responses, loaded most heavily on questions such as checking who a partner was following or who was following them, and viewing who had liked their posts. This factor was named 'Surveillance Behaviors'.

Factor II accounted for 12.7% of the variance in responses and predominately clustered together questions which involved active, shared experiences that occurred directly between partners and that were not accessible to others. This factor included behaviors such as sharing a video chat or sending pictures directly to each other, and so was named 'Direct Communication'.

Factor III accounted for 8.9% of variance in responses and largely grouped together behaviors that would be visible to others outside of the relationship such as posting a message publically about a partner, and liking or commenting on their pictures. The factor was therefore, named 'Public Displays of Contact'. Since all items loaded negatively on this factor, indicating the factor rotation aligned with an absence of these behaviors, all question items were reverse scored before calculating the scale total, so that a higher factor total corresponded to a greater tendency to engage in public displays of contact in the subsequent analyses reported.

Table 1. Factor loadings for participants' social media behaviors towards their partners and percentage of respondents engaging in each behavior. Values in bold indicate parent factor.

Social media behaviour	Participants engaging in behaviour (%)	Factor loadings		
		Factor I	Factor II	Factor III
Check who is following them	38.1%	**.85**	−.19	−.08
Check who they are following	41.5%	**.84**	−.18	−.08
View who has liked their pictures	42.4%	**.75**	−.14	−.23
View pictures they have liked	55.5%	**.64**	−.08	−.12
Check your partners social media page	73.3%	**.64**	.13	−.22
Check when your partner is online	66.9%	**.45**	.39	.11
Use partner's social media without them knowing	3.8%	**.44**	.43	.26
Share a video chat	72.0%	−.07	**.60**	−.06
Send a picture to each other	97.5%	.01	**.59**	−.28
Send a message to each other	98.7%	−.23	**.53**	−.24
Send a voice note to each other	35.2%	−.12	**.53**	.06
Check your partner's location	45.3%	.27	**.40**	.02
Use partner's social media with them knowing	19.9%	.33	**.40**	.14
Send them a link	73.7%	−.12	**.35**	−.24
Comment on their picture	79.7%	.11	.06	**−.73**
Like their picture	94.9%	.19	.07	**−.73**
Tag them in a picture	89.4%	−.05	.13	**−.67**
Post about your partner	84.7%	−.05	.13	**−.67**
View your partners 'stories'	87.3%	.00	−.01	**−.63**
Show partner social media posts when together	97.5%	.06	−.10	**−.43**
Factor Eigenvalue		4.50	2.54	1.79

3.2   Importance of Social Media to Relationships

To evaluate participants' attitudes towards the use of social media to support different aspects of communication and engagement with their partners, a Factor Analysis with oblique rotation was performed on the 14 attitude statements assessing the importance of social media in relationships (Table 2). A three factor solution was extracted using PCA which was confirmed by parallel analysis as being the most appropriate solution for the data (Minimum random Eigenvalue = 1.43, KMO = .79).

Table 2. Factor loadings for perception of social media importance to relationships items and percentage of participants reporting each attitude. Values in bold indicate parent factor.

Attitude component	Participants reporting attitude (%)	Factor loadings		
		Factor I	Factor II	Factor III
I feel unappreciated when my partner does not post pictures of me on social media	42.4%	**.77**	−.02	.15
I feel jealous seeing my partner like other people's pictures	34.3%	**.77**	−.06	−.17
I feel paranoid seeing who my partner follows on social media	24.2%	**.72**	−.01	−.17
I obsess over checking my partner's social media	14.8%	**.71**	−.21	−.15
I am disappointed when my partner does not comment on or like my pictures	56.4%	**.67**	.06	.22
My partner posting about me on social media helps me to feel like I am more included in their life	73.7%	**.62**	.23	.21
If I see my partner is active on social media but has not contacted me, I feel annoyed	57.2%	**.56**	.25	−.05
Sending my partner messages on social media makes me feel closer to them	89.0%	.10	**.81**	.10
I believe social media helps my partner and I to communicate more efficiently	88.1%	−.02	**.79**	.22
Social media helps my partner and I to share common interests	93.6%	.08	**.74**	.00
I do not feel the need to socialize with my partner on social media	56.8%	.06	**−.61**	.34
Social media does not adversely affect my relationship with my partner	73.3%	−.09	−.07	**.75**
It does not bother me seeing my partner communicate with somebody online that I do not know	64.0%	.14	−.06	**.68**
I feel happy seeing my partner post pictures online with other people, as I know they are having fun	94.5%	−.14	.22	**.53**
Factor Eigenvalue		3.69	2.45	1.48

Factor I accounted for 26.4% of the variance in participants' responses and loaded most heavily on questions relating to feeling unappreciated, jealous or paranoid about their partner's behavior on social media. This factor was named 'Online Jealousy' (7 items). Factor II comprised questions which related to the positive benefits of using social media to communicate with their partner such as increased closeness, sharing interests and efficiency of support, and accounted for 17.5% of the variance in responses. This factor was named 'Relationship Facilitation' (4 items). Factor III accounted for 10.6% of the variance in participants' responses and consisted of questions which indicated participants felt social media had no bearing on their relationship, or that they were unaffected by or felt benevolent towards their partners social media behavior. This factor was named 'Online Disinterest' (3 items).

Online jealousy correlated strongly and positively with social media surveillance behaviors ($r(234) = .58$, $p < .001$), but was not related to the use of social media for direct communication. Online jealousy also correlated negatively with public shows of contact via social media ($r(234) = -.29$, $p < .001$). Relationship facilitation correlated positively with the use of social media for direct communication ($r(234) = .41$, $p < .001$) and correlated negatively with public shows of contact via social media ($r(234) = -.29$, $p < .001$) but was not related to surveillance behaviors. Online Disinterest was weakly correlated to the use of social media for direct communication ($r(234) = .18$, $p = .006$) and was not related to surveillance behaviors or public shows of contact between partners.

3.3 Social Media Use and Attitude Differences by Relationship Distance

To compare differences in online behaviors and perceptions regarding the importance of social media within relationships as a function of geographical distance between partners, a one-way multivariate analysis of covariance was performed, with length of relationship as a covariate (Table 3).

Table 3. Mean (± 1 SD) subscale totals for social media behaviors and perception of importance of social media to relationships as a function of relationship type.

Social media behaviours and attitudes	Relationship type			F	p	η^2
	CC	GCR	LDR			
Surveillance behaviors	1.76 (0.65)	1.73 (0.67)	1.64 (0.64)	0.55	.58	.01
Direct communication	2.24[a] (0.54)	2.58[a] (0.54)	2.78[a] (0.43)	15.09	<.001	.12
Public displays	2.11[a] (0.75)	2.20 (0.64)	2.41[a] (0.70)	3.20	.04	.03
Online jealousy	1.56 (0.52)	1.63 (0.57)	1.69 (0.52)	0.83	.44	.01
Relationship facilitation	2.51[a] (0.55)	2.84[a] (0.68)	3.17[a] (0.61)	13.81	<.001	.11
Online disinterest	2.57 (0.66)	2.51 (0.73)	2.59 (0.73)	0.35	.70	.00
Frequency of social media partner contact	6.94[a] (2.97)	7.89[b] (2.42)	8.85[ab] (1.68)	9.10	<.001	.07

[ab]Group means with the same letter differ significantly at $p < .05$ (Bonferroni comparisons).

A significant multivariate effect was found between the three relationship groups ($F(14,454) = 5.38$, $p < .001$, $\eta_p^2 = .14$, Wilks' $\lambda = 0.72$). Significant univariate differences were found for 3 of the subscale measures. Results indicated that participants in long-distance relationships were more likely to use social media for direct communication with their partner and overt public displays of contact with their partner, when compared to other relationship types. The perception of social media as a relationship facilitator also differed as a function of geographical distance between partners, with participants in long-distance relationships regarding social media as being more beneficial than those in geographical close relationships or those who lived together. The frequency with which participants used social media to contact their partners also differed significantly as a function of geographical distance; those in long-distance relationships used social media to communicate more frequently with their partners compared to those in other relationship types. However, there was no difference in the frequency of social media communication between those in geographically close relationships or those who lived together.

3.4 Correlations Between Social Media Behaviors, Perceptions of Social Media Importance and the Quality of Relationships

Pearson correlation coefficients were calculated to explore the relationships between social media behaviors, attitudes towards the importance of social media within relationships and the QRI measure of relationship quality (Table 4).

Table 4. Pearson's correlations between social media behaviors, attitudes towards the importance of social media, partner contact and relationship quality.

Social media behaviours and attitudes	Quality of relationship (QRI)		
	Support	Conflict	Depth
Surveillance behaviors	.14*	−.01	.23**
Direct communication	.16*	.16*	−.04
Public displays of contact	−.21**	−.14*	−.04
Online jealousy	.08	−.04	.32**
Relationship facilitation	.08	.16*	−.01
Online disinterest	.03	.17**	−.18**
Frequency of face-to-face partner contact	.06	.04	.05
Frequency of social media partner contact	.08	.08	.04

*$p < .05$, **$p < .01$ (2-tailed)

Significant positive correlations were found between surveillance behaviors with relationship support and depth, suggesting participants who reported engaging in greater monitoring of their partner online also experienced a greater sense of relationship support and deeper more meaningful relationships. Greater use of social media for direct, personal communication between partners was associated with a greater perception of relationship support, but also greater relationship conflict. Whereas greater public displays of contact between partners was associated with reduced relationship conflict, but also a reduced sense of support.

Somewhat paradoxically, participants who reported experiencing feelings of jealousy as a result of their partner's behavior online reported greater relationship depth. However, the belief that social media facilitated relationships showed no correlation with relationship support or depth, but was related to greater relationship conflict. Those who believed social media played no role in their relationship (online disinterest) also reported greater relationship conflict and reduced relationship depth. No significant correlations were found between either the frequencies of face-to-face or social media contact reported by participants with their partners and any aspect of relationship quality.

4 Discussion

The current study identified three common patterns of social media behaviors reported by those in romantic relationships: surveillance without a partner's knowledge; direct private communication between partners; and indirect public displays of contact to communicate partnerships that are visible to others. The study also identified three consistent attitudes in the responses of participants regarding the perceived importance of social media to their relationships: the belief that social media positively facilitates relationships, the belief that social media has no real bearing on relationships with partners, and the belief that social media use invokes feelings of jealousy and relationship insecurity. Several patterns emerged where online jealousy was more strongly associated with social media surveillance, whilst the belief that social media facilitated relationships was more strongly associated with more direct, private communication. Public displays of contact between partners were associated with reduced relationship facilitation, but also reduced jealousy.

With respect to the geographical distance between partners, LDR participants were found to communicate more frequently with their partner via social media, were more likely to use direct private communications and were more likely to believe social media facilitated their relationship than GCR participants or CC participants. LDR participants also engaged in more public displays of contact between partners than CC participants, but not GCR participants. Since direct communication between partners was associated with greater perceived relationship support, this may be taken as partial evidence to support the idea that communication via social media is beneficial to long-distance relationships. However, it should be noted that greater direct communication, and the belief that social media helps to facilitate relationships were also both associated with increased relationship conflict. Public displays of contact between partners, which were greatest in LDR participants were also associated with lower perceived relationship support. It follows that not all aspects of online behavior used by individuals to communicate with their partners in distance relationships may improve relationship satisfaction.

One explanation for these seemingly contradictory findings could be the assumption that increased online communication invariably creates positive outcomes. Braiker and Kelley [5] argue that couples who are more interdependent also tend to experience greater conflict within their relationship. With constant access to social media, it is possible that individuals can also use direct communication to send more harmful messages. Contextually less rich forms of communication such as those provided by social media may also provide couples with greater opportunities to miscommunicate or misinterpret intentions, or to prolong previous arguments online. Consistent with this view, Coyne et al. [8] found that individuals who perceived their relationship to be more satisfying used social media in order to express affection towards their partner, whereas those who were less satisfied with their relationship were more likely to use social media for the purposes of confrontation.

Zhao, Sosik, and Cosley [30] propose that public displays of affection do not have the purpose of benefiting the individuals in a relationship, but are instead primarily used to address third parties. Where individuals use social media to promote their partner instrumentally to highlight that they are in a relationship, rather than aiming to satisfy their partner's needs directly, it follows that such behaviors may not lead to a greater sense of support in relationships, consistent with present findings. This may also account for the negative correlation observed between public displays of contact and reduced relationship conflict within the current study; where individuals choose to present a positive image of their relationship with their partner to support their own ends [30], a consequence of this could be that their partner also feels more appreciated. Whilst this may hypothetically serve to reduce conflict, online public displays of partnership appear to show no association with relationship depth within the current study, indicating that the interpersonal bond shared by couples is not related to the publically shared content they chose to present via social media.

The use of social media for partner surveillance was positively correlated with greater social support and a greater sense of relationship depth, but was not related to relationship conflict. Moreover a greater sense of online jealousy and insecurity within participants' relationships was also associated with greater perceived relationship depth. These findings appear to contradict previous research which found surveillance on social media to be associated with a dissatisfying relationship [12]. A possible corollary to the current pattern of results might be the use of online mate-retention tactics by participants [7] which are used to 'guard' against potential rivals where a partner is particularly invested in their relationship. Individuals who care more about their partner are more likely to experience online jealousy within their relationship if the feel their relationship could be threatened by external factors [1]. This may provide an explanation as to why individuals who experience greater online jealousy, can also feel a greater sense of depth within their relationship.

Results from the current study showed a positive association between disinterest in participants' attitudes towards their partner's social media use and feelings of relationship conflict, and a negative association with relationship depth. General perceptions of relationship quality are thought to be derived from a set of expectations that individuals hold about the perceived assistance, commitment and acceptance they receive from their partner [22]. The impact of these expectations on the relationship depends on the values of both parties involved, and not only affects the individual's experience of the relationship but also influences their interactions within the relationship [21]. It follows that a person whose values communicate disinterest about their partner's online actions, where these are dissimilar to the partner's own expectations about the use of social media, may be more likely to experience conflict within their relationship and the bond within the relationship itself may be perceived as less emotionally deep.

5 Conclusion

The findings of this study provide partial support for the idea that social media platforms may provide an effective mechanism to support and maintain long-distance romantic relationships, which can compensate for the absence of face-to-face contact. However, the overall frequency of social media use was not an important factor in maintaining a satisfying relationship, whether couples were long-distance, geographically close or living together. In addition, social media use was not effective as a means of reducing relationship conflict in any form of relationship. Constant access to social media might result more readily in the use of communication media to facilitate arguments, or for couples to misinterpret each other's intentions. Further research is therefore needed to examine the potential loss of communication effectiveness via social media and impact this may have on relationship quality.

References

1. Barelds, D.P.H., Barelds-Dijkstra, P.: Relations between different types of jealousy and self and partner perceptions of relationship quality. Clin. Psychol. Psychother. 14(3), 176–188 (2007). https://doi.org/10.1002/cpp.532
2. Belus, J.M., Pentel, K.Z., Cohen, M.J., Fischer, M.S., Baucom, D.H.: Staying connected: an examination of relationship maintenance behaviors in long-distance relationships. Marriage Family Rev. (2018). https://doi.org/10.1080/01494929.2018.1458004
3. Billedo, C.J., Kerkhof, P., Finkenauer, C.: The use of social networking sites for relationship maintenance in long-distance relationships and geographically close romantic relationships. Cyberpsychol. Behav. Soc. Netwo. 8(3), 152–157 (2015). https://doi.org/10.1089/cyber.2014.0469
4. Bowe, G.: Reading romance: the impact Facebook rituals can have on a romantic relationship. J. Comp. Res. Anthropol. Sociol. 2, 61–77 (2010)
5. Braiker, H.B., Kelley, H.H.: Conflict in the development of close relationships. In: Burgess, R.L., Huston, T.L. (eds.) Social Exchange in Developing Relationships, pp. 135–167. Academic Press Inc., University Park (1979)
6. Brandtzæg, P.B., Heim, J.: Why people use social networking sites. In: Ozok, A.A., Zaphiris, P. (eds.) OCSC 2009. LNCS, vol. 5621, pp. 143–152. Springer, Heidelberg (2009). https://doi.org/10.1007/978-3-642-02774-1_16. Online ISBN 978-3-642-02774-1
7. Brem, M.J., Spiller, L.C., Vandehey, M.A.: Online mate-retention tactics on Facebook are associated with relationship aggression. J. Interpers. Violence 30(16), 2831–2850 (2015). https://doi.org/10.1177/0886260514554286
8. Coyne, S.M., Stockdale, L., Busby, D., Iverson, B., Grant, D.M.: "I luv u :)!" A descriptive study of the media use of individuals in romantic relationships. Interdiscip. J. Appl. Family Sci. 60(2), 150–162 (2011). https://doi.org/10.1111/j.1741-3729.2010.00639.x

9. Dainton, M., Aylor, B.: Patterns of communication channel use in the maintenance of long-distance relationships. Commun. Res. Rep. **19**(2), 118–129 (2002). https://doi.org/10.1080/08824090209384839

10. Dargie, E., Blair, K.L., Goldfinger, C., Pukall, C.F.: Go long! Predictors of positive relationship outcomes in long-distance dating relationships. J. Sex Marital Ther. **41**(2), 181–202 (2014). https://doi.org/10.1080/0092623x.2013.864367

11. Du Bois, S.N., Sher, T.G., Grotkowski, K., Aizenman, T., Slesinger, N., Cohen, M.: Going the distance: Health in long-distance versus proximal relationships. Family J. **24**(1), 5–14 (2016). https://doi.org/10.1177/1066480715616580

12. Elphinston, R.A., Noller, P.: Time to face it! Facebook intrusion and the implications for romantic jealousy and relationship satisfaction. Cyberpsychol. Behav. Soc. Netw. **14**, 631–635 (2011). https://doi.org/10.1089/cyber.2010.0318

13. Hampton, A.J., Rawlings, J., Treger, S., Sprecher, S.: Channels of computer-mediated communication and satisfaction in long-distance relationships. Interpersona: Int. J. Pers. Relat. **11**(2), 171–187 (2015). https://doi.org/10.5964/ijpr.v11i2.273

14. Holt, P.A., Stone, L.S.: Needs, coping strategies, and coping outcomes associated with long-distance relationships. J. Coll. Stud. Dev. **29**, 136–141 (1988)

15. Juhasz, A., Bradford, K.: Mobile phone use in romantic relationships. Marriage Family Rev. **52**(8), 707–721 (2016). https://doi.org/10.1080/01494929.2016.1157123

16. Lee, Y., Chang, C., Lin, Y., Cheng, Z.: The dark side of smartphone usage: psychological traits, compulsive behavior and technostress. Comput. Hum. Behav. **31**, 373–383 (2014). https://doi.org/10.1016/j.chb.2013.10.047

17. Mansson, D.H., Myers, S.A.: An initial examination of college students' expressions of affection through Facebook. South. Commun. J. **76**(2), 155–168 (2011). https://doi.org/10.1080/10417940903317710

18. Muise, A., Christofides, E., Desmarais, S.: More information than you ever wanted: does Facebook bring out the green-eyed monster of jealousy? CyberPsychol. Behav. **12**(4), 441–444 (2009). https://doi.org/10.1089/cpb.2008.0263

19. Pierce, G.R., Sarason, I.G., Sarason, B.R.: General and relationship-based perceptions of social support: are two constructs better than one? J. Pers. Soc. Psychol. **61**(6), 1028–1039 (1991). https://doi.org/10.1037/0022-3514.61.6.1028

20. Roberts, A., Pistole, M.C.: Long-distance and proximal romantic relationship satisfaction: attachment and closeness predictors. J. Coll. Couns. **12**, 5–17 (2011). https://doi.org/10.1002/j.2161-1882.2009.tb00036.x

21. Sarason, I.G., Pierce, G.R., Sarason, B.R.: Social support and interactional processes: a triadic hypothesis. J. Soc. Pers. Relat. **7**(4), 495–506 (1990). https://doi.org/10.1177/0265407590074006

22. Sarason, B.R., Shearin, E.N., Pierce, G.R., Sarason, I.G.: Interrelations of social support measures: theoretical and practical implications. J. Pers. Soc. Psychol. **52**(4), 813–832 (1987)

23. Stafford, L.: Maintaining Long-Distance and Cross-Residential Relationships. Routledge, New York (2005). https://doi.org/10.4324/9781410611512

24. Stafford, L., Merolla, A.J.: Idealization, reunions, and stability in long-distance relationships. J. Soc. Pers. Relat. **24**(1), 37–54 (2007). https://doi.org/10.1177/0265407507072578

25. Stewart, M.C., Dainton, M., Goodboy, A.K.: Maintaining relationships on Facebook: associations with uncertainty, jealousy, and satisfaction. Commun. Rep. **27**(1), 13–26 (2014). https://doi.org/10.1080/08934215.2013.845675

26. Tokunaga, R.S.: Social networking site or social surveillance site? Understanding the use of interpersonal electronic surveillance in romantic relationships. Comput. Hum. Behav. **27**(2), 705–713 (2011). https://doi.org/10.1016/j.chb.2010.08.014

27. Turkle, S.: Alone Together: Why We Expect More from Technology and Less from Each Other. Basic Books, New York (2017)

28. Turner, M., Love, S., Howell, M.: The importance of mobile telephone communication medium to the maintenance of social relationships. In: AHFE International (2nd International Conference on Applied Human Factors and Ergonomics), Las Vegas, USA, 14th–17th July 2008 (2008)

29. Utz, S.: Media use in long-distance friendships. Inf. Commun. Soc. **10**(5), 694–713 (2007). https://doi.org/10.1080/13691180701658046

30. Zhao, X., Sosik, V.S., Cosley, D.: It's complicated: how romantic partners use Facebook. Paper presented at the SIGCHI Conference on Human Factors in Computing Systems (2012). https://dl.acm.org/citation.cfm?id=2207788

Technology-Based Social Skills Learning for People with Autism Spectrum Disorder

Katherine Valencia[1]([⊠]), Virginia Zaraza Rusu[1], Erick Jamet[1],
Constanza Zúñiga[2], Eduardo Garrido[1], Cristian Rusu[1],
and Daniela Quiñones[1]

[1] Pontificia Universidad Católica de Valparaíso,
Av. Brasil 2241 2340000 Valparaíso, Chile
katherinevalencia25@gmail.com,
rusu.virginia.zaraza@gmail.com, erickjamet@gmail.com,
eduardo.garrido.libro@gmail.com,
{cristian.rusu,daniela.quinones}@pucv.cl
[2] Universidad de Valparaíso, Av. Angamos 655, 2520000 Viña del Mar, Chile
constanzazunigaprado@gmail.com

Abstract. Autism spectrum disorder (ASD) affects a significant number of people who have difficulties with communication and socialization. The Diagnostic and Statistical Manual of Mental Disorders, DSM-5, defines ASD as a condition characterized by deficits in two core domains: (1) social communication and social interaction, and (2) restricted repetitive patterns of behavior, interests, and activities. Several authors examined the use of technology and computer-based interventions to teach people with ASD language and social skills. The use of technological advancements provides a comfortable, predictable, and structured environment that promotes constant learning for people with ASD, since they show affinity to technology. This paper explores: (1) how technology related papers to teach skills to people with ASD characterize the difficulties of these people, (2) how these characteristics have been considered to design their technological solutions and (3) which are the results obtained in these studies, in order to determine design guidelines and a structure and preliminary design for a future technological intervention that cover specific needs in people with ASD related to the area of socialization.

Keywords: Autism Spectrum Disorder · Technology-based learning · Social skills

1 Introduction

Autism spectrum disorder (ASD) is a developmental disorder that affects people's communication and behavior [1]. Several studies have compiled the conditions presented by people with ASD and addressed these through different methods and/or systems. Most of the studies reviewed highlight the difficulties that people with ASD have regarding their social skills, specifically to maintain relationships and identify emotions, as well as their affinity with the use of technology. Studies such as Escobedo et al. [2] Milne et al. [3] and Sturm et al. [4] highlight the need to generalize these skills

© Springer Nature Switzerland AG 2020
G. Meiselwitz (Ed.): HCII 2020, LNCS 12195, pp. 598–615, 2020.
https://doi.org/10.1007/978-3-030-49576-3_44

in daily life beyond an intervention with technology, so that these skills are applied not only during interventions. Other studies such as those by Christinaki et al. [5], Sturm et al. [4] and Lorenzo et al. [6] recommend the use of non-tactile interfaces to encourage interaction, since it is important to take into account the difficulties in the motor skills of the participants. In addition, studies such as Lorenzo et al. [6], Harrold et al. [7], Christinaki et al. [5], Hourcade et al. [8] and Romero [9] highlight the importance of interventions being predictable and structured, as these are better adapted to the characteristics of people with autism spectrum disorder. It is also important to note that many of these studies such as Ribeiro and Raposo [10], Christinaki et al. [5], Boyd et al. [11] and Bernardini et al. [12] are based on traditional interventions in people with ASD to design their technological solutions, such as the use of the Picture Exchange Communication System (PECS) [13], ABAB [14], SCERTS [15], TEACCH [16] intervention and social stories [17].

Taking into account the information collected through the review of 11 papers related to technology interventions to develop social skills in people with ASD, in this paper we have detailed: (1) the way in which these studies characterize the difficulties of people with ASD, (2) how these characteristics have been considered to design their technological solutions and (3) which are the results obtained in these studies, in order to determine design guidelines and a preliminary design for future technological intervention that applies what was learned in this research and that will be useful to determine and validate good practices that cover specific needs in people with ASD. Section 2 analyzes relevant related work. Section 3 synthetizes some design guidelines for technological interventions for people with ASD. Section 4 proposes a technological intervention focused on teaching social skills for people with ASD. Finally, Sect. 5 highlights conclusions and future work.

2 Related Work

In order to guide our work and determine our preliminary design for a new technological intervention to teach social skills to people with ASD, we reviewed 11 papers related to this topic of interest. These papers were selected based on a previous systematic literature review [18], where we classified them as technological interventions that aimed to teach social skills. For each of these studies, we identified how the authors characterize the difficulties of people with ASD, how they considered those characteristics to design their technological solutions, the results obtained in these studies, and also useful recommendations that can be helpful to design our solution. The contributions of each of the 11 papers is detailed in the following paragraphs.

Ribeiro and Raposo [10] mention that "at about 50% of the people diagnosed with autism have problems in developing any kind of functional language", and that most of their reviewed studies try to teach people with ASD to develop social skills such as vocabulary, but no communication skills between people with autism, and even more with people with severe autism. For this reason, they developed and validated the effectiveness of the ComFiM software, an educational and collaborative software that focuses on helping children with severe autism to promote communication between them.

ComFiM is based on the Picture Exchange Communication System (PECS) intervention [13], through which children can communicate by creating sentences or by selecting images that represent objects and actions, in order to develop essential actions to start a communication such as "I give" and "I want". The software has three levels of difficulty, where children must interact with a tablet to comply with what is indicated by the software through a screen in front of them. In the first level the player has to exchange messages with the tutor to perform some tasks, request or give an object to achieve the objectives. In the second level two children are participants in the interaction, and they should seek or give an object between them through messages in tablets, where the tutor fulfils the role of mediator. In the last level, players must fulfil each of the roles during interaction with the tablets and get to the goal in one movement (the tutor plays the role of mediator), thus requiring a greater degree of communication.

The authors indicate that the results obtained demonstrate that the software has allowed the development of communicational intentions in children such as gestures, short phrases, signs and looks among the players. The players during the course of time understood the role that the tutor was playing during each of the levels and sessions.

Boyd et al. [11] mention that people with ASD experience difficulties in developing social skills [19], which leads to social isolation [20]. Additionally, the authors mention that studies show that people with ASD are more susceptible to depression, indicating that this may occur due to lack of friendships [21]. For this reason, it is that an ABAB study [14] was conducted in order to evaluate how technology could increase the development of social skills in children, thus maximizing the impact of the results on the participants [22]. Subsequently, the authors have formed four dyads (giving a total of 8 children), in order to develop membership skills (the child's ability to participate in a group physically, contributing to the activities generated within it), partnership (the ability of how two people, with specific responsibilities, achieve a common goal mutually) and friendship (two individuals have mutual interests and mutual affinity). In order to develop these skills, they worked on sessions with children using Legos and with the application Zody, a collaborative game for iPad, which has four mini-games, each of these are interconnected through the plot of the game.

The results highlight that: (1) Membership can be strengthened with the careful design of the physical space provided to children, the small dimensions of the iPad generated a physical proximity between the players, and the assignment of well-defined roles encouraged the participation of participants. Although the authors mention that the lack of fulfilment of roles and that the physical space to interact, sometimes generated discomfort in some participants. (2) Partnership is supported by the careful use of cooperative gestures [23], such as "serial gestures" which provides a structure where couples have the ability to take turns, and "simultaneous gestures", where players coordinate their actions on time. (3) Friendship is supported by the joys shared after "wins" and the empathy that occurs after a "loss" made the players generate understanding and friendship between them.

Bernardini et al. [12], indicate that people with autism spectrum conditions (ASC) have three main areas of difficulty, known as the "triad of impairments" [24], which includes: (1) communication, which refers to problems with verbal and not verbal language, (2) social interaction, which refers to the problems to recognize and understand the emotions of other people, as well as to express their own emotions, and

(3) patterns of restricted or repetitive behaviors, which exposes problems to adapt to new environments. For this reason, the authors present the design and implementation of a serious game called ECHOES, which focuses on helping young children with ASC to develop social communication skills.

ECHOES is based on recommendations of best practices of autism and the SCERTS framework [15], a framework that aims to identify the essential skills for successful social communication, from which they have taken into account supporting children in the subcomponents of communication: (i) Joint attention, ability to share attention, emotions and intentions with their peers, and (ii) Symbol use, ability to use objects, images, words or signs to represent things. The system is composed of a cognitive layer provided by FAtiMA [25] and a fragment of the Makaton language system [26], each of which forms a virtual agent called Andy. This agent plays different roles depending on the situations and/or actions that occur in the course of the child's interaction with the system, he acts as a partner and as a tutor.

After conducting a large-scale intervention, in which they deployed the application in five special needs schools, the authors documented children behaviour in a pre-test with a tabletop game activity and using ECHOES. They also assessed the generalization of communication skills by conducting a final test with the tabletop activity. The authors found no significant evidence of transfer of skills, but saw evidence of children benefited from their exposure to ECHOES and its virtual agent Andy. The number of interactions from kids to Andy was significantly less than the ones done to their teachers at the beginning, but the difference disappeared at the end. Teachers highlight that ECHOES allowed children to show their communicative skills in a comfortable environment.

The authors highlight that having heterogeneity in the target populations can have a big impact on the intervention, as it makes difficult to create an environment suitable for all users, and that some degree of flexibility in the technology used is needed, as the intended use of a piece of technology such as a serious game will not necessarily be reflected in its actual use.

Christinaki et al. [5] highlight difficulties to understand and express emotions [27], the importance of early interventions [28], and the delay in fine motor skills which causes difficulties the interaction [29]. Considering this, they designed and tested a serious game to teach emotions identification to pre-schoolers with autism using a no-touch user interface (NUI) that reads hand gestures with Kinect. Their game is based on three levels: labelling emotions from images, recognizing emotions from descriptions and facial features, and recognizing causes of emotions in social stories [17]. For its design they incorporated practices from traditional interventions for people with ASD such as one to one intensive play-based intervention from DIR/Floortime [30], visual support from PECS [13], positive reinforcement and rewards from ABA therapy [31], and a structural and predictable learning environment from TEACCH [16]. They considered the user needs for serious games for teaching people with ASD emotions [32]: repetition, matching instead of learning the features, lack of holistic face processing and deliberately incorrect selection. They also followed game design frameworks, identifying six relevant elements for game design for people with ASD: matching, recognition, observation, understanding, generalizing and mimicking.

After observing their experiments and conducting surveys, they concluded that NUI devices enhance game acceptance, game recognition and player involvement and participation, the player's emotional state is affecting its learning abilities in such a way that sometimes it makes the learning process impossible, and that minor changes in where the game is played affect dramatically the game acknowledgement, game acceptance, and game interaction but have a small or no effect on the NUI device avatar acknowledgement.

Sturm and et al. [4] mention the importance of computerized education, which can be more motivating than in-person education for autistic people [33] as it is well-aligned with the processing styles of many autistic people [34]. The authors highlight the relevance of generalizing skills learned from a computer interaction to in-person interactions. Whyte et al. [35] speculated that problems in generalization may be attributable to flaws in game design, and recommended the use of hybrid computer and in-person interactive opportunities. Taking in account the generalization of skills, they included people with ASD in a participatory design process, as this is engaging and promote generalization [36], of ConnectingTK, a serious game that focuses on teaching emotion recognition of complex emotions through collaboration between players and using body movements through Kinect. In this game, two players stand side by side using hand gestures to move the pieces of a puzzle, which shows an emotional face that is related to a relevant social situation.

After the participatory design process and applying surveys their results showed that students have difficulties to recognize complex emotions, users show better results when paired with non-ASD users, and that participatory design was well received, as the students felt involved and they recommend their experience. The authors also recommend to improve the communication channels in their participatory design, and provide more engagement in their solution using shared discoveries, not imposed by the game.

Lorenzo et al. [6] describes some characteristics of people with ASD, such as their emotional incapacity to maintain empathic relationships and to identify emotions [37], and that they have a tendency towards visual and structured thinking [38]. Baron-Cohen [39] indicate some aspects that characterize the difficulties related to the empathic capacities of people with ASD, such as minor joint attention frequency, less imaginary games and more activities with clear rules, a reduction in intuitive comprehension, impairment in the capacity to understand the meaning of things and/or predict other people's behavior, a high capacity to pay attention to details, and a significant retardation in the perception and comprehension of emotions and as a consequence, an inappropriate response to other people's emotions. Considering this, the authors developed an IVRS (Immersive Virtual Reality Systems) to stimulate the notably visual cognitive processing that characterizes students with ASD for the purpose of improving the student's emotional skills. IVRS allows repetition and systematization, which can lead to a reduction of this emotional deficit. In this application they used the IVRS to recreate situations, in the form of social stories [17], which allows the recognition of expression and emotions as well as the training of appropriate emotional behavior. Their experiment consisted in two phases: (1) Identification of the situation and the emotions, where the evaluator explains the social situation and asks the child about the components of the situation and about the different characters' emotions, and (2) implementation of the emotional script, where there is an established common emotional script for all the social stories, in which the users need to follow and select appropriate behaviors. They also included a computer vision system to follow and assess the user's emotion automatically. The results of their experiments showed that training helps the child to adapt to the virtual environment and improves the identification in the IVRS more than in the traditional VR, students that carry out the social stories in the immersive environment show significant improvements related to the emotional behaviors and the compliance with the guidelines, and users reduce their inadequate emotional behaviors in the IVRS, according to the automatic computer vision assessment. They also assessed the generalization of the skills through surveys directed to the teachers of the children, where they noted improvement in their social skills in the school environment.

Escobedo et al. [2] characterize people with ASD as people with social skills impairments [24], that struggle with making eye contact when interacting with others, and are more willing to initiate play and to interact appropriately when using entertainment-based assistive technologies, as it also helps them to maintain concentration. They also highlight the need of generalizing skills beyond the classroom. Considering this, they developed MOSOCO, a mobile assistive application that uses augmented reality and the visual supports of a validated curriculum, the Social Compass (A behavioral and educational curriculum), to help children with autism practice social skills in real-life situations. The minimal social skills required for social interaction are addressed by six lessons from the Social Compass curriculum: eye contact, space and proximity, start interaction, asking questions, sharing interests, and finishing interaction. Using augmented reality MOSOCO encourages them to make eye contact, maintain appropriate spatial boundaries, reply to conversation initiators, share interests with partners, disengage appropriately at the end of an interaction, and identify potential communication partners.

Students received MOSOCO positively, finding it useful, fun, and helpful. The application increases quantity and quality of social interactions, reduces social and behavioural missteps, and enables the integration of children with autism in social groups of neurotypical children, which interacted physically more when using the application. The authors recommend to have more game-like interactions, as they were engaging, and also use context-aware tools, that can recognize interaction contexts and react accordingly.

Hourcade et al. [8] characterizes children with ASD, as people that are unlikely to live independently when reaching adulthood, have impairments in social interactions and communication [24] and show strong interest in computers. They favour local over holistic processing [40]. Considering this, they developed computer supported activities to enhance the social skills of children with ASD with an emphasis on collaboration, coordination, creativity, compromising one's interests with the interests of others, and understanding emotions, enabling them to better collaborate, be creative, express themselves, compromise their interests, and understand emotions. For this, they used multi-touch tablets as a platform to support face-to-face activities. They considered their applications to be mistake-free, not showing errors, or system states, in order to reduce frustration. They used four different applications: (1) Drawing, where they used stylus to draw and express themselves, how they feel, and share with others. They also did collaborative interventions related to storytelling through drawings. (2) Music Authoring, where they created music in a harp-like interface. This allowed them to create something to share, and have fun with something out of their interests. They also included a collaborative activity where they passed the tablet to create together. (3) Untangle: a puzzle to encourage communication, collaboration, coordination and visuospatial thinking. (4) Photogoo: which enables children to distort images by dragging their fingers on the screen, allowing them to modify faces of cartoons to express emotions. The users improved their prosocial behaviours such as collaboration, coordination, augmented appreciation of social activities, and provided new forms of expressions, which also helped nonverbal children to express their thoughts and emotions.

The authors recommend to use a toolbox of activities instead of only one computer intervention, that users should reach a level of personal comfort on a new activity before doing it in groups, and create safe and predictable environments to help the comfort of the children.

Milne et al. [3] characterize children with autism as people with difficulties with social skills for which is challenging understanding nonverbal cues and social behaviors [41], have affinity with technology [42], and have difficulties when generalizing skills to real-world contexts [43]. Considering those difficulties, they used autonomous virtual humans to teach and facilitate practice of basic social skills in the areas of greeting, conversation, listening and turn taking. Those virtual human characters guide the learner in tasks and social scenarios, together with a teacher, a peer with strong social skills and a peer developing social skills. Being a technology-based approach, this benefits from immediate feedback and prompting, allowing the students to work at their own pace, reducing frustration. The solution also includes a three-tiered extrinsic reward system, to engage the participants. The authors recommend that assessment should be integrated in the overall learning, rather than being a separate activity, and should be used to continually inform and adjust activities presented to learners [44], and also highlighted that rewards and punishment only has a small influence in educational outcomes [45], but feedback with helpful suggestions can be beneficial for learners.

In [9], Romero determines that people with ASD have difficulties interpreting and or predicting emotions of others, which affects their social competence. Social competence can have a positive effect on the quality of people's life [46], including maintaining mutually satisfying relationships, and increasing the ability to hold to a job [47]. Poor Theory of Mind abilities have been linked to difficulties interacting with others, especially in emotion recognition [48] social competence [49] and anxiety in social situations [50]. The Ability to attribute mental states to others is important for people with ASD and requires awareness and attention to facial expressions [51]. Facial expressions provide important clues to an individual's mental state.

The authors considered the difficulties related to emotion recognition to develop a computer intervention program, "The Transporters". This program consists of 15 episodes, each focused on an emotion or mental state: happy, sad, angry, afraid, disgusted, surprised, excited, tired, unfriendly, kind, sorry, proud, jealous, joking, and ashamed, where users can learn to understand each expression with real life characters grafted onto vehicles that are presented with limited movement, to be predictable. The program also includes quizzes related to each episode.

The authors performed pre-assessments of the emotion recognition elements, and then the users were presented with scenarios to play, that consider the interests of the child, to increase the likelihood that they would like and watch the scenario to play out. They used narrators in order to not distract the users from the emotions of the characters. In the interventions they conducted a quiz which had three types of questions: (a) matching faces with faces (match the two characters that are feeling the same); (b) matching faces to an emotion (identify the face that portrays a specific emotion); (c) matching situations with faces (identify the correct emotion that might be displayed in a given situation).

After their interventions, the authors observed changes in the ability to process information from local to global processing of faces, and improvements of the ability to attribute mental states to others. They also showed improvement in emotion recognition in faces, generalized their knowledge and maintained the gains after the intervention.

Harrold et al. [7] considered their intervention, CopyMe, an early intervention for people with ASD, which is crucial to ease their struggle. As stated in other studies, people with ASD tend to like the use of technology, as it represents a structured and predictable environment to learn. CopyMe is an iPad serious game to learn emotions through observation and mimicry which combines automatic facial expression recognition technologies with real-time feedback for players performances. The players observe a photo of a human face, then attempt to copy it using the tablet camera, and a score is calculated to record successes without penalties for failed attempts, aiming to reinforce desired behaviors without causing stress. They tested their interventions with six children, 2 with ASD, aged 8 to 10, having 5 min of playtime and then 5 min of post-session interview, where they were asked 13 questions about the usefulness of the game to teach emotions. All the participants liked the use of iPad, and the ASD affected participants demonstrated enjoyment of the predictability of the game repetition, showing high levels of motivation and performance during gameplay.

The authors recommend using simple and uncluttered interfaces, as it's helpful to engage children with ASD, having scenarios to associate emotions and step-by-step or animated approach to demonstrate how to form an expression. They also highlight the importance of having visual rewards and achievement systems to enhance the experience and engage children for longer periods of time.

The reviewed studies present common ideas, such as having predictable and structured environments, or using tablets or Kinect to promote interactions. As the selected studies were focused on teaching social skills, most of the presented activities were related to emotion recognition, as this is a fundamental skill for social interactions. The authors also provided insights, good practices and lessons learned, which we have compiled as a set of design guidelines that consider the most relevant design elements that we discovered during the review phase.

3   Design Guidelines for Technological Interventions for People with ASD

After reviewing the 11 studies, identifying how they characterize difficulties of people with ASD, how they designed their technological solutions considering those difficulties and their results, we propose a structure and preliminary design for a future technological intervention to teach social skills to people with ASD. For this we propose a set of design guidelines that considers techniques successfully tested and applied in the reviewed interventions, lessons learned and good practices that the authors recommend, such as (1) having a structured and predictable learning environment, (2) provide ways to generalize skills to daily life, (3) consider different learning dynamics: individual and collaborative, (4) set engaging activity cycles through game elements: progress, feedback, rewards, (5) managing error, (6) have a variety of activity types, (7) using no-touch and technological-real hybrid interfaces. Using these elements, we defined a technological intervention based on PECS [13] which we aim to implement and validate in future works. In this section we first detail each of the 7 design guidelines considered, and then we describe our technological intervention proposal.

3.1   Structured and Predictable Learning Environment

Considering that according to DSM-5 [1], people with ASD have restricted and repetitive patterns of verbal and nonverbal behavior, interests, or activities, in order to design interventions that cover needs in individuals with ASD, it is necessary a certain accommodation to these modes of functioning. Thus, it is important that these interventions offer a structured and predictable learning environment [5–9]. As Lorenzo et al. [6] and Ribeiro and Raposo [10] indicate, it becomes relevant that people with ASD who participate in different types of activities are presented with the instructions in a clear, short, concise, simple and explicit way.

In this sense, incorporating technology can help an intervention with greater structuring and predictability, also increasing the attention, interest, engagement, and enjoyment [8] of individuals with ASD, since they exhibit high technology usage patterns and report a significant affinity for technology [42, 52].

In regard to socialization, as people with ASD find real social interactions to be stressful and intimidating because of their unpredictability [12], as well as initially frightening, challenging, and even undesirable, Hourcade et al. [8] explain that paired with technology, the process of enhancing social skills, might be a reward within itself. In order to improve the quality of social bonding, technology may be enough of an incentive, being also able to provide instead of the usual open-endedness of social relations, that inconvenience individuals with ASD, a more structured narrative for their interaction patterns [8].

3.2   Generalization to Daily Life

The patterns of restricted or repetitive behaviors that characterize people with ASD leads to problems with adapting to novel environments [1]. Considering that the transfer and generalization of skills learned from virtual or computerized contexts to the real world [3, 4, 6, 43] and from classroom learning to novel contexts and real-life situations [2, 53] are a known difficulty and a significant limitation for these people [9], these aspects are widely recognized issues in relation to interventions of any kind [3], that should be addressed from the design of the interventions.

In order to apply and transfer what individuals with ASD learn to daily situations outside the context of the interventions and to natural environments that involve family members and peers [2, 3], it is necessary to design situations with elements known by the students, which are as real as possible [6]. In addition, it is important to consider that facing to the practice of several behaviors or aspects to be taught or improved in different contexts, can help people with ASD to extrapolate and generalize the skills learned to a wider range of capacities, situations and contexts [12].

3.3   Learning Dynamics: Individual and Collaborative

As recommended by Ribeiro and Raposo [10], we considered to use a two-phase model, where the student could start learning in an individual intervention where the participant can get acquainted with the activity and have its own progress, to later move towards a group activity. It is important to note that this first phase a tutor will be supporting the process. The second phase could include group activities, which can be based on improving over three social phases, membership, partnership and friendship as stated in [11]. In membership, the participant who wants to enter the group must perform a symbolic act as an entry, such as sitting at the same table. In this form of organization there is no clear division of duties or responsibilities. Partnership involves two people who have specific responsibilities to achieve a mutual objective, and the responsibility is divided, and the individuals are interdependent in relation to the performance of the activity. Finally, friendships are based on sharing mutual interests and that often involves having fun together, which can lead to lasting relationships. In addition to these forms of organization of the group activity, there are additional elements that are important to consider, such as *symmetry, parallelism, proxemic distance, additivity, identity awareness* and the *number of users* [11].

In the case of *Symmetry*, the activities to be carried out are considered equivalent in effort and importance. The above can be obtained by having each participant perform the same activity or by making them equivalent in difficulty.

With regard to *Parallelism*, this can be done in two main ways: making the participants carry out the activity in the same period of time or in a chain, where an activity begins, and at the end of it, the next participant continues. This would imply that the participants were obligated to take and respect turns if they want to achieve the objectives.

On the other hand, the *Proxemic Distance* between the participants is an element that must be taken into account. For this we must consider both the construction of the software and the means where it will be installed. An example of this is, if a small tablet is used for more than one person to interact simultaneously, they may be forced to get too close to each other to be able to access the activity at the same time. Otherwise, if proximity it is not wanted, a larger architecture can be used, or the use of the Internet can be allowed, so that people can participate while not being in the same physical place.

In addition, *Additivity*, as a key element, implies that when more than one participant performs a specific action, a synergy is generated in the result. This could mean that a certain number of participants perform an action such as pressing a button that would unlock or give access to a new item or activity. In a similar range is *Identity Awareness*, however, in this case the participants have different roles and must work together to obtain a result that would otherwise be impossible.

Finally, the *Number of Users* and number of devices would determine the complexity in learning and the level of organization that might need it to perform it. The management of these structural elements could define which skills or abilities are worked within the device, for example, taking turns, teamwork, tolerance, empathy among others.

3.4   Engagement Through Activity Cycles and Game Elements

Studies such as Boyd and Kapp [11, 54] indicate that games provide a proper environment to develop social skills in people with ASD. Additionally, studies such as Werbach's [55] indicate that the use of game elements in non-game contexts can generate an attractive and motivating environment for users. Concepts such as motivation, rewards, feedback and progress are interesting to consider when designing game interventions for people with ASD.

Motivation encourages users to achieve objectives and develop expected behaviors. This motivation can be extrinsic and intrinsic. Extrinsic motivation is based on the theory of behaviorism, which indicates that humans and animals respond to external stimuli in predictable ways [56], so these types of stimuli encourage people to achieve things. On the other hand, intrinsic motivation is based on the theory of self-determination [57] and indicates that humans are inherently pro-active, with a desire to develop.

Rewards can be powerful incentives for continued participation [11]. However, offering a high amount of external rewards such as real-world prizes or benefits, produces a "Displacement Effect" [58]: an increase in extrinsic motivation thus dissipating intrinsic, so it is important to have a balance when applying these concepts.

Accurate and helpful feedback can be beneficial when working with people with ASD [3]. Feedback can come from different places such as progress towards an objective, from a peer, or as a response to an action within the context [55], thus helping to generate autonomy within the system, generate intrinsic motivation and originate possible friendships between people with ASD. Feedback is a key element for games to be effective and motivating. The use of concepts such as feedback, motivation and rewards generate what is known as the activity cycle, important to generate a greater commitment in users. The activity cycle indicates how motivation is capable of generating an action, which receives immediate feedback through rewards or points, and then motivates the user to perform more actions [55].

It is important to consider a progression system in the design, as activity cycles do not capture user progression. Progression, can be designed as progression stairs [55], which consider the use of levels and difficulty scaling. Having a way for the users to visualize the progress during the interaction is important to increase interest in the system, engage and motivate users, especially when considering that people with ASD have the ability to process and search visually [59, 60]. Establishing challenges that eventually increase in difficulty, followed by periods of rest or consolidation are relevant to consider.

3.5 Error Managing

People with ASD tend to be more susceptible to depression and frustration [21]. Many of the people with autism spectrum disorder get frustrated at not being able to express their emotions, thoughts and needs. Studies such as Hourcade et al. [8] recommend that systems should be free of errors, error messages, incorrect answers and unclear instructions, so as not to cause frustration in people with ASD.

Having feedback focused on constructive suggestions, such as the use of positive and concise expressions such as "oh, you were wrong, try another card", or facial expressions and obvious gestures for people with ASD [12], encourages the search for solutions, thus regulating frustration.

3.6 Mixed Activities

People with ASD have traditionally demonstrated a certain ease and ability to interact with computers, an aspect that can open doors to new treatments thanks to the application of technology [61], Regarding the development of activities, it is necessary to consider that many of the distractors or everyday elements that can disorient people with autism, disappear when they enter a controlled environment, such as therapy. In addition, when using a digital platform, the adaptation of the various levels or degrees of difficulty in the activities is facilitated when considering the user's own characteristics, since, the tasks can be adjusted to the level of progress or development that the person possesses. Particular learning rhythms could be stimulated by accompanying through a higher rate of individualization, in order to promote active learning, with flexibility and adaptability [62].

With regard to diversity in activities, there is a need to create a platform that allows a balance between different guided activities and free activities based on exploration and on spontaneity [63]. As for the possibility of repeating levels or activities, it could be counterproductive if they are identical, since it could encourage memorization. Some students may also use repetition as a way to avoid working: play past levels instead of solving the current problem or move on [64]. That is why presenting alternative forms or proposing a system that only promotes progress, over repetition, could be a favorable alternative.

3.7 No-Touch and Hybrid Interfaces

Studies such as Boyd et al. [11] mention that the use of tablets provides an effective and efficient platform when it comes to developing social skills in people with ASD, since these are portable, low-cost, generate a fun environment and do not require human mediators. The same study [11] cites that touch screens and/or interactive surfaces "allow face-to-face interaction and multiple simultaneous inputs from individuals acting independently or as part of a group" [65].

However, studies such as Strum et al. [4] highlight the use of technologies such as Kinect, as this provides tools to recreate social interactions that arise in the real world, where people generally must interact with each other using body movements, thus generalizing what has been learned to everyday life. Also, studies such as Christinaki et al. [5] highlight the delay in fine motor skills in people with ASD, causing difficulties to grab and manipulate objects [29], such as interacting with a mouse. Additionally, in [5] it is mentioned that the use of non-tactile systems controlled by hand gestures allows users to focus on learning and not be distracted by the use of complex interaction devices for them. It is important to consider the use of no-touch interfaces and hybrids between technological and not-technological interaction interfaces in the solution design, as they can provide an extra layer of accessibility and encourages the generalization of skills.

4 Intervention Proposal

Considering the design elements detailed in Sect. 3, we propose a preliminary design for a technological intervention focused on teaching social skills for people with ASD. The core of our proposed hybrid intervention will be based on the traditional intervention PECS [13], and will include the recommendations detailed in the previous section. We aim to implement and validate this proposal in future works.

Within the communicative difficulty of people with ASD, an intervention method for the language area is through augmentative - alternative communication systems (AAC) [66]. These communication systems can be sign language, voice generating devices or exchange-based communication [67]. For example, one of the most commonly used ACC is PECS, a method where they are taught to exchange symbols or images for specific elements instead of pointing them out on a communication monitor [68]. The use of these symbols is intended to clarify and accelerate communication without texts or words [69], increasing understanding by eliminating dependence on abstract words and concepts such as physical or spatial objects [70]. Studies have been carried out to analyze this type of behavior and it has been concluded that people with autism have superior visuospatial processing, activating more brain areas when listening to everyday language [70]. Another type of investigation revealed that people with autism have difficulties in following instructions, which is enhanced by the use of images. [71, 72].

PECS it is widely known and used for learning activities for people with ASD, and could be improved through the use of a hybrid technological implementation to support its use, such as integrating a tablet to display images and gamification-elements with physical objects like the image cards used in the traditional PECS intervention. An interesting approach to achieve this could be the use of NFC cards as physical objects to interact with the tablet software. These cards can include images related to emotion-recognition or other objects that are relevant to teach social skills in general.

Creating a hybrid intervention between the software application and physical interactive cards, will allow us to include all the design guidelines discussed in this study, such as different learning dynamics and types of activities, gamified progression and rewards, and error managing.

5 Conclusions

In this study we have reviewed 11 papers in which technological interventions have been created to develop social skills in people with ASD. After identifying how the authors characterize difficulties of people with ASD, how they are addressing these difficulties with their interventions and which were the results obtained, we have compiled and proposed design guidelines, considering common approaches, author recommendations and lessons learned in the reviewed studies. Our set of 7 design guidelines are expected to be a solid starting point for the design of new technological interventions to teach social skills to people with ASD.

Technological approaches to teach skills for people with ASD are a promising field to explore, and setting up design guidelines can be relevant to facilitate the development of new interventions, thus also helping the skill learning for people with ASD.

Considering our design guidelines, we proposed the base structure for a new technological intervention based on the PECS traditional intervention, which we aim to implement and validate in future works, helping us to also validate the guidelines established in this paper.

Acknowledgments. Katherine Valencia is a beneficiary of the CONICYT PhD Scholarship in Chile 2019, number: 21191170.

References

1. American Psychiatric Association: Diagnostic and Statistical Manual of Mental Disorders, 5th edn., pp. 853–854. American Psychiatric Publishing, Arlington (2013)
2. Escobedo, L., et al.: MOSOCO: a mobile assistive tool to support children with autism practicing social skills in real-life situations. In: Proceedings of the 30th ACM Conference on Human Factors in Computing Systems, CHI, Austin, TX, United States, pp. 5–10. ACM (2012)
3. Milne, M., Raghavendra, P., Leibbrandt, R., Powers, D.M.W.: Personalisation and automation in a virtual conversation skills tutor for children with autism. Multimodal User Interfaces 12(3), 257–269 (2018)
4. Sturm, D., Kholodovsky, M., Arab, R., Smith, D.S., Asanov, P., Gillespie-Lynch, K.: Participatory design of a hybrid kinect game to promote collaboration between autistic players and their peers. Hum. Comput. Interact. 35(8), 706–723 (2019)

5. Christinaki, E., Vidakis, N., Triantafyllidis, G.: A novel educational game for teaching emotion identification skills to preschoolers with autism diagnosis. Comput. Sci. Inf. Syst. **11**(2), 723–743 (2014)

6. Lorenzo, G., Lledó, A., Pomares, J., Roig, R.: Design and application of an immersive virtual reality system to enhance emotional skills for children with autism spectrum disorders. Comput. Educ. **98**, 192–205 (2016)

7. Harrold, N., Tan, C.T., Rosser, D., Leong, T.W.: CopyMe: a portable real-time feedback expression recognition game for children. In: Proceedings of the 32nd Annual ACM Conference on Human Factors in Computing Systems, CHI EA, Toronto, ON, Canada (2014)

8. Hourcade, J.P., Bullock-Rest, N.E., Hansen, T.E.: Multitouch tablet applications and activities to enhance the social skills of children with autism spectrum disorders. Pers. Ubiquit. Comput. **16**(2), 157–168 (2012)

9. Romero, N.I.: A pilot study examining a computer-based intervention to improve recognition and understanding of emotions in young children with communication and social deficits. Res. Dev. Disabil. **65**, 35–45 (2017)

10. Ribeiro, P.C., Raposo, A.B.: ComFiM: a game for multitouch devices to encourage communication between people with autism. In: 3rd International Conference on Serious Games and Applications for Health, SeGAH, Rio de Janeiro, Brazil. IEEE (2014)

11. Boyd, L.E., Ringland, K.E., Haimson, O.L., Fernandez, H., Bistarkey, M., Hayes, G.R.: Evaluating a collaborative iPad game's impact on social relationships for children with autism spectrum disorder. ACM Trans. Access. Comput. **7**(1), 1–18 (2015)

12. Bernardini, S., Porayska-Pomsta, K., Smith, T.J.: ECHOES: an intelligent serious game for fostering social communication in children with autism. Inf. Sci. **264**, 41–60 (2014)

13. Charlop-Christy, M.H., Carpenter, M., Le, L., LeBlanc, L.A., Kellet, K.: Using the picture exchange communication system (PECS) with children with autism assessment of PECS acquisition, speech, social-communicative behavior, and problem behavior. Appl. Behav. Anal. **35**(3), 213–231 (2002)

14. Kazdin, A.E.: Single-case Research Designs: Methods for Clinical and Applied Settings, 2nd edn. Oxford University Press, New York (2011)

15. Prizant, B., Wetherby, A., Rubin, E., Laurent, A., Rydell, P.: The SCERTS Model: A Comprehensive Educational Approach for Children with Autism Spectrum Disorders. Brookes, Baltimore (2006)

16. Mesibov, G.B., Shea, V., Schopler, E.: The TEACCH Approach to Autism Spectrum Disorders. Springer Science, New York (2004). https://doi.org/10.1007/978-0-306-48647-0

17. Gray, C.A., Garand, J.D.: Social stories: improving responses of students with autism with accurate social information. Focus Autistic Behav. **8**(1), 1–10 (1993)

18. Valencia, K., Rusu, C., Quiñones, D., Jamet, E.: The impact of technology on people with autism spectrum disorder: a systematic literature review. Sensors **19**(20), 4485 (2019)

19. Baron-Cohen, S.: Social and pragmatic deficits in autism: cognitive or affective? Autism Dev. Disord. **18**(3), 379–402 (1988)

20. Ghaziuddin, M., Ghaziuddin, N., Greden, J.: Depression in persons with autism: implications for research and clinical care. Autism Dev. Disord. **32**(4), 299–306 (2002)

21. Leyfer, T.O., et al.: Comorbid psychiatric disorders in children with autism: interview development and rates of disorders. Autism Dev. Disord. **36**(7), 849–861 (2006)

22. Sears, A., Hanson, V.L.: Representing users in accessibility research. ACM Trans. Access. Comput. **4**, 2235–2238 (2012). TACCESS. ACM, Vancouver, Canada

23. Morris, M.R., Huang, A., Paepcke, A., Winograd, T.: Cooperative gestures: multi-user gestural interactions for co-located groupware. In: Conference on Human Factors in Computing Systems, SIGCHI, Montréal, Canada, pp. 1201–1210. ACM (2006)

24. American Psychiatric Association: Diagnostic and Statistical Manual of Mental Disorders, 4th edn. American Psychiatric Publishing, Arlington (2000)
25. Dias, J., Paiva, A.: Feeling and reasoning: a computational model for emotional characters. In: Bento, C., Cardoso, A., Dias, G. (eds.) EPIA 2005. LNCS (LNAI), vol. 3808, pp. 127–140. Springer, Heidelberg (2005). https://doi.org/10.1007/11595014_13
26. Walker, M., Armfield, A.: What is the makaton vocabulary? Spec. Educ. Forward Trends **8**(3), 19–20 (1981)
27. White, S.W., Keonig, K., Scahill, L.: Social skills development in children with autism spectrum disorders: a review of the intervention research. J. Autism Dev. Disord. **37**, 1858–1868 (2007)
28. Tzanakaki, P., Grindle, C.P., Hastings, R., Hughes, J.C.: How and why do parents choose Early Intensive Behavioral Intervention for their young child with Autism? Educ. Train. Autism Dev. Disab. **47**(1), 58–71 (2012)
29. Jasmin, E., Couture, M., McKinley, P., Reid, G., Fombonne, E., Gisel, E.: Sensori-motor and daily living skills of preschool children with autism spectrum disorders. Autism Dev. Disord. **39**(2), 231–241 (2009)
30. Pajareya, K., Nopmaneejumruslers, K.: A one-year prospective follow-up study of a DIR/floortime parent training intervention for preschool children with autistic spectrum disorders. Med. Assoc. Thail. **95**(9), 1184–1193 (2012)
31. Axelrod, S., McElrath, K.K., Wine, B.: Applied behavior analysis: autism and beyond. Behav. Interv. **27**(1), 1–15 (2012)
32. Abirached, B., Zhang, Y., Park, J.H.: Understanding user needs for serious games for teaching children with autism spectrum disorders emotions. In: Proceedings of World Conference on Educational Multimedia, Hypermedia and Telecommunications, Denver, Colorado, pp. 1054–1063 (2012)
33. Moore, M., Calvert, S.: Brief report: vocabulary acquisition for children with autism: teacher or computer instruction. Autism Dev. Disord. **30**(4), 359–362 (2000)
34. Media in Transition. http://web.mit.edu/m-i-t/articles/index_blume.html. Accessed 27 Jan 2020
35. Whyte, E.M., Smyth, J.M., Scherf, K.S.: Designing serious game interventions for individuals with autism. Autism Dev. Disord. **45**(12), 3820–3831 (2015)
36. Benton, L., Johnson, H., Ashwin, E., Brosnan, M., Grawemeyer, B.: Developing ideas: supporting children with autism within a participatory design team. In: 30th ACM Conference on Human Factors in Computing Systems, CHI, Austin, Texas, United States, pp. 2599–2608 (2012)
37. Ehrich, J.A., Miller, J.R.: A virtual environment for teaching social skills: AViSSS. Comput. Graph. Appl. **29**(4), 10–16 (2009)
38. Schopler, E., Mesibov, G.B.: High-Functioning Individuals with Autism. Springer, New York (1992). https://doi.org/10.1007/978-1-4899-2456-8
39. Baron-Cohen, S., Richler, J., Bisarya, D., Gurunathan, N., Wheelwright, S.: The systemizing quotient: an investigation of adults with Asperger syndrome or high-functioning autism, and normal sex differences. Philos. Trans. Royal Soc. Biol. Sci. **358**(1430), 361–374 (2003)
40. Mottron, L., Dawson, M., Soulieres, I., Hubert, B., Burack, J.: Enhanced perceptual functioning in autism: an update, and eight principles of autistic perception. Autism Dev. Disord. **36**(1), 27–43 (2006)
41. Kroncke, A.P., Willard, M., Huckabee, H.: What is Autism? History and Foundations. Springer, Cham (2016). https://doi.org/10.1007/978-3-319-25504-0_1
42. MacMullin, J.A., Lunsky, Y., Weiss, J.A.: Plugged in: electronics use in youth and young adults with autism spectrum disorder. Autism **20**(1), 45–54 (2016)

43. Neely, L.C., et al.: Generalization and maintenance of functional living skills for individuals with autism spectrum disorder: a review and meta-analysis. Rev. J. Autism Dev. Disord. **3** (1), 37–47 (2016)
44. Black, P.: Assessment: friend or foe of pedagogy and learning. Past as Prologue (2015)
45. Hattie, J., Timperley, H.: The power of feedback. Rev. Educ. Res. **77**(1), 81–112 (2007)
46. Hall, L.J.: Autism Spectrum Disorders: From Theory to Practice. Pearson, London (2009)
47. Cotugno, A.J.: Social competence and social skills training and intervention for children with autism spectrum disorders. Autism Dev. Disord. **39**(9), 1268–1277 (2009)
48. Ashwin, C., Chapman, E., Colle, L., Baron-Cohen, S.: Impaired recognition of negative basic emotions in autism: a test of the amygdala theory. Soc. Neurosci. **1**(3–4), 349–363 (2006)
49. Bosacki, S., Astington, J.W.: Theory of mind in preadolescence: relations between social understanding and social competence. Soc. Dev. **8**(2), 237–255 (1999)
50. Coupland, N.J.: Social phobia: etiology, neurobiology, and treatment. Clin. Psychiat. **62**, 25–35 (2001)
51. Baron-Cohen, S., Wheelwright, S., Jolliffe, T.: Is there a "Language of the Eyes"? Evidence from normal adults, and adults with autism or asperger syndrome. Vis. Cognit. **4**(3), 311–331 (1997)
52. Putnam, C., Chong, L.: Software and technologies designed for people with autism: what do users want? In: 10th International ACM SIGACCESS Conference on Computers and Accessibility, Nova Scotia, Canada, pp. 3–10. ACM (2008)
53. Betz, A., Higbee, T.S., Pollarda, J.: Promoting generalization of mands for information used by young children with autism. Res. Autism Spectr. Disord. **4**(3), 501–508 (2009)
54. Kapp, K.M.: The Gamification of Learning and Instruction: Game-Based Methods and Strategies for Training and Education. Pfeifer, San Francisco (2012)
55. Werbach, K., Hunter, D.: For the Win: How Game Thinking Can Revolutionize Your Business. Wharton Digital Press, Philadelphia (2012)
56. Skinner, B.F.: The Behavior of Organisms: An Experimental Analysis. Appleton-Century, New York (1938)
57. Ryan, R.M., Deci, E.L.: Self-determination theory and the facilitation of intrinsic motivation, social development, and well-being. Am. Psychol. **55**(1), 68–78 (2000)
58. Kohn, A.: Punished by Rewards: The Trouble with Gold Stars, Incentive Plans, A's, Praise and Other Bribes. Mariner Books, New York (1999)
59. Kaldy, Z., Kraper, C., Carter, A.S., Blaser, E.: Toddlers with autism spectrum disorder are more successful at visual search than typically developing toddlers. Dev. Sci. **14**(5), 980–988 (2011)
60. Gonzalez, C., Martin, J.M., Minshew, N., Behrmann, M.: Practice makes improvement: how adults with autism out-perform others in a naturalistic visual search task. Autism Dev. Disord. **43**(10), 2259–2268 (2013)
61. Alcantud, F.: Las Tecnologías de la Información y de la Comunicación y los Trastornos Generalizados del Desarrollo (2004)
62. Fernández, J., Miralles, F.: Formación en los trastornos de desarrollo. Utilización de metodología eLearning. Psicogente **17**(32), 283–293 (2014)
63. Carrillo, E., Pachón, C.M.: Creación, diseño e implementación de plataforma eLearning utilizando mundos 3D para los niños con Trastorno del Espectro Autista (TEA). Educación y Desarrollo Social **5**(1), 70–80 (2010)
64. Liu, Z., Cody, C., Barnes, T., Lynch, C., Rutherford, T.: The antecedents of and associations with elective replay in an educational game: is replay worth it? In: 10th International Conference on Educational Data Mining, EDM, Wuhan, China, pp. 40–47 (2017)

65. Morris, M.R., Huang, A., Paepcke, A., Winograd, T.: Cooperative gestures: multi-user gestural interactions for co-located groupware. In: Conference on Human Factors in Computing Systems, Montreal, Canada, vol. 2, pp. 1201–1210. ACM (2006)

66. Mirenda, P.: A back door approach to autism and ACC. Augment. Altern. Commun. **24**(3), 220–234 (2008)

67. Ganz, J.: AAC interventions for individuals with autism spectrum disorders: state of the science and future research directions. Augment. Altern. Commun. **31**(3), 203–214 (2015)

68. Mirenda, P.: Toward functional augmentative and alternative communication for students with autism: manual signs, graphic symbols, and voice output communication aids. Lang. Speech Hear. Serv. Schools **34**(3), 203–216 (2003)

69. Clara, S., Wirania, S.: Pictogram on signage as an effective communication. J. Sosioteknologi **16**(2), 167–176 (2017)

70. Kana, R.K.: Sentence comprehension in autism: thinking in pictures with decreased functional connectivity. Brain **129**(9), 2484–2493 (2006)

71. Manti, E., Scholte, E., Van Berckelaer-Onnes, I.: Exploration of teaching strategies that stimulate the growth of academic skills of children with ASD in special education school. Eur. J. Spec. Needs Educ. **28**(1), 64–77 (2013)

72. Gomez, J., Jaccheri, L., Torrado, J.C., Montero, G.: Leo Con Lula, introducing global reading methods to children with ASD. In: 17th ACM Conference on Interaction Design and Children, IDC, Trondheim, Norway, pp. 420–426. ACM (2018)

A Personalized and Context Aware Music Recommendation System

Champika H. P. D. Wishwanath, Supuni N. Weerasinghe,
Kanishka H. Illandara, A. S. T. M. R. D. S. Kadigamuwa,
and Supunmali Ahangama[(✉)]

Faculty of Information Technology, University of Moratuwa,
Moratuwa, Sri Lanka
champikawishwanath@gmail.com,
supuni.14@itfac.mrt.ac.lk,
kanishkaillandara@gmail.com, dskadiya@gmail.com,
supunmali@uom.lk

Abstract. People listen to music as it expresses and induce emotions. Considering millions of songs available in online streaming services, it is difficult to identify the most suitable song for an emotion of a user. Most of the music recommendation systems available today, are based on user ratings and acoustic features of the songs. Those systems are unable to address the cold start problem and rating diversity. Furthermore, song preferences will be altering based on the current mood of the users. If these problems were not addressed, then these online services will fail to achieve user satisfaction. To cope with those problems, this paper proposes a novel music recommendation approach that utilizes social media content such as posts, comments, interactions, etc. and recommend them with the most relevant songs to relax their mind considering the current mood (happy, sad, calm and angry). The current mood and the preferences are extracted from the social media profile of the users. Then the songs were classified to moods based on the lyrics and audio of the songs.

Keywords: Music recommendation · Social media · Personalized recommendation

1 Introduction

With the hectic schedule in the day to day life, everyone lives in different states of moods at different times of the day. These moods will alternate time to time. Based on the individual mood and preference, people tend to listen to different types of music [1] to change their mood, relax their minds and improve their existing pleasant feelings. Due these "emotional powers" of music, people have been attracted to music [2]. Music can have a great impact on both the emotions and the human body. For an instance, fast tempo music can make a person more alert while slow tempo music can calm and relax the mind and body. Moreover, music can be effectively used for relaxation and stress management. People will listen to music that suits their individual preference and situation. It is suggested that different individuals perceive different emotions from the

© Springer Nature Switzerland AG 2020
G. Meiselwitz (Ed.): HCII 2020, LNCS 12195, pp. 616–627, 2020.
https://doi.org/10.1007/978-3-030-49576-3_45

same piece of music [2]. Therefore, it is important to determine individual listening patterns and preferences.

As Social Network Sites (SNS) and streaming services had become the distribution channel of digital music, millions of music tracks are accessible to people. For example, more than 50 million songs are available in Apple Music stores [3]. Thus, it is merely impossible for a user to select the most suitable songs and it would take many hours to decide the most appropriate song for the current mood. To select the user preferred songs with less time, automated music recommendation systems (MRS) are required and MRS are extensively used by online music streaming services like Spotify. To suggest songs based on the user's emotion/mood, it is necessary to classify songs suitable for different moods. However, most of the existing playlists categories the songs based on the public opinion or meta data of the songs. In view of music recommendation, these states of moods should be significant for building proper user preferences to choose suitable music. Music recommendations are extensively used by online music streaming services like Spotify. Most of the recommendation systems consider content-based information [4] and context-based information [5, 6]. However, they do not provide personalized recommendations based on user mood. As such, in this study, the authors have developed a personalized recommendation system based on current mood of the user.

This paper proposes a MRS, that uses song features (lyrics and audio) to classify songs to four types of moods (as happy, sad, calm and angry) and recommends songs based on the current mood of the person. In the proposed MRS, there will be a music player and a playlist of recommended songs. Moreover, the user listening patterns will be captured to improve the recommendations further. The current mood of a person is captured from the individual profiles in SNS. SNS has become an essential part of life of individuals in different age levels and geographic areas. Among them Facebook has unique features which created virtual communication platform open to anyone to express their opinions and feelings. Thus, this study is based on the Facebook user data. Most of the SNS users freely share their own opinions through his/her social media account. From user's profile in Facebook, it is possible to extract attributes such as person's mood, activities, thinking style, and interactions. Moreover, music listening preferences of users can be identified by analyzing the user profile. Thus, it is be possible to get a complete idea of the user's natural behavior.

The primary motivation for researching this area was to provide an easier way for music listeners to queue up songs based on their current moods. Thus, various alternative approaches to recommend mood fixing songs that enrich initial music preference of user based on artist and songs will be evaluated considering various factors. In the proposed recommendation system, there will be a music player and a playlist of recommended songs. Moreover, the user listening patterns will be captured to improve the recommendations further (learning process).

The remainder of the paper is arranged as follows. In the next section, a review of the related literature will be given. Subsequently, the approach followed will be explained along with the results of the evaluation. Finally, the discussion and conclusion are available.

2   Literature Review

Recommendation Systems' role is to provide users with the most relevant items based on their preferences or by their past evaluations and interactions [7, 8]. This information can be acquired explicitly or implicitly [8]. Explicit information is provided by the users themselves. For an instance, giving an opinion, a rating or a like on an item could be considered as explicit information. Implicit information is gathered from the user interaction with the service without users themselves giving the information. For an instance, information such as viewing and playing times are considered as implicit information.

The most used option in music recommendation is collaborative filtering (CF) [9]. Prominent services like Last.fm or iTunes Genius are using CF techniques [10, 11]. In CF, it is important to consider the interaction between users and song items. For an instance, recommendations in Last.fm are computed using user behavior and user generated content (feedbacks, tags) regarding a song. Similarly, Genius by iTunes uses user feedback. However, with the limited user preference data, music recommendations tend to fall short of human expectations. Furthermore, traditional CF approaches do not consider social media data [12].

Nowadays, music recommendation strategies are mostly based on content, that is available as low-level features (audio features like tempo, harmony, pitch, sound level) [13], or high-level features (metadata or social tags) [14] in order to provide recommendations. Rather than using CF, the content-based filtering recommendation (acoustic-based music recommendation) has been able to address the problems like cold start problem, that is, newly released or unpopular music when the music production continuously flowing in an uncontrolled manner. As content-based methods like matrix factorization, neighborhood-based methods, and Markov model are commonly used [15]. For example, Pandora is a popular music services that uses these approaches [11]. These recommender systems have considered audio features and the user ratings. To further improve the performance of the online music services, social media data has been used in addition to acoustic based content of the songs [12]. Moreover, there is a huge potential in using context-aware music recommendations [16]. Specifically, contextual situations like time, weather data, current mood of a person, users' physical location, age, gender and all the other impacting variables should be considered in music recommendation. However, some modern music providers like Spotify, Hungama and YouTube do not fulfil their systems to handle these situations.

In conventional music players, a listener had to manually search the playlist and select songs that would suit his/her mood. Music square can classify the songs manually according to four basic emotions; namely, passionate, calm, joyful and excitement. Today, there have been many advancements in the music players including features like streaming, local playback, fast forward, reverse, and grouping based on genre. Even though, these features might satisfy some of the requirements of the listeners when browsing through the playlists, still it is a manual and time-consuming process. Thus, developing a playlist that automatically recommends a song from his/her playlist, according to his mood and preferences will be useful [17].

Emo player was developed by [17, 18] uses facial emotions of the users and based on the current emotions, the songs are played. However, it is difficult to capture the facial emotions of the users. There are some of the playlists created using special hardware to measure the EEG or by analyzing the user speech. However, they are slow in processing and computationally expensive [18].

3 Approach

Even though there are many popular online streaming services with millions of subscribers, a truly personalized way of listening to music is missing in the music streaming industry. Many services have tried to handle this problem by adding features such as mood stations or a "radio" mode for discovering new music. However, none of these options are dynamically changing along with the user's mood. This proposed approach aims to solve this problem. As shown in Fig. 1, there are three (3) main parts of the system. They are (1) user profile analysis, (2) song profile analysis and (3) music recommendation. There will be a music player and a playlist of recommended songs as the final output of the proposed MSR. Moreover, user's listening behavior (number of times the user has listened, context and rating given) were captured to improve the recommendations.

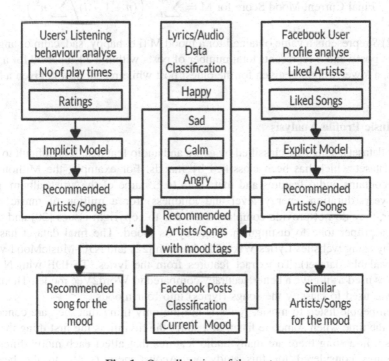

Fig. 1. Overall design of the system

3.1   User Profile Analysis

Current mood of a person is detected using recent (e.g. within a 24-h period) posts, comments, text in images and emoticons shared in Facebook by a user. The current mood will be determined only if there are recent posts in the Facebook profile of the user. After pre-processing the text extracted from text posts and image posts, a mood classification will be performed using 1D CNN Model through Tensorflow (with 85% accuracy). Overall current mood level for a post (if there are text and emoticons) is computed as in (1) using both text content and emoticons extracted from a post of a user [19].

$$\text{Score for a mood in a post} = 0.6 \times \text{emoticon score} + 0.4 \times \text{text content score} \quad (1)$$

If only emoticons or textual content is available, then the (1) would not be used. The individual score obtained would be used as the overall mood score for a specific post.

If there are multiple posts within the time period, a time-based approach is used to calculate the score for the current mood. A weight is added to each post based on the posted time so that the most recent post will get a higher weight compared to other posts.

$$\text{Final Current Mood Score for M} = \sum_{i=1}^{n} \left((n+1-i) \Big/ \sum n^{S_i} \right) \quad (2)$$

In (2) S represents a value obtained for a mood M (i.e. happy, sad, calm or angry) in a specific post i and n represents total number of posts within a 24 h period for a mood M. Thus, a lower weight is given for the oldest post while recent post is given a higher weight.

3.2   Music Profile Analysis

In many datasets, songs are classified by genre and audio features. It is difficult to find a proper dataset which has been classified by moods. For example, the Million Song Dataset contains audio features and meta data (e.g. name of the artist, album, genre, created year, duration, energy level and loudness) for a million of music tracks. However, they do not provide complete track due to copyright issues [20] and do not provide a proper tone to distinguish songs by its mood. The final dataset has been created by using websites Lyrics Wiki [21], Last.fm [22] and NJU-MusicMood-v1.0 (a freely available dataset). To extract features from the lyrics, TF-IDF with N-Gram model was used as it gave a better accuracy compared to Word2Vec model. Then SVM model was used to classify the songs (lyrics) into four moods.

When people listen to music, lyrics is not the only thing that they are concerned. Most of the time when someone listen to a song, the rhythm is the first thing that they will grasp. In a song there are many audio features that affect each mood differently. The features considered for this study are Acousticness (sense to the hearing), Danceability (suitability to dance), Energy (intensity and activity of the music track), Loudness (quality of the sound), Tempo (beats per minute) and Valence (positiveness of a track, where high valance sound are more positive) [22]. For example, a happy mood can be represented by fast and small tempo, medium-high sound level, small sound level variability, and small timing variability [2]. These features for music tracks were extracted from the developer API for Spotify. The list of songs was obtained from the Million Song Dataset. Random forest was used to predict the mood for each song based on the dataset developed using the low-level features extracted from the music tracks.

Finally, the overall mood for each song is identified based on the moods predicted for lyrics data and audio data. If both lyrics and audio features predict a certain mood that will be considered as the mood of the music track. However, human intervention is used if different moods were predicted as per the lyrics and audio features.

As illustrated in Fig. 1, the recommendation system will map the music tracks to users based on the current mood of the users.

3.3 Music Recommendation

Recommendation systems work by collecting data on the preferences of its users for a set of items. This data can be acquired explicitly or implicitly. Explicit data is provided by the users themselves such as giving an opinion, a rating or a like on an item. For example, a song can be given a rating from 1 to 5; where closer to 1 indicates that the user dislikes the song and closer to 5 indicate that the user like the song very much. However, most of the time users do not rate the songs they listened or purchased. As it is difficult to capture explicit data, implicit data like user behavior or things that the user has consumed would be considered (e.g. number of times a song is played). Implicit data is gathered from the user interaction with the service without users themselves giving the information. In the proposed system we have considered the number of times a user listened a song.

The proposed recommendation system was created considering both CF and content-based filtering approaches and the songs were predicted based on the real time current mood updates of the users. The proposed system is accessing Last.fm service through its public API. For each artist, name, titles of their most popular tracks, play count of those tracks and a set of tags that describe the artist were accessed from Last. fm. Subsequently, these artist related data were mapped with the user preferred artist list identified through the recommendation system. To identify the user preferences, user's music playing histories or sequences were examined.

We have considered implicit model and explicit model. Implicit model finds similar items and make recommendations to users while explicit model suggests the most appropriate songs and artists for the current mood by analysing the Facebook user profile.

Implicit Model. As the initial step, a matrix was created with number of times a user played a song. Each user will have listened only to a subset of songs. Therefore, for each user, number of times a song is played will be available only for a subset of the songs. Since all the users have not listened to all the songs available, it is not possible to know the entries in this matrix. In a sparse matrix for implicit data, the missing values may represent a user's dislike for a song or song is unknown to the user (but they might have liked the song if they had known it). Thus, a missing value has a value or a meaning.

With CF, the idea is to approximate the matrix by factorizing it as a product of two matrices: one that describes properties of each user, and one that describes properties of each song. Thus, even if two users have not listened to the same song; still, they can be mapped to each other based on the common properties of the songs. When selecting the two matrices, it is important to reduce the error for the values for user/song pairs where the correct number of times a song is played is known. The Alternating Least Squares (ALS) algorithm was used to accomplish matrix factorization. Initially, user's matrix was filled with values randomly and then iteratively optimizing the value of the songs such that the error is minimized. It holds the song's matrix constant and optimizes the value of the user's matrix. Given a fixed set of user factors (i.e., values in the user's matrix), a known number of plays will be used to find the best values for the song's factors using the least squares optimization. Then "alternate" and can pick the best user factors for given fixed songs factors.

Here, as suggested by Hu et al. [8], the aim is to merge the preference (p) for an item with the confidence (c) for that preference. In this model, the missing values as a negative preference with a low confidence value and existing values as a positive preference with a high confidence value will considered [8]. The confidence can be calculated using interactions like play count or time spent listening to a song. The preference is taken by considering whether the user listens to a song or not (r). That is, preference (p) would be a binary value of 1 or 0 based on the feedback data (e.g. count of playing a song), r.

$$p_{ui} = \begin{cases} 1, & r_{ui} > 0 \\ 0, & r_{ui} = 0 \end{cases} \tag{3}$$

If the user listens to a song (feedback r is greater than 0), then p is set as 1 or else it set as 0 as given in (3).

Then the confidence can be calculated as follows:

$$C_{ui} = 1 + \alpha \cdot r_{ui} \tag{4}$$

Where in (4), C is the confidence, r is the feedback (e.g. play count) and α is the linear scaling factor. As per Hu et al. [8], $\alpha = 40$, gives the best results.

If a user has played, viewed or clicked a song more times, then this confidence score will increase. For example, if user listens to a song 100 times there will be a higher confidence value compared to listening only once. If the user has not listened to the song, still the confidence value would be 1.

To find similarities between two items, the equation given below was used.

$$\text{Similarity score} = V \times V_i^T \tag{5}$$

Where in (5), V_i is song item vector, V_i^T is the transpose of song vector. In this study, we have used (5) to find the similarity between artists.

To make recommendations, the equation given below was used.

$$Score = U_i \times V^T \qquad (6)$$

Where in (6), U_i is the User vector and V^T is the transpose of item vector. Thus, recommendation score will be calculated for a specific user for each song item.

To improve the performance, three different implicit ALS functions were considered.

Explicit Model. To make recommendation without the impact of "cold start problem" [23], the liked artists of users available through Facebook user profiles were considered. If a new user joins the proposed recommendation system, the most appropriate songs and artists for them should be suggested. To handle that, the nearest neighbor search method was used to identify artists and songs for these new users. Various algorithms were proposed to improve efficiency and accuracy of nearest neighbor search. Most popular methods that can be used are metric-tree, ball-tree, cover tree, Brute-force, and KD tree. After comparing accuracies for using these popular methods, KD tree was selected as the explicit model algorithm for recommendation.

4 Analysis

Performance is evaluated for the implicit model and the explicit model. The performance was evaluated considering various approaches to identify the most suitable approach to be used in the recommendation system.

4.1 Performance Evaluation of Implicit Model

The evaluation of the model was performed using three different functions for implicit data (Fig. 2).

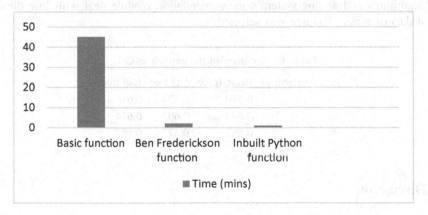

Fig. 2. A comparison of execution time for basic ALS function, Ben Frederickson ALS function and inbuilt python ALS function.

Those implicit ALS functions used are basic implicit ALS function, implicit ALS Ben Frederickson function and inbuilt Python ALS function. As illustrated in Fig. 2, inbuilt Python ALS function performs better than the other two functions based on the execution time. Thus, it was used in the proposed MRS. Therefore, inbuilt python implicit library was used to get the similar artists according to a score. As shown below, higher value of the score hold for the most suitable artists.

Similarity scores are given below.

```
                               artist       score
        0                brian wilson    1.141458
        1              the beta band     1.130788
        2              harry nilsson     1.120744
        3                    buck 65     1.112741
        4                  sam cooke     1.111302
        5         sly & the family stone 1.110645
        6                  the onion     1.108948
        7  elvis costello & the attractions 1.102296
        8                    donovan     1.100646
        9                        npr     1.097487
```

4.2   Performance Evaluation of Explicit Model

To check the explicit model accuracy, the authors of this paper used various methodologies as indicated in Table 1. Accuracy is compared by changing the neighbor size against the three models. Based on experimental observations, it can be concluded that the KD tree performs faster than the ball-tree when constructing the tree and solving the problem. Moreover, accuracy of the KD tree is comparable to other models. Since KD tree performs well in low dimensional data when compared to other two algorithms and as this system's recommendation module deal with low dimensional data of music, KD tree was selected.

Table 1. Accuracy of the explicit model

No of neighbors	Brute-force	KD tree	Ball tree
45	0.589	0.624	0.610
60	0.688	0.695	0.674
90	0.597	0.577	0.567

5   Discussion

The proposed recommendation system is created considering both CF and content-based filtering approaches. Based on the real time current mood updates of the users, music tracks were predicted. To predict music tracks for a given user, the implicit model with ALS algorithm was used. It was noted that there are many songs that have only been listened once, as a result, had to compare models that include and exclude those songs that have been listened only once. The model including those songs returns a slightly lower root-mean-square deviation on the test dataset compared to the model excluding them. Since the training set includes more songs, it may be more reflective of their listening profiles.

One of the main challenges in the recommendation model was how to address the songs that have been never heard by a user. To handle this, implicit function with matrix factorization was used, where, unseen items are treated as negative with a low confidence. As the implicit model, the inbuilt python ALS function was used based on the execution time as shown in the Fig. 2.

For any recommendation system, another problem is providing a recommendation when there is a new user. When a new user enters the music recommendation system, it should recommend those users with the most appropriate songs according to their current mood. In order to face this problem, the proposed system used Facebook user profile data including liked artists based on their preferences. With this option, the system can generate a personalized playlist based on the mood of a user. Based on the evaluation results, KD tree with nearest neighbour search algorithm was used.

Since a music player needs to perform as a real time application, the proposed model should actively run on every state of the system. As such, algorithms that execute instantly were selected.

As future work to improve the results of the recommendation system, it is important to develop a context aware recommendation system. For example, need to consider the time of the day as user preferences changes with the time of the day and based on the weather user moods will change. Through social media it is important to gather more details about the user personalities, thus, it will improve the recommendations further. In addition, through other online streaming services like YouTube history and online playlist logs.

6 Conclusion

The proposed recommendation system will be considering various factors in developing a personalized MSR. Music tracks were categorized to types of user moods based on the lyrics and acoustic features of the music tracks and current mood of the users were captured through the image and textual posts in Facebook. Subsequently, songs were recommended to users based on the user preferences and their current mood. Based on the accuracies and execution time, inbuilt Python ALS function and KD tree were used in the proposed MSR.

Acknowledgements. This research was supported by the Faculty of Information Technology, University of Moratuwa and the Senate Research Committee, University of Moratuwa.

References

1. Kim, J.-Y., Belkin, N.J.: Categories of music description and search terms and phrases used by non-music experts. In: Proceedings of the 3rd International Society for Music Information Retrieval Conference (ISMIR 2002), pp. 209–214 (2002)
2. Juslin, P.N., Laukka, P.: Expression, perception, and induction of musical emotions: a review and a questionnaire study of everyday listening. J. New Music Res. **33**(3), 217–238 (2004). https://doi.org/10.1080/0929821042000317813
3. Apple Music - Apple. https://www.apple.com/lae/apple-music/. Accessed 29 May 2019
4. Wang, X., Wang, Y.: Improving content-based and hybrid music recommendation using deep learning. In: Proceedings of the 22nd ACM International Conference on Multimedia, pp. 627–636 (2014)
5. Rendle, S., Freudenthaler, C., Schmidt-Thieme, L.: Factorizing personalized Markov chains for next-basket recommendation. In: Proceedings of the 19th International Conference on World Wide Web, pp. 811–820 (2010)
6. Forbes, P., Zhu, M.: Content-boosted matrix factorization for recommender systems In: Proceedings of the Fifth ACM Conference on Recommender Systems, RecSys 2011, p. 261 (2011)
7. Park, M.-H., Hong, J.-H., Cho, S.-B.: Location-based recommendation system using bayesian user's preference model in mobile devices. In: Indulska, J., Ma, J., Yang, Laurence T., Ungerer, T., Cao, J. (eds.) UIC 2007. LNCS, vol. 4611, pp. 1130–1139. Springer, Heidelberg (2007). https://doi.org/10.1007/978-3-540-73549-6_110
8. Hu, Y., Koren, Y., Volinsky, C.: Collaborative filtering for implicit feedback datasets. In: 2008 Eighth IEEE International Conference on Data Mining, Pisa, pp. 263–272 (2008)
9. Li, Q., Myaeng, S.H., Kim, B.M.: A probabilistic music recommender considering user opinions and audio features. Inf. Process. Manag. **43**(2), 473–487 (2007)
10. Chen, Y.X., Boring, S., Butz, A.: How Last.fm illustrates the musical world: user behavior and relevant user-generated content. In: CEUR Workshop Proceedings, vol. 565 (2010)
11. Sunitha, M., Adilakshmi, T.: Music recommendation system based on unsupervised discretization. Int. J. Comput. Appl. **145**(7), 22–25 (2016)
12. Bu, J., et al.: Music recommendation by unified hypergraph: combining social media information and music content. In: Proceedings of the 18th ACM International Conference on Multimedia, pp. 391–400 (2010)
13. Logan, B.: Music recommendation from song sets. In: Proceedings of the 5th ISMIR Conference, pp. 425–428 (2004)
14. Nanopoulos, A., Rafailidis, D., Symeonidis, P., Manolopoulos, Y.: Musicbox: personalized music recommendation based on cubic analysis of social tags. IEEE Trans. Audio Speech Lang. Process. **18**(2), 407–412 (2009)
15. Wu, X., et al.: Personalized next-song recommendation in online karaokes. In: RecSys 2013, pp. 137–140 (2013)
16. Schedl, M., Knees, P., Gouyon, F.: New paths in music recommender systems research. In: RecSys 2017, pp. 392–393 (2017)
17. Hemanth, P., Adarsh, Aswani, C.B., Ajith, P., Kumar, V.A.: EMO PLAYER: emotion based music player. Int. Res. J. Eng. Technol. **5**(4), 4822–4827 (2018)
18. Nathan, K.S., Arun, M., Kannan, M.S.: EMOSIC—an emotion based music player for Android. In: 2017 IEEE International Symposium on Signal Processing and Information Technology (ISSPIT), Bilbao, pp. 371–376 (2017)

19. Weerasinghe, S., Ahangama, S.: A method to identify the current mood of social media users. In: 2019 IEEE International Conference on Industrial and Information Systems, ICIIS 2019, pp. 1–6 (2019)
20. Million Song Dataset: Code | Million Song Dataset. https://labrosa.ee.columbia.edu/millionsong/pages/code#datacreation. Accessed 19 Sept 2019
21. Wecome to Lyrics Wiki - Lyrics Wiki. http://lyricswiki.com/. Accessed 19 Sept 2019
22. Last.fm: Last.fm | Play music, find songs, and discover artists
23. Lam, X.N., Vu, T., Le, T.D., Duong, A.D.: Addressing cold-start problem in recommendation systems. In: Proceedings of the 2nd International Conference on Ubiquitous Information Management and Communication, ICUIMC 2008, p. 208 (2008)

Author Index

Printed in the United States
By Bookmasters